ORGANIZATIONAL REALITIES

ORGANIZATIONAL REALITIES

STUDIES OF STRATEGIZING AND ORGANIZING

WILLIAM H. STARBUCK

With contributions from

MICHAEL L. BARNETT
ARENT GREVE
BO L. T. HEDBERG
JOHN M. MEZIAS
FRANCES J. MILLIKEN
PAUL C. NYSTROM
P. NARAYAN PANT
VIOLINA P. RINDOVA
SUSAN REILLY SALGADO
E. JANE WEBSTER

OXFORD
UNIVERSITY PRESS

OXFORD

UNIVERSITY PRESS

Great Clarendon Street, Oxford OX2 6DP

Oxford University Press is a department of the University of Oxford.
It furthers the University's objective of excellence in research, scholarship,
and education by publishing worldwide in

Oxford New York

Auckland Cape Town Dar es Salaam Hong Kong Karachi
Kuala Lumpur Madrid Melbourne Mexico City Nairobi
New Delhi Shanghai Taipei Toronto

With offices in

Argentina Austria Brazil Chile Czech Republic France Greece
Guatemala Hungary Italy Japan Poland Portugal Singapore
South Korea Switzerland Thailand Turkey Ukraine Vietnam

Oxford is a registered trade mark of Oxford University Press
in the UK and in certain other countries

Published in the United States
by Oxford University Press Inc., New York

British Library Cataloguing in Publication Data

Data available

Library of Congress Cataloging in Publication Data

Data available

Typeset by SPI Publisher Services, Pondicherry, India
Printed in Great Britain
on acid-free paper by
Biddles Ltd., King's Lynn,
Norfolk

ISBN 0–19–928851–8   978–0–19–928851–9

3 5 7 9 10 8 6 4 2

Contents

Preface: Realistic Perspectives on Organizing and Strategizing

The idea for this book came from an observation by Jim March. I noticed that Jim had published a couple of books composed of his previously published articles, so I asked him whether he had found such republication to be worthwhile. He said it appeared that people were using the books because articles in the books were being cited more often than they had been when they originally came out in journals.

Ten of the articles in this book have received many citations. However, much of the value of this collection arises from the articles that have not been cited frequently because they appeared in books or journals with low visibility. Although these articles are likely to be unknown to many readers, I judge them to deserve more attention than they received where they appeared earlier, and I am hoping that this book will bring these articles more attention.

One reason for the low visibility of some articles is that I have often published in journals that most Americans have ignored and Americans constitute the largest audience for academic journals. A few of these less visible journals have been devoted to marginal topics that I have wanted to support, such as the interactions between human behavior and information systems or qualitative studies of organizations. More of these less visible journals have been ones published outside the United States. I have been employed by academic institutions in seven countries, I have visited briefly institutions in eight other countries, and I have attended academic meetings in another nine countries. These experiences have impressed me with the wisdom and diverse insights of people from different societal and academic traditions. Many societies have long traditions of excellent scholarship by very intelligent and perceptive people, and I believe academic researchers from every country can benefit from trying to understand these alternative viewpoints. I see publishing in non-American journals as a way to show my appreciation for intellectual contributions by people other than Americans.

My research has dealt with various topics at different times. This pattern deviates from the focused one often advocated for career success, and I have heard colleagues advocate repeatedly that a researcher should focus on a specialized domain so as to achieve expertise and fame. I blame my deviance on other people, of course. My parents taught me that the main requirement for becoming very good at anything is to work at it hard enough, and my parents and teachers encouraged me to explore a wide range of talents, so I delve into diverse research topics as if hard work gives me license to do so. Such explorations have demonstrated my limitations without damping my enthusiasm for further explorations. Numerous colleagues have presented me with interesting opportunities or

challenges. Almost every research project I have undertaken originated with someone else. However, I have enjoyed the consequent variety, I have been able to inject
my personal biases and interpretations into my research, and I recoil from the
thought of a life dedicated to career success and focused obsessively on one topic.

The articles chosen for this book discuss aspects of organizations—how organizations behave and how life looks to the people within organizations. The
articles are otherwise somewhat diverse in that some review research literature,
some report empirical findings, some propose conceptual reformulations, and
some offer advice to managers; some are quite short and others quite long. Like a
father who cherishes the different qualities of his varied children, I take pride in
these articles in different ways depending on what they attempt to do. Each
reflects to some degree the time and circumstances of its composition.

My research has three properties that make it somewhat unusual. First, because
some of my research topics would be classified as organizational behavior, some
as organization theory, and some as strategic management, an enacted consequence has been that my projects have often crossed boundaries between these
subjects. My studies of managers have related to their behaviors with respect to
organization or strategy; my studies of organizations have related to their strategic development and their dependence on managerial inputs; my studies of
strategic management have treated strategies as products of individual managers
and of organizational development. My studies treat organizations as integrated
social systems that choose actions, some more innovative than others, and that
develop and learn over time. The articles that focus on individual people view
them as actors within organizational settings and as contributors to organizations' actions, especially strategic actions.

Second, my research has often focused on activities within organizations and
the development of individual organizations. These foci contrast with much of
the research about organizations, which has concentrated over the last two
decades almost exclusively on populations of organizations and has ignored
intraorganizational activities and, indeed, ignored individual organizations. Naturally, I think that activities within organizations and the development of individual organizations are interesting in their own right and that they warrant more
attention than they have been receiving. Readers can put this issue into concrete
terms by examining the first chapter in this book. Written over forty years ago,
the chapter expressed confidence that research would soon provide more and
better data about the growth and development of organizations. Yet, the unanswered questions of forty years ago remain unanswered today because researchers have largely ignored what happens inside organizations above a workgroup level. I hope that this book will stimulate renewed interest in activities
within organizations and the development over time of individual organizations.

Third, my research has usually been data-driven rather than theory-driven.
Contemporary methodological teaching says researchers are supposed to derive
hypotheses from previous studies and then gather data to test these hypotheses.
Journals generally decline to publish studies that fail to confirm their hypotheses,
so it is essential that data should produce no surprises. Thus, research has the

character of demonstrating that researchers have nothing to learn. To me this seems to be either dishonest pretence or a waste of research resources. I do not have the wisdom and expertise to formulate only correct hypotheses, and in fact, most of the time, I am prepared to believe that contradictory hypotheses might be true. I also feel pleasure when data surprise me and force me to reexamine my assumptions.

I have sequenced the chapters of this book chronologically partly because they show some of the evolution of my thinking over forty years. Although this evolution may interest no one except me, none of the alternative sequences have a significantly stronger rationale, and subheadings within the Table of Contents suggest alternative perspectives. Of course, any appearance of development over time is as much a reflection of my changing coauthors as of changes in my interests or beliefs. Many of these articles reflect the ideas and hard work of colleagues with whom I have collaborated—Mike Barnett, Arent Greve, Bo Hedberg, John Mezias, Frances Milliken, Paul Nystrom, Narayan Pant, Violina Rindova, Susan Salgado, and Jane Webster.

HUMAN DIMENSIONS OF ORGANIZING AND STRATEGIZING

To me, the characteristic that unites these articles is their consistent emphasis on real-life human beings. Much social science research portrays people as incredibly logical and knowledgeable and organizations as incredibly efficient and fore-sighted. The organizations I have studied have not been perfect. They have not always matched their environments. They have not been well-oiled machines that always functioned smoothly. They have not been free of internal politicking and contests between interest groups. Their attempts to develop competitive strat-egies have sometimes been impressively effective and sometimes ludicrously self-destructive, and competitive strategies have reflected the idiosyncratic preferences of the people who designed them. Efforts to improve have typically succeeded for rather short times and then begun to degrade performance. The people in these organizations have distrusted each other, struggled for dominance, and served their personal interests to the detriment of their colleagues. Managers and decision-makers have misperceived their own organizations and their organiza-tions' environments, they have imitated the wrong models, and they have chosen actions that they later regretted.

Awareness of human limitations and scheming arises from consciousness of my own fallibility as well as from various educational and research experiences. My graduate studies at Carnegie Institute of Technology revolved around the topic of human imperfection. Nearly every seminar, no matter what the an-nounced topic, turned into a debate between two great social scientists, Franco Modigliani and Herbert Simon. Modigliani and Simon differed sharply about the degrees to which actual behavior approximates the ideal. Modigliani held that it is possible to make accurate predictions about behavior by assuming perfect reasoning, whereas Simon saw reasoning as having limitations imposed by human physiology. As well, working for Dick Cyert and Jim March, I ran an experiment in which I saw people deciding to extract personal rewards at the expense of their teammates. Another student at the time, Ollie Williamson, was arguing that managers divert slack resources to obtain benefits for themselves. Cyert and March themselves wrote about conflicts of interests within organizations, perceptual biases that reflected the perceivers' goals, and the effects of limited resources on firms' strategies. Later, after I began teaching, I ran experiments in which I saw human decision-makers making errors, and I participated in a project to try to remedy the high error rates in hospitals. Many further experiences reiterated the themes of human error, lack of foresight, perceptual biases, political coalitions, and conflicts between individual benefits and collective ones.

One emerging theme has been a concern with imperfect cognition: What do people perceive? How do organizations capture knowledge? Do strategies achieve the results expected by their formulators? Gradually over the years, I have come to see people and organizations as blundering along half-blind to events and situations around them. Efforts to act in one's own interests often produce unpleasant surprises. A corollary theme has been the survival of organizations, which fare poorly. Organizations have high failure rates, and nearly all of them have short lives. I suspect that managerial jobs and strategic policies also have high failure rates and short lives, but I have not studied these statistically.

Several of these properties of people and organizations appear in the first chapter of the book, which is the oldest one. This chapter starts by pointing out that the people who guide organizations typically pursue many different goals and they generally act as if they are giving priority to about three goals simultaneously. The chapter then proceeds to describe the development of organizations over time as resulting from conflicting forces—forces that are seeking change and ones that are striving to preserve the status quo. Formalization is a natural consequence of organizational aging and it produces subunits that vie with each other; formalization also makes organizations less capable of dealing with short-run fluctuations in the problems the organizations are trying to solve. Next, the chapter describes various models of organizational growth, some of which attribute growth patterns to biased decision-making, to managers' misperceptions, and to limited resources for managers' attention.

I originally became interested in organizational development because Dick Cyert suggested that I should attempt to create a computer simulation of a large division of an even larger company. I eventually abandoned this project because I found that the data in files at factories differed significantly from the data that the factories had sent to headquarters. I was unable to decide whether I should be modeling the company that existed at the factory level or the company that existed at headquarters. Meanwhile, Herb Simon had pointed out a methodological issue with an idea about administrative hierarchies published by Haire (1959). This induced me to draft a long review article and to attempt two empirical studies relating to organizational size, one of which yielded so few data I did not even write it up. Knowing of these activities, Jim March suggested that I should write about organizational growth and development for a handbook he was editing. Never even considering the possibility that the handbook might have no visibility, I worked sixteen-hour days, seven days a week, for eighteen months. Chapter 1 is the result. It was widely cited and led to an invitation to write Chapter 2, which was also widely cited. I composed most of Chapter 2 during 1970–71, several years before it appeared in print.

Two events influenced much of my research during the 1970s. A project for a German government agency started me thinking about how organizations could remain up-to-date and appropriate for current technologies (Starbuck 1974, 1975), and a debate with Bo Hedberg initiated a series of studies of organizations that were confronting serious crises (Starbuck 1989). These two themes interacted, as my colleagues and I wrote several articles about organization design, how learning from success causes organizations to fail, and what organizations and managers should do to avoid trouble. This book includes five chapters on these topics.

Both of the reviewers who evaluated 'Camping on Seesaws' rejected it completely on the ground that it did not look the way an academic article ought to look. The article lacks statistics, it has a poetic quality that reflects the personality of Bo Hedberg, and the language in the article manifests its authors' efforts to write in a style that symbolizes the vitality of organizations. The journal's editor said he was accepting it for publication solely because he had more confidence in me than in the reviewers. Then, the journal's copy editor expressed the opinion that what this article says is so obviously true that she could not figure out why no one had ever said these things before. We authors regarded this as a begrudging acknowledgment that we had made our case in a compelling way. This chapter has subsequently received more citations than anything else I have published.

The other four chapters in this section have also been cited frequently, and three of these involved strange editorial experiences. 'Organizations as Action Generators' and 'Acting First and Thinking Later' originated as parts of a single manuscript that was rejected outright by the journal's editor and one of the people who reviewed it for publication. Since one of the two reviewers had liked the manuscript and I thought I could address the concerns of the negative reviewer, I revised the article and resubmitted it to the same journal, but satisfying the reviewers' demands had expanded the manuscript to 64 pages. Again the reviewers were split, one positive and the other negative, whereupon the journal's editor told me he would publish exactly half of the article. When I asked him which half, he said he would leave decisions about what the final article would say to me but the final manuscript must not exceed 32 pages. At one point, I telephoned the editor, told him I had cut it to 34 pages, and asked if that length would be acceptable. He said I must cut it to 32 pages and suggested that I delete the word 'the' from the manuscript. Readers will find very few instances of 'the'. Having finally cut 'Organizations as Action Generators' to 32 pages, I was left with a residual 32 unpublished pages. These later became the core of 'Acting First and Thinking Later', so the two chapters are siblings.

Paul Nystrom and I composed 'To Avoid Organizational Crises, Unlearn' because an editor for *Harvard Business Review* wrote to us saying that she had read and liked a paper we had presented at a convention, and asked us to turn this document into an article for the *Review*. After we sent her a draft, she asked for many revisions. After we made the revisions, she said the article met her approval and she would submit it to an editorial board of Harvard professors who were specialists in organizational behavior. Based on the professors' reactions, the editor then asked for more revisions. After we made these revisions, the editor told us she would now submit the article to the entire editorial board of the *Review*. The editorial board then rejected our article. We received no explanation, but it was our conjecture that the core problem was that our article had said managers make mistakes. We had the impression that the *Review* of that era did not recognize managers' fallibility. Only a short time later, the editor of another journal with a very large managerial readership wrote to us, saying he had enjoyed 'Camping on Seesaws' and he wondered if we would write an article for managers on a similar theme. We sent him the manuscript that the *Harvard Business Review* had rejected, which he published without revision.

Our studies of crises demonstrated the importance of organizational perception systems, and the next cluster of chapters focuses on perceptions. Of course, since we had been studying crises, perception systems seemed mainly to limit what organizations perceive. An article by Meyer and Rowan (1977) stimulated Paul Nystrom and me to submit a paper about organizational facades to the annual meeting of the Academy of Management. This unnoticed paper, which we have updated somewhat for this book, describes a phenomenon that deserves more attention than it has received—managers' attempts to misrepresent their actions and achievements. The other two chapters in the first section on perceptions drew more attention. The chapter about executives' perceptual filters states some generalizations about biases in sense-making but also makes a case for the importance of biases in 'noticing'. Noticing has received much less attention than sense-making, yet it may exert more influence on what people do. Noticing is crucial because sense-making cannot affect interpretations of stimuli that people have overlooked. The chapter about the explosion of the Space Shuttle Challenger describes a situation in which incremental learning from ongoing activities led to erroneous inferences, as efforts to squeeze slightly more productivity from the Shuttle had unanticipated and poorly understood consequences. The article also points out the potential value of conflicting subcultures within organizations. Although our studies of crises had made us aware that organizations normally encompass diverse, conflicting perceptions that link to the perceivers' training and jobs, the Challenger story showed how conflicting occupational groups express organizations' inconsistent goals.

Bo Hedberg initiated another research theme by inviting me to speak at a conference about 'knowledge-intensive firms'. To gather material for my talk, I visited several firms that might be described as knowledge-intensive, where, of course, I mainly noticed behaviors relating to the themes on which I had been writing—organizational learning, strategic development, interactions between organizing and strategizing. I also organized a faculty seminar on knowledge as a strategic asset. Every single speaker at this seminar, without exception, offered a different definition of knowledge, so it was not hard to see how research on this topic might reflect researchers' biases.

One of the most interesting products of my venture into knowledge-intensive firms was a study of a very successful law firm. This study astounded me by showing how well the ideas we teach in management courses can work. The law firm does, to a large extent, exactly what management professors try to teach their students to do. Of course, our students do not go forth and do what we try to teach them to do, and the lawyers had not studied management and they had developed their ideas entirely without reference to the contents of management courses. One of the unusual characteristics of this law firm is that it has learned useful things from its experience. As general patterns, organizations learn from their successes but these lessons gradually turn into liabilities, and large organizations, at least, learn nothing from their failures. The law firm has extracted useful lessons from both successes and failures. A key factor seems to have been a core group of senior partners who placed high value on learning: They made consistent efforts to extract lessons, and they had enough political power to apply their lessons.

Despite my various exposures to strategic failures, I remained a believer in formal strategic planning until sometime in the late 1970s or early 1980s. Then, an article by Grinyer and Norburn (1975) raised questions in my mind. They had found that profitable business firms are as likely not to do formal strategizing as to do it, and that the same is true of unprofitable firms. Because I had been assuming that strategizing was achieving its claimed purposes of increasing profits, this finding surprised me but started reflection. I had earlier noticed studies that had suggested that managers misperceive their business environments and misperceive the capabilities of their own organizations. If strategists misperceive both organizations and the organizations' environments, they would have little chance of matching organizations to environments in a fashion that would be anything but random. A few terms teaching forecasting had shown me that forecasting techniques are generally capable only of extrapolating simple, obvious trends for brief periods. Since it normally takes firms substantial time to put strategies into effect, the premises for strategies are likely to become obsolete by the time the strategies take effect. Furthermore, the injunctions of strategic management skate close to the illegal or immoral because they say firms should seek to create and exploit monopolistic positions. Laws bar most of the tactics available for such purposes or the public sees them as antisocial. 'Strategizing Realistically in Competitive Environments' articulates these issues, and proposes that organizations should use strategic planning activities to help the participants gain more realistic perceptions of their organizations and their organizations' environments. Then 'Trying to Help S&Ls' describes a situation in which strategic efforts that were intended to benefit banks contributed to the failure of many of them. The somewhat misguided efforts of different actors interacted to amplify and create problems for the S&Ls, and eventually for Americans in general. Again, this story showed strategies producing unexpected consequences when economic and legal environments changed.

In 1993, Derek Pugh asked me to edit a book of readings on 'premodern management thought', explaining that this meant works written before 1880. I agreed to attempt this, not as an expert in premodern thought, but to learn about it. A few weeks of reflection brought me to wondering about very ancient management practices—long before Niccolò Machiavelli or Robert Owen. I had seen descriptions of ancient practices only in George's (1968) history of management thought. Therefore, I asked the students in a doctoral seminar to investigate ancient management practices. I asked each student to dig out evidence about actual management practices in one society. To keep the students from sliding too easily into well-known works and to push them toward earnest library research, I told them to limit their searches to times before the year 0 BCE. Violina Rindova, my coauthor of the two chapters in this book, looked at ancient China, and I investigated Egypt and Mesopotamia. Later, Violina and I spent many months producing modern interpretations of ancient writings from China, Egypt, and Mesopotamia, which are the regions with the oldest surviving records. The first chapter in this small cluster reveals that even the most ancient documents point to difficult relations between superiors and subordinates. Superiors distrust their subordinates, and subordinates distrust their superiors, yet each has to depend on the other. The other chapter traces the history of Chinese theories about control, leadership, management, and organization. The ancient theories are as complex as modern ones and they were supported by reasoning that we find easy to understand today.

Also in 1993, John Mezias asked me to suggest some readings about managers' perceptions, especially studies of the accuracy of managers' perceptions. I told him of the studies I knew—three somewhat-inappropriate studies from the mid-1970s. John asked me why I had only suggested studies from long before. Where were the recent studies? I knew of none, and despite months of searching, we were unable to find any. We were both astonished at this null result. Our analysis of the extant research left us debating what conclusions we ought to be drawing. The old studies from the 1970s had to be misleading, we thought, because managers could not possibly be so far out of touch with their environments. So, we decided to study perceptual accuracy. We initially conjectured that we could design a study that would find much smaller perception errors than those older studies, and we expected to be able to discover patterns in the errors that would make it possible for organizations to minimize or compensate for many errors. In no way did we anticipate that we were starting a project that would stretch out ten years.

We found this to be a very difficult topic for study. It was difficult to locate appropriate people to study because we wanted data about people who had job experience. It was difficult to create appropriate questions because we were seeking information that would be relevant for academic theories whereas managers' worlds are wholly alien to academic concerns. Because we could obtain only small numbers of observations, our data did not satisfy the assumptions of standard statistical techniques and we had to investigate unfamiliar and poorly understood alternative techniques. Indeed, the first output from our project was an article about how difficult it was to study the accuracy of managers' perceptions (Starbuck and Mezias 1996).

We also found it very difficult to publish our findings. Our project's second output was an article intended for reading by managers. We augmented our research by trying to think of techniques organizations could use to compensate for perception errors and then documenting instances where organizations had tried such techniques. However, after three rounds of revisions, we finally gave up trying to persuade the referees and editor that our work deserved publication. Again, a key problem appeared to be the unacceptability of research that says managers make mistakes. Research on academic publishing indicates that reviewers use comments about research methodology in order to promote ideas they like or to suppress ideas they dislike (Mahoney 1977, 1979). So it seemed with our research. Reviewers would raise issues, we would address these issues, the reviewers would raise more issues, we would address these additional issues, the reviewers would raise still more issues, and so on. Eventually, we just gave up trying to publish that manuscript.

Thus, the chapter in this book is the third one we attempted. This chapter describes two studies because we were dissatisfied with the quality of our first study, so we made a second one that required elaborate negotiations with a large company and involved quite a few managerial personnel in its design. Although we were finally confident we had asked appropriate people appropriate questions and had found appropriate objective data to compare with these people's perceptions, our research did not turn out as we had hoped. We did not show that managers have more accurate perceptions than prior research had suggested and we did not discover patterns that would help organizations compensate for perception errors. Both of our studies said that only three-eighths of managers have fairly accurate perceptions, and in both studies, we were unable to distinguish more accurate managers from less accurate ones based on their job experience. 'Studying the Accuracy of Managers' Perceptions' describes our research adventure, and 'The Accuracy of Managers' Perceptions' discusses implications of inaccurate perceptions for firms' behavior. Under new editors and new policies, the *Harvard Business Review* published a synopsis of this research (Mezias and Starbuck 2003).

'Which Dreams Come True?' is the only chapter in this book that follows a methodology resembling that prevalent in the U.S.—hypotheses, statistical analyses, and significance tests. However, a closer look at this chapter reveals some differences from prevalent practices. First, the regressions weight observations so that estimated parameters will resemble those obtainable from controlled experiments rather than from random samples. Second, distributions are graphed rather than described by summary statistics. Most consumers of research, including those who actually do research, have greater comprehension of graphs than of numerical tables, and graphs can communicate nonlinear relationships. Third, the statistical calculations use robust regression to limit the influence of low-probability observations on the inferences, and thus to make the inferences more likely to represent the population. Fourth, the chapter reports effect sizes and does not report statistical significance. That the calculations have statistical significance is obvious from the fact that the analyzed data comprise high proportions of the population. Thus, the study illustrates how I think researchers ought to perform and report statistical analyses. The study shows support for the idea that powerful organizations can influence future values of some of the variables that shape their success. However, these effects are not large.

LONG-RUN LESSONS

I have found the doing of research to be humbling in at least two ways. First, although it is widely believed that research clarifies, that it answers questions and sharpens perceptions, this has not been my experience. Rather, for every question that my research has answered, it has raised several new questions, and rather than clarifying my perceptions, research has complicated them. Second, the new questions have challenged both the topics investigated and the methods used to investigate them, and the revealed complications have undermined my confidence that I comprehend fully. My collaborative effort with John Mezias to assess the accuracy of managers' perceptions illustrates these phenomena. We entertained different hypotheses at various times and our data contradicted almost all of them. We discovered that familiar statistical methods yield misleading inferences and that producing fully convincing inferences would require more data than we knew how to gather. In the end, we found ourselves puzzling about grander issues than we had imagined before we began.

One consequence of the foregoing consequences of research is that others have sometimes classified me as a 'critical theorist'. It is unquestionably correct that I have occasionally discovered deficiencies of widespread research methods and my studies have sometimes contradicted generally accepted beliefs. I enjoy making such discoveries. As I see it, I find problems in widespread beliefs because I have cultivated habits of mind that compel me to look at propositions from multiple perspectives, and I enjoy finding out that widespread beliefs are wrong or incomplete because I do not want to hold incorrect beliefs. Similarly, I find deficiencies of widespread research methods because I am constantly questioning the validity of my research methods, and I enjoy discovering deficiencies in research methods because I want to use better methods. Criticizing as such seems petty, whereas finding better ways seems useful.

Doing research over many years has also demonstrated the degree to which my thinking reflects my environment. There have been several times when I have read an article or book and seen close parallels with something I had written at approximately the same time as the material I was reading. I do not suspect the authors of these articles and books of using my ideas without giving me credit. Rather, I conjecture that a common social environment influenced these other people as well as me, and it seems entirely likely that each of us believed we were autonomously thinking innovative thoughts. These perceptions of innovativeness might have been correct in that we had not seen ideas similar to our own in print, yet our thoughts were expressing logical inferences from widespread premises. Someone was destined to draw these inferences eventually. To discover that more than one person drew similar inferences should surprise no one.

Some years ago, around the time I wrote the first version of 'Strategizing Realistically in Competitive Environments', I told my colleague Bill Guth, who had taught strategic management for many years, that I was doubting the value of our teaching strategic management. Because it was so difficult to make accurate predictions and competitors could respond to each others' strategic actions, I said, it seemed that strategies were only meaningful when conceived in retrospect. I speculated that strategies served mainly to give people confidence that their completed actions have formed understandable sequences. Bill astonished me when he replied, 'That is a very important function.' Thus, this book has given me confidence that my various research projects have created coherent, intertwined threads and that I am wiser today than 40 years ago.

ACKNOWLEDGMENTS

Mike Barnett, Joan Dunbar, Arent Greve, John Mezias, David Musson, and Paul Nystrom offered useful advice about this preface.

List of Figures

List of Tables

Credits

01 'Organizational Growth and Development' was published in J. G. March (ed.), *Handbook of Organizations*. Rand McNally, 1965, 451–583. James G. March has granted permission to republish it, and it has been edited and shortened for this book.

02 'Organizations and Their Environments' was published in M. D. Dunnette (ed.), *Handbook of Industrial and Organizational Psychology*. Rand McNally, 1976, 1069–1123. Marvin D. Dunnette has granted permission to republish it, and it has been shortened and slightly revised for this book.

03 'Camping on Seesaws: Prescriptions for a Self-designing Organization' was published in *Administrative Science Quarterly*, 1976, 21: 41–65. *Administrative Science Quarterly*. Bo L. T. Hedberg, and Paul C. Nystrom have granted permission to republish it. It has been edited lightly for this book.

04 'Responding to Crises' was published in the *Journal of Business Administration*, 1978, 9(2): 111–137; this also appeared simultaneously in C. F. Smart and W. T. Stanbury (eds.), *Studies on Crisis Management*, 1978. Institute for Research on Public Policy, Toronto. Arent Greve and Bo L. T. Hedberg have granted permission to republish it, as has Daniel F. Muzyka, Dean of the Sauder School of Business at the University of British Columbia, which published the *Journal of Business Administration*. It has been edited lightly for this book.

05 'Organizations as Action Generators' was published in the *American Sociological Review*, 1983, 48: 91–102. The American Sociological Association has granted permission to republish it, and it has been edited lightly for this book.

06 'To Avoid Organizational Crises, Unlearn' was published in *Organizational Dynamics*, 1984, 12(4): 53–65. Both Elsevier Ltd and Paul C. Nystrom have granted permission to reprint it. It has been edited lightly for this book.

07 'Acting First and Thinking Later: Theory Versus Reality in Strategic Change' was published in *Organizational Strategy and Change*, by J. M. Pennings and Associates (including me). Jossey-Bass, 1985, 336–372.

08 An earlier version of 'Organizational Facades' was published in the *Academy of Management, Proceedings of the Annual Meeting, Boston*, 1984, 182–185. It has been revised and updated for this book. Both the Academy of Management and Paul C. Nystrom have given permission to publish it.

09 'Executives' Perceptual Filters: What They Notice and How They Make Sense' was published in D. C. Hambrick (ed.), *The Executive Effect: Concepts*

and Methods for Studying Top Managers. JAI Press, 1988, 35–65. Both Elsevier Ltd and Frances J. Milliken have granted permission to republish it.

10 'Challenger: Changing the Odds Until Something Breaks' was published in the *Journal of Management Studies*, 1988, 25: 319–340. Both Blackwell and Frances J. Milliken have granted permission to republish it. It has been very slightly updated for this book.

11 'When Is Play Productive?' was published in *Accounting, Management & Information Technologies*, 1991, 1: 1–20. Both Elsevier Ltd and E. Jane Webster have granted permission to republish it. It has been edited lightly for this book.

12 'Learning by Knowledge-Intensive Firms' was published in the *Journal of Management Studies*, 1992, 29(6): 713–740. Blackwell has granted permission to republish it.

13 'Keeping a Butterfly and an Elephant in a House of Cards: The Elements of Exceptional Success' was published in the *Journal of Management Studies*, 1993, 30(6): 885–921. Blackwell has granted permission to republish it. The version in this book has been expanded and updated from the original.

14 'How Organizations Channel Creativity' was published in C. M. Ford and D. A. Gioia (eds.), *Creative Action in Organizations*. Sage, 1995, 106–114. Sage has granted permission to republish it.

15 An earlier version of 'Strategizing Realistically in Competitive Environments' was published as 'Strategizing in the Real World' in the *International Journal of Technology Management, Special Publication on Technological Foundations of Strategic Management*, 1992, 8(1/2): 77–85. Inderscience Enterprises Ltd has granted permission to republish it.

16 'Trying to Help S&Ls: How Organizations with Good Intentions Jointly Enacted Disaster' was published in Z. Shapira (ed.), *Organizational Decision Making*, Cambridge University Press, 1996, 35–60. Cambridge University Press and P. Narayan Pant have granted permission to republish it.

17 'Unlearning Ineffective or Obsolete Technologies' was published in the *International Journal of Technology Management*, 1996, 11: 725–737. Inderscience Enterprises Ltd has granted permission to republish it.

18 'Distrust in Dependence: The Ancient Challenge of Superior–Subordinate Relations' in T. A. R. Clark (ed.), *Advancements in Organization Behaviour: Essays in Honour of Derek Pugh*. Ashgate Publishing, 1997, 313–336. Both Ashgate and Violina P. Rindova have given permission to republish it.

19 'Ancient Chinese Theories of Control' was published in the *Journal of Management Inquiry*, 1997, 6: 144–159. Both Sage Publishers and Violina P. Rindova have given permission to republish it.

20 'How Organizations Learn from Success and Failure' was published in M. Dierkes, A. Berthoin Antal, J. Child, and I. Nonaka (eds.), *Handbook of Organizational Learning and Knowledge*. Oxford University Press, 2001, 327–350. Oxford University Press and Bo L. T. Hedberg have given permission to republish it.

21 'The Accuracy of Managers' Perceptions: A Dimension Missing from Theories About Firms' was published in M. Augier and J. G. March (eds.), *The Economics of Choice, Change and Organization: Essays in Memory of Richard M. Cyert*. Cheltenham, UK: Edward Elgar Publishing, 2002, 168–185. Elgar, John M. Mezias, and Susan Reilly Salgado have granted permission to republish it.

22 'Studying the Accuracy of Managers' Perceptions: A Research Odyssey' was published in the *British Journal of Management*, 2003, 14: 3–17. Both Blackwell and John M. Mezias have granted permission to republish it.

23 'Which Dreams Come True? Endogeneity, Industry Structure, and Forecasting Accuracy' was published in *Industrial and Corporate Change*, 2003, 12(4): 653–672. Oxford University Press, Michael L. Barnett, and P. Narayan Pant have granted permission to republish it. The version in this book omits measures of statistical significance that appeared in the original version solely because an editor demanded them.

Part I

Organizational Growth and Development and Environmental Relations

1

Organizational Growth and Development

1. INTRODUCTION

This chapter defines growth as change in an organization's size when size is measured by the organization's membership or employment, and it defines development as change in an organization's age. The chapter considers why and how organizations grow and develop, and it examines effects of growth and development on organizational structure and behavior.

Many words have been written about growth and development. The bibliography includes over two hundred items. The chapter's primary goal is to review this literature. In some cases, it is a critical review, but it is also an optimistic review. Some of the work is interesting, imaginative, empirically based, and methodologically sound. There have been attempts to construct theories and to make predictions. There is even some consistency among studies.

One reason growth and development evoke research interest is the possibility of uncovering characteristics that apply generally to organizations of various kinds. One can measure organizational size and age in comparable units (people and years) in business firms, military units, social movements, government agencies, and hospitals. Whether a four-year-old business firm having eighty employees can be compared with a government agency of the same size and age is debatable, but much research in this area assumes that such comparisons are valid and are likely to yield significant generalizations. Certainly, if one believes that common denominators exist among large classes of organizations—and there is no point in studying organizations if one does not believe this—then comparing organizations in terms of straightforward independent variables like size and age is a sensible start. Further, such comparisons often produce sizeable correlations.

However, discovering that certain organizational characteristics correlate with size and age still leaves one a long way from being able to attribute these characteristics to size and age. One can usually find other factors that might explain the observed differences and that correlate with size and age. Thomas' study of welfare bureaus provides an example. He found that large bureaus differ from small ones, but then observed that:

Most of our results may be accounted for plausibly in terms of the population and the community setting of the county in which the welfare bureau was located. The size of the bureau itself depends largely upon the population size of a county.... (1959: 35)

The association of the workers' personal characteristics with the size of welfare bureaus probably indicates that the pool of potential employees in the counties with large populations differs from those with small populations. Available information indicates that some of the contrasts between workers in the smaller and the larger bureaus parallel those between rural residents and residents of cities. (1959: 36)

Unfortunately, not all researchers are as conscientious as Thomas was. Researchers often report correlations as if correlation were proof of causal relation, leaving readers the problems of posing alternative hypotheses and searching for corroborative studies. This chapter may make the latter task less difficult by providing information about previous research and indicating areas in which further research might be especially useful.

Inevitably, this chapter overlooks some studies. I am most familiar with work published in the United States and having direct relevance for business firms. Beyond those biases, three rules guided selection of studies for review:

First, the chapter emphasizes descriptive studies and theories in preference to normative ones. Although it is important to develop prescriptions about how an organization *should* grow and develop, current knowledge is so rudimentary that prescriptive statements seem premature.

Second, the chapter emphasizes the 'formal' aspects of organizations rather than the 'informal' aspects. One characteristic that distinguishes organizations from other collections of people is a commitment to achieving members' goals by means of explicit and stable task allocations, roles, and responsibilities. Mobs and informal social groups are not organizations. Social and service clubs, like Rotary and Kiwanis, are organizations only part of the time. The study of organizations should not and cannot ignore interactions and behaviors that depart from structural norms. However, so long as one is concerned with organizational behavior and not with social behavior in general, one should emphasize those modes of behavior in which organizations specialize.

Third, the chapter ignores experimental studies of small groups. These studies have produced interesting data that have potential relevance to the study of organizations. However, the experimental studies concern groups of 3–12 people over short periods of time, and the concern here is with groups of 30–12,000 people over long periods. The fallacies of extrapolating from one category to the other are self-evident. One can look to small-group studies for hypotheses, but researchers need to investigate these hypotheses independently in large, persistent organizations. In the absence of such supporting data, the results of the small-group studies are as likely to mislead as to contribute to understanding. This objection might not apply to all applications of small-group data to organizations, but in this instance, potential differences due to group size and time span have special significance.

The core of this chapter has four sections.

'Motives for Growth' considers, from the viewpoints of various organizational members, some advantages of large organizations over small ones, and of old ones over young ones, or vice versa. This section discusses ten organizational goals that relate to growth. Other goals may be relevant, but these ten include all the goals that have received extensive treatment in the literature, and until additional empirical studies have assessed the importance and consequences of various organizational goals, any list involves guesswork. Only one study is reviewed that attempted to find out how often managers express certain goals and to correlate managers' goals with the sizes, structures, and growth rates of their firms.

'Adaptation and Growth' examines some determinants of an organization's ability to establish viable relationships with its environment. Discussed are the effectiveness of different kinds of behavior strategies in producing growth, organizational members' attitudes toward change, and the evolution of an organizational structure that is adapted to the environment. The preceding discussion of motives stresses organizational size because desire for an exogenously controlled variable like age cannot affect behavior (except in the sense of a desire for survival). The discussion of adaptation shifts emphasis to organizational age because organizations must learn adaptive responses and learning takes time. Size is not wholly ignored, and size and age are usually correlated, but the basic nature of adaptation is such that the longer an organization survives, the better prepared it is to continue surviving.

'Models of Growth' focuses on relations between size and age as they have been expressed in theories of why growth occurs and what happens inside growing organizations. The models range from ones that describe patterns in an organization's size and structure over time without paying much attention to processes that generate these patterns, to models that describe decision processes inside an organization without paying much attention to patterns in size and structure that these processes generate.

'Administrative Structure and Growth' has been greatly abbreviated for this republication. It surveys theoretical discussions of the effects of organizational size on administrative efficiency. Then it summarizes observations about administrative employment, spans of control, hierarchical levels, and managerial employment.

2. MOTIVES FOR GROWTH

Growth is not spontaneous. It is a consequence of decisions: decisions to hire or to not fire, decisions to increase output in response to demand, decisions to stimulate demand, and so forth. Relationships between specific decisions and ultimate expansion of the organization may be tenuous, but expansion necessarily depends upon some decisions and actions that follow them. These decisions are, in turn, functions of goals pursued by members of the organization. Thus, organizational growth can take place only if increased size relates positively to achievement of the organization's goals or goals of individual members of the organization (McGuire 1963: 3).

This is not intended to suggest that organizations and their members make decisions that achieve desired outcomes. Organizational growth may work contrary to the interests of some, or even most, members of the organization. Growth may not be the best way to achieve goals it is intended to achieve. On occasion, growth may be a transient exploration of an organization's environment that, proving to be unrewarding, is subsequently abandoned. The point is simply that the growth of an organization is not a random event.

Increased organizational size may be a goal itself, in at least two senses. First, growth may be valued as a symbol of achievement. Growth is often difficult to accomplish because growing organizations must deal with intraorganizational stresses and overcome external forces. Society recognizes obstacles to growth and awards prestige and admiration to members of organizations that have expanded successfully, particularly those members who were instrumental in the expansions. These people also receive internal rewards in the form of feelings of success and pride in their achievement (Nourse 1944). Second, increased size may be an operational goal, a benchmark for progress. The size of an organization is easily measured and easy to talk about—characteristics that recommend it as an operational goal. However, use of size as an operational goal does not necessarily mean that increases in size per se are valued. There is usually an implicit assumption that size correlates with attainment of goals having more basic relevance to the organization's purpose or holding more immediate interest for some organizational members.

By far the most widely accepted approach to growth has been that growth is either a means of attaining other goals or a side effect of such attainment, rather than an end in itself. The literature describes a number of goals that, with varying degrees of face validity, relate to growth. Ten of these are described here.

(1) 'Organizational Self-Realization'

To quote Katona (1951: 205–206):

> ... the going concern is commonly viewed as a living entity of itself. Self-realization of a business concern represents, then, a topic worth further study. A corporation is not conceived by its executives simply as an organization making money, or making automobiles. It has to carry out its functions, complete the tasks taken up, and expand to justify itself. It has been recently pointed out that here may be found one of the most important explanations of the fact that our large corporations are continuously expanding in diverse fields that are often foreign to their original activity. Small investments may be made, for instance, in order to study the use of by-products or waste products. When some progress has been achieved, the task once begun is pushed toward completion. There is a drive, perhaps even a compulsion to follow through after one has begun.

Newman and Logan (1955) summarized a round table discussion by nineteen executives that came up with five reasons for growth, all of which have the aesthetic flavor of 'self-realization'. The five reasons were: (*a*) customers demand complete service, for example, plants in all parts of the country; (*b*) firms attempt to master their technologies, that is, to become vertically integrated; (*c*) research laboratories develop products outside existing product lines; (*d*) in order to attract retail dealers, a manufacturer must offer a complete product line, for example, all kinds of major appliances; and (*e*) if firms do not expand, they contract; they cannot stand still.

In his review of *Parkinson's Law*, Galbraith (1957) remarked that bureaucratic expansion results from narrow specialization and a 'tendency to create organizations on the basis not of need but of plausibility'. One wonders if this is not Katona's 'self-realization' viewed cynically.

(2) Adventure and Risk

Organizations may grow because executives like to gamble on new activities. Gordon (1945: 310–311) found that some executives are motivated by 'the urge for adventure and for "playing the game" for its own sake', and one executive compared the desire to risk capital and effort on expansion with the compulsion that draws people to Nevada. This could explain why an entrepreneur who has reached a point of satiation with respect to wealth and power might continue to be aggressive. Within specific organizations, it may be a powerful motive, but it would be surprising to find that compulsive pursuit of risk was a major factor in most organizations.

More pervasive, perhaps, than pursuit of adventure and risk, is avoidance of boredom. Blau (1955) reported a study of civil servants in which boredom of personnel who had mastered their tasks favored change, and Argyris (1957) reviewed numerous studies with similar implications.

(3) Prestige, Power, and Job Security

In addition to the prestige that follows from successful expansion, there is prestige attached to supervision of a large number of people. The more people an executive supervises, the greater the executive's prestige. Ordinarily, this supervisory prestige accompanies some degree of power over the persons supervised, autonomy, and job security (subordinates being more expendable than their superiors are). Gordon (1945: 305–307, 311) stated that the urge for personal power and prestige is one of the most important nonfinancial motives of business executives, and Hanson (1961) found that superintendents of large hospitals have more responsibility relative to hospital boards than do superintendents of small hospitals.[1]

Parkinson is probably the best-known exponent of the prestige-power-security motive complex. He (1957: 4–5) wrote, 'An official wants to multiply subordinates, not rivals', and went on to explain:

... we must picture a civil servant, called A, who finds himself overworked. Whether this overwork is real or imaginary is immaterial, but we should observe, in passing, that A's sensation (or illusion) might easily result from his own decreasing energy: a normal symptom of middle age. For this real or imagined overwork there are, broadly speaking, three possible remedies. He may resign; he may ask to halve the work with a colleague called B; he may demand the assistance of two subordinates, to be called C and D. There is probably no instance in history, however, of A choosing any but the third alternative. By resignation he would lose his pension rights. By having B appointed, on his own level in the hierarchy, he would merely bring in a rival for promotion to W's vacancy when W (at long last) retires. So A would rather have C and D, junior men, below him. They will add to his consequence and, by dividing the work into two categories, as between C and D, he will have the merit of being the only man who comprehends them both.... When C complains in turn of being overworked (as he certainly will) A will, with the concurrence of C, advise the appointment of two assistants to help C. But he can then avert internal friction only by advising the appointment of two more assistants to help D, whose position is much the same. With this recruitment of E, F, G, and H the promotion of A is now practically certain.

(4) Executive Salaries

Roberts (1956, 1959) showed that the salary of the highest paid executive in a firm was independent of the profit earned by the firm, and increased exponentially with the firm's sales volume. This implies that, to increase his salary, the top executive should be more interested in increasing the firm's size than its profits. Simon (1957*b*: 34–35) then argued that economic variables alone did not adequately explain Roberts's result. His model yielded Roberts's empirical result on the basis of three mechanisms: '(*a*) economic determination, through competition, of the salaries at the lowest executive levels where new employees are hired from outside the organization; (*b*) social determination of a norm for the "steepness" of organizational hierarchies (usually called the span of control); and (*c*) social determination of a norm for the ratio of an executive's salary to the salaries of his immediate subordinates.' Simon pointed out that his model explained, not only the salary of the top executive, but also the numbers of executives at various salary levels throughout a hierarchy.

Williamson (1963: 240–241) took a logical next step when he constructed a model of a firm in which management expanded itself in order to increase its salaries:

Modern organization theory treats the firm as a coalition (managers, workers, stockholders, suppliers, customers) whose members have conflicting demands that must be reconciled if the firm is to survive. In the sense that each group in the coalition is essential to the firm's continuing existence, the members of the coalition can be regarded as 'equals.' This view, however, is more useful when observing the firm in a period of crisis than when survival is not a pressing problem. Where survival is not a current concern, restoring a hierarchy among the members based on the attention they give to the firm's operations may lead to more productive insights. From this viewpoint, management emerges as the chief member of the coalition; its role as the coordinating and initiating agent as well as its preferred access to information permit it quite naturally to assume this primacy position. Thus, although in certain circumstances it may be necessary to give special attention to shifts in demands made by members of the coalition other than managers, under 'normal' conditions it may be entirely appropriate to take the demands of the other members (for wages, profits, product, and so forth) as *given* and leave to the discretion of the management the operation of the firm in some best sense. . . .

In the present model, managers are held to operate the firm so as to maximize a utility function that has as principal components (1) salaries, (2) staff, (3) discretionary spending for investments, and (4) management slack absorbed as cost. This utility function is maximized subject to the condition that reported profits be greater than or equal to minimum profits demanded.

Williamson defined 'management slack absorbed as cost' as the difference between 'reported profits' and 'actual profits'. How he would measure this quantity is unclear.[2]

(5) Profit

Profit maximization has been the catchall motive in the traditional economic theory of the firm. Although this theory has been the center of considerable controversy, the notion that profit is a motive is not in question (Cyert and March 1963; Penrose 1959). As any perusal of business journals will confirm, business executives are concerned about profit and, other things being equal, prefer more profit to less.

One controversial characteristic of the theory of the firm is the assumption that profit is the *only* motive for business behavior. This assumption seems incredible, as there is much evidence that business executives pursue other motives in addition to profit. It is common now to find the theory of the firm stated in terms of utility maximization rather than profit maximization.[3]

Even if firms ignore nonprofit goals like prestige, security, and so forth, one would expect to find firms pursuing goals other than profit as defined by financial statements. One reason is that accounting procedures often tell incomplete stories, either because there are distortions inherent in accounting 'conventions' or because financial statements reflect the past more than the future. Most business managers try to look beyond financial statements when they set goals and evaluate performance and, in the process, they may give functional autonomy to components of profit like overhead cost or advertising expense. Cyert and March cited six operational goals as being adequate to explain 'most price, output, and general sales strategy decisions'. They are: (*a*) the volume of production; (*b*) the stability of production; (*c*) the minimum finished inventory level; (*d*) sales volume; (*e*) market share; and (*f*) profit (1963: 40–43). Dent's (1959) study suggests a somewhat different list that is discussed below.

Profit, even if broadly defined as the difference between the value of services performed and the cost of these services, is not a major factor in the operation of nonprofit organizations like governmental agencies, hospitals, trade associations, or labor unions. One suspects that, over long periods and in informal ways, society assesses the 'profit' from such organizations in that organizations that cost more than they are worth disappear. Churches are a good example; they depend on voluntary contributions and fail if the 'take' is not sufficient. One theory of trade associations is that they operate on demand and cost variables outside the control of individual firms, and so maximize total profit to an industry. However, this may be a tautological statement. The 'revenues' of such organizations, the value of the services that they perform, are only partially measurable and not in units directly comparable with cost: numbers of licenses issued, numbers of students in school, students' average scores on scholastic achievement tests, numbers of complaints received. Therefore, attempts to construct all-inclusive measures of net yield are not very fruitful.

(6) Cost

The major components of profit, revenue and cost, may become operational goals in their own rights. It makes no sense to minimize cost in the strictest sense because the cheapest organization is the one that does not exist, but it may be useful to minimize cost per unit of output subject to constraints (e.g. the requirement that the organization exist).

There are at least three a priori reasons for believing that cost per unit decreases as the size of an organization increases, assuming that output also increases. First, there is the advantage in being able to hire and fully utilize specialists. Florence (1953: 50–52) called this 'The Principle of Multiples':

Specialized men and machines must...be used in their speciality up to capacity. But the capacity of different specialists and special machines is very different and they are indivisible; thus arises a difficult problem in 'balancing' production...the smaller the scale of operation (or production) and the fewer the total number of persons dividing and diffusing their labor, the less chance there is of all of them being fully made use of as specialists.

Second, there is Florence's 'Principle of Bulk Transactions':

...the total monetary, physical or psychological costs of dealing in large quantities are sometimes no greater (and in any case less than proportionately greater) than the costs of dealing in small quantities; and hence the cost *per unit* becomes smaller with large quantities.

And third, there is the statistical phenomenon that Florence labelled 'The Principle of Massed (or Pooled) Reserves':

...the greater the number of similar items involved the more likely are deviations to cancel out and leave the actual average results nearer to the expected results.

That is, increasing the size of an organization increases the sample sizes of random variables and therefore decreases the variances of the means.[4]

Increasing employment does not necessarily decrease cost. Given a level of output, the relation between cost and employment may be U-shaped. Having too few employees leads to heavy dependence on overtime and higher wages; having too many employees wastes labor resources. Thus, an optimum level of employment may exist for a given level of output. Holt et al. (1960) employed operations research techniques in an attempt to specify such an optimum.

Suppose that an organization's level of output increases. The optimum level of employment will also increase (though less than proportionately if Florence's 'Principles' are taken seriously). In this sense, output and organizational size rise and fall together, and cost per unit can vary with size.[5] The functional relationship between cost and size is unclear. Very small firms probably achieve definite cost savings by expansion; several studies support this view. Excepting that one point, the most balanced conclusion seems to be Osborn's (1951: 92): 'Considering all the uncertainties involved, the unsatisfactory conclusion is reached that we do not know very much about relative efficiency [as measured by cost] in relation to size.' Cost per unit may decrease uniformly as size increases, or it may decrease and then increase again as organizations get very large.[6]

In a sense, the actual relationship between cost per unit and size is irrelevant. The relevant relationship is the one that executives believe holds true. Eiteman and Guthrie (1952) asked business executives what they thought their products' average cost curves looked like. Table 1.1 gives their results in abbreviated form.

The argument for increasing cost in the largest organizations rests on three notions. The first states that managerial problems become inordinately complex as size increases, producing progressively higher production costs. Section 5 below examines this proposition. The second states that large organizations produce so much output that the demand for their products is nearly saturated, and each additional unit of output requires progressively higher selling expense. This is probably a serious consideration for some organizations but not for others. The third reason for hypothesizing high costs for large organizations is membership apathy. Baumgartel and Sobol (1959), Indik (1963), Revans (1958), Talacchi (1960), TAST (1953, 1957), Warner and Low (1947), and Worthy (1950a, 1950b) concluded that morale is lower in large organizations, and Gouldner (1954) pointed out that use of standard operating procedures, as occurs in large bureaucracies, allows employees to perform near minimum-acceptable levels.

Table 1.1. Cost per unit[a]

Cost per unit as output increases	Number of firms	Number of products
Uniform increase	0	1
Short decrease, then a long increase	1	5
Long decrease, then a short increase	130	438
Uniform decrease	20	638
Totals	334	1082

[a] From Eiteman and Guthrie (1952).

On the other hand, Newman and Logan (1955) concluded that 'size by itself is not a major determinant of morale,' and Sills (1957) reported that 'the factor of size has not led to membership apathy' in an organization that was decentralized and managed participatively. In general, research on morale has concentrated on measures of employee satisfaction without tracing consequences of satisfaction or dissatisfaction for costs, profits, and productivity. March and Simon (1958) observed that satisfaction and productivity are not perfectly correlated, and it is conceivable that low morale is a symptom of high efficiency. Further, researchers have often confounded the sizes of primary work groups with the sizes of whole organizations. The literature suggests that morale depends more on the size, structure, and management of the work group than on organizational size.

When cost is viewed as a function of output, output is measured as a production rate, for example, units of output per annum. However, cost also depends upon cumulative output, the number of units produced since production began (Alchian 1959). This relationship between cost and cumulative output is a matter of learning: People correct difficulties in production processes; workers waste fewer motions; errors occur less frequently; people see opportunities to reduce costs and to increase productivity.

Alchian (1949), Asher (1956), Hirsch (1952), Nadler and Smith (1963), and Searle and Gody (1945) all found that the labor required to produce an additional unit of product decreased significantly with each successive unit produced. This learning curve approximated an exponential function. Specifically, working hours per unit equaled

$$Az^{-B};$$

where A and B are positive parameters and z is cumulative output. One interesting characteristic of these studies is that despite variations in products studied—from cargo ships to machine tools—B was consistently close to 0.3. (The confidence limits ranged from 0.25 to 0.36.)

Cooper and Charnes (1954) used learning to explain some apparently illogical data. They observed that empirical studies of total cost (C) as a function of output (Y) often yielded a negative coefficient A for the cubic function

$$C = A \cdot Y^3 + B \cdot Y^2 + D \cdot Y + E.$$

For A to be negative was illogical because it implied that total cost would decrease for a large enough output. Cooper and Charnes argued that $A < 0$ was consistent with a model of the type

$$C = C^*(Y,T) + f(t,T) \cdot g(Y)$$

where t is time; $C^*(Y, T)$ is a long-run cost function that can be achieved at some future date T, $f(t, T)$ is a learning curve that expresses a decrease in cost as time passes, and $g(Y)$ is a perceptual function that expresses an increase in the number of opportunities to economize as output increases.

(7) Revenue

Griffin (1949: 158) observed that 'increased volume, to a considerable extent, is an end in itself, not merely (as it is often described) a means of increasing profit rates'. However, Baumol (1959: 47–48; 1962) placed the strongest emphasis on revenue as a goal. He proposed that oligopolists' behavior resembled revenue maximization subject to a minimum profit constraint:

> The evidence for my hypothesis that sales volume ranks ahead of profits as the main object of the oligopolists' concern, is again highly impressionistic; but I believe it is quite strong. Surely it is a common experience that, when one asks an executive, 'How's business?', he will answer that his *sales* have been increasing (or decreasing), and talk about his profit only as an afterthought, if at all. And I am told the requirements for acceptance to membership in the Young Presidents Organization (an honorific society) are that the applicant be under 40 years of age and president of a company whose annual volume is over a million dollars. Presumably it makes no difference if this firm is in imminent danger of bankruptcy.
>
> Nor is this failure to emphasize profits a pure rationalization or a mere matter of careless phrasing. Almost every time I have come across a case of conflict between profits and sales the businessmen with whom I worked left little doubt as to where their hearts lay. It is not unusual to find a profitable firm, in which some segment of its sales can be shown to be highly unprofitable. For example, I have encountered several firms who were losing money on their sales in markets quite distant from the plant where local competition forced the product price down to a level which did not cover transportation costs. Another case was that of a watch distributor whose sales to small retailers in sparsely settled districts were so few and far between that the salesmen's wages were not made up by the total revenues which they brought in. When such a case is pointed out to management, it is usually quite reluctant to abandon its unprofitable markets. Businessmen may consider seriously proposals which promise to put these sales on a profitable basis. There may be some hope for the adoption of a suggestion that new plant be built nearer the market to which current transportation costs are too high, or that watch salesmen be transferred to markets with greater sales potential and a mail order selling system be substituted for direct selling in little populated regions. But a program which explicitly proposes any cut in sales volume, whatever the profit considerations, is likely to meet a cold reception. In many cases firms do finally perform the radical surgery involved in cutting out an unprofitable line or territory but this usually occurs after much heart-searching and delay.

As with cost, it is theoretically possible for very large organizations to be less well-off than medium-sized organizations, for revenue to decrease as output and employment increase. The logic behind this view is: (*a*) demand depends on price; (*b*) in order to sell more output one must reduce price, especially if output is extremely high; and therefore (*c*) revenue, being the product of output and price, may decrease when output increases (Boulding 1953).

Price reductions and increasing sales expense both imply that organizational growth is constrained to a single market, or a narrow range of markets; neither factor seriously restricts organizational size unless a specific organization chooses, or is forced, to confine itself. Most organizations can find plenty of opportunities for expansion in terms of new products and new markets, and a point of diminishing returns with respect to any single product or market is not binding. Chandler (1962: 391) observed in his study of large corporations—particularly DuPont, General Motors, Standard Oil of New Jersey, and Sears, Roebuck:

> As the market became more saturated and the opportunities to cut costs through more rational techniques lessened, enterprises began to search for other markets or to develop other businesses that might profitably employ some of their partially utilized resources or even make a more profitable application of those still being fully employed.

Further, the idea that price decreases can decrease total revenue assumes that all customers buy at the same price. Many organizations that are chartered to narrow product lines, such as Community Chest and United Fund organizations, can discriminate among customers—collecting larger amounts from some and smaller amounts from others. Likert (1961: 153–160) studied the effectiveness of Leagues of Women Voters as a function of League size, defining effectiveness primarily in terms of revenue-oriented variables.[7] His data indicated that total effectiveness was a monotone increasing function of size; although effectiveness per member declined in large Leagues, there was no indication that total effectiveness ever decreased. One of Likert's interesting findings was that participation by central members (leaders) increased with League size, and participation by peripheral members decreased. It suggests that relationships between group size and participation in small groups may generalize to voluntary organizations.[8]

(8) Monopolistic Power

There has been a traditional argument that one reason for increasing organizational size is the power of a large organization as a monopolist or monopsonist. This argument has less force today than it did in the early twentieth century. In the first place, antitrust legislation and enforcement have made exercise of monopoly power dangerous; unless a monopolist stays within tight legal constraints, the monopolist gets into trouble. In the second place, empirical studies of pricing behavior suggest that monopolists probably do not take full advantage of their potential power because they are uncertain what the limits of their power are and because they shy away from the social stigmas attached to using it (Cyert and March 1963; Hall and Hitch 1939). In the third place, there are too many large firms. Monopolistic power depends more upon relative than absolute size; if a monopolist's customers and suppliers are as large as the monopolist is, the monopolist may have no power at all (Galbraith 1952).[9]

Size and power generally do go together and executives appreciate power. Increased power is unquestionably a consideration in many decisions to expand, but it is doubtful that Katona was right when he (1951: 204–205) said: 'There are indications that the prevailing institutional set up has greatly enhanced the desire for power among American businessmen.'

Large size and monopoly power can be fatal to business firms. The American economic system depends upon competition among many firms to keep prices low and efficiency high. However, beginning about 1870, single firms or coalitions of firms came to dominate many industries. Among the industries so controlled were coal, gunpowder, lead, matches, meatpacking, petroleum, sugar, tobacco, and whiskey. The tactics used by monopolists to obtain their power, and the exploitation that they practiced after they obtained it, eventually led to disciplinary action by society at large. The Sherman Act was enacted in 1890, the Clayton and Federal Trade Commission acts in 1914, and the Robinson-Patman Act in 1936; each law was more severe and explicit than preceding ones.[10]

The basic pattern of antitrust legislation and enforcement has been to penalize offensive acts and practices by monopolists—like deception, collusion, discriminatory pricing, restraint of trade, and 'unfair' competition—not to penalize monopoly itself. However, courts have recognized that size and power are inseparable. In his 1945 opinion in the case of *United States* v. *Aluminum Company of America*, Judge Learned Hand (1945: 427–428; or 1948: 57682) held that a distinction between latent power and exercised power is 'purely formal; it would be valid only so long as the monopoly remained wholly inert; it would disappear as soon as the monopoly began to operate; for when it did—that is, as soon as it began to sell at all—it must sell at some price and the only price at which it could sell is a price which it itself fixed. Thereafter the power and its exercise must needs coalesce.'

One of the most interesting facets of the Alcoa case is Hand's implication that, for a monopoly, growth itself is offensive. The company had argued that it had not actively sought a monopolistic position through merger, conspiracy, or other overt acts, but that it had simply expanded in response to demand for its products. Hand replied (1945: 431; or 1948: 57685):

It was not inevitable that it should always anticipate increases in the demand for ingot and be prepared to supply them. Nothing compelled it to keep doubling and redoubling its capacity before others entered the field. It insists that it has never excluded competitors; but we can think of no more effective exclusion than progressively to embrace each new opportunity as it opened, and to face every newcomer with new capacity already geared into a great organization, having the advantage of experience, trade connections and the elite of personnel.

There are two types of nonprofit organizations where desire for monopolistic power is most evident as a legitimate and size-dependent motive. One is the labor union: the more members, the greater the union's bargaining power. The other is the military defense organization: the more troops, planes, and ships, the greater the retaliatory power. Otherwise, there is certainly no consensus that power increases uniformly with the size of the organization. Analysts have argued that union bargaining power rests with specific subgroups of employees and that once these employees have organized, there is no advantage, and there may be disadvantages, in organizing other employees. One major change in United States defense policy was recognition that 'massive retaliation' was an inflexible strategy.

(9) Stability

As pointed out above, large organizations tend to face more stable environments than do small ones, the basis for this statement being that the variance of a sample mean decreases as the sample size increases. This has some obvious consequences for capacity-oriented costs like warehouse space; it has even more immediate consequences for the peace of mind of organizational members. In large organizations, daily variations in the numbers of orders processed, numbers of letters typed, labor used for production, and so forth are proportionately less than the corresponding variations in smaller organizations. This means work loads can be more balanced and scheduling less painful.

A desire for stability may be a very important consideration in choosing a direction for growth. Diversification of activity is often sought in expansion, whether by business firms or by military organizations. Katona (1951: 204) observed that:

We engage in business in order to make money, which we desire, need, and plan to use for the sake of other more basic or more immediate satisfactions. In certain circumstances, the means may become ends, and we may strive for profits for the sake of profits themselves. More generally, however, the desire for security implies striving for continuous, regular income rather than short-period maximum profits.

Stability is one goal that has active support from nonownership elements in an organizational coalition. Labor unions seek stable employment in collective bargaining, and contracts with suppliers may call for stable usage of raw materials. Although a desire for stable production rates and workloads does not necessarily imply expansion, it tends to block contraction and to focus expansion choices on contracyclical alternatives.

That large organizations actually achieved more stable levels of income was shown by Osborn (1951: 93), who found that:

... both the rate of profit for the income corporations and the rate of loss suffered by no-income corporations vary inversely with size. Which size group is the most profitable depends to a considerable degree on the proportion of corporations of each size which falls in the no-income category. During the shift from depression to prosperity the percentage of unprofitable small firms decreases the most rapidly and the most profitable over-all size likewise declines.

In short, large corporations were the most profitable size group during a depression and the least profitable during a boom; small corporations were the most profitable size group during a boom and the least profitable during a depression.

(10) Survival

The importance of survival to an organization cannot be overstated—at least as a logical necessity. An organization may not maximize profit or minimize cost. It may not impart prestige, power, and security to its members. It may not do many things. However, one thing that it must do, if it is to be an organization at all, is survive. As Barnard (1938: 251–252) pointed out:

Thus in every organization there is a quadruple economy: (1) physical energies and materials contributed by members and derived by its work upon the environment, and expended on the environment and given to its members; (2) the individual economy; (3) the social utilities related to the social environment; and (4) a complex and comprehensive economy of the organization under which both material services and social services are contributed by members and material things are secured from the environment, and material is given to the environment and material and social satisfactions to the members. The only measure of this economy is the survival of the organization. If it grows it is clearly efficient, if it is contracting it is doubtfully efficient, and it may in the end prove to have been during the period of contraction inefficient.[11]

A statement like Barnard's implies that survival is difficult, and hence that a high level of efficiency is required. This can soon lead to a 'survival of the fittest' point of view (Alchian 1950; Enke 1951; Winter 1964). Nearly all organizations find survival easy nearly all the time.[12]

When survival is at stake, large size can be advantageous. Business failures occur primarily among small firms (Steindl 1945). An error that a large organization might take in stride can wipe out the resources of a small one (Whitin and Peston 1954). It may be that large organizations are no more profitable than small ones because they absorb potential profits as 'slack' and thus have cushions against the shocks of adverse events (Williamson 1963). One might conjecture that small firms take commensurately small risks and that the average loss incurred is proportionate to organizational size. Two points discount this. First, average loss is not important. What matters is a very large loss in the tail of the probability distribution—like the statistician who drowned in a creek that averaged only six inches in depth. Second, small organizations are neither more omniscient nor wiser than large ones in choosing low-risk alternatives, and may very well be less so. Small businesses indicate that this is a source of concern to them.

One reason survival correlates with size is the relation between size and age. Large organizations tend to be older than small ones; they have accumulated more knowledge about the problems they are likely to encounter and they employ personnel that are more experienced. Woodruff and Alexander (1958: 117) reported in their study of small firms that 'new and untried management was a worse longevity risk than management with a number of years experience behind it. The median age of the unsuccessful management was about three years, whereas the median age of successful management was about 22 years.' Crum (1953: 105) concluded that there was 'overwhelming support for the conclusions that young corporations are more liable to suffer deficits than older corporations, and that the age structure of corporations showing a deficit is younger—more steeply J-shaped—than that of corporations showing a profit'.[13] Crum (1953: 135) also found that 'the chance of death generally declines with increasing age until age reaches more than fifty-five years'.

When an organization gets into trouble, it often needs support from outside sources. Older, larger organizations find such support easier to obtain than do younger, smaller ones. This applies in particular to capital. Small firms often find borrowing difficult even when they are profitable (Steindl 1945; Woodruff and Alexander 1958). When the going gets rough, capital markets may disappear altogether (Heller 1951). Old, large organizations benefit from customary financial relationships, long-time customers who pay their bills quickly, and long-time suppliers who extend credit.[14]

Goals and Results

Ten goals have been reviewed, attainment of which may depend upon organizational growth or may produce growth as a by-product. Three of these goals are rooted in the self-interest of individual organizational members: an urge for adventure and risk; a desire for prestige, power, and job security; and a desire for higher executive salaries. Three are rooted in the problems and aesthetics of managing an organization: the desires for a stable environment, for 'organizational self-realization', and for organizational survival. Four are rooted in organizational purpose and effectiveness: the desires for high profit and revenue, for low cost, and for monopolistic power.

Some of these goals likely characterize certain types of organizations and not others, and some goals may be more highly correlated with growth than others. Certainly, such relationships must exist. However, the data are fragmentary and the methodological problems are great. In particular:

1. Rarely do people speak frankly of their motives. One is more likely to get answers about mores than motives. Suppose a minister is asked why she wants her church to grow. The probability that she would say 'large churches pay more than small ones' is practically zero, whatever her personal feelings.

2. It is difficult to compare the goals of diverse organizations. Voluntary organizations often talk as if members' time is a free good, and as if numbers of members indicate revenue. Yet these organizations decide not to undertake activities because 'they would take more time than they're worth' and leaders debate whether to appoint committees 'to get more people involved' or to do tasks themselves 'to get them done'. Do such discussions suggest that members' time has a cost? Is a profit goal implicit?

3. To distinguish cause from effect is all but impossible. The relations between goals and results integrate environmental effects, and people learn to pursue realistic goals. If growth is difficult, the organization will tend to pursue goals that are not growth-oriented, whereas if growth is easy, the organization will learn to pursue growth-oriented goals. What one observes are the learned goals. Do these goals produce growth, or does growth produce these goals?

Dent (1959) attempted to relate the goals of business firms to organizational size, structure, and growth rate. His study raised questions rather than answered them, but it indicated interesting relationships exist. Dent asked 145 chief executives: 'What are the aims of top management in your company?' He took responses at face value. Table 1.2 shows the frequencies of various responses.

The second response (to provide a good product; to provide a public service) is ambiguous. Dent seems to have interpreted it as an expression of altruism, and Gordon (1945) reported that some executives have altruistic motives. However, conversations with business people suggest that this may have been a statement about sales strategy—about product quality as a subgoal that contributes to high revenue. For example, a banker said he was in business to provide a public service, but the banker's actions revealed this to be an injunction to himself about the best frame of mind for dealing with customers and not a reason for being in business.

Dent correlated the goal responses with three variables: (*a*) total employment; (*b*) the proportion of employment that is white-collar, professional, or supervisory; and (*c*) the average annual increase in total employment. Noteworthy correlations were as follows:

1. The proportion replying 'to provide a good product, etc.' increased with total employment. This proportion was essentially the same for all size categories greater than 100. The correlation with employment arose because firms with less than 100 employees gave this response much less frequently than did firms with more than 100 employees.

2. Among unionized firms, the proportion replying 'to provide employee welfare' increased with total employment.

3. Among nonunionized firms, the proportion replying 'to provide employee welfare' decreased as total employment increased.

4. The proportion replying 'to make money or profit' decreased as the percent white-collar increased.

Table 1.2. Executives' goals[a]

Goal	Percentages of executives mentioning goal	
	First goal mentioned	Among first three goals mentioned
To make money or profit	36	52
To provide a good product; to provide a public service	21	39
To provide employee welfare	5	39
To grow	12	17
To run or develop the organization	9	14
To meet or stay ahead of the competition	5	13
To be efficient	4	12
To pay dividends to the stockholders	1	9
Miscellaneous	7	18

[a] From Dent (1959).

5. The proportion replying 'to grow' increased with the percent white-collar. The decrease in 'to make money' responses and the increase in 'to grow' responses might have represented a transfer; Dent did not report the proportion giving both responses, but the sum of the proportion replying 'to make money' and the proportion replying 'to grow' was almost constant. This suggests the two responses were partially synonymous.

6. The proportion replying 'to provide a good product, etc.' increased with growth rate.

7. The proportion replying 'to meet or stay ahead of the competition' increased with growth rate.

8. The proportion replying 'to run or develop the organization' decreased as the growth rate increased.

9. In an unpublished reanalysis of these data, Dent found that the proportion replying 'to make money or profit' decreased as the growth rate increased.

Each of Dent's findings has several interpretations, but without further data, one can only conjecture. Consider for example the eighth finding: Executives in organizations that were growing slowly or declining in size said they were trying to run or develop the organization; executives in organizations that were growing rapidly did not mention this problem. One possibility is that slow-growing organizations had organizational problems and the stockholders had chosen executives who were conscious of these problems. This would imply that Dent was interviewing remedial managements and reported a consequence, not a cause, of slow growth. A second possibility is that slow-growing organizations had outlived their economic usefulness and had found no new functions, and that their executives were trying to hold the organizations together as long as possible, perhaps in the hope of finding new functions. Again, this would imply that the goal responses were a consequence of slow growth, but one should interpret the word 'develop' loosely. A third possibility is that organizational development was not an effective goal to pursue from the viewpoint of growth; perhaps when executives devoted their attention to developing the organization, they were diverting energy from the more effective goals 'to meet or stay ahead of the competition' and 'to provide a good product, etc.' This would imply that the goal 'to run or develop the organization' was a cause of slow growth. A fourth possibility is that organization-conscious executives were poor managers, more concerned with methods than results. Woodward (1958: 38–39) concluded from case studies of three firms:

The 'organization conscious' firms tended to draw on the concepts of management theory, irrespective of how appropriate they were to the technical situation. . . .

The most successful firms are thus likely to be the 'organization conscious' firms, in which formal organization is appropriate to the technical situation. Next would come the less 'organization conscious' firms, where informal organization mainly determines the pattern of relationships. The least successful firms are likely to be the 'organization conscious' firms, where formal organization is inappropriate and deviates from informal organization.

This interpretation implies that the goal responses correlated with a cause of slow growth.

Other conjectures are possible about the nature of Dent's eighth finding, and the number of conjectures that could be advanced about all nine findings is enormous. One can even ask why certain relationships were *not* visible. What is needed are data that untangle the causal relationships.[15]

3. ADAPTATION AND GROWTH

The presence of growth-oriented motives is not sufficient to produce expansion. For such motives to find expression in the organization's behavior strategies, they must overcome other motives that imply decreasing organizational size or maintaining the status quo. The ultimate behavior patterns arise from bargaining and problem solving in which motives that promote growth conflict with motives that inhibit growth.

An organization's environment stages this conflict and decides its resolution. The environment supplies the human raw materials and determines their mores and aspirations, their standards for the conduct of conflict, their attitudes toward authority. Even taking organizational personnel and their goals as given, the environment determines whether these goals can best be satisfied by expansion or by contraction. For instance, the relationship between profit and employment depends on the firm's demand and cost curves, which in turn depend on characteristics of the consuming population, actions of competing firms, available technologies, alternative markets for raw materials, and so forth.

Clearly, environmental effects are ubiquitous. One can say nothing about an organization without also saying something about its environment, and an organization's need for satisfactory interactive relationships with its environment is inescapable. For example, to attempt a thorough review of effects of geographic location on organizations would require another chapter at least as long as this one.[16]

This section discusses some specific determinants of an organization's ability to establish effective and viable relationships with its environment, to adapt. Adaptation is an obvious precondition for survival, and survival is an obvious precondition for growth. All aspects of organizations that affect adaptation are relevant, which means everything written about organizations is relevant. To bound the subject, three constraints are observed. First, discussion concentrates on topics that relate directly to organizational size and age. Second, only long-run, gross adaptation is considered. Third, the focus is on an organization itself rather than its environment. As Dill (1962: 96) pointed out:

... our best strategy for analyzing the environment is probably not to try to understand it as a collection of systems and organizations external to the one we are studying. We seldom have enough data to do an adequate job of this. Instead, we can view the environment as it affects the organization which we are studying. We treat the environment as information which becomes available to the organization or to which the organization, via search activity, may get access.

The Effectiveness of Behavior Strategies

Because an organization's environment determines the effectiveness of behavior strategies, most organizations, at one time or another, attempt to manipulate their environments to make them more munificent. They advertise new products, train new employees, and undertake research to improve manufacturing techniques (Brown 1957). Some, like the Communist party in Russia, have sufficient power and longevity to begin educating an entire nation in values consistent with increased organizational size and power.

Large organizations have more leverage over their environments than small organizations do. As Carter and Williams (1959: 69) put it: 'A big firm can change or ignore its environment; a small firm depends much more on the existence of facilities provided by others.'

At least for innovation of manufacturing techniques, one can document the advantage of large firms. Their advantage begins with spending for research and development. They spend more per employee; they employ more scientists; they spend more per scientist; and they give each scientist more technical assistance.[17] Mansfield traced results of this spending: Spending on research and development correlated with the numbers of innovations introduced (Mansfield 1964). Hence, 'the length of time a firm waits before using a new technique tends to be inversely related to its size', and in fact, 'as a firm's size increases, the length of time it waits tends to decrease at an increasing rate' (Mansfield 1963*b*: 291–292).[18] Apparently, size of firm was the only organizational characteristic correlated with readiness to innovate; the firm's growth rate, its profitability, its liquidity, and the age of its president did not correlate with innovation (Mansfield 1963*b*).[19] A lack of correlation between innovation and growth rate only applied to firms' growth rates *before* they introduced innovations; although innovators had the same growth rates as noninnovators before they innovated, they grew faster than noninnovators *after* they innovated (Mansfield 1962). However, the relation between innovation and firm size was not consistent; no class of firms was always the innovating group (Mansfield 1963*b*). There seemed to be differences among industries in the innovative leadership shown by the large firms. Mansfield surmised that there would have been less innovation in the petroleum and bituminous coal industries if the large firms had been broken up into smaller firms, but there would have been more innovation in the steel industry if the large firms had been broken up into smaller ones (Mansfield 1963*c*).

Very few organizations can make major changes in their environments, especially in the short run. The impact of an individual organization is severely limited—sometimes by law, as in the case of antitrust legislation—sometimes by powerful competing organizations, as in the case of the American political parties—sometimes by ignorance, as in the case of technological innovation—and always by the massive inertia of the existing structure, as in the case of the Russian Communist party. There may be some advantage in taking an aggressive position toward the environment. As Mansfield's studies showed, aggressive organizations often gain advantages over nonaggressive organizations, but the overriding problem of all organizations is adjusting to and exploiting resources that exist.

In principle, an organization can expand as long as it discovers strategies that elicit additional resources by satisfying some need of society. Thus, an organization that can continuously generate new, successful strategies can expand indefinitely. That is in principle; in fact it does not happen.

For one thing, most organizations specialize. They voluntarily adhere to a limited range of behavior strategies: production of a specific class of products, employment of a specific type of employee, utilization of a specific production methodology. Specialization provides a degree of insulation from the actions of competing organizations (Chamberlin 1950). For instance, American Motors was able to survive and prosper by differentiating its product from those of General Motors and Ford and cultivating a consumer subgroup, whereas Studebaker-Packard persisted in trying to compete directly with larger firms, and failed. Another reason for specialization is that an organization originates to pursue specific and limited goals, examples being the Townsend Movement and the Woman's Christian Temperance Union. These limited-charter organizations often break out of their original molds and pursue what Blau (1955: 195) called a 'succession of organizational goals'.

The attainment of organizational objectives generates a strain toward finding new objectives. To provide incentives for its existence, an organization has to adopt new goals as its old ones are realized.

However, not all organizations that might benefit from a change in the bases for their specialization actually do change. McGuire (1963: 54) reported:

There is considerably more product rigidity among manufacturing firms than many business scholars would expect. Respondents to the investigation into the growth patterns of 270 manufacturing firms were asked if substantial changes had been made in their products in the past [1950–1959]. Only 8.5 percent indicated a major change in product line; 91.5 percent noted that they had not made such alterations. To a certain extent, this rigidity may have been caused by investment in specialized equipment and plant, so that many firms could not change products except at a cost which they considered too exorbitant. In other instances, it seemed evident that businessmen simply lacked imagination to change and remained with their one product even though sales were declining, even when it appeared reasonable for them to change at least to similar but more profitable products.

Still another reason for specialization is an organization's desire for internal consistency as a basis for coordination and control. Communication among members requires a common language and comparable experiences, superiors must be able to understand their subordinates' problems, and normal managerial succession must not alter goals and operating procedures drastically. The importance of this restriction on organizational diversity becomes increasingly apparent as an organization grows. Haire (1959) stressed 'centrifugal' effects of large size, and Clark (1956) and Kaufman (1960) discussed some divisive effects of geographic dispersion. One can find 'organizations' that do not display internal consistency and that do not attempt to coordinate activities of their subunits, but the word 'organization' is misapplied in such cases.

It may be that specialization in terms of a methodology is less restrictive to growth than specialization in terms of an end product. Chandler (1962: 391) concluded that 'the enterprises whose resources were the most transferable remained those whose men and equipment came to handle a range of technology rather than a set of end products'. Moreover, Sills (1957: 270) stated:

In the final analysis, however, the most compelling reason for predicting that the Foundation will in the future make a successful adjustment to the achievement of its major goal is that the organization has in fact *already* been transformed, in large part by its Volunteers, into something other than a special purpose association. . . . Since the Foundation includes among its Volunteers so many who are able to conceptualize their involvement in terms of its ultimate implications (for themselves, or for society as a whole), rather than only in terms of a limited, pragmatic goal, it has already become an organization as deeply committed to its mode of operation as to its current purposes. In a word, it is an organization which is as committed to a means as it is to an end.

Nevertheless, there are serious logical problems in this proposition. First, changes in methodology are pervasive and gradual. There may be a tendency to overestimate the stability of methodologies and to classify observed changes as 'improvements'. If methodologies actually change as extensively and rapidly as products, one cannot say that the organization specializes in either. Second, whenever an organization changes its behavior, some characteristics of its behavior do not change and, in that sense, every organization specializes in something. There may be a tendency to classify the constants in behavior as methods and the variables as products, particularly when correlating changes in behavior with environmental changes, because one thinks of products as falling on the 'boundary' between organization and environment and thinks of methodologies as being 'internal' to an organization.

Another constraint on an organization's ability to generate new, successful strategies comes from conflict among strategies. When an organization adopts one class of strategies, it makes other strategies difficult or impossible. This situation is evident in political party platforms. When the Republican Party espoused emancipation, its subsequent adoption of a states' rights view became less than credible to Southern voters. Selznick (1949) reported another example. TVA's adoption of the 'grass-roots theory' brought the support of local agencies and helped TVA achieve local success, but the policy also alienated the Department of Agriculture, which blocked TVA's expansion outside the Tennessee Valley.

Selznick's book stressed the strategic value co-opting the environment, including forming coalitions with other organizations. Judiciously applied, co-optation can strengthen an organization's power to survive and grow. Elling and Halebsky (1961) found that voluntary hospitals that allied with their communities' social structures increased the value of their facilities greatly, whereas the value of facilities in governmentally supported hospitals tended to remain constant. Blankenship and Elling (1962) noted that it was important for voluntary hospitals to form alliances with powerful, upper-class members of a community rather than middle- or lower-class members. Co-optation can be helpful because it usually constitutes one half of an exchange. An organization gives up some of its autonomy in exchange for influence in the decisions of other organizations (e.g. protection from certain kinds of competition) or access to environmental resources (e.g. financing, technical expertise). However, co-optation can be expensive. One hospital in the Blankenship and Elling study nearly co-opted itself out of existence: Its board decided there were too many hospitals in the community.[20]

Attitudes Toward Change

Attitudes of organizational members toward change are crucial in the growth process. Growth is a type of organizational change and a growing organization must adjust to environmental change. In fact, growth may depend upon an organization's ability to exploit opportunities created by environmental change.

Organizational rigidity is rooted in the inducements–contributions balance of an organization. Members of an organization receive inducements in exchange for their contributions. These inducements include salaries and statuses, the pleasures of performing tasks in particular and familiar ways and of associating with particular and familiar people, and the satisfactions of contributing to accomplishment of specific goals and of molding organizational goals to personal value systems. Changes in an organization often imply new salaries, statuses, personnel, methods, and goals, so members who stand to lose by such changes resist them. Even changes that would have insignificant long-run effects can incur opposition because of their transient effects (Coch and French 1948).

Resistance to change can take several forms. Resisters can reduce their contributions to match the reduced inducements being offered to them. Not infrequently, those who initiate changes anticipate such reactions and view them as desirable consequences; more frequently, reduced contributions are unanticipated or considered undesirable. Resisters exit the organization; small reductions in inducements can trigger withdrawal if an affected individual perceives favorable alternatives outside the organization. Withdrawals offer an organization opportunities to enlist new members whose value systems are more compatible with the altered organizational structure, but new members must become acclimated, learn their tasks, and develop satisfactory personal relationships with other members, and the time required for this absorption delays organizational growth. Finally, resisters may take direct action to persuade or force an organization to adhere to its existing structure. When backed by sufficient power, direct resistance can be quite effective, as 'featherbedding' on railroads testifies.[21]

Overt changes in inducements are not the only way that the inducements–contributions balance may be upset. Many organizational inducements derive their values from the environment, and as the environment changes, these inducements can lose value. An example is the effect of inflation on wages. Diamond (1958) reported the case of an organization that dissolved into a society because intraorganizational statuses were the only inducements it offered and, over time, extraorganizational wealth and social mobility deprived intraorganizational statuses of their value.

Organizational rigidity can be overemphasized. In fact, gradual change may be welcome. McClelland and associates (1953) postulated that small displacements from the 'adaptation level' trigger positive affect and that large displacements trigger negative affect. This suggests that an optimum rate of change may exist and that organizational members will be unhappy in both overly stable and overly variable environments.[22] In one study, Blau found that both the 'progressive ideology' of members and boredom after mastering tasks favored change, and he (1955: 197) concluded that 'opposition to change in the organization, while apparently indicating perfect accommodation to existing conditions, is actually the result of insufficient adaptation to them. Newcomers, who had not yet become adapted, as well as less competent officials, felt threatened by change.' Sofer (1961) claimed that once an organization has changed, it is inclined to 'overvalue novelty' and to undervalue 'much that was functional and positive in their past'. This suggests that an organization's concept of its optimum rate of change depends upon its experience, and that acceleration of change, not velocity of change, is the main factor that evokes resistance.

Bonini constructed a hypothetical, computerized model of the firm and examined effects of assorted changes in this organization's structure and environment. He found that variability of the environment had very significant impacts on the organization's behavior. Firms in highly variable environments had lower costs and prices and higher sales, inventories, and profits than firms in stable environments.

It is fairly easy to postulate how large amounts of variability could lead, in the real world, to a more profitable firm. Firms existing in a relatively stable environment may be sluggish in adjusting to new conditions, in taking advantage of market opportunities, and in introducing new technology. On the other hand, firms which live in a constantly fluctuating world may be quicker to sense and seize opportunities. The existence of large downswings sometimes forces the firm to seek these opportunities or perish. (Bohini 1963: 135–136)

The proposition that young organizations are less rigid than old organizations has had wide acceptance. Certainly, the proposition sounds plausible. Young organizations are probably more accustomed to change, and the members of young organizations may not yet be enamored of specific goals, activities, and social relationships. On the other hand, Cohen (1961: 124, 128) concluded from a series of experiments with small-group communication networks:

The most important results of the six studies viewed as a unit is that problem-solving groups selectively modify their methods of dealing with a task by calling upon their preceding experiences. Transfer of training and rationality are general concepts useful in understanding these results.

Transfer of training, though used in many contexts, refers basically to the human tendency to respond to new and separate events by placing them in classes for which attitudes and procedures already exist. Previous experience is essential: If a group knows only one way of performing a task, it tends to continue this practice without critical examination. Inexperienced groups, therefore, generally have no tradition of critical evaluation, view change as disruptive and unrewarding, find sharing the responsibility for modifying the environment difficult, lack knowledge concerning alternative methods, and have no means of perceiving some other procedure as more efficient than the one which they are using.

Systematic evidence about relations between organizational age and flexibility is virtually nonexistent. As reported above, Mansfield's studies indicated that large (old?) firms were likely to try new production techniques first. However, Mansfield (1963a: 358) published another study with different implications. Considering the speed with which firms took full advantage of innovations, he found that 'small firms, once they begin, are at least as quick to substitute new techniques for old as their larger rivals'. Mansfield's work concerned the adoption of new *production* techniques. Discussions of *product* innovation have been inclined to the opinion, which Nelson (1959) summarized, that 'established firms, even progressive established firms, are usually backward about radically new inventions'. Nelson cited several case studies as examples and Jewkes, Sawers, and Stillerman (1959: 189–190) reported similar anecdotes. However, small firms may not be less myopic than large ones when it comes to 'radically new inventions'. Carter and Williams (1959: 63–65) suggested that small firms may have advantages over large firms when it comes to unradical new inventions. Thompson and Bates (1957) and Wilson (1966) posed hypotheses relating organizational structure and innovation.

Young organizations and old ones likely differ in the *kinds* of change that they resist. In particular, old organizations may be more flexible with respect to changes in their ultimate goals, and young organizations may be more flexible with respect to changes in their social structures. With the possible exception of young voluntary organizations, both young and old organizations likely resist changes in their task structures.

One can distinguish three kinds of change: change in ultimate goals, change in task structure, and change in social structure. Each corresponds to a reason for organizational membership. Members may value an organization's goals; they may value activities that they perform in its task structure; or they may value interactions they experienced in its social structure. A member who greatly values factor A is likely to resist changes in factor A and to resist changes in factors B and C that would devaluate factor A, but this member is likely to support changes in factors B and C that would enhance factor A. Thus, a member who values the goals of an organization will resist changes in these goals as well as changes in the organization's task structure and social structure that seem to impede accomplishment of these goals, but the member will support changes in the task and social structures that seem to further these goals. Task structure is usually an intervening variable between goals and social structure. Changes in goals tend to have direct effects on task structure, but to affect social structure only indirectly. Changes in social structure tend to have direct effects on task structure but to affect goals only indirectly. Changes in task structure tend to have direct effects on both goals and social structure.

Members of new organizations and new members of old organizations tend to value either goals or task structures, and they tend not to value social structures. The relative balance between interest in goals and interest in task structure varies with the type of organization. In nonvoluntary organizations like business firms, most new members value aspects of the task structures: activities they perform, statuses they hold, salaries they receive. In voluntary organizations, like the National Foundation, most new members value the organizations' goals (Tsouderos 1955). New members of nonvoluntary organizations should feel secondary commitments to their organizations' goals because of the effects of goal change on task structure, and new members of voluntary organizations should feel secondary commitments to their organizations' task structures both because changes in task structures affect goals and because they like aspects of the task structures. Although the variable that determines the natures of these primary and secondary commitments is the newness of organizational membership, one associates them with young organizations because young organizations contain many new members.

As organizations age, their members' central commitments shift toward the organizations' social structures. There are three reasons for this shift. The first is that members become acquainted with one another: friendships spring up, social roles stabilize and members incorporate them into their expectations, and positions in the task structure become associated with the individuals who hold them.

The second reason for this shift is that organizations typically try to promote organizational loyalty among their members. They set up indoctrination programs for new employees; they publish organizational newspapers that stress the accomplishments of the organizations and of individual members; they withhold responsibility from new members and reward seniority with promotions and special awards; they require members to learn organizational songs and creeds; they make intraorganizational statuses central in their inducement schemes; they put uniforms on members to distinguish them from nonmembers; they change members' geographic assignments so that extraorganizational loyalties are disrupted; they adopt paternalistic policies that provide for members' health, recreation, retirement, and death (Kaufman 1960; W. H. Whyte 1956). The net effect of most of these loyalty-inducing activities is to strengthen members' commitments to the organizations' social structures and to dilute their commitments to specific goals and specific aspects of the task structures. Simon (1957*a*: 118) observed: 'The individual who is loyal to the *objectives* of the organization will resist modification of those objectives, and may even refuse to continue his participation if they are changed too radically. The individual who is loyal to the *organ-*

ization will support opportunistic changes in its objectives that are calculated to promote its survival and growth.'[23] In addition, Blau and Scott (1962: 60–74) concluded that 'there is an inverse relationship between professional commitment and organizational loyalty'.

The third reason for shifting commitments, or possibly another aspect of the second reason, is that members who are committed to organizations' social structures tend to move into central positions for policy determination. In nonvoluntary organizations, this is a two-way process: Organizations tend to promote members who have long tenure, are well integrated in the social structures, and are strongly committed to their organizations per se. Conversely, organizations concentrate loyalty-inducing activities on central members by changing their job assignments frequently, giving special recognition to their accomplishments, and offering them greater inducements than would other organizations. Similar processes occur in voluntary organizations, but migration of inactive members out of voluntary organizations increases the emphasis on social structures; active members of voluntary organizations tend to have strong commitments to social structures and weak commitments to goals and tasks. For example, several studies have indicated that active members of labor unions had little, if any, commitment to the labor movement in general and felt no antagonism toward their employers (Dean 1954–1955; Lipset, Trow, and Coleman 1956; Spinrad 1960; and Tannenbaum and Kahn 1958). As compared to inactive union members, the active members had greater seniority in their jobs, were more highly skilled, earned higher pay, and were more satisfied with their work environments. What made the active union members active was a sense of social cohesiveness: they were long-time residents of their communities and were acquainted with their coworkers; they had no desire for social mobility and escape from their class; they enjoyed social interaction. Of course, the facilitating conditions for and manifest degrees of organizational loyalty vary greatly among cultures. Some decades ago, Abegglen (1958: 11) reported:

At whatever level of organization in the Japanese factory, the worker commits himself on entrance to the company for the remainder of his working career. The company will not discharge him even temporarily except in the most extreme circumstances. He will not quit the company for industrial employment elsewhere.

Thus, the members of old organizations, at least those who have been around awhile, tend to focus their commitments on the organizations' social structures. This tendency is probably stronger in voluntary organizations than nonvoluntary ones, but social structures are often primary commitments in both types of organizations. Also in both types of organizations, members tend to have secondary commitments to task structures because changes in task structures affect social structures. Table 1.3 summarizes the preceding analysis.

From the above, one would expect old organizations to treat their goals opportunistically. Goal-setting becomes, as Thompson and McEwen (1958: 23) characterized it, the problem of 'determining a relationship of the organization to the larger society, which in turn becomes a question of what the society (or

Table 1.3. Conjectures about resistance to change

| Type of Organization: | Types of change most likely to be resisted | | Type of change most likely to be supported |
	Primary	Secondary	
Young voluntary	Goals	Task structure	Social structure
Young nonvoluntary	Task structure	Goals	Social structure
Old	Social structure	Task structure	Goals

elements within it) wants done or can be persuaded to support'. Goal flexibility is most apparent when organizational survival is threatened, and when an old *voluntary* organization (where dominance of social structure over goals is clearest) is in danger, the changes are often dramatic. Messinger's study of the Townsend Movement is one of the best-known documentations. Originally, the movement was purely political and refused to support other groups having aims that were more conservative. After the number of members and the amount of financial support dwindled, the movement began to accept compromise of its 'full program', it undertook the merchandising of health foods and vitamins, and it emphasized social rather than business activities at meetings. Messinger (1955: 9–10) summarized his findings as follows:

In the ascendant phases, when social forces press for reconstruction and changes are still in the offing, the concern of leaders and members of social movements alike is with those things that must be done to translate discontent into effective and concerted action. An evident condition of this orientation is discontent itself. In turn, this discontent must be supplied or renewed by social forces which, it must be believed, can be ameliorated by banding together. These provide the dynamic of value-oriented social movements, as well as the characteristic missions with which their organized arms become identified.

When the movements themselves lose impetus through a shift in the constellation of social forces, their organized arms are deprived of conditions necessary to sustain them in their original form. But organizations are not necessarily dissolved by the abatement of the forces initially conjoining to produce them. They may gain a certain degree of autonomy from their bases and continue to exist. We will expect, however, that the abatement of the particular constellation of social forces giving rise to the movement will have important consequences for the remaining structure. The most general of these is, perhaps, increasing lack of public concern for the organizational mission. This is reflected in the ending of public discussion of the issues which the organization represents or, perhaps better put, with these issues in the frame of reference that they are placed by organizational representatives. Within the organization, the abatement of social forces spells dropping membership and, more serious in the long run, the end of effective recruitment. This latter may be reinforced by the development of alternative organizational structures competing for the same potential membership. The end of recruitment is quickly transformed into financial difficulty. Where the organization has been geared to financial support from its own adherents, this last consequence will be especially crucial.

The organized arms of declining social movements will tend to adapt to these changed conditions in characteristic ways. We can broadly describe this adaptation by asserting that the dominating orientation of leaders and members shifts *from the implementation of the values the organization is taken to represent* (by leaders, members, and public alike), *to maintaining the organizational structure as such*, even at the loss of the organization's central mission. To this end, leaders will be constrained to direct action toward new issues or in new ways which will attenuate the organization's identification with the particular set of aims held to be central to it. In this process, the locus of issue-selection will tend to move outside the organization, to alternative leaderships who highlighted the growing irrelevance to most of the traditional central mission. Presumably, a new mission may be found. Where this is not the case, leaders will be forced to search out new means of financing as the traditional mode of appeal and reap falls on fewer and deafer ears. In this process, members, and especially potential members, will cease to be regarded as 'converts' and will come to be seen as 'customers'. Finally, membership activities, initiated in a context of declining public interest to support a faltering organization, will work to turn what were once the incidental rewards of participation into its only meaning. This last, by altering the basis for whatever recruitment may take place, would seem to insure that the organization, if it continues to exist, will be changed from a value-implementing agency to a recreation facility. In sum, the organizational character will stand transformed.[24]

The Formalization Process

The rapid and dramatic changes in the Townsend Movement during the postwar period were not changes in goals.[25] Accomplishment of the organization's political program was a goal at the time of the organization's founding. Perhaps consensus made it the only goal. Over the years, members' commitments shifted from the political program to the organization's social structure. By the time the organization's survival was threatened, members looked upon the political program as a subgoal, as a means to organizational persistence, and not as an ultimate goal. The postwar transition would not have been possible without the gradual shifting of members' commitments that constituted the basic change in the organization's goals. When commitments to the social structure began to dominate, organizational persistence became a goal beyond and apart from any specific operations performed.

Members' commitments began shifting during the first months of the organization's existence. The shift probably began shortly after the initial expansion of membership but before income actually declined. It is during this early period that an organization starts to gel as an organization: statuses and roles are assigned; passive members begin to depart; and active members make commitments to the organization (Simon 1953). Tsouderos (1955) called this process 'formalization'. In his study of ten voluntary organizations, he found that the number of members was a leading variable in the overall pattern of expansion and contraction from organizational birth to death. Income lagged membership, and administrative expense lagged income. He hypothesized that formalization begins when the number of members starts to fall, but while income and administrative expense are still rising.[26]

Interviews by McGuire supported Tsouderos's lead-lag findings. McGuire (1963: 67) said:

There is a considerable time lag between the growth of numbers of production workers and the expansion in employment of other personnel. The majority of firms interviewed with sales under $100,000 added to their production work forces as sales mounted. Typically, however, they did not add to their managerial personnel or to their clerical staff below this level of sales, regardless of how rapidly sales were expanding.... In smaller firms, therefore, there appeared to be a much closer correlation between production workers and [sales] than between non-production workers and [sales].

However, Tsouderos's hypothesis about the onset of formalization, if correct at all, may be correct only for voluntary organizations. An initial burst of membership expansion due to newly aroused interest in the objectives of the organization is not characteristic of nonvoluntary organizations. In the latter, expansion of total employment is likely to continue for decades after formalization begins.

The formalization process continues as an organization gets older and larger, though the earliest manifestations of formalization are the most striking ones. Patterns of behavior stabilize; individuals settle into characteristic roles; standard operating procedures develop. The most significant characteristic of this advance is that it represents organizational learning—the learning of a formal organizational structure expressive of the problems that must be solved and rationales for solving them. The formal structure provides a framework for dividing labor, specializing, delegating responsibilities, systematizing routine communications, and allocating inducements. Imitation plays a part in the creation of structure and, to the extent that different organizations have unique problems, imitation may lead to inappropriate structural elements. However, organizations imitate with awareness and structural consistencies among organizations reflect similarities in problems. For instance, after interviewing the executives of 106 small manufacturing firms, Wickesberg (1961: 54) concluded:

There was hesitancy... to embark on organizational changes, such as formation of formal functional units or use of committees or outside agencies, when little or nothing was known or could be demonstrated concerning the probable net gain to the firm.

Wickesberg obtained information about the probable sequence in which formal specialization develops in small manufacturing firms. He reported on the appearance of formal internal subunits and on the employment of outside service agencies as functions of firms' sizes and ages. Since he gave no basis for separating the effects of size from the effects of age, only findings where size is the independent variable are listed here:

1. The number of formal subunits increased with size. There was a clear probability ordering over the first four subunits to appear. The first subunit established tended to be a production department; the second a sales department; the third a purchasing department; and the fourth a quality-control

department. The ordering for the fifth and subsequent subunits was more ambiguous than that for the first four.

2. The number of outside services used also increased with size. The probability ordering was clear for the first five services used, but more ambiguous for the sixth and subsequent services. The first service used tended to be an auditing service; the second a legal service; the third a personnel service; the fourth an advertising service; and the fifth a labor-relations-and-negotiations service.

Baker and Davis (1954) and Weigand (1963) also collected data on functional differentiation.

If the formalization process continues, unhindered by environmental instability, the organization ultimately becomes a bureaucracy. Merton (1957: 195–196) described this bureaucratic extreme as follows:

A formal, rationally organized social structure involves clearly defined patterns of activity in which, ideally, every series of actions is functionally related to the purposes of the organization. In such an organization there is an integrated series of offices, of hierarchized statuses, in which inhere a number of obligations and privileges closely defined by limited and specific rules. Each of these offices contains an area of imputed competence and responsibility. Authority, the power of control which derives from an acknowledged status, inheres in the office and not in the particular person who performs the official role. Official action ordinarily occurs within the framework of pre-existing rules of the organization. The system of prescribed relations between the various offices involves a considerable degree of formality and clearly defined social distance between the occupants of these positions. Formality is manifested by means of a more or less complicated social ritual which symbolizes and supports the pecking order of the various offices. Such formality, which is integrated with the distribution of authority within the system, serves to minimize friction by largely restricting (official) contact to modes which are previously defined by the rules of the organization. Ready calculability of others' behavior and a stable set of mutual expectations is thus built up. Moreover, formality facilitates the interaction of the occupants of offices despite their (possibly hostile) private attitudes toward one another. In this way, the subordinate is protected from the arbitrary action of his superior, since the actions of both are constrained by a mutually recognized set of rules. Specific procedural devices foster objectivity and restrain the 'quick passage of impulse into action.'...

The chief merit of bureaucracy is its technical efficiency, with a premium placed on precision, speed, expert control, continuity, discretion, and optimal returns on input. The structure is one which approaches the complete elimination of personalized relationships and nonrational considerations (hostility, anxiety, affectual involvements, etc.).

This is an overstatement, as the reviews by Argyris (1957) and March and Simon (1958) and Merton's own work (1940) have made clear, but it does capture the spirit behind bureaucracy.

Both Gouldner (1954) and Grusky (1961) pointed out that large organizations are less liable to disruption because of managerial succession than small organizations. They attributed this relative stability to a tendency for authority to inhere 'in the office and not in the particular person'. Grusky (1961: 269) presented data to show that 'frequency of administrative succession at the top is directly related to size of firm', and he concluded 'that succession will be rationally treated by being routinized' in large firms, and that 'because of their predispositions for stability, bureaucracies require periodic succession at the top if they are to adapt adequately to their environment'. Grusky's hypotheses make sense, but his data also are consistent with hypotheses that are more mundane. One would be that it takes longer to rise to the top in a large organization, and so people at the top are near retirement when they take office.

Bureaucracies can have irrational as well as rational characteristics. Selznick (1949) showed how delegation of authority may foster development of subunit goals that work at cross-purposes to the central goals of the organization and eventually prevent further growth. Merton (1940) pointed out that standard operating procedures can become functionally autonomous and independent of demands placed on the organization, and that impersonal reward systems can overlook individual achievement. Tsouderos (1955) noted that formalized communication procedures can be ineffective in voluntary associations. Stinchcombe (1959) and Udy (1959a) suggested that rational organizations and bureaucratic organizations are different things, although both used the term 'rational' in a highly specialized manner. Blau and Scott (1962: 206–211) provided a useful discussion of this material.

Nevertheless, such consequences fall into the 'unanticipated' category. When most organizations discover undesirable consequences of their current formal structures, they endeavor to correct these by changing their structures. One must distinguish between structural consequences that are irrational from the viewpoint of an external observer and structural consequences that are irrational from the viewpoint of the organizational members. The literature abounds with analyses of undesirable consequences by omniscient observers. Rarely do these observers recognize the possibility that their own value systems, by which they apply the term undesirable, may be quite different from the value systems of the organizational members. When such differences are recognized, the observers usually conclude that the organizational members hold the wrong values.

On the Nature of Adaptive Processes

The formalization process is fundamentally an adaptive process. As an organization grows older, it learns more and more about coping with its environment and with its internal problems of communication and coordination. At least this is the normal pattern, and a normal organization tries to perpetuate its learning by formalizing them. It sets up standard operating procedures; it routinizes reports on organizational performance; it appoints specialists in areas of consistent need; it discovers effective factorings of organizational tasks and delegates the factored components to subunits. An organization's need and capacity for formalization increase as it grows. Information that a small organization needs infrequently and can obtain informally must be supplied regularly and collected in a systematic manner. Task segments become large enough to occupy specialists. Needed supervisory activity escapes the capacity of a small group and must be delegated.

There may be evidence of organizational adaptation in Tsouderos's study. During the period of contracting membership, administrative expense, administrative employment, and the amount of property owned all rose *cyclically*. Decline in one or more of these variables could trigger adaptive changes in behavior strategies, which renew expansion. Although the variables in this hypothesis are subject to fluctuations in the economy, it seems worth investigating. Cyclical fluctuations in an organization's expansion path are predictable from the 'fire department' model of organizational decision-making that Cyert and March (1963: 119) stressed:

We assume that organizations make decisions by solving a series of problems; each problem is solved as it arises; the organization then waits for another problem to appear. Where decisions within the firm do not naturally fall into such a sequence, they are modified so that they will.

The formal structure is commonly associated with rigid and change-resistant aspects of an organization. Since one objective of the formalization process is stabilization of behavior patterns, and since formal structure includes salaries, statuses, standard procedures, and goals that offer members inducements, some association is logically necessary. However, formalization and resistance to change are not the same thing. Resistance to change is a reaction against alteration of a familiar state of affairs. Since informality and instability can become familiar and can provide inducements, they too are associated with resistance to change. That is, organizational members are inclined to resist changes that increase formality as well as changes that decrease formality.

On the other hand, every formal structure is incompatible with—or perhaps, inadequate for—certain types of change. An organization's structure is a theory. It is a model for performance of organizational tasks, and it incorporates assumptions about the causal relations in the organization and the environment. This model is at best approximate. Events will occur that the model cannot anticipate, cannot comprehend, and may not perceive. Even if these unpredicted events are perceived, the model is unlikely to suggest appropriate organizational responses. Several studies comment on this inability of organizations to predict events or to generate appropriate responses. Summarizing the opinions of nineteen experienced executives, Newman and Logan (1955: 90) wrote:

Perhaps the most striking point made regarding the need for a change is that rarely do companies foresee this need in time to prepare for it. Instead, the common situation is for firms to outgrow their old managerial practice and find a change necessary for survival.

After interviewing executives in 106 small companies, Wickesberg (1961: 53) concluded: 'Creation and designation of formalized units to perform major or related functions within the enterprise were, by-and-large, unplanned and perhaps not even anticipated in the earlier stages of organizational development.' In addition, McNulty's investigation (1962: 18) of 30 expanding firms led him to state that 'in the cases where explicit, purposeful reorganization was instituted to deal with growth in markets the results in terms of adaptation do not seem to have been clearly better than when less formal methods were used'.

Inability to foresee the future and difficulty in coping with unanticipated events are not unique to organizations. Doubtless, some organizations have better structures in that these organizations encounter unpredicted events less frequently and have less difficulty adjusting to new circumstances. Organizations cannot evolve structures that anticipate all circumstances and never confront the unforeseen, and organizations should not evolve structures that maximize flexibility and informality. A highly flexible and informal organization is poorly adapted to a stable set of problems, just as a highly inflexible and formal organization is poorly adapted to an unstable set of problems. A well-adapted organization is one that matches the stability of its problem set.

The stability of an organization's problem set is an increasing function of the organization's age. Young organizations have little experience in distinguishing important problems from unimportant ones, and few mechanisms for dealing with routine problems routinely. They perceive unstable problem sets and need flexible structures. Older organizations have learned to ignore unimportant problems, and have accumulated mechanisms for attending to routine problems. They perceive stable problem sets and need stable structures. The degree of stability that an organization tends finally to attain depends in part on the basic stability of the organization's environment and in part on the adequacy of the causal model imbedded in the organization's structure. The latter is usually a more serious constraint, but, from the organization's point of view, the two are indistinguishable.

Formalization is adaptive in still another way. It is formalization that stabilizes members' roles and positions and makes an organizational social structure possible, and it is formalization that places active, loyal members in central positions. Thus, formalization is a necessary (but not sufficient) condition for the shifting of members' commitments from specific goals and aspects of task structure to aspects of social structure. This commitment shift is adaptive. Young organizations, operating against the handicap of unstable problem sets, need strong orientations toward efficiency and goal achievement in order to survive—particularly if their larger competitors benefit from returns to scale. Old organizations, operating with stable problem sets and possibly benefiting from returns to scale themselves, do not need strong orientations toward efficiency. Old organizations risk having their original goals rendered obsolete by changing social needs, or by their success in achieving these goals, and they need to be able to look upon their original goals as changeable strategies.

Formalization is certainly not the only kind of adaptation that an organization displays. Changes in formal structure occur gradually and cannot accommodate ubiquitous short-run fluctuations in an organization's problem set. Short-run adaptation must rely on flexibilities within the decision structure and on informally evolved behavior patterns. Coalitions gel and dissolve. Operational goals shift.

Search procedures and attention rules are invented and discarded. Communication channels open and close.[27] Formal structure is like a large log floating down a turbulent stream. The log's inertia makes the log's trajectory fairly independent of swirls and eddies in the stream itself. No doubt each obstruction that the stream passes over affects the log, but what effects and how are not immediately apparent. The most obvious symptoms of adaptation are in the stream.

4. MODELS OF GROWTH

Models of organizational growth fall into four groups: (*a*) *cell-division* models and (*b*) *metamorphosis* models focus on patterns in the size and structure of an organization as it expands; (*c*) *will-o'-the-wisp* models and (*d*) *decision-process* models focus on mechanisms, internal to an organization, by which growth occurs.

This chapter discusses these model groups in a sequence corresponding to the attention they pay to adaptive processes. Cell-division models tend to concentrate on effects and to ignore causes; when described, connections between cause and effect are vague. Metamorphosis models describe both causes and effects, but again connections between cause and effect are obscure. The orientation of metamorphosis models is internal; the models describe internal problems likely to arise for organizations of different sizes and changes in organizational structure likely to result. Will-o'-the-wisp models are dynamic; they stress sequences of events and make time an explicit variable. Relative to the metamorphosis models, will-o'-the-wisp models generally give more attention to connections between cause and effect and to environmental influences. Decision-process models are at the opposite end of the spectrum from cell-division models; they tend to concentrate on causes and to ignore effects. The models detail specific processes that turn causes into effects, and the effects emerge as outputs from these dynamic processes.

Cell-Division Models

Cell-division models focus on growth as a percentage change in size. The obvious example is Haire's (1959) study that made explicit use of the biological analogy. Haire fitted data from eight firms to the equation

$$\frac{dN_t}{dt} = AN_t - BN_t^2,$$

or

$$\frac{N_t}{N_o} \cdot \frac{BN_o - A}{BN_t - A} = e^{At},$$

where N_t is the number of employees at time t, and A and B are parameters. A was estimated 'by observing the first (two or three) years' growth', and B was 'quite arbitrarily chosen'.

Biologists frequently use an equation like that above to describe the reproduction of organisms. The notion is that each organism, or pair of organisms, reproduces at a fixed frequency. At time $t + \Delta$, the total number of organisms $N_{t+\Delta}$ will be N_t plus an increment proportional to N_t and to Δ:

$$N_{t+\Delta} = N_t + A\Delta N_t.$$

Stated in terms of continuous time, the equation becomes

$$\frac{dN}{dt} = AN.$$

The coefficient A nets out births and deaths—a positive A implying more births than deaths.

The second term in Haire's equation, $-BN^2$, lowers the rate of increase in N as N grows large. N reaches a maximum at the value A/B, and decreases thereafter.[28] Haire (1959: 281–282) associated this decrease in the growth rate with 'the related state of competition in the industry and the demand for the product' and with 'the internal price paid for increase in size'.

Haire discussed two aspects of internal structure in addition to the pattern of employment over time. One fanciful analysis dichotomized employees as 'internal' and 'external' and drew an analogy between these categories and the volume and surface area of a three-dimensional solid. The second analysis traced the expansion of 'staff' and 'clerical' functions, but Haire's data suggest that organizational size per se has little effect on either the proportion of staff employees or the proportion of clerical employees.[29] These proportions appear to increase with organizational age during the first few years after founding and then to remain constant. One conjecture might be that early increases reflect the formalization process.

'To liken a firm to an organism' is not always 'an ill-founded procedure', as Penrose (1952: 809) said. However, when one uses analogies as extensively as Haire did, one should spell out why they are valid. Haire did not do this, a deficiency that was especially apparent in his internal-external analysis. If the reasons for Haire's confidence in biological analogies were obscure, Chapin's approach to growth was sheer mystique. Chapin (1957) contended that organizations develop structures and grow at rates given by the 'Fibonacci proportion'.

The Fibonacci proportion is $0.5(\sqrt{5} - 1) \approx 0.618$. This number is the $\text{Limit}_{t\to\infty} N_t/N_{t+1}$ when $N_{t+1} = N_t + N_{t-1}$. Chapin (1957: 449) wrote: 'The Fibonacci proportion, taken as a measure of integration, harmonious balance of parts, and equilibrium of structure, suggests a mathematical model with the logarithmic spiral as the principle of growth.' Chapin obtained a 'spiral' by graphing t as an angle and N as a radius. Otherwise, his model was nearly identical to Haire's. For large t, one has

$$\frac{N_t}{N_{t+1}} \approx 0.618$$

$$N_{t+1} \approx \frac{1}{0.618} N_t = 1.618 N_t$$

$$N_t \approx N_0 \cdot (1.618)^t$$

which is Haire's equation for small N and with $A = \text{Log}\ (1.618)$. Haire estimated that $A = \text{Log}\ (1.5)$.

Chapin's data were church memberships. At one point, he argued that the ratio of 'Church Membership' to Church Membership plus 'Sunday School Enrollment' tended toward the Fibonacci proportion as the organization grew older and as 'institutional strength' increased. This is probably (approximately) correct but not because the number 0.618 has magical qualities. Church Membership is essentially the number of adult participants in a church; Sunday School Enrollment is essentially the number of children. In 1920, the proportion of people over the age of nineteen in the United States population was 0.592, and in 1930 it was 0.612. Further, Chapin pointed out that the ratio increased as a church got older. This increase is consistent with the fact that new churches often are organized in areas that are newly settled and heavily populated by young families.

Haire's study was unusual in that it used time-series data on employment in individual firms.[30] Most studies use cross-section data about a number of different organizations at a given point in time. A cross-section approach generates, as Haire (1959: 292) pointed out, 'a spurious growth curve. It is not a curve of growth representing the dynamics within an organization, but a set of static measurements arranged by size.'

Haire's point is valid, but it does not justify ignoring all cross-section data. The growth process involves many variables: time, number of employees, sales volume, capital investment, and so forth. Cross-section studies ignore the time dimension, particularly as it affects the initial period of adaptation and learning in young organizations. Cross-section studies also confound organizations that have stabilized at some size with organizations that are passing through that size while growing or declining. In short, cross-section studies tend to focus on equilibrium states at the expense of transient states. In some cases, it may be useful to focus on equilibria, taking these to describe 'average' organizations after their initial surges of growth. Whether this is reasonable depends on whether one believes that individual organizations eventually conform to the pattern of 'average' organizations.

Much research on production functions by economists and operations research people falls into the cross-section pattern, sometimes a cross-section of firms in an industry and sometimes a time-independent cross-section of outputs from a given firm. A production function is a statement of the output obtainable from some combination of factors of production. In theory, a production function should state the *maximum* output from a given combination of factors, but when researchers fit parameters, they settle for the average output. Theorists have employed linear functions, quadratic functions, and a few more-complex ones. One function holds particular interest because several empirical studies have used it and it easily adapts to exponential models of growth. It is the Cobb-Douglas function:

$$P = \alpha \cdot L^{\beta} \cdot C^{1-\beta},$$

where P represents output, L represents labor, and C represents capital. When Cobb and Douglas introduced this function in 1928, they gave three reasons for their choice: (*a*) when each input is multiplied by a constant, output is multiplied by the same constant, that is, two identical plants produce twice as much as one; (*b*) if either input goes to zero, output also goes to zero; and (*c*) the function seemed to fit the data. Ease of computation adds a fourth reason. If one takes logarithms of *P*, *L*, and *C*, one can estimate the parameters by linear regression.[31] Functions of the Cobb-Douglas type appear in Section 5.

One cross-section study is of interest both because it supported the percentage-growth hypothesis and because it had implications about effects of competition on the sizes of firms. Simon and Bonini (1958: 610) described their model as follows:

Let us assume that there is a minimum size, S_m, of firm in an industry. Let us assume that for firms above this size, unit costs are constant. Individual firms in the industry will grow (or shrink) at varying rates, depending on such factors as (*a*) profit, (*b*) dividend policy, (*c*) new investment, and (*d*) mergers. These factors, in turn, may depend on the efficiency of the individual firm, exclusive access to particular factors of production, consumer brand preference, the growth or decline of the particular industry products in which it specializes, and numerous other conditions. The operation of all these forces will generate a probability distribution for the changes in size of firms of a given size. Our first basic assumption (the law of proportionate effect) is that this probability distribution is the same for all size classes of firms that are well above S_m. Our second basic assumption is that new firms are being 'born' in the smallest-size class at a relatively constant rate.

Simon and Bonini proceeded to show that this model (*a*) estimated a rate of entry of new firms close to the actual rate of entry for American firms, (*b*) predicted well the relative ingot capacities of the ten largest steel producers, and (*c*) implied minimum feasible plant sizes consistent with Bain's (1956) estimates of actual minimum sizes in thirteen industries.

Most important from the viewpoint of this chapter, perhaps, is the report that Simon and Bonini (1958: 612) gave on the validity of the proportionate effect hypothesis:

Data are now available, both in Britain and the United States, that allow us to follow the changes in size of individual firms, and to construct the transition matrices from one time period to another. Hart and Prais have published such transition matrices for British business units for the periods 1885–96, 1896–1907, 1907–24, 1924–39, and 1939–50 (1956, Tables 3, 4, 5, 6, 7). From the matrices, they have been able to test directly the first assumption underlying the stochastic processes we are considering—the law of proportionate effect. They found that the frequency distributions of percentage changes in size of small, medium, and large firms, respectively, were quite similar—approximating to normal distributions with the same means and standard deviations. We found the same to be the case with the transition matrix for the 500 largest U.S. industrial corporations from 1954 to 1955 and 1954 to 1956.

A simple, direct way to test the law of proportionate effect is to construct on a logarithmic scale the scatter diagram of firm sizes for the beginning and end of the time interval in question. If the regression line has a slope of 45 degrees and if the plot is homoscedastic, the law of proportionate effect holds and the first assumption underlying the stochastic models holds. A plot of the U.S. data shows these conditions to be well satisfied for the 1955–56 period.[32]

Small firms may not satisfy the law of proportionate effect as well as large ones do. The studies cited in Part II above by Crum (1953), Osborn (1951), Mansfield (1962), and Steindl (1945) implied that small firms are more likely to fail and have more variable growth rates. McGuire (1963) concluded from his study that young firms grow faster than old ones and that large firms grow faster than small ones, but he did not use multivariate analysis, performed no statistical tests, and handled his data in ways that might have introduced bias.

Nevertheless, the hypothesis of constant (size-independent) percentage growth does seem to be approximately correct. At least, cell-division models afford good starting points for more sophisticated models of growth.

Metamorphosis Models

Metamorphosis models express the view that growth is not a smooth, continuous process but incorporates abrupt and discrete changes in the conditions for organizational persistence and in the structures appropriate to these conditions. As Sofer (1961: 163–164) put it: 'The policies and procedures appropriate at one stage of an organization's history can become dramatically unsuited at another. . . . Just as different procedures are appropriate to the different phases of an organization's affairs, so are different sorts of people.'

An emphasis on 'different sorts of people', particularly top management people, is characteristic of this group of models. Moore's (1959: 220–222) model is typical:

The evolution of strategies in a particular business proceeds in more or less well-defined stages. The first stage is the creation of the business activity itself. . . . Someone or some small group of individuals possesses, develops, or stumbles on potential assets or resources which, when combined with certain other assets, provide the conditions favorable to the development of a business. . . .

The creative strategy of a business is frequently undeveloped and unbalanced in its initial form. It tends to emphasize the special interests, talents, possessions, behavior, and general orientation of the founding father. If the business is to survive in a competitive world, the original strategy must be consolidated.... If the first stage of a business requires a Promoter or Activity Generator, the next stage requires a Businessman or Consolidator. This is the stage when the business develops 'sound business practices'.

As the business grows and problems of adjustment increase, a new stage is reached—that of organization.... [T]he organization itself as a rationalization of means to ends becomes a strategic device for insuring an advantageous position in the socio-economic environment. This is the stage of the Manager or the Administrator.

Marshall (1920: 285) stated that a manager of a small business must display 'energy and flexibility... industry and care for small details', and then as his firm grows larger, he must 'adapt... to his larger sphere' and display 'originality, and versatility and power of initiation... perseverance, tact and good luck'. This proposition that the survival of small firms depends upon 'close attention to detail and quick adjustment to uncertain circumstances' seems to be popular. For example, Florence (1953: 64–65) wrote:

Many small firms survive because they give the precise and reliable service required by customers, particularly in 'jobbing' for producer-customers, with whom they keep in personal contact. They promise firm delivery dates, however unreasonable, and keep their promise; they produce the exact unstandard quality and design (usually unreasonably) required and attend to the customers' complaints, however wrong-headed. For this minute attention and adjustment to detail and circumstance, patiently building up goodwill with no place for mass production, a strong and direct incentive is required; the small entrepreneur, paid for his enterprise with profit, meets the demand.

Marshall paid particular attention to the consequences of an entrepreneur's old age and death. He (1920: 286) said that an entrepreneur's 'progress is likely to be arrested by the decay, if not of his faculties, yet of his liking for energetic work. The rise of his business may be prolonged if he can hand down his business to a successor almost as energetic as himself.' When the entrepreneur dies, his descendants will 'prefer an abundant income coming to them without effort on their part, to one which though twice as large could be earned only by incessant toil and anxiety' (1920: 300). So 'after a while, the guidance of the business falls into the hands of people with less energy and less creative genius, if not with less active interest in its prosperity' (1920: 316).[33]

W. F. Whyte (1948, 1961) emphasized the shifting control problems of restaurant managers as their businesses grow. He identified five stages in the growth process. Stage one is a small, informal restaurant with no division of labor and informal relations among managers, workers, and customers. Stage two involves work specialization, with the result that managerial positions entail more supervision because managers coordinate the activities of employees. Stage three involves the introduction of a supervisory level between top managers and first-line employees, and stage four begins when a second level of supervision appears. Top managers' relations with customers and employees are more formal in stages three and four; the top managers have less feedback on problems and they initiate formal procedures for controlling cost, quantities, and quality of food. In these stages, a restaurant's success depends upon the top managers' ability to manage rather than to do things themselves.

When Jones was beginning, he could state his personnel problem in very simple form: How can I get the cooperation of the workers? As the organization grew, he found he had to leave that problem more and more in the hands of his supervisors. His problem was: How can I get the cooperation of my supervisors? (1961: 86)

Stage five is reached when a single restaurant becomes a chain. At this point, managers must standardize recipes and service procedures because: 'From the customers' standpoint, there is little justification for a chain except in the advantage it gives them in knowing what type of food and service to expect, no matter which unit they patronize' (1961: 87).

Fayol (1949) and Newman and Logan (1955) viewed organizations in much the same way as Whyte. Fayol distinguished seven stages. The first is the one-person business; the second begins when employees are added; the third is marked by the introduction of a foreman to whom some supervision is delegated; in the fourth through seventh stages 'two, three, or four foremen make necessary a superintendent, two or three superintendents give rise to a departmental manager'. Newman and Logan identified three transition points (four stages). The first transition occurs when the entrepreneur becomes a manager instead of a doer; the second occurs when the manager delegates some managerial activity to subordinates; and the third, and most important, transition occurs when policy-making is decentralized.

Herbst (1957) and Starbuck (1966) suggested that there are differences between small and large retail stores. Herbst stated that the fundamental difference between small and large stores lies in their dependence on explicit administration. Small stores are 'intrinsically regulated'; they meet their control and coordination requirements without any personnel assuming administrative roles explicitly. Large stores are 'extrinsically regulated'; administrative specialists perform control and coordination functions. Starbuck distinguished between 'clerking activities' that involve interaction with customers, and 'backing activities' that do not. Small stores are 'intrinsically backed' because their employees perform both clerking and backing activities, whereas large stores are 'extrinsically backed' because some of their employees never interact with customers. Starbuck associated the transition from intrinsic to extrinsic backing with manufacturer-lot purchasing, branch operations, and the employment of backing specialists.

Perrow (1961b: 857) observed that, since the late nineteenth century, 'There has been a general development among hospitals from trustee domination, based on capital and legitimization, to domination by the medical staff, based upon the increasing importance of their technical skills, and, at present, a tendency towards administrative dominance based on internal and external coordination'. Perrow (1961b: 865) suggested that this same dominance cycle may be seen in the histories of individual hospitals and '[a]s the market and technology change, this cycle could be repeated'.

Tsouderos (1955) distinguished between the 'growth' stage of a voluntary organization, during which membership increases, and the subsequent 'formalization' stage. Filley (1963) distinguished three stages in the history of a business firm: a 'nongrowth traditional stage', a 'dynamic stage of growth', and a 'bureaucratic stage'.

The metamorphosis models clearly imply that an organization is an adaptive system capable of dealing with different problems in different ways. In fact, the metamorphosis models fit nicely into Ashby's concept of an 'ultrastable' system. Ashby was primarily concerned with biological organisms, but his analysis (1960: 136) captured some organizational characteristics as well.

[T]he disturbances that come to the organism are of two widely different types (the distribution is bi-modal). One type is small, frequent, impulsive, and acts on the main variables. The other is large, infrequent, and induces a change of step-function form on the parameters to the reacting part. Included in the latter type is the major disturbance of embryogenesis, which first sends the organism into the world with a brain sufficiently disorganised to require correction (in this respect, learning and adaptation are related, for the same solution is valid for both).

To such a distribution of disturbances, the appropriate regulator (to keep the essential variables within physiological limits) is one whose total feedbacks fall into a corresponding bimodal form. There will be feedbacks to give stability against the frequent impulsive disturbances to the main variables, and there will be a slower-acting feedback giving changes of step-function form to give stability against the infrequent disturbances of step-function form.

Such a whole can be regarded simply as one complex regulator that is stable against a complex (bi-modal) set of disturbances. Or it can equivalently be regarded as a first-order regulator (against the small impulsive disturbances) that can reorganise itself to achieve this stability after the disturbance of embryogenesis or after a major change in its conditions has destroyed this stability.

Smelser's (1959: 2) model of social change also stressed discrete shifts in structure, but he contemplated only changes in which one component of the existing structure divides into two or more new components.

When one social role or organization becomes archaic under changing historical circumstances, it differentiates by a *definite and specific sequence of events* into *two or more* roles or organizations which function more effectively in the new historical circumstances. The new social units are structurally distinct from each other, but taken together are functionally equivalent to the original unit.... Any sequence of differentiation is set in motion by specific disequilibrating conditions. Initially this disequilibrium gives rise to symptoms of social disturbance which must be brought into line later by mechanisms of social control. Only then do specific ideas, suggestions, and attempts emerge to produce the more differentiated social units.

In organizations, small, frequent disturbances include normal daily operating problems, turnover in noncentral personnel, and the like. Large, infrequent disturbances include major changes in consumer demand or production technology, turnover in central personnel, and significant increases in organizational size. The metamorphosis models talk about structural parameters of the organization's system for adapting to routine, short-run disturbances. A specific set of parameter values constitutes a stable structure for a corresponding range of short-run disturbances. As long-run shifts accumulate, the existing parameter values lose the power to provide stability and so they must change. The metamorphosis models describe probable changes in structure when the cumulative, long-run shifts are organizational growth and aging. Although one might quibble about the significance of some of the structural changes that these models described, structural changes that correlate with growth and age are worth studying.

Will-o'-the-Wisp Models

Will-o'-the-wisp models explore one kind of process that might connect the motives of organizational members to increases in organizational size. These models describe expansion in pursuit of opportunities that tend to vanish when the expansion is completed. As Penrose (1959: 2) put it, 'there may be advantages in *moving* from one position to another quite apart from the advantages of *being* in a different position'.

Andrews set forth a theory in which savings in unit costs provide a motive for growth. Economic theory distinguishes between short-run and long-run costs. In the long run, all costs are *variable*, meaning that all costs change with output. In the short run, some costs are variable and some are *fixed*, meaning that they are independent of output. Andrews (1949a: 59) noted that because some costs are fixed, 'short-run costs will normally be falling even if the long-run cost curve is rising'.[34] This implies that business expansion may be undertaken to obtain short-run cost savings. Further:

No business man would *expect* to be a less efficient manager at a larger scale; he will tacitly assume that he will remain as efficient as he is for any increase in scale that he is likely to make. Realized costs may, therefore, differ from the expected costs on which he plans, but that cannot affect his planning....

Time is of the essence of the business man's thinking. There will be a limit to the rate at which he will be prepared to grow. He normally views a new scale as a position which once taken calls for consolidation. He will expect his costs at first to be higher than they will become when he has achieved that consolidation—in fact, for any given scale, he will expect, other things being equal, that his cost curves will fall over time, that he will always be able to make some improvements in the light of experience. The idea of an optimum size of business is outside his usual way of thinking. (1949a: 79)

The short-run cost savings that Andrews's businessman pursues are illusory. In the long run, the long-run cost curve reigns. The businessman is led, by his myopia and inability to learn from experience, to seek nonexistent savings. This search does not continue indefinitely for: 'Even when one would consider them to be of equal efficiency on balance, business men usually differ in the interest that they take in particular aspects of their functions, and their personal predilections and abilities leave their mark on the business. This personal equation is especially important in determining the size to which a given business has been allowed to grow or towards which it is straining' (1949a: 55).

Penrose (1955, 1959) took an approach that is both similar to Andrews' and crucially different. She (1959: 103) made growth a pursuit of 'disappearing economies' in much the same sense that Andrews did:

The growth of firms may be consistent with the most efficient use of society's resources; the result of a past growth—the size attained at any time—may have no corresponding advantages. Each successive step in its growth may be profitable to the firm and, if otherwise under-utilized resources are used, advantageous to society. But once any expansion is completed, the original justification for the expansion may fade into insignificance as new opportunities for growth develop and are acted upon. In this case, it would not follow that the large firm as a whole was any more efficient than its several parts would be if they were operating (and growing) quite independently.

Penrose (1959: 98–99) rejected the notion that the long-run unit costs rise as a firm grows large: '... there may be an "optimum" output for each of the firm's product-lines, but not an "optimum" output for the firm as a whole. In general we have found nothing to prevent the indefinite expansion of firms as time passes.' She was ambivalent about whether large firms suffer from management difficulties. On page 19, she said: 'Apparently what has happened as firms have grown larger is not that they become inefficient, but that with increasing size both the managerial function and the basic administrative structure have undergone fundamental changes.' But then on page 206, she said:

The large diversified firms, although undoubtedly wielding much power and occupying strong monopolistic positions in some areas, do not, so far as we can see, hold their position without the expenditure of extensive managerial effort. And it is quite possible that the proportion of total managerial services required to maintain the current operations of a firm will begin to rise when it becomes large enough.

Penrose also saw growth as a means to exploit transient advantages in goodwill and managerial and technical expertise, for increasing profit as well as for reducing cost. The primary motive for growth, she (1959: 30) wrote, is maximization of long-run profits: 'from the point of view of investment policy, *growth and profits become equivalent as the criteria for the selection of investment programmes.* Firms will never invest in expansion for the sake of growth if the return on the investment is negative, for that would be self-defeating.' She added: 'There is no need to deny that other "objectives" are often important—power, prestige, public approval, or the mere love of the game—it need only be recognized that the attainment of these ends more often than not is associated directly with the ability to make profits.'

The core of Penrose's theory was the supply of managerial services. Management was both an accelerator and a brake for growth.

Under given circumstances, therefore, the maximum amount of expansion will be determined by the relevant managerial services *available* for expansion in relation to the amount of these services *required* per dollar of expansion....

If we assume that a firm is fully using its capacity to grow, the maintenance of any given rate of growth over time requires that the supply of the managerial services available for expansion increase at a rate at least equal to the rate at which the managerial services required per dollar of expansion increase; an increased rate of growth can be achieved only if the former are increasing at a rate greater than the latter; a reduced rate of growth must follow if the relevant services become available for expansion at a slower rate than the requirement for those services per dollar of expansion is increasing. (1959: 200)

The managerial services available for expansion were a residual category, 'the difference between the total services available to the firm and those required to operate it' (1959: 201). The effect of expansion on these excess services tended to be transient; 'it is clear that the creation and execution of plans for expansion absorb managerial services, and that as these services are released they become available for still further planning of expansion if they are not needed to operate the expanded concern' (1959: 50). In fact: 'If there is not scope for the full use of the capacity of individuals in the firm to perform administrative services, to plan and execute production programs, to sell the firm's products, to test new ideas, a pressure to expand will be exerted on the firm' (1959: 54). Therefore, excess services created opportunities to employ more managers.

Other things being equal, the supply of excess managerial services increased with time because 'when men have become used to working in a particular group of other men, they become individually and as a group more valuable to the firm in that the services they can render are enhanced by their knowledge of their fellow-workers, of the methods of the firm, and of the best way of doing things in the particular set of circumstances in which they are working' (1959: 52). The rate of adjustment increased with the workload. 'If a group is to gain experience in working together, it must have work to do. The total amount of work to be done at any time in a firm depends on the size of the firm's operations' (1959: 46–47). On the other hand, addition of new managerial personnel disrupted the managerial structure and forced the firm to pause for acclimation; 'if a firm deliberately or inadvertently expands its organizations more rapidly than the individuals in the expanding organization can obtain the experience with each other and with the firm that is necessary for the effective operation of the group, the efficiency of the firm will suffer, even if optimum adjustments are made in the administrative structure' (1959: 47).

Pieces of Penrose's theory have received support from others. Heller (1951: 102) quoted an executive as follows:

Perfecting a layout involves a minimum amount of managerial and technical work that you can't escape. You have to handle expansion projects in a series, because you simply don't have the necessary number of men of the required caliber around to keep up a doubled-up pace. If we had gone ahead too fast, we would not have been able to get either proper supervision or the technical brains required to get the bugs out. Also, we have to keep production up during the change-overs ... or we will be losing part of our market. So it's the scarcity and costliness of brains that slow down our rate of investment.

March and Simon's (1958: 185–188) discussion of innovation supported the idea that expansion depends upon managerial resources that are underutilized. Cyert and March (1963: 110–112, 120–122, 285–286) suggested that firms' planning is primarily of the short-run variety. Andrews (1949b: 282) pointed out that pressure to expand is sometimes due to 'the young up-and-coming men, pressing for promotion and looking for ways in which to achieve it'. W. F. Whyte (1961: 571–574) stressed the importance of 'fitting-in' as a precondition for managerial authority. Weiss (1956: 23) made this observation:

> It seems that an integration slowly develops of the expectations of the new person and those of the staff members already a part of the group; a mutual confidence in who can be relied on to do what. The new staff member learns what the co-workers expect of him, and what he can in turn expect of them. The older staff members learn to think about their units as including the new person, and to take his contributions as a matter of course, as they do the contributions of the other members of the unit.
>
> Until the new staff member is fully accepted there is a certain hesitancy in interaction involving him. Everyone is very careful. Things are to be made as explicit as possible. There may be a tendency to exclude him from group tasks requiring close co-ordination, and to count on him more than is necessary for routine work.

Other supportive evidence was cited above, including Blau's (1955) observation that task mastery produces pressure for change, McNulty's (1962) finding that planning changes in organization structure is not advantageous, and numerous reports of learning effects.

Although the dynamics of Penrose's theory stressed factors inside the firm, she attended to environmental influences like market conditions, availability of financing, competitive relationships, and opportunities. She looked upon internal processes as determinants of a hypothetical maximum rate of expansion, and treated environmental factors as constraints on a firm's ability to achieve this maximum growth rate. Which factors constrain which factors is a chicken-or-egg question, so what is important is that she considered both internal and external factors.

An Appendix to this chapter presents a mathematical treatment of Penrose's theory. Only internal dynamics are considered and they are greatly simplified, but the mathematical model questions Penrose's statement that 'we have found nothing to prevent the indefinite expansion of firms as time passes'. In particular, her theory implies that an expansion path could fall into either of two patterns, depending on such things as the productivity of managerial employees, the gross margins obtainable on products, and the 'manager-intensiveness' of the production process. One pattern corresponds to expansion into the indefinite future, as she suggested. The other pattern corresponds to expansion followed by contraction. Thus, Penrose's theory ended up where Haire's began.

Decision-Process Models

Decision-process models attempt to reproduce the fabric of organizational decisions. These models are potentially the most fruitful approach to organizational growth, but they are expensive. A model-builder must try to specify, by direct observation of individual organizations, all the major decision rules used by the organizations and then test the model against detailed data on actual behavior. Because little is known about decision processes and the processes are complex, armchair theorizing tends to be unrewarding.

The current body of knowledge on decision-process models is due almost completely to Cyert and March (1963: 19) and their associates. 'Our conception of the task we face is that of constructing a theory that takes (1) the firm as its basic unit, (2) the prediction of firm behavior with respect to such decisions as price, output, and resource allocation as its objective, and (3) an explicit emphasis on the actual process of organizational decision making as its basic research commitment.'

Cyert, Feigenbaum, and March (1959: 93–94) developed a duopoly model that, although it has a weak empirical basis, illustrates application of a decision-process model to growth. They modeled a situation in which a monopolist has been forced to permit establishment of a smaller 'splinter' firm. Their interest was the relative profitabilities and sales volumes of the two firms.

The theory we have used differs from conventional [economic] theory in six important respects: (1) The models are built on a description of the decision-making process. That is, they specify organizations that evaluate competitors, costs, and demand in the light of their own objectives and (if necessary) re-examine each of these to arrive at a decision. (2) The models depend on a theory of search as well as a theory of choice. They specify under what conditions search will be intensified (e.g., when a satisfactory alternative is not available). They also specify the direction in which search is undertaken. In general, we predict that a firm will look first for new alternatives or new information in the area it views as most under its control. Thus, in the present models we have made the specific prediction that cost estimates will be re-examined first, demand estimates second, and organizational objectives third. (3) The models describe organizations in which objectives change over time as a result of experience. Goals are not taken as given initially and fixed thereafter. They change as the organization observes its success (or lack of it) in the market. In these models the profit objective at a given time is an average of achieved profit over a number of past periods. The number of past periods considered by the firm varies from firm to firm. (4) Similarly, the models describe organizations that adjust forecasts on the basis of experience. Organizational learning occurs as a result of observations of actual competitors' behavior, actual market demand, and actual costs. Each of the organizations we have used readjusts its perceptions on the basis of such learning. The learning rules used are quite simple. This is both because simple rules are easier to handle than complex rules and because we expect the true rules to be susceptible to close approximation by simple ones. (5) The models introduce organizational biases in making estimates. For a variety of reasons we expect some organizations to be more conservative with respect to cost estimates than other organizations, some organizations to be more optimistic with respect to demand than others, some organizations to be more attentive to and perceptive of changes in competitors' plans than others. As we develop more detailed submodels of the estimation process, these factors will be increasingly obvious. In the present models we have not attempted to develop such submodels but have simply predicted the outcome of the estimation process in different firms. (6) The models all introduce features of 'organizational slack'. That is, we expect that over a period of time during which an organization is achieving its goals a certain amount of the resources of the organization are funneled into the satisfaction of individual and subgroup objectives. This slack then becomes a reservoir of potential economies when satisfactory plans are more difficult to develop.

In order to deal with these revisions, the models have been written explicitly as computer programs. Such treatment has two major values. First, simulation permits the introduction of process variables. The language of the computer is such that many of the phenomena of business behavior that do not fit into classical models can be considered without excessive artificiality. Entering naturally into the model are cost and demand perceptions within the firm in relation to such factors as age of firm, organizational structure, background of executives, and phase of the business cycle; information handling within the firm and its relation to the communication structure, training, and reward system in the organization; and the effects of organizational success and failure on organizational goals and organizational slack.

Secondly, simulation easily generates data on the time path of outputs, prices, etc. For that large class of economic problems in which equilibrium theory is either irrelevant or relatively uninteresting, computer methodology provides a major alternative to the mathematics of comparative statics.

In their model, each firm followed a decision sequence involving five basic steps: (*a*) forecast competitor's behavior, (*b*) forecast demand, (*c*) estimate costs, (*d*) specify a profit goal, and (*e*) determine whether any level of output will satisfy the profit goal. If (*e*) implied that a satisfactory profit could be obtained, the firm chose an output level. If (*e*) implied that no output level would yield a satisfactory profit, the firm (*f*) revised its estimate of costs, or (*g*) revised its forecast of demand, or, as a last resort, (*h*) revised its profit goal. They assumed the ex-monopolist and the splinter firm displayed crucial differences. When forecasting their competitor's behavior and when setting their profit goals, the ex-monopolist was more heavily influenced by past performance and the splinter by recent performance. The ex-monopolist made a pessimistic forecast of demand and was less willing than the splinter to revise this estimate; the splinter made an optimistic forecast of demand. The ex-monopolist started out with a higher unit cost than did the splinter.

The authors compared this model with actual data on 'the competition between American Can Company and its splinter competitor, Continental Can Company, over the period from 1913 to 1956', and obtained results that they felt were 'rather surprisingly good' (1959: 90–93). As they pointed out, there are serious problems in fitting this type of model to data. The number of parameters in the model was so large that, if one could find a practical computation scheme, an exact fit might have been possible. However, the model was so complex, and the relations among parameters so obscure, that no such computation scheme existed. As a result, a priori parameter estimates were as much a part of the hypothesis tested as the structure of the decision process.

After 1959, Cyert and March constructed more-elaborate models based on case studies of actual decisions. These models differed from the above duopoly model by including several independent and partially conflicting goals instead of the single profit goal. They resembled the duopoly model in emphasizing adaptation, learning, search, and dynamic interactions between the organization and its environment. One of these models was 'a summary of our understanding of the key microprocesses in price and output determination by a modern firm' (1963: 8). However, this model was too complex to discuss here, and they did not apply it to a situation relevant for growth.

One problem with most models of organizational growth is that they imply a degree of autonomy and predestination that is difficult to reconcile with one's direct observation. Decision-process models take an organization's concern with immediate and unique problems as their central theme, letting long-run patterns emerge as by-products of short-run decisions. Although this may be a promising approach, before decision-process models can make major contributions, researchers must invest much more work in them. Little is known about long-run learning. Studies have tried to capture organizational decision structures at single points in time, and virtually no evidence has been gathered about how decision structures evolve. Methods must be discovered for handling decision-process models methodologically. The stronger the empirical base of these models, the more complex they become; and the more complex the models, the harder it is to understand why they do what they do. For instance, Bonini said of his hypothetical model:

The majority of this chapter has been devoted to discussing specific mechanisms which influenced the major results. It is important, however, not to overemphasize the importance of these mechanisms in causing the results. They certainly have contributed, but there are many interactions and interconnections in the model. It is the whole system which produced the result, and we must be cautious in attaching undue importance to any specific part. (1963: 144)

We cannot explain completely the reasons why the firm behaves in a specific fashion. Our model of the firm is highly complex, and it is not possible to trace out the behavior pattern throughout the firm.... Therefore, we cannot pinpoint the explicit causal mechanism in the model. (1963: 136)

5. ADMINISTRATIVE STRUCTURE AND GROWTH

The focal question in this section is: Do old, large organizations suffer from declining administrative efficiency? This is an issue in the will-o'-the-wisp and cell-division models of growth, in the formalization process, and in such goals as cost, profit, executive salaries, and prestige-power-security. The central interest here is in what actually happens to administrative structure as organizational size and age increase, not in what should be done to make an organization efficient. Normative commentaries are relevant only because normative statements may turn out to be descriptive statements if organizations try to organize themselves efficiently. Since administrative efficiency is not the only concern, the final section considers managerial employment.

The Question of Administrative Efficiency

There is a proposition, accepted primarily among economists, that 'the difficulties of internal organization usually check the growth of individual enterprises well short of complete monopoly' (Warner and Low 1947: 113).

Economists adopted this proposition opportunistically. As Andrews (1949b: 128) observed:

Economists have found that the application to the real world of the abstract theory of pure competition requires that long-run costs should rise with increased scale. This has made it easy for the supposition to be accepted in economics that long-run costs do, in fact, rise, and, in the absence of any other plausible explanation as to why they should rise, economists have tended to call in increasing managerial inefficiency as a fairly plausible hypothesis which could not easily be refuted.[35]

Rising long-run costs are useful because the theory of pure competition assumes no market limitation on the sales of any single firm. The theory says a firm produces whatever quantity will maximize its total profit and it has no difficulty selling this quantity at the market price. Suppose that the market price is p and the firm's total cost curve is

$$c_0 + c_1 q + c_2 q^2,$$

where q represents output and c_0, c_1, and c_2 are nonnegative. The firm's profit is

$$pq - [c_0 + c_1 q + c_2 q^2],$$

and the firm would maximize profit when

$$q = \frac{p - c_1}{2c_2}.$$

The importance of a positive c_2 is evident. Only if c_2 is positive will the optimum q be finite; if c_2 is zero, the firm should produce an infinite output. Economic theorists have made managerial costs the basis for a positive c_2. The 'logical' argument has been: (*a*) A firm has a finite size. (*b*) Therefore, c_2 must be positive. (*c*) But technology implies that c_1 is small and c_2 zero (e.g. specialization of labor, quantity discounts on raw materials, stochastic returns to scale). (*d*) 'Increasing managerial inefficiency' could make c_2 positive, and it is 'a fairly plausible hypothesis which could not easily be refuted'.

Robinson (1934: 256) usually gets credit for inventing the managerial inefficiency hypothesis.

...an optimum firm with an upper limit imposed by the difficulties and costs of co-ordination is both logically satisfactory and a necessary hypothesis to explain the existing facts.

Robinson argued that managerial efficiency depended primarily on the skills of an entrepreneur at the peak of a managerial hierarchy. As a firm grew larger, this entrepreneur's talents were spread more and more thinly across the range of operations, and efficiency decreased as a result. Chamberlin took issue with Robinson, pointing out that management was not a 'fixed factor'. Others besides the entrepreneur could display managerial skill, and the organization's total managerial resources could be expanded by adding managers. Nevertheless, Chamberlin too saw the logical necessity of a positive c_2. He attributed this to managerial inefficiency, specifically, 'the greater complexity of the producing unit as it grows in size, leading to increased difficulties of coordination and management'. Chamberlin (1948: 250) was frank about the motivation for his assumption:

It is sometimes argued that a policy of decentralization may be adopted beyond the minimum point, reproducing the conditions there found in substantially independent units, and thus eliminating, almost by definition, the problems of complexity. . . . In so far as decentralization is an effective means of combating the diseconomies of size, far from being denied, it is, of course, included by definition in the envelope curve at all points. . . . and its effect may often be to postpone net diseconomies far beyond the scales of production to be found in reality. It is contended only that the curve does turn up somewhere.

Discussions by organization theorists have partially paralleled those by economists—contrasting, on the one hand, returns to scale from specialization and, on the other hand, problems of coordinating divided labor. Fordham (1957–1958) suggested that the efficiency of an individual member of an organization was the product of two functions. One was an increasing function of the span of control, implying that as the span of control increased, each subordinate became more of a specialist and developed more expertise. The other was a decreasing function of the span of control, implying that as the span of control increased, each subordinate had to spend more and more time communicating with other members of the organization.

Organization theorists' interest in the complexity assumption appears to have derived less from theoretical opportunism than from fascination with the binomial expansion.[36] Most of the complexity arguments by organization theorists and sociologists have paid homage to Graicunas (1933). Graicunas observed that a group composed of persons A, B, and C might behave differently from a group composed of A, B, and D. From this, he concluded that the 'complexity' of a group composed of n people is proportional to the total number of distinct dyads, triads, and so forth that could be formed from the group. That is, complexity is proportional to[37]

$$\sum_{k=2}^{n} C_k^n = 2^n - n - 1.$$

However, few of Graicunas' disciples adopted this formula in its full glory. They emphasized only the number of dyads in the group:

$$C_2^n = \frac{n(n-1)}{2}.$$

Herbst's (1957: 341) discussion is typical:

Let us suppose that the components of a system are independent of one another or very nearly so, then the amount of work required for control would be proportional to the number of components (n) of the system, so that the

$$\text{amount of control work} = b_1 n$$

If the component parts are interconnected, then the amount of work required additionally for the coordination of components may be taken to be a function of the number of interconnections between components. The maximum number of interdependence links between n components is $n(n - 1)/2$ so that in the simplest case

$$\text{maximum coordination work} \sim b_2 n^2$$

If we compare the amount of work in the form of control and integration in the case where there is complete interdependence between component parts with that where there is complete linkage between components, we find that this is a function of n (the number of components) in one case and of n^2 in the other. The size of the integrating unit may then be taken to be a function of the size of the system raised to the power $1 + \alpha$ where α may be taken as a measure of the degree of complexity of the system in terms of the degree of connectedness between its components.

The idea that complexity varies with 'the degree of connectedness between its components' has been a standard part of the complexity discussions. Urwick (1956) was careful to restrict his discussion of complexity to subordinates '*whose work interlocks*', and Graicunas observed that 'this factor will operate with much less force where the work done by each of various subordinates does not come into contact with that done by others'.

Herbst was one of the few organization theorists who made complexity the basis for declining efficiency in the organization as a whole. Most expressed confidence in an organization's ability to factor its tasks among work groups without producing serious coordination problems. The purpose for which Graicunas created his formula, and the purpose to which complexity arguments have typically been put, is the justification for keeping work groups small, that is, the justification for small spans of control. Graicunas argued that the span of control should be such that the number of relations supervised approximately equaled the maximum 'span of attention' of one supervisor. Thus, the specific functional form of the complexity function was irrelevant to Graicunas' argument. Since he used only one arbitrary point of the function, any increasing function of n would have been equally satisfactory.

The optimum span of control was supposed to be smaller near the top of the management hierarchy than near the bottom because there was greater need for coordination near the top. Hamilton (1921) said the span of control should be approximately three near the top, increasing to six at the bottom. Other theorists have agreed with him. Caplow (1957) justified spans between three and six on a different basis. He argued that this was the natural size range for 'groups of intimates' and he cited James's (1951, 1953) data on the size distribution of 'free-forming' small groups as evidence for his position.[38] Trist and Bamforth (1951) also stressed the importance of organizing around 'primary groups'.

There has not been consensus that spans between three and six are optimal. Likert wrote: 'The optimum size of units in local Leagues has been found from experience to be about fifteen to twenty persons. This is also true of boards. Similarly, the optimum size of resource committees is usually not more than about fifteen to twenty persons.' He (1961: 159) conceded that even below this size 'there is some decrease in effectiveness per member', but 'as the groups exceed about twenty, the decrease in effectiveness becomes more marked'. Suojanen (1955: 13) said, 'the institutionalization of the organization and the development of primary relationships among the members of the executive group together provide such a high degree of control that the area of effective supervision of the chief executive is much wider than that predicted by the span of control principle'. Argyris (1957: 66) objected that small spans 'increase the subordinates' feelings of dependence, submissiveness, passivity, and the like'.

One argument against small spans of control pointed out that, holding the size of the organization constant, small spans imply many hierarchical levels. According to Simon (1957a: 28):

The dilemma is this: in a large organization with interrelations between members, a restricted span of control inevitably produces excessive red tape, for each contact between organization members must be carried upward until a common superior is found....

The alternative is to increase the number of persons who are under the command of each officer, so that the pyramid will come more rapidly to a peak, with fewer intervening levels. But this, too, leads to a difficulty, for if an officer is required to supervise too many employees, his control over them is weakened.

Granted, then, that both the increase and the decrease in span of control have some undesirable consequences, what is the optimum point?

Dubin (1959: 229) noted that 'the greater the number of links in the system, the greater will be the probability of "noise" in functional connections among organization units'. Richardson and Walker (1948) and Worthy (1950a, 1950b) reported situations where reductions in the number of hierarchical levels correlated with heightened morale.[39]

Most theories of organization have taken the position that—provided the span of control, the number of hierarchical levels, and other variables were properly manipulated—organizational size has little effect on managerial efficiency. The self-confidence of Mooney and Reiley (1931: 504–505) is atypical, but their fundamental attitude is not:

If the principles of organization we have asserted are real and not imaginary, then their correct application must contain the solvent of all such problems. Given this application, it is impossible to conceive of any human organization too vast for organized efficiency.

This attitude has led organization theorists to search for effective factorings of organizations into departments without worrying about whether such factorings might be less efficient for large organizations than for small ones.[40] For example, March and Simon (1958: 29) said:

The problem of departmentalization ... centers on two variables: self-containment (or alternatively, coordination requirements), and skill specialization. Its central proposition is that the forms of departmentalization that are advantageous in terms of one of these outcomes are often costly in terms of the other: Process departmentalization generally takes greater advantage of the potentialities for economy through specialization than does purpose departmentalization; purpose departmentalization leads to greater self-containment and lower coordination costs than does process departmentalization. As size of organization increases, the marginal advantages accruing to process organization from the first source become smaller, while the coordination costs become larger. Hence, the balance of net efficiency shifts from process to purpose organization as the size of organization increases.

Empirical Studies of Administrative Structure

There has been a tendency, stronger among early organization theorists than among later ones, to view the administrative structure as a pyramidal hierarchy. One person comprises the top level in this hierarchy; this person has s subordinates who comprise the second level; each of these has s subordinates, giving s^2 people in the third level; and so forth. Of course, s is the span of control, and the total number of administrative employees in a hierarchy with λ levels is

$$A = 1 + s + s^2 + s^3 + \ldots + s^{\lambda-1}$$
$$= \frac{s^\lambda - 1}{s - 1}.$$

Taking σ to be the number of production workers per supervisor, there are

$$P = \sigma \cdot s^{\lambda-1}$$

production workers and

$$T = A + P = \frac{s^\lambda - 1}{s - 1} + \sigma \cdot s^{\lambda-1}$$

total employees. Only three of the four variables s, σ, λ, and T are free because:

$$\lambda = \frac{1}{\log(s)} \{\log 1 + T[(s-1)] - \log 1 + \sigma[(1 - 1/s)]\}$$

Administrative efficiency can be measured by the ratio of administrative employees to production employees. A pyramidal model implies that the ratio A/P increases very slightly as T increases. For virtually any organization of interest,

$$\frac{A}{P} > \frac{1}{\sigma}$$

and in the limit as T goes to infinity,

$$\frac{A}{P} \rightarrow \frac{1}{\sigma} \cdot \frac{s}{s-1}.$$

Figure 1.1 shows the A/P ratio as a function of T, for $s = 6$ and for two values of σ. Note that the abscissa is logarithmic.

It does not matter whether s is smaller at the top of the hierarchy than at the bottom. For example, if the chief executive had a span of 3, the executive's subordinates had spans of $3 + \alpha$, their subordinates had spans of $3 + 2\alpha$, and so forth, and if α were chosen so that the average span for all administrative employees were 6, then the A/P ratio would graph exactly as shown in Figure 1.1. The number of hierarchical levels would not be the same, however, λ being larger in this second case. Data collected by Dale (1952) and Entwistle and Walton (1961) indicated that s increases with total employment:

$$s \sim 2 \, \text{Log}_{10}(T)$$

Figure 1.2 shows how such an increase in s affects A/P. The ratio rises rapidly to a maximum and then decreases monotonically. Although A/P is rather constant over a wide range of organizational sizes, the effects of size differ from those in Figure 1.1. In the limit as T goes to infinity,

$$\frac{A}{P} \rightarrow \frac{1}{\sigma}$$

Although a greatly oversimplified model of organizational structure, a pyramid is consistent with the data on administrative employment. Studies of administrative structure can be separated into three categories: (*a*) studies taking *size* as the independent variable, (*b*) those taking *technology* as the independent variable, and (*c*) those taking *time* or age as the independent variable. When published, the chapter included long discussions of data collected by various researchers.[41]

Summary

Studies of administrative structure support the following conclusions:

1. The administrative span of control, s, probably increases with organizational size. Studies consistent with this increase are Dale (1952), Entwistle and Walton (1961), Haas, Hall, and Johnson (1963), Healey (1956), Melman (1951, 1958), Terrien and Mills (1955), Woodward (1958), as well as reanalysis of Chester's data.

2. The administrative span of control, s, may also increase with 'technological complexity', but Woodward (1958) is the only study to note such an effect.

3. The number of production workers per supervisor, σ, may increase with organizational size. Studies consistent with this increase are Anderson and Warkov (1961), Haire (1959), Terrien and Mills (1955), and Woodward (1958).

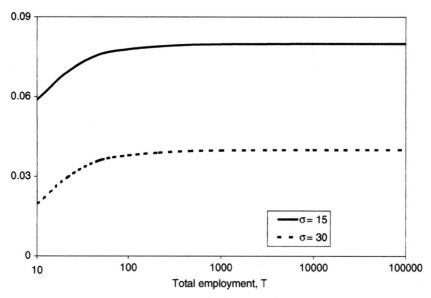

Figure 1.1. A/P for s = 6

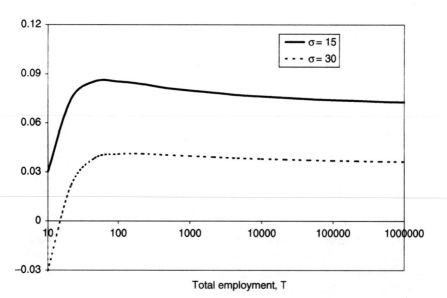

Figure 1.2. A/P for s = 2 Log$_{10}$(T)

4. The number of production workers per supervisor, σ, is probably a concave function of 'technological complexity'. Studies consistent with this view are Anderson and Warkov (1961), Blau (1957), Faunce (1958), Harbison et al. (1955), Simpson (1959), Woodward (1958), as well as reanalysis of Chester's data.

5. For organizations with more than 100 employees, the A/P ratio is essentially independent of organizational size. The only study not consistent with this conclusion is Anderson and Warkov's (1961).

   This implies that either the effects described in (2) and (4) above do not occur simultaneously or neither effect is very pronounced. It also means that the A/P ratio tends to be dominated by technological effects. A/P is probably an increasing function of 'technological complexity'. Woodward's (1958) and Chester's (1961) data are consistent with this increase.

6. There are virtually no data on the A/P ratio in organizations with less than 100 employees, but Figure 1.1 suggests that A/P is an increasing function of T in this range. One expects the A/P ratio to be highly variable in small firms; the studies by Haire (1959) and Melman (1951, 1958) indicate as much. Although Woodward (1958) found no correlation between firm size and 'technological complexity' in large firms, one should expect to find a correlation in small firms.

7. The A/P ratio is probably an increasing function of time. This may be due to increasing 'technological complexity'; it may be a consequence of changing definitions of 'administrative' work; or it may be the result of new requirements imposed on and new activities undertaken by firms.

Empirical Studies of Managerial Employment

Data collected by Chester (1961) show that the numbers of managers are not simply proportional to either the numbers of administrative employees or total employment. Consider four characteristics of the title 'manager'.

First, managers have status. They are set apart from nonmanagerial employees, and they are accepted in the managerial class. They stop eating lunch with nonmanagerial associates and start eating lunch with other managers, often in private dining rooms. Many of their nonmanagerial friendships dissolve and are replaced by friendships with managers. They are admitted to membership in social clubs that had been closed to them by convention if not by fiat. They are invited to be officers in charitable and professional organizations. Most organizations use managerial status as a formal reward. They tie status to other rewards, like salary, and they reinforce the distinction between managerial and nonmanagerial employees. Managers are given expense accounts, private secretaries, and access to the company plane. Organizations may pay their managers' dues in private social clubs or establish country clubs especially for managers. Of course, 'A title on the door rates a Bigelow on the floor'.

Second, managers have job security. They are less likely to be fired than non-managerial employees are. In fact, data from Chester (1961), Haire (1959), and Weber (1959) support the idea that the numbers of managers rarely decrease over time, irrespective of other events. Faltermayer (1961) reported some steps firms take to avoid firing managers. Some firms cut salaries; others ask managers near retirement age to retire early; large organizations can reduce the numbers of managers by not hiring replacements for those who resign or retire. The most popular alternatives appear to be those that reduce the fringe benefits of managerial status. The company stops paying club dues. Fewer long distance calls are made. Trips are canceled or made tourist class instead of first class. Secretaries are fired. Indeed, one firm required its executives to eat in the cafeteria with the rest of the employees.

Third, managers have delegated responsibility. Most managers have charge of distinct segments of the organizational tasks. In this sense, they are specialists. Most organizations endeavor to assign managerial jobs in ways that minimize coordination problems and give autonomy to individual managers. Managers are not the only responsible people, nor are they the only specialists, but there are relationships between an organization's task factorings and its managerial job assignments.

Fourth and finally, managers manage. Nearly all managers supervise nonmanagerial employees. This means that an organization is unlikely to create an additional managerial position unless the task segment associated with that position is large enough to occupy more than one person.

These four characteristics imply that the number of managers (M) increases with: (*a*) the size of the organization (T), (*b*) the age of the organization (t), and (*c*) the cumulative experience of organizational members (E). Cumulative experience is defined here as the total number of working years invested in an organization since its founding. For T measured annually,

$$E = \sum_{\tau=0}^{t} T(\tau).$$

E increases monotonically with t, but less rapidly when T is small than when T is large.

Relations between M and T are straightforward. Large organizations have enough work in many activities to occupy several employees, including a manager. Small organizations may not have enough work in any activities to occupy even one person. Thus, large organizations have more managers than small organizations.

Relations between M and t result partially from the formalization process. New organizations tend to define their tasks vaguely. They are not sure which task segments are important or necessary, and they are not sure how their overall tasks should be factored. Consequently, they tend to operate with small numbers of managers whose responsibilities overlap. As time passes and the organizations grow older, they define their overall tasks more clearly; they distinguish important task segments from unimportant ones; they discover effective task factorings;

they develop standard operating procedures that reduce the need for coordination between subunits and routinize it. All these changes create opportunities for factoring tasks into finer segments, and for appointing managers to take responsibility for the segments. Thus, one expects to find associations between M and t due to formalization primarily in older organizations. Managerial job security is another factor relating M and t. When employment in nonmanagerial categories falls, managerial employment falls less than proportionately, and may even rise. When employment in nonmanagerial categories rises, managerial employment rises, again less than proportionately. Such fluctuations reduce the correlation between M and T, and to the extent that M increases *mutatis mutandis*, they increase the correlation between M and t. In view of these considerations, one can predict that M is more closely associated with T than with t in young firms that have stable scales of operation. M is more closely associated with t than with T in older firms that have unstable or fluctuating scales of operation.

Because cumulative experience (E) combines the characteristics of T and t, M should be more closely associated with E than with either T or t in young firms that have unstable scales of operation and in older firms that have stable scales of operation.

Association among M and T, t, or E may also reflect the standards established for promotion. An organization that adheres to the organization theorists' precepts concerning span of control, without much regard for the skills and talents of promoted personnel, would tend to have M associated with T. At least among young organizations, an organization that promotes primarily on the basis of seniority would tend to have M associated with t. An organization that promotes based on 'merit', considering both the employee's native ability and the employee's experience with the organization, would tend to have M associated with E. The effects of promotion policies may not be large enough to show up in data. One might also hypothesize that firms that expand rapidly have a more difficult learning problem and thus tend to have M associated with T. The trouble is another proposition counters that one: firms that learn rapidly, expand rapidly.

Haire provided data on ten firms for analysis. These data show that the behavior of managerial employment differs among firms, but they do give weak confirmation to the above hypotheses.

6. CONCLUDING REMARKS

Most studies of organizational growth and development are typical examples of social science research, and, as such, are subject to faults common in social science research. In particular, they exhibit

1. a tendency to substitute theorizing for data collection,
2. a tendency simply to present data without formal analyses, and
3. a tendency to base formal analyses on naive assumptions.

Nevertheless, no study is perfect and poor studies often provoke better ones. Considering the bibliography as a whole, an impressive amount of useful work has been done. Many questions have been explored, and researchers have good bases for moving toward a predictive understanding of growth and development.

At this point, what is needed more than anything else is data—data on goals, data on behavior strategies, data on structural variables, data on patterns of development, data on nearly every aspect of organizational growth and development. Some areas of social science research suffer from a lack of theory, there being well-established facts and no theories adequate to explain them. The subject of organizational growth is not such an area. Indeed, the theories seem to outnumber the facts. In few instances can one point to systematic bodies of data and analysis concerning interrelated phenomena, as one can, for example, point to Mansfield's studies of technological innovation. There are many instances wherein one can point to a collection of theoretical formulations based on single case studies or on theorists' personal experiences. The worth of such contributions depends greatly on a specific theorist's genius, and an entire area of research can hardly be founded on the premise that the average researcher is a genius.

The kind of data likely to be most useful is time-series data on individual organizations. Researchers should obtain at least two observations of each organization studied, and preferably several. This is desirable because one current deficiency is the lack of effective classification schemes for organizations such that two organizations in the same class can be validly compared as if they were two observations of the same organization. Until such classification schemes are created, cross-section studies will remain inefficient. At best, they require very large samples to establish statistical significance; at worst, they produce spurious correlations due to systematic but unobserved differences among organizations. Moreover, classification schemes must follow development of an empirically based consensus about which organizational characteristics are most critical, and the field is far from that. In the interim, the best approach is to work with multiple observations of each organization, taking maximum advantage of opportunities to compare each organization with itself rather than with other organizations. This approach minimizes the number of assumptions about similarity implicit in a given comparison.

The subject of organizational growth and development needs work toward a general theory, not work on a general theory. It is a mistake to bet heavily on the ability to classify and group different organizations. Granting this, the subject appears ripe for some major advances. A lot of progress can be made in a short time if researchers will commit themselves (*a*) to build formal models, (*b*) to collect detailed time-series data on individual organizations over several years, and (*c*) to confront models with data in a rigorous way. As Cyert and March (1963: 287) said:

What we tend to forget is that uniqueness . . . is not an attribute of the organization alone; it is an attribute of the organization and our theory of organizations. An organization is unique when we have failed to develop a theory that will make it nonunique. Thus, uniqueness is less a bar to future theoretical success than a confession of past theoretical failure.

ACKNOWLEDGMENTS

Arnold Cooper, Charles Howe, James March, Genever McBain, Vernon Smith, and especially Richard Walton contributed helpful criticism and comment.

NOTES

1. Also see Copeland (1955).
2. Also see Gordon (1945: 271–304), McGuire, Chiu, and Elbing (1962), and Patton (1961).
3. For further discussion of business motives other than profit, see Berle and Means (1932), Cyert and March (1963), Gordon (1945), Hickman and Kuhn (1956), Katona (1951), Papandreou (1952), and White (1960).
4. Whitin and Peston (1954) gave bibliographic references on this topic; references with direct relevance to employment are Feller (1950), Holt et al. (1960), and Starbuck (1966).
5. The statistical problems involved in this inference are not negligible. Steindl (1952: 18–19) found that output per man increased with increasing sales volume and decreased with increasing employment. He said: 'It can easily be demonstrated that if output per worker is uncorrelated with size . . . when size is measured by output, then a negative—and spurious—correlation must obtain . . . where size is measured according to number of workers. Similarly, it can be demonstrated that if output per worker is positively correlated with size [by output], it must, under certain conditions, be negatively correlated with size [by employment].'
6. For general reviews of the empirical evidence see Blair (1948), Florence (1953), Kaplan (1948), Osborn (1951), and Staehle (1942). Specific studies of interest are Bain (1954; 1956), Crum (1939), Johnston (1955–1956), Melman (1956), Rostas (1948), TNEC (1941), and Woodruff and Alexander (1958).
7. To quote Likert (1961: 141): 'Each of the 29 women who served as judges was asked to rate the effectiveness of each of the sample Leagues. League effectiveness was defined as the extent to which a League accomplishes its goals. The general criteria used by the League in evaluating local Leagues' strengths and weaknesses were presented to guide the raters in their evaluations: size of League in relation to the size of the community, growth of League, the quality and quantity of League materials, the level of participation of members, their interest in League activities and their knowledge about them, success in fund-raising campaigns, and effect on their community.'
8. For example, the relations observed by Bales (1951), Coleman (1960), and Stephan and Mishler (1952).
9. But a monopolist may have compatibility. Warner and Low (1947) noted that large firms had the advantage of sizes and structures that matched the sizes and structures of their suppliers and customers.
10. For a readable, although argumentative, review of criticisms of big business, see Glover (1954). Wilcox (1955) has offered a technically detailed review of antitrust legislation and enforcement.
11. Stigler (1950) made a similar argument. Others who emphasized survival goals are Drucker (1958), Maurer (1955), Ross (1947), and Rothschild (1947).

12. Rothschild (1947) would probably disagree. He has argued that 'price wars, while tending to occur infrequently, are a dominant feature of the oligopolistic situation' and therefore 'the desire for *secure* profits' is 'of a similar order of magnitude as the desire for maximum profits'.

13. Also see Mansfield (1962).

14. For further references on survival by small firms and large firms, see BBRP (1958: 39–41, 67–68, 105–108).

15. A mail survey by McGuire (1963: 93–95) supports some of Dent's findings. McGuire asked firms to rank order five goals: '...the ranking in order of preference was as follows: (1) Profits, (2) Increase sales, (3) Increase or maintain market share, (4) Survival, (5) Growth....' McGuire also endeavored to relate goal preferences to the firms' growth rates. However, he considered only the firms' first choices and obtained uniform distributions. Since Dent's firms averaged over two responses each, one would expect firms to have difficulty describing their goals in terms of a single criterion, and hence expect a rank ordering over the first two or three goals to be unstable.

16. Those interested in this literature should see BBRP (1958), Blau and Scott (1962: 199–206), Form and Miller (1960), and RERP (1959).

17. See NSF (1956, Tables 5, A-28; 1959, Table A-27) and for corresponding British data, DSIR (1958).

18. See also Phillips (1956).

19. The profitability of a specific innovation also correlated with firms' readiness to adopt it.

20. Gordon (1945: 116–267) treated the firm as a coalition of executives, directors, stockholders, suppliers, creditors, labor unions, customers, government agencies, consultants, and competitors Also see Cyert and March (1963: ch. 3), Levine and White (1961), Perrow (1961a), and Stocking and Mueller (1957).

21. For normative discussions of how to effect change, see Bennis (1963), Bennis, Benne, and Chin (1961), Gardner and Moore (1955), Ginzberg and Reilley (1957), Likert (1961), Lippitt, Watson, and Westley (1958), and Mann and Neff (1961). For a discussion of ways in which labor unions resist technological changes, see Slichter, Healy, and Livernash (1960: 12).

22. See Fiske and Maddi (1961: especially chs. 2, 5, 9, 13).

23. Also see Simon (1957a: 198–219) and March and Simon (1958: 73–75).

24. Sills (1957: 254–264) discussed similar findings from three other studies; Soemardjan (1957) and Zald and Denton (1963) are also relevant.

25. Of course, any change in the organization affects its *operational* goals, and, in that sense, the described changes were changes in the movement's goals. To quote Simon (1953: 236): 'When we change the organization, we change the picture that the people in it have of the concrete tasks to be done and the concrete goals to be achieved—their concept of the program. When we change the concept of the program, we change the relative emphasis that the various parts of the complex whole will receive, we alter allocations of resources and relative priorities among goals.'

26. Clark (1962: 191–195) and Weinshall (1960–1961) contributed other discussions of formalization.

27. Cyert and March (1963), Dill (1962), Eckstein (1958), Kaufman (1960), March and Simon (1958), Selznick (1943).

28. At this point, the assumptions behind the equation become a matter for serious consideration. An equation like the one used by Haire implies that N can ultimately

become negative. At the very least one would expect $N > 0$, and in some cases it might be more reasonable to use an equation where N never decreases at all.

29. Also see Draper and Strother (1963).
30. Also see Filley (1963).
31. For a complete bibliography of studies before 1944 and a worthwhile discussion of the methodological problems, see Marschak and Andrews (1944). Phelps Brown (1957) provides another useful methodological discussion.
32. Also see Ijiri and Simon (1964).
33. Also see Christensen (1953).
34. This proposition is far from obvious at high output levels. Total short-run cost might be represented by the function $A + Bq + Cq^2$ where A, B, and C are positive parameters and q is output. Cost per unit would then be $Aq^{-1} + B + Cq$, which has the derivative with respect to q: $C - A/q^2$. As q becomes large, the righthand (fixed cost) term becomes negligible. Andrews assumed that $C = 0$. See also Alchian (1959) and Dixon (1953).
35. Ross (1952–1953: 148) made a similar statement.
36. Those who used complexity assumptions include Bossard (1945), Caplow (1957), Davis (1951), Dubin (1959), Entwisle and Walton (1961), Haire (1959), Herbst (1957), Kephart (1950), and Urwick (1956).
37. This is not the formula given by Graicunas. He used n to represent the number of subordinates; here n represents the subordinates plus their supervisor. Further, Graicunas's formulation has been corrected. He counted some dyads twice, including them under 'direct single' relationships and 'cross' relationships and also under 'direct group' relationships. The formula given is the correct one for the number of relationships 'computed on minimum basis,' that is, equating the dyads AB and BA.
38. For statistical discussions of James's data, see Coleman and James (1961), Simon (1955), and White (1962).
39. Also see Blau and Scott (1962: ch. 5).
40. There has been overlap among economists and organization theorists. Ross (1952–1953) and Andrews (1949a, 1949b) seem to have agreed with Mooney and Reiley. Conversely, Davis (1951) and Warner and Low (1947) were convinced that efficiency declined as size increased. Also see Miller (1959).
41. The section on structure as a function of size discussed data collected by Baker and Davis (1954), Blau and Scott (1962), Dale (1952), Entwistle and Walton (1961), Haas, Hall, and Johnson (1963), Haire (1959), Healey (1956), McNulty (1956–1957), Melman (1951, 1958), Terrien and Mills (1955), and Woodward (1958). The section on structure as a function of technology discussed data collected by Anderson and Warkov (1961), Blau (1957), Chowdhry and Pal (1957), Faunce (1958), Harbison and Myers (1959), Harbison et al. (1955), Simpson (1959), Udy (1959b), Walker and Guest (1952), and Woodward (1958). The section on structure as a function of time discussed data collected by Bendix (1956), Chester (1961), and Melman (1951, 1958).

APPENDIX
A MATHEMATICAL TREATMENT OF PENROSE'S MODEL

Penrose's (1959) model of growth contains logical circularities that are difficult to disentangle when the model is stated verbally. In such a circumstance, an algebraic model can be very helpful. Define:

$X(T)$ = the number of managers at time T,

$Z(T)$ = the firm's output at time T,

$V(T, \Theta)$ = the cumulative experience at time T of a manager hired at time Θ,

$Y(T, \Theta)$ = the 'managerial resources' at time T provided by one manager hired at time Θ,

$U(T)$ = the total managerial resources at time T, and

$W(T)$ = the excess managerial resources available for expansion at time T.

Considering Penrose's statement that experience is a function of work load, assume:

(1)
$$V(T, \Theta) = \int_\Theta^T \frac{Z(t)}{X(t)} \cdot dt$$

and then, because nearly all studies of learning are consistent with an exponential representation, assume:

(2)
$$Y(T, \Theta) = \alpha - \beta \cdot \text{Exp}\{-\gamma \cdot V(T, \Theta)\}$$

where α, β, and γ are all positive and $\beta > \alpha$. By definition:

(3)
$$U(T) = \int_0^T Y(T, \Theta) \cdot X'(\Theta) \cdot d\Theta$$

where X' indicates the derivative.

Penrose hypothesized some effects of size and age on the demand for managerial services for operations (1959: ch. 9). However, in the interest of simplicity, assume that the managerial services needed for operations are proportional to output:

(4)
$$W(T) = U(T) - \delta \cdot Z(T), \delta > 0$$

Similarly, assume that the rates of expansion of output and managerial employment are both proportional to excess managerial resources:

(5)
$$X'(T) = \varepsilon \cdot W(T), \varepsilon > 0$$

(6)
$$Z'(T) = \zeta \cdot W(T), \zeta > 0$$

This formulation assumes that, once employed, a manager never retires. Because a time lag must be introduced to deal with retirement, allowing for it greatly complicates the model without increasing realism commensurately.

(i) Relations (5) and (6) imply:

(7)
$$Z(T) = Z(0) + \frac{\zeta}{\varepsilon}[X(T) - X(0)].$$

(ii) Relations (4), (5), and (7) imply:

(8) $$X'(T) = \varepsilon \cdot U(T) - \varepsilon\delta \cdot Z(0) - \zeta\delta \cdot [X(T) - X(0)].$$

(iii) Relations (2) and (3) imply:

(9) $$U(T) = \alpha \cdot [X(T) - X(0)] - \beta \cdot I$$

where $$I = \int_0^T X'(\Theta) \cdot \mathrm{Exp}[-\gamma \cdot V(T, \Theta)] \cdot d\Theta.$$

(iv) Relations (8) and (9) imply:

(10) $$X'(T) = (\alpha\varepsilon - \zeta\delta) \cdot [X(T) - X(0)] - \varepsilon\delta \cdot Z(0) - \beta\varepsilon \cdot I.$$

(v) Relation (1) and the definition of I imply:

(11) $$\frac{\partial I}{\partial T} = X'(T) - I \cdot \left\{ \frac{\gamma\zeta}{\varepsilon} + \frac{\gamma}{X(T)} \cdot \left[Z(0) - \frac{\zeta}{\varepsilon} X(0) \right] \right\}.$$

(vi) Relation (11) and the derivative of (10) imply:

(12) $$X''(T) = (\alpha\varepsilon - \zeta\delta - \beta\varepsilon) \cdot X'(T) + I \cdot \left\{ \beta\gamma\zeta + \frac{\beta\gamma}{X(T)} \cdot [\varepsilon \cdot Z(0) - \zeta \cdot X(0)] \right\}.$$

(vii) Relations (10) and (12) imply:

(13) $$X''(T) + \left[\zeta\delta + \beta\varepsilon - \alpha\varepsilon + \frac{\gamma\zeta}{\varepsilon} \right] \cdot X'(T) + \frac{\gamma\zeta}{\varepsilon} \cdot [\zeta\delta - \alpha\varepsilon] \cdot X(T)$$

$$= -\alpha\gamma\zeta \cdot X(0) - [Z(0) - \frac{\zeta}{\varepsilon} \cdot X(0)] \cdot \gamma$$

$$\cdot \left\{ \frac{X'(T)}{X(T)} + 2\zeta\delta - \alpha\varepsilon + \frac{1}{X(T)} \cdot [\varepsilon\delta \cdot Z(0) - (\zeta\delta - \alpha\varepsilon) \cdot X(0)] \right\}$$

(viii) On the premise that the concern is not with starting transients, assume $X(0) = \frac{\varepsilon}{\zeta} \cdot Z(0)$ Relation (13) simplifies to:

(14) $$X''(T) + 2A \cdot X'(T) + B^2 \cdot X(T) = -\alpha\gamma\zeta \cdot X(0)$$

where $$A = \frac{1}{2} \cdot \left[\zeta\delta - \alpha\varepsilon + \beta\varepsilon + \frac{\gamma\zeta}{\varepsilon} \right] > 0$$

and $$B^2 = \frac{\gamma\zeta}{\varepsilon}(\zeta\delta - \alpha\varepsilon).$$

(ix) Relation (14) possesses the solution

$$(15) \quad X(T) = C_1 \cdot \mathrm{Exp}[(-A + \sqrt{A^2 - B^2}) \cdot T] + C_2 \cdot \mathrm{Exp}[(-A - \sqrt{A^2 - B^2}) \cdot T]$$

$$- \frac{\alpha\varepsilon}{\zeta\delta - \alpha\varepsilon} \cdot X(0)$$

where $$C_1 + C_2 = \frac{\zeta\delta}{\zeta\delta - \alpha\varepsilon} \cdot X(0).$$

(x) When $X(0) = 0$, relation (15) becomes:

$$(16) \qquad X(T) = C_0 e^{-AT} \cdot \mathrm{Sinh}\left[T\sqrt{A^2 - B^2}\right]$$

Relation (16) implies that $X(T)$ and $Z(T)$ display one of three modes of behavior:

1. When $B^2 < 0$, $X(T)$ and $Z(T)$ will grow indefinitely. $X'(T)$ and $Z'(T)$ are positive for all T. The condition $B^2 < 0$ says the total managerial services needed for production are less than the product of the maximum managerial services available from one manager times the number of managers. This requirement can always be satisfied by employing more managers if there are no financial constraints. But, of course, there always are.

2. When $0 < B^2 < A^2$, $X(T)$ and $Z(T)$ will grow and then decay. There is a T^* such that $X'(T)$ and $Z'(T)$ will be non-negative for $T = T^*$, and then will be nonpositive for $T \geq T^*$.

3. When $B^2 > A^2$, $X(T)$ will oscillate. $X'(T)$ and $Z'(T)$ will be alternately positive and negative. However, given the assumptions that all coefficients are positive, this condition can never occur.

Thus, the system has only two modes of behavior. $B^2 < 0$ corresponds to continuous growth; $B^2 > 0$ corresponds to growth and then decay. The secret to maintaining growth would be keeping B^2 negative.

2

Organizations and Their Environments

1. INTRODUCTION

This chapter is symbolized by Jonah trying to swallow the whale.

Several weeks of preparatory reading demonstrated how extensive and heterogeneous is the literature on organization–environment relations. Not only has there been no comprehensive summary of relevant knowledge, but some of the most interesting and relevant studies have appeared in journals that organization theorists ordinarily ignore. Therefore, a thorough review and synthesis would bring genuine benefits. Moreover, the literature includes many intriguing and potentially fruitful, but partially developed, notions that cry out for elaboration and theoretical cultivation, and more than a few conceptual vestibules open onto whole vistas of unexplored research terrain. It was not difficult to outline a chapter that promised to be socially useful without boring anyone.

However, the finished document deviates somewhat from its initial outline. Close examination disclosed that only a book could effectively summarize the research, and it would be quite a long book at that. Bringing immature ideas to ripeness could not be a primary objective because of time constraints. At least for this author, ideas will not mature according to a schedule. Therefore, the central thrust had to become the pointing out of portals that evidently lead to vast unexplored regions, together with enough editorial comments about theory and method to facilitate the work of exploration. However, even this restricted objective exploded into an unmanageably large task during the writing, as each opened door revealed another long gallery of doors to open. In consequence, the material to follow covers less than one-third of the originally planned content.

The chapter is composed of three main sections, each divided into several subsections. The first, titled Boundaries, is concerned with the demarcation between an organization and its environment. The second, titled Domains, Roles, and Territories, discusses the logical associations between organizational and environmental characteristics. The third, titled Adaptation, Evolution, and Research Strategy, is devoted to the dynamics over time of organization–environment relations. However, all three sections possess similar general orientations—indicating some fundamental philosophical issues and the methodological dilemmas they create, surveying alternative conceptual formulations and their implications for research strategy, and identifying topics on which research effort ought to be especially productive.

The net result cannot fail to persuade researchers that the study of organization–environment relations offers adequate scope for them to expend their time and to release their energies. One can easily avoid familiar, carefully worked out ideas and integrated sets of concepts. Unless they consciously seek contact, researchers are unlikely to find themselves even brushing against others' territories. Not only do the puzzles not unravel themselves, but many resemble Gordian knots. Very modest searches will uncover questions about which no data exist.

Merely the vision of such opportunities must be irresistibly attractive...to people with a craving for whale.

2. BOUNDARIES

One difficulty inherent in studying organizations' relations with their environments is that one must distinguish organization from environment. Even talking about an organization's environment implies that the organization differs from its environment. Yet the two are not separate, and a boundary between them is partially an arbitrary invention of the perceiver (Child 1969, 1972; Thompson 1962).

An organization displays some of the properties of a cloud or magnetic field. When one is far enough inside it, one can see its characteristics and effects all about; and when one is far enough outside it, one can see that it comprises a distinctive section of social space. However, as one approaches the boundary, the boundary fades into ambiguity and becomes only a region of gradual transition that extends from the organization's central core far out into the surrounding space. One can sometimes say 'Now I am inside' or 'Now I am outside', but one can never confidently say 'This is the boundary'.

In fact, organizational boundaries are even more ambiguous than are those of clouds and magnetic fields. One can identify a cloud or magnetic field by the presence of a single phenomenon—water droplets or magnetic force. However, one cannot identify an organization by the presence of a single phenomenon because organization implies the conjunction of several related but imperfectly correlated phenomena. Consider the variety of definitions of organization. A consequence is that an organization has different shapes and different boundaries depending on what organizational phenomena are observed and on who does the observing. Another consequence is that a specific organizational component may appear to be central as measured by some phenomena and appear to be peripheral as measured by other phenomena, and a specific environmental component may be proximate according to some phenomena and remote according to others.

At least the foregoing are conjectures based on experiential evidence. Researchers have not studied organizational boundaries in an empirically systematic fashion. Studies of intraorganizational authority, influence, and clique structures have assumed that organizational boundaries are known, and they have focused on individuals falling within the boundaries. Studies of job involvement, role conflict, and competition between organizational and professional norms have aggregated individuals from many different organizations. An apparently smooth and continuous boundary according to multiorganizational data might only signify that discrete, discontinuous boundaries occurred in different places in different organizations. The multiorganizational studies have also assumed that only persons falling within some defined boundary are relevant. Finally, existing studies have concentrated on a single organizational phenomenon or on a cluster of closely associated phenomena, searching for correlations and consistencies rather than for orthogonalities and inconsistencies. A given individual is only likely to be central on one dimension and peripheral on another if the two dimensions are distinctly different.

A Not-Entirely-Hypothetical Example

To see whether his conjectures about centrality and peripherality make sense, and to see what might emerge from systematic studies, the author fabricated measurements from case evidence about a manufacturing firm with which he has had extensive contact. He listed specific people with whose work he was familiar, wrote down what he knew about their behaviors, and estimated the measurements that a real study might yield. Unfortunately, the list of people was short and it contained people having similar jobs, so the author drew up a supplementary list of other people whose activities were familiar and who worked in or dealt with firms like the one being approximated. To provide weak insurance against the author's prejudices, all of the fabricated measurements were components of scales—such as frequencies, percentages, upper and lower bounds, and rates per unit of time—and not the scales themselves.

Figure 2.1, based on these fabricated measurements, shows the positions of various people on four scales that one can interpret as measuring distances from the organization's center. Exponential transformations give all four scales approximately the same range. Obviously, many other scales are possible, and some alternatives probably represent more important dimensions than those in Figure 2.1. For example, one could examine hours spent in prescribed role activities or pay received from the firm. If one can define the sets of insiders and outsiders meaningfully, one could look at social visibility within the set of insiders, or at the ratio of inside to outside visibility (Haire 1959). The four dimensions in Figure 2.1 were chosen because they show rather different patterns and they do not assume a known set of insiders.[1]

The subsets labeled Boundary one are those including both people who are conventionally regarded as members of the firm (a member of the board of directors, a typist, an operations research analyst) and people who are conventionally regarded as members of other organizations (the union's bargaining representative and shop steward, a competing firm's president and salesman). One possible rule to distinguish insiders from outsiders is that an insider is inside

Distance from company's center	Dimension 1 Psychological job investment (Hours spent on activities directly affecting the company, times job involvement)	Dimension 2 Social visibility (Hours spent on social interaction relevant to company, times numbers of people[1] talked to at one time)	Dimension 3 Influence on resource allocation (Expected[2] increments in the values of the company's resource flows)	Dimension 4 System response speed (Reciprocal of the median time for decisions to take effect)
1 –	Vice president heading division President	Telephone switchboard operator	President	Telephone switchboard operator
	Plant manager Sales manager at plant level Production scheduler at plant level Analyst on operations research staff Accountant on corporate staff	President	Vice president heading division Plant manager	
3 –	Department foreman in plant Salesman Production planner at plant level	Vice president heading division Plant manager Sales manager at plant level Department foreman in plant	Sales manager at plant level	
	Unskilled worker in plant Corporate lawyer, part-time	Analyst on operations research staff Salesman Typist in secretarial pool	Production scheduler at plant level	
	Telephone switchboard operator	Production scheduler at plant level Production planner at plant level Corporate lawyer, part-time	Union's bargaining representative Competing firm's president.	Unskilled worker in plant
10 –	Typist in secretarial pool Competing firm's president. Competing firm's salesman —Midpoint of boundary two	—Midpoint of boundary two Accountant on corporate staff Unskilled worker in plant	—Gap within boundary one	
32 –	Union shop steward, part-time Competing firm's production scheduler	Competing firm's salesman Competing firm's president. Union shop steward, part-time —Midpoint of boundary one —Gap within boundary one	Corporate lawyer, part-time —Midpoint of boundary two Department foreman in plant Production planner at plant level Accountant on corporate staff	Typist in secretarial pool Department foreman in plant
	—Midpoint of boundary one	Competing firm's production scheduler Outside member, board of directors Union's bargaining representative	—Midpoint of boundary one Salesman Large regular customer Telephone switchboard operator Agent for internal revenue service Outside member, board of directors Analyst on operations research staff	
100 –	—Gap within boundary one			
316 –	Union's bargaining representative Outside member, board of directors agent for internal revenue service		Union shop steward, part-time Unskilled worker in plant Competing firm's production scheduler Competing firm's salesman	—Midpoint of boundary two
	Large, regular customer		Typist in secretarial pool	Union shop steward, part-time
1000 –				Production scheduler at plant level
		Large, regular customer	Banker	Large, regular customer
	Banker	Agent for internal revenue service	Property assessor, local government	Salesman Accountant on corporate staff
3162 –	Property assessor; local government	Banker		—Gap within boundary one
	Small, infrequent customer	Property assessor, local government		Competing firm's salesman Sales manager at plant level Corporate lawyer, part-time. Plant manager Vice president heading division Competing firm's production scheduler
10,000 –		Small, infrequent customer	Small, infrequent customer Member of local zoning commission	—Midpoint of boundary one Banker
		Member of local zoning commission		Small, infrequent customer Union's bargaining representative President
31,623 –				Member of local zoning commission
				Agent for internal revenue service Small stockholder
				Property assessor, local government
	Voter, local elections			Outside member, board of directors Production planner at plant level Analyst of operations research staff Competing firm's president
100,000 –	Small stockholder Member of local zoning commission	Voter, local elections	Voter, local elections	Voter, local elections
	Small stockholder	Small stockholder		

[1] All people are counted equally, independent of their affiliations with the subject firm.

[2] The expectation allows for the probability that taken decisions will actually be implemented.

Figure 2.1. Distances, on four dimensions, from a manufacturing firm's center

on all dimensions and an outsider outside on all dimensions. As shown in Table 2.1, this rule implies that none of the twenty-eight people is an insider and that only the voter in local elections is an outsider. A second rule would be

Table 2.1. Insiders and outsiders among the people listed in Figure 2.1

Criterion	Insiders	Outsiders
Above the Boundary one subsets on all four dimensions, or below the Boundary one subsets on all four dimensions	None	Local voter
Above the midpoints of the Boundary one subsets on all four dimensions, or below the midpoints of the Boundary one subsets on all four dimensions	Department foreman Divisional vice president Plant manager Sales manager Production scheduler Staff accountant Corporate lawyer	Local voter Small stockholder Zoning commissioner Small customer Property assessor Banker IRS agent Outside director
Above the midpoints of the Boundary two subsets on all four dimensions, or below the midpoints of the Boundary two subsets on all four dimensions	None	Local voter Small stockholder Zoning commissioner Small customer Property assessor Banker IRS agent Outside director Large customer Competitor's scheduler Union's steward
Above the largest gaps in the Boundary one subsets on all four dimensions, or below the largest gaps in the Boundary one subsets on all four dimensions	Production scheduler	Local voter Small stockholder Zoning commissioner Small customer Property assessor Banker IRS agent Outside director

that an insider is inside the midpoints of the boundaries on all dimensions and that an outsider is outside all the boundary midpoints. If one takes Boundary one as a premise, this rule identifies seven insiders and eight outsiders, and leaves thirteen people in the boundary category. However, identifying new sets of insiders and outsiders calls for redefining the boundary. A new boundary implies further changes in the sets of insiders and outsiders, and further changes in the boundary itself. The results of following these iterative cycles to their logical conclusions are shown as Boundary two. According to the midpoints of the Boundary two subsets, there are no insiders and eleven outsiders.

Boundary two implies that, although one can identify some people who fall outside a given organization, no one is an insider with respect to all of the organization's activities. This is partly a consequence of the inverse relationship between a decision's magnitude and its time-span of implementation. Small decisions take effect promptly; large decisions concern the future and may never take effect because the farther into the future one plans, the lower the chance that one's plans will prove useful. The lack of insiders may also partly result from the curvatures of the four scales. The midpoint of a scale segment is sensitive to the scale's metric properties, and nonlinear transformations of the scales shift the boundary midpoints.

Boundary two has the advantage that it relies on observed behaviors rather than social conventions, but the midpoints criterion has the disadvantage that it ignores the possibility of a discrete organizational boundary. A discrete boundary would not necessarily fall near the center of a boundary region. If there were discrete boundaries between the firm and its environment, they would appear as gaps in the scales of Figure 2.1. A gap implies that everyone is either unambiguously inside and above the gap, or unambiguously outside and below the gap. Unfortunately, however, one cannot say that a gap exists until one has enumerated everyone, because one cannot say no one falls within a given region until one can say where everyone does fall. This is a practically insurmountable hurdle, given that *everyone* must encompass people in the organization's environment and given that the people surrounding gaps would not traditionally be organizational members. Nevertheless, Figure 2.1 illustrates this idea by identifying the largest gap within each instance of Boundary one. In addition, Table 2.1 shows that the gaps criterion identifies the same outsiders as did the midpoints criterion, but the gaps criterion identifies the production scheduler as the sole insider.

Some Research Problems Suggested by Centrality Measurements

If the empirical hurdles to discovering gaps in the organization-environment transition can be overcome, a payoff would be the sorting out of various conceptualizations of organization–environment relations. For example, Dill (1958), Emery and Trist (1965), Evan (1965, 1966), Haire (1959), Levine and White (1961), Normann (1971), and Terreberry (1968) have assumed that perceivers can distinguish organization from environment and they can classify environmental components as relevant or irrelevant. This implies that there should be at least two gaps in each organization–environment dimension: one gap identifying everyone unambiguously as an insider or outsider, and another gap separating relevant outsiders from irrelevant ones. The example of Figure 2.1 suggests that neither gap exists in an absolute sense, and that organization–environment dimensions are either continua or so different from each other that composite dimensions are continua (Hoiberg and Cloyd 1971). Child (1972), Guetzkow (1966), Litwak and Hylton (1962), Miller (1972), Thompson (1962), and Weick (1969) have taken the latter view.

Gaps or no, measures of the organization–environment transition are a necessary first step toward discovering conditions making organizations more or less independent of their environments. For instance, Beesley (1955) and Stinchcombe (1965) have argued that organizations breed more organizations by training organization founders and by creating demands for the outputs of organized activities. Stinchcombe also proposed that the prevalence of organizations increases with the society's literacy and schooling rates, with its degree of urbanization, and with its utilization of monetary transactions.[2] If new organizations do not always replace old organizations, more organizations per capita imply more organizational memberships per capita. Moreover, if nearly everyone belongs to some organization, or if organization memberships are restricted to an elite subpopulation, more memberships per capita imply more organizational interdependence. Therefore, organizations might become more interdependent as their societies become more literate, monetary, and the like.

On the other hand, the logic linking the preceding propositions becomes binding only in extreme cases, and all real societies may fall into the nonextreme ranges where logical necessity fades into ambiguity. Two important contingencies are the society's norms about role compartmentalization and about organizations' purposes. It could be that organizationally sparse societies create broad-purpose organizations and insist that role behaviors in different organizations be logically compatible; and it could be that organizationally dense societies create narrow-purpose organizations and encourage membership schizophrenia (Stinchcombe 1965: 146). Societies also differ in the constraints they impose on organizational memberships. Centrally planned economies ordinarily require that the focal political parties have representation on all economically relevant policymaking bodies, whereas the United States (at least officially) proscribes overt participation in business firms by members of the federal government and members of competing firms (Berle and Means 1967; Chatov 1971; Gordon 1961; Pfeffer 1972). Bennis (1970) forecasted, 'This idea of the mono-organizational commitment will likely erode in the future where more and more people will create pluralistic commitments to a number of organizations', but he did not explain why.

The argument that organizational density induces organizational interdependence emphasizes the importance of people and roles, and it is essentially opposite to the argument usually put forth about the differences between oligopolies and purely competitive markets. The latter emphasizes the importance of information and perception, saying that interdependence only affects behavior when the total number of interdependent organizations is small enough for one organization to perceive the others as unique individuals and small enough to enable stable coalitions (Caves 1967; Stigler 1968). When the total number of interdependent organizations becomes very large, interorganizational perceptions diffuse and generalize, and the potential impacts of one organization on another dwindle in relative importance. An organization in a densely populated sector should behave in terms of the sector's general properties, and should assume that its own behaviors will not change the sector's properties. When the number of interdependent organizations becomes very small (but greater than one), interorganizational perceptions differentiate among the other organizations, and the potential influences of one organization on another become more significant. An organization in a sparsely populated sector should forecast other organizations' behaviors, including the other organizations' responses to its own acts. Since such forecasts are neither easy nor reliable and since the small number of relevant parties makes direct negotiation feasible, sparsely populated sectors tend to form coalitions (Aiken and Hage 1968; Caves 1967; Friesema 1970; Levine and White 1961; Litwak and Hylton 1962; Pfeffer 1971).

In the late nineteenth and early twentieth centuries, many large business firms emerged either as voluntary coalitions of small firms or as attempts by some wealthy owners to impose control. Ever since, it has been popular to predict that industry is becoming more concentrated and interdependent (Emery and Trist 1965; Terreberry 1968). Economic statistics suggest that some industries (automobiles, flour, glass, malt liquors) have clearly increased in concentration, some industries (cement, chemicals, fertilizers, paper and pulp) have clearly decreased in concentration, and the overall trend across all industries has been negligible (Caves 1967: 32–35; Steindl 1965: 187–221; Stigler 1968: 74–88; Weiss 1965). However, the economic time-series describe artificially defined industries that may or may not exist in the real world of organizational behavior. The time trends might look quite different if researchers would use data such as those in Figure 2.1 to measure the relative influences of competitors, customers, suppliers, government agencies, and so forth, and then would identify organizations as interdependent based on actual behaviors. Indeed, Levine (1972) has mapped some networks of banks and industrial firms created by interlocking directorates. This is precisely the kind of analysis needed, but interlocking directorates are only one form of interorganizational relationship and far from being the most important form.

Centrality data analogous to Figure 2.1 offer the opportunity for at least two more lines of research. First, one could establish an empirical weighting function for measures of organizational effectiveness (Seashore and Yuchtman 1967; Yuchtman and Seashore 1967) or at least, one could discover how weighting functions vary with measures of effectiveness. If an organization has different shapes and different boundaries from the viewpoints of different observers, effectiveness depends on the observer's frame of reference (Friedlander and Pickle 1968). Second, the scales of Figure 2.1 describe people in an unsatisfactory way because one supervisor may do quite different things from another. From centrality data, one could establish job taxonomies based on similar role profiles, establish organizational taxonomies based on similarities in the ways influences are distributed, and probably eliminate (explain) a lot of the variance in present observations of job involvement, morale, pay, status, and the like.

The most important consequence of such data would be a revised concept of what organizations are. If the fabricated measures in Figure 2.1 approximate reality, this would be more a revolution than a revision, for the fabricated measures imply that one should stop thinking of organizations as distinguishable subsets of society, and start thinking of them as hills in a geography of human activities (Pock 1972). Social groups and networks would appear as mounds and ridges on the organizational hills, and societies and economies would appear as islands and continents (Crozier 1972; Hoiberg and Cloyd 1971; Levine 1972).

Since there are many activity dimensions, one must choose the dimensions one wishes to map—just as geographers must choose whether to map altitudes, climates, population densities, or transport networks—and the shapes of organizational hills will shift as functions of the dimensions mapped. Based on Figure 2.1, a map of psychological job investment would show a set of interdependent organizations as a cluster of plateaus separated from each other by shallow valleys, and separated from the general population of organizations by deep valleys; a map of response speed would show each organization as a steep spire rising from an undulating plain. In either case, some people conventionally classified as organization members would be undifferentiated from the population at large, and other people would be difficult to assign to a specific organization.

This view of organization is hardly new. It is latent in many texts on organizations, social psychology, social anthropology, and industrial structure (e.g. Katz and Kahn 1966: 30–70), and the maps one could draw are kindred to the organization chart and the sociogram. However, no one has yet collected the data to convert a general orientation into a perceptual frame of reference, and when someone does this, it will transform the topography of organization theory.

At present, virtually all organizational research assumes organizations can be sharply distinguished from their environments. A given person or phenomenon is inside or outside, or relevant or irrelevant. This practice is analogous to trying to develop a physics of gases based on a dichotomy like breathable–unbreathable that scrambles variables together and ignores fine gradations in temperature, pressure, and chemical composition. The dichotomy makes such strong monotonicity assumptions and discards so much information that it is nearly valueless, and yet its acceptability as a measurement standard blocks systematic observations of temperature, pressure, and composition. Such simple and useful relations as Boyle's and Avogadro's Laws may indefinitely remain undiscovered.

3. DOMAINS, ROLES, AND TERRITORIES

Studies of organization–environment relations also draw complexity from the ambiguous, relativistic character of organizational environments (Barker 1968; Weick 1969). To no small degree, an organization's environment is an arbitrary invention of the organization itself. The organization selects the environments it will inhabit, and then it subjectively defines the environments it has selected.

Environmental Selection

Because environments can vary on multitude dimensions and each dimension can assume many values, an organization has potential access to a vast number of environments. Since the organization occupies just a few of these environments, it effectively selects some alternatives. At least, that is an abstract conceptualization. Actual selection processes are neither explicit, thoughtful, nor orderly.

Organizations exclude many environments from consideration by imposing constraints unreflectively or unconsciously, through assumptions and values that are inherent in decision-making procedures (Buck 1966; Starbuck and Dutton 1973). One reason criteria are implicit, rather than explicit, is that the organization acquired them by imitating other organizations in its social reference group. Since the tendency is to imitate choices rather than rules for choosing, the organization does not have to consider what the rules are; and even if it imitates rules, there is no contrast with neighboring organizations to make the organization consider why it does what it does. Another reason for criteria being implicit is that selection processes progress incrementally (Mintzberg 1972; Normann 1971). An organization only examines its environmental choices because external pressures, such as the actions of competing organizations, raise doubts about the viability of its present environment (Hedberg 1973, 1974; Terreberry 1968); and the organization only reevaluates those environmental segments that are under attack. Selection criteria supporting unthreatened environments remain implicit, even though they may be logically inconsistent with the criteria explicitly applied in threatened domains.

Implicit selection criteria depend less strongly on an organization itself than on its neighbors—the surrounding system of organizations that Evan (1966) called the organization-set. Members of the organization-set provide the examples for imitation (Chandler 1962; Richman and Copen 1972; Starbuck and Dutton 1973; Stinchcombe 1965). They make the attacks that instigate environmental reassessments, and then they constrain the directions incremental revisions can take (Clark 1965; Levine and White 1961; Maniha and Perrow 1965; Thompson and McEwen 1958; Weick 1969). They set prices, costs, and available resources, and they preserve and transmit managerial traditions. Since implicit criteria filter out nearly all environmental alternatives and leave only a few for explicit consideration (Cyert, Simon, and Trow 1956), an organization's ultimate environmental selections strongly reflect the properties of its organization-set. As a result, the degrees to which specific organizations occupy appropriate environments partially reflect organizational social systems as wholes (Hirsch 1972; Levine and White 1961).

Once an organization has explicitly identified environmental alternatives, it must select some to inhabit. However, organizations' choices among explicit alternatives are none too systematic (Cohen, March, and Olsen 1972; Cyert, Simon, and Trow 1956; Normann 1971). Some environmental alternatives possess special prominence because they predate the choice question and even the organization or because they come with unusually large amounts of information. Other alternatives appear promising or unpromising based on a priori theories that owe as much to folklore and myth as to analysis and evidence. Organizations tend to evaluate alternatives with whatever data they can acquire easily and quickly. They reject some alternatives because of initial impressions that would not survive investigation, and they make other alternatives final contenders on equally superficial grounds.[3] Not infrequently, evaluation data come from other organizations that are advocating the selection of particular alternatives—potential customers or suppliers, communities seeking industrial employers, and so on.

Of course, noise and disorder in the selection process degrade the association between organizational and environmental properties. Even if an organization would attempt to choose environments that match and complement its idiosyncratic strengths and weaknesses, it would likely end up in environments whose properties correlate only loosely with its idiosyncrasies. In addition, nearly all organizations find it impossible to assess themselves and to choose matching environments (Starbuck and Dutton 1973; Wildavsky 1972). They find it difficult to acknowledge and to discuss their own inadequacies and incompetences. They avoid strategic specialization, both because they see diversification as a hedge against risk and because specialization concentrates intraorganizational power in the hands of persons having appropriate expertise. They seek reassurance in goals and solutions that have the endorsement of universal acceptance and use. In addition, insofar as possible, they avoid talking about ultimate goals and values at all, preferring to escape interpersonal conflict and to maintain an atmosphere of cooperative problem solving. The result is that organizations rarely achieve even the degree of environmental compatibility attainable with badly conducted selection processes, and the overwhelming majority of organizations inhabit environments characterized by extremely weak appropriateness (Bell 1974; Starbuck and Dutton 1973).

Environmental Perception

The second aspect of the environmental invention process is perceptual relativity. The same environment one organization perceives as unpredictable, complex, and evanescent, another organization might see as static and easily understood.

Interorganizational perception differences are partially analogous to the differences between two individual humans. Every perception system encounters difficulties in discovering reality inductively; and to learn an environment's causal structure solely through observation of naturally occurring phenomena is virtually impossible because autocorrelations among successive observations can be produced either by a variable's dependence on its own past values or by interdependence among groups of variables. The abstract feasibility of sorting out correct from incorrect explanations becomes practically relevant only after perceivers have accumulated literally tens of thousands of successive observations, and by that time, the causal structure may well have shifted to a new form.

Consequently, perceivers' ability to organize and interpret their observations depends very strongly on the theories and beliefs they hold a priori, and they tend to learn what they already believed (Clark 1970, 1972; Dill 1962).

The degree to which an environment is simple and predictable is especially contingent on prior beliefs. Suppose, for example, problem solvers start out with the premise that their environments are fundamentally simple—being decomposable into just a few broad classes of phenomena that follow smooth, easily expressed trends—but that actual events are to some extent randomly determined in the sense that they include erratic components unique to a specific time and circumstance. These problem solvers set about discovering continuous, readily understandable patterns, and because that is what they seek, any observational components implying complexity and discontinuity appear as random deviations about average patterns. They also aggregate their observations across different times and circumstances in order to distill out generally valid truths. They perceive competing problem solvers, for instance, as specific realizations of a large, general class, and these competitors are individually uninteresting because the problem solvers characterize competitive behavior on the basis of its uniformities across different individuals.

The chance such problem solvers will ever have to question their initial preconceptions is very small. Their every experience, having both general, explicable components and unique, random components, fits neatly into their perceptual frameworks and confirms the wisdom underlying their prior beliefs. If the accuracy of their predictions is low, it is nevertheless as high as the environment allows, and they need only look to their neighbors to see that their predictions have comparable accuracy. Of course, their neighbors obtained their prior beliefs through the same socialization process as the problem solvers and they use similar analytic methods.

However, organizational perceptions are even more relativistic than are those of individuals. One reason is that organizations are exceptionally conscious of and inclined to accept social reality. They hire personnel from neighboring organizations and imitate their methods; they form coalitions (e.g. trade associations) with other organizations for acquiring environmental data and influencing environmental variables; they send personnel to interorganizational training programs and conventions; they encourage personnel to belong to professional associations and to adopt professionally approved methods. They also devote substantial resources to consensus development and distill out the common elements from members' heterogeneous experiences. Such collective socialization processes homogenize perceptions across different organizations and reduce each organization's sensitivity to the unique and unusual characteristics of its own environments.

Consensus production has the additional effect of eliciting affective commitments to existing, socially approved perceptions, and so heightening the dependence of organizational perception systems on prior beliefs. Yet, consensus production is only one of several processes that reduce the amount of ambiguity an organization can assign to its current knowledge in anticipation of future learning, that create inertia against the incorporation of new perceptions, and that institutionalize data-collection formats that reinforce prior beliefs. For example, organizations tend to crystallize and preserve their existing knowledge whenever they set up systems to routinely collect, aggregate, and analyze information, whenever they identify and allocate areas of responsibility, whenever they hire people who possess particular skills and experiences, and whenever they plan long-range strategies and invest in capital goods (Aguilar 1967; Child 1972; Dill 1962; Mintzberg 1972; Normann 1971). It is literally as well as poetically true that organizations cast their prior beliefs in steel and concrete.

Finally, organizations normally play influential, active roles in their own environments (Weick 1969). Partly because they seek environments that are sparsely inhabited by competitors (locating one's fish-and-chips shop at least 200 yards from the existing ones), partly because they subjectively define their products and outputs in ways that emphasize distinctions between themselves and their competitors (the only one of the Chinese restaurants in Lafayette, Indiana, that specializes in Northern Cantonese cuisine), partly because they infer what environmental possibilities exist based on past and present experiences (young people are more likely than middle-aged ones to use marijuana), and partly because they must impose simplicity on extremely complex interrelationships (eight competitors might be treated as distinct individuals, but 800 cannot be), organizations perceive their environments as systems in which they themselves constitute important components. Moreover, to no small extent, these perceptions validate both themselves and organizations' beliefs about environmental structure. It is primarily in domains where an organization believes it exerts influence that the organization attributes changes to its own influence, and in domains where an organization believes itself impotent, it tends to ignore influence opportunities and never to discover whether its impotence is real. Of course, someone who launches a marriage agency on the premise that people have difficulty finding suitable mates is likely to observe that clients have found it difficult to find suitable mates. Moreover, it is the beliefs and perceptions founded on social reality that are especially liable to self-confirmation. A lone baker who increases his flour inventory because he thinks the flour price will rise for a few weeks and then fall might well be wrong, but if many bakers respond to a shared, collective forecast by increasing their inventories, their expectations will quite probably be confirmed.

Analytical Strategies and Environmental Dimensions

The foregoing discussion implies that organization–environment relations constitute highly complex and ambiguous stimuli to persons who are trying to observe them. Naturally, enough, these ambiguous stimuli have evoked heterogeneous responses from different observers.

Organization theorists have taken at least five different approaches toward describing the environmental elements that have direct, immediate effects on organizational behaviors. One group of theorists has emphasized primarily the effects of interorganizational relations, whereas another group has adopted inclusive viewpoints in which interorganizational relations are merely components. Within each of these general groups, there have been subgroups differing in the emphases they placed on data obtained from organizational members versus data obtained from outside observers, and differing in the emphases they placed on prescriptive versus descriptive information. Various theorists have elaborated these perceptual orientations into at least twenty terminological variations.[4]

The complexity of organization–environment relations and the ambiguity of organizational boundaries imply also that different perceivers will disagree about what dimensions characterize organizations versus what dimensions characterize environments. For example, this author would argue that an organization's technology, its perceptual characteristics, or its ability to predict future events are more properly dimensions of an organization itself than dimensions of its environment. However, Dill (1958), Evan (1966), Khandwalla (1973), Normann (1969), and Thompson (1967) have classified as environmental dimensions such technological characteristics as the disruptiveness of environmental inputs or the range of technology used. Duncan (1972, 1973), Emery and Trist (1965), Khandwalla (1973, 1972), Lawrence and Lorsch (1967), McWhinney (1968), and Thompson (1967) have treated an organization's inability to predict future events as environmental uncertainty. In addition, Dill (1958), Duncan (1972), Lawrence and Lorsch (1967), and Thompson (1967) have put into the environmental category such perceptual characteristics as clarity of information or time span of feedback.

This kind of conceptual disagreement is, to some extent, irresolvable. Phenomena involving interactions between organization and environment necessarily reflect the characteristics of both. Consider, for instance, an organization (or whose environment) has a long time span of feedback for price changes; that is, after a price change, a rather long time elapses before the organization notices such responses as changed product demand or changed prices sought by competitors. If the long time lapse occurs because customers and competitors are price-insensitive and do not even notice that the price changed, one could argue that slow feedback is an environmental property. On the other hand, one could argue that slow feedback is an organizational property if the long time lapse occurs because the organization has inadequate and insensitive perceptual mechanisms, as in the classic case of a manufacturing firm that attends only to the orders it receives from wholesalers and ignores what happens at the retail level. Of course, such pure cases do not occur in reality. Every organization has some perceptual mechanisms that are less effective and sensitive than they might be, and every environment ignores some organizational activities.

Nevertheless, organization theorists could reduce the frequency of conceptual confusion and disagreement by avoiding concepts that include interactions between organization and environment. Time span of feedback, for example, could become two concepts: the environment's reaction speed and the organization's reaction speed; and there would probably be stronger consensus that an environment's reaction speed is an environmental characteristic and that an organization's reaction speed is an organizational characteristic. However, even this split would not fully resolve the debate. An environment's reaction speed to price changes could be substantially different from its reaction speed to advertising changes, and hence an aggregated reaction speed to marketing changes would depend on the organization's propensities for price or advertising changes. Again, researchers can reduce confusion through more detailed specification ('the environment's reaction speed to . . .'), but they can never erase the residual ambiguity entirely because interactive phenomena depend intrinsically on both participants in the interaction.

It would also help if concept formulators adhered to the principle that measures based solely on subjective data provide information about the informant, not about the informant's environment. If the only data in a study of Harry Brown's relation to his 'environment' were Harry's self-reports, one would expect to find concepts like cognitive balance (or congruence or consonance) appearing prominently in the analysis. In the absence of corroborating evidence, one would not accept Harry's description of his environment as being objectively realistic. Even if Harry were multiplied into all the inhabitants of a town, one would expect the analyst to make statements of the form 'The inhabitants of Brownville perceive their environment as offering equal opportunity to all', rather than 'The Brownville environment offers equal opportunity to all'.

By contrast, studies that have tried to measure organizations' environmental uncertainty (Duncan 1972, 1973; Khandwalla 1972; Lawrence and Lorsch 1967) have depended entirely upon subjective data obtained from the organizations' members, and yet they have spoken as if environmental uncertainty were a characteristic of some objectively real environment. There is a strong case for saying that uncertainty is inevitably a characteristic of a perceiver rather than of a perceived situation, and hence that studies of environmental uncertainty are inevitably studies of ideology and attitude structure. A similar observation applies to any study that measures both organizational and environmental properties with reports from organization members. The logic of reality becomes comparatively irrelevant and the logic of ideology dominates. Moreover, even if researchers measure organizational properties in some objective fashion, the realism of environmental perceptions may be irrelevant. Organization members should adapt their organizations to the environments that they believe exist, whether their perceptions would be objectively confirmed or not. Therefore, the usefulness of subjective perceptions, including environmental uncertainty, is not in question. What is in question is whether researchers should treat data about perceived environments as if they were data about real environments and whether researchers should consider uncertainty to be an environmental characteristic.[5]

4. ADAPTATION, EVOLUTION, AND RESEARCH STRATEGY

The many questions on which little or no systematic research exists suggest that the topic of organization–environment relations offers opportunities for dramatic research progress. Although this promise appears real, its fulfillment will depend strongly on judicious choices of research questions and methods. The complexity and richness of organization–environment relations imply high frequencies of logical ambiguities, simultaneous relations, and spurious correlations. Statistically significant correlations will probably be prevalent, substantively significant correlations will probably be rare, and truly profound discoveries will probably require research techniques radically different from those organization theorists presently use.

Few Organizations or Many?

One strategic choice a researcher faces is whether to study just a few organizations or many. Assuming the total resources available for data collection are predetermined and independent of the number of organizations studied, observing more organizations means observing fewer characteristics of each organization or obtaining fewer consecutive observations of each variable. Therefore, someone seeking to build and document a complex, dynamic theory should investigate comparatively few organizations at one time, and someone working toward a simple, static theory should observe many organizations simultaneously (Starbuck 1968).

One can debate whether organization theorists ought to be giving first priority to complex, dynamic theories or to simple, static theories, of course; but so many research topics remain unexplored that assigning priorities among them is substantially an act of faith. It is as if, based on their first impressions, the blind men tried to decide which part of the elephant should have first priority for further investigation. For the time being, there is latitude to indulge the personal preferences of leg-men, tail-men, and trunk-men.

Still, it is important to recognize that apparently superficial choice criteria—like the number of organizations studied—may embody rather profound substantive issues. A researcher who opts for trunks is likely to study elephants; one who opts for tails is likely to study peacocks; and the two may find themselves with much greater comparability problems than the legendary blind men faced.

As normally conducted, studies of many organizations reveal the general behavioral propensities that permeate cultures, industries, and similar aggregates; but the disclosures are so macroscopic and diffuse that an analyst glimpses only the grossest causal relationships, and one suspects that the composite pattern is as much an artificial product of aggregation techniques as a valid insight into real behavior. For example, if guided by average statistics, one might get the impression that small corporations grow into middle-sized ones, and eventually into large corporations (Crum 1953; Steindl 1965). However, nearly all small corporations simply go out of business before they are ten years old, the highest percentage of middle-sized corporations are less than two years old, and a large proportion of the largest corporations are essentially new births. The implication (neither supported nor denied by published statistics) is that most large corporations were at least middle-sized at birth, and only a very small portion of them grew from small beginnings.

Researchers can reduce this aura of artificiality—and partially replace it by a sense of immediate, live, causally connected activity—through intensive studies of one or two organizations. However, case studies normally impress observers with the high proportion of organizational resources devoted to apparently unique, idiosyncratic, or nonrecurring activities, thereby casting suspicion that the studied organization is unrepresentative. Even a case example chosen to typify a large class of organizations would almost certainly persuade an intimate observer that it possesses enough atypical properties to render it a poor basis for generalization. So people who study just one or two organizations tend to observe deviant and peculiar details characterizing single organizations, whereas people who study many organizations simultaneously tend to discover aggregate, general propensities to which few, if any, organizations conform exactly.

Large-sample studies are also comparatively effective sources of information about environmental constraints, such as legal restraints on organizational forms and behaviors, natural resource limitations, or technological feasibilities. Truly operational constraints must manifest themselves in the behaviors of large numbers of organizations, since a law that few observe is not an effective constraint. On the other hand, it is very difficult to think of environmental constraints that are not (or cannot be) violated by specific, individual organizations. Sometimes the violations are surreptitious and clandestine, as in the case of most criminal activities, and sometimes the violations are overt and socially sanctioned, as in the case of most patented production techniques. In any event, one cannot depend on case studies alone to reveal the existence and forms of environmental constraints, because a studied case may violate some, or even many, of the constraints that bind other organizations.

A constraint creates both a limitation and an opportunity at the same time. Laws forbidding the sale of heroin present quasi-monopolistic opportunities for organizations that are prepared and able to behave illegally; a patent advantages the patent holder precisely because it restricts the behaviors of other organizations. Moreover, analogous dualities are implicit in many of the aggregate behavioral propensities exposed by large-sample studies. Substantial returns to scale in automobile manufacture contribute to market domination by high volume, semistandard products; but this mass market also, by leaving some customers unsatisfied, makes possible the existence of such small-volume manufacturers as Morgan, Bristol, and Stutz. One cannot expect large-sample studies to disclose how people identify and exploit such idiosyncratic opportunities because large-sample methodology has difficulty coping with nonrandom deviations from aggregate patterns. Studies of carefully selected individual organizations are far more effective for that purpose.

In summary, large-sample studies show the anatomy of conformity whereas small-sample studies show the anatomy of deviance. To the extent one must understand deviance in order to comprehend conformity—and conversely—the two types of studies complement one another. However, they are not simply two sides of the same coin.

Dynamic Adaptation Versus Static Evolution?

Interlocked with the issue of how many organizations to study is the question of whether a researcher perceives organizations as relatively long-lived, dynamic systems that adapt themselves to environmental changes, or the researcher perceives them as relatively short-lived, static structures that are selected for environmental fitness through survival-of-the-fittest competition.

Researchers who undertake small-sample studies tend to develop models in which an organization shifts continuously from one form to another. Some of these shifts are responses to intraorganizational stresses and learning; some are reactions to such environmental pressures as competitors' behaviors, technological changes, and governmental policies; and some represent initiatives in which the organization seeks to redefine its strategy and its environment. Yet, they all take place concurrently, interacting with one another, so that observers never perceive systems developing in controlled environments and displaying properties that clearly generalize to many environments, and more importantly, so that descriptions of how organizations look at one time are about as representative and meaningful as single frames from reels of motion picture film. Researchers find themselves trying to assemble complete motion pictures of highly flexible, nearly fluid systems that display more persistence and cohesion than structure and form.

Clearly, it is no trivial task simply to describe this sort of adaptive system. Verbal characterizations tend to vibrate between painfully detailed anecdotes and poetic ambiguities. Although mathematical methods can describe quite complex dynamic systems, these methods require expertise in topics that most mathematical social scientists have ignored or de-emphasized. If a researcher invests the massive effort to create a realistic mathematical model, almost no one else will understand what the model says. Computer simulation offers a compromise between the verbal and the mathematical, but the promise remains potential. The handful of published computer simulations have concentrated on microscopic subsystems of real, observed organizations or have generalized vaguely about the qualitative properties of hypothetical, abstract organizations. Moreover, computer simulations often lure researchers into Bonini's paradox—the more realistic and detailed a model, the more the model exhibits the complexity and ambiguity of the modeled organization.

If describing the adaptation of a flexible, dynamic system is difficult, gathering the data to document an insightful description is even more challenging. To maximize a theory's potential for generalization, a researcher must distinguish among the various kinds of changes mentioned above: those instigated by intraorganizational stresses and learning, those instigated by environmental forces, and those representing the organization's strategic initiatives. Yet the data available combine all of these phenomena in a single, intermingled, reproducible, and uncontrollable stream, and truly, the only appropriate statistical tools are those designed for samples of size one.

Data gathering strategies vary along many dimensions, of course, but two strategic dimensions appear to be particularly critical during the present stage of organization theory's development. An analyst must decide whether to emphasize the postdictive explanation of events that have already taken place, or to attempt the predictive extrapolation of events that are going to occur. The analyst must also choose between passively observing events that transpire naturally and actively intervening to force certain events to happen (Starbuck 1974).

Sciences (and organization theory has been no exception) seem inevitably to begin in the passive-postdictive mode. The doctor collects a patient's medical history; the geologist records earth movements and the patterns generated by past movements; the economist compiles the periodic statistics that add up to an economic history. Then the investigator advances one or more theories to explain the observations—a tentative diagnosis, a conjecture about the earth's development, a macroeconomic model.

These passive-postdictive biases are healthy for a science's early development. They highlight the most prominent, nonpathological phenomena. They reduce distortions arising from scientists' observational activities. They minimize the costs of proposing erroneous theories and thereby stimulate the invention and unbiased evaluation of alternative hypotheses. They discourage the premature rejection of partially deficient theories and promote processes of revision, modification, correction, combination, and elaboration. They decrease personal associations between specific scientists and specific observations, concepts, or philosophies. They permit standards of scientific achievement to develop in relative autonomy from extra-scientific payoffs.

However, it is important that a science start diverging from its initial passive-postdictive mode as soon as it grows strong enough to do so. For one thing, until the doctor acts upon a diagnostic conjecture and prescribes a treatment, the patient can receive no benefit. However, intrinsically scientific reasons are of equal or greater importance.

Firstly, as long as the costs associated with promulgating erroneous theories remain low, there is little incentive to eliminate erroneous theories and hence to discriminate carefully between better hypotheses and worse ones. Defective hypotheses tend to hang around long after their deficiencies have become obvious; comparisons among alternative theories tend to be inconclusive; data measurement can remain vague; and scientists generally behave as if they do not take their science seriously.

Secondly, because people proposing postdictive theories know in advance what phenomena their conjectures must explain, all serious proposals are consistent with the most prominent empirical facts and all appear to perform almost equally well. Differences between postdictive theories always lie in their abilities to explain comparatively unimportant phenomena, or what the theories' proponents believe to be comparatively unimportant phenomena; and postdiction must give way to prediction before the differences between theories emerge clearly and unambiguously.

Thirdly, autonomous scientific development gradually shifts from fertility to sterility. Scientific disciplines develop social structures and codes of behavior that, for all of their fundamental virtues, can become intellectual prisons that stifle innovation, creativity, and progress. Therefore, to prevent this progression toward sterility from actually coming about, the autonomy of disciplinary development needs to be moderated and disrupted by extra-disciplinary influences (Gordon and Marquis 1966; Starbuck 1974). One of the most obvious ways to inject extra-disciplinary values is to transform the science into an actively interventionist activity that seeks to bring about desired states of affairs, because criteria of desirability are extra-scientific and evoke influence attempts by any affected, nonscientific, social systems.

Fourthly, an exclusive emphasis on naturally occurring phenomena produces data distributions dominated by uninteresting events—nearly everyone has brown eyes, nearly all rock formations are stable, nearly all prices are the same as they were last week. In order to acquire the kinds of data that facilitate comparisons among theories, in quantities that make these comparisons conclusive, a researcher must achieve some degree of experimental control over that which the researcher observes. At the very least, a researcher must be able to select settings likely to yield interesting, revealing observations—meaning that the researcher has predicted what the researcher will observe—and to demonstrate convincingly a theory's effectiveness and completeness, a researcher must extrapolate a trajectory from past events and then intervene and engineer events that deviate from the predicted trajectory. The latter endeavors put science all the way into an active-predictive mode.

Finally, a point that is especially relevant for organization theorists who perform small-sample studies: the passive-postdictive mode contravenes analyses of organizations as flexible, adaptive systems. An adaptive system is both reactive and selectively active. It reacts to changes in and signals from its environment, and possesses a characteristic repertoire of response patterns. It also selects environmental settings to which it is capable of responding, and either learns new reaction patterns that match its environment's requirements, or undertakes to modify its environment's properties to bring them into line with its own capabilities (Normann 1971). To analyze such a system effectively, a researcher must strive to distinguish among and to comprehend individually the system's short-run immediately programmed reactions, its flexibilities for learning new reaction patterns or rigidities for preserving old ones, and its long-run strategies for selecting or creating appropriate environmental settings.

A researcher can use several analytic approaches to gathering separate data about each of these adaptive subsystems. The researcher can observe the system's reactions to regular oscillatory inputs of different frequencies; observe its reactions to sudden, step-like shocks; observe its reactions to introductions of informational noise; observe its reactions to disruptions of internal and external information channels; and so on. However, naturally occurring phenomena do not often match one of these analytic approaches, partly because almost all events are merely sequences of routine and expected behaviors by both an organization and its environment, and partly because the various observational conditions mix in an uncontrolled, but nonrandom, mélange. Either researchers must depend on having the good luck to observe natural events of unusual sorts—implying acceptance of a slow and decelerating rate of scientific progress—or they must intervene and exert some degree of experimental control. The net result is that organization theorists will have to undertake experimental manipulations simply to ensure that their science maintains a reasonable rate of progress. And since organizations are purposeful systems that do not tend to accept interventions purely for the sake of scientific progress, that tend to demand plausible forecasts of the consequences of proposed interventions, and that tend to place evaluations on alternative interventions, experimental manipulations are virtually certain to be amplified into full-scale, active-predictive investigations.

In sum, the organization theorists who perceive organizations as relatively long-lived, dynamic, and adaptive systems confront major methodological challenges that are calling for innovations in research strategy. A gradual transition from the traditional passive-postdictive mode of data gathering to an active-predictive mode appears inevitable, although this transition may occur very slowly. Another potential transition lurks in the deficiencies of current descriptive methods. That no truly adequate descriptive medium exists seems clear, but no one knows what alternative media are going to become available.

Static, Evolutionary Models

On the other hand, one does not have to emphasize organizations' adaptive properties. Most researchers who undertake large-sample studies take the position, at least implicitly, that organizations are relatively stable, static structures. They stress the properties each organization displays right now, and the similarities and differences among comparable organizations, without regard for trajectories of change within the histories of single organizations.

This is not to suggest that it is plausible for organization theorists to ignore social change. After all, change is constant (to coin a phrase). It is plausible, however, to perceive any given organization as having a static structure at any given time, and then to perceive social change as a birth and death process that alters the population of existing organizations.

One can even view the life history of a single organization in terms of birth and death processes. That is, one can think of a social system that is continuously the same organization by legal, geographic, or other criteria as also being an envelope containing a sequence of discretely different organizations at different times, according to other criteria for organizational existence. Consider, for example, a small manufacturing plant that is sold to a large, conglomerate corporation, the former owner being retained as plant manager and no sudden, drastic changes being made in who is employed or what is manufactured. Based on distributions of customers, products, and inventories, on assignments of activities among employees, or on geographic location, one might argue that the original organization still survives. However, based on who receives the profits, on the legal form of organization, or on methods of accounting, one might argue that the previous firm no longer exists and a new organization has been born.

Death and rebirth has traditionally been an accepted description for bankruptcies, mergers, ownership changes, and similar legally demarcated transitions. Very modest extrapolation will extend this description to cover large-scale turnovers in managerial personnel, major reorganizations of operating divisions, or drastic strategic reorientations. From there, it begins to appear reasonable to characterize as death and rebirth virtually any kind of reorganization, reassignment of roles, or revision of decision rules. One soon finds oneself perceiving organizations as evanescent structures indeed, static at any given time, but often on the brink of being discarded and replaced by newer forms.

The birth and death viewpoint brings forth once again the centrality of two dilemmas that have perennially plagued organization theory. Since the organization that died long ago according to one definition probably still exists according to another, how one operationally defines an organization strongly affects what one learns about organizations. It also makes a great deal of difference what criteria one uses to measure the magnitudes of social changes, because a process that appears as a smooth, continuous flow by one set of criteria appears as a sequence of discrete and distinct stages by other criteria. However, long histories of debate have produced little, if any, movement toward consensus about how these issues should be resolved, and the solutions individual researchers endorse remain very much matters of personal preference. It would be unrealistic to forecast any imminent revolutions.

The birth and death viewpoint also implies that organization theorists can assign low priority to understanding adaptation within the life history of a single organization, and can concentrate instead on macroscopic views of adaptation. Researchers should assign high priorities to understanding what tasks and rules a society imposes on its organizations, how these task and rule assignments translate into organizational birth and death rates and into measures of survival fitness, and what frequency distributions across different types of organizations result. All societally important adaptive processes manifest themselves by shifting whole populations of organizations, and the central task is to comprehend these population motions rather than the motions of individual organizations within their subpopulations. It is not even essential to understand how individual organizations are able to violate aggregate rules or to deviate from aggregate trends for brief periods. These are merely noise in the overall development of a large-scale social system, and researchers should first seek to perceive the total system with such noise filtered out.

Stepping back and getting a macroscopic perspective makes any single organization appear ephemeral. The very high death rates among newly created organizations are striking. Among industrial firms, approximately half survive less than two years and four-fifths less than ten years (Crum 1953; Marcus 1967; Steindl 1965). Then one also realizes that even lifetimes of 50–100 years may appear short in comparison to the speeds with which organizational populations shift (Stinchcombe 1965). Statistically, it probably makes little difference whether existing organizations adapt to extend their life spans or they fail and new organizations emerge (although the organizations' members undoubtedly have opinions about the more desirable course).

A macroscopic perspective also suggests that population movements may fit into an evolutionary model. Evolution is essentially a matching process by which an environment acquires appropriate residents. The environment's properties translate into fitness criteria that influence the birth and survival probabilities of various potential residents, gradually reducing the proportions of less-fit residents and raising the proportions of more-fit residents. Some environmental properties, such as the presence or total absence of certain resources, determine fitness criteria directly—for example, people having large lung capacities are better suited to living at high altitudes. Other environmental properties, such as limitations on the total supplies of certain resources, determine the basis on which residents compete with each other for survival—for example, limited water supplies imply competition for water. This second type of population shift has been labeled survival-of-the-fittest.

Evolutionary concepts have the potential to contribute significantly to our understanding of organizations. Organizational environments clearly differ in their propensities to give birth to various types of organizations, in the rules they require organizations to obey, in the tasks they reward organizations for performing, and in their criteria for organizational existence. Organizations often compete with each other for environmental resources; imitation evidently produces an inheritance-like transmission of characteristics from one generation to the next; and births and deaths are statistically important organizational phenomena. In fact, it is astonishing that organization theorists have not built up a substantial body of research on organizational evolution. However, such is the case. Aside from Stinchcombe's work (1965), the main writings on organizational evolution have come in domains that most organization theorists ignore: empirical studies by economists of long-run changes in industrial composition (e.g. Beesley 1955; Downie 1958; Esposito and Esposito 1971; Mann 1966; Marcus 1967; Qualls 1972; Scherer 1970; Stigler 1968; Weiss 1965) and theoretical discussions, also by economists, of the effects of competition and financial constraints on firms' internal decision rules (Alchian 1950; Downie 1958; Nelson 1972; Winter 1964, 1971). One of the most stimulating analyses from an organization theorist's vantage point is Levins's (1968) *Evolution in Changing Environments*, a purely biological treatment that has not yet filtered into the social sciences. Therefore, in principle, organizational evolution is another vein of high-grade intellectual ore awaiting exploitation.

Before plunging enthusiastically ahead, one should recognize that evolutionary models have limitations that are capable of disillusioning the overly optimistic. Not only do previous attempts to apply evolutionary concepts in the social sciences (e.g. Alland 1970; Sahlins and Service 1960) imply that evolutionary propositions have strong propensities for degenerating into vacuous tautologies, but the inferences one can draw have at least one fundamental limitation. The constraints imposed by environmental properties are not, in general, sufficiently restrictive to determine the characteristics of their organizational residents uniquely.

For example, one attempted application of evolutionary theory was the argument that survival-of-the-fittest implied that all firms maximize profits. Any firm that did not use profit-maximizing decision rules would be at a competitive disadvantage in comparison to firms that did use them, would lose financial support, and would go out of business. Extensive debates—in which Alchian (1950) and Winter (1964) presented the key counterarguments—demonstrated that such inferences are too strong. Firms only compete with other firms, and it is far from obvious that any existing firms have discovered profit-maximizing decision rules. Some firms might accidentally hit on nonoptimal decision rules that produce the same behaviors as profit-maximizing decisions, and thus maximize profits for fallacious reasons. Because there is continuous change in the environment and in the behaviors of the competing firms, a profit-maximizing firm must adapt both ceaselessly and erratically, and the kinds of incremental adaptation used by firms are unlikely to maintain accurate tracking. Since financial supporters such as stockholders, suppliers, and bankers do not shift their resources quickly, a non-profit-maximizing firm can survive for quite a long time; and in addition, a study by Simon (1956) suggests that a firm holding a modest resource inventory might survive indefinitely. Financial sources, not being omniscient, might mistakenly withdraw their support from firms that are maximizing long-run profits, and support instead firms that are maximizing short-run profits, with the result that all true profit maximizers would go out of business. And so on. The list of contingencies is quite long.

Evolutionary propositions should contain information about intraorganizational behaviors in the sense that evolution should make some behaviors more prevalent and other behaviors less so. Nevertheless, evolutionary selection will not ordinarily be strong enough that only one mode of intraorganizational behavior will enable an organization to survive, and survival may be achievable through many, many different modes of behavior.

Such ambiguity should be especially characteristic of organizational evolution. For one thing, organizations actively manipulate and restructure their environments. They try to change environmental properties that are constraining them and impeding their survival. For another thing, organizations' environments are themselves largely composed of other organizations that are all changing at the same time, so that both organizations and their environments are evolving simultaneously toward better fitness for each other. Since neither knows the other's ultimate state, there is certain to be a great deal of exploratory behavior, and this variation becomes itself a constraint on the pattern of evolution; a constraint that increases the range of possible outcomes. Consequently, models of organizational evolution are likely to be composed of weak statements about change propensities such as inequalities involving partial derivatives, rather than statements about what changes will definitely occur.

Nevertheless, evolutionary models remain one of the more promising topics that organization theorists have not thoroughly explored, and evolutionary models should be especially attractive to those organization theorists who perform large-sample studies. Because organizational populations evolve more slowly than individual organizations adapt, it may be possible to make stronger predictions about large systems of organizations than about single cases. In addition, one could reasonably argue that good theories about organizational populations should be a high priority objective because of their applicability to social policies and their potential for benefiting whole societies.

NOTES

1. The range of possible dimensions is suggested by Barker's (1968) inventory of the behaviors in a Midwestern city and by Aguilar's (1967) descriptions of the allocations of information gathering tasks among managers.
2. Stinchcombe's propositions are far from self-evident, and they are difficult to document. Relevant statistics do not exist for most societies; the available statistics are often noncomparable; and there is a high probability one will only discover that literacy, schooling, and so forth increase the accuracy and exhaustiveness of a society's record-keeping. Moreover, an unpublished pilot study by Carlos Bertero suggested that nations fall into at least three distinct subsets (highly developed economies, highly undeveloped economies, and two-class societies composed of a small, affluent class and a large, impoverished class). The correlations representing Stinchcombe's propositions were very small within each subset; the functional forms differed from subset to subset; and correlations across all three subsets were suppressed by confounding of the highly developed and the two-class societies. It is also doubtful that Stinchcombe's propositions are valid when the variables reach their upper ranges. In the United States, for example, monetary transactions have become abnormal and are becoming rare. One pays with a promise, which is an individualistic rather than a universalistic good, but affluence has become so high that the individualistic character of promises is no longer a dominating liability. As well, the social norms about management practice have become so stringent that literacy has become nearly irrelevant. Organization founders are no longer expected to be able to read the legal or even the financial documents an organization must have; they hire lawyers and accountants to read for (not to) them.
3. There is some evidence that people lack effective heuristics for deciding how much data to acquire before making a decision (Beach 1966; Phillips, Hays, and Edwards 1966; Starbuck and Bass 1967).
4. As originally published, this chapter included two tables describing the terms various theorists had used.
5. As originally published, this chapter included two large tables that pointed to numerous research studies about the effects of environments on organizations and the effects of organizations on environments.

3

Camping on Seesaws: Prescriptions for a Self-Designing Organization

Coauthored with Bo L. T. Hedberg and Paul C. Nystrom

1. INTRODUCTION

An organization's history can be broken down into segments of all kinds. One can focus upon single members' activities in their jobs or upon the activities involving single functional or geographic units, like the purchasing department or the European division. One can discuss social and intellectual domains, such as chemistry, supervision, or theology. One can attend to contiguous events, such as what happened during January 1962.

Although prevalent, these analyses portray an organization as static, and do not reveal its developmental capabilities. Designing an organization to fit society's needs implies that it is less important to discover where an organization is than to understand how it got there, and where it can go tomorrow. Analyses that give footholds in time are the appropriate components for assembling trajectories into the future.

Stories, such as myths, sagas, and legends, are one method of portraying dynamics (Clark 1972; Mitroff and Kilmann 1976). Some stories describe critical events and other stories summarize unobtrusive long-run developments, but both types derive from interpretations made after the fact and both distort what has happened. Stories can spin out desired futures only if the distortions are consistent with an organization's unknown future needs and environment. If a story describes an organization and environment that no longer exist, the story's predictions will fail, and its power to generate behavior will undermine the organization's effectiveness.

An alternative method for analyzing dynamics is to concentrate on the generators of behavior—processes. Processes are the media by which an organization creates future acts out of its experiences. Yesterday surges in and tomorrow gushes out.

Processes are difficult to comprehend because their visages shift with the events streaming through them. Processes' strength and usefulness rest on their adaptability to heterogeneous demands. Yet understanding processes warrants effort, because principles that generalize across diverse circumstances are the keys to both scientific comprehension and effective designs.

This chapter discusses what kinds of processes exist, how processes interact with one another, and how organizational designs incorporate interacting processes. First, it is necessary to assess designers' role and the objectives designers pursue.

2. WHY DESIGNERS SHOULD HELP OTHER PEOPLE ERECT AN ORGANIZATIONAL TENT

Designing is widely thought to belong outside the stream of routine activities. Designers are technical specialists who value their noninvolvement. They enter a situation, inventory the problems and capabilities, go off and explore alternative solutions in the abstract, return with an optimal solution, and finally implement their solution. Since implementation requires changes, effective designers initiate and control changes. If the organization adopts these changes, people judge the designers successful.

Even if one accepts this perception of designers, understanding of processes is designers' most precious skill. Formulating and then implementing designs take time. The organization that existed when designing began will endure only in myths by the time a design is being implemented (Brooks 1963). Therefore, designers can achieve greater success by thinking in terms of an organization that will come into being while they are creating a design for it.

Designers can be even more successful if they will discard this generally accepted concept of their role. One reason is that changes start complex causal chains that are hard to predict and discrete interventions set off reactions that are still harder to predict (Churchman 1971). An organization persists by developing feedback signals that heighten its resilience to abnormal internal events and to shocks originating in its environment, and abrupt interventions instigate reactions by these feedback systems. Predicting an organization's future well enough to control it reliably requires greater analytic capability than designers, or any other people, possess.

Another reason designers can benefit from a new role is that their direct influence over organizational participants' behaviors is weak. Although it is possible to influence activities by setting such premises as choice criteria, information flows, and spans of responsibility, nonparticipant designers have only sporadic, marginal opportunities to alter these premises. Activities are ultimately controlled by those who perform them, and participants often begin repealing designers' manipulations as soon as the designers withdraw (Nystrom 1977).

Designing Process Hierarchies

Rather than seeking to shift how an organization behaves, designers can concentrate on altering the processes that accomplish changes (Beer 1972; Starbuck 1975). Processes can be more reliably extrapolated than the behaviors they generate, because they are more versatile and inertial. Designers' modifications of processes will adapt to most variations in an organization's capabilities and internal politics or in environmental constraints and opportunities. Indeed, truly effective modifications of processes would improve an organization's propensities to learn, to correct flaws in its design, and to experiment with alternative structures and strategies.

Designs can be composed of processes—as generators of dynamic sequences of solutions, in which attempted solutions induce new solutions and attempted designs trigger new designs.

Process designs will both enhance an organization's flexibility and responsiveness and enhance the aesthetics of design activities. The perception of design as a problem-solution-implementation sequence misrepresents how solutions evolve; and the notion that designs require implementation leads designers astray. Transplanted designs arouse rejection mechanisms that thwart implementations. Moreover, while nonparticipant designers are off inventing solutions, the problems may change or even disappear. For example, defining a problem for a consultant may redefine the problem for the organization's members, who then begin alleviating the original problem (Hedberg 1975*b*).

When designs become processes generating streams of solutions, implementations become second-order processes that enable organizations to learn first-order processes. Because those who execute first-order processes must take responsibility for second-order learning (Emery and Thorsrud 1969; Starbuck 1975), designers can at best catalyze an organization's self-designing. Not only would the organization's members define problems for themselves and generate their own solutions, but they would also evaluate and revise their solution-generating processes.

Designers have the opportunity to focus on ideologies and other third-order strategies for carrying out second-order learning. Steplike changes in processes can instigate more troubles than abrupt changes in behavior can. Attempts to force discrete shifts in processes amplify behavioral errors, establish contradictions across parallel processes, and elicit rejection mechanisms, so processes need to be modified gradually in social contexts that acknowledge the transience of what is being done at any time. A self-designing organization functions most smoothly if its ideology cherishes impermanence.

Erecting Tents or Palaces?

This redefined role for designers accompanies revised specifications for the well-designed organization.

Designers, and especially management scientists, have long promoted skill specialization, integration, clear objectives, and unambiguous authority structures. These widely accepted values assert that an organization should be internally differentiated and yet harmonious, should use explicit communication channels and explicit decision criteria, and should act decisively and consistently.

Such properties could improve the performance of an organization if it inhabited an unchanging environment. Routine activity programs could replace unprogrammed strategic analyses and coordinating messages (J. R. Galbraith 1973; Hedberg 1975a; Landau 1973; Miller and Mintzberg 1974; Thompson 1967). Activity programs could be multiplied and pared to their essential elements, then preserved in capital equipment and standard operating procedures (Gershefski 1969; McGuire 1963; Starbuck and Dutton 1973; Thompson 1967). Communications could be abbreviated with efficient codes, and responsibilities could be sharply delineated (Bennis 1965; J. R. Galbraith 1973; Khandwalla 1974; Miller and Mintzberg 1974; Starbuck 1965; Thompson 1967). In constant surroundings, one could confidently assemble an intricate, rigid structure combining elegant and refined components—an organizational palace.

Yet change is one of the world's dominant properties (Beer 1974; Bennis 1970). An organization's environment does change. Evolving cause-effect relations render today's methods obsolete, so what has been learned has to be replaced (Terreberry 1968). Ansoff (1965) summarized some pressures forcing changes in products, competitive relations, and governmental controls on business enterprises. Hedberg (1974) described how the development of solid-state electronic technology forced revolutions within the business-machines industry. Grinyer and Norburn (1975) found no evidence that consensus about objectives, clearly defined roles, or formal planning correlated positively with financial performances across twenty-one companies. Instead, financial performances correlated positively with reliance on informal communication and with the diversity of information used to assess company performance.

Designers who erect an organizational palace had better anticipate problems caused by shifting subsoils. Carter (1971) and Miller and Mintzberg (1974) showed how pursuing stability and avoiding uncertainty interfere with an organization's long-run adaptation and survival. Thompson (1967) observed how difficult it is for an organization to devote enough resources to searching its environment for opportunities, because defensive responses to newly recognized problems consume too many search resources (Cyert and March 1963). Normann (1971) found that business firms that used formal power and mechanistic procedures to couple subunits were apt to undertake too few product reorientations, and those undertaken often were based on little except advocacy by a single, powerful executive.

One approach to eliminating mismatches between a rigid structure and a changing environment is systematic remodeling. March and Simon (1958) proposed that top executives establish programs for periodically reviewing their organization and its environment. The program-planning and strategic-planning movements represent attempts to routinize organizational reassessments (Gilmore and Brandenburg 1962; Hitch 1966; Steiner 1969). However, systematic procedures offer weak protection against unpredictability, just as increased rigidity does not effectively prepare a building for earthquakes. Some flaws of systematic procedures are inherent in the concept of strategic planning. Drafting plans, dismantling an old structure, and erecting a new structure take so long that designers need to forecast how the environment will shift. Since forecasts are only conjectures derived from experiences, greater reliance on forecasts induces greater design errors (Beer 1974; Grinyer and Norburn 1975; McNulty 1962). Systematic procedures also sap an organization's flexibility by strengthening its rationality. Interdependence originates when harmony is imposed on contradictory subgoals and disordered activities, and a change in part of an interdependent structure requires changes throughout. The result is an organization that embodies more forecasts and that responds more sluggishly when its forecasts manifest their errors.

Camping in a Tent

Residents of changing environments need tents. An organizational tent places greater emphasis on flexibility, creativity, immediacy, and initiative than on authority, clarity, decisiveness, or responsiveness; and an organizational tent neither asks for harmony between the activities of different organizational components, nor asks that today's behavior resemble yesterday's or tomorrow's. Why behave more consistently than one's world does?

An organizational tent actually exploits benefits hidden within properties that designers have generally regarded as liabilities. Ambiguous authority structures, unclear objectives, and contradictory assignments of responsibility can legitimate controversies and challenge traditions (White 1969). Incoherence and indecision can foster exploration, self-evaluation, and learning. Redundant task allocations can provide experimental replications, and partial incongruities can diversify portfolios of activities. Jönsson (1973) found that unbalanced resources and crises were major forces driving growth and survival in Swedish investment development companies, and that problem solving during crises relied on informal communications. Since the industrial development companies that grew smoothly in balanced increments displayed more concern with conserving their past gains than with developing investment opportunities, Jönsson inferred that an organization should incorporate imbalances. Similarly, Burns and Stalker (1961) and Normann (1971) observed that ambiguous role definitions and amorphous communication networks help an organization adapt to marked changes in its environment. J. R. Galbraith (1973) proposed that an organization in a rapidly changing environment should divide itself into self-contained units so as to prevent information overloads. Miller and Mintzberg (1974) observed that companies operating successfully in turbulent markets had intensive internal communications, managed themselves participatively, utilized coordinative committees, delegated discretion to components that had to cope with the environment, and devoted considerable effort to scanning the environment.

Those who live in an organizational tent can use good alarm clocks, wash-and-wear clothes, and the ability to plan itineraries quickly. They invent sensors for alerting themselves to significant events, and ceaselessly question their present assumptions and habits (Landau 1973). They remain ready to replace old methods, and they discard even adequate old methods in order to try new ones, looking upon each development as an experiment that suggests new experiments. They hear descriptions of what exists as statements about the past, and fantasies about what might happen as opportunities to create reality. They regard their organization as a means, not an end (White 1969). They avoid anchoring their satisfactions in the roles and procedures that are specific to the existing organization, and instead, they draw satisfactions from the skills and relationships that contribute to processes—the processes generating the organization to come.

Of course, today's organization is unlikely to resemble a tent, and few organizational members act like campers. McGuire (1963) discovered that only 8 percent of manufacturing firms changed their product lines substantially during the 1950s, even though many of the static 92 percent suffered declining sales. Wildavsky (1972) has masterfully summarized the difficulties an organization confronts when trying to evaluate its own achievements and capabilities.

Sections 3, 4, and 5 of this chapter discuss how processes interact to facilitate or to block changes; then the final section describes properties of successful organizational designs.

3. HOW PROGRAMS TETHER AN ORGANIZATION TO ITS ENVIRONMENT

When environmental activities seemingly threaten, an organization can adjust its behaviors to accommodate the environment. Processes by which an organization maps its environment into itself can be labeled adaptive. The adaptive processes include selecting environments, monitoring and predicting environmental changes, consulting outsiders, learning, and buffering fluctuations in the flows of resources across organizational boundaries (Normann 1971; Starbuck 1976; Starbuck and Dutton 1973; Thompson 1967). Alternatively, when an organization sees opportunities arising or believes its environment is pliable, it can undertake to remodel environmental elements. Processes by which an organization impresses itself into its environment can be called manipulative. The manipulative processes include constructing desirable niches and negotiating domains, forming coalitions, educating clients and employees, advertising to potential clients and customers, and resolving conflicts (J. K. Galbraith 1973; Starbuck 1975, 1976; Weick 1969).

Conventional usage implies adaptation and manipulation also differ in timing and psychological orientation. Adaptation occurs after an environmental stimulus, and the adapter defends, conforms, or submits; manipulation is an aggressive, proud, perhaps selfish, act that instigates environmental reactions.

Timing distinctions between adaptation and manipulation are not merely uninformative, they often deceive. Stimulus–response pairs break behavioral chains into segments so short that a perceiver loses perspective; and vanishing with perspective, goes awareness of subtle maneuvers and unexploited opportunities. An environmental happening only elicits reactions if preparations for it were inadequate. For instance, universities can hire temporary teachers as hedges against having to fire tenured faculty when enrollments drop. Conversely, an environment only calls for remodeling insofar as an inhabitant has erroneously adapted to it. For example, investments in equipment can substitute for programs to add skilled workers to the labor market.

Psychological distinctions between adaptation and manipulation are more elusive than timing distinctions, but they can be just as deceptive. Manipulation need not be arrogant or aggressive: An organization may propose a coalition so as to escape impending disaster. Similarly, adaptation is not solely defensive or submissive: Learning can prepare for the future as well as accommodate to the past. Unfortunately, an organization may avoid acts labeled manipulative so as not to appear hostile or may endorse them to demonstrate independence. An organization may undertake acts labeled adaptive to present a cooperative image or may spurn them to evade subservience. When organizations choose acts because of expected effects, the key step is forecasting these effects. Since environmental components do not know whether an organization's members intend to adapt or to manipulate, the members' intentions, as such, have insignificant effects.

Tethering with Programmed Chains

Real processes are never purely adaptive or purely manipulative, of course, and since an organization always misunderstands itself and its environment to some degree, processes inevitably spawn unanticipated effects. An intended manipulation is only the first link in a vaguely forecasted chain of adaptations and manipulations.

Over time, these chains of intermingled adaptations and manipulations transform both an organization and its environment. Many organizations create, or migrate into, benevolent environments; many other organizations find environmental benevolence springing up about them. A benevolent environment allows an organization to standardize and program many of its activities, with cues automatically evoking different activity programs. Activity programs make efficient use of perceptual and problem-solving capacities (J. R. Galbraith 1973; Thompson 1967). Resources are not wasted solving familiar problems, and creative talents can focus where innovation is sought (Penrose 1959; Starbuck 1965).

However, programmed behaviors loosen the tethers between an organization and its environment. Activity programs supply little self-doubt and few occasions for reconsidering conventional reactions. The cues triggering activity programs neglect inconsistent, but supposedly unimportant, stimuli, so that some variations in perceived events are absorbed (Cyert and March 1963; Tuchman 1973). Because every organization ignores event variations that satisfy the tolerance limits of the programs in use, the organization adheres to programs after the conditions for which they were developed no longer hold. Events also merely provoke switches among previously learned programs unless they violate the tolerance limits of every program in the organization's repertoire (Nystrom 1975a). When the situation differs radically from any encountered before, trying out old programs delays attempts to generate entirely new modes of behavior. In essence, an organization has to unlearn its previous activity programs by exhausting the processes that keep behaviors static, before it starts analyzing an unfamiliar situation and devising appropriate new activity programs.

The contents of programs and the ways programs are applied reduce perceptual sensitivity further. Organizations train members to accept approved beliefs and to conform to standardized role prescriptions (Clark 1972; Denhardt 1969; Kaufman 1960; Starbuck 1976; Wynia 1972). Buffers—such as inventories, intermediary agents, and contingencies in routine decision rules—mediate the boundaries between organization and environment and interfaces between workflow stages inside an organization (Cyert and March 1963; March and Simon 1958; Nystrom 1975; Thompson 1967). Organizations allow slack resources to build up when affluence rises, then pursue economies and efficiencies aggressively when affluence wanes (Bonini 1963; Cyert and March 1963; Lewin and Wolf 1972; Nystrom 1975).

An organization can choose how it uses programs as tethers between itself and its environment. An unusually dynamic organization shifts products, clients, technologies, or territories because it sees its environment as benevolent. It perceives and investigates abundant opportunities; it develops new products, services, clients, and suppliers; it creates new subunits and realigns old ones; it continuously changes methods, technologies, and task assignments. However, even the dynamic organizations tend to turn these searches for opportunities and migrations into new niches into programs (Carter 1971); difficulties induce revisions of activity programs much more frequently than do opportunities (March and Simon 1958; Newman and Logan 1955).

Another sort of organization—the usual one—makes changes, but makes as few as possible, and does so only to satisfy environmental pressures. The organization sees its environment as rather static and minimally benevolent, offering few opportunities, but erecting many constraints, and emitting just enough threats to disrupt complacency (Maniha and Perrow 1965; Normann 1971; Starbuck 1976). This is partly a self-confirming perception, for nonadaptation is a form of manipulation. Because the organization responds lethargically and with the least innovative responses feasible, its environment must threaten and constrain to elicit action; and because the organization does not exploit opportunities, opportunities are offered to it fleetingly and diffidently, if at all. To the organization, proposals for changes are criticisms of how things are, its environment appears to change little, and programmed behaviors appear fully adequate to cope with the changes that occur. The organization can elaborate its program repertoire into a palatial hierarchy. However, the palace sits on a bit of flotsam in a sea of social and technological changes, and the flotsam is constantly being eroded by impinging events.

Drifting into a Decaying Backwater

Every so often, a bit of flotsam washes out of the mainstream. An organization drifts along in an environment that it believes is placid and somewhat more than minimally benevolent—until one day it bewilderedly realizes its environment has evolved into a stagnating backwater. Unperceived changes have carried the organization into niches that are decaying and becoming infertile. Even though the niches are not yet totally stagnant, the organization's continued survival suddenly depends on making drastic changes. Processes tethering the organization to the stagnating environment have become dangerous and must be dismantled. The organization needs new processes, first for creating or discovering a vital environment, then for mating together organization and environment, and later for reestablishing a dependable, nutrient equilibrium. Although this new equilibrium, if achieved, may not bring forth such extremely self-confident insensitivity as characterized the former equilibrium, the organization will have metamorphosed out of a nonreflective state in which manipulative processes were comparatively dormant and adaptive processes automatic. It will have generated pervasive efforts to manipulate and to adapt, and will have extinguished the most extreme and disruptive processes.

The reactions of an organization in a stagnating environment can disclose how it creates processes, revises them, and fits them together. Although a stagnating environment results from abnormalities, an organization in a stagnating environment is only marginally and quantitatively abnormal. The usual organization displays properties qualitatively similar to those of an organization in a stagnating environment, and many an organization only escapes environmental deterioration through the intervention of forces beyond its control. Moreover, there are organizations in stagnating environments to observe, and because so many problems reveal themselves simultaneously, such situations constitute an efficient context for discovering how an organization diagnoses its difficulties and how it reprograms itself.

The next section of this chapter describes how an organization in a stagnating environment reacts, and the sections following draw inferences from these reactions.

4. HOW TO CONVERT A CRISIS INTO A LETHAL TRAGEDY AND OCCASIONALLY SURVIVE

Since activity programs foster perceptual insensitivity, there is risk that an organization will see its behaviors as succeeding long after their effectiveness fails.

Success, or the appearance of it, breeds somnolence. Sensors for scanning the environment wither away (Miller and Mintzberg 1974; Thompson 1967). The organization no longer perceives gradual, evolutionary changes in the environment, and it resists gradual, evolutionary changes in itself. The organization's structure rigidifies, as coordination relies on planning, and as the communication channels linking subunits atrophy (J. R. Galbraith 1973; Khandwalla 1972; Miller and Mintzberg 1974). Activity programs are rationalized through embedding in organizational ideologies and myths (Clark 1972; Mitroff and Kilmann 1976). Confidence in myths and programs grows stronger as success appears to continue. Motivation to undertake strategic innovations evaporates, because managers measure their achievements by criteria for administrative maintenance rather than by entrepreneurial criteria (Miller and Mintzberg 1974; Thompson 1967). Past success is interpreted as readiness for the future (Thompson 1967), and a prototypic prescription is 'Don't change a winning team'.

These properties reach pathological acuteness in an organization in a stagnating environment. The organization gradually slides so far out of touch with what is happening, both within itself and in its environment, that a potentially fatal disaster develops unseen. Then when reality begins to intrude, the organization misapprehends its difficulties and responds in ways that amplify the crisis. Of course, a stagnating environment is a diagnosis by an organization that is nearly blind: The critical defects do not lie in the environment at all, and environmental deterioration is only ordinary technological and social evolution that the organization meets ineptly.

Studies of organizations in stagnating environments—primarily case studies conducted by Hedberg (1973, 1974, 1975a) and by Miller and Mintzberg (1974)—suggest that an organization's reactions divide into three heuristic phases.

Weathering the Storm

At the outset, an organization does not entertain the notion that its environment has irreversibly changed. The environment is only temporarily deviating from its usual, benevolent state. Sales have declined, applications are lower, the currency has been devalued, competition is fiercer than usual, fuel is more expensive, perhaps hard to find. This deviation presents something of a challenge: Everyone must pull together, work as a team, and tolerate temporary constraints. However, the trouble originates outside the organization, and a return to normal is imminent. Since the organization itself remains strong, the challenge can be overcome through intensified efforts—do as before, but more. A marketing-oriented company increases its advertising and sales efforts, and a production-oriented company acquires new equipment. The organization strengthens quality and cost control systems and budgeting procedures, follows standard operating procedures strictly, and suppresses innovations and informal communications outside approved channels.

As time passes, the spirit of jauntily facing a challenge together fades. Shortages of liquid funds force more stringent economies, and people take actions to improve the accounting statements. Excised are superfluous goals, such as intercollegiate athletics, job tenure, egalitarian decision-making, high wages, organizational image, high admission standards, pollution control, full product lines, or equal employment opportunities. Managers seek short-run improvements at the expense of long-run progress. They postpone investments, defer maintenance, and cut costs; they slash advertising, education, recruitment, research, and training; they do not replace retirees and resignees; they lay off some people; they reduce wages; they try to renegotiate contracts. Friendly camaraderie vanishes and dissension develops. Members, especially low-level ones, are alienated. Those in charge are criticized, and some people or subunits become scapegoats. Management centralizes decision-making, adds controls to compensate for dissension, emphasizes vertical communications up and down the hierarchy, and demands a strong task orientation (Beer 1974; Hall and Mansfield 1971; Thompson 1967; Vickers 1959).

An organization's initial diagnoses are remarkably simplistic. Managers make only superficial attempts to understand the root causes of difficulty, and they aim actions instead at removing the symptoms. Since the symptoms are communicated by the accounting system, the focus is on promptly improving the accounting reports. What is required is a better bank balance, a better income statement, a better balance sheet. Many of the steps taken to achieve such improvements undermine the organization's future viability by squandering resources to gain time and by abrading already precarious relations with the environment. Buildings, land, and equipment are sold to obtain operating cash. Management terminates projects to modernize products or to develop new products, discontinues even well-advanced efforts to attract new categories of clients, and stops advertising. Experimental curricula are deleted; long-time clients are denied credit; equipment is not repaired; investments in know-how, such as groups of specialists, are foreclosed; and prices and tuition fees are raised.

Moreover, if an organization succeeds in eliminating the signs of distress from its formal reports, it decelerates its efforts to reform and discounts the need for fundamental strategic changes over the long run. Things are improving. Not only have the temporary obstacles been overcome, but the primary means to this achievement have been centralized control and adherence to those activity programs that have traditionally formed the strategic core. The effectiveness of activity programs and the wisdom of top management have been demonstrated once again. The organization's structure has been pared of unproductive and burdensome fat—redundant machines and buildings, nontraditional products and services, excessively skilled personnel, the football team, advertising and research specialists, preventive medicine and diagnostic clinics, and informal communication channels.

Unlearning Yesterday

Perhaps the funds shortages, negative profits, and falling revenues never cease, or perhaps they disappear and then reappear in an organization that no longer has the resources to buy delay. In either case, the permanence of change manifests itself, and the organization's members must decide what permanent actions to take.

The first step toward new behaviors is unlearning old behaviors. The effectiveness of existing activity programs and traditional strategies is disconfirmed, and the processes binding the organization to today's behavioral patterns are disengaged.

Unlearning actually began, but was not recognized as such, while the organization was weathering the storm. Stress engendered feelings of uncertainty (Kahn et al. 1964). People were displaced from familiar roles and forced to reconcile competing roles. Trust in and affection for leaders diminished. Snarling quarrels over the shrinking resource carcass built up antagonisms between people and between subunits. Favorite activities were deleted and cherished goals dropped; the organization's goal structure may have been stripped to a skeleton composed only of cynicism and opportunism (Vickers 1959).

When members discover that their organization may not survive, unlearning mounts: Doubts multiply concerning the organization's appropriate domain, and followers abandon their leaders, especially the leaders associated with past programs and strategies.

This collapse of faith brings the potential benefit of opening the way for new viewpoints (Normann 1971; Thompson 1967). The organization's survival will depend on transferring influence to leaders having entrepreneurial propensities and possessing expertise related to new strategic alternatives. However, new leaders and new ideas escalate conflict in an already conflicted organization. The perilous financial condition limits strategic experiments to a few, at most, and new activities cannot be added without subtracting old activities. Priorities have to be set, and there must be losers as well as winners. Unfortunately, an organization that has continuously inhabited a benevolent environment probably lacks processes for resolving conflicts on the basis of substantive criteria, because growth in its resources allowed it to escape conflicts by distributing a little more to almost every claimant (Olofsson, Schlasberg, and Swalander 1973).

It is nearly impossible for an organization to survive through this nadir. Changes in structure, strategy, personnel, and ideology must now be revolutionary; marginal, gradual modifications that fit into historical trends will no longer suffice. The organization must discover reality. It must find a new environment and restyle itself to match this environment (Khandwalla 1972; Starbuck and Dutton 1973). Yet the organization was riddled with defects before the recent threats demonstrated themselves, and since then, the organization has not only been centralized and further routinized, but also stripped of its creativity, heterogeneity, and mutual trust. Almost no human or financial resources can now be marshaled for information gathering or experimenting.

Inventing Tomorrow

Nonetheless, a rare organization does make it. To do so, it must act swiftly and decisively. It realistically assesses today's desperate plight, yet simultaneously arouses the courage to seek out tomorrow's opportunities (King 1974). It emphasizes contests to wrest more resources from external sources instead of intraorganizational contests over the limited resources already at hand. It shoots out sensors for perceiving potential new niches, and strives boldly to manipulate its environment. It finds entrepreneurial personnel, gives them discretion, and avoids punishing them for taking risks. Disregarding precedents, it takes on a fluid and ambiguous structure in which there is much communication and minimal consensus. It sets priorities and makes wise choices about the projects that should come first. It counteracts dissension and inefficiency with participation, coordination, and trust (Normann 1971; Schendel, Patton, and Riggs 1975; White 1969).

Both adaptive and manipulative strategies are fundamentally inadequate. An organization in a stagnating environment dare not adapt to its present niches, for that would reinforce its burdens. Yet paradoxes inhere in matching an organization to a future environment that has still to be defined: Curricula cannot be tailored to the unique needs of unknown students; unspecified customers or suppliers cannot influence strategic planning. On the other hand, there are paradoxes in significantly manipulating an environment that has yet to be explored. Premature attempts to persuade may evoke undesired interpretations; innovative products or methods may not survive the transition from controlled experimentation to regular, large-scale operation.

Adaptation and manipulation are interspersed, and manipulative efforts predominate when the turnaround begins. First, experiments are tried to construct a potentially nutrient environment or to wedge the organization into existing niches; then the organization is modified in the direction of its projected future; then more experiments are run. Problem solving alternates back and forth between present capabilities and idealizations of what ought to be.

A further complication is the organization's struggle against desires for certainty. Having been immersed in stress and change for some time, the organization's members feel very uncertain even before they acknowledge that the organization's former environment has been stagnating. Facing up to reality adds further uncertainty. Exploring unknown, possibly hostile, alternative environments, while simultaneously trying out new roles, new methods, and new structural arrangements inside the organization, adds even more uncertainty. Members with low tolerances for ambiguity are likely to leave voluntarily, but the remaining members and new arrivals exhibit generalized propensities for reducing uncertainty. They conduct surveys, install computerized information systems, make sophisticated statistical analyses, assemble simulation models, and consult outsiders who seem knowledgeable about potential environments.

Insofar as such methods bring in valid information and alleviate fright, they facilitate survival. However, benefits do not always materialize. Analyses of available data may absorb labor and funds that could more usefully go to experimenting and to gathering data with greater relevance. Formalized information systems tend to be mechanistic and inflexible, and they incorporate assumptions that their designers have already identified the organizational and environmental properties deserving attention. People who invest time and energy in solving problems develop commitments to the solutions they generate; and in turbulent situations, they are likely to become committed to solutions for the wrong problems (Mitroff and Featheringham 1974). People often reduce uncertainty by stressing the elegance of methods used to solve problems rather than the importance of the problems themselves, but an organization in a stagnating environment needs imaginative suggestions more than it does concrete, documented answers. Consultants hired to provide data often go on to interpret the data, to reformulate the problems, to suggest solutions, and to manipulate the organizational client for their personal ends (Normann 1971).

Methods for reducing uncertainty become increasingly plausible as an organization achieves mastery within its new environmental niches. People can routinize surveillance of the environment. They can reflect on frequently arising situations and develop activity programs for dealing with them, thus ensuring that the heterogeneity of solutions matches the heterogeneity of problems. People can make activity programs that arise spontaneously compatible with one another. They can set up subunits to encompass crucial contingencies in the flow of activities and to manage the boundaries between organization and environment. They can tailor subunits' capabilities to tasks they regularly perform. Plans, programs, and inventories can replace informal communications as the primary means of coordination. Consensus can be fostered among members as to what goals the organization will pursue and how it will develop over the long run (Beer 1972; Khandwalla 1974; Normann 1971; Starbuck and Dutton 1973; Thompson 1967).

Of course, someone who stayed with an organization while it drifted into a stagnating environment and then had to fight its way out, might wonder, 'Are we going to go through it all again?'

5. HOW AN ORGANIZATION CAN FLY WITHOUT FLYING APART

The reactions of an organization in a stagnating environment suggest several inferences about the ways processes interact with one another, about the guidelines these interactions follow, and about the rules for effectively managing processes.

Different processes hold different potentials for change. Change often accelerates through such processes as enlisting new members, appointing new leaders, acquiring subsidiary organizations, buying complete packages of methods, or consulting outside experts. These accelerators either increase the speed of change in present directions or divert change into new directions; they enable an organization to absorb new experiences and concepts rapidly, they reinforce or inhibit forces acting on an organization's environment, and they stimulate new visions and experiments. Active processes, such as evaluating the past performances of people or subunits, retiring, firing, or retraining members, competing with other organizations, or consulting outside experts, often decelerate by reducing the speed of change in present directions. These active decelerators erase memories of past events and weaken organizational traditions; they sever links between an organization and its environment; they confront fantasy with reality and raise doubts about the usefulness of today's practices. Many other decelerator processes act passively, in that they tie an organization to its past states but do not aggressively oppose the accelerating forces. Some processes that can passively decelerate are indoctrinating new members, accounting, investing pride in the skills used to perform current tasks, and mythmaking. Finally, some processes stabilize speeds and directions of change and weave strands of consistency through behaviors at different times. These stabilizer processes characteristically include reinforcing the use of activities that seem to succeed, standardizing procedures, training, switching around among activity programs, limiting people and subunits to specialized activities, and ignoring small variations in perceived events.

Interactions between accelerator, decelerator, and stabilizer processes generate contests in which coherence struggles against fragmentation. An organization does not automatically travel along as one compact cluster of activities; it tends to separate into fragments flying at different speeds in divergent directions. Continued viability requires that an organization remain coherent without becoming rigid, and requires that an organization's speeds and directions of change approximate those of its environment. Outlying fragments have to be restrained, diverted, stimulated, or chopped off, and dynamic balances must be struck among the diverse forces.

However, an organization has much discretion among ways to achieve viability. It can strive to adapt promptly to the motions of its present niches, or it can set out to construct, through manipulative acts, a sequence of environments that will nurture its evolution along a planned flight path. Neither of these extreme strategies is likely to succeed, because adaptive and manipulative acts complement one another. Somewhere between the extremes is a balanced organization that regards its environment as partly an unknown to be discovered, partly a set of constraints to be satisfied, partly an alternative to be selected, and partly a setting to be resculptured.

An organization generally has similar discretion about the balance between processes furthering long-run goals and those furthering short-run goals. Some goals of both sorts deserve to be pursued simultaneously: Crises are eluded by meeting urgent needs, and self-determination comes from discovering long-run options. However, apparently pressing needs often disappear if ignored, most plans never work out, and many efforts to develop future options yield no lasting results (Cohen, March, and Olsen 1972; McNulty 1962; Grinyer and Norburn 1975). Therefore, beyond some essential minima, emphasizing either short-run goals or long-run goals wastes resources.

An organization also has latitude for choosing how coherent to be. Each strategic maneuver can be systematically echoed throughout the organization; subunits can be left free to develop autonomously with only minimal concern for their interdependencies; or, somewhere between these two extremes, members can endlessly debate whether subunits should be more or less coherent, and debate which subunits should be more or less autonomous.

Nonetheless, the prevalence of organizational failure demonstrates that discretion is largely an illusion that forms when a single behavioral dimension is examined in isolation. Not only is it possible to swerve too far in one dimension, but the many dimensions of behavior interact. For example, the studies of organizations in stagnating environments suggest that shifts in emphasis toward adaptive processes and away from manipulative ones accompany shifts toward coherence and increased emphases on short-run goals; and if any of these shifts extend too far, either absolutely or relatively to the others, troubles start multiplying. Such complex interactions among dimensions greatly narrow the dynamic fulcra on which processes must balance. Although the fulcra are not knife-edges, they are also not really the broad plateaus seen from the perspective of one-dimension-at-a-time.

An organization finds itself in a stagnating environment because it failed to stay balanced on fulcra. The organization thought its environment was not optional, not unknown, not constraining, and not in need of manipulation; and it believed so strongly in its long-run goals that it ignored daily changes in itself and its environment. This perceptual insensitivity drew nurture from a lack of conscious attention to choices about coherence; it relied on mechanistic communication procedures to coordinate subunits.

Suddenly, the organization decides that a short-run emergency exists. All efforts concentrate on adapting to this temporary crisis; long-run goals and resources are sacrificed to obtain immediate relief; and control is centralized. The imbalances that allowed the organization to disregard environmental deterioration have now been supplanted by new imbalances, characteristically fatal ones. Survival becomes possible only if the organization finally discovers fulcra and dynamically balances its processes.

6. HOW TO RECOGNIZE FLYABLE SEESAWS

Processes should balance on six fulcra—more or less. All six fulcra are so closely related that adjacent ones could be merged; yet each of the six could be partitioned into two or more components.

The six fulcra share influence over organizational inertia: an organization's ability to uncouple stabilizer processes, to install or to terminate accelerator and decelerator processes, to recognize the need for accelerations or decelerations. Inertia is not always undesirable; it has an optimum value that varies with the organization's strategy and its environment. The usual organization probably has too much inertia. Moderately excessive inertia causes an organization to respond a little too slowly, to gloss over situations that deserve some attention, or to adopt slightly inadequate remedies. Moderately deficient inertia compels an organization to respond somewhat too quickly, to respond to relatively unimportant signals, or to take inordinate corrective measures. Gross deviations from optimum, however, produce truly serious consequences. Massive inertia is one reason an organization drifts into a stagnating environment.

To emphasize the difficulties of staying balanced, we state the fulcra as if an organization ought to seek minimal amounts of desirable characteristics. However, it would be equally correct to say an organization should seek minimal amounts of the opposite characteristics, but this latter approach might be misinterpreted as reaffirming values that an organizational palace upholds.

Minimal Consensus

An organization can extract advantages from both consensus and dissension simultaneously. Balance implies that consensus does not become regimentation and dissension does not become warfare.

Since the usual organization seeks more consensus than is useful, since it often settles for superficial symbols that subordinates are properly submissive, and since it suppresses conflicts that could be genuinely resolved, additional dissension would confer benefits.

Every organization is blind to some phenomena, of course, but a better organization perceives more, comprehends more of what it perceives, and brings more of its comprehension to bear on decisions (Grinyer and Norburn 1975; Starbuck 1965). Perceptions broaden through sources of dissension such as heterogeneity across personnel and subunits, delegating responsibilities to autonomous people and subunits, redundant and partly inharmonious assignments of responsibility, and diversified portfolios of activities (Jönsson 1973; Starbuck 1974, 1976; White 1969). Diverse perceptions are more likely to be used effectively if the heterogeneous personnel participate in decision-making, if information flows are intense and not rigidly channeled, if deviations are sometimes permitted from standard operating procedures, if authority is diffused, and if dissent and debate are prevalent and tolerated (Landau 1973; Mason 1969; Miller and Mintzberg 1974; Mitroff and Betz 1972; Wildavsky 1972). Participative decision-making and delegation of responsibility also make policies more practical and more likely to be followed (Dunbar 1971; Locke 1968; Pressman and Wildavsky 1973).

Dissension stimulates reconsideration of implicit or conventional assumptions, encourages strategic diversification, and deters maladaptive stresses from aggregating into crises (Coser 1956; Smith 1966). However, excessive dissension debilitates. Autonomous subunits, ambiguous goals, and nonuniform perceptions generate competing claims that have to be settled by assigning priorities; they also foster disagreements, some of which deserve constructive resolution. However, conflict resolution is blocked by distrust, insufficient communication, and personal criticisms. Extremely ambiguous authority structures or lack of confidence in leaders may prevent arbitration, and generalized disputes about long-run goals may preclude disagreements being settled on substantive grounds.

Therefore, there is a lower bound below which the level of consensus must not fall if the organization is to control its coherence (Etzioni 1968; Moore and Tumin 1949; Schneider 1962; Wildavsky 1972).

Minimal Contentment

The usual organization seeks happy, contented members. At least, this is the policy enunciated for public consumption. An organization strives to satisfy its members, and its failures to make everyone completely contented result from unavoidable competitions among claimants, from inexorable constraints imposed by the environment, or from the unrealistic demands of some members. Observers voice doubts about this overt policy after noting that people who allocate resources often behave selfishly. Unions bargain for higher wages than labor's productivity deserves, managers pay themselves excessive salaries and sit smugly in plush offices, and faculties assign themselves light teaching loads. However, these doubts concern the ways satisfactions are distributed; though the doubters suggest some members ought to receive smaller or larger pieces of the satisfaction pie, they do not challenge the desirability of an organization satisfying its members.

It is vital that people be at least minimally contented with their personal rewards, with their current activities, and with the organization's long-run goals and prospects. An organization loses essential heterogeneity if members grow so discontented that they refuse to participate (Hirschman 1970). Although voiced opinions may say an organization is doing the right things, consensus appears merely because dissenters have withdrawn physically or psychologically. Moreover, risk taking, initiative, and experimentation depend on contentment. Members will only experiment if they believe their organization can continue to exist, believe their own membership can continue, and believe unsuccessful experiments will not cause organizational failure (Thompson 1967). Experimentation also hangs on members being satisfied that their fellow members have talent and skill, that cooperation and joint problem solving can yield good solutions, that leaders can be trusted to promote the mutual welfare, and that the visible decision procedures and criteria resemble the real ones (Schneider 1962). In effect, minimal contentment can buffer against the short-run reductions in satisfactions and expectations that changes involve.

On the other hand, excessive contentment incubates crises. Low levels of contentment sharpen an organization's perceptions. Changes in an organization and its environment are signaled primarily by processes for monitoring what is going wrong; the more sensitive these error monitoring processes, the better able an organization is to perceive gradual changes (March and Simon 1958; Newman and Logan 1955). Although error monitoring can be programmatic and impersonal, programs are liable to overlook subtle unanticipated events or to misinterpret them. The important unprogrammed processes for monitoring errors utilize discontent and emit signals through dissent, complaint, disagreement, and controversy (Mason 1969; Mitroff and Betz 1972; Starbuck 1975). Sufficient discontent to induce people to speak up about what they think is going wrong provides crucial insurance against surprises of crisis proportions, because the higher the basal levels of discontent, the more likely it is that small errors will trip off alarms (Coser 1956; Pettigrew 1974).

Minimal Affluence

Discontent generally decreases as an organization gains affluence. Slack resources build up (Bonini 1963; Cyert and March 1963; Hedberg 1975a). Everyone can receive a little more, mutual self-satisfaction grows, and self-confident complacency sets in. Insensitivity toward environmental and organizational happenings accumulates and spreads. Since the usual organization is seeking as much affluence as possible, it can be charged with striving to maximize its unawareness of reality.

Affluence does offer advantages. It affords a margin that absorbs consequences of failure and that loosens the tethers between organization and environment. Opportunities can be given to display initiative and to experiment. Long-run goals can be pursued and strategies analyzed, and decisions need not be made immediately, without reflection. Members can be retrained and their knowledge updated. Alternative structures can be tried within the organization.

Therefore, a small buffer of flexible resources is an asset. However, excessive affluence can be as serious a liability as is poverty. An organization requires reminding that its environment is partly unknown, evolves, and sometimes turns hostile. Outdated activity programs have to be explicitly proven ineffective and then purposefully unlearned; inadequate paradigms must be actively disconfirmed, perceptual frameworks clearly shown invalid, and dysfunctional political coalitions undermined (Hedberg 1973, 1974). Not every claimant deserves a share of resources.

The case studies of organizations in stagnating environments suggest that insufficient affluence is the most frightening signal emitted by error monitoring processes, and that insufficient cash rouses special excitement. This doubtless indicates that an organization in a stagnating environment has such rudimentary monitoring processes that it does not realize something is awry until it has run out of cash. Such an organization relies inordinately on formal accounting—which is a decelerator process—and fails to use virtually all of the other monitoring processes it might use. However, concern about affluence is not always pathological. Every organization measures its financial states and flows much more precisely than it measures its other characteristics; and societies as wholes develop elaborate technologies for measuring wealth accurately, for keeping track of wealth positions, and for transferring wealth from one social unit to another. They do so because money is the commodity that substitutes and does not rot. Although money changes in value over time, it can be stored in totally abstract form, and it embodies the cumulative efforts of civilizations to invent a commodity that exchanges for all other commodities. The consequence is that wealth can inventory flexibility as protection against an uncertain future.

Minimal Faith

An organization should plan its future but not rely on its plans. Plans and long-run goals allow an organization to anticipate what will be required tomorrow, and the more realistic the organization's problem-solving processes, the more tomorrows it can accurately anticipate (Vickers 1959). Challenging current practices on the basis of plans is a means of creating the lead times needed for abrogating commitments, for unlearning, and for inventing new methods before they are required. Plans also serve as the key premises for appraising potential environments, for constructing performance measures that take account of future costs and benefits, for deciding which short-run demands actually warrant attention, for reacting to immediate problems in ways that do not destroy desired opportunities, and for reassuring members that changes will turn out well.

However, an organization needs balanced criteria for developing plans and goals. Because every organization fails to predict some events, extremely detailed plans or plans extending far into the future waste problem-solving capacities and discourage responsiveness (McNulty 1962; Newman and Logan 1955; Starbuck 1965; Wickesberg 1961). Moreover, plans and goals are frequently too systematic and rational; useful goals are somewhat unclear, and useful plans are somewhat disorganized, erratic, and uncertain (Moore and Tumin 1949; Schneider 1962).

A realistic organization keeps itself ready to replace plans and goals in order to match and to exploit environmental unpredictability (Beer 1972, 1974; Starbuck 1965, 1975). Since events that disprove invalid hypotheses or suggest useful conjectures might emerge at any time, alertness snares knowledge and flexibility captures opportunities. Experiments can breed opportunities and expose nascent challenges; they help an organization alternate between practical assessments of what it is and ideas about what it can become. Diversified, inharmonious activities can hedge against misunderstandings and erroneous beliefs. Unexpected strategic reorientations remind members that explicit plans and goals are merely images of evolving aspirations (Landau 1973; Wildavsky 1972).

Minimal Consistency

The usual organization behaves as if it prefers revolution to evolution.

Some changes can be postponed but not escaped; other changes are desirable. If an organization avoids changes, its effectiveness degrades, its capacity to accept changes weakens, and needs for change build up. By the time changes can no longer be held off, needs may have accumulated to revolutionary proportions, and the organization may have lost most of its ability to take changes in stride. Yet the usual organization systematically avoids changes through inflexible policies, strict conformity to standard procedures, indoctrination programs for new personnel, clear and rationalized goals, reward structures that discourage risk taking, sharply delineated responsibilities, blocked communication channels, punishment of dissent, insistence upon overt consensus, and centralized control. Activities and strategies are reinforced, rewarded, inhibited, or eliminated because of consequences they seemingly have already produced, or because of their consistency or inconsistency with precedents. Monitoring processes are carefully turned to the signals from current and former environments, and internal communications are channeled for efficiently executing former and current tasks (Clark 1972; Hedberg 1975a; Starbuck 1976).

What an organization should be avoiding is drastic revolutions. Since sudden changes do not allow enough time for each subunit to adjust to the recent behavioral changes of other subunits, coordination efforts may founder (Starbuck 1974). Task forces and committees set up to cope with emergencies expose conflicts among goals, values, and responsibilities. Consequently, doubts escalate about the legitimacy of entrepreneurial experiments by others, heterogeneity and unplanned diversity are deleted from activity portfolios, conformity and dependence increase, responsibility is depersonalized and transferred to groups, and fewer higher-risk experiments replace more lower-risk experiments. Stress elicits simplistic analyses and uses up much energy on behavior that serves no purpose beyond emotional tension release. Needs for quick action drive out problem-solving modes of behavior and interfere with the development of priorities founded on substantive analyses. Instead, issues are resolved through bargaining between coalitions that are rooted in the past rather than the future. If levels of conflict exceed the conflict-resolution capacities of the available communication channels, interpersonal warfare breaks out and inflicts lasting damage.

Costs such as hostilities, demotivation, wasted energies, ill-founded rationalities, and foolish risks can be lowered by nurturing small disruptions and incremental reorientations—by substituting evolution for revolution.

The primary requirements for evolutionary change are ideological, conceptual, and procedural. An organization can never be satisfied to continue behaving as it has, for perfection itself justifies dissatisfaction. Even in the face of apparent optimality, the organization needs incremental experiments to sharpen perceptions, to test assumptions, and to keep learning processes vital (Box and Draper 1969; Starbuck 1974). Long-standing traditions handicap, and precedents and sunk costs are bad reasons for future behaviors. Being prepared for the future implies that major investments are carefully screened for prompt payback and for adaptability to unexpected events, that technologies use labor rather intensively and avoid specialized skills, that task assignments and statuses change frequently, and that training programs diversify members' skills and prepare members for continued learning (Kaplan 1967; Wilson 1966). Only when new products are easily introduced, when freedom from competition is assured, and when long-term pools of customers are reliably forecast, is it safe to delete redundancies and to standardize products (Starbuck and Dutton 1973).

At the same time, an organization can generally avoid abrupt leaps to radically different procedures (Braybrooke and Lindblom 1963; Cartwright 1973; Lindblom 1959; Starbuck 1974; Vickers 1959). Improving procedures as quickly as possible ultimately produces less benefit than does breaking down major improvements into small increments spread out over time. When each increment is small enough to leave intact most of the activities and perceptions of most people, and small enough to uncover only partial conflicts of interest and only marginal contradictions among goals and responsibilities, an organization avoids the mammoth losses that revolutions impose. Incremental changes also limit the trust placed in current knowledge, leave time for analyzing the results of experiments, and preserve latitude for taking advantage of new discoveries. Balanced and continuous innovation aims at rates of acceleration and deceleration that interpolate between what the organization has been assimilating and what it expects. An organization needs either awareness of its unique past or, better, a stable concept of its destiny, because these help it attain identity as a distinct subculture and focus members' loyalties toward this subculture.

On the other hand, shifting responsibilities mean that tasks are given to inexperienced people who make naive mistakes and that people are trained to fill positions already occupied by persons having skill and experience. Shifting responsibilities also increase misallocations of resources, inefficiencies, and uses of crude problem-solving methods. Inconsistencies over time expend effort undoing what has just been achieved, and ceaseless experimenting sets aside optimal solutions so as to try suboptimal ones. Breaking down major improvements into small ones delays benefits. Nevertheless, these costs of evolution are more than offset by the savings from avoided revolutions (Day and Tinney 1968).

Minimal Rationality

The organization has traditionally been viewed as a vehicle for rationality, and bureaucracy has been characterized as the most rational of social systems. The self-designing organization advocated here is anything but bureaucratic, however. In a self-designing organization, objectivity should be fostered, responsibilities delegated, and conflicts resolved impersonally on substantive criteria; but also, expertise should be diluted, authority ambiguous, statuses inconstant, responsibilities overlapping, activities mutually competitive, rules volatile, decision criteria varying, communication networks amorphous, behavior patterns unstable, analytic methods unsophisticated, subunits conflicting, and efficiency a subordinate goal.

Indeed, rationality itself warrants cautious pursuit. One danger lies in oversimplifying models. The models used to choose rational solutions inevitably abstract from reality, and usually, the more explicit and manipulable they are, the more detail they omit. Models also incorporate false assumptions introduced for analytic convenience. Although an exceptionally talented model builder can oversimplify and distort and still retain the essential characteristics of reality, an organization cannot count on having exceptional model builders, and even very good models beget mistakes after the modeled situation evolves. When adopting a model means suppressing alternative formulations, as it nearly always does, an organization binds itself to fallacy (Lindblom 1959).

A related danger is emphasizing means to the exclusion of ends. When solutions are generated and evaluated, criteria of excellence often have more to do with how analyses are conducted than with what results the analyses produce. Are measurements accurate? Are statistical coefficients significant? Is the computational algorithm efficient? Analyses conducted by professional specialists are especially prone to this corruption. The crucial issues, frequently ignored, include: Is the problem important? How realistic are the assumptions? How much does the solution alter when the problem varies slightly? Are the pursued goals really in the organization's long-run interest?

Still another related danger is developing rational answers to the wrong questions. Questions may be asked solely because ways appear for answering them (Cohen, March, and Olsen 1972); then the people who invent answers shackle themselves to their answers. Large-scale projects produce many commitments that do not hinge on how good answers are. Power struggles to get a project launched and social relations among staff members generate strong emotional bonds to the project's outputs, yet the outputs may be distinctly suboptimal, or may be transient local optima. Questions may be incorrectly stated, or the key questions may not even have been conceived (Mitroff and Featheringham 1974). Wise decisions about what questions to leave unanswered probably contribute more to an organization's viability than do wise decisions about what questions to answer (Starbuck 1975).

The general point is that rationality is not easily identified. The usual organization pursues a superficial image of rationality that understates the value of imperfection. Not only can every organization expect imperfection, a self-designing organization should seek it. An optimal degree of imperfection attaches no more certainty to assumptions than their credibility deserves, converts imbalances into motivators, and uses unclear goals to keep an organization as ready for change as its environment is (Baumol and Quandt 1964; Day, Aigner, and Smith 1971; Hedberg 1974; Jönsson 1973; Landau 1973; Starbuck 1974). A self-designing organization can attain dynamic balances through overlapping, unplanned, and nonrational proliferations of its processes; and these proliferating processes collide, contest, and interact with one another to generate wisdom.

ACKNOWLEDGMENTS

The authors are indebted to Kathleen S. Christoffel, Richard H. Franke, Tiffany H. Lee, Thomas M. Lodahl, J. Robert Moore, C. Edward Weber, and Antoinette M. Wilkinson for constructive criticism.

Part II

Organizational Learning and Strategizing Part I

4

Responding to Crises

Coauthored with Arent Greve and Bo L. T. Hedberg

1. INTRODUCTION

For nearly fifty years, Facit was regarded as a successful manufacturer of business machines and office furnishings. Facit grew until it operated factories in twenty cities and it maintained sales units in fifteen countries. Employment reached 14,000. Suddenly, this success metamorphosed into impending disaster. For three consecutive years, gross profits were negative and employment and sales declined. Plants were closed or sold. Again and again, top managers were replaced and the managerial hierarchy was reorganized. Consultants were called in: they recommended that more operations should be closed and more employees should be fired. But after numerous meetings, the top managers could not decide whether to do what the consultants recommended.

Handelstidningen had succeeded for more than a century, and it had become one of Sweden's most prestigious newspapers. It was especially known for high-quality journalism about culture, business and politics, having served often as a forum for debates about social policies. Readers commended *Handelstidningen's* thoroughness, seriousness, consistency and credibility. Then circulation stopped growing and began to decline. Advertising revenue also declined. But wages and materials costs continued to rise, so new printing equipment was bought and costs were tightly controlled. The top managers decided to reemphasize the newspaper's traditional virtues: sports reporting ceased; less space was devoted to reporting crimes, accidents, and local news; business news, international politics, and cultural events were highlighted. But circulation and advertising revenue continued falling, costs continued rising, and losses became substantial. The new printing equipment was sold to get money to pay operating costs.

Kalmar Verkstad originated as a repair workshop that was jointly owned by several railroad companies, but its activities expanded to encompass the production of new rolling stock as well as repairs. Some years later, most railroad companies were bought up by Swedish Railroad, the large nationalized system. Swedish Railroad became Kalmar Verkstad's dominant owner as well as its primary customer. Behind the shield of its ownership, Kalmar Verkstad enjoyed a comfortable, if constrained, existence for nearly ninety years. In the early 1960s, the Swedish government announced that the bulk of Swedish Railroad would receive no more subsidies, and the railroad announced that its suppliers would receive no more large orders for new rolling stock. Kalmar Verkstad's board of directors, which included several executives from Swedish Railroad, decided that its primary customer had, indeed, stopped buying. To evaluate strengths and weaknesses and to search for new products, the board appointed a management committee that included an outside consultant. This committee reported that Kalmar Verkstad was good at welding, at building structures of steel sheet, and at woodworking; they proposed eleven new product lines fitting these capabilities. However, the committee also reported that Kalmar Verkstad had no sales personnel, no engineers who could design new products, no experience in bidding, and no reputation outside the railroad industry.

Facit, *Handelstidningen*, and Kalmar Verkstad exemplify organizations that encounter crises. Crises are times of danger, times when some actions lead toward organizational failure.

Based on several case studies of organizations facing crises, this chapter explains what makes some organizations especially prone to encounter crises, it describes how organizations typically react to crises, and it prescribes how organizations ought to cope with crises.

2. WHY DO CRISES OCCUR?

One initial conjecture was that crises originate as threatening events in organizations' environments. A competing conjecture was that crises originate from defects within organizations themselves. Analyses of actual crises suggest that both conjectures are partly true and both are partly false.

Organizations facing crises do perceive the crises as having originated in their environments. For example, Facit's top managers attributed many difficulties to temporary depressions of the firm's economic environment, and they often complained about the fierceness of market competition. At first, Facit's top managers thought that electronic calculators would replace mechanical calculators only very gradually; later, they saw electronic calculators as a technological revolution that was progressing too quickly for Facit to adapt to it (Starbuck and Hedberg 1977).

And it was, in fact, true that national economic growth was sometimes faster and sometimes slower. There were indeed competing firms that were wooing Facit's customers. Electronic calculators actually did challenge and ultimately replace mechanical calculators. So the observations of Facit's top managers had bases in reality. But one would have to be quite gullible to accept such reasons as completely explaining Facit's crisis.

Organizations' perceptions are never totally accurate. Organizations decide, sometimes explicitly but often implicitly, to observe some aspects of their environments and to ignore other aspects. They also interpret, in terms of their current goals, methods and competences, what they do observe. Such interpretation is evident in the statements about electronic calculators by Facit's top managers.

There are special reasons to question the perceptions of the top managers in organizations facing crises. If crises result partly from defects within organizations, these defects could distort the organizations' perceptions. Because distorted perceptions appear in all organizations, it may be overstatement to say that distorted perceptions alone are sufficient to cause crises. However, perceptual distortions do seem to contribute to crises by leading organizations to take no actions or inappropriate actions. The perceptions of top managers are highly influential because perceptual distortions cannot have strong effects on actions unless the top managers accept these distortions. Top managers' perceptions are also highly susceptible to being distorted in conservative directions. Promotions are earned partly through seniority and partly through ascribed success during the past, so the top managers usually understand best the traditional technologies and the long-standing customers. Further, because top managers generally believe that they chose their organizations' current goals and methods, they want to rationalize and defend these choices (Wildavsky 1972). One wonders, for instance, whether the conviction that mechanical calculators would continue to have a strong market in spite of competition from electronic calculators was shaped by the fact that Facit had just completed a massive program of investments in equipment for manufacturing mechanical calculators.

Defects in organizations not only affect perceptions; they also affect the realities that are there to be perceived. Organizational defects are translated into environmental realities when organizations choose their immediate environments—by choosing suppliers, product characteristics, technologies or geographic locations—or when they manipulate their environments—by advertising, training employees, conducting research or negotiating cooperative agreements (Starbuck 1976). For example, the top managers decided that *Handelstidningen*'s customers would not miss the sports news, so they deleted sports reports from the newspaper and they eliminated sports reporters from the staff. An inevitable consequence was that, after this deletion, no customer bought *Handelstidningen* in order to read sports news. Similarly, Kalmar Verkstad assumed that they could not sell rolling stock outside Sweden, so they made no effort to sell outside Sweden, and they made no sales outside Sweden.

Learning to Fail

Talk of organizational defects can, however, easily create misimpressions about the differences between those organizations that encounter crises and those that avoid crises. The organizations that encounter crises do not have qualitatively unusual characteristics, and they are not fundamentally abnormal. Probably the great majority of organizations have the potential to work themselves into crises, and the processes that produce crises are substantially identical with the processes that produce successes (Hedberg et al. 1976).

These ironies arise from how organizations learn and from how they use their successes. The key process for organizational learning is programming: when organizations observe that certain activities appear to succeed, they crystallize these activities as standardized programs. These programs are built into the formalized roles assigned to organizations' members. Both programs and roles make activities consistent across different people and across different times. Programs generate activities that resemble those leading to good results in the past, and they do so efficiently. Organizations respond quickly to most environmental events because these events activate previously learned programs. However, programs also loosen organizations' connections to their environments. Because environmental events fall into equivalence classes according to which programs they activate, organizations fail to perceive many of the small differences among environmental events. Because organizations indoctrinate their members and train them to perform roles, organizations fail to accommodate or utilize many of the differences among members who are recruited at various times in diverse locations (Nystrom et al. 1976).

Programming often facilitates success, and success always fosters programming. Success also produces slack resources and opportunities for buffering—both of which allow organizations to loosen their connections to their environments (Cyert and March 1963; Thompson 1967). Customers are clustered into equivalence classes, and products are standardized. Raw materials and products are stored in inventories, work activities are smoothed, and work schedules are stretched out into the future. Programs and roles are added rather frequently and discarded less frequently. Technologies are frozen by means of large capital investments. Such buffers make possible efficiencies that create slack resources, which in turn can make organizations less dependent upon their environments. Similarly, programming can make it less necessary to expend analytical resources on responses to environmental events, and analytical resources can be used to make organizations less dependent on their environments.

Programming, buffering, and slack resources are tools that cut on two sides. On one side, these tools enable organizations to act autonomously—to choose among alternative environments, to take risks, to experiment, to construct new environmental alternatives—and autonomous actions are generally prerequisites for outstanding successes. But on the other side, these tools render organizations less sensitive to environmental events. Organizations become less able to perceive what is happening, so they fantasize about their environments, and it may happen that realities intrude only occasionally and marginally on these fantasies. Organizations also become less able to respond to the environmental events they do perceive: they too rarely reflect before they act, they believe too strongly in the rightness of their programs, they are too confident of their abilities to act autonomously (Hall 1976; Starbuck and Hedberg 1977). Because strategies interact with organizational politics, strategic reorientations generally induce changes in who holds power, so those people who currently hold power tend to resist strategic reorientations (Normann 1971; Wildavsky 1972).

For example, success enabled *Handelstidningen* to attract outstanding personnel to its editorial staff and to establish a reputation for serious, credible reporting about culture, business, and politics. The newspaper's top managers rightly perceived that the readers placed high values on these characteristics. But the idea was sheer fantasy that the readers cared very much about culture, business, and politics, and that they cared very little about sports.

Handelstidningen's top managers did not even question the newspaper's product strategy until the crisis had been underway for two years. Then one member of the board of directors proposed conversion from daily to weekly publication. This proposal was rejected without debate.

A year later, after *Handelstidningen* had become a financial disaster, a task force was appointed to propose strategic reorientations. The task force submitted five proposals, two of which involved conversion to weekly publication. The proposal that the board of directors endorsed was to strengthen those pages from which the newspaper's reputation arose, and to obtain the resources to do this by excising the pages about which readers supposedly did not care (Nystrom et al. 1976).

In summary, it is argued that organizations take advantage of their successes to loosen their connections to their environments. Loose connections give organizations the freedom to exercise some self-determination—to choose immediate environments with desirable characteristics and to manipulate environmental characteristics. But choices involve risks: organizations may inadvertently try to inhabit nonviable environments. In particular, organizations may try to stabilize characteristics of their immediate environments in patterns that are incompatible with generalized societal trends. Such risks are amplified by faulty perceptions of environmental events, and organizations with loose connections to their environments are prone to perceive erroneously. Thus successes instigate processes that nurture crises.

Crises do occur because organizations make mistakes, and these mistakes can be attributed to certain organizational characteristics. For example, both Facit and *Handelstidningen* sought to remain in obsolete markets; and in both firms, these strategies were supported by top managers over the protests of managers at low levels and of representatives of the blue-collar workers. The organizations that encounter crises may be marginally extreme: they may allocate too much influence to top managers; they may rely too strongly on formal procedures, formalized communications, and standardized programs; they may feel unwarranted complacency; they may stringently filter their perceptions of their environments; they may have unusually fanciful beliefs about reality; they may initiate imprudent experiments (Grinyer and Norburn 1975; Hedberg et al. 1976; Miller and Mintzberg 1974). However, these organizations are marginally extreme at most. Many organizations exhibit these characteristics, all organizations have some disadvantageous characteristics, and all organizations make mistakes. Environmental events pick out the specific organizations that come face-to-face with their mistakes.

3. WHAT REACTIONS DO CRISES EVOKE?

Explaining Crises Away

It seems that conventional accounting reports, and the ideology asserting that such reports should be bases for action, are among organizations' major liabilities. The more seriously organizations attend to their accounting reports, the more likely they are to encounter crises, and the more difficulty they have coping with crises.

Accounting reports are intentionally historical: at best they indicate what happened during the previous quarter, and even recent reports are strongly influenced by purchases of goods and equipment dating back many years, and by inventories of unsalable products and obsolete components. The formats of accounting reports change very slowly. Accounting reports also intentionally focus upon formalized measures of well-observed phenomena; the measures are always numerical, the importances of phenomena are appraised in monetary units, and the observations are programmatic. Much of the content in every report is ritualized irrelevance.

Accounting reports could be more helpful and less misleading, but accounting reports do not themselves cause crises. Rather, concern for accounting reports is one symptom of a generalized pattern of organizational behavior. The organizations that take their accounting reports very seriously are assuming that their worlds change slowly—that precedents are relevant to today's actions, that tomorrow's environments will look much like yesterday's, that current programs and methods are only slightly faulty at most (Hedberg and Jönsson 1978; Thompson 1967). Such organizations devote few resources to monitoring and interpreting unexpected environmental events; they do not tolerate redundant, ostensibly inessential activities; they guide their development by means of systematic long-range planning. Concern for formal reports may testify that there is little spontaneous, informal communication: activities are coordinated through planning and programming, performances are evaluated solely by the measures in formal reports, areas of responsibility are clearly demarcated, authority is hierarchically systematic (Miller and Mintzberg 1974).

All of these characteristics make it difficult for organizations to see unanticipated threats and opportunities. Indeed, many unanticipated events are never perceived at all, whereas others are only perceived after they have been developing for some time. Then, when unanticipated events are perceived, these characteristics introduce perceptual errors. One consequence is that organizations overlook the earliest signs of developing crises, because the earliest signs are changes in poorly observed variables and are communicated orally in informal reports. Another consequence is that, after signs of crises are seen, organizations underestimate the needs for action. Remedies are not attempted when crises are newly born and mild remedies might yet suffice.

Those organizations that are strongly wedded to their pasts, naturally enough, fear rapid changes. They expect abrupt changes to produce undesirable consequences. This logic is often reversed when undesirable events occur: the undesirable events are hypothesized to be the consequences of rapid changes. The early signs of crises are attributed to the organizations' injudicious efforts to change—new markets, capital investments, inexperienced personnel, or product innovations. Such interpretations imply that no remedies are needed beyond prudent moderation, because performances will improve automatically as operations stabilize.

The idea that organizations ought to be stable structures also fosters another rationalization for early signs of crises—that poor performances result from transient environmental pressures such as economic recessions, seasonal variations in consumption, or competitors' foolish maneuvers. This rationale implies that no major strategic reorientations are called for; on the contrary, the current strategic experiments ought to terminate. Organizations decide that temporary belt-tightening is needed, together with some centralization of control and restraints on wasteful entrepreneurial ventures, but these are portrayed as beneficial changes that focus attention on what is essential (Beer 1974; Nystrom et al. 1976; Thompson 1967).

Statements by the top managers at Tandberg exemplify efforts to explain crises away. After forty years, the company had established a reputation as a manufacturer of good-quality consumer electronics—television receivers, radios, tape recorders, loudspeakers, teaching machines, and so on. Tandberg operated five factories in Norway and one in Scotland; it employed about 3,000 people; its sales had been more than doubling every three years; and its future looked bright. But the top managers worried that costs, especially labor costs, were rising even faster than sales, so they authorized large investments in new production facilities, including two new factories. While these new facilities were still under construction, sales growth decelerated somewhat to 20 percent. Profits were chopped in half that year. The top managers blamed the low profits on high costs of parts and labor, but they expressed confidence that the new production facilities would counterbalance these pressures.

However, the next year brought no improvement: Tandberg's sales rose only 10 percent, costs continued to rise rapidly, and profits became losses. The top managers publicly attributed the deceleration of sales growth to economic recessions in foreign markets even though Tandberg's domestic and foreign sales were behaving identically. The top managers also stated that the company needed better budget control, long-range planning, and more automatic equipment to save labor costs. Improved performance was predicted for the next year as a result of planning, budgeting, and rationalized production.

Once again, the ensuing year brought no improvement to Tandberg. In fact, it was disastrous. Sales went up less than 6 percent. There was a large loss that the top managers attributed to increased competition, to devaluation of the British pound, to high research costs, to high labor costs, and to delays in bringing the new automatic equipment into use. The top managers also pointed out that 'The figures for [this year and last year] cannot be compared to the preceding years because of changes in accounting procedures'.

Then the losses became so serious during the year following that the Norwegian government loaned Tandberg approximately $50 million in order to save the company from collapse.

Denials that crises are developing and that strategic reorientations are needed arise, to no small degree, from sincere conviction (Gundhus 1977). There is widespread endorsement of the idea that actions ought to be determined by rational analyses, and this idea implies that organizations ought to be stable bureaucracies. The managers who rely upon accounting reports really do believe that they should base actions only on reliable information and that communications should flow through channels. Of course, managers who have helped to formulate strategies are likely to be convinced that they have formulated good strategies that should not be changed merely because of transient difficulties. And it is a normal human characteristic to adhere to one's prior beliefs in spite of evidence that they are incorrect.

But not all denials of crises arise from sincere conviction. Managers who have helped to formulate strategies often expect—rightly—that they will be blamed if these strategies are judged faulty. These managers resist strategic reorientations in order to retain power and status, and they try to persuade themselves and others that their strategies are appropriate. Crises induce skilled personnel to depart, financial backers to desert, and suppliers to withhold credit. Anticipating such problems, managers may launch propaganda campaigns that deny the existence of crises. These propaganda efforts always include distortions of accounting reports: accounting periods are lengthened, depreciation charges are suspended, gains from sales or reevaluations of assets are included with operating profits. But it is inconsistent to assert that no crises exist while also initiating changes to remedy crises. So, to make their propaganda credible, these managers argue that major strategic reorientations are unnecessary.

Facit's top managers made numerous efforts to persuade stockholders, employees, and the public that no crisis existed, that the crisis was not serious, or that the crisis had ended. When poor performance first intruded into Facit's accounting reports, the top managers explained that this poor performance was the temporary product of currency devaluations and fierce competition. 'Facit is well equipped to meet future competition.... Improvement is underway, but has not affected this year's outcome.' Later, as the crisis deepened, Facit's managing director was replaced several times: each new managing director reported sadly that the situation was actually worse than his predecessor had publicly admitted, but he was happy to be able to announce that the nadir had been passed and the future looked rosy. Again and again, Facit's top managers announced that their firm was in sound condition and that improved performances were imminent; the chairman of the board and the managing director made such announcements even while they were secretly negotiating to sell the firm. After two years of serious difficulties, when plants were being closed, when hundreds of employees were losing their jobs, and when the top managers were privately in despair, the top managers announced that they intended to expand Facit's product line by 60 percent (Starbuck and Hedberg 1977).

In many situations, managers find delay to be an effective tactic: delays frequently render overt actions unnecessary, and delays may clarify what actions are desirable. Thus, when managers fail to react to the early signs of crises, they are behaving in a way that would be effective in many situations. But those situations for which delays produce improvements are not crises. In fact, situations are not crises if normal behaviors produce improvements. Crises are dangerous, in part, because normal behaviors make them worse.

Crises call for strategic reorientations, but delays increase both the magnitudes of these reorientations and their urgencies. Reorientations that could have been achieved gradually with moderate stress escalate during delays into major upheavals that are nearly impossible to bring off successfully. Delays are bought at the cost of tight budgets, asset consumption, centralized control, and restrictions on entrepreneurship (Nystrom et al. 1976; Stinchcombe 1974). However, if the top managers who exercise centralized control had the ability to take corrective actions, there would be no crises. So, in crises, centralization transfers control to inappropriate people (Starbuck and Hedberg 1977). Tight budgets and restrictions on entrepreneurship halt strategic experimentation and drive away ambitious, creative managers, with the result that organizations lose both the knowledge to guide reorientations and the people to implement them. Asset consumption means that organizations have nothing to fall back on when delays fail and needs for action are finally acknowledged.

Living in Collapsing Palaces

The organizations that encounter crises resemble palaces perched on mountaintops crumbling from erosion. Like palaces, these organizations are rigid, cohesive structures that integrate elegant components. Although their flawless harmonies make organizational palaces look completely rational—indeed, beautiful—to observers who are inside them, observers standing outside can see that the beauty and harmony rest upon eroding grounds.

Organizational palaces are rigid because their components mesh so snugly and reinforce their neighbors. Perceptions, goals, capabilities, methods, personnel, products, and capital equipment are like stone blocks and wooden beams that interlock and brace each other. There are no chinks, no gaps, and no protruding beams because careful reason has guided every expansion and remodeling. Rationality is solidified in integrated forms that are very difficult to move: the components that blend smoothly in one arrangement fit badly in another, components that mesh tightly must be moved simultaneously, and movements fracture tight junctions. So the inhabitants' first reactions to crises are to maintain their palaces intact—they shore up shaky foundations, strengthen points of stress, and patch up cracks—and their palaces remain sitting beautifully on eroding mountaintops.

However, shoring up affords only temporary remedies against crumbling mountains, and eventually, the palaces themselves start falling apart. People begin to see that the top managers have been making faulty predictions: doubts arise that the top managers know how to cope with the crises, and the top managers usually end up looking like incompetent liars. Idealism and commitments to organizational goals fade; cynicism and opportunism grow; uncertainty escalates (Jönsson and Lundin 1977; Kahn et al. 1964; Vickers 1959). Budget cuts and reorganizations stir up power struggles that undermine cooperation.

These processes of disintegration reinforce themselves. Organizations' abilities to achieve depend strongly on expectations (King 1974): when people expect failures, failures become more likely, and expectations of failure multiply. Achievements also depend upon ability and effort. People who see job opportunities elsewhere gain reasons to take them, and the people who are most able are offered more job opportunities, so the average level of ability falls. Those people who remain are told to work harder while taking on unfamiliar tasks and receiving fewer rewards, so their job performances degrade and their satisfactions slide downward. Cynical, opportunistic acts by subordinates elicit exhortations from their superiors—but the exhorters are seen as being untrustworthy cynics. Conflicts and power struggles stimulate additional centralized control by top managers who are themselves seen as grasping power even though they do not know how to use it.

Many of the organizations facing crises start disintegrating and never manage to pull themselves together. *Handelstidningen* was one. Circulation and advertising revenue spiraled downward year after year. For a time, costs were reduced in proportion to income, and losses were kept under control. But cost reductions became increasingly difficult and losses escalated. Staff attrition became a serious problem. A subsidiary was sold. Then the printing equipment was sold, and the newspaper was printed in a competitor's plant. The chief editor resigned. Finally, *Handelstidningen* stopped publishing ... six years after the crisis began (Nystrom et al. 1976).

Other organizations are unable to help themselves, but they are saved by outside interventions. Facit was such a case.

Two or three years after Facit's crisis became obvious, the top managers reached a state of paralysis. The managerial hierarchy had been reorganized repeatedly. Several small plants had been closed, and the main office furnishings plant had been sold. But the situation had continued to get worse and worse. Efforts to sell a subsidiary failed completely. Manufacture of voting machines stopped after Facit was unable to produce machines of satisfactory quality. Every division but one was losing money, and the chief executive of this division resigned. Public statements by the top managers grew increasingly erratic: claims that Facit confronted no serious hurdles alternated with solemn appraisals that Facit still had to surmount very serious hurdles. Local politicians publicly criticized Facit's managers and asked Sweden's Minister of Industry to intervene. The news media expressed doubt that Facit had a future.

Facit's board of directors called in McKinsey & Company. The consultants recommended further drastic retrenchments: more plants should be closed and 2400 more people should be fired. The board of directors discussed these recommendations for many hours and could not reach a decision one way or the other. The board felt strong commitments to maintaining high levels of employment.

Finally, the board invited an executive who had been working in another firm to become Facit's managing director and to decide whether to retrench further. The man turned their offer down.

At this point, Electrolux bought Facit and achieved a dramatic turnaround. Eight-hundred employees were laid off right away, but these people were being rehired within three months. It was discovered that Facit possessed a large, unfilled demand for typewriters: a mechanical-calculator plant was converted to typewriters, and the typewriter plants were expanded. The demand for office furnishings was also found to exceed production capacity. Facit's research had developed electronic calculators, small computers, and computer terminals that had never been marketed aggressively: substantial demands existed for these products. During the second year after Electrolux stepped in, Facit's employment went up 10 percent, production increased 25 percent, and Facit earned a profit.

Facit's turnaround was made possible by the disintegration that preceded it. The impediments to learning usually grow very strong in organizations. Because organizations are intricate, they fear that changes would produce unforeseen disadvantages. Because organizations are logically integrated, they expect changes to initiate cascades of further changes. Because organizations are rational, they buttress their current programs and roles with justifying analyses. These impediments to learning grow strongest in the organizational palaces that emphasize rational analyses, reliable information, and logical consistency. Palaces have to be taken apart before they can be moved to new locations, and organizations have to unlearn what they now know before they can learn new knowledge. Organizations have to lose confidence in their old leaders before they will listen to new leaders. Organizations have to abandon their old goals before they will adopt new goals. Organizations have to reject their perceptual filters before they will notice events they previously overlooked. Organizations have to see that their old methods do not work before they will invent and use new methods (Cyert and March 1963; Hedberg 1981; Nystrom et al. 1976).

Unfortunately, crisis-ridden organizations may learn that their old methods do not work, and yet they may not learn new methods that do work.

4. HOW TO COPE WITH CRISES

Crises are dangerous, by definition. After crises have fully developed, organizations face serious risks of failure. To eliminate these risks is often difficult, and the remedies bring pain to some people. Consequently, the best way to cope with crises is to evade them.

Avoiding Excesses

It is not easy to prescribe how organizations should evade crises. Because crises are partially caused by environmental events that organizations cannot control, events might inflict a crisis upon any organization, and no prescriptions can render crises utterly impossible. Moreover, insofar as crises are caused by defects within organizations, these causes have deep roots: the people in organizations believe that they are using good methods and pursuing sound strategies. Thus, prescriptions advocating different methods are received as advocating poorer methods, and prescriptions of different strategies are received as recommending less sound strategies.

Organizations are right to receive prescriptions skeptically. Their complexities make organizations very difficult to manage as complete systems, whereas prescriptions for managing organizations have to be simple in order to be understandable. When prescriptions describe methods and strategies that are easily translated into actual behaviors, these prescriptions oversimplify, they ignore contingencies, and they state half-truths. When prescriptions specify methods and strategies applying to complete, complex systems, these prescriptions read like poems that express verities but that have obscure applications to actual behaviors. Both kinds of prescriptions induce the people who follow them to misinterpret what is prescribed. Thus organizations should never adhere strictly to any prescription... including this one.

Yet, even difficulties created by uncontrolled environmental events need not lead to organizational failures: Organizations can pick up and attend to early-warning signals, and so begin remedial actions in time to prevent crises from maturing. And the case studies suggest that many organizations adhere too strictly to those prescriptions that favor rationality, reliability, formality, logical consistency, planning, agreement, stability, hierarchical control, and efficiency. All of these properties can bring benefits when they appear in moderation: organizations need some rationality, some formality, some stability, and so on. But excessive emphases on these properties turn organizations into palaces— palaces on eroding mountaintops. Organizations also need moderate amounts of irrationality, unreliability, informality, inconsistency, spontaneity, dissension, instability, delegation of responsibility, and inefficiency. These properties help to keep perceptions sharp, they disrupt complacency, and they nurture experimentation and evolutionary change (Hedberg et al. 1976; Miller and Mintzberg 1974).

One sensible operating rule is that whenever organizations adopt one prescription, they should adopt a second prescription that contradicts the first. Contradictory prescriptions remind organizations that each prescription is a misleading oversimplification that ought not to be carried to excess. For example, organizations should work toward consensus, but they should also encourage dissenters to speak out; organizations should try to exploit their strategic strengths, but they should also try to eliminate their strategic weaknesses; organizations should formulate plans, but they should also take advantage of unforeseen opportunities and combat unforeseen threats. It is as if each prescription presses down one pan of a balance: matched pairs of prescriptions can offset each other and keep a balance level. There is no evidence in the case studies that these balances have to be exactly level. Small imbalances apparently do not cause serious difficulties, and even large imbalances take long times to produce crises. Organizations err mainly by failing to recognize that good prescriptions become bad prescriptions when they are carried to excess.

But balancing prescriptions is a defensive tactic that cannot rescue the organizations that already face crises. These organizations have been defending themselves—unsuccessfully—too long; they need to go on the offensive. The remainder of this chapter prescribes how organizations can terminate their crises and begin to rebuild themselves in viable forms.

Replacing Top Managers

When Electrolux took over Facit, it promptly fired all of Facit's top managers. This is exactly what Electrolux should have done. If Electrolux had not taken such drastic action, its intervention would probably have failed.

Similar, but less complete replacements took place at Ferry Cap and Set Screw Company. Ferry was a family-owned firm that had been rather profitable during World War II and the immediate postwar period, but that began to fail in the early 1950s. Facing stiff competition in the manufacture of ferrous screws, Ferry did not make sufficient profits to be able to replace its aging machinery. So year after year, Ferry's machines grew less dependable and more expensive, and profits grew smaller and smaller. Then several Japanese firms entered the ferrous-screw industry with new, efficient factories. Many American firms responded to the Japanese challenge by borrowing capital and rebuilding their own factories, but Ferry could not take this course because it could not borrow the necessary capital.

Ferry's principal owner, the widow of the founder, appealed to her son for help. He left his own business and became Ferry's president. He also brought in a new vice president for marketing, and the two men began searching for a viable strategy. This search was greatly facilitated by students of marketing research at a local university: Ferry made itself available as a source of data for the students' research projects, and the firm thereby obtained hundreds of man-hours of marketing research—and useful ideas—at negligible cost.

Because Ferry's machines were in terrible condition, repairs had to be made frequently, and large orders were nearly as expensive to produce as were small orders. If Ferry were to sell large orders at competitive prices, it would make no profits. On the other hand, Ferry could produce small orders profitably because machines could be maintained and repaired while they were being set up. Small orders meant custom designs of stainless steel or nonferrous metals; this, in turn, meant new manufacturing techniques, new sales techniques, new suppliers, and new customers.

After struggling for two or three years, Ferry's two new top managers finally concluded that many of their colleagues in top management had to be replaced because these people were persistently adhering to the firm's traditional methods. Gradual reeducation was taking more energy than the two top managers could muster, and the firm's financial condition left no room for complacency.

Indiscriminate replacements of entire groups of top managers are evidently essential to bringing organizations out of crises. The veteran top managers ought to be replaced even if they are all competent people who are trying their best and even if the newcomers have no more ability, and less direct expertise, than the veterans.

By the time crisis-ridden organizations face up to their needs for major, long-run remedies, the organizations are teetering on the brink of failure. They lack disposable assets. No slack remains in their costs, yet they are losing money. Their debts are high, and creditors will lend them no more. Creative, entrepreneurial managers have left. Cooperation has broken down. Subordinates no longer believe what their superiors say. Everyone expects failure. No one has the energy and enthusiasm to try experiments. There are no resources to support further delays, and no insiders can argue convincingly that they know what actions should take the place of delays.

Remedies are needed urgently. Perhaps the greatest need is for dramatic acts symbolizing the end of disintegration and the beginning of regeneration. Because propaganda and deceit have been rife, these symbolic acts have to be such that even skeptical observers can see they are sincere acts; and because the top managers represent both past strategies and past attempts to deceive, these symbolic acts have to punish the top managers. In addition, however, the organizations need new perceptions of reality, fresh strategic ideas, and revitalization. Since no one really knows what strategies will succeed, new strategies have to be discovered experimentally. Experimenting depends upon enthusiasm and willingness to take risks; people must have confidence their organizations can surmount new challenges and exploit discoveries. Experimenting also depends upon seeing aspects of reality that have been unseen, and upon evaluating performances by criteria that differ from past criteria. Crisis-ridden organizations have already tried those experiments that look promising within their past perceptual frameworks, and the experiments they have not tried are ones they perceive as foolish.

Even crisis-ridden organizations are not undifferentiated wholes. They incorporate multiple, conflicting perceptions and disparate evaluation criteria. For example, Facit contained many managers and union officers who disagreed with the firm's overall strategic thrust and who were striving to be heard by the top managers. However, such heterogeneities are buried in the lower echelons of hierarchies with monolithic tops. Consensus among top managers is one reason these organizations drift into crises in the first place. Then when crises bring on centralized controls and criticism by outsiders, the top managers coalesce further into unified groups. Dissidents among the top managers rarely dissent publicly. Thus, the top managers filter the heterogeneities out of the ideas, proposals, and opinions of their subordinates.

Before regeneration can proceed, these filters have to be broken up, and replacements of one or two top managers at a time are not enough. Such gradual replacements happen spontaneously while crisis-ridden organizations are disintegrating: if gradual replacements were sufficient to end crises, the crises would already have ended. But when top managers are replaced gradually, the newcomers are injected into on-going, cohesive groups of veterans, and the newcomers exert little influence on these groups, whereas the groups exert much influence on the newcomers.

Group cohesion also impedes the veterans' own efforts to adopt remedies. Each member of a group is constrained by the other members' expectations, and cohesion draws these constraints tight. A group as a whole may bind itself to its current methods even though everyone in the group is individually ready to change; when a group includes one or two members who actively resist change, these resisters can control what happens. Group cohesion at Ferry doubtless contributed to the managerial rigidities that impeded change until the group of top managers was replaced.

Rejecting Implicit Assumptions

One reason groups of top managers find change difficult is that many of the assumptions underlying their perceptions and behaviors are implicit ones. Explicit assumptions can be readily identified and discussed, so people can challenge these assumptions and perhaps alter them. But implicit assumptions may never be seen by the people who make them, and these unseen assumptions may persist indefinitely.

For example, the top managers of Kalmar Verkstad found reorientation extremely difficult in spite of sincere, energetic attempts to change (Gezelius and Otterbeck 1977).

After Swedish Railroad's announcement in 1963, Kalmar Verkstad's top managers decided to find new product lines to replace railroad rolling stock. First, the company bought the rights to manufacture a line of mining equipment. Second, it began to design an automobile—the Tjorven—that would have advantages for postal deliveries. Licenses were purchased so that the Tjorven could utilize an engine and chassis built by DAF in the Netherlands. Third, a management committee was set up to develop product alternatives. From eleven alternatives initially proposed by this committee, the top managers chose two for aggressive pursuit: Kalmar Verkstad would build buses and it would construct interiors for boats, ships, and camping vehicles.

Over the ensuing year, the management committee expanded its list to fifteen alternatives, but its investigations dimmed the promise of these alternatives. Kalmar Verkstad lacked the technical know-how to produce some of the product lines. Other product lines elicited no enthusiasm from potential buyers and sellers. Still other product lines would confront fierce competition. After several months, no buses or interiors had been sold, although one order had been received for fifty trucks. The Tjorven, however, continued to look promising. The Swedish postal service had approved the Tjorven's design, and the postal services of six other countries had said they might buy the Tjorven.

But Kalmar Verkstad really did not need new product lines as yet because rolling stock was being produced for mines and for the Stockholm subway as well as for Swedish Railroad. In fact, rolling stock was using up 90 to 95 percent of production capacity, and the other products and contract work were keeping capacity filled.

The orders for rolling stock continued to come in year after year, and other products began to crystallize. Cooperation with DAF led to Kalmar Verkstad's becoming the Swedish distributors of DAF automobiles. For the first time, Kalmar Verkstad hired a sales manager: the sales manager's assignment was to put together a sales-and-service network for the DAF automobiles. A subsidiary was created to build automated parking garages, and another subsidiary was created to construct wooden interiors. The Swedish postal service ordered 1000 Tjorvens to be delivered over four years, but there was not enough space in the plant for this added production, so Kalmar Verkstad bought an empty building and converted it into an automobile factory.

During the six years after Swedish Railroad's announcement, Kalmar Verkstad's employment more than doubled, sales multiplied two and half times, and Kalmar Verkstad began turning itself into an automobile manufacturer. The top managers planned to make the Tjorven the springboard for a range of small automobiles and trucks that would attract mass demand for driving in urban traffic. The 1969 budget called for production of 2500 Tjorvens and 300 Tjorven trucks, and the 1970 budget anticipated production of 1700 Tjorvens and 800 trucks. Prototypes were built for two additional versions of the Tjorven, one an electric model. Swedish Railroad sold most of its stock shares in Kalmar Verkstad to the Swedish government, and new stock was issued and sold to Statsföretag, the governmental agency that supervises the nationalized enterprises in Sweden. In fact, Kalmar Verkstad's stock account was twelve times as large in 1969 as it had been in 1967, and Statsföretag ended up owning 86 percent of this stock.

Not everything was progressing satisfactorily however. Kalmar Verkstad had lost money in 1965 and 1966 and had made only small profits during the other years, so before-tax profits averaged only 0.8 percent of sales from 1964 to 1969. The 1970 budget predicted that sales would grow by a phenomenal 80 percent but that profits would be only 0.5 percent of sales. Tjorven production was lagging far behind schedule—only 720 vehicles were actually completed in 1969 against the budget of 2500 vehicles. Moreover, the Tjorven was costing a lot more than had been expected—actual costs per vehicle were 185 percent of budget during 1969.

Kalmar Verkstad's performance during 1970 did not come up to expectations. Sales rose only 29 percent, and there was no profit. Indeed, losses totaled an unbelievable 40 percent of sales!

The losses during 1970 exceeded the company's sales for any year before 1967. Every product line—even rolling stock—lost money, although 70 percent of the losses originated in automobile production.

Kalmar Verkstad continued to lose money during 1971 at the same, horrendous rate as during 1970. The subsidiary that constructed wooden interiors was sold in January 1971. An effort was made to enlist Volvo's help in producing the Tjorven, but Volvo refused; so in March 1971, Kalmar Verkstad stopped producing automobiles. The second largest stockholder, a bank, made a gift of its stock to Statsföretag. The board of directors reviewed the situation in June 1971: the board concluded that both rolling stock and the remaining new products faced dismal futures, and that large losses could continue indefinitely. Therefore, the board decided to close the company. Before 1971 ended, half of the employees had been fired, and five of the six top managers had departed. The only person remaining from the group of top managers, the 34-year-old manager of export sales, was promoted to managing director and was ordered to shut the company down by the middle of 1974.

Evidently, in attempting to cope with the crisis visualized in 1963, Kalmar Verkstad had charged blindly into another crisis that the company could not survive.

But Kalmar Verkstad did survive. Instead of shutting the company down, the new managing director sparked a resurrection.

The managing director started the resurrection by enlisting help: he formed a consultative group composed of union officers, blue-collar workers, foremen, the personnel manager, and a newly hired assistant managing director. This consultative group set out to stop the large losses and to raise productivity. The group decided that many difficulties were originating in the system of paying piece-rate wages because these encouraged workers to maximize their wages as individuals, even when the results were production bottlenecks and imbalances. Moreover, the time studies and discussions to set piece rates were wasting the time of blue-collar workers and managers alike. The consultative group asked forty workers to evaluate various jobs, and on this basis, the group assigned an hourly wage to every job. The alternative wage systems were submitted to the workers for a vote, and 65 percent of the workers said they wanted to shift to hourly wages.

The consultative group also sent delegations and written petitions to the Swedish government, with the result that the company received a stopgap order from Swedish Railroad to repair some old rolling stock and to scrap some old locomotives.

The chairman of Kalmar Verkstad's board of directors had been quite pessimistic about the company's future. At the end of 1972, this man left Statsföretag and the chairmanship. His replacement as chairman of the board expressed interest in the company's survival.

Kalmar Verkstad's potential market for rolling stock was the subject of considerable debate. The managing director believed that a large export market existed. Also, of six Swedish firms that competed with Kalmar Verkstad in 1963, five had given up. The only remaining Swedish competitor was a small subsidiary of Swedish Railroad. Yet even this small competitor might be too much. In March 1973, Sweden's Department of Transportation received a consulting report that said Swedish Railroad would have no need to place orders outside its own subsidiary for at least three years, and perhaps five years. This report greatly discouraged the people at Kalmar Verkstad.

But only one week later, morale surged upward. Statsföretag postponed the company's closing for an indefinite period and said that firings could stop. The big losses had ended. Statsföretag had faith, despite the negative consulting report, that Kalmar Verkstad could obtain orders for rolling stock because several large orders were actually being negotiated. Above all, Statsföretag was impressed with the way Kalmar Verkstad was operating as an integrated team under the leadership of its managing director.

The decision to keep Kalmar Verkstad in business was made permanent in October 1974. Employment had been cut to only 69 percent of the 1963 level, but productivity was nearly twice as high as it had been in 1963, and so production during 1974 was 36 percent higher than during 1963. There was a two-year backlog of orders for rolling stock. Many of these orders were coming from outside Sweden, but two very large orders had come from Swedish Railroad. Furthermore, only 60 percent of production capacity was being used for rolling stock. The company was also making plastic bodies for automobiles and large forklifts, and the latter were proving to have a substantial export market.

Kalmar Verkstad's profit in 1975 was nearly six times as large as the largest profit the company had ever earned before.

The resurrection altered at least three assumptions that had been implicit in Kalmar Verkstad's behavior up to 1971. One assumption was that rolling stock could be sold only inside Sweden. Believing this to be so, the company had not solicited export orders for rolling stock. In fact, no sales personnel sought export orders until 1969 when the future managing director was hired as manager of export sales, and even after 1969, it was assumed that the only export product would be the Tjorven. As the manager of export sales traveled around Europe, however, he concluded that there was little demand for the Tjorven but much demand for rolling stock. Of course, his conclusion was not welcome in a company that was busily moving out of the rolling stock business and into the Tjorven business. But he got a chance to test his conclusion's accuracy after he became the managing director, and he proved to be right. Kalmar Verkstad began exporting rolling stock to Africa as well as to Europe.

A second implicit assumption was that remedies for Kalmar Verkstad's difficulties lay within production rather than within sales. The company had long been owned by its major customer, and it employed no sales personnel. Its top managers thought of it as a factory. When Swedish Railroad announced the end of large orders, Kalmar Verkstad's top managers inferred that their factory would have to find new products to replace rolling stock. They began immediately to investigate new products. They did not ask how rolling stock could continue to be sold, they did not mount an effort to sell rolling stock, and they did not ask how rolling stock could be sold to the Swedish Railroad in spite of its announcement. Although the top managers recognized that Kalmar Verkstad lacked capability in sales, they did not try to correct this deficiency. The company did not even have a sales manager until 1968 when a man was hired for the purpose of building a sales and service network for DAF automobiles.

The orientation of top management shifted abruptly at the end of 1971 because there was only one top manager left and he had been a salesman. In fact, he was a brilliant salesman. He sold cooperation and teamwork to Kalmar Verkstad's employees. He sold the desirability of Kalmar Verkstad's survival to Statsföretag.

He sold rolling stock throughout Europe and Africa, including big sales to Swedish Railroad. He gave Kalmar Verkstad a sales capability to balance its production capability.

A third implicit assumption was that managers should manage the company. Before 1972, Kalmar Verkstad was organized on the premise that managers should form a hierarchical social class that dominates other workers. Top managers were supposed to make the basic decisions; middle managers and foremen were to implement these decisions by controlling the activities of blue-collar workers; blue-collar workers were to pursue their personal self-interests within the controls set by managers. This system did not work well. Indeed, it is ironic, in view of the top managers' emphasis on production, that they could not make their factory produce. The large losses occurred because the managerial hierarchy could not control what was happening: actual production fell far below the planned levels, and actual costs soared far above budgets.

The new managing director began to alter this arrangement when he enlisted union officers and blue-collar workers into his consultative group. His premises were that managers and other workers should collaborate with each other, that all workers should have influence upon basic decisions, that blue-collar workers know how to make a factory productive, and that managers do not have to control other workers. These premises apparently have some validity, for the unions and the blue-collar workers did take responsibility for making the factory produce, and productivity went way up. Not everyone at Kalmar Verkstad has equal say about everything, but the company has grown progressively more and more democratic since 1972, and success has accompanied this democracy.

Experimenting with Portfolios

Kalmar Verkstad was behaving sensibly during 1974 insofar as its management committee was investigating many alternative product lines. The top managers could not identify new product lines that were certain to succeed—as they demonstrated when they initially chose to build buses and wooden interiors. So they should have been hedging their bets by developing diverse alternatives simultaneously. And they actually did start to develop a diversified portfolio of activities. They tried to build wooden interiors, automated parking garages, and several versions of the Tjorven, and they tried to sell DAF automobiles. In retrospect, however, it is clear that this portfolio tilted out of balance. Because the Tjorven captured the imaginations of the top managers, the company put too little effort into wooden interiors, parking garages, and DAF sales, and too much effort into the Tjorven. When the Tjorven's basket fell apart, too many eggs were in it.

In order to escape from crises, organizations have to invest in new markets, new products, new technologies, new methods of operating, or new people. Diversification plays the same role in these investments as it does in other investments: expected returns are traded for protection against mistaken predictions.

If an organization had perfect foresight, its optimal strategy would be to invest all of its efforts in a single activity—an activity that is both certain to remedy the crisis quickly and certain to provide a sound basis for future development. However, this single-activity strategy is only optimal for an imaginary organization with perfect foresight. If an organization makes small errors of prediction, it might misjudge the relative merits of several activities that all look good. Such an organization must invest effort in several activities in order to be confident that its portfolio includes the best alternative. If an organization's predictions contain large errors, it might mistakenly invest in activities that look promising but really are not. Such an organization must invest in several activities merely to be confident that its portfolio includes even one good alternative (Landau 1973). Of course, crisis-ridden organizations have highly distorted perceptions, so they are prone to make enormous prediction errors.

But crisis-ridden organizations find it difficult to pursue several alternatives simultaneously because they lack resources. Not many organizations start to develop alternatives while they are still as affluent as Kalmar Verkstad was in 1963. Most organizations, like Ferry, delay until they have sold their disposable assets, until their credit is stretched to the limit, until their people are demoralized and overworked, and until their operations have been cut to bare essentials.

By 1972, Kalmar Verkstad had lost its affluence, but it dealt effectively with its impoverishment through democracy. In essence, democracy enlarged the company's resources by eliciting involvement and enthusiasm and by raising productivity. The resulting teamwork and profitability impressed Statsföretag, which restored the company's credit. The company's delegations and petitions to the Swedish government also got hearings because they came from a democratic base.

By contrast, Ferry conserved its selling resources by means of centralized data analysis and centralized control. Ferry's vice president for marketing obtained detailed business statistics from the American government, and then he culled through these statistics for companies that were using stainless steel and non-ferrous metals. His premise was that these companies might purchase the kinds of screws Ferry could make profitably. He put potential customers into geographic clusters. Then to get his salesmen to call on desired customers instead of familiar ones, he gave the salesmen schedules that specified what companies they should contact each day and what kinds of screws these companies might buy.

Organizations may have less difficulty obtaining tangible resources than obtaining the equally essential intangible resources, because organizational disintegration subjects people to tremendous stress. Stress amplifies uncertainty (Kahn et al. 1964), and so people have had their fill of uncertainty long before organizations start to investigate alternatives. Consequently, people want to believe that surefire remedies have been found—they do not want to hear about prediction errors, and they do not want to invest themselves in experiments that might fail.

Nevertheless, experimentation is the right theme to engender. Crisis-ridden organizations do not know surefire remedies, so they have no choice but to experiment, and some of their experiments will fail. Kalmar Verkstad's losses from 1970 to 1972 were so large mainly because the company had stopped treating the Tjorven as an experiment. Since the company had invested psychologically as well as financially in the Tjorven, the project's failure totally discouraged both the top managers and the owners.

When people recognize that they are experimenting, they can manage their experiments in ways that cut down losses that failures would produce. Experimenting people can also accept the inconsistency of searching for remedies among activities that looked unpromising in the frameworks of their organizations' former perceptions and beliefs. Of course, an experimental theme brings the danger that people will not take their activities seriously enough and that experiments will fail solely because people lack faith in them. This danger is serious, but it is a danger arising from realistic skepticism and it can be combated. Moreover, an experimental theme offers long-run advantages in that experimenting people are unlikely to be satisfied by the first indications of success: they keep on trying for improvements because experiments never come out perfectly (Hedberg et al. 1976; Starbuck and Nystrom 1983).

Managing Ideology

Top managers are often the villains of crises. They are the real villains insofar as they steer their organizations into crises, and insofar as they intensify crises by delaying actions or taking inappropriate actions. And they are symbolic villains who have to be replaced before crises end. But top managers are also the heroes when their organizations escape from crises. They receive the plaudits, and they largely deserve the plaudits because their actions have been the crucial ones.

Sometimes top managers contribute to escapes from crises by inventing new methods and strategies. Top managers have the best chance to do this effectively in small organizations like Ferry, because small organizations do not make sharp demarcations among managers at different levels and they do not sharply distinguish managers from staff analysts. However, even in small organizations, the top managers should beware of relying on their own strategy-making skills. In large organizations where top management is a specialized occupation, it is generally a mistake for the top managers to act as strategy-makers.

Especially in large organizations, there are usually staff analysts who are better than the top managers at formulating strategies and inventing new methods. People are promoted to top management partly because they have been given credit for past successes. But these successes are characteristically organizational achievements that blend contributions from several individual people; the leaders of organizational successes often lose their ascribed abilities when their followers or tasks change. The people who have been credited with successes overestimate the generality of their past decision rules and their past analytic techniques, so they underestimate the speed with which their expertise grows obsolete. People are also chosen as top managers partly because they can skillfully manage other people. But managing differs from analyzing, and managers' work is fragmented into brief episodes that leave few opportunities for thoughtful reflection (Mintzberg 1973).

Furthermore, when top managers are occupied with strategy-making, they are not doing the more important work that is their special responsibility: managing ideology. The low-level and middle managers do attend to ideological phenomena to some extent, but they focus their attentions upon visible, physical phenomena—the uses of machines, manual and clerical work, flows of materials, conferences, reports, planning documents such as schedules and blueprints, or workers' complaints. Top managers have the complementary responsibility: although they have to attend to visible, physical phenomena to some extent, they should concentrate their attentions on ideological phenomena such as morale, enthusiasm, beliefs, goals, values, and ideas. Managing ideology is very difficult because it is so indirect—like trying to steer a ship by describing the harbor toward which the ship should sail. But managing ideology is also very important because ideological phenomena exert such powerful effects upon the visible, physical phenomena.

Electrolux's turnaround of Facit was wrought almost entirely by managing ideology (Starbuck and Hedberg 1977). Except for the replacements of top managers, Electrolux left Facit's organization largely alone. Electrolux did loan Facit approximately $2 million so that actions would not have to be taken solely out of financial exigency, but this was a small sum in relation to the size of the company. What Electrolux did was to reconceptualize Facit and Facit's environment. Electronic calculators were no longer a technological revolution that was leaving Facit behind: Facit was making and selling electronic calculators. Typewriters and office furnishings became key product lines instead of sidelines to calculators. Competition stopped being a threat and became a stimulus. As Electrolux's managing director put it: 'Hard competition is a challenge; there is no reason to withdraw.' A newspaper remarked: 'Although everything looks different today, the company is still more or less managed by the same people who were in charge of the company during the sequence of crises. It is now very difficult to find enough people to recruit for the factories.... All the present products emanate from the former Facit organization, but still, the situation has changed drastically.'

Kalmar Verkstad's resurrection, too, was overwhelmingly produced by managing ideology (Gezelius and Otterbeck 1977). Kalmar Verkstad metamorphosed from a factory that made products to a company that made and sold products. The company's market expanded beyond Sweden's borders, and rolling stock acquired a growing demand instead of a declining demand. Union officers and managers discovered that they shared mutual interests and that they could benefit from collaboration. Workers were magically transformed from selfish individuals trying to get around managerial controls into responsible members of a team striving to increase productivity.

The processes of disintegration make shambles of the ideologies in crisis-ridden organizations, and the top managers confront the task of building new ideologies on these shambles. These new ideologies should encourage people to break with precedents and to root out implicit assumptions. The best way to disconfirm implicit assumptions is to substitute experiments for analyses, to evaluate proposed strategies and methods by trying them out rather than by speculating about their outcomes. Experiments depend upon enthusiasm and willingness to take risks, and risk taking depends, in turn, upon the penalties for failure being mild.

The penalties for failure dropped precipitously in both Facit and Kalmar Verkstad. Before Electrolux appeared on the scene, Facit's crisis was being portrayed as a national tragedy in which tens of thousands of jobs were being lost and several towns were being destroyed. People could not risk making such a serious tragedy worse. But then Facit became merely 30 percent of a massive conglomerate, and its financial and goodwill buffers were augmented. It would no longer be a national tragedy if an experiment failed. At Kalmar Verkstad, the worst possible tragedy occurred when the board of directors decided in June 1971 to shut down the company. No experiment thereafter could make the situation noticeably worse, and modest experiments would be inadequate even if they succeeded. Radical experiments became possible... if not inevitable.

Equally striking, and perhaps more important, were the revolutions in enthusiasm at Facit and Kalmar Verkstad. Facit was infused by an atmosphere that a newspaper labeled parochially 'the Electrolux spirit'—optimism, confidence, search for opportunities, fast action, and energy. But a union officer may have made the most insightful statement about Facit's transformation; he said: 'It is again fun to work.' A manager at Kalmar Verkstad made virtually the same statement. Two academic observers, Gezelius and Otterbeck (1977), described the resurrected Kalmar Verkstad as '350 optimists who all are very intimately acquainted with the dangers of unabashed optimism'.

Facit, Ferry, and Kalmar Verkstad are three organizations that have rediscovered the truth of an ancient, Chinese insight. The Chinese character for crisis combines two simpler symbols, the symbol for danger and the one for opportunity. Crises are times of danger, but they are also times of opportunity.

Organizations can benefit from crises if they can perceive their opportunities and can marshal the courage and enthusiasm to pursue them. Whether organizations do this is largely up to their top managers. With little more than words, the top managers can shape ideological settings that reveal opportunities, nurture courage, and arouse enthusiasm. As Edmund Leach rightly observed: 'The world is a representation of our language categories, not vice versa.'

ACKNOWLEDGMENT

Leah Taylor suggested useful editorial revisions.

5

Organizations as Action Generators

1. INTRODUCTION

Managers, management scientists, and organization theorists generally assert that organizations are, and ought to be, problem-solvers. Problem-solving is activity that starts with perception of a problem. Although often equated with decision-making, problem-solving is defined by its origin, whereas decision-making is defined by its ending—a decision. Problem-solving can stop without decisions having been made, if problem-solvers can find no solutions or if problems just disappear. Some analysts have reported that decision making usually starts before decision-makers perceive problems (Mintzberg, Raisinghani, and Théorêt 1976). Many decisions lead to no actions, yet they may solve problems; many decisions may be imputed in hindsight (Weick 1979); and many actions occur without anyone thinking they solve explicated problems.

Problem-solving involves repetitive cycles of activity. A seminal study remarked that 'the "problem" to be solved was in fact a whole series of "nested" problems, each alternative solution to a problem at one level leading to a new set of problems at the next level' (Cyert, Simon, and Trow 1956: 247). However, that study ended when a committee voted for an action, as if this vote ended the process. Subsequent studies have portrayed decisions as endings, but they have not insisted that all decision processes begin with problems. Cyert and March (1963: 121), for example, noted that problems may be excuses: 'Solutions are also motivated to search for problems. Pet projects (e.g. cost savings in someone else's department, expansion in our own department) look for crises (e.g. failure to achieve the profit goal, innovation by a competitor).'

Cohen, March, and Olsen (1972) argued that decisions result from interactions among streams of problems, potential actions, participants, and choice opportunities. When a choice opportunity arises, participants bring up pet problems and propose actions unrelated to any visible problems, so the choice opportunity comes to resemble a garbage can filled with unrelated problems and potential actions. Participants may perceive a decision (*a*) when an action is taken, even if this action solves no problems in the garbage can; (*b*) when a problem is removed from the garbage can, even if no action has been taken to cause its removal; or (*c*) when an action is mated with a problem and called a solution. Cohen, March, and Olsen asserted that events (*a*) and (*b*) predominate and event (*c*) occurs infrequently.

This chapter backtracks the trail blazed by Cohen, March, and Olsen, and then sets off in a different direction. The backtracking occurs because the garbage-can model understates cause–effect attributions, de-emphasizes the activities preceding decisions, and ignores the activities following decisions. When Cohen, March, and Olsen claimed that decisions infrequently mate problems with solutions, they were letting the participants judge whether decisions occur, whereas they themselves were judging whether actions solve problems. Participants generally think actions do promise to solve problems; most problems are generated or remodeled to justify intended actions. Participants also see logic in problem-solving activities despite their disorganization, and participants react to actions' results.

Organizations' activities categorize in at least two modes: a problem-solving mode in which perceived problems motivate searches for solutions, and an action-generating mode in which action taking motivates the invention of problems to justify the actions. The problem-solving mode seems to describe a very small percentage of the activity sequences that occur, and the action-generating mode a large percentage.

The view I propose both decomposes and generalizes. The phenomena others have called problems are separated into four concepts: symptoms, causes of symptoms, needs for action, and problems. Actions are distinguished from needs for action and solutions. At the same time, opportunities, threats, and successes strongly resemble problems.

Although this view integrates ideas from many sources, two especially influential ancestors are Hewitt and Hall (1973). They pointed out that people collectively appraise a shared problematic situation by talking in stylized language. The appraisal talk continues until participants agree on a cure. Then the participants generate a core problem that the agreed cure will solve. The next step is to build a theory relating the core problem to its cure; theory building is iterative and includes tests of the theory against past events and concocted examples. The theory (a) defines the essential, real elements of the core problem and excludes peripheral, illusory elements, (b) explains why the core problem arose and how the agreed cure will solve it, (c) generalizes to numerous situations so that the stimulus situation becomes a specific instance, and (d) founds itself on widely accepted, societal ideologies.

2. PROGRAMS AS ACTION GENERATORS

Case studies of organizations facing crises (Nystrom, Hedberg, and Starbuck 1976; Starbuck, Greve, and Hedberg 1978) teach several lessons—among them, that normal organizations may manufacture crises for themselves by choosing to inhabit stagnating environments. The organizations do not foresee the results of their actions: they misperceive environmental opportunities and threats, impose imagined constraints on themselves, and expect rational analyses to produce good strategies. Organizations create behavior programs to repeat their successes, but these programs turn into some of the main causes of crises. Programs focus perceptions on events their creators believe important, so the programs blind organizations to other events that often turn out to be more important. Within the frames of reference created by and inherent in programs, they appear to be working well. However, evaluation data are biased, and programs are not updated as rapidly as they should be.

For example, Facit AB grew large and profitable while making and selling business machines and office furnishings (Starbuck and Hedberg 1977). Although Facit made many products, the top managers believed the key product line to be mechanical calculators: they saw products such as typewriters, desks, and computers as peripheral. In fact, the top managers declined to authorize production of computers and electronic calculators designed by a subsidiary. Facit concentrated on improving the quality and lowering the costs of mechanical calculators, and it created behavior programs to facilitate production and sale of mechanical calculators. Technological change was seen as slow, incremental, and controllable. In the mid 1960s, Facit borrowed large sums and built new plants that enabled it to make better mechanical calculators at lower costs than any other company in the world. Between 1962 and 1970, employment rose 70 percent and sales and profits more than doubled. By 1970, Facit employed 14,000 people who worked in factories in twenty cities in five countries, or in sales offices in fifteen countries.

Facit's focus on mechanical calculators was self-reinforcing. Electronics engineers were relegated to a small, jointly owned subsidiary. The engineers within Facit itself concentrated on technologies having clear relevance for mechanical calculators, and Facit understood these technologies well. Top, middle, and lower managers agreed about how a mechanical-calculator factory should look and operate, what mechanical-calculator customers wanted, what was key to success, and what was unimportant or silly. Behavior programs were pared to essentials; bottlenecks were excised; no resources were wasted gathering irrelevant information or analyzing tangential issues. Costs were low, service fast, glitches rare, understanding high, and expertise great.

But only within the programmed domain! One loyal customer finally cancelled a large order for voting machines after Facit had failed repeatedly to produce machines of adequate quality. Although some lower-level managers and engineers were acutely aware of the electronic revolution in the world at large, this awareness did not penetrate upward, and the advent of electronic calculators took Facit's top managers by surprise. Relying on the company's information-gathering programs, the top managers surmised that Facit's mechanical-calculator customers would switch to electronics very slowly because they liked mechanical calculators. Of course, Facit had no programs for gathering information from people who were buying electronic calculators.

Actual demand for mechanical calculators dropped precipitously, and Facit went through two years of loss, turmoil, and contraction. The top managers' contraction strategy aimed perversely at preserving the mechanical-calculator factories by closing the typewriter and office-furnishings factories. With bankruptcy looming, the board of directors sold Facit to a larger firm. The new top managers discovered that demand for typewriters was at least three times and demand for office furnishings at least twice the production capacities: sales personnel had been turning down orders because the company could not fill them.

Such observations dramatize the power of behavior programs to shape reality. Programs are not merely convenient and amenable tools that people control. Programs construct realities that match their assumptions—by influencing their users' perceptions, values, and beliefs, by dictating new programs' characteristics, by filtering information and focusing attention (Rosenhan 1978; Salancik 1977; Starbuck 1976). Most importantly, programs act unreflectively. March and Simon (1958: 141–142) remarked:

Situations in which a relatively simple stimulus sets off an elaborate program of activity without any apparent interval of search, problem-solving, or choice are not rare. They account for a very large part of the behavior of all persons, and for almost all of the behavior of persons in relatively routine positions. Most behavior, and particularly most behavior in organizations, is governed by performance programs.

Indeed, research shows that programs account for almost all behavior in non-routine positions as well (Mintzberg 1973; Mintzberg, Raisinghani, and Théorêt 1976; Tuchman 1973). Behaviors get programmed through spontaneous habits, professional norms, education, training, precedents, traditions, and rituals as well as through formalized procedures. Adults cope with new situations by reapplying routines they already know, and one would be hard pressed to find unprogrammed behavior in a supermarket, a business letter, a courtroom, a cocktail party, or a bed.

Organizations amplify the general human propensity to create behavior programs, because programming is organizations' primary method for coordinating activities, learning, and hierarchical control. Indeed, organizations frequently create action generators—automatic behavior programs that require no information-bearing stimuli because they are activated through job assignments, clocks, and calendars. Consequently, organizations act unreflectively and nonadaptively most of the time. A manufacturing organization does not produce goods at ten o'clock on Tuesday morning because some problem arose at nine o'clock and careful analysis implied that a solution would be to start producing: its founders created the organization to produce goods; funds were solicited with promises that goods would be produced, then spent on production equipment; personnel were chosen for their capabilities to produce goods; people arrived at work on Tuesday expecting to produce goods. Similarly, organizations advertise, make budgets, maintain inventories, answer letters, and hold annual picnics whether or not these actions can be interpreted as solving any immediate problems. Even if actions first begin because of specific needs, they become automatic when assigned to specialists, written into budgets, and given floor space. Most likely, however, action generators do not even originate because of specific needs: they are traditional, copied from other organizations, taught in schools of management, or legitimated by managerial literature and talk (Beyer 1981; Starbuck 1976).

Although new organizations inherit and imitate, old organizations undoubtedly have larger repertoires of action generators than do new ones. Because formalization produces action generators, bureaucracies have larger repertoires than nonbureaucratic organizations; bureaucratization correlates with organizational size. Similarly, the newer subunits of organizations tend to possess fewer action generators, as do the less bureaucratized subunits. Some subunits, such as those that conduct ceremonies or those with great autonomy, participate in activity domains that evaluate conformity to programs legitimated by societal ideologies; and self-selection and socialization may make members of these subunits especially respectful of societal ideologies (Beyer 1981; Meyer and Rowan 1977). Such subunits would use action generators more often than entrepreneurial subunits or subunits that participate in illegitimate domains. Thus, old, bureaucratic banks, churches, and public-accounting firms contrast with new, nonbureaucratic, and deviant organizations such as criminal associations or entrepreneurial firms.

People see actions as producing results, including solutions to specific problems, so organizations sometimes modify or discard action generators to obtain different results. Failures and difficulties may provoke changes, whereas successes heighten complacency (Hedberg 1981); successful organizations seem to depend strongly on action generators (Nystrom, Hedberg, and Starbuck 1976). However, actions and benefits are loosely associated. Actions occur even if not stimulated by problems, successes, threats, or opportunities that exist here and now; and action generators may continue operating without change through periods when no problems, successes, threats, or opportunities are acknowledged. This stability has evoked proposals for zero-based budgeting and sunset laws.

3. JUSTIFYING ACTIONS

Societal ideologies insist that actions ought to be responses—actions taken unreflectively without specific reasons are irrational, and irrationality is bad (Beyer 1981; Meyer and Rowan 1977). So organizations justify their actions with problems, threats, successes, or opportunities. Bureaucrats, for instance, attribute red tape to legal mandates or to sound practice.

Expecting justifications to be self-serving, audiences discount them; and so organizations try to render justifications credible. Examples range from falsified reports by police officers, through military reports portraying all personnel as superior, to workers who behave abnormally during time studies (Altheide and Johnson 1980; Edelman 1977). Such examples show organizations interpreting, classifying, and labeling ambiguous data as well as recording biased data, but they also show that organizations encompass contending interest groups.

Actions may be justified unintentionally, because brains involuntarily alter current beliefs so as to fit in new information (Loftus 1979). People cannot avoid revising their memories or perceptions to make them match; and in particular, an actor's brain highlights memories justifying that action and suppresses memories making the action appear irrational or wrong (Salancik 1977; Weick 1979: 194–201).

Problems as Justifications

After observing managers, Kepner and Tregoe (1965: 7–17) concluded that differing meanings of the word problem engender a lot of confusion, disagreement, and wasted talk. Managers use problem to denote: (*a*) evidence that events differ from what is desired; (*b*) events that cause discomfort or effort; (*c*) conjectures about why events differ from what is desired; (*d*) possible sources of events that cause discomfort; and (*e*) actions that ought to be taken to alter events. Managers also use problem synonymously with such words as issue, question, trouble, and situation.

To avoid such confusions, I denote usages (*a*) and (*b*) with the term symptoms, usages (*c*) and (*d*) with the term causes of symptoms, and usage (*e*) with the term needs for action. Needs for action also include statements advocating inaction. I reserve the word problem for molecular concepts to which people give distinctive labels, such as 'the quality-control problem' or 'the problem of production'.

I have analyzed every problem-solving transcript I could find. These analyses suggest that people avoid problem labels with negative connotations and adopt labels with positive or neutral connotations. Taken literally, most problem labels imply that no symptoms exist. Very few labels specify symptoms (the problem of absenteeism) or causes of symptoms (the crime problem). Some labels name sites, observers of symptoms, or potential problem-solvers (the Watergate thing, Mitchell's problem). More labels describe variables used to measure what is going on (the market-share problem, the population problem). Many labels describe desired states of affairs (the President's credibility problem, the need for a better corporate image). Thus, problem labels conform to the widespread tendency to sterilize organizational communication with euphemisms.

The cash problem might refer to any amount of cash that the speaker considers problematic, and the credit problem to any level of credit. Such ambiguity enables problem labels to be used over and over while people generalize and rationalize problems. A problem is an ideological molecule that integrates elements such as values, causal beliefs, terminology, and perceptions. Over time, people expand one of these molecules to include fitting ideological elements, and they edit out inharmonious elements. Being an ideological element itself, a problem's label helps to determine which ideological elements fit in. The problem evolves toward an ideal type that matches its label and rational logic, but deviates more and more from immediate realities. Evolution may also change the problem label, to a more general or more positive one; but a sufficiently general and positive label persists as an increasingly accurate designation.

For example, Facit's top managers viewed their company as a harmonious system that evolved slowly by conforming to plans, and they perceived their industry as focusing on price competition over technologically stable products. For many years, their central challenge had been competitive threat, and they interpreted electronic calculators as a new aspect of competitive threat. This marginal revision left the central challenge basically the same, so it could be met through the familiar planned evolution. Two years of plant closings, managerial transfers, and financial losses convinced the top managers that planned evolution no longer met the challenge of competitive threat. But, they thought, their company was designed to change slowly so it could not change quickly, and a harmonious system for producing mechanical calculators might never be able to produce electronic calculators. The top managers could see that competitive threat had become an unmeetable challenge. After Facit was sold, the new top managers did not even see competitive threat. Indeed, Facit faced weak competition in the sale of typewriters and office furnishings and its subsidiary had designed electronic calculators and computers. The company turned around in less than a year, including the addition of electronic products.

Because action generators are stable and nonadaptive, they require stable, nonadaptive justifications; and ambiguous labels and generalized problems afford such justifications. Thus, for Facit to keep on producing mechanical calculators, the top managers had to categorize electronic calculators as elements of competitive threat.

Growing crystals in complex fluids. The ideological molecules called problems resemble crystals: they form incrementally; their elements array in logically congruent patterns; and as rationalization fills the logical gaps, problems grow perfect and hard like emeralds or rubies.

People mix symptoms, causes of symptoms, and needs for action into conceptual and conversational hodgepodges that also include situation statements, goals, values, expectations, plans, symbols, beliefs, and theories; and consequently, problems may begin to crystallize around diverse initial elements. Advocates of rational problem-solving react to this by prescribing systematic procedures for growing problem crystals. Kepner and Tregoe (1965), for instance, advocated first defining symptoms precisely, next identifying causes of these symptoms, and then spelling out goals and values before proposing needs for action.

Because brains create new categories on slight pretexts and apply logic so enthusiastically that they remember fictional events, one might ask why people do not spontaneously form problem molecules in a systematic, rational way such as Kepner and Tregoe and others have prescribed. One reason is that ideological elements have meaning only in relation to other elements. Defining symptoms requires describing the symptoms' contexts: the symptoms can be identified as A and B only if C, D, and E can be excluded. Defining symptoms also reveals goals, values, and expectations; Kepner and Tregoe themselves prescribed that problem-solvers should identify symptoms by comparing actual performances with expected ones. Both contextual distinctions and expectations rest upon causal beliefs. Hodgepodges help people surmount the self-deceptions of their compulsively logical brains and grow problem crystals that mirror some of the complexity of their environments.

People also deviate from systematic, rational problem-solving because justifying actions requires tight integration between needs for action, symptoms, and causes of symptoms; and to justify actions strongly, problem crystals must emphasize needs for action (Brunsson 1982). Needs for action talk about symptoms indirectly, by asserting that certain actions should be taken to correct symptoms, or by arguing that corrective actions are unnecessary: 'I wonder if our real problem isn't what we're going to do about stepping up production' rather than 'Production is too low'.

Then too, people behave as they do because they believe: (*a*) that results are good or bad; (*b*) that results have discernible causes; and (*c*) that results should evoke statements about needs for action. Small children learn that results are rarely neutral, that reward and punishment are ubiquitous, and that adults react to results by taking actions. Older children learn that even if rewards, punishments, and responsive actions cannot be observed immediately, they will occur eventually and perhaps subtly. Because children are asked to solve mysteries with answers that look obvious to their parents and their teachers, children learn that adults solve mysteries easily, that mysteries arise mainly from inexperience or stupidity. Of course, some people learn these lessons better than others.

Contemporary, industrialized societies encourage people to create large problems with crystalline structures. Complexity, rapid change, and floods of information impede learning: When faced with overloads of mediated information about intricate cause–effect relations, people form simple cognitive models having little validity (Hedberg 1981). At the same time, these societies advocate rationality, justification, consistency, and bureaucratization: people are supposed to see causal links, interdependencies, and logical implications; to integrate their ideas and to extrapolate them beyond immediate experience; to weed out dissonance and disorder (Beyer 1981; Meyer and Rowan 1977). Bureaucratization reinforces rationality, justification, and consistency as well as hierarchical cognitive models.

Successes, Threats, and Opportunities as Justifications

Problems justify negatively by indicating that symptoms warrant correction; and insofar as problems emphasize perceived or remembered symptoms, they justify currently or retrospectively. Therefore, problems can be viewed as a subset of continua in at least two dimensions. Successes, threats, and opportunities are other subsets of these continua: successes justify actions retrospectively and positively by implying that continuation of past actions will yield continued successes; threats and opportunities justify prospectively in terms of possible symptoms and expected needs for action. (The term symptom encompasses events that cause pleasure as well as discomfort.)

Record keeping, contending interest groups, and weak socialization can make organizational memories intractable—as Richard M. Nixon and his colleagues demonstrated—so problems and successes sometimes fail to justify actions. Threats and opportunities offer more latitude for fantasy and social construction, but may lack credibility because they are merely predictions, or may lack immediacy because they lie in the future. To justify strongly, threats and opportunities have to be larger than life, possibly too large to be taken seriously. Moreover, most societies frown on opportunism, so opportunities are mainly used confidentially inside organizations. For external audiences, organizations sometimes try to legitimate pursuits of opportunities by disclosing their altruistic motives: oil companies have been portraying their exploration activities as societally beneficial responses to OPEC's control of oil prices. Many societies also disapprove of exercises of power unless they correct undesirable conditions, so organizations characterize powerful actions as responses to problems or threats rather than as responses to opportunities or successes. The United States has a Department of Defense, not of Armed Aggression and Control by Force.

Dissolution Through Unlearning

A small problem, success, threat, or opportunity dissolves gradually. A symptom disappears; an expectation changes; a goal evolves; a causal process becomes visible. Each change propagates within the ideological molecule, influencing logically adjacent elements, strengthening some logical bonds between elements, and weakening others. Because adjacent elements need not be completely congruent, the secondary effects of a change attenuate as they propagate and parts of the molecule remain unaffected. Thus, a sequence of reinforcing changes may erode the molecule, but leave one or more fragments that become nuclei of new molecules. A solved problem may leave behind it a success and an opportunity that justify continuing the same actions; the opportunity may eventually turn into a threat or another success.

A large, general molecule picks up new elements as rapidly as it loses old ones, so instead of dissolving, it evolves. Organizations amplify this dynamic stability by creating action generators that add new elements to old molecules. Quality control might accurately be named defect discovery; annual reports and newsletters augment success records.

Organizations have great difficulty dissolving the problems, successes, threats, and opportunities that hold central positions in their top managers' ideologies, because these molecules are so big and so crystalline. Organizations facing crises demonstrate this. The organizations find it hard even to notice that anything is amiss, but symptoms do eventually attract attention and percolate up to the top managers, who attribute the symptoms to temporary environmental disturbances such as recessions, fickle customers, or random fluctuations. The managers talk of trimming the fat, running a tighter ship; and they seek short-term relief through such tactics as unfilled positions, reduced maintenance, liquidated assets, and centralized control. In true crises, the symptoms reappear, and unlearning begins. Some people try to persuade colleagues that current behavior programs no longer work. Subordinates set out to overthrow leaders. Bankers and governmental and union officials try to exert influence. Many people depart, distrust and stress escalate, conflicts amplify, and morale collapses (Nystrom, Hedberg, and Starbuck 1976).

Unlearning seems to be a distinctly social phenomenon, and it may be predominantly organizational. Theories about individual people omit unlearning: the theories say a brain can replace a stimulus–response pair immediately by learning a new stimulus or a new response. But organizations wait until stimulus–response pairs have been explicitly disconfirmed before they seriously consider alternative stimuli or responses, at least for the central molecules in their top managers' ideologies.

The need for unlearning arises from ways organizations typically differ from individual people: (*a*) Organizations rely on action generators, which add inertia and impede reflection. (*b*) Organizations emphasize explicit justification, which rigidifies and perfects their rationality. (*c*) To facilitate documentation and communication, organizations use perceptual categories that destroy subtlety and foster simplification (Axelrod 1976; Bougon, Weick, and Binkhorst 1977). Language defines reality, and objectively perceived realities do not make small changes (Nystrom, Hedberg, and Starbuck 1976). (*d*) Organizations not only use perceptual programs, they concretize these programs in standard operating procedures, job specifications, space assignments, buildings, and contracts (Starbuck 1976). (*e*) Organizations' complexity engenders fear that significant changes might initiate cascades of unforeseen events. (*f*) The conjunction of complexity with differentiation allows organizations to encompass numerous contradictions. Disparate ideological molecules can coexist. (*g*) Hierarchies detach top managers from the realities that their subordinates confront, so top managers' ideologies can diverge from the perceptions of low-level personnel. (*h*) Top managers' macroscopic points of view let them see more ideological elements than their ideologies can incorporate, and their secondhand contact with most events and their spokesperson roles encourage them to simplify and rationalize their ideologies (Axelrod 1976). Public statements encourage distortion while committing the speakers to their pronouncements. (*i*) Organizations punish dissent and deviance, thus silencing new arrivals who have disparate ideologies or low-level personnel whose ideologies are more complex and less logical than their superiors' (Dunbar, Dutton, and Torbert 1982). (*j*) Their members see organizations, especially successful ones, as powerful enough to manipulate their environments. (*k*) Organizations buffer themselves from their environments, so they interact loosely with their environments and have scope to fantasize about environmental phenomena. The foregoing properties correlate, of course, with organizational size, age, success, and bureaucratization.

4. WATCHING RESULTS

Problems, successes, threats, and opportunities crystallize while people are result watching, which happens intermittently. Much of the time, people simply continue acting without watching the results. However, societal ideologies say that organizations should set goals and record progress toward these goals (Dunbar 1981; Meyer and Rowan 1977), so organizations create action generators that routinely gather and evaluate data about goal achievement.

Both performance data and their evaluation are ritualistic. Numerical coding makes it easy for people to bias data; and standards for what to collect and how to categorize and interpret data are designed to make managements look successful (Boland 1982; Halberstam 1972). Societies put priorities on some kinds of data, primarily by assigning monetary valuations, and these priorities assign no value to other kinds of data. Consequently, organizations record almost no data about the causal processes operating in everyday life, and the recorded data confound attempts to infer practical lessons (Dunbar 1981; Hopwood 1972). Yet people attend to these data because they influence social statuses, pay, autonomy, and freedom from supervision.

Laboratory experiments suggest some hypotheses about result watching. If laboratory behaviors extrapolate to natural settings, people see nonexistent patterns, pay too much attention to exciting events and too little to familiar events, accept data readily as confirming their expectations, interpret competition or talk about causation as evidence that they can control events, attribute good results to their own actions, and blame bad results on chance or exogenous influences such as people they dislike. Consequently, bad results rarely elicit basic changes in actions: what is needed is to reinforce the actions with more effort and money and to document better the good results (Staw and Ross 1978).

Result watching produces many scenarios. People may perceive symptoms and proceed to crystallize new problems. They may see action alternatives and debate whether these actions would solve any problems or defend against any threats. They may discover causal processes that suggest revisions in their theories. Revised theories or new action alternatives may imply revised goals and expectations. Revised goals may disclose different symptoms. And so on.

Some of these scenarios correspond to the conventional notion of problem-solving: perceive a problem, consider alternative actions, choose a solution. Thus, organizations exhibit a problem-solving mode. Such scenarios are unusual: in one study, only 4 of 233 decision processes conformed closely to problem solving (Witte 1972). Moreover, attempts to conform to a problem-solving scenario tend to be self-defeating. Insisting that problems be solved before actions are taken renders actions impossible, because people rarely have enough information and understanding to feel sure they have found solutions. Considering alternative actions makes it difficult to arouse the motivation and commitment to carry out actions, because people see risks and liabilities of the chosen actions (Brunsson 1982). Defining problems without regard for potential actions may yield problems that have no solutions (Watzlawick, Weakland, and Fisch 1974). Even scenarios that approximate to problem solving include activities—such as learning, experimentation, and feedback from actions to problems—that fall outside the notion of problem-solving.

Observers have seen diverse scenarios (Hewitt and Hall 1973; Mintzberg, Raisinghani, and Théorêt 1976). What is striking about the published reports is not that result watching follows consistent scenarios but that all kinds of scenarios occur. The patterns observers discern are better explained as artifacts of the observers themselves or of the (often artificial) situations they observe than as characteristics of spontaneous activities in familiar settings.

Explanations of why people start problem-solving tend to be tautological. Hewitt and Hall (1973: 368), for instance, held that people classify a situation as problematic 'if the behavior seems atypical, unlikely, inexplicable, technically inappropriate, unrealistic, or morally wrong'. But any situation could be interpreted as violating at least one of those criteria, because people readily alter their goals, expectations, moral standards, and perceptions. A meaningful explanation has to consider minute events that determine whether particular people will regard a specific situation as problematic. Among the organizational action generators are periodic meetings in which people make sense of performance data, periodic meetings in which people agree to plans and evaluation criteria, and documents that arrive routinely and demand signatures or data. Also, outsiders may ask for data or point out problems or request actions. All of these initiate result watching. Knowing that result watching calls for statements about symptoms, causes of symptoms, and needs for action, people make such statements, and it is these statements that explicate disorder and render situations problematic. Ensuing scenarios operate primarily to mesh the disorder-making statements into pre-existing problems, successes, threats, and opportunities (Lyles and Mitroff 1980).

Talking About What to Do

People generally spend little or no time on pure description before they evaluate results and propose actions (Kepner and Tregoe 1965; Witte 1972). Talk about results usually begins with someone stating a need for action, a symptom, or a cause of a symptom; and overtly descriptive statements nearly always imply certain causal interpretations or certain needs for action (Mehan 1984). However, hearers do not interpret these statements as definitive conclusions even if the speakers evince confidence. Rather, the statements initiate social rituals that build up collective definitions of reality, and stylized language plays central roles in these rituals.

People vote for or against proposals in many ways, including nods, mumbles, and skeptical looks; but two especially interesting media for voting are rephrasings and causal clichés. These enable people to contribute to social construction and to reinforce their organizational commitments without advancing alternative proposals: people can participate without risking their interpersonal statuses. Rephrasings purport merely to echo previous proposals: 'You're saying it's time we did something about quality control' (which was actually a subtle reorientation of what had been said). Causal clichés endorse or reject proposals indirectly by commenting on causal models that, the clichés imply, underlie the proposals: 'He who hesitates is lost.' Although clichés portray their speakers as inane and imitative, the clichés' value lies in their unoriginality and emptiness: unoriginal, empty statements are not to be mistaken for alternative proposals, so hearers know they should interpret them as votes. In fact, clichés' unoriginality implicitly disavows their overt meanings, as if to disclaim, 'I haven't thought about it very much, but....' Rephrasings announce quite explicitly that they are only votes, and they disown their overt meanings overtly: 'This is what you said, so you are to blame if it isn't what you meant.'

People in organizations must not only choose actions, they must arouse motivation and elicit commitments to take actions; and group discussions facilitate both (Brunsson 1982). When only one or two people contribute, participation is inadequate to support collective actions; but there would be too much ideological diversity if many participants injected unique contributions. Clichés and rephrasings enable many to participate with not very much uniqueness, and unoriginality signals commitments to cooperation and organizational membership (Schiffrin 1977). Because groups and organizations rarely endorse needs for action when they are first proposed (Fisher 1980: 149–154), rephrasing is essential to winning endorsements.

Although the participants in group discussions frequently mention a core, real, or main problem (Hewitt and Hall 1973), these phrases rarely reflect consensuses about priorities. People may speak this way to remind others that they met to discuss a specified problem, to designate their problem as the most important problem, to follow prescriptions that advocate solving the most important problem first, or even to express confusion. Groups hardly ever agree on a core symptom, a core cause of symptoms, or a core need for action (Fisher 1980; Kepner and Tregoe 1965). Most actions are justified by more than one problem, and most problems justify more than one action.

Nor do people generally seek or believe they have found guaranteed solutions. They regard agreed needs for action as conjectures to be tested experimentally. This frame of reference helps them accept: (*a*) that participants disagree about needs for action; (*b*) that many agreed needs for action are never acted upon; and (*c*) that few actions solve problems.

Figure 5.1 summarizes the foregoing discussion by diagramming the main causal processes that regulate the cognitive frameworks of organizations. The dashed arrows denote inverse processes that can produce negative feedbacks. For example, the inverse process between expected results and discovery can decelerate crystallization as ideological molecules grow larger—the illusion that learning becomes unnecessary because so much is already known.

5. TRYING TO STABILIZE CHANGE

Change and stability coexist in dialectical syntheses (Giddens 1979: 131–164). Stability may occur in the structural facades that legitimate organizations in terms of societal ideologies, while changes appear in behaviors, technologies,

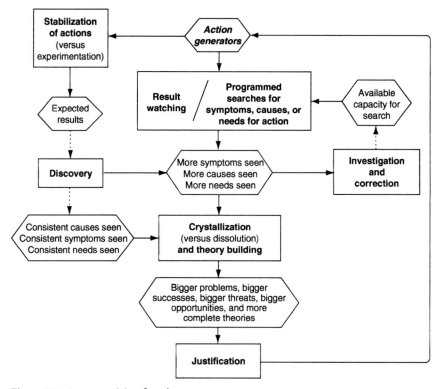

Figure 5.1. A summarizing flowchart

and environments. Everyday programs and relations may remain stable during dramatic changes in long-run goals, expectations, and values. The stability of programs and relations may bring on revolutionary crises that end in organizational demise. Stable action generators can generate changes in actions.

Normann (1971) observed that organizations react quite differently to variations, which would modify the organizations' domains only incrementally, than to reorientations, which would redefine the domains. Variations exploit organizations' experience, preserve existing distributions of power, and can win approval from partially conflicting interests. Reorientations take organizations outside their familiar domains and alter the bases of power, so reorientation proposals instigate struggles between power holders and power seekers (Rhenman 1973; Wildavsky 1972). For example, Facit's top managers did not understand electronics, and they doubtless feared the younger managers who spoke enthusiastically of an electronic future. The top managers also expected (rightly) to be blamed for committing Facit to mechanical calculators.

Watzlawick, Weakland, and Fisch (1974) emphasized the relativity of perception. Reorientations seem illogical because they violate basic tenets of a current cognitive framework, whereas variations make sense because they modify actions or ideologies incrementally within an overarching cognitive framework that they accept. Thus, Facit's top managers thought it sensible to close the unimportant typewriter and office-furnishings factories so as to save the important mechanical-calculator factories. The top managers viewed electronic calculators as reorientations even though other managers classed them as mere variations on a large product line.

The conceptual filtering of reorientation proposals and power struggles over them are dramatic versions of pervasive, everyday processes. People appraise their proposals before enunciating them: they put forth only real symptoms, only plausible causes of symptoms, and only needs for good actions. Real symptoms concern variables that high-status people hold important, describe deviations from legitimate goals or expectations, or describe discomforts, pleasures, efforts, or benefits that people can properly discuss in public (Lyles and Mitroff 1980). Plausible causes mesh into current theories, blame people instead of rules or machines, and enemies or strangers rather than friends, and define accidents in terms of what legitimate theories could have predicted, or what authorities did predict. Good actions follow precedents, harmonize with current actions, resemble the practices in other organizations, use resources that are going to waste, fit with top managers' values, or reinforce power holders (Mehan 1984; Starbuck 1976; Staw and Ross 1978). Although people apply these appraisal criteria implicitly, the criteria remain rather stable from situation to situation; and stable criteria for appraising allow people to shift their criteria for choosing.

Managerial ideologies cherish variations. Executives believe organizations should grow incrementally at their margins. Variations, like searches for symptoms, are often programmed: research departments generate opportunities for complementary actions; sales personnel report on competitors' actions within current domains. Companies that managers regard as well run 'tend to be tinkerers rather than inventors, making small steps of progress rather than conceiving sweeping new concepts' (Peters 1980: 196).

Emphasis on variations may be essential in normal situations because of the gross misperceptions people suffer. Programs, buffers, and slack resources dull organizations' perceptions of what is happening, so organizations fantasize about their environments and their own characteristics. Business firms' profits correlate not at all with their managers' consensus about goals and strategies, and formal planning by business firms is as likely to yield unprofitable strategies as profitable ones (Grinyer and Norburn 1975). Managers' perceptions of their industries correlate zero with statistical measures of those industries (Downey, Hellriegel, and Slocum 1975; Tosi, Aldag, and Storey 1973). Members of organizations agree with each other and with statistical measures about whether their organizations are large or small; but about all other characteristics of their organizations, they disagree with each other as well as with statistical measures (Payne and Pugh 1976). Formal reports are filled with misrepresentations and inadvertent biases (Altheide and Johnson 1980; Hopwood 1972), and organizations that take formal reports seriously either get into trouble or perform ineffectively (Grinyer and

Norburn 1975; Starbuck, Greve, and Hedberg 1978). Ritualistic result watching encourages people to tolerate deviant observations that make no sense and to accept superficial, incomplete causal theories. Such misperceptions mean that reorientations would generally be foolhardy, whereas incremental variations keep low the risks of unpleasant surprises.

However, variations are also inadequate. People choose variations and interpret results within the frameworks of their current beliefs and vested interests, so misperceptions not only persist, they accumulate. Because organizations create programs to repeat their successes, they want stable environments, and so they try to choose variations that will halt social and technological changes. Such variations can succeed only to small extents and briefly, but the organizations perceive more environmental stability than exists.

Hierarchies amplify these tendencies. Top managers' misperceptions and self-deceptions are especially potent because top managers can block the actions proposed by subordinates. Yet top managers are also especially prone to misperceive events and to resist changes: they have strong vested interests; they will be blamed if current practices, strategies, and goals prove to be wrong; reorientations threaten their dominance; their promotions and high statuses have persuaded them that they have more expertise than other people; their expertise tends to be out-of-date because their personal experiences with clients, customers, technologies, and low-level personnel lie in the past; they get much information through channels that conceal events that might displease them; and they associate with other top managers who face similar pressures (Porter and Roberts 1976: 1573–1576). Thus, organizations behave somewhat as Marx ([1859] 1904) said societies behave. Marx argued that ruling social classes try to preserve their favored positions by halting social changes, so technologies grow increasingly inconsistent with social structures, until the ruling classes can no longer control their societies. For organizations, the issue is less one of technologies versus social structures than one of internal versus external events: Top managers can block technological changes inside their organizations, but they have little influence on either technological or social changes outside their organizations.

Marx said that when a ruling social class can no longer control events, a revolution installs a different ruling class and transforms the social structure. His observation generalizes only partly to organizations. Reorientations do punctuate sequences of variations, and reorientations do activate and broaden political activities, but few reorientations transform organizational structures (Jönsson and Lundin 1977; Normann 1971; Rhenman 1973; Starbuck 1973). Facit's reorientation, for instance, began with the replacement of a dozen top managers, but the overwhelming majority of members occupied the same positions after the reorientation as they did before. Indeed, hierarchies generally mean that large behavioral and ideological effects can result from changing just a few top managers.

Many organizations drift along, perceiving that they are succeeding in stable environments, until they suddenly find themselves confronted by existence-threatening crises. Most of the organizations my colleagues and I have studied did not survive their crises; but in every case of survival, the reorientations included wholesale replacements of the top managers, and we infer that survival requires this. Crises also bring unlearning when people discover that their beliefs do not explain events, that their behavior programs are producing bad results, that their superiors' expertise is hollow. Although this unlearning clears the way for new learning during reorientations, it so corrodes morale and trust that many organizations cannot reorient.

Crises evidently afflict all kinds of organizations, although they may be more likely in bureaucracies that have recently enjoyed great success. Some organizations facing crises unlearn, replace their top managers, reorient, and survive. More organizations unlearn and then die. Thus, nonadaptiveness turns organizations into temporary systems, nearly all of which have short lives. The fifty-year-old corporations represent only 2 percent of those initially created, and fifty-year-old Federal agencies only 4 percent (Starbuck and Nystrom 1981). Although older organizations are more likely to survive, even elderly organizations are far from immortal. Approximately 30 percent of the fifty-year-old corporations can be expected to disappear within ten years, as can 26 percent of the fifty-year-old Federal agencies.

ACKNOWLEDGMENTS

This article benefited from the suggestions of Scott Greer, Tiffany H. Lee, Michael Moch, Paul Nystrom, and anonymous reviewers.

6

To Avoid Organizational Crises, Unlearn

Coauthored with Paul C. Nystrom

1. INTRODUCTION

Organizations learn. Then they encase their learning in programs and standard operating procedures that members execute routinely. These programs and procedures generate inertia, and the inertia increases when organizations socialize new members and reward conformity to prescribed roles. As their successes accumulate, organizations emphasize efficiency, grow complacent, and learn too little. To survive, organizations must also unlearn.

Top managers' ideas dominate organizational learning, but they also prevent unlearning. Encased learning produces blindness and rigidity that may breed full-blown crises. Our studies of organizations facing crises show that past learning inhibits new learning: Before organizations will try new ideas, they must unlearn old ones by discovering their inadequacies and then discarding them. Organizations in serious crises often remove their top managers as a way to erase the dominating ideas, to disconfirm past programs, to become receptive to new ideas, and to symbolize change.

This chapter begins by describing some organizational crises and the ways in which top managers' past learning only made the crises worse. The following section shows how clever managers have executed remarkable turnarounds by changing their organizations' beliefs and values. After considering why organizations unlearn by the drastic step of replacing top managers en masse, the chapter urges top managers to accept dissents, to interpret events as learning opportunities, and to characterize actions as experiments.

2. LEARNING FROM CRISES

Many managers and scholars think that organizational survival indicates effectiveness. Survival is an insufficient measure of effectiveness, but the organizational survival rates are so low that there is clearly much room for improvement. Table 6.1 gives some approximate statistics for American corporations: Only 10 percent survive twenty years. Moreover, of those that do survive twenty years,

Table 6.1. Survivals by U.S. corporations

Ages in years	Percentages surviving to various ages	Percentages surviving at least five years after various ages
5	38	55
10	21	65
15	14	70
20	10	73
25	7	76
50	2	83
75	1	86
100	0.5	88

more than a fourth disappears during the ensuing five years. The statistics for U.S. federal agencies look much like those for corporations.

A crisis is a situation that seriously threatens an organization's survival. We have spent several years studying organizations in crises—why crises arise, and how organizations react (Hedberg 1981; Nystrom, Hedberg, and Starbuck 1976; Starbuck and Hedberg 1977; Starbuck and Nystrom 1981; Starbuck, Greve, and Hedberg 1978). Our studies suggest that most organizational failures are quite unnecessary. The following two cases illustrate typical patterns.

Company H successfully published a prestigious daily newspaper for more than 100 years. Circulation reached a new peak in 1966, and the managers invested in modern printing equipment. The following year, circulation leveled off and advertising income dropped, while costs increased. Despite altered accounting procedures, the next year brought losses and a severe cash shortage. The board reacted by focusing even more intensely on cost control; it rejected with laughter a proposal to change the product a bit. Another bad year led the managers to raise prices radically and to form a task force to study corrective actions. Of five alternatives proposed by the task force, the board chose the only one that avoided all strategic reorientation. That is, the board decided to concentrate on those things the organization had always done best and to cut peripheral activities. Many key staff departed. Financial losses escalated. In 1972, the managers sold the printing equipment to pay operating costs, and Company H disappeared altogether a year later.

In the late 1960s, Company F made and sold mechanical calculators as well as typewriters and office furnishings. The company had succeeded consistently for nearly fifty years, and its top managers believed that no other company in the world could produce such good mechanical calculators at such low costs. These beliefs may have been accurate, but they soon proved irrelevant, for an electronic revolution had begun. Although some of the company's engineers had designed electronic calculators and computers, the board decided against their production and sale. The board understood how to succeed with mechanical calculators, the company had invested heavily in new plants designed specifically to manufacture mechanical calculators, this industry had always evolved slowly, and the board believed that customers would switch to electronic calculators only gradually. However, sales began a dramatic decline in 1970, and profits turned into losses. The board retrenched by closing the factories that manufactured typewriters and office furnishings in order to concentrate on the company's key product line: mechanical calculators. After three years of losses, bankruptcy loomed and the board sold Company F to a larger company. What happened next is reported later in this chapter.

These cases illustrate that top managers may fail to perceive that crises are developing. Other people see the looming problems, but either their warnings do not reach the top, or the top managers discount the warnings as erroneous. When top managers eventually do notice trouble, they initially attribute the problems to temporary environmental disturbances, and they adopt weathering-the-storm strategies: Postpone investments, reduce maintenance, halt training, centralize decision-making, liquidate assets, deny credit to customers, raise prices, leave positions vacant, and so forth. During this initial phase of crises, top managers rely on and respond to routine formal reports, particularly accounting statements, that present only superficial symptoms of the real problems. A major activity becomes changing the accounting procedures in order to conceal the symptoms.

In real crises, weathering-the-storm strategies work only briefly. Then the symptoms of trouble reappear; only this time, the organizations start with fewer resources and less time in which to act. The second phase in organizations' reactions to crises involves unlearning yesterday's ideas. People in organizations rarely abandon their current beliefs and procedures merely because alternatives might offer better results: They know that their current beliefs and procedures have arisen from rational analyses and successful experiences, so they have to see evidence that these beliefs and procedures are seriously deficient before they will even think about major changes. Continuing crises provide this evidence. People start to question the conceptual foundations of their organizations, and they lose confidence in the leaders who advocated and perpetuated these concepts. Conflicts escalate as dissenters, voicing new ideas, challenge the ideas of top managers.

3. REORIENTING BY CHANGING COGNITIVE STRUCTURES

Some people see potential crises arising and others do not; some understand technological and social changes and others do not. What people can see, predict, and understand depends on their cognitive structures—by which we mean logically integrated and mutually reinforcing systems of beliefs and values. Cognitive structures manifest themselves in perceptual frameworks, expectations, world views, plans, goals, sagas, stories, myths, rituals, symbols, jokes, and jargon.

Not only do top managers' cognitive structures shape their own actions, they strongly influence their organizations' actions. King (1974) conducted a field experiment that reveals the power of a top manager's expectations. A top manager of Company J told the managers of plants 1 and 2 that he expected job redesigns would raise productivity, and he told the managers of plants 3 and 4 that he expected job redesigns would improve industrial relations but would not change productivity. What actually happened matched the top manager's initial statements. In plants 3 and 4, productivity remained about the same, and absenteeism declined. In plants 1 and 2, productivity increased significantly, while absenteeism remained the same. What makes the experiment even more interesting is that different types of job redesign were used in plants 1 and 3 than in plants 2 and 4. Plants 1 and 3 implemented job enlargement whereas plants 2 and 4 implemented job rotation, yet both types of job redesign produced the same levels of productivity and absenteeism. Thus, differences in actual job activities produced no differences in productivity and absenteeism, whereas different expectations did produce different outcomes.

Expectations and other manifestations of cognitive structures play powerful roles in organizational crises, both as causes and as possible cures. The Chinese exhibited great wisdom when they formed the symbol for crisis by combining the symbols for danger and opportunity: Top managers' ideas strongly influence whether they and their organizations see opportunities as well as dangers. For example, Company F, one of the companies described earlier in this article, surmounted its crisis primarily because a change in its top managers introduced different beliefs and perceptions.

Its top managers and board saw Company F as being designed to adapt to slow, predictable changes in technologies and markets. They initially predicted that electronic calculators would have slow, predictable effects, and the sudden electronic revolution both bewildered and terrified them. They decided that, for their company, the electronic revolution posed an insurmountable challenge. As it floundered at the brink of disaster, Company F was acquired by Company E, which promptly fired all of F's former top managers.

The top managers of Company E soon discovered opportunities that seemed obvious to them: Demands for typewriters and office furnishings were two to three times production capacities; sales staff had been turning down orders because the plants could not fill them! Also, the company's engineers had designed good electronic calculators and computers that the previous board had refused to put into production. The new top managers talked optimistically about opportunities rather than dangers, challenges rather than threats. They borrowed a small amount of money from the parent company with which to experiment, they converted plants producing mechanical calculators into ones making typewriters and office furnishings, and they authorized production and energetic marketing of electronic products. Within a year of acquisition, losses converted into profits, production and employment began rising, and optimism prevailed again.

Top managers' cognitive structures also block recoveries from crises. In Company H, the newspaper described earlier, the top managers' beliefs intensified their commitment to a faulty strategy, generating actions and inactions that sealed the company's fate.

Top managers who clung steadfastly to incorrect ideas also undermined the success of Company T, which made and sold consumer-electronics equipment such as television receivers, tape recorders, loudspeakers, and radios. Sales had doubled about every three years over its forty years' existence. The top managers invested in two new plants in order to replace labor with capital because they thought that labor costs were rising too rapidly relative to sales revenues. Sales growth slowed substantially while these new plants were under construction. The top managers attributed this deceleration to various environmental factors even though available evidence contradicted each of their attributions. The top managers asserted that these problems would be solved by the new plants with low labor costs that would enable lower prices. In the fourth year of this crisis, the national government lent Company T many millions of dollars to save it from collapse. But the loan only postponed the collapse for two years... and increased its cost.

A Harsh Way to Unlearn

Organizations succumb to crises largely because their top managers, bolstered by recollections of past successes, live in worlds circumscribed by their cognitive structures. Top managers misperceive events and rationalize their organizations' failures. Some top managers, like those in Company F, admit privately that they do not understand what is happening and do not know what to do, while publicly they maintain facades of self-assurance and conviction. Other top managers, like those in Company T, never doubt that their beliefs and perceptions have more validity than anyone else's.

Because top managers adamantly cling to their beliefs and perceptions, few turnaround options exist. And because organizations first respond to crises with superficial remedies and delays, they later must take severe actions to escape demise. They must replace constricting, hopeless cognitive structures. But if only one or a few new managers join an ongoing group, either they adopt the prevailing cognitive structure or the other managers regard them as deviants with foolish ideas. Crises intensify these social processes by creating a wagon-train-surrounded-by-Indians atmosphere. So the top managers must be removed as a group, except for the rare individuals who dissented from the prevailing beliefs and perceptions. Moreover, revitalizing a crisis-ridden organization requires enthusiasm and energy... these from people who have grown cynical after hearing their top managers make failed promises and hollow excuses for several years. Before they will replace their cynicism with effort and vision, the people have to be convinced that this time, at last, someone is serious about making real changes. One way to do this, usually the only way, is to turn the former top managers into scapegoats.

Cognitive reorientations spark corporate turnarounds. Some enterprising people take over ailing corporations and successfully convert losses into profits by seeing opportunities that the former managers overlooked. Conversely,

William Hall reported that turnaround efforts generally fail when firms in stagnating industries get subsidies from their parent corporations or from governments. The difference in outcomes seems to spring from infusions of new ideas, not solely infusions of financial resources. Indeed, the financial infusions are usually small in successful turnarounds. Strategic reorientations are rooted in cognitive shifts, and turnarounds almost always involve both significant changes in top management and changes in overall strategies.

Company S, which made ferrous screws, lapsed into persistent losses caused by aging machinery and brisk competition. A new president and vice president for marketing embarked on a strategic reorientation: shifting from large orders of ferrous screws to small orders of nonferrous screws. But two years of persuasion failed to loosen the other top managers' adherence to old modes of acting and thinking. Because the two new managers could not afford to waste more time, they replaced their colleagues. Company S subsequently achieved substantial success.

Removing people is a quick, effective way of erasing memories. Our colleague, Bo Hedberg, reviewed the psychological literature and concluded that unlearning must precede the learning of new behaviors. But top managers show a quite understandable lack of enthusiasm for the idea that organizations have to replace their top managers en masse in order to escape from serious crises. This reluctance partially explains why so few organizations survive crises.

4. UNLEARNING CONTINUOUSLY

Top managers might try to keep emerging crises from becoming serious, by reacting promptly to early symptoms of trouble and by avoiding weathering-the-storm strategies and superficial cover-ups. But not all symptoms warrant prompt reactions, and weathering-the-storm strategies can be useful. The top managers we studied all believed that they were acting wisely (at least when they took the actions), but they were misled by their faulty beliefs and perceptions. Faulty cognitive structures do not always plunge organizations into crises, but they do always keep managers from controlling their organizations' destinies.

To stay in control of their futures, top managers have to combat the inevitable errors in their own beliefs and perceptions. This is, of course, very difficult. It demands exceptional objectivity and humility as well as enough self-confidence to face errors within oneself. But it is easier to keep managers' cognitive structures continuously realistic and up-to-date than to try abruptly to correct errors that have added up and reinforced each other. And it is easier to correct cognitive structures while things are going well than to do so after troubles develop.

Top managers can stimulate their own unlearning and new learning in at least three ways: They can listen to dissents, convert events into learning opportunities, and adopt experimental frames of reference. The next three sections give examples of ways in which top managers can use these methods to benefit themselves and their organizations. However, we intentionally stop short of offering how-to-do-it prescriptions. Managers often get into trouble by trying to follow prescriptions that were formulated by someone else in a different situation. For one thing, obeying someone else's prescriptions requires a partial substitution for one's best judgment. The simpler and more practical prescriptions sound, the more trust one puts in them, and so the more danger they pose. For another thing, effective methods of getting things done respect the constraints and exploit the opportunities that distinguish specific situations. We also question the view: 'If managers knew how to do it, they would already be doing it.' Many managers exhibit great skill at creating pragmatic techniques and procedures to achieve the goals they are pursuing. Top managers who want to unlearn will likely find ways to do it, ways that mesh with the other aspects of their jobs. But the top managers we studied never looked upon their past learning as impediments and they never tried to unlearn.

Listening to Dissents

Complaints, warnings, and policy disagreements should cause reflection that sometimes leads to unlearning. Because such messages assert that something is wrong, top managers ought to respond by reconsidering their beliefs and practices. However, well-meaning colleagues and subordinates normally distort or silence warnings and dissents. So top managers receive only some of the messages sent, and even these messages arrive in watered-down forms, often accompanied by defensive rationalizations.

Moreover, research shows that people (including top managers) tend to ignore warnings of trouble and interpret nearly all messages as confirming the rightness of their beliefs. They blame dissents on ignorance or bad intentions—the dissenting subordinates or outsiders lack a top manager's perspective, or they're just promoting their self-interests, or they're the kind of people who would bellyache about almost anything. Quite often, dissenters and bearers of ill tidings are forced to leave organizations or they quit in disgust, thus ending the dissonance. For example, after Company F had struggled with its crisis for two years, the head of the typewriter division quit in protest over his colleagues' decisions to sell typewriter plants in order to get funds to subsidize the production of mechanical calculators. His division was the only division earning a profit.

Porter and Roberts (1976) reviewed research showing that top managers do not listen carefully to their subordinates. People in hierarchies talk upward and listen upward: They send more messages upward than downward, they pay more attention to messages from their superiors than to ones from their subordinates, and they try harder to establish rapport with superiors than with subordinates. People also bias their upward messages to enhance good news and to suppress bad news, yet they overestimate how much real information they transmit upward. Although these communication patterns are understandable, they are also harmful. In every crisis we studied, the top managers received accurate warnings and diagnoses from some of their subordinates, but they paid no attention to them. Indeed, they sometimes laughed at them.

After studying twenty corporations enmeshed in crises, Dunbar and Goldberg (1978) concluded that the chief executives generally surrounded themselves with yes-sayers who voiced no criticisms. Worse yet, the yes-sayers deliberately filtered out warnings from middle managers who saw correctly that their corporations were out of touch with market realities. Many of these middle managers resigned and others were fired for disloyalty (also see Hall 1980).

Top managers might maintain more realistic cognitive structures if they would personally interview some of the people leaving their organizations. But why wait until people exhaust their loyalty and decide to leave? Top managers should listen to and learn from dissenters, doubters, and bearers of warnings. Not all dissents are valid, and warnings are often wrong, but dissents and warnings should remind one that diverse worldviews exist, that one's own beliefs and perceptions may well be wrong. Indeed, top managers should worry if they hear no such messages: long silences signal distortion, not consensus. Although consensus sometimes occurs within top-management groups, we have found no organizations in which strong consensus pervaded the managerial ranks. Furthermore, Grinyer and Norburn (1975) conducted careful research that found no benefits from strategic consensus: Firms in which managers disagree about goals, policies, and strategies earn just as much profit as firms in which managers agree.

How are top managers to know which dissents and warnings to consider seriously? They certainly dare not rely on their own judgments about ideas' validity because everyone's beliefs and perceptions contain errors. Messages that sound obviously correct add little to knowledge. On the other hand, messages that sound fanciful can highlight defects in one's knowledge, because they arise from premises quite different from one's own.

We recommend this screening procedure: First, assume that all dissents and warnings are at least partially valid. Second, evaluate the costs or benefits that would accrue if messages turn out to be correct: Fanciful messages typically entail high costs or benefits; realistic messages likely entail low costs or benefits. Third, try to find some evidence, other than the messages' content, about the probabilities that messages might prove to be correct. For instance, have the messages' sources acted as if they truly believe what they are saying? Are the sources speaking about their areas of special expertise? Fourth, find ways to test in practice those dissents and warnings that might yield significant costs or benefits. Launch experimental probes that will confirm, disconfirm, or modify the ideas.

Exploiting Opportunities

Changes induce people to question their worldviews. One very successful organization, Company C, actually appointed a vice president for revolutions, who stepped in approximately every four years and shook up operations by transferring managers and reorganizing responsibilities. When asked how he decided what changes to make, he answered that it made little difference so long as the changes were large enough to introduce new perceptions. Statistics show that productivity rose for about two years after each shakeup, then declined for the next two years, until another shakeup initiated another productivity increase.

Company C's practice should be imitated widely. The vice president for revolutions injected unexpected and somewhat random question marks into operations that, otherwise, would have grown smug and complacent through success and would have lost opportunities and alertness through planning. Indeed, Company C itself might have benefited from more frequent doses of its own medicine: Shouldn't the shakeups have happened every two years, when productivity had peaked and before it began to decline?

However, managers would not have to generate so many question marks if they turned spontaneous events into question marks. Managers can create unlearning opportunities by analyzing the consequences of such events as new laws, technological innovations, natural disasters, disrupted supplies, fluctuating demands for outputs, and recessions. Meyer (1982) learned a lot about the dynamics of hospital organizations because he happened to be studying some hospitals when they were jolted by a doctors' strike. To his surprise, he found that ideologies were more powerful than structures as forces guiding organizational responses. The hospitals that took best advantage of the strike were ones with ideologies that cherish dispersed influence in decision-making, frequent strategic reorientations, and responsiveness to environmental events. Such hospitals both anticipated the effects of the strike and used the strike as a stimulus for long-run improvements.

One of the most successful adaptations to the doctors' strike was made by Hospital C. This hospital's culture values innovation, professional autonomy, and pluralism; its administrator urges the subunits to act entrepreneurially and to maintain bonds with the community. The administrator himself devotes 70 percent of his time to outside relationships, and he predicted the strike two months before it began—well before other hospitals anticipated it. Because he purposely avoids codifying procedures and formalizing relationships, he subtly encouraged the (overtly spontaneous) coalescing of an informal group to consider the strike's impacts. This group sent all supervisors a scenario of what might happen and asked them to write up plans for response. When the strike occurred, Hospital C cut costs and reallocated resources so quickly that it continued to earn a profit; and after the strike ended, the hospital easily adapted back. The administrator said, 'We learned that we could adapt to almost anything—including a drastic drop in our patient load—and, in the process, we discovered some new techniques for cutting our operating costs.'

Experimenting

Experimentation offers many benefits as a central frame of reference for top managers. People who see themselves as experimenting are willing to deviate temporarily from practices they consider optimal in order to test the validity of their assumptions. When they try out other people's ideas that they themselves expect to be suboptimal or foolish, they create opportunities to surprise themselves. They also manage experiments in ways that cut down the losses that failures would produce; for instance, they attend carefully to feedback. Because they place fewer personal stakes on outcomes looking successful, they evaluate outcomes more objectively. They find it easier to modify their beliefs to accommodate new observations. And they keep on trying for improvements because they know experiments never turn out perfectly.

A team from McKinsey & Company studied ten companies that executives think are unusually well run. Experimenting tops the list of characteristics they have in common. To quote Thomas Peters' conclusion from *Business Week* (July 21, 1980): Controlled experiments abound in these companies. The attitude of management is to 'get some data, do it, then adjust it', rather than wait for a perfect overall plan.

Managers can program some searches for better ideas. For example, evolutionary operation (EVOP) is a well thought-out method for continual experimentation. The basic idea is to run experiments that entail little risk because they deviate only incrementally from what the experimenters believe to be optimal operation. The experiments should be planned and interpreted by committees that are carefully designed to meld technical expertise and political clout. Although Box and Draper (1969) created EVOP as a way to improve manufacturing processes, the basic ideas generalize to repetitive activities in finance, marketing, personnel management, and office procedures.

Experiments need not be carefully designed in order to be revealing, and they need not be revealing in order to stimulate unlearning, but it is better to use experiments fruitfully. Company K's experience suggests some of the differences between fruitful and unfruitful experiments.

Company K had successfully made and repaired railroad rolling stock for almost ninety years; then, in 1963, the nation's major railroad announced that it would buy no more new rolling stock from anyone for the foreseeable future. Company K's managers saw the railroad industry collapsing about them, so they studied several possibilities and chose three new product lines for development. After two years, however, the Company had achieved no sales whatever in two of these lines. The managers launched two more experimental product lines, but they concentrated their efforts on the one new product line that looked most promising: a small automobile. Sales multiplied two and a half times over the next five years, but profits were only 0.8 percent of sales! Despite frequently repeated dire predictions, railroad rolling stock was accounting for 95 percent of sales; and despite frequent hopeful predictions, the automobile had not yet gotten into production and was generating high costs. When the automobile finally did come into production in 1970, the result was horrendous losses in both 1970 and 1971—so horrendous that the directors decided to close the company.

Why did Company K's experiments turn out so badly? One reason was too many eggs in one basket. The managers poured all their energies and most of their company's money into the automobile; their experiments with other new product lines were halfhearted and ritualistic. A second reason was an absence of feedback. The managers ignored evidence that the automobile project was developing badly and evidence that the rolling-stock business was doing well. Nor did they learn from their failures. Recall that two of their experimental product lines yielded zero sales: Might this have occurred because Company K had no sales personnel, not even a sales manager? Might it have forewarned what would happen when the automobile came into production? Company K did add a sales department to promote the automobile: a sales manager and one sales representative!

Shortly after the directors decided to close Company K, five of the six top managers and half of the lower-level employees departed voluntarily. The board appointed the remaining senior manager president, with orders to continue shutting the Company down. Instead, the new president (who had nothing to lose) launched some new experiments. These disclosed substantial foreign demand for railroad rolling stock—the previous managers had ignored foreign markets. The experiments also showed that the blue-collar workers could run the factory themselves with very little assistance from managers—the previous managers had created a competitive game in which managers and workers were trying to outsmart each other. In fact, after they took charge, the blue-collar workers doubled productivity: By 1974, production was 36 percent higher than in 1963 even though employment was only 69 percent of the earlier figure. Two new product lines were tried, and one of these became as important as rolling stock. By then, the directors had decided to keep the company in business. Profits in 1975 were six times the highest profits the company had ever earned previously, and they have continued upward since.

Why did the second wave of experiments turn out so differently? The directors' decision to close Company K initiated unlearning: The people who departed took with them their convictions about how the Company should operate and what opportunities the environment offered; the people who remained became ready to abandon their past beliefs. No longer sure they knew what to do, people tried some experiments that they would previously have rejected as outrageous or silly. The company had no resources to squander on experiments that were turning out badly, so everyone paid close attention to how the experiments were turning out: Feedback quickly had real effects. Not least, the new president was an unusually wise man who knew how to engender enthusiasm, entrepreneurship, and a team spirit.

5. CONCLUSION

Our studies underline top managers' dominance of their organizations' survival and success. Top managers are the villains who are blamed for steering organizations into crises, and they are the heroes who get the credit for rescuing organizations from crises. Such blaming and crediting are partly ritualistic, but also partly earned. Top managers do in fact guide organizations into crises and intensify crises; they also halt crises by disclosing opportunities, arousing courage, and stirring up enthusiasm.

The top managers who instigate dramatic turnarounds deserve admiration, for they have accomplished very difficult tasks of emotional and conceptual leadership. Even greater heroes, however, are the top managers who keep their organizations from blundering into trouble in the first place. To do this, they have had to meet the still more difficult challenge of conquering the errors in their own beliefs and perceptions.

7

Acting First and Thinking Later: Finding
Decisions and Strategies in the Past

'Gaiety is the most outstanding feature of the Soviet Union.'

—Joseph Stalin (1935)[1]

'The only thing science has done for man in the last hundred years is to create
for him fresh moral problems.'

—Geoffrey Fisher, Archbishop of Canterbury (1950)

'I don't believe in aeroplanes, science and progress, in railway timetables or in
economic law. I cannot think of them as real, and there will be none of them
in my future. There is no room for them.'

—Bernard Fay, philosopher (1933)

1. INTRODUCTION

Social science research has demonstrated a few truths quite convincingly. One of
these is that people behave in very diverse ways, so one can find at least a few
instances that match or contradict virtually any assertion about human behavior.
Another truth is that realities are as numerous and different as their perceivers.
Thus, social scientists should feel no surprise upon learning that other people see
realities somewhat different from their own. But some realities diverge so greatly
from my own perceptions that they do surprise me. Consider the following
observations about organizational decision-making:

- Organizations' members make conscious decisions that determine their actions. A contrasting observation attributes the power to determine organizations' actions mainly to decision-making by top managers; subordinates
  supposedly act as their superiors decide.

- Organizations' members make decisions by engaging in problem-solving, and
  they expect their organizations' actions to solve problems. Steiner (1969: 322)
  stated one version of this view: 'A business decision is made in the course of and
  grows out of the lengthy, complex, and intricate process of problem discovery,
  exploration of methods to resolve it, and analysis of means.'

- Actions that begin after the actors construct sturdy rationalizations produce more benefits than would actions lacking strong prior rationalizations. More elaborate rationalizations—such as operations-research models—yield greater benefits. For instance, Hofer and Schendel (1978: 5) asserted that 'organizations need formalized, analytical processes for formulating explicit strategies'. Similarly, Christensen, Berg, and Salter (1980: 13) said, 'An evaluation of both the strategy itself as well as the progress of the organization in carrying out that strategy is made easier if the strategy formulation process and the underlying logic and assumptions are made explicit.'

- In similar circumstances, actors (whether people or organizations) that behave in highly consistent ways get greater benefits from their actions than do actors that behave quite inconsistently. Thus, actors should increase the consistency of their actions through strategies and policies. Before taking any actions, organizations' members ought to choose strategies and policies, and then use these to constrain their organizations' subsequent actions. Actions that adhere to pre-formed strategies yield greater benefits than would actions occurring in an absence of preformed strategies or those deviating from preformed strategies. Similarly, actions that conform to preformed cross-unit policies produce more benefits than would actions that occur in an absence of cross-unit policies or those that violate preformed policies. Chang and Campo-Flores (1980: 29–30), for example, listed four benefits of strategy making: 'Strategic actions . . . replace brute force and hasty actions. Second, strategy offers a mentality, a discipline, and a technique to manage changes. . . . Third, strategy . . . provides a systematic and decisive method of problem solving. . . . Last, strategy generates directional action.'

- In similar circumstances, actors that try to predict the long-range future get greater benefits from their actions than do actors that make no long-range predictions. Newman and Logan (1981: 34), for instance, prescribed, 'To adjust most effectively, central management should try to predict important changes before they occur.' To get the benefits, however, actors must turn their predictions into formal plans and take the plans seriously; actions that adhere to formalized long-range plans generate more benefits than would actions occurring without formalized long-range plans or those diverging from formalized plans. Newman and Logan (1981: 537–538) said that long-range programming yields three advantages: 'Long-cycle actions are started promptly. . . . Executives are psychologically prepared for change. . . . Actions having long-term impact are coordinated.'

The foregoing summary is no straw man. Not only does it describe the general thrust of the literature on strategic decision-making, but such a reality attracts me. I wish I inhabited it! How nice it would be to predict the future accurately, to formulate strategies that are much more likely to yield more benefits than costs, to see only rational causality in my environment, even to be sure I think before

I act. But research evidence, personal experience, and logic compel me to live elsewhere. Stated concisely, my reality looks like this:

- People, including organizations' members and top managers, act unreflectively nearly all of the time because they adhere to well-established behavior programs. Indeed, most organizational actions originate in action generators, which are automatic behavior programs that are activated by job assignments or clocks rather than by informative stimuli.

- People often take actions without saying or thinking that they solve explicated problems, but some actions do arise from reflective problem-solving. Problem-solving can be identified by its origin—the perception of a problem. Normative theories assert that perception of a problem should instigate a unidirectional sequence of activities: a problem-solver should identify alternative actions that would solve the problem, and then evaluate these alternatives, choosing the best. Such tidy, unidirectional sequences occur very infrequently in actual behaviors, however.

- Decision-making can be identified by its termination—a decision. Thus, decision-making and problem-solving do not always coincide. In fact, Mintzberg, Raisinghani, and Thèorêt (1976) inferred that the decision makers usually perceive no problems when decision-making starts. Decisions may solve problems even though they lead to no actions; and problem-solving can end without decisions having been made, if the problem solvers can find no solutions or if the problems disappear while the problem-solvers are still searching for solutions.

- People make many of their decisions, perhaps a great majority of them, after they have begun to act and have seen some of the consequences of their actions. When they begin courses of action, people normally see themselves as following the only sensible courses, not choosing among several plausible courses. They may not even realize that they are embarking on distinct courses, partly because organizations decompose big actions into multitude increments, and partly because the individual actors in organizational actions merely follow banal programs. But looking back, the people can see that alternative courses did exist and so they must have chosen. Thus, decisions are often retrospective reenactments that misrepresent actual sequences of events.

- Because strong rationalizations make behaviors inflexible, actions that begin with only tentative and quick rationalizations produce more benefits than do actions that begin after the actors construct sturdy rationalizations. All actions evoke retrospective rationalizations, and these retrospective rationalizations grow stronger as the actions get repeated.

- People and organizations do act consistently in that their actions resemble preceding and successive actions: most actions repeat familiar patterns, and most innovations are no more than incremental variations on familiar patterns.

However, this consistency arises because people unreflectively follow behavior programs, because powerful people have vested interests, and because settings for action remain stable, rather than because people are striving consciously to conform to preformed strategies.

- Strategies are behavior patterns that remain consistent over time, and policies are intended behavior patterns that remain consistent either through time (strategies) or across organizational subunits. To be the objects of decision-making, strategies and policies have to be conscious. But very few of organizations' members and very few top managers choose strategies or policies consciously on a regular basis. The choices that do occur reflect the choosers' interests as individuals as well as their organizations' interests as collectivities.

- People formulate many strategies and policies, perhaps a great majority of them, only after they have acted and seen some of the consequences of their actions. The general consistency of organizational actions makes strategies and policies easy to invent. Thus, like decisions, strategies and policies are generally retrospective reenactments.

- The processes by which people articulate strategies and policies often involve rationalization. But people perceive their environments inaccurately, and logic injects large amounts of fantasy into rationalizations. So articulated strategies and policies render actions less realistic and less responsive to environmental events. Consequently, actions occurring in an absence of preformed strategies and those deviating from preformed strategies generally yield greater benefits than would adherence to preformed strategies. Similarly, actions that violate cross-unit policies and those taken in an absence of cross-unit policies generate more benefits than would conformity to cross-unit policies.

- Partly because they misperceive their environments and themselves, partly because they apply rational logic to situations that lack rationality, and partly because they generate predictions through processes of social construction, people predict their alternative futures inaccurately. Predictions about long-range futures incorporate much larger errors than predictions about short-range futures. People revise formalized plans less often than informal plans, and they formalize plans through social interactions, so formalized plans incorporate larger errors than do informal plans. Thus, actions that diverge from formalized long-range plans and those taken without formalized long-range plans usually generate more benefits than would continued adherence to formalized long-range plans.

This chapter explains why I find this second reality more realistic than the first. The discussion loosely follows the sequence in which I have just summarized my views, but it is organized around the consequences of three powerful tools. Generally speaking, tools that can cause no harm also lack power, whereas powerful tools have correspondingly strong disadvantages. Three of humans' most powerful tools are rational thought, programmed behavior, and social interaction. These enhance humans' effectiveness tremendously, but they also circumscribe actions sufficiently to become serious handicaps.

2. RATIONALITY

'Prediction is very difficult, especially about the future.'
—Niels Bohr

Rationality is defined by human physiology. Human brains use rational logic, although imperfectly and inconsistently; and from a human's perspective, rational logic seems to aid understanding. Indeed, human philosophers, logicians, and mathematicians have abstracted this propensity and generated rules that they prescribe normatively.

But physical and social universes probably act nonrationally. There is no reason for confidence that human physiology has evolved a logic that matches the physical universe. A social system may behave nonrationally in the aggregate even if every one of its human members acts rationally at all times—an implausible assumption itself. Thus, it is an empirical question how accurately rational logic can predict the future states of humans' worlds. Experience suggests, however, that rational logic produces disappointingly inaccurate interpretations of and predictions about social phenomena.

Further, human brains often apply rational logic inappropriately. People cannot avoid revising their memories to make them match their perceptions, because brains involuntarily alter the information they already hold in order to make new information fit in (Kiesler 1971; Loftus 1979). And brains revise perceptions to make them match memories; laboratory experiments suggest that people update their beliefs much more slowly than statistical models say they should (Edwards 1968). Brains also invent memories and perceptions of events that never occurred but that rational logic says ought to exist, and they resolve logical inconsistencies by creating new categories. Awareness that one has contributed to an action stimulates one's brain to justify that action (Salancik 1977; Weick 1979: 194–201).

Singer and Benassi (1981: 50) have concisely summarized the findings from laboratory experiments investigating how people interpret information:

When presented with an array of data or a sequence of events in which they are instructed to discover an underlying order, subjects show strong tendencies to perceive order and causality in random arrays, to perceive a pattern or correlation which seems a priori intuitively correct even when the actual correlation in the data is counterintuitive, to jump to conclusions about the correct hypothesis, to seek confirmatory evidence, to construe evidence liberally as confirmatory, to fail to generate or to assess alternative hypotheses, and, having thus managed to expose themselves only to confirmatory instances, to be fallaciously confident of the validity of their judgments.

Wanting to control events and to claim credit for good results, people interpret very weak clues as indicating that their actions influence what happens—the existence of competition, the mere hypothesis that skillful actors do better, or talk about causation (Dunbar 1981; Langer 1975). Such clues can be injected into virtually any situation. But despite their reluctance to concede that situations may be beyond their control, people tend to blame bad results on chance or on exogenous influences such as people they dislike (Berkowitz and Green 1962; Frankenberg 1972; Langer and Roth 1975; Maier 1963).

> 'And while I am talking to you mothers and fathers, I give you more assurance; I have said this before, but I shall say it again and again: Your boys are not going to be sent into any foreign wars.'
>
> —Franklin D. Roosevelt (1940)

> 'In all likelihood, world inflation is over.'
>
> —The Managing Director of the International Monetary Fund (1959)

> 'Rock 'n' roll is phony and false, and sung, written and played for the most part by cretinous goons.'
>
> —Frank Sinatra (1957)

Industrialized societies promote rationalization and bureaucratization. The ideologies of these societies say that organizations should operate consistently, should make plans and monitor their progress toward fulfilling these plans, should obey hierarchical superiors, and should only take actions they can justify (Dunbar 1981; Meyer and Rowan 1977). The societal ideologies also tell people to eliminate inconsistencies and disorder; to integrate their perceptions and beliefs; to look for causes, interdependencies, and implications; and to extrapolate their experiences (Beyer 1981; March 1971; Sproull 1981; Thompson 1967).

At the same time, industrialized societies make rational logic less effective. Large, complex societies flood their members with information, confound them with tangled causal relations, and assail them with numerous changes, many of which cannot be predicted with rational logic. Faced with too much information, information that comes through intermediaries, and intricate cause–effect relations, people find learning difficult and they develop oversimplified beliefs that have little validity (Hedberg 1981; Hewitt and Hall 1973; Schroder, Driver, and Streufert 1967). Simpler frames of reference omit more contingencies and make cruder distinctions.

> 'Nay, if a woman, even in unlawful copulation, fix her mind upon her husband, the child will resemble him though he did not beget it.'
>
> —Aristotle

Organizations too promote rationalization: they encourage people to make rational logic more perfect and to justify actions explicitly. Explicit rationality is the essence of bureaucracy. However, explication makes rationality more rigid; easily communicated and recorded concepts oversimplify and distort perceptions; social pressures induce people to espouse positions somewhat dishonestly; and large organizations' complexity makes it more likely that changes will produce unforeseen consequences (Axelrod 1976; Bougon, Weick, and Binkhorst 1977). Because organizations create buffers between themselves and their environments (Thompson 1967), they have more scope than individual people to misperceive environmental events. Although most organizations encompass numerous and contradictory viewpoints, many organizations punish dissent and deviance, so the disparate views remain unspoken, and top managers dominate beliefs and perceptions (Dunbar, Dutton, and Torbert 1982; Janis 1972). Unfortunately, top managers experience most events at secondhand, and their spokesperson roles encourage them to simplify their beliefs and to filter out logical inconsistencies, so they frequently have less realistic beliefs than many of their subordinates, and their public pronouncements and vested interests make them slower to accept new views (Axelrod 1976; Bougon, Weick, and Binkhorst 1977; Hart 1976, 1977; Starbuck, Greve, and Hedberg 1978).

> 'I think there is a world market for about five computers.'
> —Thomas J. Watson, President of IBM (1948)

Ideological Molecules

Rational logic creates systems of interdependent ideas that resemble molecules. Each molecule integrates diverse elements—such as goals, values, beliefs, perceptions, theories, plans, expectations, labels, and symbols—that interlock through logical bonds.

Advocates of rational problem-solving have consistently prescribed unidirectional procedures for growing ideological molecules (Weick 1983). For example, in their comparatively sophisticated book, Kepner and Tregoe (1965) prescribed a sequence of fourteen activities that start with identifying whether a problem exists. People, they said, should give the label 'problem' to an issue or situation only if and insofar as it involves a deviation of actual performance from desired performance; and they should identify and describe this deviation precisely. The problem definition should become the foundation for searching out possible causes of the problem and choosing the single most likely cause. The next steps ought to be laying down criteria for a desired action, developing and evaluating alternative actions, and choosing the single best action. However, the best action may produce bad side effects, so possible adverse results should be predicted, and the solution should be expanded from one action into a cluster of simultaneous actions. The final step should be making sure that actions are carried out.

Behaving quite at odds with such prescriptions, people naturally make unclear distinctions between problems and related ideological elements such as goals, expectations, descriptive statements, threats, opportunities, and labels. Kepner and Tregoe (1965: 7–17) and Maier (1963) have observed that people treat the word 'problem' as interchangeable with issue, question, trouble, and situation; and that people apply these concepts variously: (*a*) to evidence that something differs from what is desirable; (*b*) to events that are causing discomfort, effort, or stress; (*c*) to possible reasons why something differs from what is desirable; (*d*) to possible sources of events that are causing discomfort; and (*e*) to actions that ought to be taken.

Furthermore, natural behaviors flow in complex streams that environmental events stimulate and perturb. Witte (1972) and his colleagues analyzed the documents generated by 233 decision processes: only four of these processes flowed unidirectionally from problem definition to solution selection. Even the decision processes that approximate to a unidirectional sequence include activities such as learning, experimentation, and feedback from actions to problems (Mintzberg, Raisinghani, and Théorêt 1976); and the four unidirectional processes observed by Witte (1972) and his colleagues were no more efficient or thorough than most other processes. A new molecule may begin to form around various kinds of elements (Beyer 1981); and thereafter, it gains and loses elements in an erratic sequence—a plan forms; a goal fades; a relationship clarifies. Rational logic expands the molecule to include other elements that fit in, it edits out or distorts elements that are hard to integrate, and rationalization fills in the logical gaps. Thus, the molecule tends to generalize and simplify as time passes, growing more complete and more stable (Pettigrew 1979). Each incremental change propagates through the molecule, influencing the logically adjacent elements, and weakening or strengthening some of the logical bonds between elements. Because adjacent elements can remain slightly incongruent, the effects of a change attenuate as they propagate; and a sequence of changes that erode a molecule may leave fragments that become the nuclei of new molecules.

As rational logic grows stronger, bad results lose the power to instigate changes. Our current programs have strong justifications, and they would have produced good results if accidents had not happened or enemies had not acted malevolently. Rather than abandon our programs, we should strengthen them with more effort or more money, and give them enough time to yield good results (Salancik 1977; Staw and Ross 1978).

> 'The fundamental business of the country...is on a sound and prosperous basis.'
>
> —Herbert Hoover, Black Friday, 1929

Altheide and Johnson (1980), Edelman (1977), and Manning (1977) have described explicit, intended efforts to manufacture evidence that justifies organizations' actions. The examples range from television ratings based on viewers who volunteer to participate and on periods of special programming, through military reports that portray all battles as victories and all personnel as superior, to falsified police reports. Recognizing that the people to whom justifications are addressed may discount them, organizations that seek public support sometimes go to elaborate efforts to render their justifications credible. A clean example is the research and politicking that enabled Crest toothpaste to win an endorsement from the American Dental Association, and a horrible example is the campaign of propaganda and false accusations through which the Nazis aroused hatred of Jews.

Even though people have to interact with and respond to complex and unpredictable environments, the ambiguity and inconsistency of natural behaviors pose a mystery in part. Brains' enthusiasm for rational logic suggests that people might naturally draw clear distinctions between concepts, and might naturally form ideological molecules in orderly ways such as Kepner and Tregoe and others have prescribed. So what explains the deviations between prescribed rationality and natural rationality? Are the prescriptions right, and do people naturally think poorly? Or does natural behavior offer advantages over prescribed rationality?

Attempts to follow unidirectional problem-solving sequences tend to be self-defeating, because such sequences make very weak provisions for correcting ignorance, and ideological elements have meaning only in relation to other elements (Bobrow and Norman 1975; Schank 1975). To infer what is wrong, for example, people must perceive other aspects of their situations: they can identify *A* and *B* as wrong only if they can also see *C* and *D*. And to infer what is wrong, people must consider their goals, values, and expectations; Kepner and Tregoe themselves said that people should identify problems by comparing actual performances with expected performances. But to form expectations and to set realistic goals, people need causal beliefs and perceptions. People rarely have enough information and understanding to feel certain that they have actually solved problems, so they dare not postpone taking actions until they have found solutions. Looking at alternative actions exposes the potential difficulties accompanying the actions, and usually shows that the best actions differ little from other good alternatives, and so makes it more difficult to take chosen actions (Brunsson 1982). Problems defined without regard for possible solutions often have no solutions (Watzlawick, Weakland, and Fisch 1974).

Outside of laboratory experiments and training sessions, people do not generally know that they ought to be solving problems because they do not know whether problems exist. They simply act and do not always reflect on their actions or watch the results of their actions. Result watching, when it occurs, might take them in various directions. They may, in fact, perceive new problems, but they may see successes, threats, or opportunities instead (Mintzberg, Raisinghami, and Théorêt 1976). They may think of potential actions and wonder whether these actions would block any threats or exploit any opportunities. They may discover causal processes or notice changes in contingency variables (Hedberg 1981). New causal beliefs or potential actions may lead to new goals and expectations. And so on. Cyert, Simon, and Trow (1956: 247), for example, remarked that 'the "problem" to be solved was in fact a whole series of "nested" problems, each alternative solution to a problem at one level leading to a new set of problems at the next level. In addition, the process of solving the substantive problems created many procedural problems for the organization: allocating time and work, planning agendas and report presentations, and so on.' The diverse elements of an ideological molecule are truly interdependent, and effective thinking acknowledges this interdependence by recalculating iteratively.

Another reason for people to deviate from the prescriptions for rational logic is that rational logic itself makes them justify their actions (Salancik 1977; Staw 1980; Weick 1979: 194–201). For actions to seem rational, people must have ideological molecules that include and highlight 'needs for action' (Brunsson 1982). These justifying molecules may be problems, successes, threats, or opportunities.

'If God had intended that man should fly, He would have given him wings.'
—George W. Melville, Chief Engineer of the U.S. Navy (1900)

Some Suggested Terminology

Needs for action are ideas stating that certain actions ought to be taken, or need not be taken, to correct what is wrong. 'I got to get an answer back to these guys!' 'Well then, our problem seems to 've turned to how to get the maximum amount of feedback from the participants' instead of 'The participants might not express their opinions.' 'It's my job to manage, and I must do something. How can I motivate them?' 'We shouldn't count on it until they put up some money.'

To avoid confusion, I distinguish needs for action from *symptoms* and from *causes of symptoms*. Symptoms are ideas describing aspects of the world that are undesirable or causing discomfort, effort, or stress. To allow for positive outcomes, the concept of symptom encompasses: (*a*) evidence of results that are better than satisfactory as well as worse than desirable and (*b*) events that cause pleasure as well as discomfort. Of course, causes of symptoms are ideas that conjecture about the reasons symptoms exist.

The word *problem* itself denotes a distinct ideological molecule. Problems comprise one subset of continua in at least two dimensions: other subsets of these continua can be called successes, threats, and opportunities. Problems justify actions negatively by emphasizing symptoms; and problems justify currently or retrospectively by emphasizing perceived or remembered symptoms. Successes also justify actions currently or retrospectively, but they justify positively by suggesting that repetition of past actions will continue to produce successes. Threats and opportunities justify prospectively by pointing to predicted symptoms or future needs for action (Staw 1980).

Threats and opportunities offer more latitude for fantasy and social construction in that people need only suppress dissonant predictions rather than memories. But threats and opportunities may lack credibility because they are only predictions, or may lack immediacy because they lie in the future. To justify strongly, threats and opportunities have to be somewhat larger than life, with the risk that they are too large to be taken seriously. Moreover, societal ideologies frown upon opportunism, so opportunities are mostly used confidentially. For external audiences, people sometimes try to legitimate their pursuits of opportunities by announcing their altruistic motives (Mills 1940).

'... the President's program will begin to bear fruit even before it is enacted.'
—Donald Regan, U.S. Secretary of the Treasury (1981)

Rationalizing Actions

Many of the activities that people label *problem solving* are mislabeled in that they do not start with problems and end with solutions. At least as often as they solve problems, probably much more often, people build rationales for actions they have taken or intend to take.

Emphasizing that people construct problems, solutions, and theories collectively, Hewitt and Hall (1973) pointed out that people often create theories by backward inference from cure to core problem to theory. The participants in 'problem-solving' frequently start by appraising a shared situation and stating needs for action, and they continue such appraisal talk until they agree upon a cure. They then make the agreed cure the basis for defining a core problem, and construct a theory that explains why the core problem arose and how the agreed cure will solve it. The theory also (*a*) distinguishes the essential, real aspects of the core problem from the peripheral, illusory aspects; (*b*) incorporates widely accepted values and beliefs; and (*c*) portrays the stimulus situation as a specific instance of a general class of problems. The participants build their theory iteratively, testing it against past events and concocted examples, and their interactions make extensive use of stylized language.

Such backwards reasoning has roots in widespread methods of child rearing and schooling. Children learn: (*a*) that results are generally good or bad, not neutral; (*b*) that results call for statements that actions are, or are not, needed; (*c*) that results have discernible causes; (*d*) that correct explanations for results have social legitimacy whereas incorrect explanations do not; and (*e*) that one can depend on other people, especially experts, to provide legitimate explanations for mysterious results. Because adults reward or punish them frequently, small children learn that results are normally good or bad, that rewards and punishments are ubiquitous, and that adults react to results by taking actions promptly. Older children discover that results, rewards, and punishments may be delayed and subtle. Because their parents and teachers nearly always know the answers to children's mysteries, children learn that adults can see the causes of mysteries and that mysteries look mysterious mainly because of inexperience or ignorance.

Thus, as adults, people spend very little time observing and describing situations before they start judging them good or bad and start proposing needs for action, they expect to be able to discern causes, and they construct theories that arise as much from societal ideologies as from direct evidence (Beyer 1981; Kepner and Tregoe 1965; Maier 1963; Mintzberg, Raisinghami, and Théorêt 1976; Sproull 1981). They often explain mysterious results with quasi theories—prevalent and legitimate causal attributions that are difficult to disconfirm with evidence (Hall and Hewitt 1970; Hewitt and Hall 1973). The quasi theory of time holds that events occur at natural or preordained times—for example, that getting visible results takes at least a minimal, but unknown, amount of time; or that organizations go through certain distinct developmental stages at appropriate, but ambiguous, times. The quasi theory of antisocial conspiracy implies, for instance, that journal editors block the publication of innovative research that would revolutionize their disciplines. The quasi theory of communication blames mistakes, crises, arguments, and wars on insufficient communication—thus, communication training is supposed to integrate into harmonious teams managers who face disparate pressures; or decisions to refuse tenure result from incomplete understanding of the merits of specific cases.

Labels and categories guide the editing of ideological molecules by helping to determine which elements fit in. Most labels and categories imply that these particular labels and these specific categories are the only right and proper ones; and some labels and categories make it improbable, even impossible, for actions to produce bad results (Golding 1980; Leach 1964). Who would hire a 'dropout' or an 'unskilled worker'? Would an 'innocent' person refuse a 'fair hearing' that metes out 'justice'? Edelman (1977: 38) has observed:

> Ever since it was established, the Federal Communications Commission (FCC) has given paramount weight in choosing among competing license applicants to the financial resources available to the applicant, so that wealthy individuals and successful corporations easily make a persuasive case, while people of moderate means, including minorities, dissenters, and radicals are easily rejected. The Commission's justification is that radio listeners and television viewers will be hurt if the licensee uses poor equipment or goes bankrupt; the weighing of comparative financial resources therefore promotes 'the public interest, convenience, or necessity', as required by the Communications Act of 1934. Paramount weight to a more equal representation on the air of political perspectives could obviously be justified on the same ground.

3. BEHAVIOR PROGRAMS

> 'The Americans have need of the telephone, but we do not. We have plenty of messenger boys.'
>
> —William Preece, Chief Engineer of the British Post Office (1876)

As long ago as 1958, March and Simon (141–142) remarked that behavior programs 'account for a very large part of the behavior of all persons, and for almost all of the behavior of persons in relatively routine positions'. This turned out to be an underestimate of behavior programs' pervasiveness: research has subsequently revealed that behavior programs account for nearly all of the actions of all people, no matter what positions they occupy (Mintzberg 1973b; Mintzberg, Raisinghami, and Théorêt 1976; Newell and Simon 1972; Tuchman 1973). People get their behavior programs through spontaneous habits, professional norms, education, training, precedents, traditions, rituals, and organizations' standard operating procedures. By adulthood, people have acquired large repertoires of behavior programs that comprise the essence of behavior.

Behavior programs amplify humans' capabilities greatly. When people perceive that situations fall into familiar categories—which happens most of the time— they do not waste time and effort discovering appropriate actions all over again: they simply follow familiar programs. The behavior programs demand little or no reflection by the actors, and they quickly produce actions like those that succeeded in the past (Weick 1987). Then when people perceive novel situations, they create new behavior programs by reassembling segments taken from existing programs. Their inventive efforts can focus on major issues rather than minor details, because reused segments fill in the details. Thus, behavior programs conserve humans' analytic resources, allowing people to allocate these resources where they can yield large benefits.

> 'The bow is a simple weapon, firearms are very complicated things which get out of order in many ways...a very heavy weapon and tires out soldiers on the march. Whereas also a bowman can let off six aimed shots a minute, a musketeer can discharge but one in two minutes.'
>
> —Colonel John Smyth, advising the British Privy Council (1591)

Behavior programs do free people from having to stay constantly alert and responsive to impinging events, but the other side of this is that behavior programs encourage people to misperceive their worlds. Firstly, much perception happens automatically, without reflection, because it is itself programmed. Organizations formalize perceptual programs in standard operating procedures, job specifications, and contracts; and they concretize them in space assignments and buildings (Starbuck 1976). Secondly, behavior programs focus perceptions: events form natural equivalence classes corresponding to the behavior programs they initiate, so people attend to the distinctions between classes and ignore the distinctions within classes. One consequence is that people generally fail to notice gradual trends until these have grown so large that no existing behavior program works, and these oversights occasionally turn out to be very important (Hedberg, Nystrom, and Starbuck 1976). Thirdly, behavior programs constitute frames of reference, so people base their information gathering and interpretation on these frames of reference (Berger and Luckmann 1966; Rosenhan 1978; Salancik 1977; Starbuck 1976; Tuchman 1973). Data tend to confirm what the programs assume to be true: the gathered data may show mainly good results even when poor results prevail, because people are gathering few data where poor results show up. For instance, people do not monitor events that they believe to be tangential or phenomena that they assume to be stable. Even with plentiful data, however, people misunderstand the causes and implications of events that violate their frames of reference (Starbuck and others 1978; Watzlawick, Weakland, and Fisch 1974).

> 'The trade of advertising is now so near to perfection that it is not easy to propose any improvement.'
>
> —*The Idler*, a newspaper (1759)

> 'Atomic energy might be as good as our present-day explosives, but it is unlikely to produce anything very much more dangerous.'
>
> —Winston Churchill (1939)

Why Programs Persist

Rather than create new programs, people reuse existing behavior programs whenever possible (Dunbar 1981; Hall 1976; Newell and Simon 1972). Consider, for example, Charlie Strothman's reactions to a research project that reduced one of his intricate behavior programs to a simple, linear equation. Although not about strategic decisions, the story does show some characteristics of a real-life behavior program, and it exposes some reasons why behavior programs exhibit stability.

John Dutton and I (Dutton and Starbuck 1971a) spent five years studying how Charlie created production schedules, including one entire year investigating how he estimated run time. Many times each day, he would look at a schedule and estimate how many hours of work it represented. We got interested in how he did this; and Charlie, who was very intelligent and had had some engineering training, took as much interest as we did. He donated his weekends to experimentation at the university, seventy miles from his home. He also made numerous useful suggestions about experimental design.

At the outset, Charlie could not say how he estimated run time. Although he had words to describe his thought processes, his words did not match what actually went on in his head. No one had taught him an explicit procedure; he had just learned from experience, and he doubted that he always used the same procedure. We and he eventually discovered that he did adhere to a single procedure. When estimating a schedule's run time, Charlie first added up the schedule's total length in feet. Then he examined several characteristics of the schedule according to a consistent sequence. One peculiarity was that he did not always estimate the number of setups, but he did always scan a column of numbers showing the length of each setup, and then estimate the average length per setup. We discovered that he could estimate average length per setup much more accurately than he could estimate the number of setups without actually counting. Both estimates gave similar information in that:

number of setups = length/average length per setup

but Charlie did not actually calculate this equivalence.

Charlie used a schedule's characteristics to select a machine speed from his memory. His memory astonished us. He had preserved his experience by memorizing approximately 5,000 machine speeds, together with the characteristics of the schedule or schedules that had produced them. Finally, he would calculate:

time = length/speed

Charlie could interpolate between the speeds in his memory, and he could make general statements about the kinds of schedules that ran faster or slower, but he had no detailed understanding of why a certain speed would occur in certain circumstances. Interpolation or extrapolation made him extremely uncomfortable, and he distrusted time estimates based on interpolated speeds. From his viewpoint, the memorized speeds were discrete observations. We, however, wondered whether there might be patterns and an implicit rationale. If Charlie's observations were accurate, we conjectured, the memorized speeds should form patterns corresponding to the machines' characteristics. Through calculations and experiments—577 experiments, we learned that his memorized speeds fitted remarkably closely to the equation:

$$\text{time} = A \times (\text{number of setups}) + [B + C \times (\text{density of material})] \times \text{length}$$

where A, B, and C represent constants. Charlie had been using two nonlinear equations and an amazing memory to compute production times that he could compute with one linear equation.

The linear equation predicted Charlie's speed estimates so accurately that he himself could not distinguish its estimates from ones he had actually made. The linear equation also provided a rationale for interpolating and extrapolating beyond Charlie's actual experiences. He had contributed as much as we to discovering the linear equation, and he understood its logic. He was no conformist and he liked to innovate: he had introduced several innovations to his job even though his immediate superiors distrusted and criticized them. So we naïvely expected him to start using the linear equation in his daily work.

Not so. Six years of habit and the frame of reference that went with it were too strong. The familiar program worked, and he trusted it. Who knows what errors lurked in an unfamiliar program? The linear equation conspicuously ignored several characteristics of schedules that his familiar program took into account, and it used a strange new characteristic—density of material. Moreover, the familiar program meshed with other programs used by other people: the whole organization talked and reported data in terms of speeds, not times. Times make little sense within a speed frame of reference: to convert times to speeds, one needs to know lengths, which might be arbitrary. If Charlie were to shift to a time frame of reference, he would isolate himself from other people in his organization, and their talk about speeds would lack meaning for him. It was no accident that he had earlier told us: 'When I first came to work here, I was told what the average speeds were.'

Action Generators

Some behavior programs—action generators—are executed automatically and unreflectively and activated by job assignments or clocks. I did not get up early this morning because some problem had appeared and careful analysis had convinced me that a good solution would be to get up: I get up early every morning, even after I have gone to bed unusually late.

Although everyone has a few action generators, they seem to perform mainly peripheral functions when people are acting as individuals. Organizations, however, use action generators prolifically and assign them central functions. Organizations operate to a great extent on the basis of repetition and expectations instead of analyses and communications, and programs of various types afford the main means by which organizations learn, coordinate activities, and control actions hierarchically. Action generators minimize the need to communicate, and people who are following action generators do not disobey or behave unpredictably. For instance, large organizations produce budgets and performance reports at regular intervals whether or not they face any difficulties that can be surmounted through budgets or performance reports: the organizations appoint budget specialists whose sole responsibility is to produce budgets, they set up procedures for recording performance data, they employ accountants who are supposed to tabulate performance data, and they provide budgets and floor space for budgeting. Likewise, organizations fabricate products, monitor product quality, conduct research, and advertise without regard for whether these actions can solve immediate problems.

The term 'organization' homogenizes a very diverse spectrum of forms and practices. Not only do some organizations use action generators more extensively than others, but some subunits within a single organization make greater use of them. Past research suggests several hypotheses:

- Older organizations and subunits likely use more action generators, because new organizations and subunits lack programs, and formalization increases over time (Starbuck 1965).

- Bureaucratization correlates with organizational size, and bureaucratization produces formal job descriptions and standardized procedures, so larger, more bureaucratic organizations and subunits have more action generators (Pugh et al. 1969).

- More successful organizations and subunits probably depend more strongly on action generators, because successes breed complacency whereas failures and difficulties encourage reflection (Hedberg 1981).

- Action generators likely proliferate in organizations and subunits that conduct ceremonies and those that are supposed to conform to legitimate practices, because self-selection and socialization would make the members of these subunits especially respectful of societal ideologies (Beyer 1981; Kaufman 1960; Meyer and Rowan 1977).

- Industrialized societies encourage programming and bureaucratization, so they also nurture action generators.

In many organizations, enough programs take the form of action generators to make unreflective, automatic action the dominant mode of behavior.

> 'The war in Vietnam is going well and will succeed.'
> —Robert McNamara (1963)

Justifying Stability and Understanding Change

Both individual people and organizations sometimes change their behavior programs and action generators in order to get better results. But because behavior programs generally, and action generators especially, let people act without reflecting, they also stabilize behaviors, impede adaptation, and produce the strategies and policies that people impute to their actions in retrospect. Moreover, people tolerate extremely loose and flexible associations between actions and benefits: they may retain their programs unchanged despite trouble and turbulence (Hedberg, Nystrom, and Starbuck 1976). Indeed, behavior programs and action generators make stability, strategies, and policies appear realistic by keeping people from seeing problems, successes, threats, or opportunities that would justify changes.

Stability is more easily justified by larger problems that have more general and more robust labels (Starbuck 1982, 1983). For example, the U.S. government has fought the challenge of international Communism on many fronts: at home through loyalty oaths, Senator Joseph McCarthy, and the House Un-American Activities Committee; in Korea, Cuba, Berlin, Vietnam, Chile, Guatemala, El Salvador, Grenada, and the skies over the Soviet Union. It is hard to imagine how the United States could have justified massive expenditures on armaments, far-flung espionage, and internal-security investigations that infringe citizens' Constitutional rights if the challenge had been defined less abstractly or less generally. Halberstam (1972: 151), for instance, observed:

It was one thing to base a policy in Southeast Asia on total anti-Communism in the early 1950s when the Korean War was being fought and when the French Indochina war was at its height, when there was, on the surface at least, some evidence of a Communist monolith, and when the United States at home was becoming locked into the harshest of the McCarthy tensions. But it was another thing to accept these policies quite so casually in 1961 (although McCarthy was gone and the atmosphere in which the policies had been set had changed, the policies remained much the same), when both the world and the United States were very different. By 1961 the schism in the Communist world was clearly apparent: Khrushchev had removed his technicians and engineers from China.

In many organizations and societies, the top managers develop central problems, successes, threats, and opportunities that are extremely stable because they are so big and so perfect in logic. Because a large, general ideological molecule picks up new elements as rapidly as it loses old ones, it just evolves instead of dissolving; and organizations and societies amplify this natural stability by creating specialized subunits that are assigned to look for new elements to add to their central molecules (Ditton 1979). For instance, the challenge of international Communism did not diminish in 1972 when the United States recognized and began trading with the People's Republic of China, when the United States and the Soviet Union signed a nuclear-arms-limitation agreement, and when Bobby Fischer defeated Boris Spassky; for Chile had recently expropriated the Anaconda and Kennecott copper mines, Communist athletes dominated the 1972 Olympic Games, and North Vietnam was continuing to win the Vietnam war. Partly because they have large central molecules, organizations and societies exhibit a phenomenon called unlearning: the members wait until events have explicitly disconfirmed their central beliefs before they seriously consider alternatives (Hedberg 1981; Hedberg, Nystrom, and Starbuck 1976).

More generally, people find reorientations difficult. Reorientations are large strategic changes that would redefine individuals' or organizations' domains in some fundamental respects. People lack experience outside their domains, so proposed reorientations evoke confusion and uncertainty. Reorientations may seem illogical and paradoxical because they violate basic tenets of people's frames of reference (McCall 1977; Watzlawick, Weakland, and Fisch 1974). It is clear, however, that reorientations imply changes in power distributions, so they instigate struggles between those who have power and those who seek it (Argyris and Schön 1978; Normann 1971; Pettigrew 1973; Rhenman 1973; Wildavsky 1972).

On the other hand, people react rather positively to variations, which are small strategic changes that appear to modify individuals' or organizations' domains only incrementally. Newman and Logan (1955) listened to business executives discussing why firms grow: the five reasons they noted all fit the prescription that organizations should change incrementally at their margins. People can make sense of variations because they alter actions or beliefs moderately within over-arching frames of reference, without challenging the frames of reference themselves (Watzlawick, Weakland, and Fisch 1974). Variations also take advantage of experience, they do not threaten current power holders, and they can draw support from divergent interests (Lindblom 1959; Normann 1971). Organizations program many variations: industrial engineers discover problems that call for slightly different actions; sales personnel report on market trends within current domains. A team from McKinsey & Company analyzed ten companies that managers regard as being especially well run: the study's main conclusion was that 'Controlled experiments abound in these companies. The attitude of management is to "get some data, do it, then adjust it", rather than wait for a perfect overall plan. The companies tend to be tinkerers rather than inventors, making small steps of progress rather than conceiving sweeping new concepts' (Peters 1980: 196).

Unhappily, 'small steps of progress' often fail to keep actions up-to-date. Even when variations are generated by random processes or mechanistic rules, people postpone reconceptualizations until the evidence piles up to uncontestable levels (Box and Draper 1969; Edwards 1968; Tversky and Kahneman 1974). But people do not ordinarily generate variations randomly or mechanistically. They choose variations on the basis of their current beliefs and vested interests, so the variations do not challenge their prior beliefs or rattle the status quo; and people interpret the results of variations within the frameworks of their current beliefs and vested interests, so their interpretations support their prior beliefs and reinforce current organizational structures (McCall 1977; Wildavsky 1972). Misperceptions persist and accumulate. Indeed, successful people and organizations create programs to reproduce their successes, and they want these programs to operate in stable environments, so they try to choose variations that counteract social and technological changes (Starbuck 1983). Such variations succeed only temporarily at best. One consequence is that smooth strategic trajectories made up of variations sometimes get interrupted by abrupt crises and reorientations (Hedberg and Jönsson 1977; Jönsson and Lundin 1977; Miller 1982; Rhenman 1973; Starbuck 1968, 1973).

'The day of the battleship has not passed, and it is highly unlikely that an airplane, or fleet of them, could ever successfully sink a fleet of navy vessels under battle conditions.'

—Franklin D. Roosevelt, Assistant Secretary of the Navy (1922)

'As far as sinking a ship with a bomb is concerned, you just can't do it.'

—Admiral Clark Woodward (1939)

4. SOCIAL INTERACTION IN ORGANIZATIONS

'Violence breeds violence, and it is predicted that by 1990 kidnapping will be the dominant mode of social interaction.'

—Woody Allen (1982)

Social interaction too illustrates the general proposition that powerful tools can produce much harm as well as much good. Many people cooperating in an organization can achieve results far beyond the capabilities of one person, but a large organization can also constitute a complex environment that dominates its members' actions while confusing their understanding. An organizational hierarchy can smooth coordination and enable a few wise and insightful leaders to dictate their subordinates' actions, but a hierarchy can also allow a few arrogant leaders with faulty perceptions to steer an organization into disaster, or let selfish superiors claim the money and credit from their subordinates' hard work and creativity. Organizations promote and enlarge the scales of rationality and programming, thus amplifying both the advantages and disadvantages of these tools.

The complexity and uncontrollability of organizational environments show up in descriptions of decision-making or problem-solving. Different observers have reported seeing very different behavioral sequences: Mintzberg, Raisinghani, and Théorêt (1976) alone saw seven categories of sequences that were composed of twelve categories of activities. Witte (1972) and his colleagues found: that the numbers of information-gathering operations, alternative-developing operations, and alternative-evaluating operations all maximize near the ends of decision-making processes; that the minimum numbers of these operations all occur shortly after processes begin; and that processes typically incorporate numerous subdecisions rather than building to final major decisions. Cohen, March, and Olsen (1972) explained the diversity of behaviors by saying that four distinct streams interact: a stream of problems, a stream of potential actions, a stream of participants, and a stream of choice opportunities. Because people facing choice opportunities may introduce their pet problems or propose actions that bear no relationship to the visible problems, 'Problems come to seek connections to choice opportunities that solve them, solutions come to seek problems they handle successfully' (Cohen, March, and Olsen 1976: 31).

To some degree, the reported behavioral sequences are best explained as artifacts of the observers themselves or of the unnatural situations observed.

However, the very diversity of descriptions indicates that observers are looking at a diverse range of complex phenomena, as does the prevalent observation that behaviors iterate through repetitive cycles. Numerous participants and their interactions render collective behaviors intrinsically complex and erratic. Even if autonomous individual people would follow unidirectional behavioral sequences—which seems improbable—interacting people have to respond to stimuli from their social environments. Organizational membership entails commitments to attend and respond to such environmental stimuli; and organizations increase the numbers of stimuli by integrating many people into networks, making it easy to transmit information, and creating numerous interorganizational interfaces.

Studies of decision-making or problem-solving start from deceptive premises by initially classifying certain activities as decision-making or problem-solving. Although decision-making meetings do occur, people do not enter most mundane work situations with clear expectations that new problems, successes, threats, or opportunities have arisen, or that they must make significant decisions. Often, people take actions without saying or thinking that the actions solve specific problems or meet specific threats, and people may continue acting for long periods without looking at the results of their actions. When people do watch results, they often lack strong expectations beyond ambiguity. Most of the performance information that organizations collect routinely has ambiguous significance: because organizations record very little information about causal processes, and the standards for collecting and interpreting information are supposed to help managements appear successful, the recorded information impedes understanding and confounds attempts to draw practical implications (Boland 1982; Dunbar 1981; Garfinkel 1967; Hopwood 1972).

> 'The Harkins briefings were of course planned long in advance; they were brainwashings really, but brainwashings made all the more effective and exciting by the trappings of danger. Occasional mortar rounds going off. A captured rifle to touch, a surly captured Vietcong to look at. What was created on those trips was not an insight about the country but an illusion of knowledge. McNamara was getting the same information which was available in Washington, but now it was presented so much more effectively that he thought he understood Vietnam. Afterward Arthur Sylvester, his PIO, told reporters how many miles he had flown, how many corps headquarters, province headquarters, district headquarters he had visited, how many officers of each rank. The reporters sat there writing it down, all of it mindless, all of it fitting McNamara's vision of what Vietnam should be. Vietnam confirmed McNamara's preconceptions and specifications.'

—David Halberstam (1972: 305)

Since all situations have numerous possible interpretations, colleagues decide jointly which interpretations seem realistic (Berger and Luckmann 1966; Ditton 1979; Hewitt and Hall 1973; Langer 1976; Ungson, Braunstein, and Hall 1981). As one consequence, observations about the stimuli that initiate decision-making or problem-solving tend to be tautologies. For example, Mintzberg, Raisinghani, and Théorêt (1976: 253) asserted, 'The need for a decision is identified as a difference between information on some actual situation and some expected standard', but people can change their expected standards and perceptions. Similarly, people could interpret any situation as violating at least one of the criteria stated by Hewitt and Hall (1973: 368):

People classify a situation as problematic when 'the orderly quality of the scene is questionable.... People are disposed to view a situation as orderly if they can find a basis for viewing the behavior in it as typical of its members, probable under the circumstances, applicable in the light of conditions, appropriate to the goals being sought, realistic in its direction, and morally within the norms. They view it as disorderly if the behavior seems atypical, unlikely, inexplicable, technically inappropriate, unrealistic, or morally wrong.

People believe that they are supposed to state symptoms, causes of symptoms, and needs for action when they are result watching; so they do state them; and it is these statements that explicate order or disorder, and that define situations as problematic or successful or threatening or opportunistic. The actions that ensue from such definitions may turn the definitions into self-fulfilling prophecies (Rosenhan 1978; Starbuck 1976; Weick 1983).

Social construction also frequently makes decisions, strategies, and policies the consequences of actions rather than their determinants. Cohen, March, and Olsen (1972) noted that participants in decision-making may perceive that decisions have occurred in three circumstances: (*a*) when actions are taken, even if these actions do not solve one of the visible problems; (*b*) when problems are removed from choice opportunities, even if no actions are taken to cause their removal; or (*c*) when actions are mated with problems and called solutions. Cohen, March, and Olsen asserted that events (*c*) happen much less frequently than events (*a*) and (*b*). Garfinkel (1967) and Weick (1979) have pointed out how often people reenact decisions by looking into the past and seeing that they evidently must have chosen courses of action. Process models of human behavior, whether models of individuals or organizations, have been strikingly devoid of explicit choices (Dutton and Starbuck 1971*b*). The process models indicate that people seek to design the single best actions rather than to choose among alternative actions. The process models also emphasize experimentation: people try out actions to see how they work, shifting to alternatives only if they get bad results. Because behavior programs govern both the designing and the experimenting, people seem to exercise little choice even at tactical levels.

Complex social environments give people good reason to simplify their worlds, and they can do this by acting tentatively, following precedents, adhering to social rituals, speaking in stylized language, anticipating others' reactions, and choosing to whom they listen. People edit their statements before making them, and they hedge their voiced observations and proposals with disclaimers (Hewitt and Stokes 1975). They emphasize symptoms that high-status people say are important, and deviations from legitimate goals or expectations (Lyles and Mitroff 1980). They define accidents as deviations from the predictions of authorities, and they blame people instead of rules or machines, and enemies instead of friends

(Dunbar 1981). They appeal to accepted theories and quasi theories. They propose conventional and accepted actions that would harmonize with current actions, that imitate other organizations' actions, that use wasted resources, or that reinforce current power holders (Alexander 1979; Mehan 1984; Starbuck 1976; Staw and Ross 1978). They vote on proposals and endorse observations via neglect, skeptical looks, clichés, and rephrasings among other means (Starbuck 1983). Of course, they follow confident leaders, defer to authority or presumed expertise, and give high priority to social solidarity (Janis 1972; Milgram 1974). Although rituals and editing do have the intended effect of simplifying complex worlds, they also foster misinformation and misperception (Argyris and Schön 1978).

> 'I won't be involved in the day-to-day operations of the team. I'm too busy with the shipping business.'

> —George Steinbrenner (1973)

> 'I thank God there are no free schools, nor printing, and hope we shall not have them these hundred years; for learning has brought disobedience and heresy and sects into the world, and printing has divulged them and libels against them.'

> —William Berkeley, Royal Governor of Virginia (1670)

Hierarchies too simplify complexity, and the stories of Alexander the Great, Napoleon, Henry Ford, and Thomas Watson show how successful hierarchical control can be. Hierarchies generally mean that replacing just a few top managers can induce large behavioral and ideological changes. Unfortunately, top managers tend to misperceive what is happening even more than many of their subordinates do: top managers' direct personal experiences with clients, customers, and technologies occurred years ago; they receive much of their information through second-hand reports that systematically avoid displeasing them; they interpret their promotions and high statuses as evidence that they have more expertise than their subordinates; and they listen mainly to other top managers who are subjected to similar pressures (Porter and Roberts 1976: 1573–1576). Top managers' influential positions make their perceptual errors quite serious. Top managers also tend to resist, more than their subordinates do, strategic reorientations within their organizations: significant social and technological changes threaten their dominance and high social statuses; and they fear, with reason, that they will become scapegoats if current programs and strategies are judged failures (Normann 1971; Starbuck, Greve, and Hedberg 1978). But top managers can exert little influence upon social and technological changes beyond the boundaries of their organizations, so their efforts to regulate and decelerate change may simply steer their organizations into stagnating backwaters (Hedberg, Nystrom, and Starbuck 1976).

> 'Most of the ideas in IBM have come from me personally, but our inventors did the actual inventing, and it is their names which are on the patents.'

> —Thomas J. Watson, President of IBM, 1946 (Belden and Belden 1962: 260)

5. BLUNDERING IN THE DARK

'I cannot imagine any condition which could cause this ship to flounder. I cannot conceive of any vital disaster happening to this vessel.'

—E. J. Smith, Captain of the *Titanic* (1912)

Top managers may be more prone to erroneous perceptions than some other people, but the great majority of people struggle along with numerous and large perceptual errors, and their beliefs incorporate substantial amounts of fantasy (Hall 1976; Singer and Benassi 1981; Starbuck, Greve, and Hedberg 1978; Tversky and Kahneman 1974). All people have limited ranges of experience: most have worked in one or two occupational ladders, in a few organizations, in fewer industries, over a couple of decades. Programs and buffers have blurred their perceptions. So they depend on colleagues and schooling to extend their experiences and to provide contexts for interpreting them. They believe that they are working in competitive industries or decentralized firms or whatever, not because these judgments have firm foundations in their own experiences, but because other people have told them so or because they have read it in a trade magazine. The other people, of course, have no wider personal experiences than themselves, and are mainly repeating what they in turn have heard—filtered and rationalized. Some people do, of course, have clearer visions and more relevant experiences, or they have done careful research. But perceivers' influence probably correlates not at all with their realism—misguided leaders fill human history (Antonio 1979), and listeners impute expertise on the basis of superficial cues such as speakers' white coats, enthusiasm, and self-confidence (Milgram 1974). The various pressures upon top managers might even make the influence-realism correlation negative. Social pressures and ritualistic formal-reporting systems encourage all people to tolerate observations that contradict their beliefs, and to accept explanations, such as quasi theories, that explain nothing. Thus, not only do organizational and societal mythologies shape frames of reference, but these mythologies perpetuate themselves somewhat autonomously of actual events.

'Heavier-than-air flying machines are impossible.'

—Lord Kelvin, renowned physicist (1890)

'X-rays are a hoax.'

—Lord Kelvin (1900)

Payne and Pugh (1976) reviewed numerous studies of organizational structures and climates, and contrasted objective and subjective measures. They found that organizations' members disagree strongly with each other: 'Perceptual measures of each of the structural and climate variables have varied so much among themselves that mean scores were uninterpretable' (1976: 1168). With understatement, Payne and Pugh (1976: 1167) also concluded that 'Relationships between perceptual and objective measures of structural variables were not strong', although people do seem to know whether they are working in large organizations or small ones. The disagreements among people correspond in part with their different occupations and hierarchical statuses. However, the disagreements cannot be explained completely by differences in valid information and expertise, for intergroup differences are much smaller than interindividual differences, and the intergroup differences clearly include the effects of rationalization and contagion. For instance, members holding higher statuses have generally more positive views of their organizations.

> 'That is the biggest fool thing we have ever done. ... The [atomic] bomb will never go off, and I speak as an expert in explosives.'
>
> —Admiral William D. Leahy, speaking to Harry S. Truman (1945)

Members also misperceive their organizations' environments. Tosi, Aldag, and Storey (1973) asked 102 middle and top managers from various firms in diverse industries to describe their environments' stabilities; then they correlated the managers' perceptions with volatility indices calculated from their firms' financial reports and industry statistics. The correlations between subjective and objective measures ranged from −0.29 to 0.04. In a similar study, Downey, Hellriegel, and Slocum (1975) elicited the perceptions of 51 division heads in a large conglomerate, and correlated these perceived environmental stabilities with the variabilities of industry projections made by the Department of Commerce. Correlations of the objective measure with various subjective measures ranged from −0.17 to 0.11.

Research generates Rorschach inkblots—findings that people interpret differently. Tosi, Aldag, and Storey (1973: 35) viewed their findings as proof that the questionnaire they used to obtain subjective measures 'is not methodologically adequate'; and Downey, Hellriegel, and Slocum (1975: 623) too concluded that 'the results do not support the construct validity of the two' instruments they had used. I draw another inference—that both studies show how frequently subjective observations diverge from objective ones. Some people do perceive some facets of their worlds accurately, at least some of the time; but enough people misperceive seriously that, averaged across many people, subjective data correlate hardly at all with objective data. A later study by Downey, Hellriegel, and Slocum (1977) suggests that people's characteristic ways of thinking may exert stronger effects on their perceptions than do properties of the things perceived.

> 'There can be no whitewash at the White House.'
>
> —Richard H. Nixon (1973)

Organizations' formal reports contribute to misperceptions and encourage people to rely on mythologies instead of on data. Quite a few studies have pointed to the misrepresentations and inadvertent biases that perforate formal reports: formal reports encourage and reflect game playing, and they mislead their readers by emphasizing financial and numerical data, by highlighting successes and rationalizing failures, and by crediting good results to superiors (Altheide and Johnson 1980; Boland 1982; Dunbar 1981; Edelman 1977; Hofstede 1967; Hopwood 1972). It may be that those organizations that rely primarily on formal reports either perform poorly or drift into crises (Grinyer and Norburn 1975; Starbuck, Greve, and Hedberg 1978). If so, the correlation probably does not arise because formal reports themselves cause problems, but because formal reports are so manifestly unreliable and inadequate that only very unrealistic people depend on them.

'You can predict things only after they've happened.'

—Eugene Ionesco

Numerous studies have sought to assess the effectiveness of formal planning (Armstrong 1982; Bresser and Bishop 1983).[2] In spite of Armstrong's conclusion (1982) to the contrary, I believe the results show that the worst studies find the strongest relationships between planning and performances, whereas the best studies find no important relationships between planning and performances.

Nearly all of these studies gathered their data by mail questionnaires that could be filled out quickly and that were filled out by self-selected respondents who had little reason to respond accurately and who may not have known what they were talking about. The data concerning planning activities were extremely sketchy, and the very low response rates imply that these data were biased. In effect, the planning-is-profitable studies found that people in profitable, fast-growing firms say they have long-range goals and plans, whereas people in unprofitable, slow-growing firms say they are unsure of their long-range goals and plans. Is it not probable that profitability makes people confident of their futures? Because deviation from long-range plans implies disappointment with performance whereas adherence to long-range plans implies satisfaction, the consequences of planning ought to be evaluated longitudinally, not cross-sectionally, and the plans should be identified before observing their consequences.

In what is probably the best study of formal planning to date, Grinyer and Norburn (1975) discovered that firms' profitability correlates only very weakly with the formality of planning ($r = 0.22$). That is, profitable firms are about as likely to plan informally as formally, and the same is true of unprofitable firms. Profitability also correlates inconsistently and meaninglessly with the degrees to which senior executives agree about objectives or responsibilities: the correlations range from 0.40 to -0.40. Thus, formalized plans seem to be inferior to informal plans nearly as often as they are superior, and consensus can be as harmful as it is beneficial when there is no way to assure that the objects of consensus are good.

Grinyer and Norburn also found that profitability correlates weakly but perceptibly with reliance on informal communication ($r = 0.40$), and moderately with the use of diverse information when evaluating performance ($r = 0.68$). Both correlations relate to formal reports: managers in more profitable firms make greater use of informal communication channels, whereas managers in less profitable firms communicate primarily through formal reports; and managers in more profitable firms use diverse kinds of information when evaluating their firms' performances, whereas managers in less profitable firms get their information mainly from formal reports. I know of no studies that have assessed the consequences of adhering to or deviating from long-range plans. But I can predict what they would say.

> 'The Nazi threat to unleash U-2 bombs on London is just a meaningless publicity stunt.'
>
> —Lord Cherwell, advising Winston Churchill (1940)

> 'Everyone acquainted with the [incandescent] lamp will recognize it as a conspicuous failure.'
>
> —Henry Morton, President of Stevens Institute of Technology (1880)

> 'You'd better learn secretarial work or else get married.'
>
> —Emmeline Snively, head of Blue Book Modeling Agency, speaking to Marilyn Monroe (1944)

So people blunder along, partially blind, acting before thinking, and fortunate to stay out of trouble. No wonder they normally avoid strategic reorientations— drawing strong inferences from undependable perceptions and faulty beliefs can lead to unpleasant surprises. Behavior programs and strategic variations keep actions close to the familiar and their consequences close to the expected. And like whistling in the dark, retrospective decisions and strategies maintain the confidence to keep on acting. But with perseverance, a series of variations can add up to a revolution.

> 'Not within a thousand years will man ever fly.'
>
> —Wilbur Wright (1901)

NOTES

1. Except where otherwise attributed, the quotations that appear throughout this article were compiled by Coffey (1983).
2. In related studies, Thune and House (1970) and Herold (1972) concluded that formal planners grow faster and increase their profits faster than informal planners: both studies gathered data with mail questionnaires; Thune and House got 36 usable responses after contacting 145 firms, and Herold analyzed more data about 10 of these firms. Malik and Karger (1975) inferred that formal planners have higher sales and earnings than informal planners: they gathered their data by a mail questionnaire that 'a CEO could answer in a few minutes'; after mailing their questionnaire to 273 companies in six industries, they got 38 usable responses distributed across three industries. All three studies gathered quite superficial data concerning the formality of planning, and their response rates range from 7 to 25 percent.

   Two studies are somewhat superior to the foregoing ones, but these studies too depended on questionnaires and had low response rates. Rue and Fulmer (1974) surveyed 1,333 firms about their planning practices and got 386 usable answers: 29 percent. Rue and Fulmer classified firms into four categories of formality, got financial data from the Compustat tapes, and found 'no simple, across the board relationship between completeness of long-range plan and financial performance' (1974: 72). Wood and LaForge (1979) asked a number of questions about specific planning practices, and received 41 usable responses out of 150 banks surveyed: 27 percent. Wood and LaForge classified banks in three categories of formality, and found that the comprehensive planners and the partial planners had higher profits than the informal planners, but the comprehensive and partial planners had similar profits.

Kudla (1980) had a response rate of 59 percent: 328 usable responses out of 557 firms surveyed. He too created three categories based on questionnaire responses, but for no apparent reason, he discarded all of the partial planners and half of the formal planners, and so ended up with only 129 firms: 23 percent. He went to considerable effort to develop credible statistics, but focused on rates of return that depend on volatile stock prices, and found no differences between formal and informal planners.

Grinyer and Norburn (1975) studied only 21 firms, a stratified 30 percent of the 71 firms chosen for their sample frame; they did not say how many of the 71 firms they actually contacted. They gathered data about planning practices, goals, and organizational structures through long, structured interviews with 91 executives; then they classified planning by both formality and regularity. Grinyer and Norburn obtained a variety of performance data, but focused on return on assets; they stated each firm's profitability as a Z-score relative to that specific industry. They made careful statistical calculations.

A few studies have been interpreted as proving that strategies raise profits: because these studies identified strategies retrospectively, they only show that dissatisfied people are more likely to change their behaviors.

Part III

Perceptions and Learning Part 1

8

Organizational Facades

Coauthored with Paul C. Nystrom

1. INTRODUCTION

Organizational facades enable managers to justify actions, to acquire resources, and to gain discretion. Facades help managers to achieve these objectives by creating the appearance of competence. Prevailing ideologies define what competence means, and in modernized societies, ideologies generally equate managerial competence with rationality. Since rationality connotes purposiveness and consistency, organizational facades tend to present such appearances.

One dictionary (World 1960: 519) defines a facade as 'the front part of anything: often used figuratively, with implications of an imposing appearance concealing something inferior'. Another dictionary (Merriam 1971: 811) defines a facade as 'a false front' and 'a false, superficial, or artificial appearance or effect'.

Organizational facades have gained importance from four historical developments: Firstly, an increasingly prevalent separation of management from owners creates opportunities for managerial motives to deviate from those of owners (Pondy 1969; Starbuck 1965) and it compels owners to evaluate managers based on performance measurements that managers can manipulate. Various scandals have revealed that some managers have used facades to create misleading impressions that their firms have been exceedingly successful, thus benefiting the managers personally. Secondly, collegiate schools of business and various professional associations encourage managers to emulate more established professions. Professionals expect to exercise autonomy as a logical consequence of their technical expertise, so techniques become symbols of professionalism that reinforce the separation of management from ownership. Facades also help managers to seek resources from sources other than owners, either to augment the resources owners can or will provide or to reduce managers' dependence upon owners. Thirdly, organizations have grown in size and complexity, with one result being less and less direct supervision and more and more supervision through goal setting and performance measurement. Studies show that goal-setting systems can trigger the falsification of performance reports (Degeorge, Patel, and Zeckhauser 1999; Schweitzer, Ordóñez, and Douma 2004). Fourthly, organizations are emphasizing performance-based compensation for managers, especially senior ones. Stock options and performance bonuses encourage managers to create the appearance that they are meeting or exceeding formal performance targets.

Institutionalized Organizations

In an influential article about structures as myths and ceremonies, Meyer and Rowan (1977) suggested that institutionalized organizations enhance their stability and survival by mirroring rules that are valued by their institutional environments. Stability and survival depend on resource acquisition, which, in turn, depends on these organizations appearing legitimate to those who control needed resources. Meyer and Rowan provided several examples describing schools, hospitals, and other governmental agencies. They implied that institutionalized organizations form a distinct category because their environments make demands that the organizations can satisfy ceremonially. They contrasted institutionalized organizations with production organizations, which, they said, must satisfy the demands of markets.

This chapter focuses on business organizations and it points out that business organizations also offer opportunities to gain advantage by meeting environmental demands ceremonially.

Business Organizations

This chapter argues that managers of business organizations can and do benefit by appearing to conform to ideologies that their environments prefer. In some of the examples that follow, managers were seeking more discretion (Finkelstein and Hambrick 1990). However, managers can also benefit financially or in terms of their organizational statuses. For instance, a recent study reported finding that major companies adopting fashionable management techniques do not perform better financially, yet they do garner superior reputations and pay their CEOs higher compensation (Staw and Epstein 2000).

Business organizations often deal with situations characterized by ambiguous goals or unclear means–ends relationships (March and Olsen 1976). When confronted by ambiguities, managers and other stakeholders tend to shift their action criteria away from actual activities and toward symbolic indicators of results (Thompson 1967; Westphal and Zajac 1998). For instance, the owners of multidivisional corporations typically do not receive information that enables them to assess the performance of different product lines or semiautonomous organizational units. Managers report financial data in aggregates that do not communicate these relative performances, and external auditors certify these reports as adequate and legitimate. Whether intended or not, these practices enhance managers' discretionary powers and they give managers strong influence over evaluations of their activities.

2. KINDS OF FACADES

Facades abound. Work processes, organizational structures, and managers' pronouncements may all become media for organizational facades. Because managers construct facades to deceive targeted people and institutions, facades mirror the norms and expectations relevant to these targets: professions, universities, industry and trade associations, competitors, customers, governmental agencies and laws, and societal traditions. Of course, facades also influence other people who were not targets.

The examples of facades that follow provide a sampling from these diverse media and targets. Readers undoubtedly will think of additional examples, thereby corroborating our main thesis that organizational facades are prevalent and diverse.

Work Processes

Given prevailing norms of organizational rationality, one might expect that managers employ computers to improve information processing and decision-making. However, organizations may purchase and display computers as facades rather than use them to enhance workflows. Possessing the most fashionable computer hardware and software signals to outsiders that managers are devoted to rationality and innovation, and attests that managers' competencies are up to date. People often infer that those who possess complex technologies know how to use them, and that they actually do use them. Such inferences may be incorrect. A recent example was the energy-trading room that Enron personnel created to impress visiting financial analysts. Managers drafted personnel into this room at the last minute from various departments around the company, the computers had no connections to a LAN or the Internet, and the telephones did not actually work.

Computer applications sometimes reflect political rather than economic aspects of organizational life. For example, engineers in a multinational firm switched from simple hand calculations to fancy computer simulations because the simulations helped to convince clients that they had purchased good engineering designs. 'The computer calculations appear precise, accurate, and sophisticated' (Kling 1980: 74). Furthermore, the simulations' proprietary nature frustrated attempts by clients to audit the designers' assumptions or reliability. In another analysis of several simulation models, researchers concluded that such modeling might be initiated 'to justify decisions already made, [to] add a sheen of technical sophistication to their reputations' (Greenberger, Crenson, and Crissey 1976).

Accounting firms perpetuate myths about the rational and impersonal nature of their profession's techniques. They emphasize ceremonial procedures and they strive to divert clients' attention away from evaluations of their outputs.

Even the vaunted Program Evaluation and Review Technique (PERT) served as a façade for the management of the Polaris missile project. Because PERT bolstered the management team's image of competence, external review boards intruded less. Behind this facade, the team reportedly did not actually use the technique to manage schedules and costs. 'PERT did not build the Polaris, but it was extremely useful for those who did build the weapon system to have many people believe that it did' (Sapolsky 1972: 125). Thus, PERT and associated managerial innovations provided 'a protective veneer' (Sapolsky 1972: 246).

Other managerial work processes also can serve as facades. Managers may install formal planning systems to assure important stakeholders that the managers care about the future. Again, people often infer that the more sophisticated the techniques, the more competent the managements. However, the effectiveness of formal planning systems remains dubious because they fail to eliminate several well-known limitations and biases inherent in human judgmental processes (Hogarth and Makridakis 1981). One detailed study of corporations found that the formality of planning does not correlate with financial performance (Grinyer and Norburn 1975). Indeed, their results suggest that firms achieving better financial performance rely on informal sources of information and informal channels of communication.

Managers also construct facades to deceive their superiors. These facades transcend the well-documented filtering and distorting of upward-flowing communications (Dunbar 1981; Porter and Roberts 1976). Managers typically construct facades at crucial interfaces, such as an interface between a division and its corporate headquarters. For example, while studying a headquarters-backed program of management by objectives (MBO), Nystrom (1977) found that some divisional managers feigned compliance; they filled out forms ritualistically, but these exercises did not affect their actual decisions and actions. Some other divisions openly defied the corporate MBO program, yet they covertly developed and enthusiastically used somewhat different MBO techniques to manage their operations.

Managers occasionally hire outside consultants to augment internal work processes. A managerial clique may hire consultants as a ploy to forestall changes, or to endorse changes they favor. Even when consultants strive to remain value-free, they can find themselves entangled in political intrigues (Rhenman 1973).

Structures

Even the broad structural configurations erected by organizations reflect prevailing norms (Lee and Pennings 2002; Stinchcombe 1965; Thornton 2002). Some managers adopt fashionable structures—such as product divisions or matrix forms—simply to appear contemporary. Are these managers satisfied to continue operating as before, but behind new structural facades?

A few years ago, to obscure the ethical conflicts between their advisory services from their auditing services, public accounting firms adopted structural facades that appeared to uncouple these activities (Boland 1982). Behind these facades of independence, however, their managers were urging auditors to sell advisory services to their clients.

Similarly, organizations operating in foreign countries may uncouple structures from actions so that their structures align with norms prevailing in the host cultures. A study of Japanese firms operating in California concluded that an organization may be wise 'to make its public face conform as best it can to prevailing ideological or normative currents and cope in an ad hoc fashion with the strains' created by slippage between official structures and actual actions (Lincoln, Olson, and Hanada 1978: 845).

Job titles become facades that mask substantial differences in behaviors and expectations. Someone who supervises two subordinates with the same job title will generally allow the less experienced subordinate less discretion. Titles may be identical, yet role relationships and freedom to act may differ. Furthermore, these differences in discretion correlate strongly with people's expectations about what constitutes equitable pay for that work (Jaques 1961).

Pronouncements

Organizations' mission statements typically use ambiguous terms that emphasize general, abstract values held by relevant publics. These mission facades provide managers with considerable latitude to alter their actions over time while professing to act consistently and purposively (Mintzberg 1994). Ethics statements promulgated by corporations (Chatov 1979) and by societies of scientists and engineers (Chalk, Frankel, and Chafer 1980) often do not contain meaningful procedures to monitor compliance and to impose sanctions.

Managers' statements to customers or clients can serve as facades. Advertising agencies need such facades because of the difficulty of proving advertising's impact on sales and of judging the relative effectiveness of proposed messages. Agencies' managers cope with clients' uncertainties by portraying their agencies' activities as routine and derived from past successes (Comanor, Kover, and Smiley 1981). To make matters more difficult, these managers must also attempt to persuade clients that the agencies' advertising campaigns are novel and innovative.

Studies of organizations in crises reveal that managers' pronouncements ringing with tones of self-assurance sometimes mask their doubts, even utter bewilderment (Nystrom, Hedberg, and Starbuck 1976; Starbuck, Greve, and Hedberg 1978). Such statements prolong and escalate crises because they mislead and lull employees and outside stakeholders.

Myths about heroic acts during trying times sometimes crystallize into sagas that influence believers' behaviors. Organizational sagas create a sense of distinctive history, mission, and pride (Clark 1972). Sagas are facades in the sense that they embellish upon actual events and in the sense that members look to myths rather than realities as guides for action. Other myths arise because history seems unclear and people want explanations for significant events (March and Olsen 1976).

Managers sometimes promulgate myths about new strategies or new technologies to enthuse members and to justify their actions (Jönsson and Lundin 1977).

3. IMPLICATIONS OF FACADES

Several implications ensue from the proposition that managers construct facades. After examining some dysfunctional consequences of facades, this chapter concludes by offering prescriptions to managers.

Dysfunctional Consequences

Organizational performance can deteriorate when managers fail to understand that organizational processes, structures, and pronouncements may be facades. Managers seek to appear competent by using the latest management techniques, but they may imitate facades. For instance, managers of a conglomerate firm may install integrating devices that have improved coordination between divisional and headquarters levels in vertically integrated firms, then find that performance deteriorates because their own divisions need greater autonomy (Lorsch and Allen 1973). Managers may also imitate the wrong organizations simply because those organizations' facades mask underlying deficiencies that one would not wish to replicate or hidden idiosyncratic advantages that one could not duplicate (Lippman and Rumelt 1982; Starbuck and Nystrom 1981*a*). Sometimes, late adopters may mimic firms that will soon experience performance declines and abandon the structures that were being imitated. Consider the rise and fall of matrix structures in multinational firms (Chi and Nystrom 1998). For example, the CEO of European-headquartered ABB extolled their matrix structure as a key to their financial success, which subsequently declined dramatically; ABB then replaced the matrix structure.

Managers wishing to appear progressive may adopt all innovations available (Mohr 1969), but indiscriminate adoption of numerous innovations can undermine organizational adaptability (Kimberly 1981). Thus, organizations that appear more innovative may actually be less effective.

Conforming to societal ideologies can lead to other dire consequences. Starbuck and Nystrom (1981*b*) related how a company manufacturing chemical instruments reaped continued successes by deviating from industry practices. When a larger firm acquired this company, they were aghast to find an absence of many systems and procedures. As they proceeded to remedy these perceived deficiencies by installing conventional systems and procedures, their costs increased. However, when they raised prices to cover the higher costs, product demand fell and losses replaced profits. These managers apparently failed to realize that organizations can reap comparative advantages through idiosyncratic practices.

Managers convert accounting data into facades. Studies of organizations in crises reveal a prevalent pattern: Managers alter reports in order to eliminate the symptoms of problems (Nystrom, Hedberg, and Starbuck 1976). For instance, managers boost short-term profitability by changing the method of accounting for inventories. Such manipulations of formal reports cover up the true extent of difficulties, misleading others and falsely reassuring the managers themselves that they have addressed the crises effectively. Altering reports seems analogous to applying fresh paint on a building that termites are devouring.

Formal reporting systems require managers to allocate time to justifying the rationality of their past actions. Ironically, negative feedback often escalates managers' commitments to faulty policies (Campbell 1969). Managers allocate additional attention and resources to the measured phenomena, thereby slighting or overlooking issues that are more relevant. In this way, retrospective rationality diminishes prospective rationality (Staw 1980).

Educational and training programs that perpetuate organizational facades exacerbate personnel turnover, especially of new members. Newcomers feel disillusioned when organizational realities do not match prior expectations (Van Maanen 1976).

Facades have dysfunctional consequences for organizational scientists who fail to recognize their real nature (Scott 1995). Consider, for instance, the many efforts to discover correlates of organizational structures—and the meager results. Structures do not correlate strongly and consistently with either environments (Starbuck 1981) or technologies (Gerwin 1981). In contrast, organizational size shows relatively consistent, strong correlations with organizational structure (Payne and Pugh 1976). These findings may imply the existence of a societal norm prescribing different structures for organizations of different sizes. More broadly, organizational size also correlates substantially with adoption of innovations (Damanpour 1992; Nystrom, Ramamurthy, and Wilson 2002) and with formal systems for environmental scanning (Yasai-Ardekani and Nystrom 1996). Such empirical findings may reflect imitation of similar-sized organizations in order to enhance legitimacy when dealing with ambiguity.

Prescriptions for Managers

Managers who construct facades should not insist that actual activities conform to the facades. To do so would undermine the strengths obtainable by understanding the shortcomings of prevailing ideologies and the advantages available by acting contrary to these prevailing ideologies. For instance, organizations can benefit by fostering dissension because this sharpens awareness of environmental shifts (Hedberg, Nystrom, and Starbuck 1976). Similarly, although organizations should engage in some planning activities, they should put low reliance on the resulting plans in order to avoid measuring performances in terms of conformity to plans and to keep alert for emerging dangers and opportunities.

Problems arise when managers actually believe in the value of prevailing ideologies and facades. They see that real-life activities deviate from these ideologies, and they interpret these discrepancies as deficiencies requiring correction. If their actions reduce these discrepancies, their organizations often become worse off. For instance, managers can undermine organizations by running them by the book, adhering to all the rules and procedures in official manuals. Difficulties with new employees who recently graduated from college frequently stem from their interpreting discrepancies as deficiencies.

Wise managers understand that they gain discretion when they allow conflicting prescriptions to coexist. For example, avoid red tape but document activities. Innovate but act consistently (Bourgeois and Eisenhardt 1988). Respect the norms of the professional employees but maintain control through the managerial hierarchy. Work toward consensus but encourage dissenters to voice their divergent views. Managers can offset the deficiencies in any one prescription by adopting a second prescription that contradicts the first. Contradictory prescriptions legitimate discretion because they highlight the existence of choices and the need for judgments.

9

Executives' Perceptual Filters: What They Notice and How They Make Sense

Coauthored with Frances J. Milliken

1. INTRODUCTION

Management magazines, academic journals, and textbooks almost always presume that analyses of past events reveal how those events actually unfolded. Such writings also frequently portray strategy formulation and implementation as a causal sequence, in which executives perceive some reality, analyze the options offered by this reality, decide to pursue one or more of these options, and obtain results when their organizations' environments react. Thus, according to this causal sequence, organizations' environments act as impartial evaluators of executives' perceptions, analyses, and actions. When the results are good, executives receive credit for accurately perceiving opportunities or threats, for analyzing these correctly and for taking appropriate actions. When the results are bad, executives get blamed for perceiving erroneously, for making analytic mistakes, for taking inappropriate actions.

This chapter argues that, prevalent though they are, retrospective explanations of past events encourage academics to overstate the contributions of executives and the benefits of accurate perceptions or careful analyses. Because retrospective analyses oversimplify the connections between behaviors and outcomes, prescriptions derived from retrospective understanding may not help executives who are living amid current events. As Fischhoff (1980: 335) observed: 'While the past entertains, ennobles and expands quite readily, it enlightens only with delicate coaxing.'

The chapter describes some of the influences on the perceptual filtering processes that executives use as they observe and try to understand their environments. It has four major sections. The first of these explains how retrospection distorts people's understanding of their worlds by emphasizing one or the other of two logical sequences. The ensuing section characterizes perceptual filtering, and argues that filtering can provide a nonjudgmental framework for looking at past, present, and future events. The next-to-last and longest section reviews evidence about how filtering processes vary with executives' characteristics—such as their habits, beliefs, experiences, and work settings. This review divides perception into noticing and sense-making. The chapter ends by considering how a focus on perceptual filtering changes one's understanding of the noticing and sense-making tasks of executives. Noticing may be at least as important to effective problem solving as sense-making: Sense-making focuses on subtleties and interdependencies, whereas noticing picks up major events and gross trends.

2. RETROSPECTION

'The French people are incapable of regicide.'
>—Louis XVI, King of France (1789)

'The Army is the Indian's best friend.'
>—General George Armstrong Custer (1870)

'I don't need bodyguards.'
>—Jimmy Hoffa (June 1975)

'Nobody can overthrow me. I have the support of 700,000 troops, all the workers, and most of the people. I have the power.'
>—Mohammed Reza Pahlevi, Shah of Iran, March 6, 1978

Observers of the past can discern executives:

> who drew erroneous inferences from their observations,
> who sensibly diversified and spread their risks, or
> who saw meaningful connections where everyone else saw unrelated events.

By contrast, observers of the present and future have less confidence that they can identify executives:

>> who are failing to anticipate important trends,
>> who are not implementing effectively strategies that might work, or
>> who are putting all of their eggs into the right baskets.

People seem to see past events as much more rationally ordered than current or future events, because retrospective sense-making erases many of the causal sequences that complicate and obscure the present and future (Fischhoff 1975; Fischhoff and Beyth 1975; Greenwald 1980; Hawkins and Hastie 1986). The past seems to contain fewer of the sequences in which

>> the goodness or badness of results remains unclear, or
>> incorrect actions by executives yield good results, or
>> correct actions by executives yield bad results, or
>> executives' actions have no significant effects on results, or
>> bad analyses by executives lead to correct actions, or
>> good analyses by executives lead to incorrect actions, or
>> analyses by executives do not significantly affect their actions, or

inaccurate perceptions by executives undermine good analyses, or
accurate perceptions by executives get lost in bad analyses, or
executives' own perceptions exert no significant effects on their analyses.

For instance, in a study of a large government project, Ross and Staw (1986) noted that public declarations of commitment to the project became occasions for erasing information that had cast doubt upon it. Such erasing may occur quite involuntarily as people's memories automatically take account of subsequent events (Fischhoff 1975; Loftus 1979; Snyder and Uranowitz 1978; Wohlwill and Kohn 1976). As Fischhoff (1980: 341) put it, 'people not only tend to view what has happened as having been inevitable but also to view it as having appeared "relatively inevitable" before it happened'.

Observers who know the results of actions tend to see two kinds of analytic sequences:

Good results→ Correct actions→ Flawless analyses→ Accurate perceptions
Bad results→ Incorrect actions→ Flawed analyses→ Inaccurate perceptions

Knowing, for example, that bad results occurred, observers search for the incorrect actions that produced these bad results; the actual results guide the observers toward relevant actions and help them to see what was wrong with these actions (Neisser 1981). Knowing that actions were incorrect, observers seek flawed analyses; the incorrect actions point to specific analyses, and the actions' incorrectness guarantees the presence of flaws in these analyses. Knowing which analyses contained flaws, observers look for inaccurate perceptions; observers inspect the perceptions that fed into the flawed analyses, feeling sure that some of these perceptions must have contained errors.

Thus, after the space shuttle exploded and destroyed the Challenger spacecraft, a Presidential Commission searched for the human errors that caused this disaster. Physical evidence from the seabed laboratory tests, and television tapes ruled out several initial hypotheses and focused attention on design flaws in the wall of the solid-rocket booster. Confident that mistakes had occurred when NASA decided to continue using this booster, the Presidential Commission could then review these processes and identify the mistakes. The Commission did spot some data that should have been taken more seriously, some rules that should have been enforced more stringently, some opinions that should have been given more credence, some communication channels that should have been used, and some specific people who had played central roles in the faulty decision processes. Many of these same actions had occurred before previous flights—the same rules had been bent, the same kinds of discussions had taken place, and the same communication channels had been ignored. But, after previous flights, no participant said these actions had been mistakes; and when inspectors noted defects in the solid-rocket boosters, NASA personnel concluded that these defects were not serious.

Retrospective perceivers are much more likely to see bad results, and hence mistaken actions and analyses, if they did not themselves play central roles in the events; and perceivers are much more likely to see good results if they did play central roles (Nisbett and Ross 1980). Festinger, Riecken, and Schachter (1956) observed a religious cult that waited expectantly for a flying saucer to arrive and carry them off so that they would be safe when the world came to an end at midnight. At dawn, facing the fact that the expected events had not transpired, the cult members retreated in confusion and disappointment to their meeting house. But they soon emerged with revitalized faith, for they had realized that it was their unquestioning faith the night before that had convinced God to postpone Armageddon.

The two dominant analytic sequences not only simplify observers' perceptions, they put executives' perceptions at the beginnings of causal sequences and imply that executives' perceptual accuracy strongly influences their organizations' results. For example, nearly all explanations of crisis, disaster, or organizational decline focus on how executives failed to spot major environmental threats or opportunities, failed to heed well-founded warnings, assessed risks improperly, or adhered to outdated goals and beliefs (Dunbar and Goldberg 1978; Mitroff and Kilmann 1984; Starbuck, Greve, and Hedberg 1978). On the other hand, explanations of organizational success generally cite executives' accurate visions, willingness to take wise risks or refusals to take foolish risks, commitments to well-conceived goals, or insightful persistence in the face of adversity (Bennis 1983; Peters and Waterman 1982). In foresight, however, one is hard pressed to distinguish accurate perceivers from inaccurate ones. Examples abound, of course. In 1979, Harding Lawrence, Chairman of the Board of Braniff Airlines, was hailed for 'his aggressive response to deregulation . . . another brilliant, strategic move that should put Braniff in splendid shape for the 80s' (*Business Week*, March 19, 1979); a few years later, industry experts were blaming Braniff's bankruptcy on Lawrence's overly aggressive response to deregulation. In 1972, James Galton, publisher of the Popular Library, told Macmillan that Richard Bach's best-selling novel, '*Jonathan Livingston Seagull* will never make it as a paperback'; Avon Books bought the rights and sold seven million copies in ten years. Immediately after World War II, IBM offered computers for sale, but looked upon this offer as merely a way to publicize the company's participation in an avant-garde wartime project at that time, Chairman of the Board Thomas J. Watson speculated, 'I think there is a world market for about five computers.'

The two dominant kinds of analytic sequences also conform to norms about what ought to happen in a rational world:

> Accurate perceptions ought to go with flawless analyses, and
> flawless analyses ought to lead to correct actions, and
> correct actions ought to yield good results.

This rationalization helps observers to understand their environments and it gives observers the comfort of knowing that their worlds are working as they should work. Unfortunately, such understanding can only exist after results have occurred and the results' goodness or badness clarifies, because good and bad results may arise from very similar processes. For example, executives who insightfully persisted in the face of adversity may also have failed to heed well-founded warnings that nearly came true. Their research led Starbuck, Greve, and Hedberg (1978: 114) to conclude that 'the processes which produce crises are substantially identical to the processes which produce successes'.

Of course, even hindsight usually leaves the past complex and ambiguous. Some results manifest themselves much later than others, and results have numerous dimensions that elicit different evaluations from observers who hold divergent values, so observers disagree about results' goodness and see multiple and inconsistent interpretations of their causes. Retrospection only makes the past clearer than the present or future; it cannot make the past transparent. But the past's clarity is usually artificial enough to mislead people who are living in the present and looking toward the future. In particular, retrospection wrongly implies that errors should have been anticipated and that good perceptions, good analyses, and good decisions will yield good results.

The present is itself substantially indeterminate because people can only apprehend the present by placing it in the context of the past and the future, and vice versa. Imagine, for instance, that this is Thursday, October 24, 1929: Stock prices plummeted today. Is this an exceptional opportunity to buy under-priced stocks that will rebound tomorrow, or does today's drop portend further declines tomorrow? To understand today's prices, one needs a forecast of tomorrow's, and this forecast derives from one's past experiences. But the past has already been reconstructed to fit the present; and as future events unfold, the past will be reconstructed again and again. Not only is the future unclear, it is fundamentally unpredictable. Indeed, a prediction that is 'correct' in the sense that some highly probable events could bring the predicted situation into being may actually invalidate itself by triggering reactions that make the projected events highly improbable. For example, the Club of Rome sponsored a computer-simulation study of the future, titled *The Limits to Growth* (Meadows et al. 1972). This study predicted that if current trends would continue, then before the year 2100 major ecological catastrophes would bring an end to civilization as we know it, because resources are being consumed so rapidly, populations are expanding so rapidly, and ecological problems are escalating. This forecast evoked furor; it alerted people by dramatizing the ecological trends; and it stimulated some immediate, superficial, short-run efforts toward conservation. But the forecast may not have triggered enough fundamental and long-run changes in human behavior to render itself incorrect.

3. PERCEPTUAL FILTERING

One thing an intelligent executive does not need is totally accurate perception. Such perception would have no distortion whatever. Someone who perceived without any distortion would hear background noise as loudly as a voice or music, and so would be unable to use an outdoor telephone booth beside a noisy street, and would be driven crazy by the coughs and chair squeaks at symphony concerts. A completely accurate perceiver might find it so difficult to follow a baseball's path that batting or catching would be out of the question. The processes that amplify some stimuli and attenuate others, thus distorting the raw data and focusing attention, are perceptual filters.

Effective perceptual filtering amplifies relevant information and attenuates irrelevant information, so that the relevant information comes into the perceptual foreground and the irrelevant information recedes into the background. The filtered information is less accurate but, if the filtering is effective, more understandable. People filter information quite instinctively: for example, a basketball player can shoot a foul shot against a turbulent backdrop of shouting people and waving hands, and a telephone user can hear and understand a quiet voice despite interference from street noise that is many times louder.

In complex environments, effective perceptual filtering requires detailed knowledge of the task environment. Systems engineers sometimes try to design filters that minimize the errors in perceived information—errors might include extraneous information, biases, noise, static, or interference between simultaneous messages (Sage 1981). To design an error-minimizing filter for some task, an engineer would make assumptions about the possible sources of stimuli, and would distinguish relevant from irrelevant sources. An error-minimizing filter makes predictions about where errors are going to occur in perception and then either removes these errors or prevents them from occurring. In a task environment as complex as most real-life environments, an error-minimizing filter would incorporate numerous complex assumptions (Ashby 1960), and for the filter actually to minimize perceptual error, these assumptions must be correct.

In real life, people do not know all of the sources of stimuli, nor do they necessarily know how to distinguish relevant from irrelevant information. They must discover the characteristics of sources and tasks experimentally. Some combinations of tasks and task environments occur often enough and with enough consistency that people learn to make useful discriminations. For example, batters can practice tracking baseballs until they develop good models of baseball trajectories and learn to distinguish baseballs from other stimuli. Even though batters may move around from one ballpark to another, they encounter enough consistency that their learning transfers. Batters also see immediate consequences of their actions, so they get prompt feedback concerning the effectiveness of their perceptions.

Executives, by contrast, find it difficult to practice strategizing: Long lags may intervene between executives' actions and the visible outcomes of those actions, and these outcomes have multiple causes; so executives lack clear feedback about the effectiveness of their perceptions and the relevance of information. Constant changes in their environments mean that executives' knowledge grows rapidly obsolete and that they gain few benefits from practice. Executives' experience may even be deceptive. Some research indicates that industries and strategic groups change bimodally: long periods of gradual incremental development get interrupted by occasional bursts of radical change (Astley 1985; Astley and Fombrun

1987; Fombrun and Starbuck 1987; Tushman and Anderson 1986). Therefore, executives' learning mainly occurs during the periods of relative stability, but their strategic skills are mainly tested during the bursts of change. It is during the bursts of change that executives most need to act creatively rather than on the basis of experience, and that perceptual errors may cause the greatest damage.

The theories about effective perceptual filtering assume that it occurs within perceivers, not their environments, and that the unfiltered stimuli are facts. However, perceivers are inseparable from their environments because each depends on the other, and perceptions can either validate or invalidate themselves when people act on their environments (Ittelson, Franck, and O'Hanlon 1976). For example, people in hierarchies pay more attention to messages from their superiors than to ones from their subordinates, so they actually receive more information from their superiors even though more messages originate from their subordinates (Porter and Roberts 1976). Another example was suggested by Hayek (1974), who argued that an emphasis on quantitative measures and mathematical models caused economists to develop mistaken beliefs about macroeconomic systems, and that these erroneous beliefs led them to formulate policies that produced unexpected consequences and actually made the macro-economic systems less manageable and less self-correcting. In particular, at one time, economists generally taught that inflation and unemployment worked against each other: an economic policy could achieve full employment only if it suffered some inflation, or it could suppress inflation by maintaining a high level of unemployment. In the 1960s, economists moved into governmental policy-making positions and began creating institutions that were designed to control inflation while minimizing unemployment. One result, said Hayek, was an economy in which unemployment rises whenever inflation stops accelerating.

Perceivers who act on their environments need perceptual filters that take account of the malleability of task environments. Perceptual errors have smaller consequences in environments that resist change, and larger consequences in more malleable environments. But errors may yield benefits as well as costs—as when faulty perceptions lead people to pursue energetically goals that would look much less attainable if assessed in utter objectivity, but the pursuers' enthusiasm, effort, and self-confidence bring success. Brunsson pointed out that actions are more likely to succeed if they are supported by strong commitments, firm expectations, and high motivation. He (1985: 27) said:

Organizations have two problems: to choose the right thing to do, and to get it done. There are two kinds of rationality corresponding to the two problems: decision rationality and action rationality. Neither is superior to the other, but they serve different purposes and are based on different norms. The two kinds of rationality are difficult to pursue simultaneously, because rational decision-making procedures are irrational in an action perspective. They should be avoided if action is to be more easily achieved.

It is generally impossible to decide, at the time of perception, whether perceptions will prove accurate or inaccurate, correct or incorrect, because perceptions are partly predictions that may change reality, because different perceptions may lead to similar actions, and because similar perceptions may lead to different actions. Many perceptual errors, perhaps the great majority, become erroneous only in retrospect. Even disagreement among people who are supposedly looking at a shared situation does not indicate that any of these divergent perceptions must be wrong. People may operate very effectively even though they characterize a shared situation quite differently, and people's unique backgrounds may reveal to them distinct, but nevertheless accurate and valid, aspects of a complex reality.

Trying to learn from past errors oversimplifies the complexity and ambiguity of the task environments that people once faced, and it assumes that the future will closely resemble the past. Furthermore, although in the present people can distinguish their perceptions from the alternative actions they are considering, people looking at the past find such distinctions very difficult because they revise their perceptions to fit the actions that actually occurred (Loftus 1979; Neisser 1981). Therefore, it makes sense to de-emphasize errors and to analyze perception in a nonjudgmental, nonaccusatory framework. One way to do this is to emphasize filtering processes.

Table 9.1 identifies some filtering processes that may be important in understanding environmental scanning and strategy formulation (McArthur 1981; Taylor and Crocker 1981). All of these filtering processes distort the raw data that executives could perceive: In some situations, these distortions enable executives to operate more effectively in their environments by focusing attention on important, relevant stimuli; whereas in other situations, these same distortions make executives operate less effectively by focusing attention on unimportant, irrelevant stimuli. Further, these types of filtering may persist over time and so characterize organizations or individual executives.

4. INFLUENCES UPON FILTERING PROCESSES

Executives who work in the same organization frequently disagree about the characteristics of that organization, and executives whose firms compete in the same industry may disagree strongly about the characteristics of that industry (Downey, Hellriegel, and Slocum 1977; Duncan 1972; Payne and Pugh 1976; Starbuck 1976). The stimuli that one executive receives may be precisely the same stimuli that another executive filters out. Furthermore, executives who notice the same stimuli may use different frameworks to interpret these stimuli and therefore disagree about meanings or causes or effects. Understanding how organizational and individual characteristics influence executives' filtering processes may both help executives themselves to behave more effectively and help researchers to predict the types of filtering processes that executives use (Jervis 1976).

The analyses to follow divide perception into noticing and sense-making. This is admittedly a difficult distinction in practice because people notice stimuli and make sense of them at the same time, and each of these activities depends upon the other. For instance, what people notice becomes input to their sense-making,

Table 9.1. Types of perceptual filtering

Distortions in noticing (where to look and what to see)

Paying too much or too little attention to stimuli with certain properties

    stimuli in certain environmental domains

    changes or regularities

    familiar or unusual stimuli

    expected or unexpected stimuli

    desirable or undesirable stimuli

    dramatic or undramatic stimuli

Letting some stimuli draw too much attention to themselves, and other stimuli evade attention

Distortions in sense-making (what it means)

Distortions in framing

    Perceiving or classifying events in the wrong frameworks (schemata)

    Applying existing frameworks in radically novel situations

    Perceiving illusory stimuli that fit evoked frameworks, or ignoring stimuli that violate evoked frameworks

    Assigning high credibility to stimuli that fit evoked frameworks, and discounting stimuli that violate evoked frameworks

    Assigning importance to covariations that fit evoked frameworks, and discounting covariations that violate evoked frameworks

Distortions in predicting

    Forming expectations by applying the wrong frameworks (schemata)

    Amplifying good events and attenuating bad events

        Underestimating or not seeing serious, imminent threats

        Overestimating insignificant, remote, or doubtful opportunities

    Amplifying bad events and attenuating good events

        Underestimating or not seeing significant, immediate opportunities

        Overestimating minor, very distant, or improbable threats

    Underestimating or overestimating

        the effects of environmental changes

        the ranges of environmental events likely to occur

        the ranges of probable outcomes from proposed actions, policies, or strategies

        risks associated with proposed actions, policies, or strategies

Distortions in causal attributions

    Making attributions by applying the wrong frameworks (schemata)

    Attributing outcomes produced by many causes to only a few causes, or vice versa

    Amplifying or attenuating the influence of

        environmental causes

        an organization's actions

        executives' actions

    Failing to notice or allow for

        contingency variables

        feedback loops

    Perceiving uncontrollable events as controllable, or vice versa

---

and in turn, the sense that people have made appears to influence what the people notice (Goleman 1985). Noticing involves a rudimentary form of sense-making in that noticing requires distinguishing signal from noise, making crude separations of relevant from irrelevant. Similarly, sense-making involves a form of noticing when a perceiver reclassifies remembered signal as noise, or remembered noise as signal, in order to fit a new interpretive framework.

Nevertheless, like others (Daft and Weick 1984; Kiesler and Sproull 1982), we believe a distinction between noticing and sense-making sometimes exists and has theoretical value. For example, Daft and Weick (1984) distinguished scanning, a process that collects data, from interpretation, a process that gives meaning to data. Thus, Daft and Weick's scanning corresponds to noticing, and their interpretation corresponds to sense-making. We prefer the term noticing to scanning on the ground that scanning seems to imply formal and voluntary actions, whereas noticing may be quite informal and involuntary; and we prefer the term sense-making to interpretation because sense-making seems more self-explanatory.

Noticing: Where to Look and What to See

> The range of what we think and do
> is limited by what we fail to notice.
> And because we fail to notice
> *that* we fail to notice
> there is little we can do
> to change
> until we notice
> how failing to notice
> shapes our thoughts and deeds.
> —R. D. Laing (Goleman 1985: 24)

Noticing is an act of classifying stimuli as signals or noise. Noticing results from interactions of the characteristics of stimuli with the characteristics of perceivers. In particular, some stimuli are more available or more likely to attract attention than others (McArthur 1981; Taylor and Crocker 1981; Tversky and Kahneman 1974). However, the characteristics of perceivers, including their current activities, strongly affect both the availabilities of stimuli and the abilities of stimuli to attract attention (Wohlwill and Kohn 1976); even colorful or loud stimuli may be overlooked if people are used to them or are concentrating on critical tasks, and novel events or sudden changes may remain unseen if people are looking elsewhere. Furthermore, executives tend to have more control over their own behaviors than over the stimuli that interest them most. Therefore, we emphasize the characteristics of perceivers, either as individuals or as members of organizations, more than the characteristics of stimuli. Noticing is influenced by perceivers' habits, their beliefs about what is, and their beliefs about what ought to be.

People classify stimuli by comparing them either to other immediately available stimuli or to standards arising from their experiences and expectations. Psychologists call the smallest differences that people can detect reliably 'just-noticeable differences', and they have devoted extensive research to ascertaining just-noticeable differences in laboratory settings.

In the 1830s, E. H. Weber studied people's abilities to identify the heavier of two weights, and posited that just-noticeable differences are approximately constant percentages of the absolute magnitudes of stimuli. By this hypothesis, a just-noticeable difference in wealth, for example, would be some percentage of a person's wealth, so a rich person would be much less likely to notice a $1 difference in wealth than a poor person. Studies indicate that Weber's hypothesis seems to describe hearing and vision accurately over a wide range of stimuli, but it describes touch, smell, and taste less accurately (Luce and Galanter 1963). It does, nonetheless, suggest some ideas about executives' perceptions. For instance, an executive in a volatile industry might be less likely to notice absolutely small changes in prices or sales volumes than an executive in a stable industry. Similarly, an executive in a small firm might tend to be more sensitive to the needs of an individual employee than an executive in a large firm.

Psychologists' studies of just-noticeable differences measure what people can perceive under controlled conditions, and these studies emphasize comparisons between simultaneous or nearly simultaneous stimuli. In real life, people not only compare stimuli to standards arising from nearly simultaneous stimuli, they also compare stimuli to standards evolved over long periods, and to models and enduring expectations about their environments. Furthermore, a yes-no characterization of noticing seems to misrepresent its subtlety and continuity. If need be, people can often recall stimuli that they had been unaware that they had noticed or that they had classified as background noise; this recall suggests that people perceive unconsciously or subliminally as well as consciously. You may, for instance, have had the experience of hearing a question but not quite hearing it, so you ask the questioner to repeat her question; but before she does so, you suddenly realize that you know the question and you answer it.

Bargh (1982) pointed out that people seem to have two modes of noticing, one of them controlled and volitional, and one automatic and involuntary. Although the two modes interact on occasion, they operate independently of each other most of the time. Bargh observed that people who are fully absorbed in performing tasks nevertheless notice it when someone speaks their names. Nielsen and Sarason (1981) found that someone can virtually always capture another person's attention by speaking sexually explicit words.

The standards that determine what people notice in real-life seem to be of several not-entirely-distinct types: People notice familiar and unfamiliar stimuli, as well as what they believe to be relevant, important, significant, desirable, or evil.

Looking for the Familiar or Overlooking the Familiar

Helson (1964) observed that perceptual thresholds reflect experience, but that adaptation both sensitizes and desensitizes. On the one hand, people grow less sensitive to stimuli as these stimuli become more familiar. For example, an executive who moves into a new industry would initially notice numerous phenomena, but many of these would fade into the background as the industry becomes more familiar. On the other hand, some sensory functions improve with practice (Gibson 1953), and as people become more familiar with a domain of activity, they grow more sensitive to subtle changes within that domain (Schroder, Driver, and Streufert 1967). Thus, an executive who moves into a new industry would initially overlook some phenomena that seem unimportant, but would gradually learn to notice those phenomena as experience clarifies their significance. Although these two processes produce opposite effects that may, in fact, counteract each other, they generally interact as complements: decreasing sensitivity pushes some stimuli into the background, while increasing sensitivity brings other stimuli to the foreground.

Helson studied the relative effects of foreground and background events on what it is that people do not notice. He (1964) argued that experience produces standards for distinguishing or evaluating stimuli, and he called these standards 'adaptation levels'. People do not notice the stimuli that resemble adaptation levels, or they act as if they are indifferent to such stimuli. In studies of vision and weight-sensing, Helson found that the adaptation level associated with a sequence of alternating stimuli resembles an average in which the foreground stimuli receive around three times the weight of the interspersed background stimuli, implying that foreground events actually exert much more influence on not-noticing than background events do. Nonsimultaneity evidently helps perceivers to concentrate on foreground events and to de-emphasize background events in cognition. On the other hand, Helson's experiments showed that the adaptation level associated with a combination of simultaneous stimuli resembles an average in which the background stimuli have around three times the weight of the foreground stimuli, implying that simultaneous background events actually exert much more influence on not-noticing than foreground events do. Simultaneous background events impede perceivers' abilities to concentrate on foreground events, and so the background events gain influence in cognition; where background events greatly outnumber foreground events, as in an ordinary photograph, the background events dominate the adaptations that determine not-noticing. An extrapolation might be that general, societal events (occurring simultaneously with events in executives' task environments) affect the executives' expectations about what is normal and unremarkable more strongly than do the specific, immediate events in their task environments.

Because simultaneous background stimuli strongly influence what people do not notice, people tend not to notice them. In particular, people tend to notice subtle changes in foreground stimuli while overlooking substantial changes in background stimuli, and so background stimuli may have to change dramatically to attract notice (McArthur 1981; Normann 1971). One reason is that familiarity enables people to develop programs and habits for noticing foreground stimuli, whereas they attend less systematically and consistently to background stimuli. Like experience, moreover, programs and habits may have complementary effects, in that they may also deaden sensitivity and convert foreground events into background events (Tuchman 1973). Programs and habits make noticing less reflective, and by routinizing it, inject extraneous detail.

Lyles and Mitroff (1980: 116) found that 'managers become aware of significant problems through informal sensing techniques'; they surmised that either 'the formal reporting systems do not identify the relevant indicators or, more possibly, ... managers tend to ignore the indicators when they are formally reported'. Formalized information systems often try to make up for inflexibility by providing extensive detail, so they bog down in detail and operate slowly: Irrelevant detail becomes noise, and slow processing makes the data outdated. For instance, in the late 1950s, executives in the Tar Products Division of the Koppers Company decided that computers could provide inputs to operating decisions, so they purchased a computer-based system that produced weekly and monthly reports of the plants' daily inventories and outputs. The collected data were voluminous but riddled with large errors, both unintentional data-entry errors and intentional misrepresentations of the plants' situations. But personnel at divisional headquarters remained quite unaware of these errors because they paid almost no attention to the computer-generated reports. The headquarters personnel in production scheduling could not wait for the computer-generated data, so they maintained daily contact with the plants by telephone; the headquarters personnel in purchasing and sales looked mainly at annual totals because they bought and sold through annual or longer contracts.

Successful experience may tend to make foregrounds smaller and backgrounds larger. For instance, IBM, which dominated the mainframe computer business, virtually ignored the initial developments of minicomputers, microcomputers, and supercomputers; these developments were obviously foreground events for Digital Equipment, Apple, and Cray. Success gives individual people and organizations the confidence to build upon their experience by creating buffers that insulate them from environmental variations, and programs that automate and standardize their responses to environmental events. The buffers and programs identify certain stimuli as foreground events and they exclude other stimuli from consideration. Starbuck (1976: 1081) observed: 'organizations tend to crystallize and preserve their existing states of knowledge whenever they set up systems to routinely collect, aggregate, and analyze information, whenever they identify and allocate areas of responsibility, whenever they hire people who possess particular skills and experiences, and whenever they plan long-range strategies and invest in capital goods'. Thus, organizational scanning systems formalize their members' beliefs and expectations as procedures and structures that may be difficult to change.

However, like sexually explicit words, social and technological changes may make themselves difficult to ignore: IBM did eventually enter the minicomputer and microcomputer businesses.

Looking for What Matters

People also define foregrounds and backgrounds on the basis of their definitions of what phenomena are relevant, important, insignificant, desirable, or evil (Goleman 1985). For instance, in recent years, two amateur astronomers, one

Australian and one Japanese, who specialized in this activity, have spotted a great majority of the known comets; presumably professional astronomers assign lower value to comet spotting in comparison to alternative uses of their time. Rosenhan (1978) remarked that the staff members in psychiatric hospitals tend not to notice that patients are in fact behaving normally; possibly these staff members would notice the normal behaviors if they saw them outside of the hospital context.

Weick (1979) pointed out that people 'enact' their environments; by this, he meant that people's beliefs and expectations define what they regard as relevant, and so beliefs and expectations define what parts of task environments draw people's notice. Deciding that certain markets and prices are worth scanning, executives may assign subordinates to monitor these markets and prices, thereby making them part of their organization's foreground. But no organization can afford to monitor everything, so by not assigning subordinates to monitor other markets and prices, the executives are implicitly defining a background (Normann 1971). For example, Mitroff and Kilmann (1984) argued that business firms overlook saboteurs, terrorists, and other 'bizarre characters' in their environments because managers find it 'unthinkable' that anyone might commit sabotage or terrorism against their firms. Another example occurred at the Facit company, a manufacturer of mechanical calculators: When Facit's top managers wanted to assess the threat posed by electronic calculators, they instructed their salesmen to interview Facit's customers about their attitudes toward this new technology: The salesmen continued to report that Facit's customers almost unanimously preferred mechanical to electronic calculators even while the number of customers was plummeting.

Executives' values about how their businesses should be run also influence their definitions of foregrounds and backgrounds. Donaldson and Lorsch (1983) for instance, commented that executives' values about organizational self-sufficiency seem to influence their organizations' actions; in particular, CEOs who believe that long-term debt indicates inadequate self-sufficiency tend to avoid strategies that require borrowing. One reason executives' values have such effects on actions is that they influence what the executives and their organizations notice. Thus, executives who believe in the no-debt principle are likely to relegate potential lenders and financial markets to the background, and so remain uninformed about available loan terms or changes in interest rates.

The influence of executives' definitions of what matters may gain strength through the uncoupling of executives' decisions about what to observe from their subordinates' acts of perception. This uncoupling and the asymmetry of hierarchical communications impair feedback, and so executives' perceptions adapt sluggishly to the actual observations made by their subordinates. Organizations encourage the creation of formalized scanning programs; they assign specialists to monitor foreground events, and they discourage subordinates from reporting observations that fall outside their assigned responsibilities. Even when subordinates do notice events that have been formally classified as background, they tend not to report these upward, and superiors tend to ignore their subordinates' messages (Dunbar and Goldberg 1978; O'Reilly 1983; Porter and Roberts 1976). For instance, on the morning of the Challenger disaster, a crew was dispatched to inspect ice formation on the shuttle and launch pad: The crew noticed very low temperatures on the solid rocket boosters, but this observation was not relevant to their assignment, so they did not report it (Presidential Commission 1986).

Sense-Making: What it Means

'On the day following the 1956 election in which a Republican President and Democratic Congress were elected, two colleagues remarked to me that the voters were becoming more discriminating in splitting their ballots. But the two individuals did not mean the same thing by the remark, for one was a staunch Republican and the other a strong Democrat. The first referred with satisfaction to the election of a Republican President; and the second approved the election of a Democratic Congress.'

—Harry Helson (1964: 36)

Daft and Weick (1984: 286) remarked: 'Managers . . . must wade into the ocean of events that surround the organization and actively try to make sense of them.' Sense-making has many distinct aspects—comprehending, understanding, explaining, attributing, extrapolating, and predicting, at least. For example, understanding seems to precede explaining and to require less input; predicting may occur without either understanding or explaining; attributing is a form of explanation that assigns causes. Yet, concrete examples seem to illustrate the commonalities and interdependencies among these processes more than their differences.

What is common to these processes is that they involve placing stimuli into frameworks (or schemata) that make sense of the stimuli (Goleman 1985). Some sense-making frameworks seem to be simple and others complex; some appear to describe static states of affairs and others sequential procedures; some seem to delineate the boundaries between categories and others to describe central tendencies within categories; some seem more general and others more specific; some appear more abstract and others more concrete (Dutton and Jackson 1987; Hastie 1981). These sense-making frameworks, like the frameworks for noticing, reflect habits, beliefs about what is, and beliefs about what ought to be.

Perceptual frameworks categorize data, assign likelihoods to data, hide data, and fill in missing data (Taylor and Crocker 1981). At the least frameworks often imply that certain data ought to exist or ought not to exist. Sherlock Holmes was, of course, remarkable for his ability to draw elaborate inferences from a few, seemingly trivial and incongruous clues. Nonfictional people, however, should contemplate the probabilities that the filled-in data may actually exist but not be seen until sought, or they may be seen in fantasy but not actually exist, or they may not actually exist until sought. Errors seen in retrospect often exemplify the latter. For instance, the faults in the space shuttle's solid-rocket booster were only a few of multitude design characteristics. Before January 28, 1986, NASA had classified some of these design characteristics as not dangerous and others as dangerous; dangerous characteristics were not errors, however. The investigation of the disaster categorized a few of these design characteristics as errors, but doing so involved making some tests and ruling out some alternatives.

Similarly, nonfictional people should allow for the probabilities that existing data may not be taken into account because they violate perceptual frameworks or may be distorted badly to make them fit perceptual frameworks. In March 1961, shortly before the U.S. Central Intelligence Agency launched an invasion of the Bay of Pigs, the CIA private internal reports stated: 'Many people in Camaguey believe that the Castro regime is tottering and that the situation can at any moment degenerate into bloody anarchy' (Report CS-3/457: 630). 'It is generally believed that the Cuban Army has been successfully penetrated by opposition groups and that it will not fight in the event of a showdown' (Report CS-3/470: 587).

In spite of their propensities for seeing what ought to exist, people do some-times strive to see beyond their blind spots. They get opportunities to discover their blind spots when they observe incongruous events that do not make sense within their perceptual frameworks (McCall 1977). Management-by-exception is an action strategy that depends on spotting situations in which current events are diverging from familiar patterns. Such observations may be either very disorient-ing or very revealing, or both. Incongruous events are disorienting as long as they make no sense, and they become revealing when they induce perceivers to adopt new frameworks that render them explicable. For instance, Starbuck (1989) and his colleagues set out to discover the abnormalities that cause a few organizations to run into serious, existence-threatening crises. But the researchers were inun-dated with examples, and so it gradually dawned on them that they were seeing normality because crises are common. Facing this incongruity brought the researchers to see that the causes of crises are essentially the same as the causes of success.

Watzlawick, Weakland, and Fisch (1974) said that all perceptual frameworks have blind spots that prevent people from solving some problems and that link behaviors into self-reinforcing cycles (Goleman 1985; Masuch 1985). To solve problems that blind spots have made unsolvable, people need new perceptual frameworks that portray the problematic situations differently. Watzlawick, Weakland, and Fisch proposed four basic strategies for reframing such problem-atic situations: (*a*) redefine undesirable elements to make them appear desirable, or vice versa; (*b*) relabel elements so that they acquire new meanings; (*c*) ignore elements that you cannot change; and (*d*) try overtly to achieve the opposite of what you want. For example, a man with a bad stammer had to work as a salesman, but this role heightened his worries about his speech defect and so made it worse. His psychotherapists advised him that potential customers gen-erally distrust salesmen precisely because of their slick and clever spiels that go on insistently, whereas people listen carefully and patiently to someone with a speech handicap. Had he considered what an incredible advantage he actually had over other salesmen? Perhaps, they suggested, he should try to maintain a high level of stammering even after experience made him feel more at ease and his propensity to stammer abated.

Framing Within the Familiar

Normann (1971) pointed out that people in organizations can understand and readily respond to events in the domains with which they interact frequently, but that they are likely to misapprehend events in unfamiliar domains, or to have difficulty generating responses to them. Different parts of organizations are familiar with different domains, and these domains both shape and reflect organizations' political systems and task divisions: Hierarchical, functional, geographic, and product differentiations affect the ways people interpret events, and these differentials foster political struggles that interact with strategic choices and designs for organizational perception systems (Dearborn and Simon 1958).

For instance, people with expertise in newer tasks tend to appear at the bottoms of hierarchies and to interpret events in terms of these newer tasks, and they welcome changes that will offer them promotion opportunities and bring their expertise to the fore. Conversely, people at the tops of organizational hierarchies tend to have expertise related to older and more stable tasks, they are prone to interpret events in terms of these tasks, and they favor strategies and personnel assignments that will keep these tasks central (Starbuck 1983). Some research also suggests that people at the tops of organizational hierarchies tend to have simpler perceptual frameworks than their subordinates. One reason is that top executives have to span several domains of expertise, each of which looks complex to specialists (Schroder, Driver, and Streufert 1967). Another reason is that top executives receive so much information from so many sources that they experience overloads (Ackoff 1967; Hedberg 1981). A third reason is that top executives receive much of their information through intermediaries, who filter it (Starbuck 1985). Still another reason is that their spokesperson roles force top executives to put ideas and relationships into simply expressed terms (Axelrod 1976; Hart 1976, 1977).

Repeated successes or failures lead people to discount accidents as explanations, to look for explicit causes, and eventually to expect the successes or failures to continue. Repeated failures may lead people to view themselves as having weak influence over events and to blame the failures on external causes such as bosses, enemies, strangers, foreign competition, economic cycles, or technological trends (Langer and Roth 1975). By contrast, repeated successes may cause people to see themselves or their close associates as having strong influence on events. NASA, for instance, experienced many years of successes in meeting technological challenges. It would appear that this made people at NASA grow confident that they could routinely overcome nearly insurmountable technological hurdles. They became used to the technologies with which they were working, and they gradually grew more complacent about technological problems as more flights worked out well. Thus, the NASA personnel came to see the space shuttle as an 'operational' technology, meaning that it was safe enough to carry ordinary citizens such as Senators and school teachers.

Framing Within the Expected

Expectations may come from extrapolating past events into the future. In a world that changes slowly and in which everyone else is deriving their expectations incrementally and so behaving incrementally, most of the time it is useful to formulate expectations incrementally oneself. It also appears that simple extrapolations generally work better than complex ones. Makridakis and Hibon (1979) tested 22 mechanistic forecasting techniques on 111 economic and business time series. They found that simple rules do surprisingly well in comparison to complex rules, and in particular, that the no-change rule

$$\text{next period} = \text{this period}$$

provides excellent forecasts. Another effective forecasting rule is a weighted average in which more recent events receive more weight. Simple rules extrapolate well because they 'hedge' forecasts towards recent experience and therefore they make fewer large errors. Complex forecasting rules amplify short-term fluctuations when they project and thus make large errors more often.

Because extrapolations normally deviate no more than incrementally from experience, they set up past-oriented perceptual frameworks that do not encourage innovation. Expectations, however, may also come from models and general orientations that are transmitted through socialization, communication, or education; and the expectations that come from transmitted models may differ radically from experience. For example, members of the religious cult observed by Festinger, Riecken, and Schachter (1956) obviously had no experience indicating that they would be carried off in a spaceship before the world came to an end at midnight. Thus, transmitted models have the capacity to generate expectations that correspond to other people's experiences, that encourage innovation, that enable people to see problems from new perspectives, or that interrupt cycles of self-reinforcing behaviors. Unfortunately, transmitted models may be difficult to disconfirm. During World War II, the Germans developed a secret code that they believed to be unbreakable (Winterbotham 1975); but the Allies broke the code early in the war, with the result that the Allied commanders often knew of the Germans' plans even before the German field commanders heard them. The Germans never did discover that their code had been broken, partly because the Germans believed so strongly in their cryptographers, and partly because the Allies were careful to provide false explanations for their successes.

Stereotypes are categorical expectations, or central-tendency schemata. People transmit stereotypes to one another, and labels enable people to evoke stereotypes for one another; so to facilitate communication, organizations tend to foster labeling and to make labels more definitive. A stereotype may embody useful information that helps a person decide how to behave in new situations or with new people; an effective stereotype enables a person to act more appropriately than if the person had no information. On the other hand, a stereotype may caricature situations or people and become a self-fulfilling prophecy (Danet

1981). At best, a stereotype describes the central tendency of a group of situations or a group of people, and specific instances deviate from this central tendency.

Fredrickson (1985) investigated the degrees to which the labels 'problem' or 'opportunity' may represent shared schemata. In strategic-management courses, he presented two strategy cases to MBA students and to upper-middle-level executives; the cases sometimes labeled the described situations as problems and other times as opportunities. He found that the labels correlated with differences in the problem-solving processes recommended by MBA students, but not by the executives. Fredrickson traced these differences to the MBA students' extensive experience with teaching cases, as compared to the executives' relative inexperience with them. It might appear that the strategic-management courses had taught the MBA students that these two labels denote stereotypes, but that executives at large had not been influenced strongly by the courses, do not hold these stereotypes, and do not assign these labels shared meanings. However, Jackson and Dutton (1987) found evidence that the labels 'threats' and 'opportunities' do evoke shared schemata among executives. Jackson and Dutton asked participants in an executive-development program to think of experiences that they would classify as opportunities or as threats, and then to characterize these experiences in terms of fifty-five attributes. The participants tended to agree that opportunities and threats differ in at least three attributes: opportunities are positive and controllable, and they offer possible gains; whereas threats are negative and uncontrollable, and they portend possible losses. The participants also perceived opportunities and threats to have seven attributes in common, including pressure to act, urgency, difficulty, and importance. Thus, problems, threats, and opportunities may possess more attributes that are similar than attributes that are different. Jackson and Dutton (1987: 34) observed: 'These simple labels do not have simple meanings.'

Fredrickson's study suggests that labeling a situation as a problem or threat might have no discernible effects on the way an executive perceives it; but Jackson and Dutton's study suggests that labeling a situation as an opportunity might lead an executive to perceive it as more controllable and to notice its positive aspects, whereas labeling the situation as a threat might cause the executive to see its negative potentials and uncontrollable elements. However, both Fredrickson and Jackson and Dutton imposed labels on the participants in their studies, the participants did not choose or generate these labels themselves, so these studies say nothing about how often executives use various labels spontaneously. Kepner and Tregoe (1965) observed managers who participated in training programs to improve group problem-solving skills. They noted that managers use the label 'problem' to denote: (*a*) evidence that events differ from what is desired, (*b*) events that cause discomfort or require effort, (*c*) conjectures about why events differ from what is desired, (*d*) possible sources of events that cause discomfort, and (*e*) actions that ought to be taken. Managers also use this label interchangeably with other labels such as 'issue', 'question', 'trouble', and 'situation'. Kepner and Tregoe concluded that the differing labels and the differing meanings of these labels engender a lot of confusion, misdirected disagreement, and wasted talk (Maier 1963; Starbuck 1983). One implication might be that, expecting labels to be used inconsistently, executives treat them as ambiguous; another implication might be that by developing shared stereotypes, organizations would improve group problem-solving.

Rotter related controllability itself to noticing and sense-making. After reviewing various studies, he (1966: 25) concluded that

the individual who has a strong belief that he can control his own destiny is likely to ... be more alert to those aspects of his environment which provide useful information for his behavior ... and [to] place greater value on skill or achievement reinforcements and [to] be generally more concerned with his ability, particularly his failures.

Rotter defined locus of control as 'a generalized expectancy' about who or what controls rewards and punishments; supposedly, a person with an internal locus of control sees herself as exerting strong influence over outcomes, whereas one with an external locus believes she has weak influence. As one driver reported to an insurance company, 'The telephone pole was approaching. I was attempting to swerve out of its way when it struck my front end.' However, research indicates that the behavioral consistencies associated with generalized personal characteristics, such as locus of control or dogmatism or cognitive complexity, are much smaller than the behavioral variations associated with different situations (Barker 1968; Goldstein and Blackman 1978; Mischel 1968).

Framing Within What Matters

'... a nuclear war could alleviate some of the factors leading to today's ecological disturbances that are due to current high-population concentrations and heavy industrial production.'
—Official of the U.S. Office of Civil Defense (Schell 1982: 7)

Beliefs about 'what matters' not only define what phenomena are relevant, important, insignificant, desirable, or evil, they also influence sense-making by determining the frames of reference that give meaning to phenomena (Jervis 1976). These beliefs include both generalized images of how the world should be and more specific ideas about what should be organizations' missions, structures, and strategies. For example, CEOs who believe that long-term debt indicates inadequate self-sufficiency may also tend to see borrowing as risky and burdensome, debt as constraining, and lenders as controlling (Donaldson and Lorsch 1983). Similarly, in 1962, Joseph F. Cullman III, the President of Philip Morris, advised his company's stockholders that 'There is growing evidence that smoking has pharmacological ... effects that are of real value to smokers'.

Because values and norms differ considerably from one arena to another, perceivers may discover that the beliefs that guided them well in one arena take them astray in another. In 1985, for instance, the U.S. Department of Justice indicted General Dynamics Corporation and several of its current and former top executives. The prosecutors charged that one of General Dynamics' defense contracts required it to absorb costs above a $39 million ceiling, but the company had fraudulently charged $3 million of the work on that project to two other contracts, one for general research and development and one for the preparation of bids and proposals. Eighteen months later, the Department of Justice withdrew these charges and explained that the contract in question was far more flexible than the prosecutors had originally surmised; in particular, the contract did allow General Dynamics to charge additional costs to other defense contracts. Evidently, the actual words of the contract were not at issue. Rather, the prosecutors had originally assumed that the contract provisions meant what they would mean outside the context of defense contracting, but the prosecutors later discovered that the language of defense contracts often appears to say something other than what it actually says. Thus, even though this contract appeared to set a ceiling on costs, both General Dynamics and the U.S. Department of Defense understood that costs above this ceiling would be paid through other channels.

Jönsson and Lundin (1977) found that organizational sense-making frameworks evolve cyclically. They observed that Swedish industrial-development companies went through waves of enthusiasm that were punctuated by intermittent crises. Each wave was associated with a shared myth, or key idea, that appeared as the solution to a preceding crisis. A new myth would attract adherents, filter perceptions, guide expectations, provide rationalizations, and engender enthusiasm and wishful thinking; vigorous action would occur. But eventually, new problems would be seen arising, enthusiasm for the prevailing myth would wane, and alternative 'ghost' myths would appear as explanations for what was wrong. As alternative perceptual frameworks, these ghost myths would highlight anomalies connected with the prevailing myth, cast doubt upon its relevance, and so accelerate unlearning of it. When enough anomalies accumulated, organization members would discard the prevailing myth and espouse one of the ghost myths.

5. LIVING WITH COMPLEXITY

A focus on filtering processes makes it clear that the past, present, and future intertwine inseparably. Familiar events, expectations, and beliefs about what matters form overlapping categories that cannot be cleanly distinguished from one another. Expectations about the future, for instance, grow out of past experience and simultaneously express models that verge very close to wishful thinking, these expectations also lead people to edit their past experience and to espouse goals that look feasible. Such complexity matches the worlds in which people live. Simon (1957: 20) pointed out that 'principles of administration... [are] like proverbs, they occur in pairs. For almost every principle one can find an equally plausible and contradictory principle.' For instance, the injunction to minimize spans of control runs up against the injunction to minimize the number of hierarchical levels. Simon pointed out that if one tries to render one of these injunctions more valid by narrowing its scope, the injunction no longer solves so many problems. Hewitt and Hall (1973) remarked that societies offer numerous 'quasi-theories', which are widely accepted recipes that can explain observed events and that apply to very diverse situations. For example, the quasi-theory of time claims that events can be expected to occur at certain times, and so an occurrence can be explained by saying that its time has come, or a nonoccurrence can be explained by saying that its time has not yet come. Edelman (1977: 5) argued that:

In every culture people learn to explain chronic problems through alternative sets of assumptions that are inconsistent with one another; yet the contradictory formulas persist, rationalizing inconsistent public policies and inconsistent individual beliefs about the threats that are widely feared in everyday life.

He illustrated this point by asserting that everyone, whether poor or affluent, learns two contrasting characterizations of the poor, one as victims of exploitative institutions and one as independent actors responsible for their own plight and in need of control to compensate for their inadequacies. Westerlund and Sjöstrand (1979) identified numerous myths that organizations sometimes bring forth to frame problem analyses. Most of these myths occur in mutually contradictory pairs. For example, the myth of organizational limitations states that an organization has boundaries that circumscribe its abilities; but this myth contradicts the one of the unlimited environment, which claims that the organization's environment offers innumerable opportunities. Similarly, the fairy tale of optimization convinces organization members of their competence by asserting that the organization is acting optimally; but it contradicts the fairy tale of satisfaction, which says that satisfactory performances are good enough.

Fombrun and Starbuck (1987) explained that such contradictions are so prevalent because processes affecting social systems inevitably call forth antithetical processes having opposing effects. For instance, laws forbidding certain businesses make it highly profitable to engage in these businesses illegally, so law enforcement unintentionally fosters criminality. One ubiquitous antithetical effect is that the handicaps of individuals motivate the creation of compensating social supports, and another prevalent antithetical effect is that organizations' strategic choices create opportunities for their competitors. Antithetical processes mean that social systems tend to remain stable, complex, and ambiguous. A process that tends to displace a social system from its current state gets offset by processes that tend to restore that current state; a process that tends to eliminate some characteristics gets offset by processes that tend to preserve the existing characteristics or to add new ones; and so the social system remains a complex mixture.

Facing such a world, realistic people have to have numerous sense-making frameworks that contradict each other. These numerous frameworks create plentiful interpretive opportunities—if an initial framework fails, one can try its equally plausible converse, or try a framework that emphasizes different elements. Thus, meanings are generally cheap and easily found, except when people confront major tragedies such as divorces or the deaths of loved ones... and even these often become 'growth experiences'. People have confidence that they can eventually make sense of almost any situation because they can.

Of course, some sense-making frameworks lead to more effective behaviors than others do, but the criteria of effectiveness are many and inconsistent, and perceivers usually can appraise effectiveness only in retrospect. The most accurate perceivers may be either ones who change their minds readily or ones who believe strongly enough to enact their beliefs, and the happiest perceivers may be the least accurate ones. The ambiguity and complexity of their worlds imply that perceivers may benefit by using multiple sense-making frameworks to appraise events; but perceivers are more likely to act forcefully and effectively if they see things simply, and multiple frameworks may undermine organizations' political structures (Brunsson 1985; Wildavsky 1972). Malleable worlds imply that perceivers may benefit by using frameworks that disclose opportunities to exert influence, but people who try to change their worlds often produce unintended results, even the opposite of what they intended. Perceivers who understand themselves and their environments should appreciate sense-making frameworks that recognize the inevitability of distortions and that foster beneficial distortions, but such wise people should also doubt that they actually know what is good for themselves, and they should recognize that the most beneficial errors are often the most surprising ones. Fortunately, people seem to have a good deal of latitude for discretion. People investigate hypotheses from the viewpoint that they are correct and as long as results can be interpreted within current frameworks, the frameworks need not change, or even be evaluated (Snyder 1981). Further, sense-making may or may not determine whether people respond appropriately to environmental events: sometimes people act first and then later make sense of the outcomes (Starbuck 1983; Weick 1983).

Because sense-making is so elusive, noticing may be at least as important as sense-making. Perhaps sense-making and noticing interact as complements in effective problem-solving: sense-making focuses on subtleties and interdependencies, whereas noticing picks up major events and gross trends. Noticing determines whether people even consider responding to environmental events. If events are noticed, people make sense of them; and if events are not noticed, they are not available for sense-making. Thus, it makes a great difference how foregrounds, backgrounds, and adaptation levels adjust to current stimuli and experience. Insofar as people can control these adjustments voluntarily, they can design noticing systems that respond to changes or ignore them, that emphasize some constituencies and de-emphasize others, or that integrate many stimuli simultaneously or concentrate on a few stimuli at a time.

In the late 1950s, residents of Seattle noticed small pits scarring their automobile windshields. As time passed, more and more auto owners reported finding these pits, and public concern escalated. One widespread hypothesis held that recent Soviet atomic-bomb tests had hurled radioactive salts into the atmosphere; and upon being captured by Seattle's moist atmosphere, these salts were creating a glass-etching dew on windshields, where their damage was highly visible.

Another popular hypothesis was that rain and macadam from extensive new highway construction were creating acid salts, with the result that autos were throwing droplets of acid onto each other. As the reports of pitting multiplied, the officials of Seattle finally appealed to Governor Rosollini for help; the Governor in turn appealed to President Eisenhower; and the President dispatched a team of investigators from the National Bureau of Standards. The Federal investigators spent no time pursuing either of the prevalent hypotheses: Instead they measured the frequency of windshield pits and discovered that they were no more common than ever. Seattle had not experienced a plague of windshield pitting, but an epidemic of windshield noticing.

ACKNOWLEDGMENTS

We thank Janice Beyer, Janet Dukerich, Jane Dutton, and Donald Hambrick for contributing helpful comments and suggestions.

10

Challenger: Changing the Odds Until Something Breaks

Coauthored with Frances J. Milliken

1. TRAGEDY FROM THE COMMONPLACE

On January 28, 1986, the space shuttle Challenger disintegrated, killing all seven of its crew, including 'America's teacher in space', Christie McAuliffe. Those who watched are unlikely to forget their feelings of disbelief and horror. The disaster destroyed more than a space shuttle: it destroyed a part of America's vision as well (Schwartz 1987).

The American public, like NASA's managers, had grown complacent about the shuttle technology. We assumed the twenty-fifth launch would succeed because the previous twenty-four launches had succeeded. NASA had produced a long string of successes in the face of hypothetically low probabilities of success, and one result seems to be that both NASA and the American public developed a conviction that NASA could always succeed. The disaster suddenly reawakened us to the technology's extreme complexity and high risk. The ensuing investigation into the causes of the accident reminded us how unrealistic and error-prone organizations can be.

Neither Morton-Thiokol nor NASA could be called a typical organization, but their behaviors preceding the Challenger accident had many characteristics that we find commonplace in organizations. Organizations often communicate imperfectly, make errors of judgment, and provide playing fields for control games. Organizations often interpret past successes as evidencing their competence and the adequacy of their procedures, and so they try to lock their behaviors into existing patterns. Organizations often try to generalize from their experiences. Organizations often evolve gradually and incrementally into unexpected states.

Although these patterns of behavior do occur commonly, we have good reason to fear their consequences when organizations employ high-risk technologies on a day-to-day basis (Perrow 1984). In such organizations, these normal patterns of behavior create the potential for tragedy. At the same time, the normality of Thiokol's and NASA's behaviors implies that we should be able to learn lessons from this experience that apply elsewhere.

Drawing on testimony before the Presidential Commission and reports in newspapers and magazines, this chapter seeks to extract useful lessons from the Challenger disaster. Because it has been investigated so exhaustively, the disaster affords a rich example that illustrates a variety of issues. But the authors of this chapter believe that the most important lessons relate to the effects of repeated successes, gradual acclimatization, and the differing responsibilities of engineers and managers. Both repeated successes and gradual acclimatization alter decision-makers' beliefs about probabilities of future success; and thereby, they may strongly influence decisions concerning high-risk technologies. These decisions occur in contexts that shift as people try to extract lessons from experience and in organizational arenas where engineers and managers represent somewhat conflicting points of view.

The next section frames the issues in terms of three theories about the ways past successes and acclimatization alter probabilities of future success. Two ensuing sections portray some effects of repeated successes and acclimatization at NASA: the first of these sections details the evolution of problems with joints in the cases of solid rocket boosters, and the second sketches some long-term changes in NASA's general culture. The fifth section then describes fine-tuning processes that result from engineers and managers pursuing partially inconsistent goals while trying to learn from their shared experiences. Fine-tuning reduces probabilities of success, and it goes on until a serious failure occurs. The final section comments on our ability to learn from disasters.

2. THREE THEORIES ABOUT PROBABILITIES OF FUTURE SUCCESS

Before the launch of January 28, 1986, many so-called experts had attempted to assess the riskiness of shuttle launches. For example, serious estimates of the probability that the solid rocket booster (SRB) would fail had ranged from as high as 1 in 10 to as low as 1 in 100,000 (Diamond 1986a; Feynman 1986; Sanger 1986c). The wide range of such estimates casts doubt on their validity. Probably, no one, including the estimators themselves, really believed firmly in any of the estimates: at best, they amount to hypotheses that incorporate multitude assumptions. Not only do engineers and managers have to use actual experiences to appraise these hypotheses and the assumptions underlying them, but experience produces changes in hardware, procedures, and knowledge that alter the probabilities being estimated.

Faced with such elusive targets, engineers and managers have to frame specific hypotheses about riskiness within overarching theories about the effects of experience. They might plausibly adopt any of three macro theories. Theory 1 predicts that neither a success nor a failure changes the probability of a subsequent success. Theory 2 predicts that a success makes a subsequent success less likely, and that a failure makes a subsequent success more likely. Theory 3 predicts that a success makes a subsequent success more likely, and that a failure makes a subsequent success less likely.

Theory 1: Neither Success Nor Failure Changes the Expected Probability of a Subsequent Success

Statisticians frequently use probability distributions that assume repeated events have the same probabilities. For instance, they assume that all flips of a coin have the same probability of turning up heads, or that all rolls of a die have the same probability of yielding sixes. Indeed, at one time, statisticians applied the label 'gambler's fallacy' to the idea that probabilities increase or decrease in response to successes or failures; such pejorative labeling fostered the notion that constant probabilities are not just convenient simplifications but absolute truths.

Engineers or managers who have studied statistics might well apply constant probability theories to the situations they face, and they might look with skepticism upon any interpretations that assume changing probabilities. According to Theory 1, the fact that NASA had launched shuttles successfully twenty-four times in a row ought to be disregarded when deciding whether to proceed with the twenty-fifth launch because the probability of failure by a solid rocket booster, or any other component, would be approximately the same on the twenty-fifth launch as on the first launch.

Richard P. Feynman compared shuttle launches to Russian roulette (Presidential Commission 1986, I-148). Building on this analogy, Howard Schwartz (1987: 61–62) remarked: 'In the case of Russian roulette, with one round in the cylinder, the odds are one in six that a pull on the trigger will fire the round. If the round does not fire on the first pull, and the cylinder is spun, the odds are again one in six for the next pull on the trigger. To some persons unfamiliar with the theory of probability, it may seem that the odds with each successive pull would be greater. This is of course wrong. But it is equally wrong to suppose that the odds will be less with each successive event. This is what the NASA officials appeared to believe. The question is, how can it have happened that NASA officials, knowing full well the laws of probability, could have made such an error?'

Although Schwartz cited an often-used statistical model, no laws compel probabilities to remain constant over time. The probability of an event may rise over time or fall, depending on what changes occur in factors that influence this probability. The probability of a pistol's firing may well remain constant throughout several successive spins of the cylinder if the person spinning the cylinder behaves consistently. But Russian roulette may not be a good analogy for shuttle launches because the shuttle's hardware and personnel and operating procedures do change from launch to launch, and the probability of a successful flight may not stay constant.

For the probability of success with a sociotechnical system to stay constant, either the hardware, procedures, and operators' knowledge have to remain substantially unchanged over time, or changes tending to raise the probability of success have to be offset by changes tending to lower it. When a sociotechnical system's probability of success is low, people rarely leave hardware and procedures alone. Thus, a high-risk sociotechnical system should not have a probability of success that remains constant. Although some changes may well offset each other where numerous changes occur simultaneously, as during a period of initial development, the engineers and managers guiding those changes are expecting to raise the overall probability of success, and so they are unlikely to expect the probability of success to stay constant.

Engineers or managers might, however, hypothesize a constant probability of success for a sociotechnical system that appears nearly certain to succeed. And engineers and managers who have successfully launched twenty-four consecutive shuttles might well infer that the next flight has a very, very high probability of success, either because this probability has been very high all along or because it has risen over time. A number of the statements by Thiokol and NASA personnel suggest they believed the Challenger's probability of success was already so high that they had no need to raise it further.

Theory 2: Success Makes a Subsequent Success Seem Less Probable, and Failure Makes a Subsequent Success Appear More Likely

A series of successes, or even a single successful experience, might induce engineers or managers to lower their estimates of the probability of a future success; and conversely, failures might induce engineers or managers to raise their estimates of the probability of a future success. Schwartz alluded to such a theory when he conjectured that a player might expect a slot machine that has not paid off recently to become ready to pay off. Such a player might also expect a slot machine that has just paid off to have a bias against paying off again in the immediate future.

Applied to sociotechnical systems, Theory 2 emphasizes complacency versus striving, confidence versus caution, inattention versus vigilance, routinization versus exploration, habituation versus novelty. Successes foster complacency, confidence, inattention, routinization, and habituation; and so human errors grow increasingly likely as successes accumulate. Failures, on the other hand, remind operators of the need for constant attention, caution, and vigilance; and so failures make human errors less likely. For instance, Karl Weick (1987: 118–119) pointed out: 'When people think they have a problem solved, they often let up, which means they stop making continuous adjustments. When the shuttle flights continued to depart and return successfully, the criterion for a launch—convince me that I should send the Challenger—was dropped. Underestimating the dynamic nature of reliability, managers inserted a new criterion—convince me that I shouldn't send Challenger.' Similarly, Richard Feynman interpreted NASA's behavior according to Theory 2: after each successful flight, he conjectured, NASA's managers thought 'We can lower our standards a bit because we got away with it last time' (Presidential Commission 1986, I-148).

Failures also motivate engineers and managers to search for new methods and to try to create systems that are less likely to fail, and successes may induce engineers and managers to attempt to fine-tune a sociotechnical system—to render it less redundant, more efficient, more profitable, cheaper, or more versatile. Fine-tuning rarely raises the probability of success, and it often makes success less certain. Because fine-tuning seems to be a very important process that has received little attention, a later section of this chapter looks at it again.

The participants in sociotechnical systems often espouse Theory 2 after failures, conjecturing that past failures will elicit stronger efforts or greater vigilance in the future. However, participants find it difficult to use Theory 2 to interpret their own responses to successes. One reason is that participants may not recognize that repeated successes nurture complacency, confidence, inattention, routinization, and habituation. Another reason is that, when they do notice such changes, participants tolerate them on the premise that they are merely eliminating unnecessary effort and redundancy, not making success less probable. Indeed, because accusations of complacency and inattention seem derogatory, participants might punish a colleague who voices Theory 2. Thus, when applied to successes, Theory 2 is more an observer's theory than a participant's theory. Although bosses might use Theory 2 when appraising their subordinates' actions, they would probably not apply it to themselves.

Theory 3: Success Makes a Subsequent Success Appear More Probable, and Failure Makes a Subsequent Success Seem Less Likely

The participants in sociotechnical systems espouse Theory 3 readily, because it is easy to believe that success demonstrates competence, whereas failure reveals deficiencies.

Expected probabilities of success are not well-defined facts, but hypotheses to be evaluated through experience. Even if engineers or managers believe that a probability of success remains constant for a long time, they need to revise their estimates of this probability as experience accumulates. Engineers or managers with statistical training might, for example, use hypothetical computations to formulate an initial estimate of a probability of success and then apply Bayes' Theorem to compute successive estimates of this probability: if so, each success would raise the expected probability of success, and each failure would lower this expected probability.

Furthermore, experience with a technology may enable its users to make fewer mistakes and to employ the technology more safely, and experience may lead to changes in hardware, personnel, or procedures that raise the probability of success. Studies of industrial learning curves show that people do perform better with experience (Dutton and Thomas 1984). Better, however, may mean either more safely or less so, depending on the goals and values that guide efforts to learn. If better means more cheaply, or quicker, or closer to schedule, then experience may not raise the probability of safe operation.

Explaining that experience produces both advantages and disadvantages, Starbuck (1989) commented:

These learning mechanisms—buffers, slack resources, and programs—offer many advantages: they preserve some of the fruits of success, and they make success more likely in the future. They stabilize behaviors and enable organizations to operate to a great extent on the basis of habits and expectations instead of analyses and communications. They reduce the complexity of social relations and keep people from disobeying or behaving unpredictably. They minimize needs to communicate or to reflect, and they conserve analytic resources. They also give organizations discretion and autonomy with respect to their environments. Organizations do not have to pay very close attention to many of the demands currently arising from their environments, and they do not have to formulate explicit or unique responses to most of these demands. Thus, organizations gain human resources that they can devote to influencing their environments and creating conditions that will sustain their successes in the future.

But these learning mechanisms also carry disadvantages. In fact, each of the advantages has a harmful aspect. People who are acting on the basis of habits and obedience are not reflecting on the assumptions underlying their actions. People who are behaving simply and predictably are not improving their behaviors or validating their behaviors' appropriateness. Organizations that do not pay careful attention to their environments' immediate demands tend to lose track of what is going on in those environments. Organizations that have discretion and autonomy with respect to their environments tend not to adapt to environmental changes; and successful organizations want to keep their worlds as they are, so they try to stop social and technological changes. Indeed, buffers, slack resources, and programs make stable behaviors, current strategies, and existing policies appear realistic by keeping people from seeing problems, threats, or opportunities that would justify changes.

3. THEORY 3 IN ACTION

Theory 3 offers a very plausible characterization of the beliefs of managers at Thiokol's Wasatch Division and NASA's Marshall Space Flight Center (SFC) as they tried to evaluate the risks posed by joints in the shuttle's solid rocket booster (SRB). As successful launches accumulated, these managers appear to have gradually lost their fear of design problems and grown more confident of success. One must understand their story in some detail, however, in order to appreciate the complexity and ambiguity of the technical issues, the managers' milieu, and the slow progression in their beliefs.

Thiokol's engineers based the design of the shuttle's SRB on the Air Force's Titan III because of the latter's reliability. The Titan's case was made of steel segments, with the joints between segments being sealed by rubber O-rings. The Titan's O-rings had occasionally been eroded by the hot gases inside the engine, but Thiokol's engineers did not regard this erosion as significant. Nevertheless, to make the shuttle's SRB safer, Thiokol's engineers put a second, presumably redundant O-ring into each joint.

However, a 1977 test of the SRB's case showed an unexpected 'rotation' of the joints when the engine ignited: this rotation decompressed rather than compressed the O-rings, making it more difficult for the O-rings to seal the joints, and increasing the chance that hot gases would reach the O-rings. This alarmed NASA's engineers, so they asked for a redesign of the joints. Thiokol did not redesign the joints qualitatively, but did enlarge the O-rings to 0.028 inches diameter and thicken the shims that applied pressure on the O-rings from outside. In 1980, a high-level review committee reported that NASA's specialists had 'found the safety factors to be adequate' and the joints 'sufficiently verified with the testing accomplished to date' (Presidential Commission 1986, I-125). The joints were classified as Criticality 1R: the 1 denoted that joint failure could cause a loss of life or the loss of a shuttle; the R denoted that the secondary O-rings provided redundancy. That is, the secondary O-rings served as a back-up for the primary O-rings.

Eight full-scale tests of SRBs yielded no sign of joint problems, nor did the first shuttle flight. During the second flight in November 1981, hot gases eroded one O-ring, but this event made little impression: NASA's personnel did not discuss it at the next flight-readiness review and they did not report it upward to top management. The three flights during 1982 produced no more evidence of O-ring problems.

In 1982, an engineer working for Hercules, Inc. proposed a new joint design: a 'capture lip' would inhibit joint rotation. NASA's engineers thought this proposal looked interesting, but the capture lip would add 600 pounds to each SRB, its practicality was untested, and a more complex joint might harbor unforeseen difficulties. It would take over two years to build SRBs with this design. NASA decided to continue using the old joint design and to award Hercules a contract to develop the new design in conjunction with a new case material, carbon filaments in epoxy resin (Broad 1986c).

Thiokol too was proposing changes in the SRBs, but these were intended to raise the rockets' efficiency. During 1983, NASA began using SRBs that incorporated three incremental improvements (Broad 1986c; Marbach et al. 1986). Thiokol made the SRBs' walls 0.02–0.04 inches thinner; they narrowed the nozzles; and they filled the rockets with more powerful fuel. Thinner walls saved several hundred pounds that could be replaced by payloads. More powerful fuel could lift more weight. Smaller nozzles extracted more thrust from the fuel.

These changes, however, made the SRB less durable and exacerbated the joint rotation. More powerful fuel and smaller nozzles raised the SRBs' internal pressures, and thinner walls flexed more under pressure, so the joints developed larger gaps upon ignition. Tests showed that joint rotation could grow large enough to prevent a secondary O-ring from sealing a joint and providing redundancy. Therefore, the R was dropped from the joints' Criticality classification, but the reclassification document, written by a Thiokol engineer, implied the risk was small:

To date, eight static firings and five flights have resulted in 180 (54 field and 126 factory) joints tested with no evidence of leakage. The Titan III program using a similar joint concept has tested a total of 1,076 joints successfully.

A laboratory test program demonstrated the ability of the O-ring to operate successfully when extruded into gaps well over those encountered in this O-ring application. (Presidential Commission 1986, I-241)

The Presidential Commission (1986, I-126) surmised 'that NASA management and Thiokol still considered the joint to be a redundant seal even after the change from Criticality 1R to 1'. Over the next three years, many documents generated by NASA and Thiokol continued to list the Criticality incorrectly as 1R. Neither management really thought that a secondary O-ring might fail to seal a joint. In the view of Joseph C. Kilminster, manager of Thiokol's space boosters programme, 'it had to be a worse-case stack-up of tolerances, which statistically you would not expect' (Bell and Esch 1987: 45).

Also in 1983, the ninth full-scale test of an SRB and the sixth shuttle flight both produced signs of heat damage. As with the second flight, the NASA personnel did not discuss this damage at the flight-readiness review for the next flight or report it to top management, but this damage may have triggered changes in testing procedures. Up to August 1983, NASA leak-checked both the nozzle joints and the other (field) joints with an air pressure of 50 psi in order to verify that the O-rings had been installed correctly. In August 1983, NASA raised the leak-check pressure for field joints to 100 psi; and in January 1984, they raised it to 200 psi. Similarly, NASA raised the leak-check pressure for nozzle joints to 100 psi starting in November 1983, and to 200 psi starting in April 1985. According to Lawrence B. Mulloy, manager of the SRB project at Marshall SFC, NASA boosted the test pressures in order to force the secondary O-rings into the gaps between adjoining case segments.

NASA and Thiokol finally did review the O-ring problems on flights two and six in February 1984, after the tenth shuttle flight showed erosion of O-rings on both SRBs. At that point, engineers at both NASA and Thiokol conjectured that the higher leak-check pressures were creating problems rather than preventing them: the leak checks might be blowing holes in the putty that sealed cracks in the SRBs' insulation and creating paths by which hot gases could reach the O-rings. Laboratory tests suggested, however, that larger holes in the insulating putty might produce less damage than smaller holes, and the tests indicated the O-rings ought to seal even if eroded as much as 0.095 inches. Thiokol's engineers made a computer analysis that implied the primary O-rings would be eroded at most 0.090 inches, just under one-third of their diameter. 'Therefore', concluded the formal report, 'this is not a constraint to future launches' (Presidential Commission 1986, I-128–32).

Mulloy then introduced the idea that some erosion was 'acceptable' because the O-rings embodied a safety factor (Presidential Commission 1986, II-H1). This notion was discussed and approved by NASA's top managers at the flight-readiness review on March 30, 1984.

After the flight launched, on April 6, 1984 also showed some O-ring erosion, Hans Mark, NASA's second-in-command at that time, asked Mulloy to submit a written report on joint sealing (Sanger 1986e). Mulloy, in turn, asked Kilminster to conduct this study, and especially to investigate leak checking and the material being used for insulating putty. Thiokol proposed some tests, NASA approved this proposal, but Thiokol did not carry the tests out, and Mark received no report.

Figure 10.1 graphs NASA's observations of joint problems over time. The vertical axis indicates the numbers of joints in which NASA found problems. A short bar below the horizontal axis denotes an absence of evidence. Fractional bars above the horizontal axis symbolize small traces of gas leakage or heat damage. To reflect its seriousness, damage to secondary O-rings is represented by bars that are four times as long as those for damage to primary O-rings or for blow-by (gas leakage).

In all, inspectors discovered heat damage to SRB joints after three of the five flights during 1984, after eight of the nine flights during 1985, and after the flight on January 12, 1986. Not graphed are two test firings of SRBs that also produced O-ring erosion. The inspectors found damage in all joints of the SRBs, but the nozzle joints were especially vulnerable, sustaining damage during twelve of the fifteen flights. Not only was heat damage becoming more frequent as time passed, but the inspectors were seeing larger and larger amounts of erosion, including secondary O-rings as well as primary ones. Mulloy and his Thiokol counterparts seem to have grown more and more secure in the face of this evidence. In September 1984, Mulloy spoke of 'allowable erosion'; and in February 1985, Mulloy and Thiokol characterized joint leakage as an 'acceptable risk'.

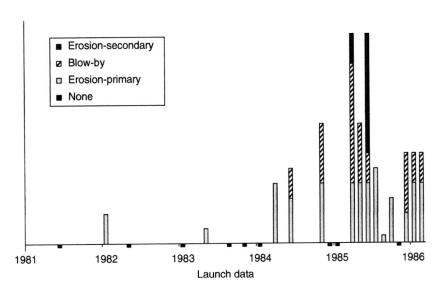

Figure 10.1. O-ring problems over time

The fifteenth flight in January 1985 experienced substantial O-ring damage: hot gas blew by the O-rings in two joints on each SRB, and the heat eroded one O-ring on each SRB. Further, this was the first flight in which a secondary O-ring was damaged. When the flight took off, the ambient temperature at the launch site was only 53 degrees. This event led Thiokol to propose that 'low temperature enhanced the probability of blow-by' (Presidential Commission 1986, I-136), which was the first time that idea had been introduced. However, even more serious O-ring damage occurred during the seventeenth flight in April 1985, when the tempera-ture at launch was 75 degrees. On this occasion, one primary O-ring eroded 0.171 inches, a substantial amount of hot gas blew by this O-ring, and so its back-up secondary O-ring eroded 0.032 inches. The 0.171 inches represented 61 percent of the primary O-ring's diameter; and the evidence suggested that the primary O-ring had not sealed until two minutes after launch (Bell and Esch 1987: 43).

One consequence of these events was that NASA's top management sent two representatives to Marshall SFC to review the O-ring problems, and these visitors asked Marshall to provide a briefing in Washington. This briefing, on August 19, concluded that 'it is safe to continue flying existing design as long as all joints are leak checked with a 200 psi stabilization pressure, are free of contamination in the seal areas and meet O-ring squeeze requirements' (Presidential Commission 1986, I-140). A second consequence was that Mulloy placed a 'launch constraint' on all subsequent flights. In NASA's jargon, a launch constraint is an acknow-ledgment that a problem of Criticality 1, IR, 2 or 2R might actually occur. The O-rings were still Criticality 1. To Mulloy, this launch constraint evidently did not mean that a flight should not occur; it only meant that each flight-readiness review should include a rationalization for waiving the constraint. During the flight-readiness review on July 2, Mulloy explained why some erosion of second-ary O-rings was also acceptable, and he described the O-ring-erosion problems as 'closed'. Mulloy proceeded to 'waive' this launch constraint for all subsequent flights up to the last one (Bell and Esch 1987: 43; Boffey 1986c). Mulloy later reflected: 'Since the risk of O-ring erosion was accepted and indeed expected, it was no longer considered an anomaly to be resolved before the next flight.... I concluded that we're taking a risk every time. We all signed up for that risk. And the conclusion was, there was *no* significant difference in risk from previous launches. We'd be taking essentially the same risk on Jan. 28 that we have been ever since we first saw O-ring erosion' (Bell and Esch 1987: 43, 47).

Kilminster seems to have concurred with Mulloy. In April 1985, NASA reminded Kilminster that Thiokol was supposed to have studied joint sealing. Kilminster then set up an informal task force that, in August 1985, proposed twenty alternative designs for the nozzle joints and 43 designs for the other (field) joints. At that point, Thiokol formalized the task force, but some members felt it was getting insufficient attention. One member, Roger M. Boisjoly, has subse-quently said that Kilminster 'just didn't basically understand the problem. We were trying to explain it to him, and he just wouldn't hear it. He felt, I guess, that we were crying wolf' (Bell and Esch 1987: 45).

Meanwhile, during the Autumn of 1984 and Spring of 1985, Hercules had successfully tested SRBs with carbon-epoxy cases and capture-lip joints. Simultaneously, laboratory tests were demonstrating that 'the capture feature was a good thing' (Broad 1986c). In July 1985, Thiokol ordered seventy-two new steel case segments having such joints; the manufacturer was expected to deliver these in February 1987. Marshall's documentation for the briefing in Washington on August 19, 1985 described the capture feature as being a 'potential long-term solution' and projected that this solution might come into effect starting in August 1988.

During a telephone call in early December 1985, someone at Marshall SFC told a low-level Thiokol manager that Marshall's Director of Engineering wanted Thiokol to 'close out' the outstanding problems, especially those that had remained unresolved for six months or more. Thereupon, this Thiokol manager wrote to Thiokol's main liaison with NASA, asking for 'closure' of all O-ring-erosion problems and stating seventeen reasons. Explaining that the problems should be closed because they 'will not be fully resolved for some time', Thiokol's liaison, in turn, relayed this request to Mulloy's immediate subordinate. A NASA 'quality assurance' administrator then marked 'contractor closure received' on all of the Problem Reports itemized in the liaison's letter. As a result, the O-rings were no longer listed as a launch constraint when it came time for the flight-readiness review on January 15, 1986, and O-rings were not even mentioned in the flight readiness documentation for the doomed Challenger. Indeed, just five days before the Challenger disaster, a NASA administrator marked these same Problem Reports 'problem is considered closed' (Presidential Commission 1986, I-142–4, II-H3).

Yet on January 16 and 17, 1986, engineers from NASA and Thiokol met to review the O-ring problems and to discuss possible solutions. By that time, NASA or Thiokol personnel had proposed at least eleven alternative hypotheses:

1. O-rings having round cross-sections did not put enough area against adjacent flat surfaces;
2. some O-rings were being installed incorrectly; or
3. some O-rings were smaller than the specified diameter; or
4. bits of dirt or metal splinters kept some O-rings from sealing, and so leak checking should occur at an air pressure high enough to force the secondary O-rings into the correct positions and to assure that they sealed properly;
5. high-pressure leak checking was displacing the primary O-rings from their proper positions, so causing them to fail to seal during launches;
6. high-pressure leak checking was creating holes in the insulating putty;
7. the primary O-rings were eroding because hot gases leaked through holes in the insulating putty;
8. the primary O-rings might not seal unless they were pressurized by hot gases that leaked through holes in the insulating putty;
9. the insulating putty had some unknown deficiencies;

10. cold temperatures stiffened the insulating putty enough to keep it from responding to the high pressures inside the engine during firing; and
11. cold temperatures stiffened the O-rings enough to keep them from sealing the joints.

4. A CAN-DO ORGANIZATION WITH AN 'OPERATIONAL' SYSTEM

Theory 3 also affords a plausible description for NASA's general culture. Ironically, participants' belief in Theory 3 may make Theory 2 a more realistic one for observers.

Success breeds confidence and fantasy. When an organization succeeds, its managers usually attribute this success to themselves, or at least to their organization, rather than to luck. The organization's members grow more confident, of their own abilities, of their managers' skill, and of their organization's existing programmes and procedures. They trust the procedures to keep them apprised of developing problems, in the belief that these procedures focus on the most important events and ignore the least significant ones. For instance, during a teleconference on January 27, 1986, Thiokol's engineers said that NASA should not launch the shuttle if the ambient temperature was below 53 degrees because no previous launch had occurred with an ambient temperature below 53 degrees. Lawrence Mulloy protested: '. . . there are currently no Launch Commit Criteria for joint temperature. What you are proposing to do is to generate a new Launch Commit Criteria on the eve of launch, after we have successfully flown with the existing Launch Commit Criteria 24 previous times' (Presidential Commission 1986, I-96). Mulloy spoke as if he had come to trust the Launch Commit Criteria that had always produced successes.

In the perceptions of NASA's personnel, as well as the American public, NASA was not a typical organization. It had a magical aura. NASA had not only experienced repeated successes, it had achieved the impossible. It had landed men on the moon and returned them safely to earth. Time and again, it had successfully completed missions with hardware that supposedly had very little chance of operating adequately (Boffey 1986a). NASA's managers apparently believed that the contributions of astronauts pushed NASA's 'probability of mission success very close to 1.0' (Feynman 1986, FI). The Presidential Commission (1986, I-172) remarked: 'NASA's attitude historically has reflected the position that "We can do anything".' Similarly, a former NASA budget analyst, Richard C. Cook, observed that NASA's 'whole culture' calls for 'a can-do attitude that NASA can do whatever it tries to do, can solve any problem that comes up' (Boffey 1986b).

As Theory 2 holds, success also erodes vigilance and fosters complacency and routinization. The Presidential Commission (1986, I-152) noted that the NASA of 1986 no longer 'insisted upon the exactingly thorough procedures that were its hallmark during the Apollo program'. But the Apollo programme called for vigilance because it was a risky experiment, whereas NASA's personnel believed that the shuttle represented an 'operational' technology. The shuttle had been conceived from the outset not only as a vehicle for space exploration and scientific research, but as a so-called Space Transportation System (STS) that would eventually support industrial manufacture in orbit. According to NASA's formal announcements, this STS had supposedly progressed beyond the stage of experimental development long before 1986. In November 1982, NASA declared that the STS was becoming 'fully operational'—meaning that the STS had proven sufficiently safe and error-free to become routine, reliable, and cost-effective. Directives issued in 1982 and 1984 specified 'a flight schedule of up to 24 flights per year with margins for routine contingencies attendant with a flight-surge capability'. NASA had actually scheduled fifteen flights for 1986.

In NASA's conception, an operational system did not have to be tested as thoroughly as an experimental one. Whereas NASA had tested equipment for the Apollo spacecraft in prototype form before purchasing it for actual use, NASA officials assumed that they had learned enough from the Apollo programme that the shuttle required no tests of prototypes. C. Thomas Newman, NASA's comptroller, has explained: 'The shuttle set out with some different objectives. To produce a system of moderate costs, the program was not as thoroughly endowed with test hardware' (Diamond 1986*c*, B4). Far from saving money or time, this strategy actually produced a great many revisions in plans, delays that added up to over six years, and operating costs fifty-three times those projected 'when Congress had approved the programme' (Diamond 1986*b*). Richard Feynman (1986) hypothesized that this strategy also contributed directly to the Challenger disaster by making the SRB difficult to test or modify. The fact is, however, that Thiokol's first eight full-scale tests disclosed no joint problems (Sanger 1986*d*)— perhaps the tests were intended to prove that the agreed design could function satisfactorily rather than to disclose its limitations and potential deficiencies.

An operational system seemingly also demanded less day-to-day care. As the shuttle became operational, NASA's top managers replaced the NASA personnel who were inspecting contractors' work on-site with 'designated verifiers', employees of the contractors who inspected their own and others' work on NASA's behalf. This increasing trust could reflect improvements over time in the quality of the contractors' work, or reflect an accumulation of evidence that the contractors were meeting specifications, but it could also be interpreted as complacency. Also, NASA cut its internal efforts toward safety, reliability, and quality assurance. Its quality-assurance staff dropped severely from 1,689 personnel in 1970 to 505 in 1986, and the biggest cuts came at Marshall SFC, where 615 declined to just 88 (Pear 1986). These reductions not only meant fewer safety inspections, they meant less careful execution of procedures, less thorough investigation of anomalies, and less documentation of what happened. Milton Silveira, NASA's chief engineer, said: 'In the early days of the space program we were so damned uncertain of what we were doing that we always got everybody's opinion. We would ask for continual reviews, continual scrutiny by anybody we had respect for, to look at this thing and make sure we were doing it right. As we started to fly the shuttle again and again, I think the system developed false confidence in itself and didn't do the same thing' (Bell and Esch 1987: 48).

5. FINE-TUNING THE ODDS

The foregoing sections show how repeated successes and gradual acclimatization influenced the lessons that NASA and Thiokol personnel were extracting from their shared experiences. These learning processes involved both engineers and managers, who were representing somewhat different points of view. The traditional differences in the responsibilities of engineers and managers give their interactions an undertone of conflict and make learning partly a process of fine-tuning the probabilities of success. Fine-tuning gradually makes success less and less likely.

Although an organization is supposed to solve problems and to achieve goals, it is also a conflict-resolution system that reconciles opposing interests and balances countervailing goals. Suppliers, customers, blue-collar and white-collar employees, executives, owners, neighbors, and governments all contribute resources to a collective pool, and then they all place claims upon this resource pool. Further, every serious problem entails real-world contradictions, such that no action can produce improvement in all dimensions and please all evaluators. For instance, an organization may seek to produce a high-quality product that assures the safety of its users, while also delivering this product promptly and earning a substantial profit. High quality and safety typically support strong demand; but high quality and safety also usually entail costs and slow down production; high costs imply high prices; and high prices and slow production may reduce revenues. Thus, the organization has to balance quality and safety against profit.

Opposing interests and countervailing goals frequently express themselves in intraorganizational labor specializations, and they produce intraorganizational conflicts. An organization asks some members to enhance quality, some to reduce costs, and others to raise revenue; and these people find themselves arguing about the trade-offs between their specialized goals. The organization's members may seek to maintain internal harmony by expelling the conflicts to the organization's boundary, or even beyond it. Thus, both Thiokol's members and NASA's members would normally prefer to frame a controversy as a disagreement between Thiokol and NASA rather than as a disagreement within their own organization. But conflicts between organizations destroy their compatibility, and an organization needs compatibility with its environment just as much as it needs internal cohesion. Intra-organizational conflict enables the organization to resolve some contradictions internally rather than letting them become barriers between the organization and its environment. Thus, on the evening of January 27, 1986, facing a conflict with NASA over the desirability of launching Challenger,

Thiokol's Joseph Kilminster asked for a recess of the teleconference with NASA, so that the Thiokol personnel could caucus among themselves.

Thiokol's caucus began with Calvin G. Wiggins, general manager of the space division, asserting: 'We have to make a management decision.' Wiggins appears to have been pointing out that, whereas it had been engineers who had formulated Thiokol's recommendation against launching, the conflict with NASA was raising nonengineering issues that managers should resolve. Two engineers, Roger Boisjoly and Arnold R. Thompson, tried to restate to the managers present why they believed cold weather would make the SRB's joints less likely to seal. After a few minutes, Boisjoly and Thompson surmised that no one was listening to them, so they gave up and resumed their seats. The decision was evidently going to be made in a managerial arena.

The four vice presidents of Thiokol's Wasatch division then discussed the issue among themselves. Kilminster and Robert K. Lund, vice president for engineering, expressed their reluctance to contradict the engineers' position. At that point, Jerald E. Mason, senior vice president and chief executive of the Wasatch operations, urged Lund: 'take off your engineering hat and put on your management hat'. The four managers then agreed to recommend launching. During this discussion, the managers agreed (*a*) that the primary O-rings possessed enough safety margin to enable them to tolerate three times the worst erosion observed up to that time and (*b*) that the secondary O-rings would provide a seal even if a primary O-ring failed. In fact, both assumptions had been contradicted in April 1985, when a primary O-ring had lost three-fifths of its diameter and neither the primary nor the secondary O-ring had sealed for two minutes.

The foregoing scenario illustrates an intra-organizational conflict that crystallizes around the differences between engineers and managers, and shows how these differences may rend a person who plays both an engineering role and a management role (Schriesheim, Glinow, and Kerr 1977).

Engineers are taught to place very high priority on quality and safety. If engineers are not sure whether a product is safe enough, they are supposed to make it much safer than they believe necessary. Facing uncertainty about safety, engineers would typically incorporate a safety factor of at least two—meaning that they would make a structure twice as strong as appeared necessary, or make an engine twice as powerful as needed, or make insulation twice as thick as required. Where failure would be very costly or additional safety would cost little, engineers might make a safety factor as large as ten. Thus, Thiokol's engineers were behaving according to the norm when they decided to put two O-rings into each joint: The second O-ring would be redundant if the shuttle's SRB operated much like the Titan's, but the design engineers could not be certain of this in advance of actual shuttle flights.

Safety factors are, by definition, supposed to be unnecessary. Safety factors of two are wasteful, and safety factors of ten very wasteful, if they turn out to be safety factors in truth. To reduce waste and to make good use of capacity, an organization needs to cut safety factors down.

People may cut safety factors while designing a sociotechnical system. Large safety factors may render projects prohibitively expensive or technically impossible, and thus may prevent the solving of serious problems or the attaining of important goals. When they extrapolate actual experiences into unexplored domains, safety factors may also inadvertently create hazards by introducing unanticipated risks or by taxing other components to their limits.

People are almost certain to reduce some safety factors after creating a system, and successful experiences make safety factors look more and more wasteful. An initial design is only an approximation, probably a conservative one, to an effective operating system. Experience generates information that enables people to fine-tune the design: Experience may demonstrate the actual necessity of design characteristics that were once thought unnecessary; it may show the danger, redundancy, or expense of other characteristics; and it may disclose opportunities to increase utilization. Fine-tuning compensates for discovered problems and dangers, removes redundancy, eliminates unnecessary expense, and expands capacities. Experience often enables people to operate a sociotechnical system for much lower cost or to obtain much greater output than the initial design assumed (Box and Draper 1969; Dutton and Thomas 1984).

Although engineers may propose cost savings, their emphasis on quality and safety relegates cost to a subordinate priority. Managers, on the other hand, are expected to pursue cost reduction and capacity utilization, so it is managers who usually propose cuts in safety factors. Because managers expect engineers to err on the side of safety, they anticipate that no real risk will ensue from incremental cost reductions or incremental capacity expansions. And engineers, expecting managers to trim costs and to push capacity to the limit, compensate by making safety factors even larger. Top managers are supposed to oversee the balancing of goals against one another, so it is they who often make the final decisions about safety factors. Thus, it is not surprising to find engineers and managers disagreeing about safety factors, or to see top managers taking such decisions out of their subordinates' hands, as happened at Thiokol. Hans Mark has recalled: 'When I was working as Deputy Administrator, I don't think there was a single launch where there was some group of subsystem engineers that didn't get up and say "Don't fly". You always have arguments' (Bell and Esch 1987: 48).

Formalized safety assessments do not resolve these arguments, and they may exacerbate them by creating additional ambiguity about what is truly important. Engineering caution and administrative defensiveness combine to proliferate formalized warnings and to make formalized safety assessments unusable as practical guidelines. In 1986, the Challenger as a whole incorporated at least 8,000 components that had been classified Criticality 1, 2, or 3. It had 829 components that were officially classified as Criticality 1 or 1R—748 of them classified 1 rather than 1R. Each SRB had 213 of these 'critical items', 114 of which were classified 1 (Broad 1986b; Magnuson 1986: 18). Since no administrative apparatus could pay special and exceptional attention to 8,000 issues, formalized Criticality had little practical meaning. To focus attention, NASA had identified special 'hazards' or 'accepted risks': The Challenger supposedly faced 277 of these at launch, 78 of them arising from each SRB. But if NASA's managers had viewed these hazards so seriously that any one of them could readily block a launch, NASA might never have launched any shuttles.

NASA's experience with the SRB's O-rings, as detailed above, looks like a typical example of learning from experience. Neither NASA's nor Thiokol's personnel truly understood in detail all of the contingencies affecting the sealing of joints. The Thiokol engineers imitated a joint design that appeared to have had no serious problems in the Titan's SRB, but they added secondary O-rings as a safety factor. The joints were formally classified Criticality 1R, and then 1, despite the Thiokol and NASA managers' conviction that a joint failure was practically impossible. Then actual shuttle flights seemingly showed that no serious consequences ensued even when the O-rings did not seal promptly and when primary O-rings sustained extensive damage and secondary O-rings minor damage. A number of managers surmised that, although an improved joint design should be adopted in due course, experience demonstrated the O-rings to be less dangerous than the engineers had initially assumed. But some engineers, at Marshall SFC as well as Thiokol, were drawing other conclusions from the evidence: Richard Cook told a reporter that propulsion engineers at Marshall had 'said to me, almost in a whisper in my ear, that the thing could blow up ... one of them said to me, "When this thing goes up, we hold our breath" ' (Boffey 1986*b*).

The 1983 changes in the SRB also made sense as fine-tuning improvements after successful experience. These looked small at the time: they trimmed the SRB's weight by only 2 percent and boosted its thrust by just 5 percent. Similar incremental changes might, in principle, continue indefinitely as people learn and as better materials become available. For instance, NASA was hoping to obtain a further SRB weight reduction by shifting to a graphite-epoxy case (Sanger 1986*a*). However, the SRB changes in 1983 illustrate also that small, incremental changes may produce small, incremental effects that are very difficult to detect or interpret.

Thus, some of the key decisions that doomed a shuttle may have occurred in 1982, when NASA endorsed Thiokol's proposed improvements of the SRBs. Thiokol's revised design had more joint rotation than the initial one, and thinner cases might have been more distorted by use. Moreover, other changes reinforced the importance of joint rotation. In particular, used segments of the SRB cases came back slightly out-of-round, so the segments did not match precisely and the O-rings were being expected to seal uneven gaps. Yet, NASA re-used case segments more often over time, and Kennedy Space Center stopped inspecting O-rings.

The Presidential Commission (1986, I-133–4) focused attention on a different sequence of fine-tuning changes: the increases in leak-check pressures from 50 psi to 200 psi. The Commission pointed out that the test pressures correlated with the frequency of O-ring problems. Using the same damage estimates as Figure 10.1, Figure 10.2 arrays NASA's observations of joint problems as functions of both leak-check pressures and the ambient temperatures at the launch site. Because the nozzle joints were tested at different pressures from the other joints,

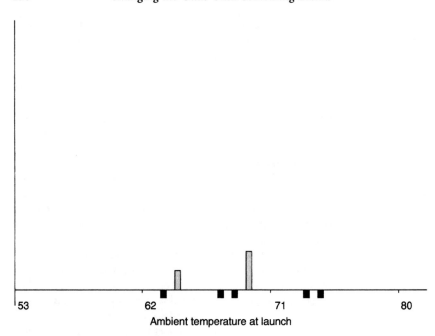

Figure 10.2a. Test pressure of 50 psi

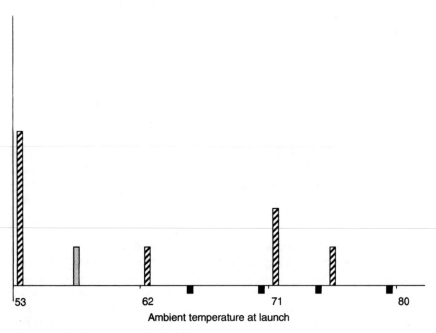

Figure 10.2b. Test pressure of 100 psi

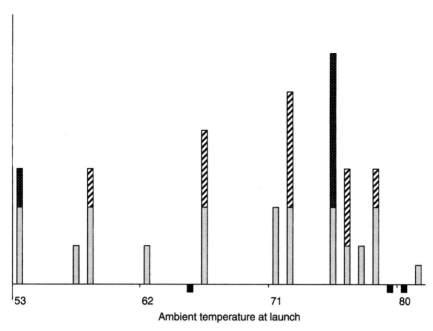

Figure 10.2c. Test pressure of 200 psi

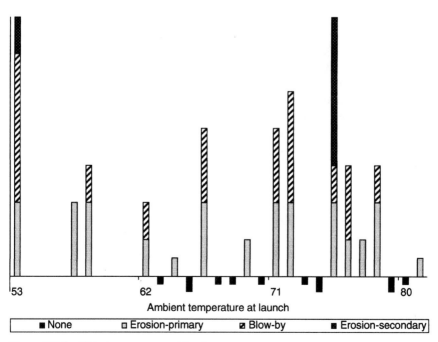

Figure 10.2d. All test pressures combined

one flight appears in both Figures 10.2a and 10.2b, and seven flights appear in both Figures 10.2b and 10.2c. Figure 10.2d aggregates the problems across all three test pressures: every flight launched at an ambient temperature below 66 degrees had experienced O-ring problems. The launch that ended in disaster began at an ambient temperature around 28 degrees, 15 degrees lower than any before.

Fine-Tuning Until Failure Occurs

The most important lesson to learn from the Challenger disaster is not that some managers made the wrong decisions or that some engineers did not understand adequately how O-rings worked: the most important lesson is that fine-tuning makes failures very likely.

Fine-tuning changes always have plausible rationales, so they generate benefits most of the time. But fine-tuning is real-life experimentation in the face of uncertainty, and it often occurs in the context of very complex sociotechnical systems, so its outcomes appear partially random. For instance, because NASA did not know all of the limitations bounding shuttle operations, the doomed shuttle might not have been the flight on January 28, 1986. An SRB joint could well have triggered a disaster earlier—say, in January 1985, when five O-rings in four joints suffered damage. Or, a disaster could have happened later, had NASA postponed the launch until the cold weather abated. Such a postponement might have turned the flight into another demonstration that the O-ring problems were not so urgent—or into a disaster at 50 degrees.

Fine-tuning changes constitute experiments, but multiple, incremental experiments in uncontrolled settings produce confounded outcomes that are difficult to interpret. Thus, much of the time, people only discover the content and consequences of an unknown limitation by violating it and then analyzing what happened in retrospect. As George H. Diller, spokesman at Kennedy Space Center, said: 'It is only after a problem that you can sometimes go back and see that you had a thread of data that is consistent with the event' (Sanger 1986*b*: 1). For example, although the NASA and Thiokol personnel had considered many hypotheses about the O-ring problems, they had not even thought of two factors that may have been important on January 28. Rain and freezing temperatures before launch could have produced ice in the SRBs' joints, and laboratory tests after the disaster showed that such ice could unseat secondary O-rings. Also, laboratory tests showed the fit between case segments to be as important as the O-rings' temperatures: O-rings failed to seal at temperatures below 55 degrees when the gap between case segments was only 0.004 inches, but they sealed at 25 degrees when case segments fitted with a 0.010-inch gap. The case segments that had to fit this precisely had diameters of 146 inches.

NASA's incremental changes in hardware, procedures, and operating conditions were creeping inexorably toward a conclusive demonstration of some kind. In retrospect, it now seems obvious that numerous launches had generated increasingly threatening outcomes, yet NASA's managers persisted until a launch produced an outcome too serious to process routinely. They seem to have been pursuing a course of testing to destruction.

NASA's apparent insensitivity to escalating threats has attracted criticism, and NASA could undoubtedly have made better use of the available evidence, but NASA was behaving in a commonplace way. Because fine-tuning creates sequences of experiments that are supposed to probe the limits of theoretical knowledge, people tend to continue one of these experimental sequences as long as its outcomes are not so bad: the sequence goes on until an outcome inflicts costs heavy enough to disrupt the normal course of events and to bring fine-tuning to a temporary halt.

6. LEARNING FROM DISASTERS

We may need disasters in order to halt erroneous progress. We have difficulty in distinguishing correct inferences from incorrect ones when we are making multiple, incremental experiments with incompletely understood, complex systems in uncontrolled settings; and sometimes we begin to interpret our experiments in erroneous, although plausible frameworks. Incremental experimentation also produces gradual acclimatization that dulls our sensitivities, both to phenomena and to costs and benefits. For instance, given the tendencies of NASA's and Thiokol's managers to interpret non-fatal O-ring erosion as evidence that O-ring erosion could be tolerated, it is hard to imagine how a successful flight could have produced O-ring erosion bad enough to persuade the NASA and Thiokol managers to halt launches for two or three years until the new SRB cases would be ready. Indeed, more erosion of secondary O-rings might have induced NASA to boost the leak-check pressure yet again.

One is reminded of Gregory Bateson's metaphor about a frog in hot water: A frog dropped into a pot of cold water will remain there calmly while the water is gradually heated to a boil, but a frog dropped into hot water will leap out instantaneously.

Because some disasters do inevitably happen, we should strive to make disasters less costly and more beneficial. Failures have to be costly in order for us to judge them disasters, but the Challenger disaster killed far fewer people than other disasters that have received much less attention. Publicity and extreme visibility made the difference. We saw the Challenger disaster live on television, and we read about it and heard about it for five months, and so we valued those seven lives highly. Also, disasters often seem more costly where the people who died were not those who chose the courses of action. This poses a practical dilemma. On the one hand, our sense of justice says that the actual astronauts should decide whether to launch. On the other hand, the Challenger disaster would probably have received less public attention if the astronauts had participated in the teleconference between NASA and Thiokol on January 27, and had themselves decided to launch at 28 degrees.

We benefit from disasters only if we learn from them. Dramatic examples can make good teachers. They grab our attention and elicit efforts to discover what caused them, although few disasters receive as much attention as Challenger. In principle, by analyzing disasters, we can learn how to reduce the costs of failures, to prevent repetitions of failures, and to make failures rarer.

But learning from disasters is neither inevitable nor easy. Disasters typically leave incomplete and minimal evidence. Complex systems in uncontrolled settings can fail in a multitude of ways; unknown limitations mean that fine-tuning terminates somewhat randomly; and incremental experiments may possess numerous explanations even in retrospect. Retrospective analyses always oversimplify the connections between behaviors and outcomes, and make the actual outcomes appear highly inevitable and highly predictable (Starbuck and Milliken 1988a). Retrospection often creates an erroneous impression that errors should have been anticipated and prevented. For instance, the Presidential Commission found that the O-ring erosion history presented to Level I at NASA Headquarters in August 1985 was sufficiently detailed to require 'corrective action prior to the next flight', but would the Commission members have drawn this same conclusion in August 1985 on the basis of the information then at hand?

Effective learning from disasters may require looking beyond the first explanations that seem to work, and addressing remote causes as well as proximate ones. With the help of the press, the Presidential Commission did try to do that: It explored quite a few alternative hypotheses, appraised NASA's administrative processes, and pointed to potential future problems. NASA's and Thiokol's reactions are also instructive: they seem to have focused on short-run changes. NASA and Thiokol replaced many managers (Sanger 1986g). NASA made more funds available for testing, and reviewed and 'resolved' 262 problems involving critical components, but decided not to modify the SRB cases to any substantial degree. With the addition of a third O-ring in each joint and the deletion of insulating putty, NASA's next launch will use the capture-lip cases that Thiokol had ordered in July 1985 (Sanger 1986g).

Two years after the Challenger disaster, one astronaut observed that it had taught lessons that NASA will probably have to learn again and again.

Part IV

Organizing and Strategizing in Knowledge-Intensive Firms, Control Systems Part 1

11

When Is Play Productive?

Coauthored with E. Jane Webster

'Anyone who has spent much time with computers knows how easy it is to get so involved that time just flies. Sometimes when at my computer, I say to my wife, "I'll be done in just a minute' and the next thing I know she's standing over me saying, "It's been an hour!" '

— Jim Collins, author (1989: 11)

'I really like my computer because it makes work more like a game. It even makes mundane tasks more like a game. I can play with logos. I can play with designs. I can play with text. I like to play. It's really good for my creativity.'

— Jane Brockett, founder of a graphics design firm (Collins 1989: 11)

'Computers remove distraction because you're not constantly going back and forth between different mediums (cutting, pasting, ink, paper, etc.). You can do it all right there at your computer and get completely lost in what you're doing.' — Marney Marris, founder of a multimedia production company (Collins 1989: 11)

Similar quotations come from Webster's (1989) interviews with white-collar workers who used computers regularly in their jobs. They described their activities with phrases such as:

> 'I'm never happier than when programming.'
> 'I feel involved, in control.'
> 'I get excited about the possibilities available.'
> 'I get mesmerized.'
> 'I'm fascinated with computers.'
> 'I like to play with computers and learn programs.'
> I like:
>> 'searching for clues',
>> 'figuring out new functions',
>> 'what if questions', and
>> 'a puzzle to be solved'.

As these quotes suggest, some computer users lose awareness of what is going on around them. Some do not notice the passage of time. Some dawdle over tasks, exploring various options. Some interact with computers instead of doing more pressing tasks (Nash 1990).

We call such behaviors playful partly because users frequently use the word 'play' to describe their experiences but mainly because theories of play help to explain people's behaviors and feelings while they work. Playful behaviors occur when children make believe, when teenagers play video games, and when adults build models, assemble puzzles, or work in darkrooms. Yet, playful behaviors also occur when adults work in their jobs, and they occur especially often when people use computers (Hiemstra 1983; Nash 1990). Seven of the fifteen users Webster (1989) interviewed talked about the enjoyment they received from using computers. Even people who perform routine, mechanical tasks without computers often try to make their work playful. For example, Garson (1977) found that some keypunchers turned their jobs into a game by synchronizing their typing, then racing each other. Roy (1960) observed horseplay by factory workers. Terkel (1974) described a supermarket checker who likened her work to playing the piano, and a waitress who felt like a ballerina on stage (Glynn 1988).

Because playful behaviors do occur often, they have significant economic consequences. Play at work may be time wasted, of course; but it may contribute to high-quality results, and it may induce workers to work longer. Webster's interviewees were not malingerers. They all took their jobs seriously, and most were career-oriented and ambitious. Five of them were secretaries with much discretion in their jobs; ten attended an MBA program part-time while they worked in financial services, in positions such as portfolio analyst. Yet, they looked on play as an aspect of their work, not as illegitimate activity in place of real work. This view of play is both interesting and profound because it contradicts the commonsense idea that play is the opposite of work.

Two factors are making play an increasingly important aspect of work: Firstly, computers foster play. Because computers follow logical rules and produce very immediate outcomes, they create work environments that resemble many recreational games, and they foster exploratory learning and what-if fantasizing. Also, users can easily convert computers from a task program such as a word processor to a game program such as Solitaire, and thus can switch rapidly back and forth between work and recreation. Secondly, by encouraging them to find new methods or solutions, play actually improves the work of highly skilled experts such as analysts, consultants, or researchers. Such jobs grow more prevalent over time because the productivity of experts rises more slowly than the productivity of less skilled workers and capital.

Thus, it is increasingly important to understand the positive and negative consequences of play at work. Play can affect productivity, product quality, and job satisfaction. It may be especially important to study play with computers (Carroll and Thomas 1988; Davis 1989; Kamouri, Kamouri, and Smith 1986; Katz 1987; Malone 1981; Ord 1989). Yet, little research has examined adults playing at work. Research on play has focused on children or college students instead of adults, or has studied adults playing games instead of working. Even the research examining playfulness in computer interactions has studied children instead of adults (Kay 1985; Malone 1981; Papert 1980; Turkle 1984), has focused on games instead of on play in a wider sense (Mehrabian and Wixen 1986), or has taken place in classrooms instead of for-profit organizations (Webster Heian, and Michelman 1990).

The first sections of this chapter look at play in general, not just play with computers, because it is not only play with computers that affects work. The next section of this chapter defines play and explains why we chose this definition over alternatives. Then it reviews several theories about motives for play and describes types of play. The ensuing section outlines the consequences of play, including effects on learning. Then attention shifts to microcomputers because these encourage play. This section suggests guidelines for when and where to play with computers. The guidelines have implications both for software designers and for people who select software, and they have analogs for work that does not involve computers. The final section contemplates the vanishing of the distinction between work and play.

1. WHAT IS PLAY?

Both laymen and researchers use the term 'play' in several ways, and failures to distinguish between different meanings produce confusion and conceptual problems (Berlyne 1969; Csikszentmihalyi 1975; Day 1981). Nearly every definition says that playful activities elicit involvement and give pleasure (Berlyne 1969; Burtchen 1987; Csikszentmihalyi 1975; Ellis 1973; English and English 1958; Gardner 1986; Glynn 1988; Levy 1983; Millar 1968; Miller 1973; Piaget 1962; Reilly 1974; Sandelands, Ashford, and Dutton 1983; Stevens 1980; Voss 1987; Webster 1989). Definitions differ, however, in what properties they add to pleasure and involvement. At one extreme, lie definitions that make play rare. At the other extreme are definitions that apply the label play to very diverse activities.

This chapter falls into the latter category. It defines play simply as activity that produces both immediate pleasure and involvement. Activity is not playful if it is pleasant but uninvolving, or involving but unpleasant (Sandelands and Buckner 1989). The pleasure must come from the activity itself, not from expectations of future pay or food or social status. In psychological jargon, play yields intrinsic rewards (Deci and Ryan 1985). Various writers have attributed such pleasure to using expertise, exercising physical skills, manipulating controls, ideating, using symbols, or exploring unknown but safe situations. When Webster asked computer users to describe playful situations, they cited: asking what-if questions, massaging data, investigating possibilities, seeing results, producing charts, discovering more efficient ways of working, figuring out new features of programs, learning new programs, receiving positive feedback from tutorials, and designing new systems. Users said that computer usage was less playful when they were using very familiar programs for routine tasks.

Many definitions go further and say that playful activities are undertaken solely for immediate pleasures arising from activities themselves, without regard for future consequences (Berlyne 1969; Ellis 1973; English and English 1958; Klinger 1969). Unfortunately, this restriction makes play quite rare and it rules out most of the activities that are generally regarded as playful. All activities have future consequences of some sort, and people rarely ignore future consequences altogether. People may enjoy immediate pleasures even though they expect to regret some future consequences, or they may seek future benefits by means that also produce immediate pleasures. Pleasant, involving activities may yield wealth, a new house, a great painting, low productivity, alcoholism, or injury. In other words, intrinsic consequences and extrinsic consequences are not mutually exclusive.

This chapter views play as a continuous variable (Day 1981; Ellis 1973). Involvement may range from none to intense. Pleasure may range from strongly positive to strongly negative, so that displeasing activities are unplayful. It then becomes a practical or empirical question what extrinsic consequences result from specific playful activities. It also becomes a practical or empirical question whether specific playful activities produce intrinsic rewards that dominate their extrinsic consequences.

One might also require that playful activities emphasize means more than ends (Miller 1973; Sandelands 1988; Wolf 1984). It is generally true that immediate pleasure and involvement make players very prone to focus on what they are doing right now. Tomorrow's consequences often fade into insignificance. Yet, immediate pleasure and involvement are themselves ends, and the theories below emphasize the rewards players receive from playful activities. There are also immediately pleasant and involving activities that people pursue to attain long-run ends—such as sexual intercourse in order to produce children. Thus, this chapter does not insist that play emphasizes means more than ends, but it does recognize that players generally pay close attention to immediate events.

Theories About Motives for Play

At least four theories help to explain why people feel immediate pleasure and involvement when they exercise skills, manipulate controls, use symbols, explore unknown but safe situations, ask what-if questions, see results, produce charts, discover more efficient ways of working, learn new programs, and so forth. Various theories say players are seeking competence, stimulation, challenge, or reinforcement.

White (1959) hypothesized that organisms (including people) explore and manipulate in order to develop competence to interact effectively with their environments. He (1959: 324–325) said:

Specimens of such behavior...demonstrate their constantly transactional nature. Typically they involve continuous chains of events which include stimulation, cognition, action, effect on the environment, new stimulation, etc. They are carried on with considerable persistence and with selective emphasis on parts of the environment which provide changing and interesting feedback.... [Such] behavior has an exploratory, varying, experimental character and produces changes in the stimulus field. Having this character, the behavior leads the organism to find out how the environment can be changed and what consequences flow from these changes.

White's theory implies that players seek moderate challenges: Activities need to be difficult enough that successes require some competence, but easy enough that successes occur regularly.

Ellis (1973) argued that people do not seek competence but instead gain competence as a by-product of fun, interesting activities. He founded his theory of play mainly on Berlyne's theory of stimulus seeking. Berlyne (1960) proposed that optimal stimulation produces pleasure: People avoid boredom as well as overstimulation. Overstimulation results from information overload, extreme novelty, or excessive task difficulty. Overstimulated people perform poorly and attempt to escape their current environments. Bored people, on the other hand, seek or create new, surprising, or complex stimuli that increase their stimulation. They try out moderately novel activities. They vary the intensity or timing of stimuli. They pursue activities that have uncertain outcomes. They construct expectations so that actual outcomes can appear surprising. They link activities to make stimuli more complex. They interact with other people.

Ellis (1973: 110) then postulated that play 'is motivated by the need to elevate the level of arousal towards the optimal'. That is, people play to gain more stimulation, and they classify activities as playful if they increase stimulation (Scott 1966). Optimal stimulation explains the pleasure players feel. He saw support for his theory in research on vigilance, sensory deprivation, and manipulative-exploratory behaviors; and Mehrabian and Wixen (1986) used this theory to explain video-game play.

Csikszentmihalyi (1975) asserted that play provides clear challenges, either through competition or uncertainty. A player feels pleasure and involvement when an activity's challenges balance the player's capabilities. Insufficient challenge causes boredom or anxiety; too much challenge creates worry or anxiety. When capabilities closely balance challenges, a player experiences a state of extreme pleasure and involvement called 'flow'. Csikszentmihalyi (1975: 72) said:

Players shift into a common mode of experience when they become absorbed in their activity. This mode is characterized by a narrowing of the focus of awareness, so that irrelevant perceptions and thoughts are filtered out; by loss of self-consciousness; by a responsiveness to clear goals and unambiguous feedback; and by a sense of control over the environment.... [I]t is this common flow experience that people adduce as the main reason for performing the activity.

Flow has been observed in studies of rock climbers, composers, modern dancers, chess players, computer programmers, basketball players, surgeons, and managers (Bowman 1982; Csikszentmihalyi 1975; Ghani 1991; Kusyszyn 1977; Csikszentmihalyi and LeFevre 1989).

A fourth theory is implicit in psychologists' findings about reinforcement. The basic findings are as follows: (*a*) The more immediate a reinforcement, the stronger its impact. (*b*) Continuous reinforcements produce faster learning that is unlearned more quickly, whereas intermittent reinforcements produce slower learning that is unlearned more slowly. (*c*) Punishments (unpleasant reinforcements) tend to discourage behaviors without encouraging alternative responses. (*d*) Punishments often elicit aggression. Thus, people receive great pleasure from activities that produce very immediate rewards (pleasant reinforcements), and such outcomes foster rapid learning. Playful activities offer players many small successes. If continuous successes stop abruptly, players first abandon their previous behaviors and try new ones, then they stop playing. Intermittent successes, on the other hand, encourage players to continue playing persistently and to stick to behavioral routines. Mixing punishments intermittently with rewards often brings out aggressive behaviors.

Similarities and Differences

All four theories are tautological insofar as they say people like pleasant situations and dislike unpleasant ones. Also, all four theories explain play by reference to players' subjective reactions: The effects of environments are moderated by people's perceptions and interpretations. An observer cannot verify independently that a player feels she has demonstrated competence, or that a player's stimulation has reached an optimum, or that a player's capabilities precisely balance the challenges of a situation, or that a specific player finds an outcome rewarding. Play is in the mind of the player. All four theories portray these subjective reactions as curved functions of various independent variables, so that very playful activities have intermediate properties: To create a feeling of competence, an activity must require some skill but not too much. To optimize arousal, stimuli must be somewhat surprising but not incredible, somewhat complex but not unintelligible. To produce flow, an activity must give clear feedback but not eliminate uncertainty. To elicit persistent efforts, reinforcements must be somewhat intermittent but not too infrequent. Thus, a curved function symbolizes an intersection between properties of an environment and of a player.

The theories make somewhat divergent statements about the kinds of activities that appear playful. White, Csikszentmihalyi, and reinforcement theory hold that players like to feel competent (Lieberman 1977), and White said that gaining competence may be sufficient motivation. According to these theories, playful activities demand some skill, but are not so demanding that failures dominate successes. Ellis, however, said gaining competence is just a side effect of performing fun, interesting activities. He asserted that players are looking for moderate amounts of novelty, surprise, uncertainty, complexity, and variation in stimuli. Reinforcement theory says players want frequent, immediate rewards, although intermittent rewards may make people play more persistently. Csikszentmihalyi said flow-producing activities have coherent requirements, follow rules, generate clear feedback, and focus players' attention within limited fields. If players can increase or decrease the difficulty of activities, they can match activities' challenges to their own capabilities.

Ellis did not make a point of players' involvement in activities, whereas White and Csikszentmihalyi did. For example, in a comparison of involved and uninvolved rock dancers, Csikszentmihalyi found that involved dancers experienced significantly fewer distractions, greater knowledge of the right things to do, greater feedback, more control of the social situation, less self-consciousness, more harmony with the environment, and faster passage of time. When involvement becomes intense, players concentrate on thoughts and perceptions relating to the activity, lose awareness of the outside world, and lose their sense of time. Involvement may itself be a source of reinforcement, both positive and negative. Csikszentmihalyi noted that intense involvement may produce mental and physical tension, anxiety, and worry. Yet, Turkle (1984) suggested that concentration on computer games, by distracting players, reduces the tension of players who have other worries.

This divergence fits with the notion that play is in the mind of the player: Not only may different people judge different activities playful, but a given person may play in very different ways at different times. To see the great variety of play activities, one need only contrast football with chess, or baroque music with pinball, or crossword puzzles with roulette.

Types of Play

None of the preceding theories puts much emphasis on fantasy or imagination. On the other hand, Malone (1981) analyzed fantasies in computer games; and Day (1981) argued that there are at least five kinds of play, three of which involve fantasy and imagination. One implication is that the theories likely overlook some types of play.

Table 11.1 suggests the wide variety of activities that have been called play. Adaptations of Day's categories comprise the first five types in Table 11.1. All the types blend into others, so they are regions of one multidimensional domain. The least prevalent type is therapeutic play undertaken at the behest of a psychotherapist. Therapeutic play may be creative, imitative, or cathartic-destructive, so it merges into creative play or mimicry. Day divided the domain addressed by Berlyne and Ellis into diversion, creative play, and exploration. Diversion has no goal except pleasure. Creative play and exploration foster learning: Creative play pursues explanations, whereas exploration pursues facts. Mimicry is Day's term for competence-developing exercises such as Csikszentmihalyi, Piaget (1962), and White discussed.

Although repetitive exercises often mimic, people (and animals) also practice behaviors that they have not observed other people perform—as when people mentally rehearse conversations that they may have or wish they had had. The properties that Day attributed to mimicry also apply to many contests in which people test their skills against inanimate puzzles. These puzzles range from largely

Table 11.1. Nine types of play

Type	Evoking conditions	Goals	Properties
Therapeutic play	Therapist Angry, anxious or hostile client	Reduction of anger, anxiety, or hostility Competence Pleasure	Fantasy Imagination Deliberate Not very pleasant May be destructive, creative, or imitative
Diversion	Too familiar environment Bored, untense player	Pleasure	Fantasy Imagination Easily disrupted Low arousal
Creative play	Interesting, but familiar, environment Confident, fanciful player	Explanations Integration Mastery Learning	Focused on stimuli Why questions Fantasy Imagination Challenging
Exploration	Novel or uncertain environment Curious player	Facts Learning	Focused on stimuli What questions Concentration Movement Tension
Mimicry	Performance standards Admiring player	Competence Learning	Formal Structured Repetitive Often social
Puzzle solving	Novel or uncertain challenge Confident player	Competence Learning	Formal Structured Repetitive Sometimes social
Competition	Opponent Uncertainty Confident player	Superiority Competence	Formal Structured Repetitive Interpersonal
Riding	Amusement park or fair	Pleasure Extreme sensations	Safe Frightening Arousing Realistic
Observing	Theater Television	Pleasure Secondhand sensations	Safe May raise or lower tension Fantasy Imagination

random ones, such as Solitaire; to entirely nonrandom ones such as crossword puzzles or piano practice; to matches against computer programs, such as Reversi or Tic-Tac-Toe. Some puzzles involve much exploration. Mathematicians sometimes call puzzles games against nature. Of course, people also play games against human opponents—competitions. Both puzzles and competitions provide frameworks for learning and competence development (Csikszentmihalyi 1975).

At least two types of play occur mainly in specialized enclaves. Rides at amusement parks and fairs allow people to feel unusual sensations such as those produced by falling, rapid turning, or exposure at great height, but to do so with little fear of actual harm. Observing plays, movies, concerts, or dances allows people to feel diverse unusual sensations at secondhand, through empathy and imagination. These sensations would be far from pleasant if felt in normal contexts, but many people find them very pleasant in contexts that signal safety and transience.

2. CONSEQUENCES OF PLAY

With play defined as activity that produces immediate pleasure and involvement, it is obvious that people prefer playful activities . . . other things being equal. Yet, other things are never equal. People with important, practical goals prefer activities that enable them to reach those goals. In particular, several studies have found that perceived usefulness is the strongest single determinant of people's attitudes toward and behaviors with computer systems (Davis 1989; Davis, Bagozzi, and Warshaw 1989; Hill, Smith, and Mann 1987; Robey 1979). Users choose playful computer systems only if these can meet their practical goals.

Together, the four theories about motives for play and the nine types of play in Table 11.1 point to many dimensions along which playful activities vary. Although play may form a unified, contiguous domain, some regions of this domain look quite different from others. One result is that different types of play may produce very diverse consequences. A second result is that research findings about 'play'—ambiguously defined and nonspecific—are very difficult or impossible to interpret.

Immediate pleasure and involvement may be the only consistent consequences of play, and even these vary greatly. In diversion, both pleasure and involvement may be very weak. Moreover, although strong immediate pleasures enhance involvement, strong involvement can create unpleasant tensions and worries that offset immediate pleasures. As a result, the effects of immediate pleasure and involvement generally reach maxima or minima when pleasure and involvement have moderate values.

Five related consequences normally accompany immediate pleasure and involvement: Three of these—emphasis on immediate reinforcements, emphasis on means more than ends, and emphasis on nearby goals instead of distant ones— are so closely linked that they can be labeled short-sightedness. The other two consequences—concentration and persistence—are also closely linked to each other. When people judge playful activities to be appropriate, they switch to them readily and try to continue doing them. Playful tasks may be so absorbing that players neglect other tasks and other social relations (Turkle 1984), and players may forget future reinforcements and long-run goals. Many authors have pointed out that people may become addicted to play.

Players often organize their activities to obtain more short-run rewards, so they follow crooked paths toward their long-run goals, and they take longer times to reach long-run goals (Miller 1973). Sandelands (1988) found that merely labeling a task as play instead of as work induces people to take longer completing it.

Consequences of play have to be described as ranges from one extreme to another. This is a result, in part, of possible variations in pleasure and involvement. Intense pleasure focuses attention on immediate reinforcements, means, and nearby goals; whereas mild pleasure allows more attention to future reinforcements, ends, and distant goals. Strong involvement elicits mental concentration and persistent effort, whereas weak involvement creates willingness to change activities. Concentration and short-sightedness reduce tensions that have arisen from other worries, but they add tensions if a player has no other worries. Some activities have strong effects on tensions; others weak. Similarly, short-sightedness, concentration, and persistence tend to decrease behavioral flexibility in a familiar task, but to foster learning and flexibility in a novel task. Crooked paths and persistence may produce discoveries, and therefore behavioral changes, even in rather familiar tasks.

Figure 11.1 diagrams the central properties of playful activities, which can be summarized by the following propositions:

- When they are low or moderate, immediate pleasure and involvement usually increase or decrease together. But, very high levels of involvement generate tensions and worries that undercut pleasure.
- As immediate pleasure increases, people become short-sighted: They put more emphasis on immediate reinforcements, on means more than ends, and on nearby goals instead of distant ones.
- Increasing involvement brings more mental concentration and more persistent effort.
- Concentration reduces awareness of time. More persistence implies less willingness to change activities.
- Short-sightedness, concentration, and persistence reinforce each other.
- Short-sightedness, concentration, and persistence may either increase or decrease flexibility or tension, depending on the activity and other factors.
- Greater short-sightedness makes people choose crooked paths toward long-run goals.
- Concentration, persistence, and crooked paths toward long-run goals make people slower to complete tasks.

Of course, the consequences of play also vary because actual consequences often differ from players' expectations. For example, therapeutic play may amplify tensions rather than relieve them. Activities that highlight competence generate

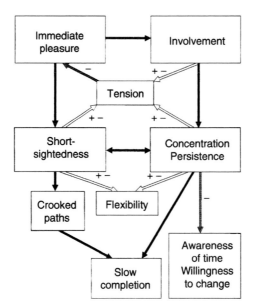

Figure 11.1. Basic relationships

pride after successes, but disappointment after failures. Competitive games make some players feel superior after successes, but make other players feel inferior after failures.

Learning

Other variations in consequences stem from the diversity of playful activities. Probably the most complex consequences relate to learning. We debated adding learning to Figure 11.1, but this would make the diagram very complicated because every box in Figure 11.1 affects learning in some way. Most types of play encourage learning because the pleasure and involvement of playful activities induces learners to expend time and effort. Exploratory play is a type of learning.

Still, both play and learning are large categories that encompass diversity, so some types of play discourage some types of learning, even as other types of play encourage other types of learning. For example, immediate pleasure and involvement may make people less willing to abandon activities that have bad consequences. Activities that encourage people to take crooked paths usually do not teach the shortest paths; but crooked paths may foster exploration and discovery, which in turn reveal short cuts. No learning occurs when players merely repeat overlearned activities. Fantasy settings encourage learners to suspend ingrained habits, but then usually give learners little help in transporting new behaviors to realistic settings.

Research findings about the effects of 'play' on learning seem to derive from the properties of specific activities or their settings. For instance, in their studies of children learning with computers, Papert (1980) and Turkle (1984) concluded that learning becomes more active and self-directed, new knowledge becomes a source of power and control, past assumptions are questioned, and interactions with other children increase because of discussions concerning computer use. Such conclusions assume that activities encourage exploration, allow social interaction, and give players discretion without risk of harm. These are prevalent properties of play, but not universal ones.

Some forms of play broaden behavioral repertoires incrementally; other forms lead players to discover or invent radically new behaviors. Both of these forms increase behavioral flexibility to varied degrees. Still other forms of play polish existing skills through repetitive practice. These forms may either reduce or increase behavioral flexibility, may make people either less or more autonomous. All forms increase some kinds of competence while interfering with others, but exploration and radical innovation may interfere with past skills while adding no significant new ones. Realistic settings help learners see real-life implications; unrealistic settings nurture fantasy and innovation.

Many other variable properties of playful activities or of players are cited in theories and research about play. Table 11.2 attempts to summarize these, but the lists could include almost every property of people or activities.

One reason it is hard to typify playful activities is 'playfulness', meaning people's predispositions to extract immediate pleasure from and to become involved in activities. Playfulness is a characteristic trait of some people, but it is also a temporary state of mind that almost everyone manifests on occasion.

Passive playfulness mainly involves reframing so that activities seem more playful; active playfulness makes a player an engineer of her activities. Lieberman (1977) argued that playfulness comes in five uncorrelated varieties: cognitive, humorous, joyous, physical, and social. Yet, variations in playfulness should be roughly as diverse as the variations in activities, and as difficult to describe. There are, after all, people who find their own pain quite pleasurable.

Consequences of Play at Work

Maximally playful tasks provide high levels of immediate pleasure and of involvement, but not extremely high levels. Such tasks elicit high, but not extremely high, short-sightedness, concentration, and persistence. People who perform very playful tasks enjoy what they are doing; they concentrate on their immediate activities and the pleasures those return; they try to continue performing those tasks and to refuse to change to other tasks; they ignore less playful tasks; they discount long-term goals and underestimate the passage of time; they choose complex methods that stretch out task-completion times. If the playful tasks are new ones, people tend to put much effort into learning them and exploring their properties; they usually try to control their own learning experiences and they

Table 11.2. Properties of play

Dimensions of playful activities	Dimensions of the interactions between activities and people	Dimensions of people
Clarity versus ambiguity	Clarity versus ambiguity	Needs for clarity versus ambiguity
Coherence of requirements	Familiarity versus novelty of task	Curiosity
Definition of rules	Credibility of stimuli	Left-brained versus right-brained
Clarity of feedback	Emphasis on why (explanations)	
Clarity of goal	Emphasis on what (facts)	Needs for consistency versus variety
Restriction of perceptual fields		Boredom
Amount of repetition	Consistency versus variety	Risk taking
	Dissonance	
Consistency versus variety	Degree of uncertainty	Simplicity versus difficulty
Amount of change in feedback	Degree of interest in feedback	Ability or skill
Frequency of reinforcement	Degree of surprise in stimuli	Cognitive complexity
Emphasis on repetition	Frequency of success	Degree of tension
Timing of stimuli	Frequency of reward versus punishment	Self-confidence
Intensity of stimuli		
	Simplicity versus difficulty	Behavioral and sensory modalities
Simplicity versus difficulty	Complexity difficulty, or challenge of activities	Various perceptual acuities
Emphasis on competence		Energy, needs for movement
Complexity of stimuli		Focus on detail
	Behavioral and sensory modalities	Liking for immediate versus delayed reinforcement
Behavioral and sensory modalities	Realism versus unrealism of context	
Emphasis on stimuli		Competitiveness
Emphasis on imitation	People's perceptions of activities' properties, such as clarity of feedback, timing of stimuli, or emphasis on imitation	Frequency of 'Playfulness'
Emphasis on human opponents		Type of 'Playfulness'
Emphasis on imagination or fantasy		
Degree of formality		Other
Amount of movement involved		Admiration for someone
Degree of control offered to player		Propensity to attribute control to self versus environment
Specialized enclave		

deviate from the courses that others prescribe. Thus, playful tasks foster creativity (Lieberman 1977).

These effects may be either good or bad, depending on the task's properties, performance criteria, and who evaluates performance. Of course, some tasks call for concentration and persistence and other tasks do not. Some situations reward swift completion or attention to long-term goals and other situations do not. Coworkers, bosses, or spouses often dispute players' choices of activities, either because they disagree with the players' preferences or because they do not themselves experience immediate pleasure and task involvement. A boss might not care whether a worker performs a task well because better performance does not produce higher profits. A boss might not want a worker to discover how to do a task better because the boss thinks hierarchical control is more important than task performance. Jarvenpaa and Dickson (1988) argued that very flexible graphics programs lower productivity because workers experiment too much. Conflicts between computers and spouses are legendary.

3. PLAYING WITH COMPUTERS

Spouses conflict with computers because computers are attractive and absorbing—so much so that some users become obsessed with computer usage.

Although some software is more playful and some less so, microcomputers make intrinsically playful partners. This playfulness owes much to computers' quickness: Microcomputers usually respond nearly instantaneously to users' actions. The mere existence of any response reinforces the preceding action, and a nonpunishing response makes the preceding action more likely to recur. The more immediate a response, the stronger reinforcement it provides. Thus, computer users receive repeated encouragement to continue pressing those keys as long as their key presses are more likely to produce desired consequences than disappointing ones. They receive these reinforcements continuously: Computers make exactly the same responses every time, and they never tire of repetition. Some software provides detailed, interactive feedback (Kay 1977). Being both pleasant and involving, these reinforcements make tasks more playful.

Interactions with Knowledge, Skill, Ease-of-Use, and Tailorability

This analysis implies that computers' playfulness depends strongly on software's 'ease-of-use' and 'tailorability', as well as on users' knowledge of computers and their skill in a specific task. Experienced and skilled users obtain desired consequences more often than inexperienced and unskilled users, of course, so they judge computers more playful. Even skilled users, however, judge very familiar tasks less playful.

High ease-of-use means that key presses are likely to produce desired consequences. Concepts about ease-of-use generally assume inexperienced users because nearly all the research on ease-of-use has concerned users who have little experience. Davis (1986) observed high correlations between ease-of-use and inexperienced users' fun. Carroll and Carrithers (1984) found that learners who are protected from making common errors learn more than unprotected learners.

However, users' notions of ease-of-use shift as they gain experience. Moderately experienced users usually think that the easiest software to use is the software they have been using. Sheppard, Bailey, and Bailey (1984) and Sheppard, Kruesi, and Curtis (1980) found that very experienced programmers who know several programming languages well prefer languages that inexperienced programmers find hard to use (Starbuck 1987).

Tailorability allows users to make computers' responses more pleasant. Many users enjoy the mere idea that they can individualize software. Rousseau (1986) proposed that programmability by users sets computers apart from other technologies. Some software lets users vary commands, speeds of response, difficulty levels, sounds, or colors. Color choices are important because some users dislike the colors that other users prefer. Silver (1988) found that ease-of-use affects users' perceptions of systems' flexibility because users fail to discover some features of difficult systems.

Tailorability may be especially important to playful software. Ghani (1990) surveyed 173 managers and professionals: The users who developed their own applications explored the capabilities of software, looked at data in different ways, spent more time, felt more involved, and enjoyed their work more.

Webster (1989) studied 43 workers who used computers 9 to 10 hours a week, had taken a Lotus course, and had used Lotus an average of 5.5 hours a week for six months. She introduced these people to two of three unfamiliar spreadsheet programs—Excel, Quattro, and VP Planner—and monitored their reactions. She did not measure users' perceptions of tailorability but she did measure their perceptions of how much control they could exercise. Table 11.3 summarizes users' perceptions of ease-of-use, control, and perceived playfulness and their preferences for the programs.

Davis (1986) studied forty MBA students' preferences for graphics programs. He observed relations between ease-of-use and three other perceptions: fun or expected enjoyment, output quality, and usefulness.

Quick responses, ease-of-use, and tailorability typify recent computers more than earlier ones and microcomputers more than mainframes (Gardner, Young, and Ruth 1989). Katz (1987) discovered much more experimenting by

Table 11.3. Ease-of-use, controllability, and playfulness of three spreadsheets

	Ease of use	User's control	Perceived playfulness	Users preferring
Quattro	28.9	16.4	1.20	81%
Excel	25.1	14.2	0.82	48%
VP Planner	24.4	11.0	−1.98	22%

microcomputer users than mainframe users. Webster (1989) found many more reports of play among users interacting with microcomputers than those interacting with mainframe systems.

Fritters

Of course, computers also offer opportunities for nonproductive play. Nash (1990) wrote of 'computer fritters', meaning activities that allow users to fritter away time at their computers. People may fritter away time by learning to use new programs, learning the details of operating systems, upgrading software or hardware, running spelling checkers, formatting text, or playing games. Fritterers as skilled as the authors of this chapter can spend weeks busily accomplishing nothing that has lasting value to others.

However, it is debatable whether frittering actually displaces activities that would have lasting value to others. Many kinds of work generate enough stress that occasional relief raises overall productivity. Some kinds of cognitive work go on while people are performing unessential chores, even while they are sleeping. Also, in domains that emphasize exploration, experimentation, and innovation, it is often difficult to figure out whether an activity is contributing to long-run results. A person who spends time graphing some data in diverse ways may be making trivial revisions, or may be discovering previously unseen relationships, and she may not know herself which description fits her activities.

When and Where to Play with Computers

Programmers have created software corresponding to all the types of play in Table 11.1. Even computer therapy has become a topic of research interest (Finkel 1990; Greist 1989).

Of course, playful software is more appropriate for certain activities and at certain times:

- Because playful software elicits more concentration and more effort, tasks should be ones in which concentration and effort can produce dividends. Two examples would be learning to type or searching through records.

- Because playful software tends to foster attention to detail, the tasks should be ones in which details can improve output quality and quality matters enough to warrant additional time and effort. Thus, playful software would be more useful for publishing a fine-art book than a newspaper. Users may need to beware of adding details that reduce output quality (Tufte 1983).

- Because playful software encourages users to explore options and to discover new paths, the tasks should be ones in which creativity might pay off in better outputs or better methods. Instances would include brainstorming, investigating poorly understood problems, and retouching photographs.

- Because playful software induces users to spend more time, the situations should be ones in which time is available and inexpensive. Overtime hours by salaried personnel generally have low marginal cost.

- Because playful software produces pleasure, the situations should be ones in which pleasure does not evoke disapproval. This implies bosses and coworkers who understand why more playful activities may be more productive. It may also imply workers who are not defensive about their productivity.

- Not all playful software injects variety or surprise. But, insofar as software does add variety or surprise, the tasks and situations should be ones that can tolerate more variety or surprise. Such software should get warmer receptions from people with predictable, consistent problems than from people with highly uncertain, erratic problems.

- Some effects can be created merely through labeling or superficial appearances. For example, learners usually become more willing to experiment if the training has the guise of play.

As discussed above, learning has complex relations to play. Some properties of playful software—such as sounds, colors, or cartoons—can encourage people who are learning to use new software. Yet, these properties may offend people who believe learning should not be fun, or they may irritate experienced users. Users should be able to mute them. Other properties of playful software—such as accelerated responses, elaborate options, or user-dictated rules—open up options that would bewilder inexperienced users. Users should be able to amplify them when they are ready for them.

4. A VANISHING DISTINCTION

Because they are simultaneously fun to use and serious tools, microcomputers are eroding the ritualized distinction between work and play.

This distinction has been pervasive in Western cultures. Huizinga (1950: 13), for example, said: 'The classic definition of play is: a free activity standing quite consciously outside "ordinary" life as being "not serious."... It is an activity connected with no material interest, and no profit can be gained by it. It proceeds within its own proper boundaries of time and space.' Erikson (1972) observed that working adults view play as recreation, and as a release from limitations imposed at work. Other authors have argued that adults view play as hedonistic and decadent (Csikszentmihalyi 1975), that socializing agents such as schools inhibit curiosity and play (Miller 1973; Voss 1987), that society puritanically views play as inferior to work (Ellis 1973), or that to accuse adults of playing is a form of ridicule (Millar 1968). Adults have tended to frown on the playing of games during working hours and to insist that play take place in specialized settings such as sports arenas.

Table 11.4a. Traditional concepts of work and play

	Unpleasant or uninvolving	Pleasant and involving
Productive	Work	Undefined
Unproductive	Undefined	Play

Table 11.4b. Modern concepts of work and play

	Unpleasant or uninvolving	Pleasant and involving
Productive	Productive chores	Playful work
Unproductive	Unproductive chores	Unproductive play

Kabanoff (1980: 60) proposed:

Industrialization resulted in a major segregation of the roles between the economic and noneconomic. Work became distinct spatially, and to some extent, socially.... Thus the previously highly integrated system of personal roles became disrupted, and this separation resulted in a clear recognition of the dualism of work and leisure.... [W]ork often has had the connotation of a chore and nonwork the connotation of play.

We suspect that the distinction is much, much older than industrialization, however. We also note that definitions of 'work' and 'play' reflect social-class distinctions. Painting or writing poetry would likely be classified as a working-class pastime and as an upper-class occupation. Anatol Rapaport once explained that he had stopped performing as a concert pianist and entered graduate study in mathematics because he did not want to remain a manual laborer all his life.

Whatever the distinction's origin, play and work have always been overlapping categories. Many people become deeply involved in and derive great pleasure from 'work' activities such as classroom oratory, exorcizing devils, farming, neurosurgery, or professional acting. Many people dislike 'play' activities such as amateur acting, listening to opera, playing chess, or riding roller coasters. 'Work' activities may produce nothing of value, either unintentionally when expectations do not come true, or intentionally when workers just put in time. 'Play' activities may yield lasting value, either intentionally or not, as when explorers discover unknown resources or an amateur painter creates a beautiful painting.

Tables 11.4a and 11.4b contrast traditional and modern concepts of work and play. The word 'chores' denotes activities that are unpleasant or uninvolving.

Economic development has been gradually breaking down the distinction between work and play. One reason is that economic development has been creating more and more jobs for legitimated experts such as consultants, medical doctors, professors, and researchers. Such occupations become increasingly prevalent for two reasons. First, industrialization creates greater wealth per capita, so more people can produce nothing. Second, it is much easier to raise the productivity of less skilled occupations. Of course, many of these experts work in specialized knowledge-intensive firms or in specialized divisions of large firms (Starbuck 1990, 1991).

Experts' high incomes place them into the upper classes, they demand high degrees of autonomy, and they have esoteric knowledge. The ambiguity of performance standards too adds discretion: Because the best methods or solutions are unclear, and innovation as such adds value, exploration and experimentation often prove fruitful. As a result, experts can do almost anything and get away with calling it work (Nash 1990). Shrewd social scientists might write an article about play and computers so that they can conduct research via computer games. Also, experts generally feel high involvement in their jobs, and they insist on receiving high job satisfaction. Most of experts' activities seem playful to experts. The division between play and work seems to vanish, although it may still be hard to convince a spouse that Pac-Man represents work.

Play is also central to the productive activities of many experts. Advertising agents, creative writers, designers, planners, and social theorists use fantasy and imagination. Athletes compete. Consultants and researchers explore. Mathematicians solve puzzles. Therapists may use therapeutic play. Such people cannot work without playing.

Yet, experts' ambiguous worlds do not challenge the populace at large. It is microcomputers that are forcing many people to rethink their concepts of work and play. Microcomputers are all over offices and they are entering factories and homes. Janitors, machinists, managers, secretaries, and spouses are having to 'deal with the temptation to play' during working hours (Nash 1990: 224). They are also having to reconcile their pleasure and involvement with the serious purposes their playful activities fulfill.

ACKNOWLEDGMENTS

The authors thank Richard Boland, Robert Gephart, Joseph Porac, Linda Trevino, and an anonymous referee for their suggestions.

12

Learning by Knowledge-Intensive Firms

1. DISCOVERING EXPERTISE

The General Manager of the Garden Company (a pseudonym) invited John Dutton and me to advise him about what he called their 'lot-size problem'. He was wondering, he said, whether Garden was making products in economically efficient quantities.

We had no idea what a strange but memorable experience this would be!

The General Manager proposed that we start with a tour of their largest plant, and assigned someone to guide us. Our guide took us first to the model shop, which produced jigs and patterns for use in the main plant. In the model shop, a skilled craftsman would start with a raw piece of metal, work on it with several different machine tools, and end with a finished component. Each successive component differed from those produced before and after, and each craftsman's tasks were shifting continually.

Then our guide took us into the plant itself. To our amazement, we found little difference from the model shop. Many workers were using several different machine tools in succession. Since each worker had several machines, most of the machines were idle at any moment.

Some workers chose to decorate castings' nonfunctional insides with patterns such as one sees on the doors of bank vaults, each worker inscribing his personal pattern. Quality standards were incredibly high, for the workers saw themselves as artisans who were putting their personal signatures on their products.

In the middle of the plant stood a wooden shack. Nails on the wall of this shack represented the distinct areas of the plant. Hanging on each nail were the production orders awaiting work in one area. We saw workers enter the shack, leaf through the orders, and choose orders to work on. Our guide said orders got processed promptly if they called for tasks the workers enjoyed, whereas orders might hang on the nails for weeks if they called for tasks the workers disliked.

Hoppers of partly finished components jammed the aisles. This, our guide explained, reflected raw-materials shortages, misplaced jigs and patterns, and missing components. After work began on an order, a worker would discover that needed raw material was out-of-stock—the order would have to wait while purchasing got the raw material. Or, a worker would be unable to find a needed jig, and a search would reveal that a subcontractor had borrowed the jig and not returned it—the order would have to wait while the jig was retrieved or replaced. Or, a product would be partly assembled and then the assemblers would discover that a component was missing—the incomplete assemblies would have to wait until the missing component emerged from production. Any of these problems might arise more than once during production of a single order. As one result, Garden was taking an average of nine months to deliver standard products that incorporated only a few hours of direct labor.

The plant tour left John and me rolling our eyes in wonder. We could not have imagined less efficient methods or greater disorder. It was hard to believe that Garden could even be making a profit! Yet the main building appeared in good condition, the office areas looked clean, and the General Manager's office had luxurious furnishings.

We told the General Manager that the plant had no lot-size problem, but we wondered whether he would not prefer to have one. A lot-size problem implied that machines would be set up for mass production and that workers would repeat specialized tasks. We suggested, however, that Garden would gain more direct benefit from production and inventory control than from mass production. A computer-based control system could keep raw materials in stock, monitor the progress of production, reduce delays, and make sure that jigs and patterns were available. Inventories could be much lower, machine usage could be much higher, and customers could receive their orders much more quickly.

The General Manager asked for estimates. We told him a control system would have a payback period of roughly two years and the inventory savings alone would cut production costs by at least 10 percent. To this, he responded, 'Why should we want to do that? Ten percent of our production costs is only 1 percent of our revenues.' He then produced Garden's financial statements for the previous year. After-tax profits had been $40 million on sales of $83.5 million. 'And that', he crowed, 'was a year in which we had a strike for ten months!'

He went on to explain that Garden made every effort to avoid direct competition. Over a third of Garden's personnel were engineers who were good at designing new products that no other firm was producing. Garden's policy was to continue making a product only as long as its gross margin exceeded 75 percent of sales. When competition drove a gross margin below 75 percent, Garden would stop offering that product for sale. The average gross margin across all products exceeded 90 percent.

Allowing for the corporate tax rate of 52 percent, we surmised that Garden employed expert tax accountants as well as expert engineers.

John and I had received several lessons in business ... and the General Manager had not even charged us tuition!

Garden's high profits did not arise from fine steel, unusually skilled craftsmen, or exceptional capital equipment. Its marketing was ordinary. Although Garden delivered high quality, it used no esoteric production technologies, and it often subcontracted production to a broad array of machine shops. It was this subcontracting that had enabled Garden to earn high profits despite a long strike. The profits also did not come from managerial competence of the sort most production firms cultivate. In that domain, Garden appeared utterly incompetent.

The remarkable profits sprang from technical and strategic expertise. The key labor inputs came not from the machinists in the plant, but from the engineers and managers in the office building. These people had created monopolistic opportunities for Garden over and over again. Garden was the only producer of many of its products, and the dominant producer of all of them.

Garden's key input was expertise. It was a knowledge-intensive firm (KIF).

Knowledge intensity has diverse meanings, partly because people use different definitions of knowledge. The next section of this chapter gives my conclusions about such issues. Two following sections then make empirically based observations about the activities inside KIFs. The first of these sections reviews the kinds of work experts do, and explains why experts find learning hard. The ensuing section then describes organizational learning: KIFs learn by managing training and personnel turnover, and by creating physical capital, routines, organizational culture, and social capital. To see the results of learning, the fifth section looks at KIFs' long-term strategic development, including multinational expansion.

2. WHAT IS A KIF?

The term *knowledge-intensive* imitates economists' labeling of firms as capital-intensive or labor-intensive. These labels describe the relative importance of capital and labor as production inputs. In a capital-intensive firm, capital has more importance than labor; in a labor-intensive firm, labor has the greater importance. By analogy, labeling a firm as knowledge-intensive implies that knowledge has more importance than other inputs.

Although the terms capital-intensive, labor-intensive, and knowledge-intensive refer to inputs, capital, labor, and knowledge also may be outputs. Why is it useful to classify firms by their inputs? A study of office-equipment or software companies groups firms by their outputs. Such a study emphasizes similarities and differences across customers and distribution channels, and it makes a good basis for analyzing relations with customers or competitors. By contrast, a study of meat packers or machine shops, groups firms by their inputs. By emphasizing similarities and differences across raw materials and personnel, such a study makes a good basis for analyzing internal structure and operations. Input classes highlight the effects of resource availabilities, and their determinants, such as governmental policies. As well, Sveiby and Risling (1986) argued that KIFs call for new definitions of ownership and new ways of controlling the uses of capital. Traditional notions of ownership, they said, assume that financial or physical capital dominates labor, whereas human capital dominates in KIFs.

Assessing the importance of knowledge is harder than comparing capital and labor, however. Economists compare capital and labor by expressing them in monetary units, but market prices mainly reflect values that many firms share. At best, prices reflect those aspects of inputs that could transfer readily from one firm to another. Prices ignore inputs' importance for intrafirm activities or for activities that are idiosyncratic to a single firm. Since much knowledge has disparate values in different situations, monetary measures of knowledge are elusive and undependable.

Knowledge itself is nearly as ambiguous an idea as value or importance, and it has many guises (Winter 1987). During a dozen seminars aimed at research about knowledge-intensive firms, almost every speaker devoted time to his or her preferred definition of knowledge. Such discussions have led me to five conclusions.

1. *A KIF may not be information-intensive.* Knowledge is a stock of expertise, not a flow of information. Thus, knowledge relates to information in the way that assets relate to income (Machlup 1962, took another view). Some activities draw on extensive knowledge without processing large amounts of current information—management consulting, for example. Conversely, a firm can process much information without using much knowledge. For instance, Automatic Data Processing (ADP) produces payroll checks. ADP processes vast amounts of information, but it is probably more capital-intensive than knowledge-intensive. Producing a payroll check requires little expertise, and many people have this expertise.

The distinction between a KIF and an information-intensive firm can be hard to draw. From one perspective, ADP merely processes data for other firms, using mainly capital in the forms of computers and software. From another perspective, ADP succeeds because it does its specialized task better than its customers can do it themselves. This superior performance likely comes from both expertise and returns to scale, so expertise and large scale reinforce each other.

2. *In deciding whether a firm is knowledge-intensive, one ought to weigh its emphasis on esoteric expertise instead of widely shared knowledge.* Everybody has knowledge, most of it widely shared, but some idiosyncratic and personal. If one defines knowledge broadly to encompass what everybody knows, every firm can appear knowledge-intensive. One loses the value of focusing on a special category of firms. Similarly, every firm has some unusual expertise. To make the KIF a useful category, one has to require that exceptional expertise make important contributions. One should not label a firm as knowledge-intensive unless exceptional and valuable expertise dominates commonplace knowledge.

Some forms of expertise may be hard to measure separately from their effects. Why, for example, does one attribute strategic expertise to the Garden Company? One might label Garden a KIF because it employed so many engineers. But many firms employ more engineers with less remarkable results, and Garden's products embodied no technological miracles. These engineers were unusual because they were using their knowledge in ways that gave Garden extraordinary strategic advantages.

Managerial expertise may pose special problems in this regard. It would make no sense to measure managerial expertise by the fraction of employees who are managers or by the wages paid to managers. To judge managers expert, one has to look either at the managers' behaviors or at the results of their behaviors. Do their firms produce unusually high profits? Do the managers show interpersonal skill?

3. *Even after excluding widely shared knowledge, one has to decide how broadly to define expertise.* One can define expertise broadly, recognize many people as

experts, and see the expertise imbedded in many machines and routines. This strategy makes KIFs less special, but it removes some blinders caused by stereotypes about expertise, and it increases the generality of findings about KIFs. Alternatively, one can acknowledge only the legitimated expertise of people who have extensive formal educations, and can emphasize high-tech machines and unusual routines. This second strategy makes KIFs appear more special, but produces findings that generalize only to the few firms that use such expertise intensively. It also accepts stereotypes about expertise.

These definitional strategies have political overtones. A broad definition of expertise obscures the influence of social class and social legitimacy, whereas a narrow definition highlights the influence of social class and social legitimacy. Legitimated expertise is normally an upper-middle-class possession. Legitimated experts usually earn wages high enough to put them into the upper-middle class. They normally gain their expertise through formal higher education, which entails at least the expense of foregone income. Higher education also may give experts entry into recognized professions.

Even jobs widely regarded as unskilled may entail much knowledge (Kusterer 1978). Skilled trades may be as esoteric and difficult to enter as the professions (Ekstedt 1989). Yet, people put other labels—such as know-how or skill or understanding—on expertise learned through primary school or on-the-job experience.

Sweden has spawned much of the public discussion and research about KIFs. In 1983, Sveiby started writing about 'knowledge companies' in one of Sweden's most prominent periodicals, and Swedish business executives expressed strong interest in this topic. Sveiby and Risling followed with a 1986 book that became a nonfiction best-seller. Probably this interest reflects Sweden's high incomes and high educational levels.

4. An expert may not be a professional, and a KIF may not be a professional firm. Professionals have specialized expertise that they gain through training or experience, and KIFs may employ people who have specialized expertise. Thus, KIFs may be professional firms.

Many KIFs are not professional firms, however. One reason is that not all experts belong to recognized professions. A profession has at least four properties besides expertise: an ethical code, cohesion, collegial enforcement of standards, and autonomy (Schriesheim, Von Glinow, and Kerr 1977). Professionals' ethical codes require them to serve clients unemotionally and impersonally, without self-interest. Professionals identify strongly with their professions, more strongly than with their clients or their employers. They not only observe professional standards, they believe that only members of their professions have the competence and ethics to enforce these standards. Similarly, professionals insist that outsiders cannot properly supervise their activities.

Management consulting and software engineering, for example, do not qualify as recognized professions. Without doubt, those who do these jobs well have rare expertise. Nevertheless, the ultimate judges of their expertise are their clients or their supervisors, and their employers set and enforce their ethical codes and performance standards. Similarly, despite talk about professional management, managers do not belong to a professional body that enforces an ethical code and insists that its values and standards supersede those of managers' employers. Employers appoint managers without regard for the candidates' memberships in external bodies. Strong loyalty to a professional body would contradict managers' roles as custodians of their employing firms.

Sveiby and Lloyd (1987) divided 'know-how companies' into categories reflecting their managerial or technical expertise. They pointed to law firms as examples of high technical expertise but low managerial expertise. To illustrate firms with high managerial expertise and low technical expertise, they cited McDonald's fast-food chain. On the other hand, Ekstedt (1988, 1989: 3–9) contrasted 'knowledge companies' with industrial companies, high-technology companies, and service companies 'such as hamburger chains'. In his schema, both high-technology companies and knowledge companies have high knowledge intensity, but high-technology companies have higher intensity of real capital than do knowledge companies.

Professional firms can exploit and must allow for all five properties of professions, not merely expertise. Health-maintenance organizations, for instance, must accept doctors' codes of ethics and must allow medical societies to adjudicate some issues. KIFs form a broader category, in which many issues reflect labor markets, interpersonal networks, and experts' individuality, self-interest, and social standing.

Yet, it could be that most KIFs have nearly all the properties that authors have assigned to professional firms. For example, Hinings, Brown, and Greenwood (1991: 376, 390) wrote:

Bucher and Stelling (1969) suggested that organizations dominated by professionals had a number of special characteristics, including professionals building their own roles rather than fitting into preset roles, spontaneous internal differentiation based on work interests, competition and conflict for resources and high levels of political activity.... The *distribution of authority* has long been identified as unique in an autonomous professional organization because of its emphasis on collegiality, peer evaluation and autonomy, informality, and flexibility of structure (Bucher and Stelling 1969; Montagna 1968; Ritzer and Walczak 1986)

Professionals are not the only experts who build their own roles, divide work to suit their interests, compete for resources, or emphasize autonomy, collegiality, informality, and flexible structures. Other occupations share these traditions, and some experts have enough demand for their services that they can obtain autonomy without support from a recognized profession.

There is another reason KIFs may not be professional firms.

5. KIFs' knowledge may not be in individual people. Besides the knowledge held by individual people, one can find knowledge in: (*a*) capital such as plant, equipment, or financial instruments; (*b*) firms' routines and cultures; and (*c*) professional cultures.

People convert their knowledge to physical forms when they write books or computer programs, design buildings or machines, produce violins or hybrid corn, or create financial instruments such as mutual-fund shares (Ekstedt 1988, 1989). Conversely, people may gain knowledge by reading books, studying buildings, buying shares, or running computer programs.

People also translate their knowledge into firms' routines, job descriptions, plans, strategies, and cultures. Nelson and Winter (1982) treated behavioral routines as the very essence of organizations—the means by which firms can produce predictable results while adapting to social and technological changes. Simultaneously, Deal and Kennedy (1982) and Peters and Waterman (1982) were saying it is cultures that perform these functions.

Describing McDonald's as a firm with low technical expertise overlooks the expertise in McDonald's technology and organization. McDonald's success stems from its ability to deliver a consistent quality in diverse environments and despite high turnover of low-skilled people. To get such results, the firm operates extensive training programs and conducts research about production techniques and customers' tastes. Although training at Hamburger University may give McDonald's managers more skill than those at most restaurants, McDonald's managers may have no more skill than those in most production firms. Ceaseless expansion forces McDonald's to concentrate training on new managers. Also, McDonald's substitutes technology and routines for in-person management.

Professional cultures too carry valuable knowledge. For instance, lawyers live amid conflict. Lawyers' culture not only supports conflict, it shows them how to conflict to maximum effect and minimum damage to their egos and reputations. Lawyers strive to advocate their clients' interests even when this might produce injustice, and they depend on conflict to foster justice by exposing all sides. Lawyers try to keep their roles as advocates for their clients separate from their interpersonal relations as members of the legal profession. They observe behavioral codes strictly, and much of their conflict concerns interpretations of and conformity to behavioral codes. When lawyers cannot themselves resolve disagreements, they seek help from above—judges in courts or superiors in law firms. The legal profession also serves as micro environments in which lawyers can cultivate long-term reputations. Some lawyers seek reputations as tough negotiators who yield little and demand much. To nurture such reputations, they may refuse to make concessions that their clients want to make.

A Starting Point

Debates about how KIFs differ from other firms persuaded me to focus on firms that would be knowledge-intensive by almost anyone's definition. As a starting point, I defined an expert as someone with formal education and experience equivalent to a doctoral degree, and a KIF as a firm in which such experts are at least one-third of the personnel. Later, Lawrence Rosenberg pointed out that some expertise takes nonhuman forms. Some KIFs may even hold most of their expertise in nonhuman forms, but I have not studied such firms.

I have not been distinguishing firms from other organizations because many KIFs operate at the boundary between government and private enterprise. They are not-for-profit firms that work mainly or exclusively for government agencies.

Although I have interviewed in eight firms satisfying the above criteria, three stand out as excellent examples.

The Rand Corporation and Arthur D. Little are the two firms that came immediately to mind when I first began thinking about the *knowledge-intensive firm*. The Rand Corporation is the prototypic think tank, located near the beach in Santa Monica. Staffed by Ph.Ds, Rand mainly makes policy studies: Rand's personnel evaluate current policies and generate policy alternatives. Rand holds long-term contracts from the US Air Force and the US Army, and it receives short-term grants or contracts from many Federal agencies. Its reports are ubiquitous in Washington, DC.

On the other coast, in a wooded campus near Harvard and MIT, Arthur D. Little is the oldest American consulting firm and an exemplary one. A. D. Little has 21 offices and roughly 1,500 consultants. In a typical year, they complete over 5,000 projects in 60 countries. The project topics range from product technology, to operations management, to economic development and strategic planning.

Partners in Wachtell, Lipton, Rosen, and Katz make more money than those in any other American law firm: It is to Wachtell, Lipton that other lawyers turn when they need the very best and they do not care how much it costs. Moreover, not only the partners do well at Wachtell, Lipton: Surveys of junior lawyers have repeatedly said Wachtell, Lipton is the best place to work.

Although quite unlike each other, all three firms share similarities, as do the other firms I have studied. Large fractions of their people have advanced degrees. They process information slowly in comparison to information-intensive firms. Their capital equipment is mainly general-purpose office space, office machines, and computers, although A. D. Little also has laboratories.

My observations come mainly from interviews. Indeed, 'interview' seems an inadequate label for fascinating conversations with very intelligent, perceptive, articulate people. I had only to point to a few issues that interested me, and they would begin to extrapolate—telling me who else I should interview, what issues *ought* to interest me, where my assumptions seemed wrong, and how their worlds look to them. I often found myself discussing topics or trying frameworks I had not considered before walking into a room.

Are KIFs Peculiar?

One critic complained that all my examples describe peculiar firms that exist solely because their environments have uncorrectable problems. An answer to this charge has three parts.

First, all firms *are* peculiar: We should look for and celebrate their individuality. There are many ways to solve most problems, more opportunities than anyone can pursue, many criteria for judging what is best. It is as important to see how individuals differ—whether individual people, or individual organizations, or individual societies—as to see what they have in common. It is as important to understand complexities as simplicities.

Second, successful firms *cause* their environments to have uncorrectable problems. Firms and their environments change symbiotically. Not only must an environment be hospitable to a KIF, but the existence of a KIF induces its environment to assume that it exists. For example, U.S. military services reassign personnel every two or three years. As a result, military personnel have little experience in their successive jobs, know little of tasks' histories or traditions, and cannot manage long-term projects effectively. Long-term projects would founder if they depended on military personnel. By providing civilian specialists who can have long tenures, the Rand Corporation and the Aerospace Corporation help the military to manage long-term projects, and they reduce the costs of retraining. Yet, having the services of Rand and Aerospace may have kept the military from developing other ways to manage long-term projects and other personnel policies.

Third, I have sought out the most successful firms, and all exceptionally successful firms exploit peculiarities. A modal firm in a competitive industry makes low profits, and it does not survive long. High profits and long survival come from monopolistic competition. Monopolistic competition arises from firms' developing distinctive competencies and mirroring their environments' unusual needs and capabilities.

Wachtell, Lipton shows how exceptional success may feed on peculiarities. The firm's founding partners had disliked their experiences in other law firms: They agreed to follow some unusual policies that would produce a better work environment. These policies have fostered collaboration and given the firm an edge in attracting new lawyers. The founding partners came from a less well-known law school whose graduates had restricted job opportunities: Much better than its reputation, this school supplied highly talented lawyers during the early years. A crisis during the firm's second year led the partners to adopt an unusual policy: Wachtell, Lipton never agrees to represent clients for long periods. This policy has had unforeseen long-term consequences for the types of cases the firm handles.

Success reinforces success, and excellence itself fends off competition. Today, with elegant offices amid New York's corporate headquarters, Wachtell, Lipton can choose among the top graduates from law schools across America. Potential clients offer the firm four to eight times as many cases than it can handle: It can pick the cases that look most interesting and best suit its abilities. The cases that potential clients bring are nonroutine ones that involve large sums, and they often concern immediate threats. Such cases draw attention, as do Wachtell, Lipton's legal innovations.

3. EXPERTS' WORK

Interactions Between Creating, Applying, and Preserving

The experts in KIFs gather information through interviews or reading; they analyze and interpret this information; and they make written and oral reports to clients and colleagues (Rhenman 1973: 161). An observer cannot overlook the strong, overt similarities across people, sites, and projects.

Nevertheless, experts themselves describe their activities diversely. Some say that they are applying old knowledge to new problems, others that they are creating new knowledge, and still others that they are preserving knowledge that already exists. Experts who see themselves as producing new knowledge emphasize the recency or originality of their data and the differences between their findings and those of predecessors. They may classify such work either as basic scientific research or as applied research on markets, products, or processes. Other experts see their work mainly as applying existing knowledge to current problems. For instance, when most lawyers do research, they analyze and interpret previous cases and they emphasize the continuity over time of knowledge and its meaning. To gain acceptance of their rulings, most judges de-emphasize the innovative quality of their reasoning.

The distinction between creating knowledge and applying it is often hard to make. Lawyers may be more successful if they reinterpret precedent cases imaginatively, or if they conceive original strategies. The Garden Company's engineers were applying known techniques, but they were applying them to products no one else had imagined. Basic research may have direct applicability, and applied research may contribute fundamental knowledge. When it comes to systems as complex as a human body or an economy, people may only be able to create valid knowledge by trying to apply it (Starbuck 1976: 1100–1103).

To my surprise, several experts described themselves as memory cells. They said their jobs are to preserve information that their clients have difficulty preserving. As mentioned above, because the U.S. military services rotate assignments frequently, military personnel lack job experience and cannot manage long-term projects. Also, military wage scales are too low to attract and retain highly educated experts. To compensate, the military services sign contracts with KIFs that provide long-term continuity of management and expertise. These KIFs employ civilian experts who do not rotate assignments frequently and who either manage long-term projects directly or advise military managers. There may be enough of these KIFs to make up a distinct, long-term-memory industry.

Creating, applying, and preserving intertwine and complement each other. At least over long periods, merely storing knowledge does not preserve it. For old knowledge to have meaning, people must relate it to their current problems and activities. They have to translate it into contemporary language and frame it within current issues. Effective preserving looks much like applying. As time passes and social and technological changes add up, the needed translations grow larger, and applying knowledge comes to look more like creating knowledge.

For new knowledge to have meaning, people must fit it into their current beliefs and perspectives, and familiarity with existing knowledge signals expertise. Evaluators assess completed research partly by its applicability, and they judge research proposals partly by the researchers' mastery of past research. Thus, Rand Corporation, which depends on research grants for some of its income, makes elaborate literature searches before writing proposals. Rand also employs

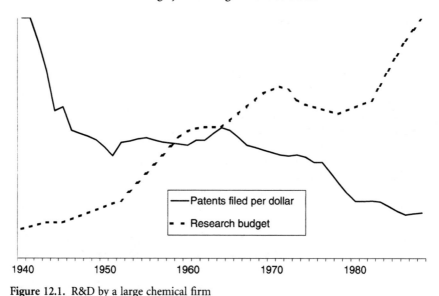

Figure 12.1. R&D by a large chemical firm

Note: Vertical axes are nominal. Data are in constant dollars. Graphs show moving averages.

public-information staff, who highlight the relevance of research findings. Similarly, A. D. Little's executives believe that having credibility with clients requires their firm to specialize in certain industries, technologies, and functions. They want new experts to have had several years experience in one of these industries and functions or technologies.

Ambiguity about the meaning of knowledge creation implies a weak tie, if any, between knowledge creation and knowledge intensity. Clearly, more input does not always produce more output. For example, Brooks (1975) pointed out how rare are the skills needed to create operating systems for computers. Adding more people to such a programing project does not accelerate it. On the contrary, more people may slow a project down, by forcing the experts with rare skills to spend more time coordinating, communicating, and observing bureaucratic routines. An example of another kind concerns R&D by a large chemical firm. As Figure 12.1 shows, this firm has spent more and more on R&D, but incremental dollars have yielded fewer and fewer patent filings.

Learning

Because experts are learned, one expects them to value learning highly. Nonetheless, many experts resist new ideas.

Such resistance has several bases. First, clients or even other experts may interpret experts' need to learn as evidence of deficient knowledge. Thus, experts find it risky to discuss their learning needs with clients or colleagues. Second, many experts get paid by the hour, and many others have to account carefully for their uses of time. Explicit learning reduces the time available for billable services. Third, expertise implies specialization, which reduces versatility and limits flexibility. To become experts, people must specialize and move into distinct occupational niches. Required years of education limit entry to these niches; and many experts belong to recognized professions that restrict entrance through licences and examinations. These niches, however, could become evolutionary deadends (Beyer 1981). Fourth, experts' niches are partial monopolies. Like other monopolists, experts hold favorable positions that confer high incomes and social statuses. These positions also give experts much to lose from social and technological changes. Fifth, expertise entails perceptual filters that keep experts from noticing some social and technological changes (Armstrong 1985; Starbuck and Dutton 1973). Even while they are gaining knowledge within their specialties, experts may overlook exciting and relevant events just outside their domains.

Knowledge creation accelerates the social and technological changes in experts' domains (Wolff and Baumol 1989). Because employers or clients often seek expertise to help them understand rapid social and technological changes, experts tend to find employment in rapidly changing domains. Thus, most experts are all too aware that expertise needs updating: They have to seek a dynamic stability in which their apparent knowledge evolves while they retain their favorable positions.

Besides, experts' scepticism about new ideas can enhance their learning. Learning is not adaptation, and it requires more subtlety and complexity than mere change. People can change without learning, and too much readiness to discard current knowledge undermines learning. To learn, one must build up knowledge like layers of sediment on a river bottom. To learn effectively, one must accumulate knowledge that has long-term value while replacing the knowledge that lacks long-term value.

The key issue that experts, like other learners, confront is how to sift out knowledge that will have little value in the future. For this winnowing, expertise itself evidently confers no advantages. Studies of many fields have consistently found that renowned experts predict future events no more accurately than somewhat informed people (Armstrong 1985; Ascher 1978; Camerer and Johnson 1991). Still, few experts know about such studies, and many experts overestimate their abilities as oracles.

4. ORGANIZATIONAL LEARNING IN KIFS

Personnel Training and Turnover

Learning generally poses different issues for firms than for individual experts. For example, the need to update leads individual experts to spend time reading or attending conferences or courses. By contrast, senior people in a firm see updating as an activity to manage more than to do. Senior people may assign their juniors to take certain courses, or to read certain journals and to summarize what they read. Senior people sometimes deny certain juniors permission to attend conferences and tell others that they must attend and report what they heard.

What individuals find hard, firms may find easy, and vice versa. In particular, individual experts learn little from changing firms, whereas organizational learning readily takes the form of personnel changes. KIFs aggressively pursue new experts with wanted knowledge, and they limit the job security of continuing experts. Since most consulting or research projects have short terms, experts must repeatedly renegotiate their relations with their firms and adapt their knowledge and skills to current tasks. Some small consulting firms give new consultants just three months in which to start bringing in enough business to cover their salaries. A would-be consultant who does not meet this target has to seek other employment. Large consulting firms may not treat each consultant as a separate profit centre, but they do ask consultants to account strictly for their time. A. D. Little, for example, expects most consultants to spend 70–75 percent of their time on activities for which clients are paying, and 20–25 percent of their time on personal betterment or soliciting new business.

Such development and personnel policies keep expertise closely aligned with environmental opportunities, so rigidity and blind spots may be more troublesome for individual experts than for KIFs. Indeed, such policies make KIFs faddish; and efforts to stay on the cutting edges of rapid technological and social changes accentuate this faddishness.

The policies also make boundaries porous. Just as KIFs may hire experts from their clients or customers, KIFs' clients or customers may add expertise by hiring KIFs' personnel (Stinchcombe and Heimer 1988). Experts at the forefront of social or technological change usually have many job opportunities. Replacing experts solely to update expertise weakens loyalty to the firm and adds variance to organizational culture. The social networks that make it easy to adopt new ideas also make in-house ideas accessible to other firms, as does the ease of transmitting information. Thus, KIFs find it hard to keep unique expertise exclusive.

Stinchcombe and Heimer (1988) described successful software firms as 'precarious monopolies'. They are monopolies insofar as they exhibit unusual abilities. Niches evolve naturally as individuals and small groups concentrate on specific streams of innovation. The firms also strive explicitly to develop and maintain unusual abilities. Unusual abilities help the firms to market their services and to avoid head-on competition.

Stinchcombe and Heimer pointed out that these partial monopolies are constantly at risk, both because technological changes may make unusual abilities obsolete and because key experts may depart. Computer technology has been changing especially rapidly, and the software firms' relations with clients and computer manufacturers repeatedly expose their experts to job offers. To sell their services to clients, software firms have to publicize the talents of their key experts, and this publicity creates job opportunities for the touted experts.

Not all KIFs control distinctive domains of knowledge. Professional firms find it especially hard to sustain monopolistic positions. The recognized professions work at keeping their control of knowledge and at preserving their members' autonomy: Firms would run into strong opposition if they would try to convert professional expertise to organizational property. Moreover, many products of professional firms are easy to imitate. For example, Martin Lipton invented the 'poison pill' defence against unfriendly corporate takeovers; but, after other law firms saw examples, Wachtell, Lipton was no longer the sole source for poison pills (Powell 1993).

Several modes of organizational learning do convert individual expertise into organizational property. These conversion processes produce at least three types of organizational property: physical capital, routines, and organizational culture. The creation of social capital, such as mutual trust with clients or customers, tends to convert organizational experience into the property of individuals.

Physical Capital

Both KIFs and individuals can gain new expertise by buying capital goods. Computer software affords obvious examples.

Not long ago, expertise was uneven across accountants who handled income taxes. Now, every accountant has low-cost access to software that makes no arithmetical errors, omits nothing, incorporates the latest changes in tax codes, and warns of conditions that might trigger audits by tax authorities.

Lawyers have recently begun to use a computer program, CLARA, to help them do legal research. CLARA helps small law firms compete more effectively against large firms, and helps novice lawyers produce results comparable to experienced lawyers (Laudon and Laudon 1991: ch. 4). Although unfinished, CLARA does research nearly as well as law professors. On reading of this achievement, one practicing lawyer sniffed: 'Too bad; maybe it will get better someday.'

In the short term, KIFs may be able to turn expertise into concrete capital. For instance, decades of experience enabled the large public accounting firms to create systematic auditing procedures. The firms then turned these procedures into checklists that novice accountants and clerical staff can complete. Similarly, Rand Corporation's research occasionally produces databases that have value beyond the projects that created them. Rand tries to exploit these databases by proposing new projects that would draw upon them.

Physical capital may be even harder to protect and retain than are people, however. Physical capital also may be less flexible than either the technologies it uses or the markets it serves. The auditing checklists created by firm A work just as well for firm B, so B can easily take advantage of A's experience.

IntelligenceWare wrote superior programs for artificial-intelligence applications. The firm has been seeking to exploit these programs by adapting them to diverse uses. Over the longer term, competing firms can analyze and imitate IntelligenceWare's programs. Also, because IntelligenceWare's programs are too complex for incremental evolution, experience will eventually force the firm to undertake a drastic rewrite.

Databases can be updated piecemeal, but they too gain or lose currency. At Rand Corporation, Brian Jenkins has compiled a database on terrorism. He began this on his own initiative, but the database became a more general asset when terrorist acts escalated and Rand began receiving inquiries about terrorism from the press. Although the press's interest in terrorism fluctuates with the incidence of terrorism, such a database requires continual maintenance.

Orlikowski (1988: 179–267) detailed a consulting firm's efforts to capture its experience as software. Over ten years and many projects, consultants built various software 'tools' that helped them plan projects and carry them out efficiently. The tools originated separately when consultants saw needs or opportunities, but the firm's general production philosophy implicitly guided these developments and rendered the tools mutually compatible. Also, at first, isolated people used these tools voluntarily, but informal norms gradually made their use widespread and mandatory. Thus, the tools both expressed the firm's culture in tangible form, and reinforced the culture by clarifying its content and generalizing its application. Generalization made the differences among clients' problems less and less important, and it weakened the contributions that clients could make to problem-solving. Generalization also reduced the influence of more-technical consultants and increased the influence of less technical consultants. In their interviews, the consultants stressed the tools' strong influence on their perceptions of problems and their methods of solving them. Eventually, the firm started to sell the tools to other firms. At that point, the firm's culture, methods, and experience became products that other firms could buy.

The ease of distributing it makes physical capital an effective way to build organizational culture, and it offers firms opportunities to expand their markets. Easy distribution also can cost firms their competitive advantages. Departing employees can easily take forms, manuals, or floppy disks with them. When firms turn physical capital into products that they sell to competitors, knowledge-intensive capital loses the character of being esoteric and advantageous. In this sense, a portable expert system is self-contradictory. Distributing an expert system renders its knowledge no longer esoteric, and thus no longer expert. It is not only tax accountants who now have low-cost access to programs for filing income taxes; millions of nonaccountants are using these programs to file their business or personal taxes.

Routines

Firms also learn by creating routines (Nelson and Winter 1982; Starbuck 1983), but formalized routines look bureaucratic. Highly educated experts dislike bureaucracy: Conflicts between professions and bureaucracies have attracted much research (Schriesheim, Von Glinow, and Kerr 1977), and some of these conflicts apply to expertise in general. Most experts want autonomy, they want recognition of their individuality, and they want their firms to have egalitarian structures.

Some experts derive independent power from their close ties with clients, so service KIFs with multiple clients look more like loose confederations than bureaucracies. Among the service KIFs, only those having long-term contracts with a very few clients seem able to bureaucratize. Even such KIFs must bureaucratize cautiously, for their expert employees have external job opportunities. Of course, a product KIF such as the Garden Company does not run into such problems because its experts have little contact with customers.

The KIFs that can enforce bureaucratic routines can draw benefits from them. Impersonal roles make programs for personnel development possible, and they ease transfers of people to meet shifting tasks. Consistent quality is essential to keeping long-term clients or customers. Bureaucratic clients or customers expect the KIFs they hire to look and behave as they do. For example, the Aerospace Corporation has a seven-layer managerial hierarchy because this structure matches the hierarchy of the U.S. Air Force.

Bhargava (1990) observed that the software firms in which developers interact closely with clients emphasize formalized documentation. These firms devote more effort to planning and systems analysis, to writing user manuals, and to recording the activities carried out and times spent on specific projects. These documents contribute to better client relations and reduce the firms' dependence on developers who might depart.

The Rand Corporation illustrates effective bureaucratization by a KIF. Rand's library staff watches for opportunities to submit proposals, and it produces bibliographies to aid technical experts' proposal writing. Some of Rand's experts review others' proposals and reports to assure that they meet Rand's standards for data gathering and statistical analysis. Copy editors suggest ways to make proposals and reports more intelligible. These activities undoubtedly improve final reports' acceptability and the odds of proposals' winning funds. Rand's research proposals have a far-above-average success rate.

Larger KIFs are better able and more inclined to bureaucratize, and larger KIFs can better tolerate and balance the opposing forces in their work. For instance, Brooks (1975) argued that 'conceptual integrity' is the key to high quality in systems design. Attaining conceptual integrity, he said, probably requires centralized control by a few key experts, whereas programming and testing a designed system may require many experts. Such work can be troublesome for KIFs with experts who see themselves as equals and substitutes. Large KIFs mitigate these problems by dividing work into projects and allowing experts to specialize in either design or implementation (Bhargava 1990). Creating routines requires persistence, and both persistence and learning may benefit from specializing with respect to technologies, markets, functions, or locations.

On the other hand, large KIFs may lack knowledge intensity. KIFs are prone to grow by adding support staff instead of experts. Adding support staff promises to increase profitability per expert by using experts more efficiently, whereas growth by adding experts may use experts less efficiently. KIFs also grow by adding activities, products, or services that promise to extract more value from the expertise already in-house. Thus, KIFs tend to lose knowledge intensity as they grow.

Some experts see this loss of knowledge intensity as desirable—a sensible way to get the maximum value from current staff. Other experts see growth as a necessity demanded by large clients or numerous customers. Still other experts see this loss of knowledge intensity as a danger to be combated—by avoiding growth, diversification, and geographic dispersion.

Routinization helps to make knowledge intensity unstable. As with physical capital, converting expertise to routines is risky. Routines may become targets of imitation, spread, and gradually lose the character of being esoteric and advantageous. A routine used by many firms confers small comparative advantages on its users.

Organizational Culture

Cultures have to be built gradually because they are delicate and poorly understood. Building a special organizational culture takes much effort as well as imagination. Imitating another firm's culture is quite difficult, if even possible, because every culture involves distinctive traditions.

Maister (1985: 4) wrote admiringly of 'one-firm firms', which stress 'institutional loyalty and group effort'. 'In contrast to many of their (often successful) competitors who emphasize individual entrepreneurship, autonomous profit centers, internal competition and/or highly decentralized independent activities, one-firm firms place great emphasis on firmwide coordination of decision making, group identity, cooperative teamwork, and institutional commitment.' According to Maister, one-firm firms:

> take very seriously their missions (usually service to clients),
> grow slowly while choosing clients and tasks carefully,
> devote much effort to selecting and training personnel,
> do R&D beyond the requirements of revenue-producing projects,
> encourage free communication among personnel,
> and give information freely to their personnel, including financial information.

Maister also warned that one-firm firms may become complacent, lacking in entrepreneurship, entrenched in their ways of doing things, and inbred.

Orlikowski (1988: 152–160) said Maister's idealization accurately describes the consulting firm she studied, except that her firm discourages R&D beyond the needs of current clients. The firm devotes 7 percent of its revenue to a training program, and each consultant spends over 1,500 hours in training during the first six years with the firm. Overtly technical in content, this training involves both self-study and classes at the firm's school. The consultants measure their career progress by their progress through this program. Nevertheless, most consultants seem to agree with the one who said: 'The biggest advantage of the school is the networking and socializing it allows. It really is not that important as an educational experience.'

Alvesson (1991, 1992) too described a consulting firm that spent much effort on formal socialization. The top managers ran a 'project philosophy course'. They also sought 'to sell the metaphor *the company as a home* to the employees'. Designed to foster informal interaction, the building has a kitchen, sauna, pool, piano bar, and large lounge area. The firm supports a chorus, art club, and navigation course. All personnel in each department meet together every second week. Every third month, each department undertakes a major social activity such as a hike or a sailing trip. The firm celebrated its tenth anniversary by flying all 500 employees to Rhodes for three days of group activities.

Interviews with software developers convinced Bhargava (1990) that larger firms work harder to build cultures. They use their cultures to promote free communication, to make them less dependent on key experts, and to ease personnel transfers. He found fewer communication problems and fewer personnel transfers in smaller firms.

Van Maanen and Kunda (1989) vividly described people's ambivalence toward culture-building efforts in a computer firm. Most people readily adopt corporate language and enjoy belonging to a supportive collectivity. Some embrace corporate values and rituals enthusiastically; more do so cynically. Most people also hold themselves aloof from group membership and protect their individual identities.

All the KIFs I have studied select experts carefully, they use teams extensively, they take their missions seriously, they manage growth cautiously, and their people talk openly. Only Wachtell, Lipton, however, comes close to the one-firm model in discouraging internal competition, emphasizing group work, disclosing information, and eliciting loyalty to the firm. The other KIFs depart from the one-firm model in having multiple profit centers, assessing the productivities of individual experts, and revealing only the financial information that laws require. All the KIFs, including Wachtell, Lipton, depart from the one-firm model in decentralizing activities, encouraging entrepreneurship, and not involving everyone in decision-making.

KIFs do downplay formal structures, and they achieve coordination through social norms and reward systems instead of hierarchical controls (Nelson 1988; Van Maanen and Kunda 1989: 70–93). One reason is experts' sense of their importance as individuals and their desires for autonomy: Close control would induce exits. Another reason is common values and norms that result from many years of formal education. KIFs appear to derive some of their properties from universities, and some KIFs employ many who could be university faculty. Third, experts have to work independently because projects involve just a few people (Alvesson 1992). The instability of projects and services provides a fourth reason: To absorb variations in demands for their services, KIFs need fluidity and ambiguity. Matrix structures are prevalent, and organization charts sketchy. Supervisors counsel nondirectively. Experts form liaisons across formal boundaries. Indeed, the Rand Corporation designed its building to foster unplanned encounters.

Still, social norms and reward systems are not equivalent to cultures. KIFs confront serious obstacles to creating and maintaining unusual cultures, especially cultures that embody organizational learning. The attributes that make hierarchical controls troublesome—autonomy, mobility, professionalization, uncertain funding—also make it hard for KIFs to integrate people and to socialize them into unusual organizational cultures. When experts join new firms, they bring with them well-developed values, standards, habits, mental frameworks, and languages. Although they have much in common with their colleagues, the culture they share is supraorganizational.

Social Capital

The Garden Company's customers can easily see whether Garden's products do what the maker claims. The customers do not buy Garden's expertise directly. One result is that Garden's relations with customers are impersonal. Another result is that these relations may be fleeting. The customers readily switch to other suppliers, and Garden itself cuts off relations with customers when it stops making products that are less profitable.

Buyers of expertise itself, by contrast, often have difficulty assessing their purchases. Clients often consult experts because they believe their own knowledge inadequate, so they cannot judge the experts' advice or reports mainly on substance. Clients may be unable to assess experts' advice by acting on it and watching the outcomes: The clients do not know what would have happened if they had acted otherwise, and it is frequently obvious that outcomes reflect uncontrollable or unpredictable influences. Clients may not even understand what their expert advisors are saying. Many experts—with awareness—use jargon that obscures their meaning. As a result, clients have to base their judgments on familiar, generic symbols of expertise. Do the experts speak as persons with much education? Have the experts used impressive statistical computations? Are the experts well dressed? Did the experts use data of good quality? Do the experts' analyses seem logical and credible? Do the experts act confident?

Successful service KIFs, therefore, pay attention to their symbolic outputs. For example, as mentioned above, the Aerospace Corporation uses seven managerial levels that match the Air Force's hierarchy. Aerospace also asks technical experts to practice briefings in-house before presenting them to Air Force officers, and it provides strong support for writing, graphics, and artwork.

Clients also hire experts to obtain legitimacy instead of expertise. In such circumstances, the client–expert relationship is a charade: The clients choose advisors who will give wanted advice. Such selection can be unconscious. For instance, when the Facit Company was in serious trouble, the board listened to presentations by several would-be advisors (Starbuck 1989). They then hired McKinsey & Company because that proposal had sounded most sensible: McKinsey's proposal had endorsed the general strategy the board had been pursuing. One result was that the board found it easy to take McKinsey's advice. Another result was that following McKinsey's advice only made the situation worse.

Rhenman (1973: 160–171) has commented perceptively from his experience:

> ...there is in the consultant–client relationship an element of conflict. A game is played with all the usual trappings: negotiations, opposing strategies, etc. The client likes to

'sound out' the consultant. The client wavers between consultant A and consultant B. He also considers the cost of a particular consultant: Will the organization really benefit? Has the consultant perhaps other purposes in mind, beyond his duty to the client? Perhaps he is seeking an opportunity for research or financial reward? The consultant may be particularly anxious to get this assignment. How can he persuade the client to engage him? Or he may be temporarily hard pressed for time. Can he persuade the client to postpone the assignment, or some particularly time-consuming part of it? And during the assignment the consultant is often sure to feel that the client is blind to his own best interests, or that he, as consultant, is becoming involved in internal conflicts....

We have already intimated that political groups may well try to use the engagement of the consultant for their own ends. Other groups may suspect and oppose the engagement on similar grounds; a long and heated struggle can easily develop. The consultant may be aware of what has been going on, or he may realize it only when he discovers that his engagement is tied to certain definite conditions....

But the political system is not simply a part of the background. Soon, whether he realizes it or not, the consultant will become a pawn in the political game: His presence will always have some effect on the balance of power, sometimes perhaps a good deal. If he is not politically aware, various interest groups will almost certainly try to use him for their own purposes.

Over the long term, service KIFs try to convert clients' satisfaction with specific projects into long-term relations. Even in contexts that are initially impersonal, repeated interactions between specific people create bonds. Firm-to-firm ties gradually evolve into person-to-person ties. An expert who repeatedly serves the same client begins to perceive 'my' client, and the client comes to think of 'my' expert.

Such personalizing can happen with any expert, but the experts having the strongest social skills are not normally those with the greatest technical expertise. Those with superb abilities in both dimensions are rare: One interviewee estimated that only ten people in the United States are 'great technical lawyers who work well with colleagues, are effective with clients, and show good judgement'.

Thus, KIFs use internal specialization, in which socially skilful experts work on building ties with a few specific clients, and technically superior experts provide specialized expertise to many clients. The KIFs offer clients familiar contact persons, who then draw upon ad hoc teams with expertise fitting specific projects. To a client, a KIF looks like a single source of diverse expertise that gives high priority to that client's problems.

Formally, American lawyers call the persons whom clients choose to contact 'originating attorneys'. Informally, they call them 'rainmakers'. Rainmaking is mysterious and magical, and rainmakers wield power. Their personal and lasting ties with clients give the contact persons divided loyalties as well as power. The divided loyalties serve a quality-control function that nurtures continuing ties between KIFs and clients. The power is a central fact-of-life that KIFs have to appreciate or risk losing long-term clients.

Keith Uncapher once worked at the Rand Corporation, designing information systems for the Defense Advanced Research Projects Agency (DARPA). Rand's top managers declared that the firm should no longer build hardware, but Uncapher believed that DARPA's goals demanded special-purpose hardware. He made a fifteen-minute oral proposal to DARPA, received an initial grant of $10 million, and started a new organization, the Information Science Institute.

As the foregoing implies they should, service KIFs favor client relations over technical expertise. If KIFs allow client relations to dominate too strongly, however, they may lose key technical experts. Instead of thinking that they work for firms, technical experts may think firms exist for their benefit and should be working for them. To remain stable, KIFs have to reconcile their client-relations specialists and technical specialists. Each of these needs the other over the long term, but their mutual dependencies may seem obscure at any moment.

5. STRATEGIC DEVELOPMENT

This chapter's second section asserts: 'Knowledge is a stock of expertise, not a flow of information.' Ironically, firms' stocks of expertise come from the flows in complex input-output systems. Knowledge flows in through hiring, training, and purchases of capital goods. Some knowledge gets manufactured internally, through research, invention, and culture building. Knowledge flows out through personnel departures, imitated routines, and sales of capital goods. Some knowledge becomes obsolete. Fluid knowledge solidifies when converted into capital goods or routines. The sequences of events resemble random walks, and the net outcomes are difficult to foresee. Thus, strategies do not evolve coherently (Greenwood, Hinings, and Brown 1990).

Diversification

For product KIFs, strategic development calls for regulating numbers of customers and numbers of product lines. Similarly, service KIFs need to regulate numbers of clients and numbers of topical foci. As with other specialization-diversification problems, high risks come from having very few clients or customers and very few topics or product lines. A KIF with very few topical foci must perform superbly in those areas, and a KIF with very few customers cannot afford customer dissatisfaction. The issues, however, do not all lie in the realms of expertise or social skills.

For a year and a half after Wachtell, Lipton began, one client accounted for 75 percent of its revenue. Then, this client asked Wachtell, Lipton to do something unethical. They replied that they could not take the wanted action. The client countered that Wachtell, Lipton must either do its bidding or lose its business. The partners refused ... and gave up 75 percent of their revenue. At that point, unsure their firm could survive, the partners adopted a policy that has had profound consequences: Wachtell, Lipton would work only one-case-at-a-time. It would never again make a long-term commitment to a client.

If Wachtell, Lipton had been more ordinary, this policy might have been deadly. But the firm became one of the rare ones to which corporations turn when their normal legal resources seem inadequate—at least, when corporations don't want to find out whether their normal legal resources would be adequate. In this status, having no long-term clients becomes an asset, for Wachtell, Lipton can be hired by whoever calls first.

Some KIFs serve a few clients contentedly. Keith Uncapher said, 'I wouldn't know how to look good to two clients'. He designed the Information Science Institute to serve only DARPA, and no other client. The Aerospace Corporation derives 99 percent of its revenues from a single long-term contract and makes no effort to change this situation.

Most KIFs that begin with narrow foci try to diversify. Like Aerospace, the Rand Corporation initially served a single client, the U.S. Air Force. At the Air Force's urging and with its help, Rand began making strenuous efforts to gain broader support and greater autonomy. These efforts have had partial success. Rand has raised an endowment exceeding $40 million, and it does research for over eighty sponsors annually. Nevertheless, three military sponsors still account for 70 percent of Rand's revenues, and 80 percent of its research deals with national security.

A. D. Little has attained broad diversification after developing incrementally for over a century. A. D. Little's precursor, Griffin & Little, began in 1886 as specialists in the chemistry of paper-making. In 1909, when the current firm incorporated, its expertise encompassed paper-making, forest products, textiles, plastics, and sugar. These industries were central to the economy of New England, the firm's home.

Over the years, as the firm expanded its geographic reach, it added a wide range of physical and biological sciences and expertise on a wide spectrum of manufacturing technologies. A. D. Little first studied regional economics in 1916, began financial studies in the 1930s, and moved into management consulting broadly in the 1950s.

These expansions sprang partly from the firm's standards about conflict of interest. After advising a client about a topic, A. D. Little will not advise a different client from the same industry about the same topic. Future projects must change either the industry or the topic.

Just as diversification regarding clients may erode a KIF's ties with its long-standing clients, topical diversification may undermine a KIF's credibility. A few years ago, A. D. Little's senior managers concluded that their firm had become too amorphous. Hiring had become hard because the firm had so few experts in any single specialty. Covering too many specialties for too many dissimilar clients was yielding neither enough profit nor enough client satisfaction. A survey revealed that clients were turning to other consultants to get 'focused depth of resources'.

Thus, the firm went through a major planning effort, and began to focus on half-a-dozen functions in a handful of industries—mainly chemicals, financial services, health care, and telecommunications. Alfred Wechsler explained, 'We try to define our expertise with verb-noun-adverb combinations. For example: we know how *to manufacture a paper cup inexpensively.'*

A. D. Little's strategic development has generally paralleled the developments in its client population—large industrial enterprises. Chandler (1962) described how single-product firms grew into multiple-product, divisionalized firms during the first half of the century: In the same period, A. D. Little was adding many product lines and decentralizing. In the 1970s and 1980s, conglomerates such as ITT decided to retrench into a few core businesses: A. D. Little was making analogous changes at the same time. After 1950, many American firms expanded overseas, and A. D. Little too became multinational.

Its initial foreign venture was an office in Zurich that opened in 1957 to serve American firms that were expanding into Europe. To their surprise, the consultants discovered that European firms also wanted their services. They now have offices in six European cities and in Mexico, Brazil, Venezuela, Saudi Arabia, Japan, Singapore, Hong Kong, and Taiwan. In 1972, they added laboratories in England; these later expanded to Germany.

Multinational KIFs

For KIFs, multinationality poses challenging issues that differ from those facing industrial firms. Many industrial firms use authority and steep hierarchies, and they can often use formal controls or hardware technology to reach performance standards. Consulting firms and other KIFs dare not resort to authority or formal controls, and they lack technological wonder pills. They have to depend on autonomous small teams to act ethically and to meet performance standards. This, in turn, means that they need cultural homogeneity.

Nonetheless, A. D. Little has found national differences to be minor problems. One reason may be careful selection of experts. Another reason may be the homogeneity arising from education. Haire, Ghiselli, and Porter (1966) found that managers with similar educations espouse similar values no matter what their nationalities. Wuthnow and Shrum (1983) discovered that education erases the ideological differences between managers and professional-technical workers. After much education, managers and professionals espouse similar values.

Perhaps because they use authority, formal controls, and technology to produce homogeneity, many industrial firms have shown insensitivity toward local values or treated host-country personnel less well than home-country personnel. Yet, insensitivity and inequity have not prevented industrial firms from operating successfully in foreign lands. Consulting firms, on the other hand, would fail if they did not allow for local values, and they are apt to treat host-country consultants more than equally.

For instance, A. D. Little is trying to deliver reliable quality across diverse sites, but its clients want services tailored to their individual needs and contexts. Tailoring calls for consultants to act differently, whereas reliable quality and teamwork call for them to act similarly. A. D. Little began its multinational expansion by exporting American experts. Experience promptly convinced the firm that a foreign office must hire primarily experts native to that country. First, devising effective solutions for problems usually requires thorough understanding of the contexts in which those solutions will be tried. Second, clients do not want to waste time explaining basic economic, sociological, or political facts to expensive foreign consultants. Thus, the consultants who staff a foreign office tend to have strong social skills and close ties with their clients. These assets, in turn, tend to give the host-country consultants high statuses within the firm.

6. LOOKING BACK AND FORWARD

Summary

Because everyone defines knowledge differently, discussions of KIFs evoke debates about proper definition. Such debates have led me (*a*) to emphasize esoteric expertise instead of widely shared knowledge, (*b*) to distinguish an expert from a professional and a knowledge-intensive firm from a professional firm, (*c*) to differentiate a knowledge-intensive firm from an information-intensive firm, and (*d*) to see knowledge as a property of physical capital, social capital, routines, and organizational cultures as well as individual people.

Highly successful KIFs exhibit uniqueness, and they reflect and exploit the peculiarities of their environments. Since they and their environments change symbiotically, their environments reflect and exploit these KIFs.

Whereas experts distinguish between preserving, creating, and applying knowledge, their daily work obscures these distinctions. Not only do preservers, creators, and appliers behave similarly, but preserving, creating, and applying are interdependent. Furthermore, experts resist new ideas—even the experts who describe themselves as creators of knowledge. Such resistance arises from self-interest and narrow perspectives. Yet, it may improve learning—by both individual experts and their firms—by making people ask whether knowledge has lasting value.

KIFs learn by hiring, training, and dismissing personnel. They also convert ideas into physical capital, routines, organizational culture, and social capital. Personnel changes and purchases of capital goods generally offer fast ways to pick up new ideas. Training, physical capital, routines, and organizational cultures can turn individuals' knowledge into collective property. Knowledge in people or in physical capital is easy to lose, and KIFs have difficulty using routines and building special cultures. Social capital transforms a series of successful relations with a client into a long-term relation, but it also converts collective successes into individual property. One consequence is that hierarchies within KIFs reflect social skills as well as technical expertise.

Three themes afford a framework for interpreting KIFs' strategic development. First, complex input-output systems for knowledge make KIFs' strategic development look erratic. Second, KIFs have to regulate numbers of customers or clients, and numbers of product lines or topical foci. Some KIFs focus on small numbers of clients, customers, product lines, or topics; but most KIFs try to diversify. Third, service KIFs often mirror prominent characteristics of their clients. These similarities are loosely qualitative, however, for KIFs differ from their clients in many ways.

Postindustrial Currents

One cliché prediction says: Future societies will have ever higher proportions of service workers, because machines will replace blue collars much more often than white collars. Perhaps KIFs are also growing more prevalent. But the future is always moot, and more interesting than the general trends are the swirling currents within them.

First, KIFs tend to grow by becoming less specialized and by adding support staff rather than experts. It nearly always *seems* that additional support staff, products, or services will extract more value from the experts already in-house. Individual experts, too, think about broadening their domains as they update their knowledge and see social and technological changes opening new opportunities. But when support staff come to outnumber experts greatly, or when KIFs claim expertise in too many domains, KIFs lose their halos of expertise and their credibility.

Second, all kinds of expertise become less profitable as they grow more prevalent. Esoteric expertise has monopoly power, and this power erodes as expertise becomes less esoteric. Neither experts nor KIFs nor KIFs' industry associations should seek proliferation. Yet, experts resist control and they have strong penchants to start new firms. Very small firms can compete successfully if they take advantage of their peculiarities and the peculiarities of their environments. The Garden Company could easily lose out to competitors with better ideas.

Third, some kinds of expertise attract consumers even though their benefits are obscure. Examples include crisis intervention, economic forecasts, investment advice, psychotherapy . . . and management science. Some obscure-benefit expertise seems to have high value partly because the experts are unusual. Such expertise may lose value as the experts come to make up higher proportions of the work force. On the other hand, such an outcome is not obvious. Placebos make effective treatments although they are very common. Mystery can be routinized. People need help with their problems even when the problems have no solutions—perhaps, especially then.

Obscure-benefit domains may be either more or less stable than the domains in which expertise yields clear benefits. Obscure-benefit domains are stable if they satisfy perennial human needs and no alternatives appear. There were probably economic forecasters before there were humans; even in recent times, the demand for economic forecasts has mounted as organizations have grown larger and more rigid. Obscure-benefit domains can be unstable if beliefs change, if human needs shift, or if more effective substitutes appear. Astrology is a case in point. Clear-benefit domains may themselves wither—as dentists are discovering.

Fourth, physical capital will displace some of experts' activities. Similar changes are occurring across the economy, within firms, and in the work of individual experts. Several new industries are distributing expertise in the form of physical capital. Both firms and individual experts are creating databases and expert systems, and they are buying or building tools to amplify experts' productivity by replacing some of their activities.

These substitutions will enable fewer experts to serve more clients or customers or to invent more products. They also will mean that many clients or customers no longer need experts, or that they can make the products they have been buying. Millions of people are already using software to do accounting, to file income taxes, to write wills, to construct leases, or to help them write articles. Computers are revolutionizing product design, manufacturing control, and computer programming. Spiraling medical costs may yet compel the use of software that diagnoses diseases and issues medical prescriptions.

To appreciate the beauty and intricacy of such currents, social scientists need to stop averaging across large, diverse categories. The average painting is flat gray, the average day is neither hot nor cold and has twelve hours of daylight, the average firm is mediocre and short-lived, and the average expert knows little about any field. In the social sciences, broad patterns oversimplify and capture only small fractions of what is happening. They leave scientists in worlds that look random. Broad patterns also tend to emphasize what is consistent with the past and to overlook subtle changes.

There is also a world of bright colours, sizzling days, exceptional firms, rare experts, and peculiar KIFs.

ACKNOWLEDGMENTS

I owe thanks to many who contributed generously their time, ideas, insights, and contacts. This chapter reflects help from Mats Alvesson, Tora Bikson, Andrew Brownstein, Mark Chignell, Jess Cook, Joan Dunbar, Roger Dunbar, Tamara Erickson, James Fogelson, Charles Fombrun, Ari Ginsberg, John Jermier, Charles LaMantia, Kenneth Laudon, Martin Lipton, Henry Lucas, Frances Milliken, Louis Miller, Theodore Mirvis, Harold Novikoff, Paul Nystrom, Anthony Pascal, Lawrence Pedowitz, Fioravante Perrotta, Joseph Post, Lewis Rambo, Donald Rice, Harland Riker, James Ringer, Stephen Robinson, David Ronfeldt, Lawrence Rosenberg, Roberta Shanman, Lee Sproull, Serge Taylor, Jon Turner, Keith Uncapher, Mary Ann Von Glinow, Herbert Wachtell, Alfred Wechsler, Elliott Wilbur, Sidney Winter, and an anonymous referee.

13

Keeping a Butterfly and an Elephant in a House of Cards: The Elements of Exceptional Success

1. WHERE TANDOORI CAN LEAD

My wife and I were eating dinner with Donna and Joe.

Joe asked what I had been doing lately.

I explained that I had been studying knowledge-intensive firms—ones that earn revenues from specialized expertise. I cited the Rand Corporation and Arthur D. Little as examples, and briefly described their work.

Joe, a partner in a prominent Park Avenue law firm, asked if I had studied any law firms.

With insufficient tact and excessive confidence, I told him I had not. I understood law firms to make most of their revenues by routinely generating standardized documents such as contracts, stock offerings, or wills. Because legal word-processing systems are widely available, because all lawyers have adequate basic knowledge, and because law firms employ lawyers with diverse skills, clients can readily substitute one law firm for another. My interest lay, I said, in firms that are renowned for their unusual expertise.

Joe replied quietly that he thought I was misjudging law firms in general, and more importantly, that some law firms do have reputations for unusual expertise.

I asked him to suggest such a firm for me to study.

He proceeded to tell me about Wachtell, Lipton, Rosen & Katz (Wachtell), another Park Avenue firm not far from his own. The very high quality of Wachtell's work and its distinctive culture had impressed him.

I did not really understand what Joe was telling me. I got the idea, which he later corrected, that he was saying Wachtell specializes in merger-and-acquisition cases and that clients seek out the firm because of this expertise. Doubting that any law firm stands out from the others, I listened to Joe's description with skepticism. As a result, it was roughly a year before I got around to writing to Martin Lipton and Herbert Wachtell, asking if I might interview them.

Had I known how exceptional their firm is, I would have waited not one day.

When I finally did interview people in Wachtell, I came away fascinated and impressed. When I later compared Wachtell statistically with other law firms, I was utterly astonished.

This chapter reports my observations.

2. A FEW OF MY MANY BIASES

While living in Berlin in the early 1970s, Wolfgang Müller and I became statistical consultants to a research project that was searching for side effects of contraceptive pills. Because it sought to find rare or unusual side effects, the project observed 30,000 women for five years.

Statistical analyses showed the main determinants of side effects to be doctors. Because some doctors noticed coronary disease, women who went to these doctors were more likely to have been diagnosed as having coronary disease and less likely to have been diagnosed as having other ailments. Other doctors noticed pulmonary disease, and women who went to these doctors were more likely to have been diagnosed as having pulmonary disease and less likely to have been diagnosed as having other ailments. And so on.

The same notion applies, of course, to social science. I tend to notice certain phenomena and to neglect others. Thus, readers need to beware of my biases.

Using Nonrigorous Methods and Focusing on Narrow Categories

During the 1960s and 1970s, many researchers attempted to find generalizations about all organizations. Widespread beliefs of that period, to which I subscribed, said that social science ought to use 'rigorous' methods to produce generalizations of very broad applicability. Unfortunately, practical experience demonstrated that these beliefs were ill-founded.

For example, the original Aston study examined eight autonomous organizations and thirty-eight subunits of organizations, and analyzed the data as if subunits were organizations.

We included manufacturing firms that made strip steel, toys, double decker buses, chocolate bars, injection systems, and beer, and service organizations such as chain stores, municipal departments, transport companies, insurance companies, and a savings bank. (Pugh 1981: 141)

Some of these organizations focused on local areas and others sold nationally. Further, the researchers carefully chose measures that would be equally meaningful in all organizations. It is the strength and the weakness of this project that no items were used unless they were applicable to *all* work organizations, whatever they did; several possible items of information had to be sacrificed to this end. Since the research strategy was to undertake a wide survey to set the guidelines, the result was superficiality and generality in the data. (Pugh et al., 1968: 69)

Of course, the drive to generalize has induced researchers to ignore or de-emphasize the properties that make organizations distinctive. Imagine comparing a hospital with a steel plant but ignoring the fact that one treats injuries and cares for sick people while the other operates blast furnaces and rolls hot steel.

Such studies showed that 'rigorous' methods contain many inherent traps. In application, methods that were labeled rigorous turned out to be formalistic, and the researchers who used rigorous methods lost sight of the commonsense content in their data. Their findings depended very strongly on assumptions embedded in their measures, assumptions of which they were unaware. The very process of following methodological prescriptions induced researchers to substitute ritual for understanding. As a result, rigorous studies had commonsense interpretations that were very different from the meanings implied by the names of variables (Starbuck 1981).

Although some might blame this outcome on the researchers, the people who did this research were bright, well educated, sincere, and among the intellectual leaders of their time. Their findings appeared in the most prestigious journals and were widely cited in other research and in textbooks. Thus, these studies showed deficiencies of rigorous methods rather than peculiarities of specific studies: So-called 'rigorous' methods are very prone to yield deceptive data that lack validity.

Thus, I generally eschew 'rigorous' methods in order to weaken the influence of my prior beliefs, to strengthen the validity of my data, and to heighten my understanding of what I observe. Most of my observations about Wachtell come from conversations with lawyers who work there. My informants are bright and articulate people who earn very high incomes because clients want the benefit of their perception and understanding: They well understand organizations and interpersonal relations. These people became my collaborators, as they not only answered my questions but told me what issues I ought to explore and with whom I should talk. Of course, my informants had agendas of their own, but their attempts to influence me afford useful data in themselves. Not only is it fun to spot inconsistencies and efforts to shape my perceptions, but the interviews I found least useful are those in which I said too much, especially at the outset. That is, I learned more by listening than by talking. One result is that I have grown even more skeptical of interviews that follow preplanned agendas.

This chapter assumes that readers also enjoy dealing with inconsistent and unprocessed information. I often let people speak for themselves. Their choices of words add to the basic information about organizational properties, but they do not portray Wachtell as a coherent, unambiguous system, and there are contradictions in what they say. I will leave these for readers to spot because I think the contradictions are rather clear and because identifying contradictions helps one to think through the issues.

Before each quotation is a letter that denotes its source, as shown in Table 13.1. The interviewed clients are all General Counsels of major corporations. The opposing lawyers include several of New York's most successful ones. The statements by associate lawyers come from questionnaires they submitted to the *American Lawyer* in 1990 or 1992 rather than from interviews.

The generalization-seeking studies have built up evidence that the properties shared by all organizations are superficial, obvious, or unimportant (Starbuck 1981). Again and again, these studies have rediscovered weak relationships that organizational researchers had observed 'nonrigorously' many years earlier—

Table 13.1. Codes identifying the sources of quotations

A An associate in Wachtell
C A lawyer who has been a client of Wachtell
L A document that Martin Lipton wrote in 1987 and then revised for the firm's 25th anniversary in 1990
O A lawyer from a competing firm who has opposed or collaborated with Wachtell
P A partner in Wachtell, including both junior and senior ones
S A member of Wachtell's nonlawyer support staff

---

possibly many centuries earlier. For instance, the strongest consistent 'finding' of the Aston studies was that larger organizations tend to be more bureaucratic. Two of the strongest consistent 'findings' from statistical studies of organizational populations have been that larger organizations have lower risks of failure than do smaller ones, and that well established organizations have lower risks of failure than do infant ones.

Even apart from the measurement methods used in studies, the properties shared by all organizations ought to be uninteresting and unimportant. One reason is that people create new organizations to pursue goals that existing organizations are not achieving. If left free, people will create organizations that complement the existing ones, and the new organizations will emphasize properties that the founders believe are both important for success and neglected by previous organizations. The overall population of organizations will grow more diverse, and diversity will increase primarily in the dimensions that are important to organizational survival or goal attainment. Many industries encompass firms that complement each other, and of course, industries complement each other (Carroll 1985; Starbuck and Dutton 1973). Thus, to see how certain properties foster success, one needs to look at the differences among organizations, and one of my goals in studying knowledge-intensive firms (KIFs) is to focus on a special category that differs from the general mass of organizations.

This chapter focuses much more narrowly yet. Far from claiming that Wachtell is a representative law firm, it argues that Wachtell's extraordinary success derives from its individuality. Not only does Wachtell differ in important ways from all organizations, it differs in important ways from the mass of law firms and it even differs in important ways from other highly successful law firms. Wachtell is quite distinctive, and other law firms have not imitated its distinctive properties.

Nor does this chapter claim to make findings that generalize to other times. A firm may have to forego some short-run profits in order to build relationships that foster longevity, so an extremely profitable firm takes some risk of transience. Also, Wachtell illustrates both the effects of passing fads and fashions and the diverse forces that undermine exceptional success—or other peculiarities. These forces promote regression to the mean and make exceptional success transitory.

Avoiding Averages

A second reason why shared properties tend to be uninteresting and unimportant is that organizations cannot gain exceptional success by imitating other organizations and exploiting shared properties (Starbuck 1992). Although not all organizations seek exceptional success, its determinants and consequences interest me.

Focusing on exceptional success had not been my explicit initial goal. I had set out to study firms having distinctive expertise. Expertise is hard to separate from its effects because clients judge advice to be good if it produces good results. Thus, after studying a few firms, I realized I had been looking at especially successful ones. This realization forced me to reexamine my goals.

North American and English social science has been paying far too much attention to averages. The study of averages has become so prevalent that social scientists do not even have to explain why they think averages are the appropriate variables to study. Other social scientists often accuse the deviates who fail to study averages of doing valueless work, as if averages were the only information of value.

A statistical principle, established over fifty years ago (Robinson 1950; Thorndike 1939), states that a correlation across a population may not recur in subsets of that population. Indeed, a true statement about averages across a population may be false for every subset of that population, including every individual in the population. For instance, in the study that introduced the concept of a strategic group, Schendel and colleagues observed a positive correlation between profits and firm size across the population of brewing companies (Schendel and Hatten 1977; Schendel and Patton 1978). But when they divided the brewing companies into size categories, they found negative correlations between profits and firm size within every size category.

Although statements about averages bother very few, they ought to bother many. For instance, scholars often state 'hypotheses' of the form 'Managers do such-and-so' and then support these hypotheses with statistically significant correlations computed across many managers. In such cases, one can nearly always point to at least one manager in the analyzed data who did not do such-and-so. Typically, many of the analyzed managers did not do such-and-so; and it is possible that none of the analyzed managers did such-and-so. Is not something wrong when analysis supports a hypothesis that is violated by most or even all specific instances? Why do scholars not specify the fraction of managers who do such-and-so? What are scholars doing when they state 'Managers do such-and-so' even though some managers do not? I suggest that they are engaging in a stylized sense-making ritual rather than science.

Social scientists not only focus on averages, they often calculate averages that lack meaning because they arise from arbitrary categories with undefined boundaries. For instance, averages across a sample of KIFs would be meaningless because no clear definition of KIFs has wide acceptance. Scholars advocate multitude definitions of knowledge and hold disparate notions about the proper definitions for KIFs (Starbuck 1992). Although one can point to specific organizations that almost everyone will agree are KIFs, the boundaries of the KIF category are obscure.

Fixation on averages makes social science blind to individuality, peculiarity, excellence, complexity, interaction, and subcultures. Similarity should not be the dominant property of people, groups, organizations, or societies because there are many criteria for what is good, many solutions for most problems, and many opportunities to exploit. All people, groups, organizations, and societies are peculiar and unique, and seeing how people, groups, organizations, and societies differ is at least as important as seeing how they look similar. In study after study, it turns out that few instances closely resemble the averages (Starbuck and Bass 1967).

Averages usually tell nothing about outlying cases such as exceptionally successful firms. In most industries, the modal firms make low profits and have short lives (Starbuck and Nystrom 1981). An exceptionally successful firm has to be unique in a way that exploits the peculiarities of its environments: It gains high profits and long survival through distinctive competencies that take advantage of its environments' unusual needs and capabilities.

Not only do its environments reflect and exploit the unique properties of an exceptionally successful firm, but the existence of a highly successful firm induces its environments to act as if the firm does exist. Thus, an observer nearly always sees marginal adjustments and rarely glimpses the complex dynamics that occur sometimes. An observer who averages across time will overlook the intricate and unusual, yet these may be the most important.

Produced by decomposition and simplification, simple relations among averages often misrepresent ecological interactions (Martin 1992). Should one describe Beethoven's Ninth Symphony only in terms of pure sine waves, as Fourier proved one can? No musicologist would do so. Should one describe Van Gogh's 'Starry Night' only in terms of cyan, magenta, and yellow, as one can in principle? No art critic or historian would attempt it.

3. STUDIES OF AVERAGES

Gilson and Mnookin (1985) reported, mainly via footnotes, that lawyers in larger law firms receive higher compensation than those in smaller firms, that more Stanford graduates had been taking jobs in large law firms, and that the largest law firms are growing larger. They then argued that law firms have been growing larger in order to diversify and that diversification helps to explain law firms' commitment to 'lockstep compensation'. Lockstep compensation makes seniority the sole determinant of lawyers' wages and of partners' profits. Gilson and Mnookin (1985: 328–329) explained: 'The lawyer cannot diversify his human capital investment. He cannot be both a securities law specialist and a bankruptcy law specialist.' Because domains of specialization become more or less lucrative as demands for their services fluctuate, lawyers find it useful to create 'full-service' firms and to agree 'that the returns to [human capital investments in different specialties] will be shared on a predetermined basis rather than in accordance with actual outcomes'.

Later, Gilson and Mnookin (1989: 585) reported:

First, firm leverage [the ratio of non-partner associate lawyers to partners] is directly related to firm profit: the higher the firm's leverage, the higher the firm's per partner profit. When one outlier is eliminated, our regression analysis of data from the *American Lawyer's* compilation of the one hundred most successful corporate law firms for 1987 discloses that differences in leverage explain 34.3% of the differences among firms in per partner profitability. Second, the degree of firm leverage appears to be determined, in part, geographically: the same data indicate that among these one hundred firms, those based in New York City had an average associate/partner ratio of 2.55, while those based outside New York had an average ratio of only 1.66; the leverage of New York firms was greater by some 54 percent....

The outlier is Wachtel [*sic*], Lipton, Rosen, & Katz, a firm specializing in hostile [*sic*] takeover work. In 1987, Wachtel was reported to have an average profit per partner of $1,405,000—the top in the nation—although its ratio of associates per partner was only 1.05. This firm bills for takeover work on a transaction, rather than a per-hour, basis, which significantly reduces the importance of leverage. If Wachtel, Lipton is included in the regression, differences in leverage explain 20.9% of the differences among firms in per-partner profits.

Note that Gilson and Mnookin based their generalizations on averages and that their wording illustrates the widespread usages cited in the preceding section.

Samuelson and Jaffe (1990: 190) remarked:

The major source of profitability for firms has traditionally been an army of associates who receive a salary equal to only a fraction of the revenues they generate, with the lion's share divided among the partners. Associates have been willing to cooperate with this system because they have had a good chance of being promoted to partnership. Thus, they anticipated that, in the relatively short period of six to twelve years, they would be sharing in the economic surplus generated by associates. Since partners have grown to expect an income based on a ratio of at least one (and ideally more) associates to each partner, firms suffer under an enormous growth imperative. Each time an associate is promoted to partnership, two or three new associates must be hired.

Price Waterhouse has been sending long questionnaires to the managing partners of 'well managed' law firms since 1961. Roughly 600 firms participate in the Statistical Survey and 300 in the Compensation Survey. Samuelson and Jaffe persuaded Price Waterhouse to allow them to analyze the responses submitted by 219 firms that responded to both questionnaires in both 1985 and 1986. These firms employed from 8 to 645 lawyers, the average being 115.

Table 13.2. Determinants of profit per partner (Samuelson and Jaffe 1990)

Variable	Incremental correlation
Number of associates	0.25
Number of partners (negative effect)	0.13
Hours billed per associate	0.10
Nonlegal staff	0.06
Computer workstations	0.02
Hours billed per partner	0.01
Being in New York City	0.01
Lockstep compensation	0.01

Samuelson and Jaffe used stepwise regression to estimate the effects of various variables on profits per partner. Table 13.2 lists the statistically significant variables.

Samuelson and Jaffe struggled with these findings because they had expected profitability to correlate with total lawyers and with leverage. They concluded (*a*) that total lawyers adds no 'explanatory value' beyond the number of associates and (*b*) that leverage adds no 'explanatory value' beyond the combination of associates and partners. One should, however, view their analysis and interpretations cautiously because of correlations among the alternative independent variables. A linear combination of associates and partners might afford a fair approximation of leverage, and associates plus partners equals total lawyers.

These studies say that law firms achieve higher profits by exploiting associates—either by exploiting more associates or by exploiting associates more.

4. HIGH-REVENUE, HIGH-PROFIT LAW FIRMS

Now consider some statistics about 20 of the United States' largest 100 law firms. As this chapter was originally published, Figures 1–6 showed four-year averages for 1988–91; the Figures below show the situation a decade later. Some of these estimates are more accurate than others because the *American Lawyer* is able to get more information or more reliable information about some firms than others. The firms shown are the ones that ranked at the top during 1999.

Figure 13.1 shows that Wachtell not only had the highest revenue per lawyer, its revenue per lawyer was far above that of any other firm. From 1988–91, Wachtell's revenue per partner averaged 55 percent higher than its nearest competitor, and in 1999 its advantage had increased to 88 percent.

Figure 13.2 indicates that Wachtell is the smallest firm in the leading group. Indeed, Wachtell is the smallest firm among the largest 100 firms.

Of course, with fewer lawyers than the others, Wachtell would likely have fewer partners, and it does. However, Figure 13.3 implies that Wachtell has more partners for its size than a few of its competitors.

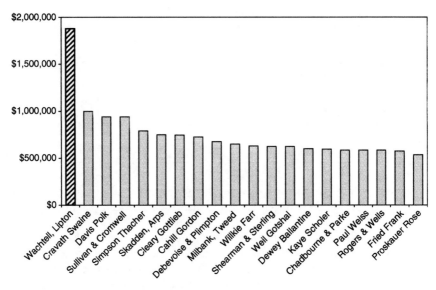

Figure 13.1. Revenue per lawyer in 1999

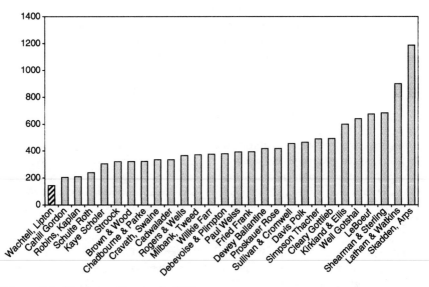

Figure 13.2. Numbers of lawyers in 1999

Figure 13.4 traces the implications of Figures 2 and 3, that Wachtell has disproportionately few associates per partner—very low 'leverage'. Indeed, from 1988–91, Wachtell averaged only 0.8 associates per partner. By 1999, this

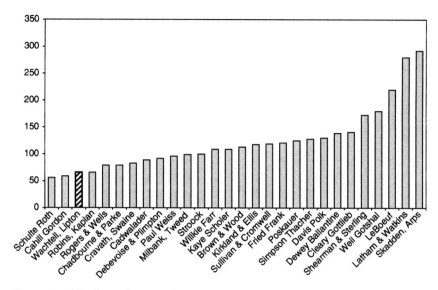

Figure 13.3. Numbers of partners in 1999

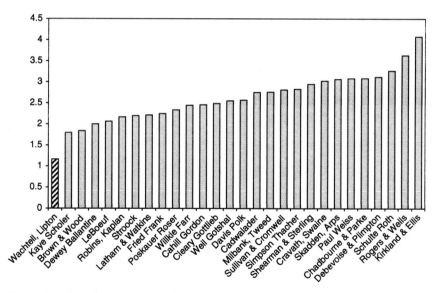

Figure 13.4. Associates per partner in 1999

ratio had risen to 1.17. Excepting Wachtell, the group averaged 2.8 associates per partner from 1988–91 and averaged 2.7 associates per partner in 1999. The two firms that most nearly resembled Wachtell in the previous Figures—Cahill Gordon and Robins Kaplan—had more than two associates per partner.

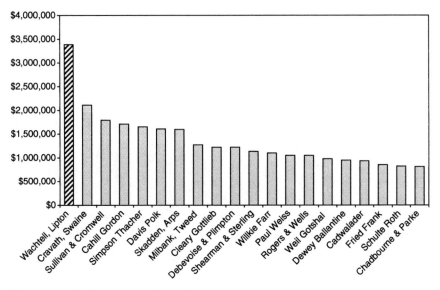

Figure 13.5. Profit per partner in 1999

Of course, the preceding statistical analyses imply that Wachtell must have very low profit per partner. According to Gilson and Mnookin, leverage determines profit per partner, and Wachtell had the lowest leverage among the largest 100 firms. According to Samuelson and Jaffe, highly profitable firms have many associates and few partners, and Wachtell has the fewest associates and disproportionately many partners. Yet Figure 13.5 says Wachtell had the highest profit per partner, fully 60 percent above its nearest competitor. It is no wonder that Gilson and Mnookin excluded Wachtell from their calculations.

Despite the firm's high ranking on this measure, Wachtell's senior partners would say profit per partner is not a good measure of their firm's performance because profit per partner places too much emphasis on partners and too little on associates. (The *American Lawyer* says its estimates of profit per partner are less reliable than other statistics, partly because some firms have various partnership classes.)

Figure 13.6 shows another astonishing differential between Wachtell and the other firms: From 1988–91, its profit averaged 68.5 percent of its revenue, which was 30 percent above its nearest competitor. In 1999, Wachtell's profit averaged 75 percent of revenue, which was 27 percent above its nearest competitor.

Wachtell stands out as a work environment as well. Each summer, large law firms employ 'summer associates' or 'interns'—students who have finished at least one year of law school. Summer employment allows the interns to see potential employers, and allows the firms to appraise prospective employees. In 1989 and 1991, the *American Lawyer* surveyed these interns, asking their reactions to the experience and to the firms. Figure 13.7 shows that the interns gave

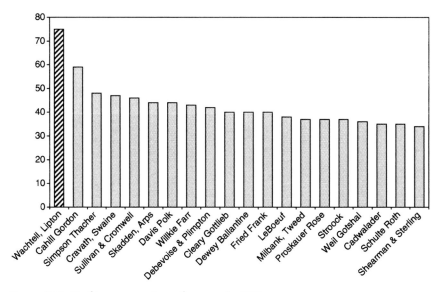

Figure 13.6. Profit as a percentage of revenue in 1999

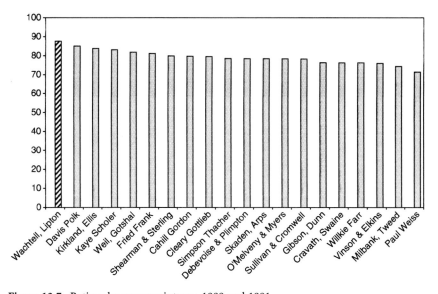

Figure 13.7. Ratings by summer interns, 1989 and 1991

Wachtell higher average ratings than any other firm in this high-revenue, high-profit group.

Similarly, in 1988, 1990, and 1992, the *American Lawyer* surveyed third-to-fifth-year associates, asking their reactions to their work experiences and to their

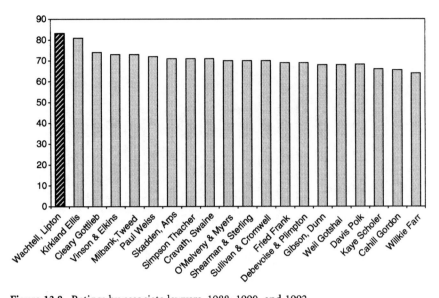

Figure 13.8. Ratings by associate lawyers, 1988, 1990, and 1992

employing firms. Figure 13.8 reveals that Wachtell's associates have given it the highest average ratings in this high-revenue, high-profit group. In 1992, Wachtell's associates rated it highly for client contact, level of responsibility, collegiality among associates, treatment of associates by partners, training of associates, associates' knowledge of their partnership chances, and compensation.

Overall, Figures 13.1, 13.2, 13.4, 13.6, and 13.8 suggest that Wachtell is in an entirely different business than the other top law firms. Although Cahill Gordon, Cravath Swaine, or Vinson & Elkins may contain subunits that generate very high revenues per lawyer, the earnings of these subunits are being averaged with much lower earnings from other subunits. Further, it is extremely unlikely that high-profit subunits in other firms have as few associates per partner as Wachtell, or associates who indicate as much pleasure with their working conditions as those at Wachtell.

5. HOW WACHTELL WORKS

The Beginning

Ironically, one of the most profitable law firms in the world was founded by men seeking 'interesting work rather than lucrative' (P).

In 1965, four friends and alumni of New York University's Law School decided to form their own law firm. Their organizing plan and early decisions portray them as idealists in headlong pursuit of financial failure. P: 'We wanted an old-fashioned partnership rather than a business.... We didn't want a hierarchy, didn't want a managed business. Our goal was a congenial home for people who can't function in a hierarchy. One early decision was better legal products at the cost of administrative waste.' This 'congenial home' would have strong egalitarian norms: Every lawyer would write his own first drafts of briefs, and every lawyer would do his own library research.

These values partly derived from personal experience. P: 'We tried to avoid the bad things. We didn't like imperious senior partners using people instead of developing a firm. We wanted to have a different relationship with our [junior] colleagues than we'd had with the people we had worked for.' They had also seen friends and former classmates working long hours for low wages while highly paid partners spent their evenings at home. P: 'In a lot of ways we didn't know what we were doing. We didn't think these things through in a logical way. We just said we don't want the unpleasantness we had and we've observed in other places.'

They vowed to refuse routine assignments even if this meant earning less money. Wachtell would not offer a full range of legal services. It would try to excel in corporate law, creditors' rights, and litigation. (Katz also did real estate.) To ensure that legal expertise would count for more than social skills, every lawyer with the same seniority would receive the same pay. There would be no special incentives to encourage the courting of clients.

O: 'They thought they could form a terrific law firm and make a lot of money. Marty Lipton is a great securities lawyer and Herb Wachtell is a brilliant litigator, so they were taking no chances. It was the next generation that took the chances—Nussbaum, Fogelson, Katcher....'

A Transactional Practice

During Wachtell's first year and a half of operation, in 1965 and 1966, one corporate client accounted for two-thirds of its revenue. Then during the firm's second year, contending groups within this key client asked Wachtell to favor them in ways that made the partners very uncomfortable. The partners resigned the relationship... and thus lost two-thirds of their income. P: 'We had to call a future employee and say "We may not be in business next year".'

The partners' immediate reaction was to 'go out and scramble' for work. However, after they had dealt with the immediate crisis, the partners adopted policies that would keep a single client from becoming so important again: P: Initially, they agreed that Wachtell would 'emphasize transactional representation rather than across-the-board general representation'. They would base relations with clients on short-term agreements about specific matters. L: 'The Firm encourages its clients to maintain relationships with other law firms.' Around 1976, after some experience, the partners adopted a more sweeping limitation: L: 'Firm does not have retainer relationships with the retainer fee applicable to any services the client desires.'

Had Wachtell become an ordinary law firm, its transactional emphasis might have been very costly. However, the firm turned out to be anything but ordinary. It has become one of the rare ones to which corporations turn when they are most desperate, when their normal legal resources seem inadequate—at least, when they do not want to find out whether their normal legal resources would be adequate, or when they do not want to risk Wachtell's aiding their opponents.

Wachtell's transactional relations with clients have become an asset. Transactional practice means that it has few conflicts of interest arising from ties to long-standing clients, so it is likely to be available to new clients. Partners in Wachtell say transactional practice also implies that other law firms can enlist Wachtell as co-counsel without fearing that it might try to steal their clients, and that clients need not fear that Wachtell will 'play politics' and disturb existing client–lawyer relations.

C: 'They are basically a litigation firm and a firm that specializes in deal making and transactions.... Where would we use them? Examples would be if we were going to make a major acquisition, or when we adopted a shareholder-rights plan (sometimes called a poison pill), or when we have shareholder suits against us.'

O: 'As an opponent and one who has been in the same area [of the legal practice], I'd rather have them against me—no, not really against me, with me as co-counsel—than any other firm because they're very bright and creative.'

O: 'I'd be afraid they'd steal the client.'

Case Selection and Innovation

Wachtell has adhered to its founders' ideal of refusing to perform routine legal chores. It does not regularly produce 'green goods' such as stock registration statements and loan agreements, and it focuses on 'a limited number of interesting and difficult specialities' (L). P: 'We are selective about cases. The partners would be bored with routine, repetitive work such as prospectuses, underwriting, due-diligence.' P: 'Wachtell is always "special counsel". It deals with unusual problems and boardroom situations, such as suits against directors. The client's CEO is involved. Such cases have high visibility.' P: 'We try to make the cases not-labor-intensive. We can't handle cases that require a lot of labor.'

Wachtell can be choosy because even in a slump, clients offer it twice as many cases as it can handle. In a boom, it turns down seven cases for each it takes. P: 'The firm could be 500 lawyers today if it took all of the work available.' P: 'We could be an 800-lawyer firm today. We chose not to do that, to keep ourselves small.' P: 'We are insulated against downturns by our small size. We've always had more work offered to us than we wanted.'

P: 'We never went 100% M&A [mergers and acquisitions]. We didn't want to do only that. The work is too intense, and the work might go away, so we always maintained a lot of other work.' P: 'The takeover and buyout businesses have declined, but bankruptcies and litigation have ballooned.' O: 'I have to believe that in the 90s, the corporate lawyers there [at Wachtell] are doing green-goods work.'

P: 'Transactional business requires a special kind of excellence—flexibility, creativity, and innovation.' L: 'The Firm encourages innovations and has been successful in developing many, such as cross-border equity mergers, mortgage-pass-through securities, the poison pill, the state business-combination-takeover laws, and innovative forms for merger and acquisition transactions.' P: 'Herb [Wachtell] has ideas that people think are crazy but they win cases.' P: 'Marty [Lipton] not only has good ideas every day, but every five years, he produces a radical innovation. He wrote the law review article about the business-judgment rule that became the basis for our M&A practice.' P: 'No one anywhere rivals him [Lipton], but a number of the younger partners have come up with innovations.'

One of Wachtell's most important innovations was the idea that, instead of being paid by the hour, lawyers' compensation should reflect their clients' benefits. P: Wachtell sometimes 'bases its fee in part on the amount involved in the transaction and Firm's contribution to the accomplishment of the client's objective'. Thus, in 1988, Wachtell received $20 million for two weeks of work defending Kraft against a takeover attempt (Cohen 1991: D6), P: 'and obtaining billions more for the shareholders than originally offered.' O: 'How they got compensated in the 80s is history. It's no longer true today. It was . . . almost an anomaly.'

O: 'Lawyers should not be partners with their clients. That type of compensation can raise questions about the lawyers' objectivity.' O: 'The two or three cases in which the courts criticized the defence all involved Lipton. In effect the courts said "You overstepped the bounds". Is it a case in which your fee arrangement makes you more aggressive?'

M&A

P: 'We would have been intellectually successful, but perhaps not as financially successful, without M&A.' P: 'M&A has evolved rapidly. Many firms have come in and dropped out. Wachtell has stayed with it every step of the way.' L: 'The Firm's success in takeover field is *not* attributable to other firms not being willing to handle takeovers—those other firms were practicing in the takeover area before the Firm—they were not successful and lost the practice because they were not structured to operate on a task force basis and were unwilling to test corporate innovations—like the poison pill—in litigation.' P: 'Takeovers are good examples of crisis-team situations. These provide good training grounds because you see a whole case from beginning to end in two months. You see two or three complete cases the first year.' O: 'It's perfectly clear to me that Marty and Joe [Flom of Skadden, Arps] saw this whole area of hostile transactions developing long before other people recognized it. They saw it coming and got into it and just out-marketed the hell other law firms. Also, what they did do was bring together the various disciplines. . . . This task-force idea was very effective in selling to clients.'

P: 'Wachtell focuses on takeover defence, Skadden on offense.' C: 'One thing I did notice. During the 1980s, the firm prided itself in only representing the targets of takeovers. And then a couple of years ago, they began to represent the other side.'

Staying on top requires staying out in front. The specific actions of law firms are easy to imitate. For example, in 1982, Martin Lipton invented the 'poison pill' defence against hostile corporate takeovers. According to Powell (1993: 439): 'Prior to the Chancery Court's decision upholding the poison pill [in 1985] ten companies had accepted the advice of Lipton and adopted his innovation, and in the eleven months between that ruling and the affirmation of the Delaware Supreme Court only an additional seventeen companies followed suit (*Corporate Control Alert* April 1986). This was a period of very cautious adoption by a few Wachtell Lipton clients who viewed themselves as highly vulnerable to a hostile takeover attempt. Law firms other than Wachtell Lipton did not recommend the pill to their clients because its future was still uncertain; it was a radical innovation, not just some minor tinkering with corporate charters. The slow diffusion of the poison pill was not due to inadequate information about the new device, however. News of Lipton's innovation spread rapidly through the legal and business presses and Lipton himself promoted the poison pill in client memoranda, interviews and addresses to lawyers.'

Once, however, the Delaware Supreme Court had put its seal of approval on the poison pill, its diffusion occurred very rapidly. Indeed, within nine months of the court's decision a total of 263 companies had poison pills in place, including many of America's largest corporations.

O: 'Gotta hand it to Marty though. That poison pill was a great thing. [Long pause.] *His* pill though didn't work! The court ruled against him in the Crown Zellerbach case. *We* added a feature to the pill that *made* it work.'

One informant opined that the poison pill changed the nature of acquisitions, by devaluing the nonmonetary components of deals and escalating the monetary values. O: 'Marty's creation, the poison pill, the courts held that it was legal because he clothed it in a garb in which the courts looked only at the formality of it and not at the substance of it.... The way the poison pill turned out was that only cash counted. Any other kind of offer could be turned down. Negotiation disappeared. Junk bonds made it possible to raise the [large amounts of] money.'

Selective Hiring

To attain and retain its status, Wachtell has had to recruit exceptional lawyers. P: 'Wachtell's strategy is rooted in personnel: Don't compromise standards. Each generation should be as good as the founders.' P: 'There is an external perception of a quality difference at Wachtell. Maintaining that perception depends on recruiting. There is only a small pool of qualified applicants.' O: 'We recently did a [very big] deal with Wachtell. They had a young tax lawyer who ran rings around my whole crew. Just beat them into the ground. He wasn't even a partner. They've got some wonderful people there.'

During Wachtell's early years, its hiring benefited from its founders' disadvantages: It looked attractive to Jews, and it had an inside track at the New York University (NYU) law school. Although discrimination had been declining since the 1940s, the large American corporations and the banks and law firms that served them had long traditions of anti-Semitism. NYU had a tradition of serving the children of recent immigrants to America; and during the decades when elite law schools were applying quotas to Jewish applicants, NYU's doors had been open equally to all. During the 1960s and 1970s, NYU's law school had very high standards and was graduating some excellent lawyers; but because the school was much less well known than the elite ones, its graduates had restricted job opportunities. The founders of Wachtell taught at NYU's law school and participated in alumni activities, and the deans of NYU's law school advised outstanding graduates to consider Wachtell. P: 'For years, two-thirds to three-fourths of the [Wachtell] lawyers were NYU' graduates. C: 'They were able to people this firm with some lawyers who might not have been acceptable at other firms—some Jews, some Irish, some Greek, some Italians, Polish—who might have been welcome as associates at other firms but would never have made partner.'

These demographic advantages gained strength from Wachtell's small size and its policies of egalitarian pay, egalitarian work, and every-associate-can-become-a-partner. P: 'I wanted a small collegially structured firm that works on the most sophisticated matters.' P: 'I joined Wachtell because I wanted a small firm with intelligent people, highly regarded people.' P: 'I was attracted by Wachtell's small size. I was also attracted by the promise that associates can make partner if they're good enough. Other firms don't do this; they reject some deserving people.' P: 'The odds of becoming partner are far higher here. This helps to attract top-notch people. We never hire people just to ease the burden of work. We've wanted the firm to grow slowly; wanted to retain collegiality.' L: 'Partnership decision is made early, with associates becoming partners at the end of six years. The basic premise is that every associate will become a partner.'

Of course, the conditions that existed when Wachtell began have all but disappeared. Discrimination against Jews has become largely insignificant in the New York law firms; NYU's law school has become highly respected; and Wachtell itself has become an icon. P: 'Wachtell is the hardest firm in the US to get a job in.' P: 'We have insanely tight criteria on whom we let in.' P: 'Most firms have many associates and few partners. The partners make money on the associates' excess value. These firms need 50–100 new associates each year. They can't hire 50–75 superstars in one year, so they hire a lot of not-so-terrific lawyers and weed out. We only take in superstars at Wachtell. No fixed number. We take as many or as few as look promising.'

Nearly all of Wachtell's hiring is out of summer jobs. Each year, around 1200 law students apply to Wachtell for jobs as interns, and the firm chooses 20–25. At summer's end, it offers long-term employment to 12–15 of the interns who are beginning the last year of law school. Six or seven accept the offers.

Associate lawyers receive appraisals after three, four, and five years. The senior partners make these appraisals quite frank so that the final partnership decision

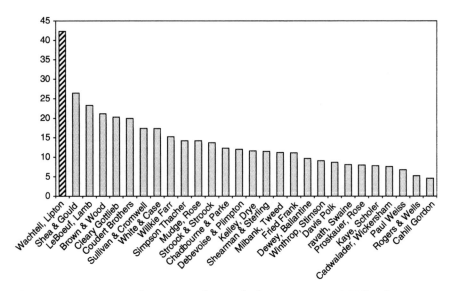

Figure 13.9. Percentages of 1979–83 graduates who became partners (NY firms)

surprises no one. The partnership decision occurs earlier than at other leading firms.

Of those who start at Wachtell, over 40 percent become partners. Figure 13.9 shows the percentages. Wachtell's percentage is three times the average and 60 percent higher than the next highest one. The data for the other firms come from the *New York Law Journal* (May 29, 1990; June 11–12, 1992). The data describe 27 of the 30 largest New York firms and lawyers who graduated from law school from 1979 through 1983.

P: 'In Wachtell's history, only one person has been brought in as a partner.'
P: 'When I joined the firm as an associate in February it was with the expectation that by year end I would be made a partner, if everything worked out. That is a euphemism for "if everyone likes you and respects you" ' (Lederman 1992: 59).

High Quality

C: 'I've had nothing but the best experiences with them and I've always had the impression that there's something they do that is unique.' P: 'The advantages of working at Wachtell are always dealing with very smart people, also highly motivated people who look further for evidence. Imaginative ideas. Good theories. It's a spectacular environment. Our clients are always amazed and happy with the people who work on their cases. Also, clients get partners, not associates, working on their matters.' P: 'People are wildly self-motivated. Their drive to do a spectacular job is so great that they'll drive themselves nuts. The success of the firm came from lousy marriages.' P: 'Wachtell is also somewhat arrogant. We believe we are as good as any firm in the US.' P: 'It is a true academic environment in the best sense of that term. There are never any political issues. The only thing to think about is what is the best way to do it. Never, never compromise anything.' O: 'I think that what has distinguished the Wachtell firm is that they have consistently gone out and hired first-class minds.' O: 'If they say "We are the best there is" and they try to behave that way, that is what makes it real.'

L: 'The Firm has not deviated from the basic premise on which it was founded twenty-five years ago—if you do a superior job there will be more demand for your services than you can meet.' P: 'People come to us because they perceive us as very good lawyers.' P: 'Wachtell's attraction to clients is basic things. People really care. They'll work 20 hours more to improve a document 2%.' P: 'Wachtell has quality consistency far higher than any other law firm.' O: 'They can be a little slovenly.' P: 'I always knew that I could work as many hours as I wanted to do the best job I could and nobody would ever second guess me.' P: 'I'm successful because I'm scared. All you have to do is screw up once or twice.'

O: 'When I was sued, they were my first choice to represent me.'

O: 'I've been involved in many situations where we've bested them. Like the...case. It was just marvelous.' So how does one go about beating Wachtell? 'There's no consistent theme to it. They don't have any glaring weakness. Marty, of course, became more doctrinaire as he matured in the practice.'

C: 'Are they better than other lawyers? I find it easier to talk about individuals. We use other firms as well. I'm enormously impressed by the associates at Cravath; I think they're the best associates I've ever met. At Wachtell, there's an enormous consistency at an exceptionally high level—mainly among the partners.' O: 'There are differences in degree in what they do, and there are differences in how hard their partners work. There is not a significant difference in the kind of work or quality of work. They have been able to do it on a more profitable basis and to have less chicken shit in what they do.'

Commitment, Stress, and Self-Confidence

Why do only half of those to whom Wachtell offers jobs accept? Who would not welcome an opportunity to work in such an organization? After all, it is a very prestigious firm that offers high pay and high probabilities of partnership, that provides an egalitarian, collegial work environment, and that practices on the leading edge of the law.

Obviously, some lawyers see a downside to working at Wachtell, but without interviews with those who turned down offers, one can only speculate about their reasons. One factor may be the lawyer's commitment to career achievement and hard work. A second factor may be the lawyer's attitude toward stress. A third factor may be the lawyer's self-confidence.

Wachtell resembles an emergency medical team. Their clients are desperate and demanding. Although willing to pay very high prices, the clients want immediate results, and they expect Wachtell to deliver products that their normal law firms cannot—legal innovations, remarkable arguments, extreme quality.

L: 'The Firm's operations are geared to the needs of its practice—24-hour-7-day full service; always prepared to do a deal, fight an injunction or give an opinion on an overnight basis.' P: 'Wachtell treats everything as a crisis. Clients get upset if lawyers slow things down.' P: 'My wife says this firm is built on failed marriages.' P: 'Our creed is being there when the client wants you, getting it done expeditiously, turning out the best possible piece of work, and being scared. You're worrying so that [the client] doesn't have to worry.' C: 'You give them something, they're interested in it. I call up at 3:30 in the afternoon, they'll be in my office at 5:30, maybe 8:30 the next morning. If I ask for Marty, he'll call me back in half an hour. He might be in Europe or on the West Coast, but he calls me back. Since most of our work is litigation, we don't use him that much, but still, I like that relationship.'

P: 'Wachtell people take a lot of pride in what they do.' P: 'Wachtell people work harder than others. They agonize over important calls and major matters.' S: 'We just *know* that it's last minute.' O: 'I suspect that they work harder than other lawyers.' O: 'Another thing I've always been impressed by over there is their dedication to hard work.'

To call these extremely self-confident people would be gross understatement. To attract Wachtell's attention initially, they had to have outstanding records in law school. They know they are brighter than almost everyone. They know they can accomplish more than almost everyone. Those who joined Wachtell before it became well known were putting their own judgments ahead of general opinion. P: 'Most law students saw Wachtell as a gamble [when I graduated]. Wachtell wasn't well known among most students at [my law school].' Even those who join Wachtell today are choosing an unconventional path.

Then Wachtell offers them positions as junior associates who have unusual responsibility. To take these positions, they have to regard themselves as ready to practice law on an equal basis with the best. They will be working among people who are at least as able as themselves.

Recall that the founders wanted a firm in which associates do not do grunt work for partners and partners work as hard as associates. As the firm developed, the founders augmented their initial ideas with three more notions: (*a*) that new graduates from law school would have major responsibilities; (*b*) that no lawyer would be hired or retained unless they expected him to become a partner; and (*c*) that major cases would be shared by teams of lawyers representing different specialties.

P: 'You're about as good a lawyer as you are ever going to be after your first year in law school.' L: 'Associates get full responsibility as soon as they are ready.' A: 'I feel I have been granted a surprising degree of responsibility.' A: 'By third year, an associate often will be the primary contact on a number of matters and negotiating major portions of transactions. I find I am given more responsibility than associates I come across at other firms—no matter what class year they are in.' A: 'It is hard for me to imagine any firm where I would get more responsibility and consistently excellent work.' A: ' "Partner" functions and roles are often not clearly distinguishable from "associate" functions and roles.' O: 'They can delegate responsibility to people who aren't ready for it.'

P: 'There is prompt feedback when you screw up.' P: 'Employees have to expect to be treated as autonomous professionals or they wouldn't join Wachtell.' P: 'You never feel afraid of telling Wachtell or Lipton "I just don't understand this. Explain it to me." ' C: 'The [Wachtell] partners have a presence. They have a certain style. It's a commanding style. They're not background people. They tend to be forceful advocates of what they think is the right legal judgment.'

P: 'The main disadvantage of working at Wachtell is not enough associates to handle matters. The partners feel overworked and complain. The partners would like more help.' P: 'Everyone drafts briefs; everyone does research; everyone deals with clients. In other firms, the senior partner goes home at 5 p.m. and leaves the work for inexperienced associates. At Wachtell, no one does that.' P: 'No one works harder than Marty Lipton.'

Egalitarian Compensation

Wachtell's compensation system reinforces its egalitarian norms.

One of the firm's most unusual policies is that it takes no markup on associates' time; clients pay proportionately less for the work done by associates. P: 'Wachtell has no leverage. Instead, we get top-dollar for what we do.'

Thus, the firm has no incentive to employ associates instead of partners. Indeed, the financial incentives promote the opposite. P: 'Partners do a lot of low-level work' but charge clients proportionately more for it. P: Wachtell is a 'bottom-loaded partnership because there are so many younger ones'. P: This strategy is 'protected by the excess demand for our services'.

C: 'We use them because they are very good. They work very hard. We can call them on a Friday afternoon and they'll work through the weekend. They're expensive, but they're not *that* expensive because they don't use so many people. They never overstaff there. Where another firm might use six or eight people, Wachtell might use two or three. The aggregate bill may be not that much higher. Why do you pay a little more? Well, the quality of the work, the timeliness.'

Partners too have egalitarian compensation in comparison with many firms. P: According to Wachtell's lockstep formula: 'The three founders get 125% of the average. Other seniors get 100%. Younger partners progress toward 100%. A new partner would get around 33%.' P: These percentages are 'determined entirely by seniority. No one is compensated for client clout.' L: 'Hours worked, client contact, firm administration, all do not affect partnership shares.'

P: This compensation system 'can only work where everyone is sharing the workload. No one is seriously considering changing the system. It requires trust among partners, sharing, beneficence by the seniors.' P: 'No one came to this firm for dollars; no one stays for dollars.' P: 'We can move associates around because no partner is responsible for a specific client. Also, there is no reticence to bring someone else into a client relationship. Lockstep is very important.'

P: 'Lockstep fosters co-operation. But the question is: can we afford it in terms of decreased entrepreneurship? Lipton gave up income to buy loyalty, but he also gained more control, more decision power.' Partners conjectured that Lipton would be making 3–6 times as much if he were in another firm. O: 'Lawyers tend to be risk-averse—even a great lawyer like Marty Lipton. If he went to another firm, would he have a senior litigator as good as Bernie Nussbaum?'

Collegiality and Culture

KIFs face serious obstacles to creating and maintaining distinctive cultures (Starbuck 1992). Although skilled experts share values, standards, habits, mental frameworks, and language, the culture they share is supraorganizational (Smigel 1964). As a result, few KIFs closely resemble what Maister (1985) called the 'one-firm firm'.

According to Maister, a one-firm firm devotes much effort to selecting and training personnel; grows slowly while choosing clients and tasks carefully; takes service to clients very seriously; stresses cooperative teamwork, group identity, and institutional commitment; de-emphasizes autonomous profit centres, entre-preneurship, and internal competition; encourages free communication among personnel; and gives information freely to its personnel, including financial information. Maister also warned that one-firm firms tend to grow complacent and habit-bound and to lack entrepreneurship and diversity.

All of the KIFs I have studied select expert personnel carefully, use teams extensively, take their missions seriously, manage growth cautiously, and encour-age open communication; and all of them depart from the one-firm model in decentralizing activities and not involving everyone in decision-making. However, only Wachtell approximates the one-firm model in discouraging internal compe-tition, emphasizing group work, disclosing information, and eliciting institutional loyalty. Wachtell's personnel disagree about whether it lacks entrepreneurship.

P: 'Wachtell is a special place. It has a culture. It is structured differently. No one is hired who is expected to leave. People treat each other well. There is no pyramid of partners and associates. There is no competition among the associ-ates.' P: 'Excellence as a lawyer is cherished. A lot of people teach [in law schools]. Education is valued. Comradeship is also valued. The one-to-one ratio lets partners spend time on associates, help them develop. There is much loyalty to the firm. The associates rated Wachtell first in New York City.' A: 'I am...im-pressed with how informal and nonhierarchical relationships between partners and associates are.' P: 'One of my surprises on becoming a partner was the very collegial atmosphere among the partners.' P: 'I came to Wachtell because it looked different—smaller, less widely known at [my law school]. The Wachtell people seemed very smart, bound together some way but not socially—young aggressive people. I didn't understand the structural difference between Wachtell and other firms.' P: 'Wachtell doesn't abuse human capital.' S: 'We all feel part of a very big family.... Every person feels that the firm cares about them. If you need money, if you need medical advice, even if you're abroad, there's always someone here.... People have been here 15–20 years. They don't leave. They feel it's just family.... People come here to be spoiled.... If someone decides they want a different soda, or a different flavor cookie, it's here. It's a firm that does everything for everybody. It's because we care.'

P: 'People like each other, and in large part, it's because the things that cause dislikes are eliminated.' P: 'Doors are open. Everyone has a first name, and people use them.' A former partner, Lederman (1992: 57), recalled: 'All office doors were always open, fostering a communal workplace. Everyone treated the office like home, and no one felt any need to knock on doors or to hesitate to cross a threshold. Lawyers would walk into your office, demand attention (almost always bringing cookies or coffee or soda from the small kitchen), and begin talking about what was bothering them, while offering you food, even though you were with someone else or on the phone.... Without any privacy, everybody knew what everyone else was doing, which meant that knowledge was shared, making the informality more effective than seminars or luncheons arranged for the dissemination of information. George Katz, one of the founding partners, embodied this family style. He visited all the offices almost every day, bringing encouragement or news or gossip, a practice which he continued until his premature death in 1989. Always optimistic, George would report on current matters and ask for advice from everyone on thorny legal questions, giving even the new junior associates the sense that their participation was valuable.'

O: 'They're pretty nice even though they're tough. There are some law firms that pride themselves on being mean. Wachtell doesn't play those games. They're not a bunch of mean pricks.' O: 'It's an interesting place and the people are fun. They're interesting people to be with.' C: 'It's a very informal firm. You walk into Cravath, it's a little bit stuffy. At Wachtell, they're in their shirt sleeves. Nothing oppressive, nothing standoffish. Some people might want more of a white-shoe atmosphere. We don't. These people are extremely smart and extremely capable. That's what *we* want.' C: 'You get a different feeling at Wachtell. Maybe collegial isn't the best word but it's the only one I can think of.'

O: 'Wachtell has limited itself to two or three disciplines, so when they talk about communication across disciplines they don't know what real communication problems are.'

L: 'The Firm is not a business; it is an old fashioned professional partnership; there is no partnership agreement—only a handshake among friends.' Lederman (as quoted by Cohen 1991: D6): 'The ethic there [at Wachtell] is, if you're in, it's your life. If you're partly in, you're out.' S: 'People here often don't understand how different other firms are. A lot of strange things happen in other firms.'

Task Forces

L: 'The Firm approaches all matters on a task force basis. An ad hoc group of tax, antitrust, litigation, creditor rights, real estate, corporate or other lawyers, as needed, is formed for each matter.... The task forces overlap with a particular lawyer leading one or more and assisting on one or more. There is considerable overlapping of the composition of the task forces so that each matter has the benefit of the best thinking the Firm can bring to bear on that matter.' P: 'Our success in takeover cases arose from marrying different kinds of expertise. In the beginning, Wachtell was a small firm working for big corporations, so we had to work together. Everyone shared every project. We had a collegial atmosphere. We learned how to create task forces. Other firms had departments, and it took them ten years to learn to make task forces.' O: 'They were a ragtag bunch of people who pulled together, bonded by the fact that they weren't tied to anything else.'

P: 'Task forces are the essence of expertise. Critical. Life and death. Other firms don't copy task forces well. People at Wachtell work together well. People know each other very well. There are few partners and they have had long relationships. Lipton is exceedingly generous.'

Management and Control

Wachtell has also applied its founders' ideas about organizing. P: 'This place would go bananas if we tried to put in systems and turn it into an efficient organization.' P: 'Our overhead costs are twice that of most firms.' Figure 13.10 graphs ratios of support staff to lawyers and indicates that Wachtell had a higher staffing ratio than any of the largest New York firms during 1990 and 1991;

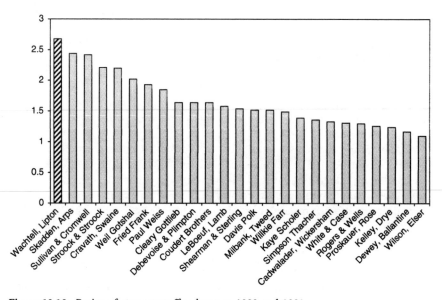

Figure 13.10. Ratios of support staff to lawyers, 1990 and 1991

Wachtell's ratio was 61 percent above the average. The data for the other firms come from the *New York Law Journal* (December 2, 1991).

Nelson (1988: 205–228) remarked on lawyers' ambivalence about power and organizational control. On the one hand, they spoke of collegiality and every partner having a say in firm governance; on the other hand, a very few lawyers dominated each firm, 'not unlike the father does in many families' (1988: 212).

P: 'Management devolves on those who will do it.' P: 'Occasionally, we lean on people.' In late 1991, four people made case assignments at Wachtell: Herbert Wachtell and Bernard Nussbaum (now Legal Counsel to President Clinton) did so for litigation, Leonard Rosen for bankruptcy and creditors' rights, and James Fogelson for major assignments and antitrust.

P: 'Three committees manage the firm. The Administration and Coordinating Committees overlap. The Recruiting Committee is the most important one.' Who is on the Recruiting Committee? P: 'Whoever wants to be on the Committee shows up.' P: 'The Administration Committee handles paper clips. At one partners' meeting, no one knew who was on it.' P: 'Wachtell is a frustrating institution sometimes. It doesn't plan very well.' P: 'We need more structuring within the firm.'

Martin Lipton says, 'I have never gone to a committee meeting.' P: 'Marty doesn't participate in management but no one can do anything without consulting him so decisions get changed. There is some grumbling about this.'

P: 'Suppose there is an issue as to whether we should take up a new matter from a nontraditional client. This produces a group discussion in the creditors' rights department. In corporate or litigation, the decision is centralized.'

P: 'Up to now, policy decisions have been made by consensus. But 60 partners makes getting everyone to agree very, very tough. Ten percent dissent can be overcome, but a 60–40 split leads to slow decisions. Ultimately some kind of smaller decision-making system will have to get put into place. Now, a lot of major decisions get made by the three main partners over lunch. If this system hadn't been benevolent, it would have been deposed.' P: 'Most decisions are made ad hoc, not at partnership meetings.' O: 'The desire to stay small is an important feature of the way they do business. It allows them to maintain control in a way that you can't do in a larger organization.'

P: 'Twice, someone at Wachtell has been involved in insider trading. In both cases, a small group made the decision and someone was dismissed. There was no partnership meeting.' (Lederman 1992: 226–261 describes both cases.) O: 'In [a small collegial firm], how did they end up with two partners within a few years who became involved in insider trading? No other firm that I know of has had two partners who did that. How did this happen?'

Rainmaking

Service KIFs generally give client relations higher priority than technical expertise (Starbuck 1992). The experts with greater social skills become client-relations specialists, and these receive higher compensation and wield greater power than other experts. Their power arises from the possibility that client-relations specialists might depart and take long-term clients with them.

Informally, American lawyers put the label 'rainmakers' on the lawyers whom clients seek out. This term symbolizes the mystery, magic, and power of client relations.

Most law firms reward rainmaking, of course, and Wachtell does not. P: 'Getting new business is irrelevant to people's performance [ratings]. The criterion is always excellent legal work.' P: 'The only thing that matters in terms of becoming a partner is whether you're any good.' C: 'Of course, by doing such good work, you don't have to market yourself. Your work speaks for itself.'

Some Wachtell personnel see the firm's disregard of rainmaking as a corollary to its transactional practice. P: 'Wachtell isn't dependent on long-term relationships with clients. Wachtell has a transactional practice.' P: 'No clients account for more than 3, 4, 5, 10% of revenues, so we don't have to worry about pissing any clients off.' P: 'We have a huge client base. Many, many more client contacts than most firms, and they are contacts at high levels. Not the assistant counsel. Usually the chief counsel, the CFO, or the CEO.' P: 'Our clients are mainly lawyers who represent corporations' and who know how to evaluate legal services. P: 'The firm tries to make all clients the firm's clients rather than individuals' clients.' P: 'Marty spreads it around. Over the years, he's succeeded in introducing the world to the rest of the firm. I think there is very little question that the firm will survive the retirements of Wachtell, Lipton, and Rosen.'

O: 'The thing that distinguishes a Cravath, Wachtell, or Davis Polk is that the clients come to them because they have big problems. They're not looking for a lawyer they can schmooze with. With the high-pressure investment banker, with the Type-A personality we usually see, there's not much room for social skills.'

Other Wachtell personnel worry that the firm may be undercutting its future. P: 'We need more people generating new business.' P: 'We haven't spread rainmaking as much as we should have. We've been too busy, so junior people haven't been encouraged to rainmake. It's happening now [during the recession] more than it was however.'

Still other Wachtell personnel are trying to make rain. P: 'Rainmaking in our kind of practice is [a matter of] doing a good job and getting to know other people. There is not a need for rainmaking [in another sense]. We get business because we do a good job. We also have to stay in touch with clients.' The latter speaker then explained how he keeps in touch with clients. He has Wachtell's library watch for ticker-tape items and articles in the business press that relate to firms he regards as his clients. When the library turns up an item on which he has insight, he telephones a senior manager or the corporate counsel, explains that he has noticed the item, and suggests that the client consider doing such-and-so. Thus, he lets clients know that he is watching out for their interests and that he has expertise relevant to their current problems; by giving advice away he implies that he could bring even greater expertise to bear.

Marty

P: 'Marty was leading. He recognized that M&A was a good way to go. We just followed him.' P: 'Marty Lipton is a business genius. He has strategic planning insight.' P: 'Marty is charismatic, confident, usually right, and he dominates. Herb is similar, yet they get along.'

O: 'Marty was one of the best securities lawyers in the country; there were maybe half a dozen others. Unlike the others, Marty was not at a firm that would necessarily frown on aggressive hostile actions. Unlike the others, Marty was willing to deploy task forces. Finally, of the great security lawyers, Marty had the best business sense.' O: 'Marty is the most honorable guy. He doesn't communicate any sleaze to anybody.' O: 'Marty has a big ego and sometimes he comes across too strong.' O: 'I have very high regard for Marty Lipton. He is a fine lawyer. He is innovative. He is superb with clients. He is the force at that firm. They have other fine lawyers, but without Marty Lipton....'

O: 'Lipton's genius was he chose to be on one side [defence against takeover]. He realized that they were prepared to pay because...they were never around afterward. You couldn't win so it was a matter of how much money you could raise for the losers. Everybody hired Marty to keep them independent, but this just wasn't possible. I believe the financial results justified the earnings, and I believe [Wachtell's] actual earnings were much higher than' the estimates made by the *American Lawyer*.

P: 'Wachtell has one phenomenal rainmaker. We've practiced in the puddle created by his rain. But he's not politically well connected or socially well connected. He's an extremely good lawyer who makes contacts because people want him to work on their cases.' P: 'Lipton would be sorely missed. His business life is interwoven with his social life. He's a genius and we all benefit from it.' P: 'Lipton is one of the most brilliant lawyers in the US, maybe the most brilliant. He's also entrepreneurial, and he networks.' P: 'No one this side of the Mississippi could replace Marty Lipton. However, many lawyers in Wachtell have close relations with various clients.' P: 'Marty is unbelievably smart. Comes up with these ideas.' P: 'Marty is unique.' P: 'Even if Lipton's not here, he's here. "What would Marty say?" '

6. WHAT LIES AHEAD?

Will Growth Drive Wachtell Back to the Mean?

P: 'We need more associates, especially in litigation. Young people are willing to do the routine work. They have more energy, more enthusiasm. Without young people you feel isolated, put upon. The young work cheaper, so there is less client complaint.'

Galanter and Palay (1991) argued that the up-or-out rule—which dictates that associates must either become partners or depart—locks law firms into exponential growth. Maintaining constant sizes requires firms to appoint new partners no faster than current partners retire or die. Maintaining leverage requires having more associates and fewer partners. But associates remain so for only a few years whereas partners remain so for many years, so to keep the same sizes, law firms must promote very few associates to partnership. When firms grow, the ratios become more severe because there are fewer partners near retirement and because firms tend to grow by adding associates rather than partners.

Galanter and Palay said that around 1960 the prominent New York City law firms were more or less in equilibrium: They had 1.36 associates per partner, and they were promoting between one-seventh and one-fifteenth of these associates to partnerships. They also allowed a few associates to hold that status indefinitely. Firms outside New York had just 1.03 associates per partner, but they were promoting about half of their associates to partnership. According to Galanter and Palay (1991: 36), 'For big firms, circa 1960 was a time of prosperity, stable relations with clients, steady but manageable growth, and a comfortable assumption that this kind of law practice was a permanent fixture of American life and would go on forever.'

Of course, what Galanter and Palay saw as comfortable stability, Katz, Lipton, Rosen, and Wachtell saw as exploitation and bureaucratization. The story of Wachtell suggests that the structure of 1960 was promoting the creation of new specialist law firms that did what they did better than their old, large competitors. In 1976, Brill (1976: 55) speculated, 'Flom's and Lipton's success seems to be part of a trend in New York that has seen younger firms spring up in the last two decades to challenge the supremacy of the old Wall Street firms. The younger firms, many of which were started by Jewish lawyers who were not as welcome then at the old-line firms, enjoy reputations among job-seeking students at major law schools as "sweatshops" or as "places where the action is," depending on the student's outlook.' Because similar developments were occurring in investment banking and financial brokerage, the new law firms could find clients who did not have established ties.

From 1960 to 1985, according to Galanter and Palay, law firms adhered to the up-or-out rule while their operations changed dramatically. Government regulations and an increasingly litigious society led corporations to search for more specialized and higher legal skills. Many corporations terminated their long-standing relationships with full-service law firms, created in-house legal departments to handle routine matters, and divided their outside legal work among specialists in governmental regulation, labour relations, mergers, pensions, taxes, and so on. The large law firms responded by bringing in former government officials as partners, by raiding each other to obtain the specialists in greatest demand, by merging with firms having complimentary specialties, and by expanding geographically. Most large law firms have opened offices in Europe and in several U.S. cities.

Nelson argued that Galanter and Palay overstated the importance of the up-or-out rule in these developments and understated the importance of lawyers' ideologies and their desire for profits. He (1992: 745–746) opined that 'corporate law firms began to mimic the aggressive entrepreneurialism of the corporate and financial actors they represented. In a corporate environment that did not value institutional loyalty, traditionally oriented law firms risked looking flabby or out-of-touch.' Furthermore, 'corporate law firms simultaneously define professional achievement in terms of status and economic returns' (1992: 747). 'Law partner-ships maintain the promotion-to-partnership tournament, not because it is the only way to arrange these exchanges, but because it is an effective surplus-producing mechanism' (1992: 746–747). (Sander and Williams (1992) also dis-agreed with Galanter and Palay's interpretation.)

Of course, Wachtell promotes associates to partnerships even though the firm does not extract surpluses from its associates.

Whatever the reasons, the large law firms grew 8 percent annually from 1975 to 1985. Since much of this growth came through recruitment at the bottom, leverage went up. Leverage probably also rose because competition among law firms for new graduates drove up starting salaries. In New York city, leverage had risen to 1.82 associates per partner by 1985; and Figure 13.4 says it had gone much higher in the top firms by 1990.

Although Wachtell has resisted an increase in leverage, it has not escaped growth. Some of its partners wonder if Wachtell has already grown too big. P: 'One hundred lawyers pose managerial problems—personnel, recruiting, space, mail, word processing.' P: 'Participatory democracy doesn't work as well with 100 lawyers as with 50.' P: 'Maintaining the culture was easier with 30 partners than with 60 partners.' O: 'I don't happen to believe that when you've got a hundred lawyers, there's that great communication!'

Others wonder how much longer the firm can continue to expand without radically altering its culture and standards. P: 'Will growth dilute the partnership interest? Will Wachtell be a victim of its success?' P: 'Can Wachtell find enough new hires who are good enough to sustain the one-to-one ratio?' O: 'The biggest problem you run into with a large law firm is: the bigger you get, the more conflicts [of interest] you get into.... It's a huge limiting factor.'

Wachtell has also resisted expansion to other sites. Responding to pressure from clients, Wachtell did experiment with an office in London, but then closed it. P: 'Our staff are "homegrown". We need to monitor quality. It's difficult to do that with just one office; multiple offices make it an impossibility. We don't want to work with people we haven't worked with before. We've been able to serve all the business by getting on airplanes. Ours is a transaction business.' P: 'We believe that to survive, you don't need 2000 lawyers all over the world. Of course, the world may pass us by; we may be an anachronism. We're not trying to do everything.'

Does Wachtell Need Long-Term Strategies?

People in Wachtell debate the need for long-term strategic planning. P: 'Wachtell needs an overall strategy as the firm gets bigger. There may be trouble in, say, 1995 when the firm has grown to 140–150 lawyers and the founders are gone.' P: 'We have no long-term strategy. Held a weekend meeting of partners. It was a bust.' P: 'We held a Retreat two years ago to talk about how to identify what is most fundamental. Everyone is struggling co-operatively with the issues. Three guys discuss the issues at lunch and agree, but they don't push their solution on others.' P: 'Do we need to plan? Yes. Lipton encourages us to plan. But he's the planner, together with Fogelson and Wachtell.'

Others see little need for long-term strategies. P: 'Our long-term strategy is "more of the same".' P: 'Fine-tuning will suffice. We have enough work for 150 partners. We think restructuring is going to be the next five years. Litigation and creditors' rights boom in a bad economy. Corporate goes the other way.' P: 'People here believe that if you're good at what you do and you do the best job you can, there will always be people who come to you. The work will always be there. There's not a whole lot of concern about the future.'

What Will Happen When the Founders Depart?

Succession is an ancient problem. For instance, Marshall (1920: 316) remarked that 'after a while, the guidance of the business falls into the hands of people with less energy and less creative genius, if not with less active interest in its prosperity'.

Wachtell's founders see this issue and aspire to create an exceptional institution that will long survive them. The L quotations above have a formal tone that reflects Lipton's vision of Wachtell as an institution. The example of Cravath Swaine proves that extreme excellence and unusual ways of organizing can memorialize those who created them (Nelson 1988: 71–73; Swaine 1946–1948). Still, no one is confident that Wachtell's excellence will survive its founders' departures.

O: 'These were four extraordinary lawyers. Emotionally, if I were part of that firm, I'd feel enormous gratitude to them.' O: 'Len Rosen—I'm told he's the best bankruptcy practitioner in the country.' P: 'It is a law-firm tradition: The original partners get diluted. The next generation is not a good as the founders. Wachtell hopes to break out of this.' P: 'There's a generation gap between the 30-year-olds and the 60-year-olds.' P: 'The organization has to get over the parental problem. Wachtell, Lipton, and Rosen stand in the parental role. The younger partners resist responsibility' for management. P: 'We have to pass relationships down to the younger generations.' C: 'I have a relationship with the two top people. I can call Marty. I can call Herb.'

James Fogelson, whom some regarded as Wachtell's likely leader for the 1990s, died in September 1991 at the age of 48. P: 'Fogelson was a great administrator. He kept track of everything.'

What Happened?

People often ask me what happened to Wachtell after I completed the study in 1993. When I interviewed them in 1992–93, several of Wachtell's opponents had predicted that the wave of mergers and acquisitions had ended, and hence that

Wachtell would no longer be able to achieve such extreme financial success. Many people, both inside and outside the firm, wondered how dependent Wachtell was on the talents and values of its founding partners.

The years 1994 and 1995 did indeed bring fewer mergers nationally and less merger work for Wachtell. But in that period, there were many corporate bankruptcies and many bank reorganizations, and Wachtell suddenly emerged as a leading U.S. firm in these two areas of practice. Leonard Rosen, one of the founding partners, had long been recognized for his expertise in Bankruptcy and Creditors' Rights, and the firm included a small group specializing in this area of practice. When bankruptcies grew prevalent in the early 1990s, this group gained prominence and took on more business. Also, one of Wachtell's partners was widely recognized for his exceptional expertise in bank reorganization. When the 1990s brought many bank reorganizations, his specialty gained prominence and the firm took on more such business.

The decline in merger activity was short-lived, and after just a few years, Wachtell again had much M&A work.

In 1999, Wachtell continued to stand out on general performance measures. Indeed, Wachtell occupied a more outstanding position in 1999 than it had in 1989–90. According to Alison Frankel (2000), 'In the last 10 years we've seen an increasing percentage of the highest-end (and best-paying) litigation and deal work consolidating at fewer and fewer elite firms—all New York-based. In fact, throughout the 1990s, just 10 firms—again, all headquartered in New York—dominated our revenue-per-lawyer and profits-per-partner rankings. They are the Winners of the Nineties, listed here in order of their dominance: Wachtell, Lipton, Rosen & Katz; Cravath, Swaine & Moore; Sullivan & Cromwell; Davis Polk & Wardwell; Cahill Gordon & Reindel; Simpson Thacher & Bartlett; Cleary, Gottlieb, Steen & Hamilton; Skadden, Arps, Slate, Meagher & Flom; Debevoise & Plimpton; and Shearman & Sterling.'

Over the decade, Wachtell expanded about 40 percent, but the number of partners increased only 10 percent, so there are now more associates per partner. Yet, Wachtell still has the lowest ratio of associates per partner among the top firms.

As the three surviving founders continued to practice law, there is no evidence about the effects of succession. But a new challenge or opportunity surfaced—'The New Economy'. As one result, in the summer of 2000, Wachtell was again considering whether to open a branch office outside New York City, this time in Silicon Valley.

7. THE ELEMENTS OF EXCEPTIONAL SUCCESS

What explains Wachtell's exceptional success? This question has many answers, all of which may be correct, and there is no way to find out whether some of these answers are truly essential. Here is a concise analysis by one of Wachtell's competitors who knows the firm well.

What factors have led Wachtell to be so profitable? The first is that Wachtell was and is a major factor in takeover work. Virtually all of the most successful firms have been major presences in takeover work.

A second factor is that Wachtell has limited lines of business. That is to me a function of its age.... Old law firms are like snowballs rolling down the hill. Not only can't you get rid of the bad business, it keeps growing. The theory that diversification is risk-averse is wrong. It's wrong because an unprofitable line is never going to become profitable again.

The third factor—Wachtell has the best work ethic of any firm in the country. A higher percentage of Wachtell's personnel have a diligent work ethic than any other law firm in the country. This too is a function of the age of the firm. Wachtell has relatively few people who are over 48–50, and the people at Wachtell who are over that age are a very diligent group. They deserve credit, a lot of credit, for maintaining that work ethic. I'd guess that 90 percent of Wachtell's lawyers share their work ethic. At a firm like this one, there might be (one seventh of the) lawyers who have that work ethic.

It takes all three factors. If they just had the other factors but not the takeover work, they'd have been very successful but not as successful as they have been. If they just had takeover but not the other factors, they'd have been very successful but not as successful as they have been.

Wachtell Is an Intricate House of Cards

The preceding analysis seems too simple. It also overstates the importance of M&A work. As the analyst observed, 'Virtually all of the most successful firms have been major presences in takeover work.' Indeed, Wachtell was far from the dominant presence in M&A cases. Powell (1993: 451) noted, 'Skadden Arps... was involved in 60% of all major mergers and acquisitions during 1985 and Wachtell Lipton in 45% (*Corporate Control Alert* February 1986).'

Every concise analysis seems too simple. Wachtell contains many elements that fit together and reinforce each other. Each element is individually a flimsy component with which to build an institution, and some elements are individually farfetched. Yet, they fit together so well that removing one element might undermine the whole structure.

I found it impossible to array the quotations in a cleanly linear fashion: For example, Wachtell's success with M&A cases arose partly from its ability to innovate, partly from its use of teamwork, partly from its willingness to practice law 168 hours a week, partly from its self-confidence, and partly from the personalities and abilities of its founders. These elements in turn interrelate with its high recruiting standards, culture, compensation systems, transactional practice, history, and social environment.

The cards forming a house stay up because they oppose each other. Likewise, Wachtell is internally inconsistent, in conflict with itself. For instance, in a profession that emphasizes individualism, it hires supremely self-confident lawyers and asks them to subordinate their individuality to teamwork. Although it specializes in difficult areas of practice and emphasizes the high quality of its work, it gives early responsibilities to associate lawyers, makes partnership decisions early, and promotes a high percentage of associates to partner. Although its policies call for transactional practice and some lawyers emphasize their independence of clients, rainmaking is on many minds. Whereas the mythology says 'management devolves on those who will do it', it is senior partners who make case assignments, who 'lean on people', and who make 'a lot of major decisions . . . over lunch'. The firm's founders say they have given low priority to income, and they seem to be foregoing personal income to build a firm. Thus, the founders are hoping to attract lawyers like themselves, yet no potential or current employee can ignore the very high incomes that Wachtell offers. Lawyers who were social underdogs have become the professional elite.

A house of cards can grow stronger as the builder adds cards, but growth also makes the structure less stable. Policies of early promotion and high rates of promotion, and possibly clients' resistance to high fees, compel Wachtell to grow; yet growth is posing serious challenges of socialization, recruiting, and demand for services. The current 100-plus-lawyer firm is probably much less integrated and less stable than the 24-lawyer firm of 1974.

Wachtell Is an Elephant

Like the blind men who tried to describe the elephant, various participants in and observers of Wachtell see different organizations. Wachtell's complexity is one cause of ambiguity, and its internal inconsistencies are another.

To explain Wachtell's success, one must point to many factors—converting disadvantages into advantages, successful recruiting, case selection, lawyers' efforts to live up to their own aspirations, a culture that promotes supreme effort, emphasis on high quality, disdain for administrative costs, the M&A fad, collegiality, teamwork, an extreme ethic of client service, founders who are willing to trade financial rewards for organizational ones, the differing personalities and values of the four founders, success that feeds on success, and luck.

It is no wonder that the partners disagree about what Wachtell should do next. The firm is not a coherent unity, and it justifies different interpretations of 'reality'. Is control more democratic in creditors' rights than in corporate law or litigation? Is there enough entrepreneurship? Does Wachtell offer a warm, collegial work environment or does it consume its personnel? Is Wachtell egalitarian or paternalistic, or is paternalism a prerequisite for egalitarianism? Does the firm's success arise from its method of organizing or from the exceptional abilities of a very few? Does Wachtell need a strategy or does it already have one? 'Task forces are the essence of expertise', and 'if you do a superior job there will be more demand for your services than you can meet'.

Law firms, and other KIFs, tend to attribute their successes and failures to individuals. For example, Gilson and Mnookin (1989: 572) wrote: 'At the time of the initial hiring decision, the law firm is unable to tell which among its pool of new associates will come to possess the knowledge and personal attributes that the firm requires in a partner. The firm is uncertain not only about an associate's legal skills, but also about more subjective personal characteristics—for example, co-operativeness, maturity, the ability to gain respect of existing clients and to recruit new ones—that traditionally have been important to the partnership decision.'

Such interpretations assume that 'personal characteristics' are indeed personal. The Wachtell case suggests that personal characteristics reflect organizational culture and policies. Wachtell has no better information about prospective employees than any other law firm, yet more of Wachtell's associates achieve partnerships and do so earlier, and Wachtell's partners have external reputations for unusually high quality and especially hard work.

Wachtell Is a Butterfly

Butterflies are elegant creatures, airy and colourful. They seem barely to touch down on flowers, branches, or leaves. Although butterflies are easily injured and short-lived, nothing lives forever. Some butterflies might choose to live longer at the cost of less beauty; others might risk their lives to attain more beauty. Wachtell too is an elegant, colourful creation that flits from one success to another, and almost no one will be surprised if Wachtell metamorphoses into something more ordinary.

Wachtell flits because it opportunistically goes where the flowers look brightest. Some observers allege smugly that Wachtell's success is a result of a fad—the M&A one. To me, this appears to be a correct statement, but not in the sense that its speakers intend.

Fads always happen. Social changes are inevitable and frequent. The important point is not that Wachtell benefited from a fad, but that Wachtell turned a fad into an opportunity. Indeed, several of Wachtell's opponents suggested that the firm both helped to stimulate the M&A fad and took actions that shaped its character. When the M&A fad faded and recession developed, Wachtell shifted to creditors' rights and bankruptcies. If emphasized, more than before, its capabilities in taxation, antitrust, and real estate; and it promoted its expertise in bank merges and in recapitalizations of and regulatory compliance by financial institutions. Then, when the recession ended, Wachtell turned to M&A work. Wachtell doesn't require a specific social current because its personnel are very proactive and very, very able; they might be able to turn almost any social current into an opportunity.

Some people protest that one should not hold Wachtell up as an example for imitation. They say the firm makes an appalling prototype because it turns an occupation into an all-consuming passion. One response to this protest is that people have the right to dedicate their lives to their occupations if they so choose and it is not only those who work at Wachtell who do this. A second response is that Wachtell cannot serve as a prototype for many firms because it is so difficult to imitate.

Wachtell Has Learned from Experience

The original version of this chapter did not give enough emphasis to one component of Wachtell's success: the firm's repeated ability to extract effective strategic policies from its experience. The founding partners' experiences as associate lawyers led them to formulate Wachtell's radical personnel policies. An early difficulty with a very important client, together with the need to surmount entry barriers, inspired an emphasis on transactional practice. Experience working together while the firm was still very small triggered an emphasis on teamwork. Interaction with investment bankers suggested the possibility of fees based on outcomes rather than hours worked. Observing that a large corporation had been unable to obtain legal service over a weekend led Wachtell to adopt a policy of 24-hour-7-day service. Success in circumventing established precedents taught lessons about surprise and innovation. After initial success with the Poison Pill, Wachtell created Poison Pills for many clients.

Although many, many law firms must have had experiences similar to Wachtell's, the other firms did not convert those experiences into ideas about how they might be able to innovate. Furthermore, after Wachtell innovated, the other firms were slow to imitate Wachtell's innovations and they usually made weak commitments to the innovations. One reason for this might be the loose, individualistic structures of most law firms. Managing partners often lack authority and they may not receive much respect; central coordination is usually weak and individual partners usually have much autonomy. By contrast, especially during the early years, the founding partners of Wachtell operated as a unified coalition that was small enough to formulate innovative policies and strong enough to control the other partners. Evidently, this coalition was also good at extracting valuable lessons from the firm's experience.

Wachtell Is More Unique

All organizations are unique, but Wachtell is more so. Although it shares many properties with other law firms, it pushes a few properties to extremes that no other law firm attains, it combines properties in a way that no other firm duplicates, and it may possess a few unique resources.

Wachtell is very much a product of a time and a place. Its founders' values fit into the 1960s, and its founding reflects the New York City legal system of the 1960s and New York City's ethnic diversity. Wachtell is also very much a product of specific people—Lipton and Wachtell with charisma and offbeat ideas, Katz and Rosen with commitments to democracy and teamwork. What if Wachtell's first major client had not posed difficulties that stimulated the founders to opt for a transactional practice? Indeed, what if Martin Lipton is truly the best corporate lawyer in America and what if the firm is basically an amplifier for his talents? How would an imitator obtain a Martin Lipton?

One strong evidence that Wachtell is difficult to imitate is the lack of a twin. Although other law firms crave Wachtell's high status and stratospheric fees, either they cannot reproduce the conditions necessary to elicit these or they have refused to make the required tradeoffs. Observers often contrast Wachtell with Skadden, Arps, Slate, Meagher & Flom. Skadden Arps opposed Wachtell in many M&A battles, and Joseph Flom's reputation for creativity and good sense equals Martin Lipton's. Skadden Arps very likely received fees for M&A work resembling those paid to Wachtell. But Skadden Arps used this injection of wealth to try to become 'a complete financial services company'. It has allied with affiliate law firms in a dozen countries, and in 1990, it employed 1,113 lawyers.

Deviance plays a powerful role in Wachtell's success. The law industry needs and can support very few firms of last resort, very few emergency medical teams. One can imagine a second Wachtell or even a third, but not five or ten. If there were five law firms with similar abilities, they would not have several times as much work as they could do, they would not be able to choose their cases, and they would not be able to charge significantly higher fees than other firms.

Nevertheless, someone could probably create a second or third law firm like Wachtell. O: 'I don't think it's a formula anybody could follow but it could happen again.' O: 'Why hasn't it been repeated? There's no question in my mind that it can be repeated. It hasn't been because lawyers are so risk-averse and we pay them so much.'

Someone could also create KIFs like Wachtell in other industries. Maister (1985) pointed to one-firm firms in accounting, consulting, investment banking, law, and the military, and one can visualize them in education, marketing research, product development, scientific research, and software. But complexity and peculiarity do make Wachtell difficult to imitate. This firm's story seems to show that it is not sufficient to assemble two or three crucial elements or to assemble many conventional elements. Those who aspire to exceptional success must integrate many elements, some of which are abnormal, and must put them together in unique combinations that may not work or that may meet environmental hostility. Indeed, the fusion of complexity and peculiarity are probably what makes exceptional success rare. Furthermore, both complexity and peculiarity offer bases for the destruction of exceptional success. Complexity means that there is a high probability of losing a few crucial elements out of many, or of opposing elements getting out of balance. Peculiarity means that there is a high probability of the peculiar elements being lost.

Wachtell's story says a great deal about what it takes to attain exceptional success, but it also says exceptional success is very difficult to attain and something most people would be unwilling or unable to attain. Like the Grand Canyon or the British Royal Family, Wachtell challenges the premise that something is only worth observing in order to imitate it.

ACKNOWLEDGMENTS

I owe thanks to many who contributed data, time, ideas, insights, and contacts. This chapter reflects help from Murray Bring, Andrew Brownstein, Joan Dunbar, William Evan, Arthur Fleischer, Joseph Flom, Blaine Fogg, James Fogelson, Stephen Fraidin, Eliot Freidson, Melvin Heineman, Dennis Hersch, Ruth Ivey, Morris Kramer, Robert Landes, Joanne Laurence, Karen Legge, Martin Lipton, Joanne Martin, Joanna Martinuzzi, Alan Meyer, Theodore Mirvis, Connie Monte, Robert Nelson, Harold Novikoff, Lawrence Pedowitz, Fioravante Perrotta, Joseph Post, James Ringer, Lawrence Rosenberg, Stephen Volk, Herbert Wachtell, Alan Whitaker, and some who asked for anonymity.

14

How Organizations Channel Creativity

The following story shows how contrasting value systems and different skills interacted to produce two important inventions (Hounshell and Smith 1988). In December 1926, Charles Stine, the Director of Du Pont's Chemical Department, wrote a memorandum advocating that his company should undertake 'pure science work'. He listed four reasons, the last and least important of which was practical applications. Three months later, after Stine had relabeled his proposal 'fundamental research', Du Pont's Executive Committee gave him money for a new building and a budget for twenty-five scientists.

By the beginning of 1928, Stine had hired only nine scientists, including just one organic chemist. The organic chemist, Wallace Hume Carothers, moved to Du Pont because it had offered him almost twice the $3,200 he had been making at Harvard. Soon after moving, Carothers told a friend: 'A week of the industrial slavery has already elapsed without breaking my proud spirit. Already I am so accustomed to the shackles that I scarcely notice them. Like the child laborers in the spinning factories and the coal mines, I arise before dawn and prepare myself a meagre breakfast. Then off to the terrific grind, arriving at 8 just as the birds are beginning to wake up. Harvard was never like this.'

Carothers espoused the then radical views that polymeric molecules were true molecules and that they could be incredibly large. He set out to create such molecules by aggregating smaller molecules. Within a year, he published a landmark paper proving his case. By the end of 1929, he was supervising eight men.

During the month of April 1930, two members of Carothers' group made important discoveries. Arthur Collins produced the first neoprene rubber, and Julian Hill made the first laboratory-synthesized fiber. The neoprene was an accidental by-product of efforts to purify another polymer, and it took Du Pont little time to turn neoprene into a commercial product. Carothers' group, however, played no part in this development, for Carothers was pursuing the implications of the synthesized fiber. This too had been an accident, a by-product of efforts to produce larger and larger polymeric molecules. While removing hot polymer from some apparatus, Hill observed that molten polymer could be drawn into filaments that turned into very strong yet very elastic fibers if they were stretched after cooling. However, Carothers' and Hill's efforts to produce useful fibers went nowhere at that time, and Carothers turned to other interests.

In June 1930, Stine was replaced by a new chemical director, Elmer Bolton, who believed that fundamental research ought to yield 'practical applications'. When Carothers was looking for new research topics in 1933, Bolton encouraged him to take another look at synthetic fibers. Carothers did so, but concluded after a time that the problem was inherently unsolvable. The goal was to produce a fiber with a high melting point and low solubility, and Carothers reasoned that these properties would make spinning impossible.

Bolton, however, kept synthetic fibers at the top of his personal priority list. In March 1934, he persuaded Carothers to make yet another stab. Carothers suggested to Donald Coffman that he try to make a fiber from an aminononanoic ester. Five weeks later, Coffman stuck a cold stirring rod into a molten polymer and observed a fine, tough, lustrous fiber adhering to the rod when he pulled it out. This was the first nylon.

All members of Carothers' group turned their efforts toward nylon. They began to repeat Coffman's work using variations of the chemicals he had used. Over the summer, they tried eighty-one chemicals, five of which looked promising. In February 1935, the U.S. Government granted a patent for nylon to Gerard J. Berchet, a member of the team.

Du Pont mounted a crash program to bring nylon into commercial production. This effort, which took five years, did not involve Carothers' group. The development team was headed by Crawford H. Greenewalt. The researchers working on it envisioned nylon replacing cellophane, leather, photographic film, and wool. But Du Pont's executives decided that development would progress faster if efforts focused on a single use. They chose women's stockings.

1. POLITICS AND UNDERSTANDING FAVOR VARIATIONS

Norman (1971) observed that organizations react quite differently to two types of change proposals: variations and reorientations. Variations would modify organizations' domains only incrementally, whereas reorientations would redefine those domains. Variations exploit organizations' experience, preserve existing distributions of power, and can win approval from partially conflicting interests. Reorientations take organizations outside familiar domains and they redistribute power to people who understand the new markets, technologies, and methods. Thus, reorientation proposals meet resistance from those top managers who stand to lose power because their expertise would become obsolete.

For example, for many years, NCR Corporation defined its domain as cash registers, adding machines, and accounting machines, all of which were electro-mechanical. It built a homogeneous group of top managers having expertise in this domain. In 1953, NCR bought a small computer company; and in 1959, this subsidiary developed the first solid-state computer in the world. But NCR's home-office managers acted as if the computer subsidiary was a threat. They warned that rapid expansion of computer-leasing would lower corporate earnings. Product-oriented sales managers told their sales staff, 'Don't waste your time on computers. Sell posting machines.' By 1968, NCR's computer hardware was lagging roughly four years behind IBM's. 'We had to resist the temptation to release it prematurely', explained one executive. 'NCR's late entry is opportune', NCR's chairman assured its stockholders. 'Our timing is perfect.' By 1971, the computer revolution had overtaken NCR. Wall Street analysts predicted that NCR could no longer compete in the computer age. NCR's top managers could not plot, let alone produce, a reorientation. Bankruptcy loomed, investors revolted, and NCR's directors finally had to replace the president (Meyer and Starbuck 1994).

Watzlawick, Weakland, and Fisch (1974) emphasized the relativity of perception. They remarked that reorientations seem illogical because they violate basic tenets of a current cognitive framework, whereas variations make sense because they modify actions or ideologies incrementally within an accepted overarching framework. The action proposals that look sensible are ones that follow precedents, harmonize with current actions, resemble the practices in other organizations, use resources that are going to waste, fit with top managers' values, or reinforce power holders (Starbuck and Milliken 1988; Staw and Ross 1978).

Managerial ideologies cherish variations. Managers believe organizations should grow incrementally at their margins. According to Peters (1980: 196), the firms that managers regard as being well run 'tend to be tinkerers rather than inventors, making small steps of progress rather than conceiving sweeping new concepts'. Variations are often programmatic: research departments generate opportunities for complementary actions; sales personnel report on competitors' actions within current domains.

Emphasizing variations may be essential in normal situations because of gross perceptual errors. Several studies suggest that most people hold highly erroneous beliefs about their organizations and about the organizations' environments (Downey, Hellriegel, and Slocum 1975; Grinyer and Norburn 1975; Payne and Pugh 1976; Tosi, Aldag, and Storey 1973). Because misrepresentations and inadvertent biases permeate formal reports (Altheide and Johnson 1980; Hopwood 1972), the organizations that take formal reports seriously either get into trouble or perform ineffectively (Grinyer and Norburn 1975; Starbuck, Greve, and Hedberg 1978). Variations mitigate the effects of perceptual errors by keeping actions close to those that have worked in the past; incremental actions are likely to produce expected results even when the actors thoroughly misunderstand their environments.

However, variations are also inadequate (Miller 1990). Because people choose variations and interpret results within the frameworks of their current beliefs and vested interests, perceptual errors both persist and accumulate. Because organizations create programs to repeat their successes, they try to choose variations that will halt social and technological changes. Such variations can succeed to only small degrees and briefly, of course. Organizations that stop innovating may not only find themselves confronting crises, they may lose the capacity to innovate (Hedberg, Nystrom, and Starbuck 1976).

2. HIERARCHIES OFTEN IMPEDE INNOVATION

Hierarchies amplify these tendencies. Porter and Roberts (1976) reviewed research showing that people in hierarchies talk upward and listen upward. They send more messages upward than downward, they pay more attention to messages from their supervisors than to ones from their subordinates, and they try harder to establish rapport with supervisors than with subordinates. People also bias their upward messages to enhance good news and to suppress bad news (Janis 1972). This bias becomes problematic because problems are much more likely than opportunities to motivate organizations to attempt changes (Hedberg 1981).

These communication biases seem to be stronger in some firms, with one result being an increased propensity to run into serious trouble. After studying twenty firms that were facing crises, Dunbar and Goldberg (1978) concluded that the chief executives in these troubled firms generally surrounded themselves with yes-sayers who voiced no criticisms. Worse yet, the yes-sayers deliberately filtered out warnings from middle managers who saw correctly that their firms were out of touch with market realities; many of these middle managers resigned while others were fired for disloyalty.

Top managers' perceptual errors and self-deceptions are especially potent because top managers can block the actions proposed by their subordinates. Yet, top managers are also especially prone to perceive events erroneously and to resist changes: Their promotions and high statuses persuade them that they have more expertise than other people. Their expertise tends to be out-of-date because their personal experiences with clients, customers, technologies, and low-level personnel lie in the past. They have strong vested interests. Reorientations threaten their dominance, and they will catch the blame if current practices, strategies, and goals prove wrong. They socialize with other top managers, who face similar pressures.

Thus organizations tend to behave similarly to Marx's (1859) observations about societies. Marx said elites try to retain their favored positions by blocking social changes. Technological changes, which elites cannot halt, make technologies increasingly inconsistent with social structures, until the elites can no longer control their societies. For organizations, however, the issues are somewhat different: Top managers can block both social and technological changes within their organizations, but they have little influence over technological or social changes outside their organizations.

Marx said that when elites can no longer control a society, a revolution transforms the social structure. This observation also generalizes only partly to organizations. Reorientations do punctuate sequences of variations (Tushman and Romanelli 1985), and reorientations also activate and broaden political activities. But, few reorientations transform organizational structures (Jönsson and Lundin 1977; Normann 1971; Rhenman 1973). Indeed, in organizations, changing just a few top managers can produce sweeping behavioral and ideological changes (Starbuck 1989).

3. CREATIVE SOLUTIONS TO UNSOLVABLE PROBLEMS

Organizations' members regularly devote creativity to trying to solve unsolvable problems (Starbuck 1993). Because societies promote inconsistent values, organizations' members try to pursue inconsistent goals. Also, some of organizations' overall goals encompass inconsistent subgoals. The organizational properties that support some goals conflict with the properties that support others, so organizations must take conflicting actions, and every 'solution' creates a new problem.

Hierarchical dominance makes a pointed example. Western societies say hierarchical control, unity, and efficiency are good, but they also say democracy and equality are good. These societies' citizens expect organizations to use hierarchical structures to coordinate actions and to eliminate waste even though hierarchical control is undemocratic and unequal. Thus, subordinates should refuse to follow superiors' commands and organizations should oppose such insubordination. One result is that organizations' members try to create 'solutions' that conceal hierarchical controls or that bring subordinates' goals into line with superiors' goals.

During the late 1940s, the solution was 'democratic' management. Then after a time, many subordinates surmised that this was feigned democracy and many managers learned that democratic choices are not always profitable. During the early 1950s, the solution became for managers to show 'consideration' while also controlling task activities. Then after a time, many subordinates surmised that their superiors' consideration was illusory. During the late 1950s, the solution became Management-By-Objectives, in which superiors and subordinates were to negotiate mutually agreed goals for the subordinates to pursue. Then after a time, many subordinates surmised that they had little say about their goals. During the 1960s, the solution became 'participative management', in which workers' representatives were to participate in managerial boards. Then after a time, many workers surmised that managers were exerting strong influence within these boards and that the workers' representatives were gaining personal benefits from belonging to these boards. During the early 1980s, the solution became 'organizational culture', by which organizations were to develop agreement about goals and methods. Then many workers resisted homogenization and after a time, many managers learned that general solidarity did not translate into operational goals and methods. During the late 1980s, the solution became 'quality circles', which broadened during the 1990s into 'total quality management'. Then after a time, . . .

Profit maximization offers another example. Firms try simultaneously to bring in as much revenue as possible and to keep costs as low as possible. To maximize revenues, the marketing personnel ask firms to produce customized products that are just what the customers want and to make these products available just when the customers want them. To minimize costs, the production personnel seek to minimize inventories and machine downtime, so they would like to deliver the same product to every customer, or at least to produce different products in optimal quantities on efficient schedules. Thus, marketing and production personnel conflict about what to do and when to do it. Seeing unpleasant conflicts, managers try to 'resolve' them. However, these efforts can only ease short-run symptoms because the conflicts are intrinsic to the goal of maximizing profit.

Unsolvable problems evoke frustration, of course, but they also present opportunities for genuine creativity. For one thing, inconsistent goals reflect the fact that people create organizations to carry out complicated, difficult, but important tasks. These tasks justify creative effort. For another thing, it sometimes happens that someone does solve an unsolvable problem—as when Carothers' group discovered nylon. Such surprises are a major reason creativity fascinates and rewards us.

Part V

Strategizing Part 2

15

Strategizing Realistically
in Competitive Environments

1. 'LET ME MAKE ONE THING PERFECTLY CLEAR...'

This chapter advances an iconoclastic argument—that formal strategizing generally makes no important contributions to profits. This argument has four bases: One is the formality with which most firms strategize; formalization undercuts formal strategizing's potential value. A second basis is the existence of fundamental barriers to achieving measurable gains through forecasting and strategizing; these barriers mean that strategizing usually cannot have visible, intended effects on profits. A third basis is the high frequency of large errors in managers' perceptions of their own firms and their market environments; when managers strategize, most of them are trying to run imaginary firms in imaginary markets. A fourth basis is the impossibility of making accurate long-range forecasts and thus of anticipating the consequences of strategies.

It is possible for formal strategizing to help firms to operate more effectively. To do so, however, the strategizing must preserve uncertainty and allow for contingencies. This, in turn, implies that strategists should not take their activities too seriously, and they should advocate common sense in a world that often shuns it.

2. WHAT DOES RESEARCH EVIDENCE SAY ABOUT THE EFFECTIVENESS OF FORMAL STRATEGIZING?

'The war in Vietnam is going well and will succeed.'
— Robert McNamara, U.S. Secretary of Defense (1963)

Everyone does some strategizing informally and strategies are often beneficial. The practical issue is: How much better is it to strategize *formally*?

Formal strategizing is a social process as well as an intellectual one. It involves meetings, discussions, negotiations, and commitments. It builds consensus about perceptions, goals, and roles and it creates rationalizations to support strategic actions. A few years ago, I ran into a surprise when I surveyed the research evidence about the benefits of formal strategizing. Many studies had examined the relationships between formal strategizing and profitability. A few of the earliest studies had found strong correlations between profitability and the degrees to which firms used formal methods of strategizing. However, these early studies had used quite poor methodology, so researchers responded by making more studies that used better methodology. As the research methods improved, the observed correlations between profitability and formal strategizing declined toward zero. The best research shows that, on the average, formal strategizing does not increase profits enough to be practically useful.

Probably the best study of this topic is one by Grinyer and Norburn (1975). They studied only twenty-one firms, but they chose these very carefully and gathered valid and extensive information from several executives in each firm. They made four key findings, two of which relate to the profitability of formal planning.

First, profitable firms are about as likely to strategize informally as formally, and so are unprofitable firms. Firms' profitability correlates only very weakly with the formality of formal strategizing ($r = 0.22$). Figure 15.1 graphs such a correlation to give a sense of its practical value.

Second, profitability correlates inconsistently and meaninglessly with the degrees to which senior executives agree about their firms' objectives or their personal responsibilities. The correlations ranged from 0.40 to -0.40.

When one first sees Grinyer and Norburn's findings, they are difficult to accept—especially if one teaches or practices formal methods of strategizing! Yet, reflection discloses that the findings do make sense: There is no reason

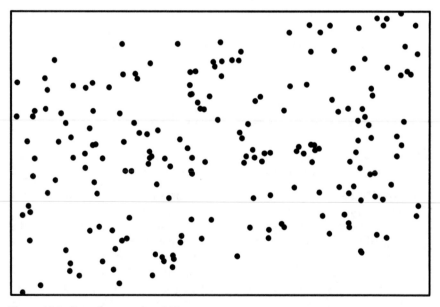

Figure 15.1. Data that correlate 0.22

strategizing should generally produce high profits. Consensus can be as harmful as beneficial when there is no way to assure that the objects of consensus are good.

Formal strategizing is a two-edged sword that is as likely to reduce profits as to raise them. One sees the beneficial edge when strategies reflect accurate forecasts of future events and accurate assessments of capabilities and everyone works together to achieve difficult, but possible, goals, while ignoring irrelevant distractions. This is the best of all worlds. But formal strategizing also can produce the worst of all worlds. One sees the harmful edge when strategies reflect inaccurate forecasts and assessments and everyone works intensely to achieve the wrong goals, while overlooking unexpected opportunities. The research studies imply that negative outcomes happen about as often as positive outcomes, and that formal strategizing has negligible effects on the average.

Chakravarthy and Lorange (1991) used the adjective 'integrative' to denote formal strategizing. They observed that 'integrative' strategizing works *only* when two conditions hold: (*a*) the business faces a predictable environment, and (*b*) the business has several distinctive competencies. When these conditions do not hold, they said, integrative strategizing is not only ineffective, it is counterproductive. Few businesses have several distinctive competencies that are large enough to yield significantly higher profits, and a later section of this chapter explains why no business can predict its environment beyond the short term.

Grinyer and Norburn made four noteworthy findings, only two of which were discussed above. The other two findings concerned strong correlates of profitability, and they imply that informal strategizing is usually more effective than formal strategizing.

> Managers in more profitable firms make greater use of informal communication, whereas managers in less profitable firms communicate primarily through formal reports ($r = 0.40$).

> Managers in more profitable firms use diverse information when evaluating their firms' performances, whereas managers in less profitable firms get their information mainly from formal reports ($r = 0.68$).

3. FEW FIRMS WILL EVER BE ABLE TO GAIN HIGH PROFITS FROM FORMAL STRATEGIZING

> 'I think there is a world market for about five computers.'
> — Thomas J. Watson, CEO of IBM (1948)

Four difficulties confront any firm that attempts to increase its profits significantly through formal strategizing.

First, most firms compete against skilled competitors that have access to very similar information. These competitors can either anticipate strategic moves or react to them promptly, so it is very difficult to gain meaningful competitive advantages through strategic moves.

Second, the strategies that can produce significant profits are illegal, immoral, or impractical; most businesses will not pursue them. High-profit strategies are all variations on monopoly power. Although these strategies have proven themselves very effective, U.S. laws bar nearly all monopolistic strategies, so American firms risk antitrust actions if they adopt them. Microsoft provides an example. The legal forms of monopoly—such as patents, first moves, and geographic locations—give either small advantages or transient ones. Patents and first moves also tend to be quite expensive, so the benefit-to-cost ratios are often poor and firms do not use these strategies repeatedly for long periods.

Third, formal strategizing often emphasizes big issues involving large sums and many people. These are nearly always long-term issues, yet the long term never unfolds as expected. Thus, strategists expend their resources on threats that never turn into actual problems and on dreams that never become real opportunities.

Fourth and most importantly, most firms use formal strategizing to build strong consensuses and to establish strong commitments. However, this use of formal strategizing makes unrealistic assumptions about people's knowledge and about their abilities to forecast accurately. Consensus is dangerous unless the strategies are very likely to produce wanted outcomes. For strategizing to produce wanted outcomes, the strategists need to have realistic perceptions of their firms' capabilities and their market environments. However, the evidence is that most managers do not have realistic perceptions of their firms or their market environments.

4. NEARLY ALL MANAGERS MISPERCEIVE BOTH THEIR FIRMS AND THEIR MARKET ENVIRONMENTS

'Gaiety is the most outstanding feature of the Soviet Union.'
— Joseph Stalin (1935)

Managers' subjective perceptions often diverge widely from objective observations. Of course, some managers see some aspects of their worlds accurately. However, most managers misperceive so greatly that, averaged across many managers, their perceptions correlate hardly at all with objective data.

Payne and Pugh (1976) compiled data that suggest that most people (including managers) see their own firms inaccurately. Payne and Pugh reviewed roughly 100 studies in which researchers had asked firms' members to characterize their firms' structures and cultures. They surmised:

Different members of a firm disagree so strongly with each other that it makes no sense to talk about an average perception.
Members' perceptions of their firms correlate very weakly with measurable characteristics of their firms.

I was reassured to learn, as you may be, that people *do* know whether they are working in large firms or small ones!

John Mezias and I (2003) observed senior managers' perceptions of quality performance in four divisions of a very large company that had made quality improvement a top priority. The company had trained nearly all managerial personnel in quality, and each business unit had a quality improvement department. The company distributed quality measures to all managers frequently, and managers met regularly to discuss quality performance in their divisions. Yet, when we asked them about current levels of quality performance in their divisions, 49–91 percent of the managers reported 'I don't know'. Although the managers who thought they knew the current levels of quality performance were often fairly accurate, the managers who specialized in quality were no more accurate than the nonspecialists.

Two studies have inadvertently produced disquieting evidence about the accuracy of managers' perceptions of their market environments. Both studies asked middle and top managers to describe the stabilities of their markets. They then compared these perceptions with stability indices calculated from the firms' financial reports and industry statistics. The correlations between managers' perceptions and objective measures were all near zero and were as likely to be negative as positive.

Tosi, Aldag, and Storey (1973) analyzed data from 102 middle and top managers from diverse firms: correlations of managers' perceptions with stability indices ranged from −0.29 to +0.04.

Downey, Hellriegel, and Slocum (1975) got data from fifty-one heads of the divisions of a large conglomerate: correlations of managers' perceptions with stability indices ranged from −0.17 to +0.11.

Mezias and I (1996) found large perception errors in data collected from seventy managers in several companies. In the best case, 39 percent of managers' perceptions of a given variable were within 50 percent of the objective measure. In the worst case, 31 percent of managers' perceptions exceeded 200 percent of the objective value. Most surprising was that managers' perceptions of variables specifically related to their areas of specialization were no more accurate than other managers' perceptions of those same variables. That is, managers with sales experience were as inaccurate in their estimates of sales-related variables as managers without sales experience.

In principle, by playing one person's error off against another's, firms might compensate for the biases of individual people. However, firms often amplify biases. First, misperceptions are often shared. Some get their unrealistic perceptions by talking with their colleagues. Second, organizations emphasize communication, and easily communicated ideas oversimplify. Third, formal strategizing encourages managers to construct rationalizations for their actions before the fact. These rationalizations then have to be reconciled with actual events, through processes that involve much distortion. Fourth, people's careers depend upon the evaluations of strategic actions, so managers strive to conceal bad outcomes. Fifth, social pressures induce managers to espouse positions dishonestly (Janis 1972). Sixth, firms' formal reporting systems foster misperceptions by emphasizing financial and numerical data, by highlighting successes and rationalizing failures, and by crediting good results to superiors. Finally, top managers' perceptions get more weight than those of subordinates even though top managers have much less contact with current markets and technologies than do their subordinates. Top managers also get much of their information through channels that bias upward messages to de-emphasize bad news and to emphasize good news. Indeed, people in hierarchies listen to their superiors more than they do to their subordinates, and they talk to their superiors more than they do to their subordinates. Thus, top managers mostly hear echoes of their own voices (Porter and Roberts, 1976).

5. WITH EVEN THE MOST ELEGANT METHODS, NO ONE CAN MAKE RELIABLE LONG-RANGE FORECASTS

> Prediction is very difficult, especially about the future.
> — Niels Bohr, renowned physicist

Although almost everyone can make accurate short-range forecasts, no one can predict accurately beyond a few months ahead. When it comes to foretelling the future, there are no true experts. In his classic book on forecasting, Armstrong (1985: 91) advised:

Expertise beyond a minimal level in the subject that is being forecast is of little value in forecasting change. This conclusion represents one of the most surprising and useful findings in this chapter. It is surprising because emotionally, we cannot accept it. It is useful because the implication is obvious and clear cut: *Do not hire the best expert you can—or even close to the best. Hire the cheapest expert.*

Since the 1950s, the U.S. government has poured many millions of dollars into intricate, computer-based economic forecasting models. The teams that developed these models have spent hundreds of man-years. They have included some of the world's most respected economists. They have used elegant statistical methods. They have not lacked financial or computation resources. Large industrial firms pay large sums for the predictions generated by these models. Thus, these models represent the very best in economic or social forecasting.

Elliott (1973) compared the four most famous of these economic forecasting models with two naive forecasts. One naive forecast, the no-change one, says that GNP in three months will be the same as GNP today. This no-change forecast was as accurate as three of the four computer models. The more accurate naive forecast, a linear trend, says that the GNP trend over the last three months will continue for the next three months. This linear-trend forecast was as accurate as the best computer model, which was the simplest one.

Surely, if these elaborate economic forecasting models say so little, one would be very foolish to expect more of any forecasting method.

Makridakis et al. (1982) compared twenty-four statistical forecasting methods by forecasting 1,001 series. They found that simple techniques generally work well. Complex methods tend to mistake random noise for meaningful events so they issue many false alarms. Complex methods forecast most poorly where situations are changing rapidly or where random noise is large. Complex methods work best for stable situations that contain little random noise— where any method would be accurate.

Makridakis et al. found that no-change forecasts beat others 38–64 percent of the time. Also, no-change forecasts were less likely to make large errors than any other method. Yet, the most accurate forecasts came from exponential smoothing with deseasonalized data. This method beat each of the others at least 50 percent of the time. Exponential smoothing is a straight-line projection that assumes data include random noise and that filters the noise by averaging. The averaging usually gives more weight to newer data.

Thus, the findings of Makridakis et al. resemble those of Elliott.

6. GETTING REALISTIC: WHAT CAN FORMAL STRATEGIZING ACHIEVE?

> I cannot imagine any condition which could cause this ship to flounder.
> I cannot conceive of any vital disaster happening to this vessel.
> — E. J. Smith, Captain of the Titanic (1912)

As the foregoing observations show, real-life formal strategizing takes place in treacherous contexts quite unlike those assumed in management textbooks. So, what can strategists realistically expect to accomplish?

Strategizing Can Sometimes Exploit Distinctive Competencies, Entry Barriers, Proprietary Information, and First Moves

Economic theory says that almost the only ways to benefit from strategizing involve using resources that other firms lack. Thus, firms should try to identify or develop competencies that make them distinctive, and then to turn these into competitive advantages. Some firms possess or can create entry barriers that protect them from competitors. Proprietary information can also give a firm an edge; firms can generate proprietary information and try to keep it proprietary long enough to extract benefit from it. A few firms can make profitable first moves.

These tactics are much easier to advocate than to execute successfully, however. It may be very expensive or technically impossible to create distinctive competencies or entry barriers. When a firm begins to put its strategy into effect, competitors can react to the actual behavior rather than to their theories about it. Proprietary information and proprietary information-processing techniques are rare. For example, even if firms do not know their competitors' costs exactly they can likely estimate those costs accurately enough. Similarly, all sensible methods of data analysis yield similar inferences. Thus, these tactics are unlikely to prove highly profitable and their profitability is short-lived.

Strategizing Can Use Forecasts to Motivate Alertness

Forecasts can be partly self-fulfilling prophecies. Because conservative forecasts may lead firms to achieve less than they could, accurate forecasting can be a mistake. Some managers use forecasts to motivate exceptional efforts. But strategists must keep balance. Consistently biased forecasts not only lose their motivation value, people learn to distrust them. Accurate forecasts, on the other hand, may help firms to identify important threats and opportunities.

Pant and Starbuck (1990) reviewed the literature about forecasting and proposed several recommendations for making accurate forecasts. Four of these recommendations are: (*a*) to allow for seasonality, (*b*) to consider 'no change' and 'no change in the trend', (*c*) to average several forecasts, and (*d*) to assume that today is not a turning point. The studies of forecasting show that it is very difficult to identify turning points while they are occurring. Every analytic framework that has the potential to say 'something quite different has begun to happen' also has the strong propensity to say this when nothing is actually happening.

To avoid some of the game playing that renders forecasts ineffective, strategists can forecast both the best that can happen and the worst and then generate strategies to suit these extreme possibilities. This approach makes people aware of the diversity of what might happen; it reduces the tendency to assume that forecasts will come true; and it motivates alertness for information about how events are actually developing. Firms often overlook important opportunities or threats simply because these were not forecast, so firms need to be alert for surprises and not just confirm their expectations.

Strategizing Can Inject Realism into Managers' Perceptions

Because most managers misperceive their firms and their market environments, there is opportunity for formal strategizing to educate managers about the actual properties of firms and market environments, by gathering and analyzing objective data. However, such education requires persuasion as well as evidence. Objective data become more valuable as managers' current perceptions become more unrealistic, yet people grow less willing to accept new information as it deviates more from their expectations. In fact, people tend to interpret nearly all information as confirming their perceptions. Because perceptions are widely shared in firms, social support often rigidifies perceptions (Nystrom and Starbuck 1984).

Formal strategizing also creates diverse opportunities to improve the flows of information upward. Porter and Roberts (1976) reviewed literature showing that top managers do not listen carefully to their subordinates. People in hierarchies talk upward and listen upward: They send more messages upward than downward, and they pay more attention to superiors than to subordinates. They also overestimate how much accurate information they do transmit upward, and they tend to tell the boss what the boss wants to hear. Formal strategizing can expose senior managers to inputs from lower levels.

In a demonstration of the usefulness of realism, Donald Regan, the U.S. Secretary of the Treasury in 1981, observed of President Reagan's economic program: '... the President's program will begin to bear fruit even before it is enacted'.

Strategizing Can Keep Strategies Flexible

Because managers do misperceive their firms and environments, and because firms tend to exaggerate these errors, explicit strategies often make actions less realistic and less responsive to unexpected events. Thus, formal strategizing should provide for changing strategies in response to new information.

1. *Strategists can avoid building strong rationales.* Strong rationalizations make behaviors inflexible and make it difficult to evaluate outcomes.

2. *Strategists can de-emphasize the long term.* Long-range forecasts incorporate much larger errors than do short-range forecasts.

3. *Strategists can avoid generalizations.* Generalizations suppress alertness, and Boland et al. (2001) found that managers make better decisions when they focus on particulars.

4. *Strategists can minimize formalization.* Formalized strategies incorporate larger errors than do informal strategies, and managers revise formalized strategies much less often than informal strategies.

5. *Strategists can emphasize informal communication.* Perhaps profitability correlates positively with informal communication because informal communication produces better understanding.

6. *Strategists can foster trust and good feelings.* Because strategies are so faulty and yield such vague benefits, only foolish managers would stake their careers on strategies or turn formal strategizing meetings into battlefields. Indeed, consensus may itself be a liability, insofar as it induces managers to focus too narrowly and to underestimate the actual uncertainty of future events.

16

Trying to Help S&Ls: How Organizations with Good Intentions Jointly Enacted Disaster

Coauthored with P. Narayan Pant

Failures of U.S. savings and loan institutions (S&Ls) in the 1980s added up to one of the largest financial disasters ever to hit the nation. The costs fell on everyone because the Federal Savings and Loan Insurance Corporation (FSLIC) insured the deposits. In 1990, the General Accounting Office estimated that the insurance losses would ultimately exceed $325 billion—over $1,000 for each resident of the United States (Barth 1991).

Since many books and articles have appeared about this disaster, a reader might wonder what else there is to say. Improbably, this chapter argues that several explanations do not work and that analysts have slighted some important factors. Analysts have ignored or de-emphasized the effects of decision processes and nearsighted analyses. Most analysts have also focused on events during the 1980s and understated the importance of long-term trends and abrupt policy changes.

The decision processes involved many organizations. Most of these were loosely coupled in that their actions only sporadically affected others, and they often acted without considering the likely impacts on others. Many organizations were also tightly coupled in that broad agreement and shared perceptions shaped most actions, and one organization's acts could sometimes profoundly affect another's future.

Because the disaster had many possible causes and involved many actors, understanding it requires a grasp of numerous details. The first section of this chapter recounts the history of the S&L industry, setting a context for events in the 1980s. The second section then assesses nine theories about what went wrong. The third section describes the disjointed interactions in decision processes. The fourth section emphasizes how long-term trends made a disaster of some size inevitable.

1. A BRIEF HISTORY OF THE S&L INDUSTRY

The Government Confers Favored Status

American S&Ls originated to support home building (Strunk and Case 1988). People wanting to build homes made deposits in S&Ls that lent funds contributed by many, and depositors could withdraw deposits only at substantial cost. Nearly all S&Ls were mutual associations owned by depositors. As White (1991: 61) explained, 'The attitude that many thrift executives had about their business could almost be described as a "calling": After all, they were actively involved in promoting home ownership and encouraging thrift. It was no accident that Jimmy Stewart's George Bailey ran a small savings and loan association in Frank Capra's 1946 film *It's a Wonderful Life*.'

S&Ls originally faced little competition. Commercial banks and mutual savings banks raised funds mainly by issuing notes payable on demand. They then made short-term loans, usually commercial ones. S&Ls made no commercial loans.

Many S&Ls failed in the 1930s. Since depositors could not withdraw funds on demand, S&Ls experienced no runs, but many depositors did make withdrawals (Barth 1991). Also, S&Ls had few or no retained earnings to cover losses. States often did not require S&Ls to maintain minimum reserves of capital, and some states forced S&Ls to distribute all earnings.

Prompted by S&L failures, Congress created twelve regional Federal Home Loan Banks (FHLBs) in 1932. These were corporations owned by the S&Ls in their districts. FHLBs were supposed to keep S&Ls liquid by judiciously advancing funds. The new Federal Home Loan Bank Board (FHLBB) would supervise both FHLBs and S&Ls.

Two years later, the government created FSLIC to insure S&Ls' deposits. Congress wanted to give depositors confidence but feared that deposit insurance might enable S&Ls to compete with commercial banks. So, Congress forbade S&Ls to accept demand deposits and restricted their assets to fixed-rate mortgages on homes. These restrictions basically continued until 1980, although Congress did authorize loans for education and housing fixtures in the 1960s and added some depository options in the 1970s.

Until 1932, all S&Ls held state charters. However, Congress authorized federal charters when it set up FHLBs. By 1993, two-thirds of all S&Ls had federal charters, and these controlled 85 percent of all assets. Thus, federal regulators gradually became much more relevant than state regulators.

FHLBB required S&Ls to have only small amounts of equity capital. In 1934, FHLBB set the requirement at 5 percent of insured deposits, about 4.6 percent of assets, which was far below the requirement for commercial banks. In 1980, Congress opined that 5 percent seemed too high, so FHLBB lowered the requirement to 4 percent and later to 3 percent. The solid line in Figure 16.1 shows that S&Ls' equity declined from 8.5 percent in the early 1940s to a reported low of 2.1 percent in 1989.

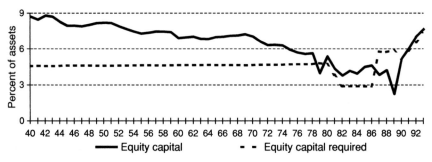

Figure 16.1. S&Ls' equity capital

S&Ls' true net worths were even below those shown in Figure 16.1 after 1981. Instead of widely accepted accounting practices, FHLBB told S&Ls to use Regulatory Accounting Practices (RAPs) that FHLBB defined. One RAP let S&Ls with deficient equity capital report capital-to-assets ratios that averaged data from more than one year—the current year plus 1–4 preceding years. This was an old RAP that suddenly began causing trouble in the 1980s. Another troublesome RAP, created in 1981, allowed S&Ls to classify losses on bad mortgage loans as 'goodwill' that they could amortize over forty years. As a result, when S&Ls sold bad mortgages, their profit statements could ignore nearly all losses, and most of the losses appeared as equity capital on their balance sheets. Barth (1991: 50) reported that by late 1983, this 'goodwill' constituted over 90 percent of S&Ls' reported equity capital. Also in 1981, FHLBB authorized S&Ls in financial trouble to issue Income Capital Certificates that FSLIC purchased. Although these were loans from FSLIC, a RAP said that they should appear as equity capital on S&Ls' balance sheets. By this means, FSLIC could make insolvent S&Ls appear solvent by loaning them equity capital. A former FHLBB staff member explained that 'there really was no capital-to-asset requirement' in the 1980s. This was literally true for new S&Ls, which could take twenty years to satisfy FHLBB's equity capital requirement.

Favoritism extended to income taxes. Until 1951, S&Ls paid no federal taxes. When they became subject to federal taxes in 1951, they could avoid paying them by deducting from income any funds reserved for bad debts. Many S&Ls did begin paying taxes in 1962, when Congress limited this deduction to 60 percent of reserves for bad debts. The deduction was cut to 40 percent in 1979, 34 percent in 1982, 32 percent in 1984, and 8 percent in 1987.

In 1966, rising interest rates led Congress to put ceilings on the rates S&Ls could pay depositors. Industry representatives protested that these ceilings suppressed deposit growth. But as Figure 16.2 shows, deposit growth began declining in 1964, two years before the ceilings; and by 1971, deposit growth resembled that during 1945–63.

Next, S&Ls faced competition from money market mutual funds that offered higher interest rates, and deposit growth dipped again in 1973–74. In response,

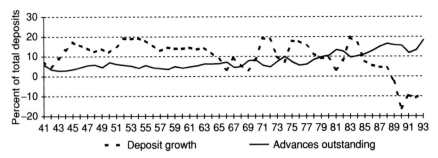

Figure 16.2. How FHLB advances varied with deposit growth

Congress let S&Ls offer depository options closely tied to short-term interest rates. These included interest-bearing checking accounts, short-term money market certificates, and small savers' accounts. However, these options did not keep pace with interest rates available elsewhere, and deposit growth sagged again in 1978–81.

FHLBs' Stabilizers Become a Steady Source of Funds

FHLBs were to ensure the availability of enough funds for home mortgages by making 'advances' whenever S&Ls faced temporary shortages (White 1986). These advances had two important properties: First, because advances came from money borrowed by the U.S. government, the advances let S&Ls borrow as if they were only as risky as the government. Second, because the S&Ls owned the FHLBs, S&Ls could strongly influence the amounts advanced.

Figure 16.2 states FHLB advances outstanding at year end as percentages of S&Ls' total deposits, and compares advances to changes in deposits. Advances did sometimes compensate for fluctuations in deposits—especially in 1966–83 when changes in advances correlated −0.53 with changes in deposits. But over the period 1940–93, changes in advances correlated slightly positively (0.14) with changes in deposits.

Figure 16.3 shows that advances became an ever larger fraction of S&Ls' funds. A former FHLBB staff member portrayed this expansion as a policy shift: 'Then when their deposits went to hell, they began to try to use advances to keep the S&Ls going.' Yet, the data show no sudden changes from a policy shift. From 1947 to 1987, outstanding advances grew at a rather steady rate that exceeded the growth rate for S&Ls' assets (Growth at a constant percentage rate generates a straight line on a logarithmic scale).

Figure 16.4 compares new advances with new mortgage loans by S&Ls. Until 1980, advances underwrote less than a quarter of S&Ls' new mortgage loans; after 1980, they underwrote over half.

Thus, FHLBs played an amazing role in S&Ls' evolution. Although Congress set up FHLBs to provide short-term liquidity for home mortgages, FHLBs

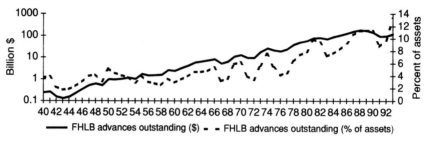

Figure 16.3. Growth in FHLB advances

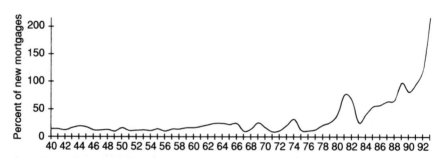

Figure 16.4. New FHLB advances

gradually became long-term sources of funds that were going into commercial mortgages, mortgage-backed securities, and nonmortgage investments. By 1993, FHLBs' new advances were more than twice S&Ls' new loans for home mortgages.

The Federal Reserve Board (FRB) Shifts Interest Rate Policies

Since the 1930s, the U.S. government has used interest rates to influence macro-economic variables such as investment, employment, and inflation. FRB's federal funds rate influences the rates at which commercial banks lend to commerce and industry, and hence affects investment and employment.

For many years, FRB had kept the federal funds rate low and changing slowly. Then, on October 6, 1979, FRB announced policies 'that should assure better control over the expansion of money and bank credit, help curb excesses in financial, foreign exchange, and commodity markets and thereby serve to dampen inflationary forces'. These policies included 'less emphasis on confining short-term fluctuations in the federal funds rate' (Document S241-6.1 of the Congressional Information Service 1980: 44).

Uncontrolled, interest rates rose rapidly. Figure 16.5 shows rates for new conventional mortgages; other rates behaved similarly. The dashed line graphs

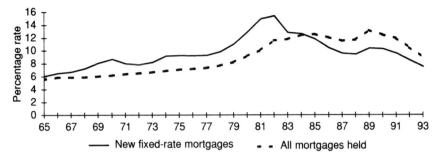

Figure 16.5. Interest rate on mortgages

S&Ls' average rates on all outstanding mortgages, which, of course, lagged the current rates.

As interest rates shot up, protests arose over FRB's policy. In mid-1982, FRB again began trying to control interest rates and dropped the federal funds rate substantially. Interest rates started to subside.

When in 1979 FRB announced its intention to let interest rates rise, it had not said that it was doing so because it was expecting a recession. It had explained that it needed to reduce inflation and that controlling the money supply was more important for that purpose than controlling interest rates. Yet, in March 1983, FRB's chairman blamed the high interest rates during 1980–82 on the recession of 1980–81 (Committee on the Budget 1983). The chairman also stated firmly in 1983 that interest rates would have to remain high as long as the federal deficit remained large. During 1982–86, interest rates dropped 33 percent while the federal deficit rose 73 percent.

When we asked former FHLBB staff members if they had forecast the interest rate rise, they said they had not seen interest rates as something to forecast. 'Short rates are cyclical; they go up and down. Who would have forecast that the Fed [FRB] would do what they did?' Furthermore, they said, no one would have believed such a forecast, let alone have acted on it. 'Everybody knows that forecasts have a risk about them, and every organization has an institutional bias.'

Congress Grants Freedoms in 1980 and 1982

The Depository Institutions Deregulation and Monetary Control Act of 1980 (DIDMCA) phased out ceilings on the interest rates S&Ls could pay depositors (Brewer et al. 1980; Garcia et al. 1983). It raised the maximum deposits that FSLIC insured from $40,000 to $100,000 and let S&Ls offer Negotiated Order of Withdrawal (NOW) accounts to individuals and not-for-profit organizations. In addition, S&Ls could issue mutual capital certificates that counted toward equity capital. S&Ls could now make credit card loans, lend for personal and commercial purposes, and lend for acquisition and development of real estate. Congress

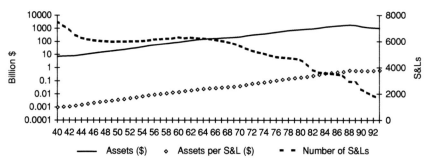

Figure 16.6. S&Ls' assets and numbers

told FHLBB to set S&Ls' equity capital requirement between 3 percent and 6 percent, implying that it should be lower than 5 percent.

In 1982, the Garn-St. Germain Act let federally chartered S&Ls offer deposit accounts that would compete with money market mutual funds. It also said S&Ls could accept demand deposits if these facilitated business relations. S&Ls gained added flexibility for commercial mortgages and consumer loans.

Even the extensive freedoms granted in 1980 and 1982 had short-term effects on S&Ls' assets and deposits. Deposit growth fluctuated but remained positive until 1989. As Figure 16.6 shows, total assets and assets per S&L rose steadily for at least fifty years until 1989, when assets turned down.

Assets per S&L increased more rapidly than total assets because the number of S&Ls kept declining. Figure 16.6 shows how the number of S&Ls declined after the early 1960s.

S&Ls Back Away from Home Mortgages

Total mortgages, the solid line in Figure 16.7, developed less linearly than assets and deposits, and they departed markedly from linearity after 1980. Lending for traditional home mortgages flattened in the early 1980s and then declined even though home ownership was booming. In 1977, S&Ls held 47.5 percent of all home mortgages; by 1993, they held only about 4 percent.

One factor in this change was mortgage securitization. Instead of holding mortgages, originators of mortgages sold them to investors as securities. In 1980, 17 percent of the new mortgages were going into securities; by 1986, this percentage had shot up to 58 percent (Brumbaugh 1988). S&Ls both sold mortgages and bought mortgage-backed securities. In many instances, an S&L sold mortgages at a discount and then bought them back as mortgage-backed securities that paid higher interest rates (Lewis 1989).

The upper portion of Figure 16.8 shows increasing commercial mortgages and mortgages on multifamily buildings, and the lower portion shows increasing

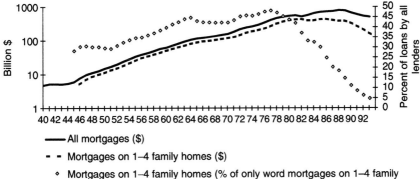

Figure 16.7. Mortgages held by S&Ls

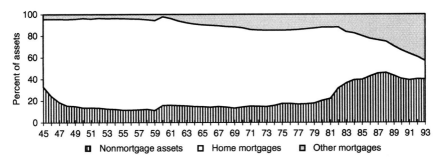

Figure 16.8. Distribution of S&Ls' assets

nonmortgage investments. In 1975–79, nonmortgage assets comprised 17 percent of the total; from 1990 to 1993 they comprised 40 percent.

These investment changes likely reflect S&Ls' ownership. By 1993 only 28 percent of S&Ls were mutual associations; 72 percent were stock companies.

New Tax Laws Take Effect in 1981 and 1986

Confronting recession, the Reagan administration tried to stimulate the economy. Two tax changes in 1981 created investment opportunities for S&Ls: The investment credit went up and the allowable depreciation on real estate doubled. These changes made real estate partnerships more profitable, and investors created many new partnerships—which sought mortgages or other loans from S&Ls.

The new real estate partnerships were willing to pay high interest rates, and they made speculative investments. Entrepreneurs created partnerships in which

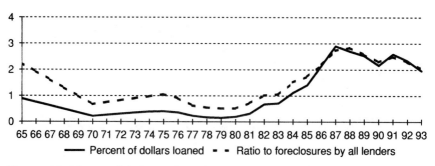

Figure 16.9. Mortgage foreclosures by S&Ls

investors would incur operating losses throughout the period of ownership but would receive capital gains (gains over what properties originally cost) when partnerships liquidated. Since investors could deduct the operating losses against ordinary income, the government was sharing the losses. Indeed, for most investors, the U.S. government was paying about half of the losses. Because the U.S. government taxed capital gains at only 40 percent of the rate on ordinary income, moderate capital gains could more than offset accumulated losses. At least, this was the plan. Most partnerships never produced gains.

These partnerships disappeared rapidly after Congress enacted tax changes in 1986 that made real estate partnerships less desirable: Capital gains lost their favored status. Maximum tax rates dropped. Depreciation periods for real estate rose again. Losses on passive activities—those in which a taxpayer plays no administrative role—could no longer offset highly taxed ordinary income. Nearly all investors in real estate partnerships had passive roles. Partnerships that might once have made after-tax profits over the long run suddenly turned into heavy financial drains with no prospect of profit. Investors lost interest in real estate partnerships, so new ventures could not attract funds and existing ventures could not find buyers for their properties. Finding themselves with unsaleable properties and the prospect of continuing annual losses, many existing partnerships declared bankruptcy. S&Ls that had lent to partnerships found themselves holding land or buildings that were very difficult to sell.

The solid line in Figure 16.9 shows the percentage of loans outstanding that S&Ls foreclosed. In the late 1970s, this rate was at or below 1 percent. After 1986, it exceeded 2 percent.

Disaster Strikes!

The number of S&Ls had declined for many years, and it was not unusual for 2 percent or even 3 percent to close in a year. But 6 percent closed in 1980 and 11 percent in 1981. S&Ls had regularly earned 10–15 percent on equity capital, and in 1978–79 their profits soared to 20–24 percent. Then their earnings dropped to only 4 percent in 1980, and they lost 22–23 percent in 1981 and 1982. Figure 16.10 graphs these shifts.

Some 1980–82 closures were due to insolvency. The insolvency rate, which had traditionally stayed below 0.1 percent, rose to 0.8 percent in 1980, 1.9 percent in 1981, and 6.6 percent in 1982. For public consumption, RAPs made it appear that insolvencies declined in 1983–87. Yet, the real situation was very different. The solid line in Figure 16.11 shows what insolvency rates would have been if S&Ls had counted only tangible assets.

Figure 16.11 also shows the public data about unprofitable S&Ls over the period 1978–89. These data show that earlier losses spread broadly: 91 percent of S&Ls shared losses in 1981–82 that equaled 43 percent of the equity capital of all S&Ls. Later losses were more concentrated: 40 percent of S&Ls shared losses in 1987–89 that equaled 75 percent of the equity capital of all S&Ls. However, after 1981, the public data understate S&Ls' losses because RAPs let S&Ls amortize losses on bad mortgage loans over many years.

In May 1987, Congress's investigative unit, the General Accounting Office (GAO) (1987: 6–7), declared that FSLIC had misrepresented its earnings. FSLIC had reported breaking even in 1985 and losing $3.6 billion in 1986; but GAO estimated that FSLIC had lost $1.1 billion in 1985, had lost $10.9 billion in 1986, and was $6.3 billion in debt.

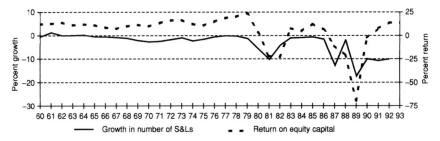

Figure 16.10. S&Ls' profits and growth

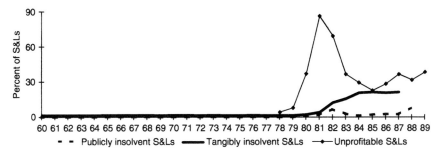

Figure 16.11. Insolvent and unprofitable S&Ls

Also in 1987, FSLIC estimated that 'the cost of providing assistance to about 280 currently insolvent institutions may range up to $21 billion. Assistance to another 100 institutions that currently appear to have little chance of recovery could add $4 billion to [FSLIC's] losses' (GAO 1987: 6). Actual events made these estimates wildly optimistic.

Congress Creates New Regulators and Imposes New Requirements

Doing something about the S&Ls was a priority of the Bush administration when it took office; and in August 1989, Congress set aside more funds for resolving insolvencies and changed the regulatory structure. It created an agency to deal with insolvent S&Ls and replaced FHLBB with two new agencies, one to regulate S&Ls and another to supervise FHLBs. Congress abolished the bankrupt FSLIC and placed S&L deposits under the agency that insures deposits in commercial banks. Congress also raised insurance premiums, set more stringent standards for equity capital, and authorized more penalties for mismanagement or criminal acts. In 1991, Congress (*a*) required annual examinations by federal examiners, (*b*) placed limits on deposits made through deposit brokers, and (*c*) said S&Ls with state charters must observe most limitations placed on S&Ls with federal charters.

These changes evidently affected many trends. The percentage of equity capital shot up (Figure 16.1). Deposit growth turned negative for the first time (Figure 16.2). Assets and deposits turned down, and assets per S&L flattened (Figure 16.6). S&Ls' investments in mortgages, especially home mortgages, turned down (Figure 16.7). Nonmortgage investments stopped increasing, and investments in commercial mortgages increased even more (Figure 16.8).

Summary

The S&L industry followed several long-term trends. Assets and deposits grew steadily until 1989, when they turned down. The number of S&Ls declined regularly, a trend that accelerated slightly after 1980, so the average size of an S&L increased until 1989. Other trends were less stable but persistent. Equity capital shrank as a fraction of S&Ls' assets until 1990. FHLB advances were a growing source of long-term funds until 1988. S&Ls invested increasing amounts in mortgages until 1989; and until 1981, they invested increasing amounts in home mortgages.

The industry also faced challenges in the 1980s. FRB let interest rates rise in 1980–82, then lowered them again. Congress let S&Ls engage in new activities, and they responded by investing in commercial mortgages and especially non-mortgage investments. New tax policies in 1981 and 1986 first encouraged and then discouraged risky real estate partnerships.

However, these short-term changes all occurred before 1989. According to the public data, long-term trends did not change much until 1989. That year, Congress passed legislation that was supposed to end the S&L disaster.

2. THEORIES ABOUT THE S&L DISASTER

Analysts have advanced at least nine theories about this disaster, all of which blame actions by the U.S. government partly or wholly. However, some theories contradict the existing evidence, and others explain only small fractions of the losses. Each theory focuses on a few phenomena while ignoring others.

Theory 1. Government regulations forced S&Ls to make long-term loans from short-term funds, thus making them vulnerable to rising interest rates. Until 1980, regulators barred S&Ls from borrowing long-term funds or making short-term loans. S&Ls offered chiefly long-term home mortgages at fixed rates of interest, whereas their depositors could withdraw on short notice. Friend (1969) pointed out that this made S&Ls vulnerable to losing money. When interest rates go up, S&Ls might have to pay more for deposits than they would receive from mortgage loans issued earlier.

Such a rate change did occur in the early 1980s (Figure 16.5), but this interest-fluctuation theory cannot explain all the losses by S&Ls in the 1980s. Figure 16.12 graphs two key interest rates: The interest rates that S&Ls received on mortgages stayed above those S&Ls paid for borrowed funds in every year except 1981.

The rates in Figure 16.12 may explain S&Ls' losses in 1981 and 1982, but even this is questionable because the recession in 1980–82 caused bad loans that lowered S&Ls' profits (Kane 1985). After 1983, S&Ls' differential between interest revenue and interest cost attained new highs. Figure 16.13 shows this differential and the industry's before-tax profit. S&Ls were suffering their largest losses in 1988–89, when the interest rate differential was setting all-time highs.

Theory 2. FRB caused S&Ls' losses by abandoning a long-standing interest rate policy that was a key basis for S&Ls' practices. The abrupt rise in interest rates in 1979–82 is the basis for a theory voiced by former officials at FHLBB. When FRB allowed interest rates to rise freely in late 1979, S&Ls were caught holding long-term fixed-rate mortgages, while depositors discovered opportunities to invest elsewhere at higher rates.

Nevertheless, S&Ls' industrywide profit turned negative for only one year, and then by only a small amount. When S&Ls issued new mortgages, they did so at

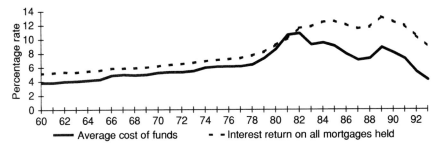

Figure 16.12. S&Ls' interest income and interest cost

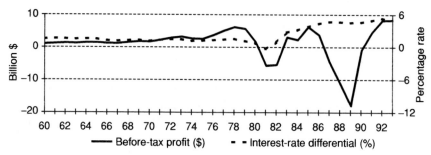

Figure 16.13. S&Ls' profit and interest-rate differential

higher and variable rates. At most, the interest rate differential may explain S&Ls' losses in 1981–82, which totaled $12 billion before taxes. Although these losses affected almost all S&Ls and consumed almost half of S&Ls' equity capital, they came to less than 4 percent of the insurance loss paid by American taxpayers.

Theory 3. FRB's allowing interest rates to rise led S&Ls to take extreme risks. S&Ls with negative implicit equity capital supposedly take extreme risks because they have nothing to lose. Friend (1969) pointed out that rising interest rates would reduce implicit market values of S&Ls' mortgage loans and thus their implicit equity capital. For example, if an S&L has loaned $100 million at an average interest rate of 6 percent, its interest income is $6 million. If the current interest rate is 8 percent, the S&L's existing loans are worth only $75 million because $75 million in new loans would yield $6 million of income. If this hypothetical transaction did occur, the S&L's equity capital would drop by $25 million.

In 1978, the equity capital of federally insured S&Ls averaged only 5.6 percent of assets, so the average S&L would have been implicitly bankrupt if the interest rate rose to 106 percent of the rate at which it had issued loans. However, this did not happen. In the worst year, 1981, S&Ls' current interest rate for new funds rose to only 103 percent of the rate at which they had issued loans.

Moreover, principles of accounting bar S&Ls from recognizing loans' market values unless they liquidate. Thus, this theory may help to explain the large insurance losses after S&Ls became insolvent, but it does not explain why S&Ls became insolvent.

Theory 4. Because the federal and state governments gave S&Ls more freedom, S&Ls pursued risky policies that caused large losses. White (1991) compared the 1985 assets of S&Ls that survived and failed in 1986–90. On average, soon-to-fail S&Ls had more nontraditional assets and less equity capital, more were stock companies rather than mutual associations, and more held state charters rather than federal ones. White also said that rapidly growing S&Ls were more likely to hold nontraditional assets and more likely to receive funds from nontraditional sources such as large certificates of deposit.

However, White did not make multivariate analyses or control for the states in which S&Ls operated. Failure rates differed greatly among states, with Texas,

California, Louisiana, Florida, and Ohio accounting for about 40 percent of the failures. Californians are among the heaviest users of S&Ls, but Louisianans are among the lightest. Thus, both failure rates and nontraditional investments might have reflected regional economic conditions or states' regulatory practices. White's argument about rapid growth focused on 1980–86; he said that growth had been much higher in 1983–84 than before or after. Although 1983–84 had a high growth rate, similarly high rates had occurred several times before, whereas unusually slow growth distinguished 1979–82 and 1985–88 (Figure 16.2).

From January 1985 through September 1986, 284 S&Ls failed. GAO (1989) 'judgmentally' selected 26 of these S&Ls that had caused 57 percent of the insurance losses and compared them with a matched sample of 26 solvent S&Ls. All the failed S&Ls had made nontraditional investments, and most had taken nontraditional deposits. Compared to 12 solvent S&Ls, 19 failed S&Ls had made loans to developers for land and construction. Compared to 5 solvent S&Ls, 21 failed S&Ls had issued 'jumbo' certificates of deposit for the insurance maximum of $100,000. The jumbo deposits had often come through deposit brokers who place clients' funds at high interest rates. GAO stressed the volatility of such deposits. However, GAO merely looked at raw frequencies without weighing alternative factors. For instance, of the 19 failed S&Ls that loaned money to developers for land and construction, 11 were in the Dallas (Texas) FHLB district, and others had made such loans in Texas.

Benston and Pant did make multivariate analyses. Focusing on 1981–85, Benston (1985) found that failing S&Ls had the same percentages of nontraditional investments and nontraditional deposits as did sound ones, and that S&Ls with state charters had lower failure rates than ones with federal charters. Pant (1991) estimated that S&Ls' aggressiveness and product diversity had little impact on financial performance. Indeed, more aggressive S&Ls may have failed less often. S&Ls with more diversified strategies after deregulation tended to be those with more diversified strategies before deregulation, and S&Ls that solicited deposits aggressively after deregulation tended to be those that had solicited deposits aggressively before deregulation.

The dubious evidence that failing S&Ls pursued riskier strategies also casts doubt on two theories that blame the S&L disaster on deposit insurance.

Theory 5. Deposit insurance keeps depositors from watching how S&L managers invest. This theory says that deposit insurance leads depositors to pay less attention to the actions of S&L managers (Barth 1991; Eichler 1989; White 1991). Thus, deposit insurance might make failures more likely when S&Ls' equity capital nears zero, for managers might take high risks then. The theory conjectures that managers would take less risk if depositors have more to lose.

Theory 6. Deposit insurance leads S&L managers to take risks because insurance premiums do not reflect risk taking (Kormendi et al. 1989). S&Ls' premiums did not vary with the riskiness of managerial practices, FSLIC did not require strict monitoring of managerial behavior, and FSLIC coverage had no practical limits. Thus, S&Ls incurred no added costs, says this theory, if they took more risks.

Theory 7. Incompetent managers squandered money and crooks stole it. In a 1988 report to Congress, FHLBB called fraud and insider abuse the most 'pernicious' causes of failures. GAO (1989) also emphasized 'unsafe practices' and 'alleged criminal activity', although it noted that failed S&Ls had made nontraditional investments and accepted nontraditional deposits. Table 16.1 lists several differences between failed and solvent S&Ls.

GAO sharply criticized supervision by FHLBB and FSLIC. Of the studied S&Ls, examiners had described all twenty-six failed ones as requiring 'urgent and decisive corrective measures'. However, in twenty of these S&Ls, examiners let over a year elapse between examinations, and five of the S&Ls had no examinations for over two years. Twenty-two of the failed S&Ls had agreed to correct problems, but eleven of these had violated the agreements and FHLBB had taken actions against only four violators. GAO remarked 'that violations and unsafe or unsound practices at these failed thrifts had often persisted for years'. Reinforcing GAO's observations, Wang, Sauerhaft, and Edwards (1987) found hundreds of S&Ls that had had no examinations between January 1984 and July 1986 (see also Kane 1989).

This theory has stronger evidential support than others. Still, GAO merely looked at raw frequencies without weighing possible causes, and GAO selected failed S&Ls with especially large insurance losses. Because GAO paired S&Ls of similar size in the same geographic areas, the comparisons suppressed effects of firm size, local regulatory practices, and local economic conditions. Pant (1991) found more evidence of criminality in larger S&Ls and in those in smaller metropolitan areas having more volatile economic conditions.

Theory 8. The government discounted problems and postponed action, thus making losses much worse. Brumbaugh (1988) asserted that FHLBB and Congress were postponing action, which was increasing costs and shifting costs from S&Ls to commercial banks and taxpayers. Barth (1991) argued that it was this delaying behavior that converted bad business judgment into insurance losses. He noted

Table 16.1. Practices at 26 failed S&Ls versus 26 solvent ones

	Failed	Solvent
Cited by examiners for recordkeeping and control deficiencies	26	9
Unsafe practices in nonlending activities, such as acquiring a subsidiary without first obtaining an appraisal	26	?
Cited by examiners for improperly analyzing borrowers' abilities to repay	24	13
Violated the regulation limiting the amount loaned to a single borrower	23	11
Violated the regulation against dealing with other firms controlled by the same officers and directors	21	Minor
Violated the regulation against conflicts of interest	20	3
Passive boards of directors	19	8
Insiders charged with crimes	19	7
Cited by examiners for excessive compensation of officers	17	3
Change in control	16	3

that most insolvent S&Ls had reported insolvency many months—indeed, years—before regulators intervened. Meanwhile, the insolvent S&Ls continued to lose money. Kane (1989: 66) argued, 'FSLIC officials (acting under constraints imposed by the politicians to whom they report) adopted a strategy of denying the problem, suppressing critical information, granting regulatory forebearances, and extending expanded powers to troubled clients. They gambled on the possibility that time alone would cure the problem.'

While agreeing with Barth and Brumbaugh, White (1991: 112) said, 'the true debacle occurred largely between 1983 and 1985; but the wave of losses, insolvencies, and closures began only in 1986'. According to White, FHLBB began raising regulatory requirements and FSLIC's insurance premiums in 1984 and began backing away from RAPs in 1987, but very gradually.

Some evidence supports White's interpretation. In 1986, FHLBB announced a higher equity capital requirement that symbolized its intentions even though few S&Ls could meet the requirement (Figure 16.1). S&Ls cut back on nonmortgage loans after 1987 (Figure 16.8), and they stopped growing after 1988 (Figure 16.6). FHLB advances leveled after 1988 (Figure 16.3). On the other hand, S&Ls foreclosed fewer mortgages after 1987 (Figure 16.9).

Theory 9. The tax laws changed. An S&L trade association, the Savings & Community Bankers of America (1994: 2), explained,

Changes in real estate tax laws in 1986 led to a rapid and unanticipated fall in real estate values in many over-built markets, causing many borrowers to default on loans. Increasing competition from banks, nonbank financial institutions, and government-sponsored housing finance agencies decreased the profitability of residential mortgage lending and worsened the growing thrift crisis. This confluence of events led to the failure of a large number of savings institutions, eventually bankrupting the federal Savings and Loan Insurance Corporation, at a huge cost to the taxpayer.

The dashed line in Figure 16.9 compares S&Ls' mortgage foreclosures to those by all lenders. Until 1983, S&Ls' foreclosure rate was the same as or less than that of other lenders. After 1986, S&Ls foreclosed at more than twice the rate of other lenders, whereas other lenders' post-1986 foreclosure rates were similar to their pre-1986 rates.

The 1986 tax changes may not have caused the higher foreclosure rates in the late 1980s. First, S&Ls' foreclosure rates started to move up in 1981, right after speculative real estate partnerships became more profitable and five years before passage of the 1986 tax law. Second, S&Ls held less than 10 percent of the commercial mortgages. Mortgages on apartments and commercial buildings were held mainly by commercial banks and life insurance companies, so these lenders should have had larger losses from the tax changes than S&Ls. They did not. However, the tax changes probably hit S&Ls' investments more heavily. S&Ls had less experience with commercial mortgages than commercial banks and insurance companies, so they invested less wisely. Some S&Ls followed poor practices (Table 16.1), and some were pawns of real estate opportunists. S&Ls had little equity capital (Figure 16.1), so small losses could make them insolvent.

An Appraisal

The disaster likely had several causes that differed over time. Figures 16.10 and 16.11 suggest that it included at least three periods: 1980–82, 1983–86, and 1987–91. A fourth period may have started in 1992, as White (1991) predicted that the 1989 legislation would cause more insolvency.

Low equity capital caused trouble through all three periods (Barth 1991). After 1979, S&Ls' economic environments became much less stable, and S&Ls made much riskier investments. Congress or FHLBB should have required much more equity capital, since companies in construction and real estate, the domains where S&Ls were investing, had equity capital that averaged 26–28 percent of assets. Instead, Congress urged FHLBB to lower the capital requirement, and it did so.

FRB's abrupt shift in interest rate policy made low levels of equity capital visibly problematic in 1980–82 because S&Ls lost money for two years. A more gradual policy change would have let S&Ls adapt to higher interest rates without incurring losses.

By 1983, S&Ls had raised interest rates, but then they ran into trouble of their own making. They had begun making more loans for apartment buildings and commercial buildings in the 1960s and stepped up this practice after 1980. They also made many more nonmortgage investments after 1980. Meanwhile, they were converting from mutual associations to stock companies. These changes not only made their investments riskier, they erased S&Ls' support from depositor-owners and their privileged status as the government-supported lender for home mortgages. That is, S&Ls voluntarily abandoned their distinctive competence and their grassroots political support.

Not only did S&Ls lack experience in appraising nonmortgage loans, their regulators assumed that S&Ls took little risk and had little criminality or corruption. Federal S&L examiners overlooked problems, and FHLBB corrected problems apathetically. Thus, self-interested opportunists came as borrowers and owners.

A combination of less competence, more risk taking, more criminality, more self-interest by S&Ls' managers, and impotent regulators invited trouble. However, the effects of these factors should have built up gradually, so they do not explain why the disaster accelerated suddenly in 1987–91. Similarly, delayed recognition of problems—due to either bureaucratic oversight or deceptive accounting standards—should have occurred gradually. The new regulatory structure authorized in 1989 probably had no effects until after the massive losses had abated.

Thus, the sudden, massive losses in 1987–91 probably had two main causes. First, stricter regulatory standards after 1986–87 may have forced S&Ls to acknowledge more bad debts and helped FHLBB to see the disaster's size. Second, tax changes in 1986–90 transformed many investments into bad loans that no longer had as much concealment from RAPs.

Government agencies caused trouble both by ignoring problems or reacting too slowly and especially by overreacting or acting too quickly. The disaster might have been much smaller if FHLBB or the Reagan administration had acted more swiftly or more forcefully. FHLBB could have raised the equity capital requirement gradually as S&Ls made riskier investments. FRB could have changed its interest rate policy in stages, allowing S&Ls to adapt incrementally. Congress tended both to overreact and to take misguided actions.

3. DECISION-MAKING BY LOOSELY COUPLED ORGANIZATIONS THAT USE DISTORTED DATA

The story of this disaster resembles a play in which some actors form groups that move together but most actors seem to ignore each other. Ropes link certain actors, and every so often, an actor who feels constrained jerks a rope and unwittingly upends another. Some actors interject fragments from other plays, and some rewrite the script. Different people play each role in each scene, bringing sundry abilities and changing emphases.

Sitting in the middle of the stage is a draped object that grows more and more immense. But not only do the actors not peek under the drapery, they ignore this object entirely. One actor constantly dances around this object without acknowledging its presence, except when he tosses more drapery over it. Mainly, this actor seems to be echoing the motions and statements of others.

Despite distractions and diversions, the motions have an overall consistency, as if specific actors and specific actions and statements do not matter all that much. Everyone gradually drifts closer and closer to the large object, until finally several bump against it and dislodge its drapery. Then all the actors assail the one who has been dancing around the object, killing him as well as a few of themselves. The survivors celebrate their triumph.

The S&L industry attracted different managers at various times. Long ago, managers were proponents of home building who saw themselves as serving their communities as well as their firms' depositor-owners. As mutual associations gave way to stock companies, some owners became managers serving their own interests. By the 1960s, managers were showing less interest in home building as such and more interest in profit-making. After 1982, the industry drew many opportunists from construction and real estate development, who used S&Ls to abet sales at inflated prices.

In Washington, the S&L industry supported two trade associations that did not always agree. One represented mainly large S&Ls, and in the 1980s it tended to argue that each FHLB district presented distinct issues that called for different treatment. The other, which represented diverse S&Ls, tended to argue that all S&Ls deserved similar treatment. A Washington insider told us that both trade associations exerted strong influence on Congress in the 1980s, and Congress's behavior is consistent with such influence until 1989.

Specific S&Ls also exerted strong influence. Brumbaugh (1988: 174) remarked:

Throughout the 1980s, for example, the industry demanded and received regulatory forbearance, primarily in the form of lower net-worth requirements, accounting forgiveness, and forestalled closure of insolvent thrifts. Each of these acts provided short-run subsidies to thrifts—insolvent and solvent. A microcosm of this behavior exists today in Texas, one of the states hardest hit by thrift insolvencies—over 40 percent of income losses for the third quarter of 1987 were in thirty-nine Texas thrifts. Powerful thrift interests successfully lobbied Congress, particularly the Texas congressman who is Speaker of the House, to make regulatory forbearance part of the scaled back FSLIC recapitalization plan [passed in 1987]. The result of the early 1980s forbearance, however, was an unintended exacerbation of thrift problems, as insolvent thrifts gambled for resurrection, fraud grew, and deflation further ravaged thrifts' portfolios.

Not only did S&Ls strongly influence Congress, they also influenced FHLBB. Presidents of the S&L-owned FHLBs met frequently with FHLBB, and FHLBB staff members told us that these presidents strongly influenced policy decisions. In an internal memorandum, a senior official in the executive branch reported in 1985, 'They [the senior officials in FHLBB] clearly feel impotent to close down insolvent thrifts as rapidly as they would like. They feel tightly bound by lack of FSLIC funding and also by opposition of the insolvent thrifts themselves, who are perceived to dominate the trade groups and to have much clout on Capitol Hill.'

Influence flowed the other direction only rarely. FHLBB occasionally toughened its rules, although FHLBB probably never took actions that most S&Ls opposed and it seldom punished rule violations. In 1989, Congress imposed heavy costs on S&Ls.

That 1989 legislation, passed shortly after a change of administration, shows how personnel changes altered policies. The Reagan administration had taken little action because of internal debate about the disaster's size and the need to close insolvent banks promptly. One side questioned FHLBB's efficacy and advocated swifter, stronger action; the dominant side insisted that the federal budget not include larger sums for this purpose. An internal memorandum stated, 'Because of deposit insurance, failure in the thrift industry is a bureaucratic decision as much as an economic fact.' Thus, stronger action did not occur until the Bush administration took office.

The Reagan administration also did not act more forcefully because formal reports said S&Ls were doing rather well. Internal memoranda observed that 'In 1984, FSLIC insured thrifts ended in the black' and '1985 may be one of the most prosperous years for thrifts'. Of course, those ideas arose from RAP profits, which understated losses from bad loans. Only later did the administration discover that they had relied on deceptive reports.

Others were also misled by RAP reports, including FHLBB, FSLIC, and the S&Ls' trade associations. Given its optimistic appraisal of the industry's condition, the Reagan administration wanted S&Ls themselves to pay for cleaning up their industry, and the trade associations endorsed this view. Because the trade associations doubted the competence of FHLBB and FSLIC, they proposed new organizations to resolve bad loans, and the Office of Management and the Budget

(OMB) refused to give FHLBB more staff to dispose of insolvent S&Ls. Within OMB, a staff member reported:

Chairman Gray [of FHLBB] stressed the point that the industry feels that FSLIC staff are incapable of solving the current problem. This has been the main reason why the industry is unwilling to capitalize the FSLIC fund.

We have talked with thrift industry trade groups and disagree with Chairman Gray. First, we believe that the distrust is not confined to FSLIC staff, but that the industry also distrusts Bank Board staff and the Board. However, we believe there is support for raising the funds needed to shore up the FSLIC fund. The industry is clearly divided on this issue. While a majority of the members favor solving the industry's problems in-house, there are a few large powerful thrifts which do not want to bear the additional costs (they would rather see the federal government pay for it).

Chairman Gray thanked OMB for having authorized FSLIC an additional 40 [employees], but mentioned that this was not enough to solve the problem. He contends that FSLIC needed flexibility from federal civil service rules to hire and retain qualified personnel. Chairman Gray indicated that the FDIC [which insures commercial banks] has 2,500 employees involved in liquidations, compared to FSLIC's professional staff of only 81. He pointed out that the average salary of a FSLIC professional was $35,800, while people on Wall Street doing equivalent work earned over $100,000. Chairman Gray believes that the only people who would work for FSLIC were the ones that could not get a job on Wall Street.

The 1986 tax changes show actors' ignoring their effects on others. According to a person who helped to design these tax changes, no one thought about their possible effects on S&Ls' solvency.

FRB's policy shifts in 1979 and 1982 also show actors ignoring their effects on others and show roles changing when new actors step in. The 1979 policy shift followed appointment of a new chairman. The 1982 policy shift, backing away from high interest rates, occurred even as Congress was passing the Garn-St. Germain Act to help S&Ls deal with high interest rates. If one takes FRB's public statements at face value, neither policy shift took account of potential effects on institutions for lending money, such as the regulatory structure for S&Ls. However, some of FRB's public statements lack credibility. It explained its 1979 shift differently at times; and although FRB did not say so publicly, its 1982 shift was likely intended to quiet complaints about high interest rates.

Apparently, key actors did not see connections between FRB's control of interest rates and FHLBB's equity capital requirement. FHLBB could get by with a low equity capital requirement as long as (*a*) S&Ls made low-risk investments, (*b*) S&Ls' economic environment was stable, and (*c*) S&Ls remained profitable. FRB's policies strongly influenced S&Ls' profits and their environment's stability. When FRB shifted policies, FHLBB needed to require more equity capital.

FHLBB was, of course, the actor who danced around the disaster while ignoring it, and in 1989 FHLBB became the scapegoat everyone assailed. But it is hard for someone sitting in the audience to see FHLBB as the villain, or to interpret FHLBB's slaying as a triumph. Congress designed FHLBB to reflect influence from S&Ls themselves; and when FHLBB attempted to restrain S&Ls,

Congress intervened on the side of S&Ls. The executive branch gave FHLBB far too few resources for it to act effectively. With the executive branch, Congress, and the trade associations all doubting FHLBB's competence and effectiveness, it certainly could not exercise moral leadership.

On occasion, FHLBB tried to use symbolism to show mastery of its environment. For example, amid the turmoil of 1980, Richard Marcis and Dale Riordan (1980) of FHLBB's Office of Policy and Economic Research made elaborate forecasts of the industry's balance sheets and income-and-expense statements for eight years. One scenario assumed that interest rates would decline from their highs reached in early 1980; a second scenario envisaged interest rates remaining steady through 1988; and a third scenario postulated interest rates increasing from current levels.

Marcis and Riordan made predictions without explaining them. They did not specify why they expected interest rates to have predicted effects. They (1980: 5) asserted that the newly passed DIDMCA would 'significantly impact S&Ls' and that S&Ls' new abilities would be 'of great significance' on both the asset and liability sides of balance sheets, but they did not describe the nature of this significance.

Yet, Marcis and Riordan described S&Ls' future in minute detail. For each scenario, they specified percentages of assets in various classes to three decimal places. They detailed assets, liabilities, income items, and expenditure items painstakingly for nine years. It seems that they intended this detail to demonstrate their understanding of the industry's condition and developmental possibilities and to legitimize their conclusion—that S&Ls would be far down the path to total recovery by 1988.

Regulatory agencies and bank examiners in fifty states and federal examiners in twelve FHLB districts played ostensibly minor roles. But some explanations of the disaster have said that these bit players were among the true villains (Kane 1989).

With all these changing actors and changing actions, it is amazing that long-run trends persisted. Yet, the disaster seems to have sprung from interactions between consistent long-run trends and erratic policy shifts. The actual character of these policy shifts appears secondary. Long-run trends were constructing an increasingly unstable situation in which a large perturbation would someday trigger disaster.

4. HOW LONG-TERM TRENDS MADE LARGE PERTURBATIONS DISASTROUS

Four long-run trends framed the disaster:

1. high and increasing favoritism by Congress;
2. escalating support from and trust by regulatory agencies;
3. low and declining equity capital requirements; and
4. declining holdings of home mortgages and declining ownership by depositors.

Ironically, three of these trends arose from others' efforts to help S&Ls, and S&Ls themselves helped to shape all four trends.

First, Congress showed favoritism toward S&Ls. Congress set up FHLBs in a way that let S&Ls borrow via the U.S. government, and it insisted that S&Ls should pay artificially low premiums for deposit insurance. Kane (1985) argued that the low premiums gave S&Ls an incentive to minimize equity capital.

One reason for Congress's attitude may have been S&Ls' standing as symbols of home ownership—almost as central to the American dream as motherhood and apple pie. Another reason may have been that S&Ls' depositors and borrowers were voters. S&Ls represented respected political constituents.

S&Ls grew more influential in Congress over time. They created active trade associations and hired effective lobbyists. The U.S. League of Savings Associations made large political contributions, along with the National Association of Realtors and the National Association of Home Builders. S&Ls focused contributions on members of the House and Senate banking committees (Kane, 1989: 52–53), and they expressed strong opinions about relevant legislation.

Second, the S&Ls had ongoing aid from regulatory agencies. FHLB advances gradually became a significant source of funds for the industry, and indirectly for home ownership and home construction. Advances outstanding were 13.3 percent of S&Ls' assets by the end of 1993, and FHLBs treated advances as support for the S&L industry rather than as funds owed to the American public. Even after the industry's deplorable condition became obvious, FHLBs did not reduce their advances.

In the early 1980s, FHLBB permitted S&Ls to portray losses on bad mortgage loans as assets and allowed S&Ls in trouble to issue Income Capital Certificates for purchase by FSLIC. Thus, insolvent S&Ls could describe themselves as solvent and continue in business with FSLIC as a silent partner.

FSLIC made perfunctory examinations of S&Ls. Rarely did an S&L have reason to fear examiners' arrival. Examiners came infrequently; they lacked competence; and when they found deficiencies, FHLBB, FSLIC, and the S&Ls ignored their complaints. S&Ls had great discretion.

Third, S&Ls had to meet no effective capital requirements. FHLBB and Congress set very low equity capital requirements, which they relaxed when S&Ls could not meet them.

Although S&Ls did not have to lower equity capital to the minima set by FHLBB, S&L managers may have assumed that FHLBB knew how much equity capital was essential. That is, some S&L managers may have thought they were behaving prudently as long as they exceeded FHLBB's requirements.

Favoritism, advances, RAPs, Income Capital Certificates, perfunctory examinations, and low equity requirements proved harmful in the long run. Low equity capital made S&Ls vulnerable to environmental changes. Escalating FHLB advances made S&Ls less dependent on and presumably less concerned about depositors. RAPs and Income Capital Certificates encouraged insolvent S&Ls to speculate recklessly and thus to multiply losses. Perfunctory examinations and nonenforcement of rules kept S&Ls from having to show competence. Congress did not question S&Ls' ability to use freedoms intelligently and prudently.

Fourth, S&Ls evolved from mutual associations that invested in home mortgages to stock companies that invested in commercial mortgages, mortgage-backed securities, and nonmortgage investments.

Not even FHLBB challenged the wisdom of S&Ls' strategic change. Through political influence and participation in governmental decision-making, S&Ls made their existence an autonomous goal. FHLBB, Congress, and the executive branch all accepted the premise that S&Ls ought to exist even if they no longer promoted home ownership. So they agreed to S&Ls' proposals for change.

But this change meant that S&Ls were politically vulnerable when the Bush administration and Congress acted in 1989. S&Ls no longer symbolized home ownership and thrift, and they no longer had widespread political support. They had become merely another financial retailer, competing with commercial banks, insurance companies, and loan companies.

Large perturbations of the 1980s caused steplike departures from long-term trends. Institutional practices had adapted to long-standing policies. Then policy shifts upset the institutional practices.

Three types of perturbations seem to have been especially important. First, many years of slowly changing interest rates shaped expectations and institutional practices. Then FRB let interest rates rise rapidly for two years. Second, for many years, S&Ls had faced tight restrictions on deposits, investments, and interest rates. Then Congress gave S&Ls much freedom. Third, tax policies toward real estate had been stable during the 1960s and 1970s. Then the government made changes that encouraged speculative partnerships. Five years later, it not only repealed the earlier changes but eliminated policies that had been in effect for a quarter of a century.

Decisions Shared by Many Loosely Coupled Organizations

Collisions between long-run trends and short-run perturbations probably typify decision processes involving many loosely coupled organizations. Because loose coupling makes communication difficult, organizations coordinate on the basis of expectations. Nearly all organizations adhere to traditions and avoid abrupt innovations, and trends tend to persist. Even nuclei of tightly coupled organizations, such as the networks of FHLBB and FHLBs, avoid abrupt innovations because they are unsure about the limits of their discretion.

But sometimes organizations do make abrupt innovations that perturb the overall system to significant degrees. The S&L disaster suggests that these perturbations have two properties: They involve unusually large actions, and the actors fail to anticipate secondary effects of their actions. FRB's 1979 policy shift stood out because FRB departed radically from recent tradition. The tax and S&L legislation called for sudden, significant changes rather than small, incremental ones. FRB forecast effects of its 1979 policy shift on inflation and employment but did not forecast the effects on S&Ls' profits. The Reagan administration forecast effects of the 1986 tax changes on taxes paid by partners but not on S&Ls' outstanding loans.

Both abrupt actions and blindness to secondary effects are prevalent in decision processes involving many loosely coupled organizations. Involvement of many participants who hold divergent views creates a need to motivate actions. Participants must achieve agreement that there is need for action and then agree on specific actions, so they are prone to define chosen actions as final solutions rather than experimental trials. Participants with divergent views need to focus on specific symptoms that are motivating them to act, so they tend to forecast only first-order results of their actions. Indeed, such decision processes often have an emotional air—as in 'the first 100 days'.

Thus, there is hope for democracy. Citizens worry about cozy relations between Congress and lobbyists, about regulatory agencies being captured by the industries they supposedly regulate, and about government support flowing to special interests. These worries would be well founded if lobbyists, special interests, and industry representatives actually knew where their long-run interests lay. But the S&L disaster suggests that they lack such foresight. Indeed, this disaster suggests that strong influence may lead special interests and industry representatives to misjudge their abilities, to give away their assets, and to make more erroneous forecasts.

Washington's political climate leads participants to lie about current goals, to reconstruct past goals, to conceal actions, to generate deceptive information, and to disclose others' secrets. Since no one dares to trust those with whom they form coalitions, cooperation becomes unreliable. Since no one can depend on public reports about what is happening, actions have unstable bases. Since dependable facts do not exist, people act on the basis of theories that contradict available facts. The powerful cannot exploit power consistently. They cannot be sure who their friends really are. When they try to help friends, they often harm them inadvertently.

ACKNOWLEDGMENTS

This chapter benefits from the insights of Joan Dunbar, Roger L. M. Dunbar, Marshall Kaplan, Richard T. Pratt, Joseph Rebovich, Harry S. Schwartz, David Seiders, and especially Kathryn Eickhoff and Lawrence J. White.

17

Unlearning Ineffective or
Obsolete Technologies

1. STICKING TO ONE'S . . . UH . . . DEPTH CHARGES

Starting in the mid-1970s, the Swedish defense forces pursued Soviet submarines lurking off the Swedish coast. Time and again, the Swedes mounted large-scale antisubmarine searches that included the dropping of grenades and depth charges and the detonating of remote-control mines.

For example, in May and June 1988, there were nine live-fire engagements between the Anti-Submarine Warfare unit and suspected foreign submarines. The Swedish Defense Ministry reacted by giving commanders on the scene authority to decide when to open fire. On one occasion, 'the prowler was detected and trapped in 282 feet of water . . . about 60 miles south of Stockholm', said a Ministry spokesman. The hunters opened up on the submarine with more firepower than Sweden had used previously. But the hunters lost contact with their prey amid the noise of exploding depth charges and underwater grenades, and the submarine apparently slipped away in the turbulence. 'When we played back the tapes, we saw that the submarine was exactly where we thought it was', the spokesman explained. He said 'it's probable' that the hunters hit and damaged the submarine although a search had failed to produce evidence of damage. 'Our anti-submarine activities have continuously improved.'

Dozens of such searches occurred every year, always during the warmer months. Yet none of these searches ended with the capture of a Soviet submarine. Only once, in October 1981, did the Swedes actually capture a Soviet submarine, and in this instance, there had been no hunt by the defense forces. Rather the submarine made a navigation error and grounded on rocks along Sweden's southern coast.

Some people theorized that the Soviets might be seeking spots where they could hide during warfare. Others posited that the Soviets might be testing their submarines' ability to evade detection. Still others speculated that the Soviets might be probing the Swedish antisubmarine defenses. The Soviets consistently denied that their submarines had been anywhere near Sweden, but these denials only reinforced the Swedes' suspicions. In 1982, in a clear reference to the Soviet Union, the chief officer of the navy, Rear Admiral Per Rudbeck, declared that 'a foreign power is preparing for war against us'.

Sweden's ineffectiveness against the Soviet submarines, although embarrassing, did not surprise them. No one really expected David to defeat Goliath. The Swedes had never intended their navy to command respect as a military power, whereas the Soviet navy was renowned for its skill and technology.

Then in February 1995, Sweden's defense chief Owe Wiktorin told a news conference that the Swedish navy had acquired new hydrophonic instruments in 1992, and these had shown that minks give off sounds similar to submarines. Earlier equipment had identified the sounds as submarines, he said, but there may never have been Soviet submarines lurking off the Swedish coast. 'The intruding submarines were not submarines but minks, or at least most likely minks.' Wiktorin said the Defense Ministry was certain that no foreign submarines had intruded into Sweden's territorial waters since 1992; defense analysts were checking sound recordings of suspected submarines from before 1992 to see if the sounds were really just small animals like minks and otters swimming from island to island. Eventually, Wiktorin reported: 'There is overwhelming evidence (technical, acoustical, and visual) that there have been five foreign submarine operations on Swedish territory since 1981', including the Soviet submarine that ran aground in 1981.

That the navy might be pursuing animals had been proposed as early as July 1987. After the navy had dropped depth charges and fired antisubmarine grenades unsuccessfully for almost three weeks in search of foreign intruders, Tero Harkonen, a Swedish seal expert, speculated that the antisubmarine hunt had been triggered by the play of young seals. 'They can play, gush through the water, and even create foam on the surface', he explained. However, navy officials maintained that the navy had surrounded a foreign mini-submarine or another type of underwater vessel with nets. They declared that there had been many 'reliable' sightings of suspected alien submarines and submarine activity in the area over the preceding two months, including air bubbles from a diver. The navy continued searching and dropping depth charges for another ten days before giving up the effort.

The Swedish Defense Ministry's recognition of error was partly the result of a change in government: A different political party had control in 1995. The recognition was also partly a result of the dissolution of the Soviet Union. The Soviet Union had collapsed, and its no-longer-so-secretive remnants no longer seemed capable of the remarkable underwater feats that the Swedes had been attributing to them. Indeed, during their 1995 review of earlier antisubmarine hunts, the Swedes consulted Russian antisubmarine experts. The Russian experts, the Swedes reported, agreed that the Swedes had been pursuing submarines but denied that the submarines had been Soviet ones.

This story illustrates three points. First, learning often cannot occur until after there has been unlearning. Unlearning is a process that shows people they should no longer rely on their current beliefs and methods. Because current beliefs and methods shape perceptions, they blind people to some potential interpretations of evidence. As long as current beliefs and methods seem to produce reasonable results, people do not discard their current beliefs and methods (Kuhn 1962).

As Henry Petroski (1992: 180–181) put it: 'Technologists, like scientists, tend to hold onto their theories until incontrovertible evidence, usually in the form of failures, convinces them to accept new paradigms.' Indeed, the Swedish navy shows that people may adhere to their current beliefs and methods despite very poor results. Even after two decades of abject failure, the leaders of the Swedish navy continued to construe their organization's failures as the logical result of an amateurish defense force from a small country competing against a highly sophisticated defense force from a large country.

Surprisingly perhaps, technical experts may be among the most resistant to new ideas and to evidence that contradicts their current beliefs and methods. Their resistance has several bases. Experts must specialize and their specialized niches can become evolutionary dead-ends (Beyer 1981). Because experts' niches confer high incomes and social statuses, they have much to lose from social and technical changes. Expertise creates perceptual filters that keep experts from noticing social and technical changes (Armstrong 1985). Even while experts are gaining perception within their domains, they may be overlooking relevant events just outside their domains.

Second, organizations make it more difficult to learn without first unlearning. People in organizations find it hard to ignore their current beliefs and methods because they create explicit justifications for policies and actions. Also, they integrate their beliefs and methods into coherent, rational structures in which elements support each other. These coherent structures have rigidity that arises from their complex interdependence. As a result, people in organizations find it very difficult to deal effectively with information that conflicts with their current beliefs and methods. They do not know how to accommodate dissonant information and they find it difficult to change a few elements of their interdependent beliefs and methods. The Swedish sailors who conducted the searches had been trained to interpret certain sounds as a submarine and rising bubbles as a diver; they had not been prepared for the sounds and bubbles made by animals. A Swedish navy that had just spent three weeks dropping depth charges and antisubmarine grenades in the belief that it had trapped an intruder was not ready for the idea that it had been deceived by playful young seals.

Tushman, Newman, and Romanelli (1986) characterized organizations' development as long periods of convergent, incremental change that are interrupted by brief periods of 'frame-breaking change'. They said 'frame-breaking change occurs in response to or, better yet, in anticipation of major environmental changes'. However, even if abrupt changes do sometimes 'break' people's old perceptual frameworks, the more common and logical causal sequence seems to be the opposite one. That is, people undertake abrupt changes because they have unlearned their old perceptual frameworks.

Third, unlearning by people in organizations may depend on political changes. Belief structures link with political structures as specific people espouse beliefs and methods and advocate policies (Hedberg 1981). Since people resist information that threatens their reputations and careers, it may be necessary to change who is processing information before this information can be processed effectively. Thus, a change in control of the Swedish government may have been essential before the Defense Ministry could concede the possibility of errors in the conduct of antisubmarine hunts. A change in control of the Soviet Union may have been essential before the Swedes could allow the possibility of Russian vulnerability or truthfulness.

Top managers' perceptual errors and self-deceptions are especially potent because senior managers can block actions proposed by their subordinates. Yet, senior managers are also especially prone to perceive events erroneously and to overlook bad news. Although their high statuses often persuade them that they have more expertise than other people, their expertise tends to be out of date. They have strong vested interests, and they know they will catch the blame if current policies and actions prove wrong (Starbuck 1989).

There is, of course, every reason for people to suspect that current beliefs and methods are wrong. Not only do new discoveries convert good current beliefs and methods into no-longer-good, but there is normally no reason to trust that current beliefs and methods ever were good. The QWERTY keyboard provides an on-going reminder of the persistence of poor methods (Gould 1987). Although C. L. Sholes had reasons for placing the keys in particular positions, he designed QWERTY for a machine that differed considerably from modern typewriters. The widespread adoption of QWERTY was fostered by a highly publicized contest between two typists in 1888. Frank E. McGurrin, the typist who used QWERTY, won by a large margin. But McGurrin had memorized the keyboard and could type without looking at his fingers whereas his competitor had to look at his keyboard in order to find the right keys.

2. HOW PEOPLE CAN FOSTER UNLEARNING

'There is not the slightest indication that [nuclear] energy will ever be obtainable. It would mean that the atom would have to be shattered at will.'
— Albert Einstein, physicist (1932)

Einstein later wrote to President Roosevelt to urge that the United States attempt to construct an atomic bomb.

This chapter suggests ways to facilitate unlearning. Since the essential requirement for unlearning is doubt, any event or message that engenders doubt about current beliefs and methods can become a stimulus for unlearning. There are at least eight viewpoints that can help people turn events and messages into such stimuli. People can start from the premises that current beliefs and methods are 'not good enough' or 'merely experimental'. They can turn surprises, dissents, and warnings into question marks. They can listen carefully to the ideas of collaborators and strangers. They can look for feedback paths and they can try to synthesize divergent interpretations of phenomena.

'It Isn't Good Enough'

Dissatisfaction is probably the most common reason for doubting current beliefs and methods. But dissatisfaction can take a very long time to produce results.

Robert Fulton launched the first commercially successful steamboat in American waters in 1807 (Petroski 1996; Ward 1989). In 1816, the boiler on a steamboat exploded and injured or killed nearly all of the boat's crew. Over the next thirty years, boilers exploded on 230 American steamboats. Thousands died; more were maimed.

Some people said these explosions were 'acts of God'; others attributed them to demons in the boilers; still others theorized that high temperatures decomposed water into hydrogen and oxygen, which then recombined explosively. In 1824, the inventors and mechanics of Philadelphia formed the Franklin Institute and this Institute sought to study the causes of boiler explosions. By 1830, boiler explosions had become the Institute's highest priority, but it lacked the funds to conduct experiments so it sent out questionnaires. However, a particularly bloody explosion in 1830 induced Congress to ask the Secretary of the Treasury to investigate, and he granted funds to the Franklin Institute. This $1500 was the first research grant awarded by the U.S. government. The Institute's experiments disproved some theories about boilers and showed some unexpected effects. It submitted a report on explosions to Congress in 1836 and a report on boiler materials in 1837.

In April 1838, a steamboat exploded and killed about 200 people, which motivated Congress to pass the Steamboat Act of 1838. Unfortunately, the law required inspection of boilers but it did not provide inspectors and it did not require that a steamboat be removed from service if it failed an inspection. Many more steamboats exploded. Finally, in 1852, Congress set up a regulatory agency with enforcement powers.

But the legislation and the regulatory agency focused solely on steamboats, although boilers had also been exploding in factories. Indeed, there were several hundred boiler explosions annually and they continued into the twentieth century. The worst was a steamboat explosion that killed 1,200–1,500 people in 1865. However, by the mid-1880s, there was general understanding that the explosions were due to excessive pressures, defective materials, or inadequate or malfunctioning equipment.

'It's Only an Experiment'

People who see themselves as experimenting are willing to deviate temporarily from practices they consider optimal in order to test their assumptions. When they deviate, they create opportunities to surprise themselves. They also run experiments in ways that reduce the losses failures would produce. For instance, they attend carefully to feedback. They place fewer personal stakes on outcomes looking successful, so they can evaluate outcomes more objectively. They find it easier to alter their beliefs and methods to allow for new insights. They keep on trying for improvements because they know experiments rarely turn out perfectly.

For example, in 1964, 3M corporation began an exploratory research program to develop new adhesives. Spencer Silver, one of the chemists working on this project, later explained: 'In the course of this exploration, I tried an experiment to see what would happen if I put a lot of it into the mixture. Before, we had used amounts that would correspond to conventional wisdom.... If I had sat down and factored it out beforehand, and thought about it, I wouldn't have done the experiment. If I had really cracked the books and gone through the literature, I would have stopped. The literature was full of examples that said you can't do this' (Nayak and Ketteringham 1986: 57). The result was that Silver found a radically new adhesive: It sticks to surfaces without bonding tightly so it removes easily without leaving traces. It was so unusual that Silver and others at 3M had great difficulty seeing how it could be applied usefully. But it eventually spawned an important new product line: Post-It note pads.

'Surprises Should Be Question Marks'

Events that violate expectations, both unpleasant disruptions and pleasant surprises, can become opportunities for unlearning. For instance, the Allies developed the tank during World War I, and most army officers viewed the tank as lethargic support for the infantry (Fleming 1995). However, George S. Patton, the commander of an American tank unit had trained as a cavalryman and he saw the tank as being able to perform the cavalry function of reconnaissance. At the battle of St.-Mihiel, a wide no-man's land developed and Patton ordered a three-tank patrol to advance until it found the enemy lines. When German cannons fired on the patrol, its commander, Ted McClure, ordered his tanks to charge, with the result that they routed the Germans and destroyed the cannons. This provided a conceptual breakthrough for Patton, and subsequently other army officers, by showing that tanks could make daring attacks.

Marcie Tyre and Wanda Orlikowski (1994) studied technological adaptation in production processes. Sixty percent of the adaptation occurred during the first 2.5 months after the introduction of new processes, but 23 percent of the adaptation occurred during a second 2.4-month spurt that started about eleven months after the introduction of new processes. These later spurts were initiated by events—such as new equipment, new production requirements, or new personnel—that disrupted routine operations and stimulated new thinking about the technology and its use. It took disruptions to induce rethinking because users rapidly came to accept the deficiencies and inadequacies of new technologies.

Too often, however, the analyses following disruptions extend only to the immediate causes of the specific disruptions. If disruptions are to affect unlearning strongly, people need to use them to reveal weaknesses in their current beliefs and methods as well as to stimulate improvements. Why didn't the original designs anticipate the events that caused disruptions? Would organizational changes or different engineering concepts have fostered more robust designs?

The North American power grid seems to illustrate ineffective unlearning. In 1964, the U.S. Federal Power Commission stated that the North American electric-power grid could deal effectively with a nuclear attack (Chiles 1985). On November 9, 1965, one of Toronto's power stations began having minor mechanical difficulties, so Toronto began drawing more power from a station at Niagara Falls. A relay at the Niagara Falls station incorrectly sensed an overload and disconnected the overloaded transmission line from the power grid. This switched 375 million watts onto four other lines that were already near capacity. They too disconnected, so 1.5 billion watts flowed onto two lines that fed into northern New York. This power surge disconnected another connection between the United States and Canada, so Ontario was both short of power and unable to receive it. Circuit breakers clicked open throughout the eastern U.S. and separated the power grid into subsystems. In a few areas, the resulting blackouts lasted less than fifteen minutes. In New York City, the blackout lasted thirteen hours. Although New York City had enough generating capacity not only to sustain itself but to supply power northward, the human dispatcher did not push the right eight buttons quickly enough. Many generators were very difficult to restart after all power had shut down because starting them required external electric power.

The blackout evoked controversy. Some argued that an integrated power grid was inherently faulty; utilities should have weak ties to prevent disruptions from cascading. Others argued that strong ties enable utilities to accommodate disruptions, so the ties should be strengthened and the grid expanded. The advocates of stronger ties carried the day. Electric power companies organized into nine 'reliability regions', and much control was transferred from humans to automatic systems.

However, in June 1967, an overloaded transmission line in Pennsylvania initiated the second biggest blackout, which affected 13 million people in four states. More procedural improvements followed, but stronger ties have called for more complex control equipment that has been more likely to fail or to produce unexpected results. Wider-scale integration has meant that events can have consequences thousands of miles away. There were more power outages during 1976 than during any previous year. Then on July 13, 1977, lightning hit Consolidated Edison's transmission lines several times in a few minutes, another human operator made another mistake, and New York City again blacked out. More procedural improvements followed, but there were more power outages during 1981 than during any previous year.

'All Dissents and Warnings Have Some Validity'

It is, of course, not literally true that every dissenter is right or that every warning should be taken seriously. There are a few loonies out there. But, for each loony, there are dozens of sensible people who see things going wrong and try to alert others. Listeners need to guard against hasty rejections of bad news or unfamiliar ideas. At a minimum, dissents and warnings can remind people that diverse viewpoints exist and that their own beliefs and methods may be wrong.

Organizational hierarchies tend to block dissents and warnings. Porter and Roberts (1976) reviewed studies indicating that people in hierarchies talk upward and listen upward. They send more messages upward than downward, they pay more attention to messages from their supervisors than to ones from their subordinates, and they try harder to establish rapport with supervisors than with subordinates. The messages that do get through enhance good news and suppress bad news (Janis 1972; Nystrom and Starbuck 1984). This bias becomes problematic because bad news is much more likely to motivate people to change than is good news (Hedberg 1981).

Morison (1966) recounted how by the U.S. Navy learned to shoot much more accurately. In 1899, many gunners on five ships fired at the hulk of a ship for five minutes and achieved only two hits. Six years later, a single gunner fired at a small target for one minute and made fifteen hits.

This improvement came from the efforts of Percy Scott, William S. Sims, and Theodore Roosevelt. Scott, a British naval officer, developed aiming techniques, gun sights, and gears that greatly enhanced gunners' accuracy. Sims, an American naval officer, met Scott, learned of his improvements, and tried them on his own ship. Impressed by the results, Sims then began to write reports to naval bureaus in Washington. First, the naval bureaus ignored Sims' reports. Then, using incorrect logic and contrived data, the Bureau of Ordnance rebutted Sims' reports. They proved with mathematics that Sims' methods could not possibly work even though he, Scott, and other officers were using them. After two years of this rejection, Sims wrote to President Theodore Roosevelt. Roosevelt listened and appointed Sims the Inspector of Target Practice. In this position, Sims taught the U.S. Navy to shoot.

How can people decide whether to take dissents or warnings seriously? Four rules seem sensible. First, assume that all dissents and warnings are at least partially valid. Second, try to find evidence, apart from the messages' contents, about the odds that messages might be correct. For instance, do the sources of the messages act as though they truly believe what they say? Are these sources speaking of topics with which they have experience? Third, evaluate the costs or benefits that would accrue if messages turn out to be correct. Fanciful messages typically entail high costs or high benefits; realistic messages likely entail low costs or low benefits. Thus, it is the fanciful messages that most deserve attention. Fourth, find ways to test the dissents and warnings that might bring high costs or high benefits. Make probes to confirm, disconfirm, or modify the ideas.

'Collaborators Who Disagree Are Both Right'

Beliefs held by qualified observers nearly always have foundations in some sort of truth. The most common problem is not to prove that one set of beliefs is wrong but to reconcile apparent contradictions by showing that they are not contradictions at all. These efforts can lead everyone to new conceptualizations. They can also produce some strange inversions.

In 1937, Hannes Alfvén wrote a theory about the origin of cosmic rays (Alfvén 1985). Showing that cosmic rays could be caused by electromagnetic effects around double stars, he pointed out that the known electromagnetic effects are not strong enough to fill the entire universe with cosmic rays. Thus, he conjectured, cosmic rays must arise in and be confined to a single galaxy. When Alfvén's paper was rejected by the most prominent physics journal, he wondered if this was because the generally accepted view at that time was that cosmic rays filled the entire universe. He published the paper in a much less visible journal.

In 1948, Alfvén attended two lectures in which Edward Teller argued that cosmic rays must arise in and be confined to one solar system. Alfvén struck up an argument with Teller, and Teller responded by inviting Alfvén to present his theory in Chicago. Alfvén went to Chicago, but by the time he arrived there, he had decided that Teller was right. Alfvén and Teller coauthored a paper about the confinement of cosmic rays to one solar system, and Alfvén went on to publish more articles and a book about this theory.

After a few years, Teller changed his mind. He and almost everyone else in astrophysics came around to agreeing with Alfvén's original theory that cosmic rays must arise in and be confined to a single galaxy. Alfvén won the 1970 Nobel Prize in Physics partly for his early work on this topic. But Alfvén himself did not believe in his single-galaxy theory: He continued to believe the theory Teller had originated that cosmic rays arise in and are confined to one solar system.

'What Does a Stranger Think Strange?'

It is usually easier to respect the views of collaborators than those of strangers. Unfamiliar with current methods and unacquainted with recent efforts, strangers are likely to make suggestions that seem naïve or ignorant or foolish. Yet, new people often introduce new perspectives. Although the newcomers may be less expert than their predecessors, they are also free of some expectations that their predecessors took for granted. Thus, strangers may be able to see peculiarities that the indoctrinated cannot see or they may be able to offer breakthrough suggestions. Indeed, 'reengineering' seems to be designed to exploit this principle (Hammer and Champy 1993).

During the 1970s, the Sony Corporation produced a small, portable, monaural tape recorder (Nayak and Ketteringham 1986). It was named the Pressman because Sony expected reporters to use it to record interviews. In 1978, the engineers who had developed the Pressman tried to upgrade it to stereo sound. They succeeded in squeezing the components needed for stereo playback into the Pressman's chassis. But there was no room left for recording components, so the engineers were left with a recorder that could not record. Of course, a stereo Pressman would also have needed a second microphone and second loudspeaker, presumably on extension cords. Unsure what to do, the engineers dropped the project and used the unsuccessful prototype to play background music in their laboratory.

Sony's founder in 1946 had been Masaru Ibuka. Although Ibuka had retired, he was called Sony's Honorary Chairman and he had the habit of occasionally roaming around the laboratories and factories. One of these tours took Ibuka into the laboratory where the tape recorder engineers were playing their unsuccessful prototype. 'And then one day, into our room came Mr. Ibuka, our Honorary Chairman. He just popped into the room, saw us listening to this, and thought it was very interesting.' Ibuka said he thought the small box was producing excellent sound. He suggested to the engineers if they had considered producing a machine that had no recording capability. Also, he suggested, if the machine had no speaker, its batteries would last much longer. He had just visited another Sony laboratory where someone had developed very small headphones that might be mated to this nonrecording recorder.

Engineers and managers in both the tape recorder division and the headphone division saw no merit in Ibuka's idea. A tape recorder that lacked both a speaker and recording capability was no recorder at all, so no one would buy it. Headphones were merely a supplement to loudspeakers; if a device had only headphones, only one person could listen.

Undeterred, Ibuka went to Sony's real Chairman, Akio Morita, and said: 'Let's put together one of these things and try it. Let's see how it sounds.' Morita could hardly refuse such a small request from his company's founder and his friend of many years. So a machine was assembled, and both Ibuka and Morita liked the way it sounded. They began carrying it with them wherever they went—on trips, to play sports—to see how much they liked it.

Morita decided that Sony should put the Walkman into production. This made the managers of the tape recorder division quite unhappy because, as they saw it, they were being ordered to produce an ineffective device that would almost certainly lose money. With the new lightweight headphones, it would cost $249. Not only was this more expensive than tape recorders with speakers that could record, but the expected teenage consumers could not possibly spend more than $170. The marketing managers said bluntly, 'This is a dumb idea'. Morita declared that the price would be $165, and he told the tape recorder division to make 60,000 of them.

The managers of the tape recorder division judged that they were being commanded to lose $35 per unit sold. 'There was no profit. The more we produced, the more we lost.' They secretly decided to produce only 30,000 units and they allotted marketing a budget of only $100,000.

Sony sold almost no Walkmans during the first month after the product's introduction. Then sales picked up, and during the third month, sales rocketed... until Sony ran out of inventory. That was when Morita found out that the tape recorder division had produced only 30,000 instead of 60,000. The tape recorder division quickly corrected its error. Six months after the product's introduction, Sony was producing and selling 30,000 units per month.

During the fourth month after the Walkman's introduction, Sony began designing the Walkman II—much smaller, with better sound and longer battery life. Sony planned its production for 200,000 units per month.

'All Causal Arrows Have Two Heads'

People can use thought processes that tend to disclose and challenge their tacit assumptions. One useful heuristic is to insist that all causal paths carry influence in both directions: Whenever one perceives that A affects B, one should also look for ways in which B feeds back and affects A. There are some causal paths that do not carry influence in both directions. However, one-directional causation is rare because systems that can converge toward equilibrium have to entail feedbacks. Searching carefully for these feedback paths can lead one to see previously over-looked causal paths.

For example, Toyota developed the concept of a Just-In-Time inventory system by inverting the causal flow. In the traditional view, production converts raw materials into finished goods. A plant turns raw materials into components that feed into in-process inventories, and the plant produces finished products by drawing components from inventories. The finished products go into finished-goods inventories, not directly to customers. Customers must buy from the finished-goods inventories. Thus, analysts view production as flows of materials through stages of conversion; inventories uncouple these consecutive stages.

According to Toyota's Taiichi Ohno, 'we reversed our thinking and considered the production process in terms of backward flow' (Nayak and Ketteringham 1986: 210). What flows backward is information about customers' desires. When customers select finished products, they create vacancies in the finished-goods inventory. As finished products fill these vacancies, they remove components from the in-process inventories. The inventory vacancies created by withdrawn components convey information about the finished products that customers want. The inventory vacancies cascading through the production process automatically decompose customers' desires into components and ultimately raw materials.

Inverting the causal flow led Ohno to see production as the conversion of customers' preferences into demands for components and raw materials. In this view, in-process inventories become barriers that delay the flows of information. To speed this information flow, Toyota set out to minimize its in-process inventories.

'The Converse of Every Proposition is Equally Valid'

Dialectic reasoning is a generalization of two-directional causation. Starting from a proposition (A affects B), one states the converse proposition (B affects A) and then one insists that both the original proposition and its converse are valid. The philosopher Georg Hegel, who advocated this mode of reasoning, called the original proposition the thesis, its converse the antithesis, and their union, the synthesis. As with causal paths, not every thesis has a valid antithesis and not every thesis can be synthesized with its antithesis. But it is possible to apply dialectic reasoning to almost all situations and the process of applying it helps one to break free of tacit assumptions.

One can see dialectic reasoning in the work of Gideon Sundback, who invented the zipper (Friedel 1994). During the latter part of the nineteenth century, the most common method of fastening shoes was hooks and eyes. These were also used to fasten women's skirts and men's trousers. But fastening them was slow work and they did not stay fastened very well. The first zipper-like patents, which emerged in 1893, proposed that a sliding 'guide' could mate hooks and eyes. These devices were rather complex and they required precise assembly, so around 1904, their inventors began attaching them to cloth tape that could be sewn into shoes or clothing. The design, however, did not work well in that the hooks and eyes tended to separate when the fastener was bent or twisted.

The company that manufactured these devices hired Gideon Sundback to improve their design. His first effort, although better than its predecessors, had similar deficiencies and it was a commercial failure. Around 1912, after pursuing improvements in the prior design for six years, Sundback came up with a radically different design. In it, a slide forced the beaded edge of a cloth tape between two rows of metal clamps—somewhat like a Ziploc fastener. Thus, Sundback had replaced the proposition 'a fastener involves hooks and eyes' with its antithesis 'a fastener has neither hooks nor eyes'.

The antithetical design also had serious deficiencies—the cloth tape wore out after only a few uses. But optimistic backers formed a new Hookless Fastener Company, and Sundback continued his experiments. In 1913, he produced a design very like the modern zipper. In it, the hooks had shrunk to small protrusions and the eyes had closed until they were indentations. It synthesized hooks and eyes with their absence, and it synthesized hooks with eyes. The two sides of the fastener were composed of identical elements.

Theories of leadership afford an example of dialectic processes operating on a large scale (Webster and Starbuck 1988). Early in the twentieth century, most managers and management theorists asserted that organizations work best if they have firm superiors and obedient subordinates. Some fortunate people, it was said, had inherent traits that made them good leaders whereas the less fortunate did not.

By the 1930s, this orthodoxy had elicited counterarguments: Barnard argued that authority is something that subordinates grant rather than something that superiors impose. Weber pointed out that organizations may depersonalize leadership and that subordinates may think their superiors lack legitimacy. The Hawthorne studies presented evidence that subordinates produce more when they have friendly superiors.

Syntheses emerged during the 1950s. Some psychologists studied democratic leadership; others documented the sharing of leadership tasks among members of work groups; and still others analyzed the distinctive personalities of different kinds of leaders. Bales distinguished leaders' social roles from their task roles. Then the Ohio State leadership studies decomposed subordinates' perceptions of their superiors into two statistically independent dimensions—initiating structure and consideration. Initiating structure embodied the essential properties of the leadership concepts of 1910, and consideration embodied the concepts of the 1930s. Thus, antithetical views had become distinct dimensions of a complex phenomenon.

3. REPRISE

'I think there is a world market for about five computers.'

— Thomas J. Watson, President, International Business Machines (1943)

Watson later helped his son lead IBM's expansion in computers.

No one should be confident that their current beliefs and methods are optimal. Optimality is unlikely. If beliefs seem accurate, someone else is probably finding other beliefs equally effective. If methods seem excellent today, better methods will appear tomorrow. Thus, one is well-advised to remain ever skeptical. 'It isn't good enough' and 'It's only an experiment' are mental frameworks that help one to stay constantly alert for opportunities to improve. 'It isn't good enough' reminds one to look for more accurate beliefs or better methods. 'It's only an experiment' helps one to feel less committed to current beliefs and methods.

Because current beliefs and methods bias information gathering, signals from one's environment tend to support these beliefs and methods. To obtain dissonant signals, one may have to be proactive. Thus, one should try to turn surprises into question marks, should respond to dissents and warnings as if they have some validity, and should act as if collaborators' ideas are as deserving as one's own.

It may be difficult to respect the views of strangers unversed in current methods and unfamiliar with recent efforts. But strangers can see errors or opportunities to which the indoctrinated are blind.

One wanting to challenge current beliefs and to discover alternative methods can apply two logical techniques. 'All causal arrows have two heads' helps one to look for neglected feedback paths. 'The converse of every proposition is equally valid' helps one to reframe current beliefs within more general schemata.

'There is no reason for any individual to have a computer in their home.'

— Ken Olson, President, Digital Equipment Corporation (1977)

Five years later, DEC began to sell microcomputers.

ACKNOWLEDGMENTS

This chapter benefits from the insights of Raghu Garud, John Hedberg, and John Mezias.

Part VI

Ancient Issues in Organizing, Control Systems Part 2

18

Distrust in Dependence: The Ancient Challenge of Superior–Subordinate Relations

Coauthored with Violina P. Rindova

1. HOW ATRAHASIS SURVIVED A FLOOD

Among the oldest records that offer practical advice for a manager are Mesopotamian stone tablets engraved with a story of a flood.[1] Scholars say the story of Noah, written around 1000 BCE, was a Judaic adaptation of this Mesopotamian story. Although the oldest substantial copy was composed around 1635 BCE, fragments of tablets suggest that the story probably goes back to at least 3000 BCE in Mesopotamia.[2]

In Mesopotamia, the man who built a boat was named Atrahasis, Ziusudra, or Utnapishtim. He lived in a city named Shuruppak (now called Fara) on the Euphrates river.

Atrahasis had to contend with quite a few gods: The most powerful god, Enlil, led the others in deciding to teach humanity a lesson by drowning everyone in Shuruppak. They chose Shuruppak because it was the 'most fortunate of cities, favored by the gods'. Although the gods agreed to keep the forthcoming flood secret, two of them broke this pact. Shamash, god of justice and truth, told Atrahasis that an evening shower would foretell the flood. Enki or Ea, god of wisdom who delighted in cunning tricks, saved Atrahasis's life by urging him to build a boat.

Atrahasis's boat was to be so massive that a single family could not build it, and Atrahasis himself had no ship-building experience. How could he induce others to help him build a massive boat? Who would believe a man who claimed that the gods intended to drown everyone? If they did believe him, would they not demand passage in his boat?

Atrahasis asked the god Enki how to handle this problem. 'I hear what you say, and I will do it in praise of you. But, I will need to explain my actions. What should I tell others? What should I tell the city, the people and their leaders?' Enki advised Atrahasis to deceive them. He should explain that he had to leave Shuruppak because it is dedicated to Enlil, and Atrahasis's own god, Enki, is quarreling with Enlil. 'Since Shuruppak is the city of Enlil, you can no longer live in the city and you can no longer gaze on the land, which Enlil rules. You must find another place to live and another god to protect you. You have therefore decided to leave Shuruppak and to seek another home. Tell them your patron will be Enki, the god who rules the deep waters, so you will dwell upon the deep waters with Enki.'

Enki told Atrahasis to tell the truth, but to do so using metaphors that hearers would misunderstand. Atrahasis should say, 'As for Shuruppak, he [Enlil, but the ambiguous antecedent allows hearers to substitute Enki] will make abundance rain down on the fortunate city: There will be a flood of bounty. The city will teem with heaven's profusion. The people will see birds and fishes unheard-of in song or story. When the new day dawns, he will pour down loaves of fresh bread and showers of wheat. He will bring a surfeit of everything, yes, more than enough. These are the things to tell the people and their leaders.'

However, for Sumerians, bread was a metaphor for darkness and wheat a metaphor for misfortune. Thus, Atrahasis's promise had a metaphorical meaning that promised doom: 'When the new day dawns, he will pour down renewed darkness and showers of misfortune.' Thus, the god Enki advised Atrahasis, in his supervisory role, to elicit work by deceiving the workers.

Atrahasis also rewarded his doomed helpers generously. 'As for the people who came to help with the work, each day was like a New Year's festival: I slaughtered bullocks for their feasting; everyday I slaughtered sheep. To drink, I gave the workers ale and beer, oil and wine aplenty, as if they came from a flowing river.' When he and his family were aboard the boat and with the storm rising, Atrahasis made his last payment: 'To Puzur-Amuru, the shipbuilder who, outside, caulked up the hatch with pitch, I gave my house with all its contents.'

Thus, what may be the oldest surviving advice about management practices concerns leaders' deceptions of followers. Tension-filled, distrustful relations between leaders and followers pervade the ancient texts. This chapter reviews these common issues and people's responses to them. The issues encompass: (*a*) how much leaders and followers should trust each other and speak forthrightly to each other; (*b*) how leaders manipulate followers and followers manipulate leaders; (*c*) how much followers respect leaders and leaders respect followers; (*d*) whether status differences are just; and (*e*) when leaders act appropriately.

The chapter draws on documents from regions with the oldest surviving documents—Mesopotamia, Egypt, and China. Although similar issues doubtless arose in many regions, only these offer records from before 1000 BCE.

We do not compare these regions because records are fragmentary and biased. To justify comparisons, one would need comparable information from all three regions. But, invasions and political upheavals created waves of mass destruction that erased disapproved documents. There is no reason to believe this historical editing operated similarly in these regions.

2. MESOPOTAMIA

Through waves of migration and invasion, Mesopotamia was home to several cultures and several languages. Invasions often involved wholesale destruction of written records. Yet quite a bit of writing survives and it gives some of the most reliable evidence about ancient practices because people chiseled cuneiform into rock or baked it into clay. Elsewhere, where words were recorded on papyrus or skins or paper, decaying documents had to be copied. Works were copied only if aristocrats approved of and valued them. Copying introduced errors, and some scribes modernized works they were reproducing. Thus, Mesopotamian documents offer better insights into attitudes of ordinary people, unfiltered by the editing of their rulers.

The records include contracts, bills of sale, grants by rulers, inventory records, and letters to and from rulers. These discuss all sorts of administrative details, from assignments of shepherds, through astronomical observations, to police investigations. However, scholars have found little writing about Mesopotamian management techniques, organization design, or strategy.

How Ordinary People Viewed Leaders

The more interesting survivors include proverbs and sayings used by ordinary people. These sayings date to at least 2000–1000 BCE and they might be much older. They reveal the ambivalence with which followers regard their leaders.[3] Some assert the necessity of leadership:

Workers without a supervisor are a canal without someone to regulate it.
Workers without a supervisor are a field without a farmer.
People without a ruler are sheep without a shepherd.

Others characterize leadership as requiring special talents or embodying special powers:

A driver of oxen should not try to be a supervisor.
To improve government, Shamash [the god of justice and truth] will speak to a ruler even if the ruler is an ignoramus.

Some sayings distinguish between rulers and administrators:

Acknowledge a lord, acknowledge a ruler, but respect an administrator.
Giving is the act of a ruler; doing a favor the act of an administrator.

And still other sayings speak cynically of rulers' doubtful value:

There are people who support spouses; there are people who support children. Rulers are people who do not even support themselves.

Protests Against a Ruler's Actions

In a society where rulers could inflict harsh punishment for disobedience or disrespect, protest could be dangerous. A protester had to find a way to tell a ruler that he had erred and yet avoid personal responsibility for this judgment.

One document dating to 1000–700 BCE seems to protest transgressions by an unnamed ruler against residents of three cities—Sippar, Nippur, and Babylon.[4] However, instead of accusing a named ruler directly of having taken or threatening to take certain actions, the document offers predictions about what would happen if an unnamed ruler would take certain actions. The actions, however, are so specific that the author was likely speaking of specific acts by a specific ruler. For example,

If a ruler denies due process to a citizen of Sippar but grants it to a foreigner, Shamash, judge of heaven and earth, will impose an alien form of due process on the state and neither nobles nor judges will have respect for due process.

If citizens of Nippur come to the ruler for justice, and the ruler accepts the customary remuneration but denies them due process, Enlil, lord of the world, will bring a foreign enemy to decimate the ruler's army and the army's commanders and officers will prowl the streets like vagabonds.

If a ruler imposes fines on citizens of Babylon that the ruler usurps as the ruler's own property, or if the ruler hears a plea from Babylonians but dismisses it as trivial, Marduk, lord of heaven and earth, will place the ruler's enemies over the ruler and give the ruler's possessions and property to these foes.

In the original language, the writing style imitated one that Mesopotamians used when describing omens of future events. Thus, the document portrays the ruler's transgressions as omens foretelling dire consequences, mainly consequences for the ruler himself but also for the society. The dire consequences are carried out by the populace, gods, or foreign invaders (who may have been seen as instruments of the gods). To find this description persuasive, a ruler would have to have believed that Sippar, Nippur, and Babylon had strong support from gods. In turn, the document had to emphasize high-minded issues that gods would support.

If a ruler does not listen to the nobles, the ruler's lifetime will be cut short.
If a ruler listens to a scoundrel, the state's morality will change.
If a ruler attempts clever deception, the great gods together will harass the ruler endlessly for the sake of justice.

3. EGYPT

Several surviving Egyptian documents are Instructions that were intended to transmit experience from one generation to another. Typically, an Instruction represented itself as having been written by a father for his sons, but they actually had much wider readership as they served as texts in schools.

It appears that Egyptians drew weak distinctions between work and other aspects of life. Their Instructions mix advice on many topics, and none focuses exclusively on management. However, the Instruction of Ptahhotep may be the oldest surviving text on organizational behavior.[5]

Ptahhotep was Mayor of the Capital and Vizier to King Isesi around 2380–2340 BCE. The Vizier was Egypt's highest appointed official, second only to the king. The Instruction states that it is offering advice to Ptahhotep's son. However, scholars debate whether Ptahhotep himself composed the Instruction because the oldest surviving copy has the writing style of works created about 200 years after Ptahhotep died. Works from Ptahhotep's day were shorter and more terse, and they used more archaic language. Surviving copies may be 'expanded and revised editions', or the work's attribution to Ptahhotep may have been a literary device to add the significance of great age. Since Egyptian schools were still using Ptahhotep's Instruction as a text around 1500 BCE, it may have been studied for 900 years.

Ptahhotep's Instruction covers such diverse topics as 'do not let your concubine starve', 'beware of greed', 'do not steal from your neighbors', and reasons children should listen to their fathers. Yet, the Instruction mainly teaches how to survive and succeed in the Egyptian social system. Its advice sometimes seems more insightful and pragmatic than advice in modern textbooks!

Being a Superior

The Instruction recognizes that rulers need support of the populace and that superiors need support of their subordinates. It advises superiors to act virtuously, modestly, and with awareness of human needs. It advocates correct behavior in terms of how people will react, not in terms of demands made by gods. There is no sign that gods intervene in human affairs in order to ensure social justice.

4. If you run into opposition from subordinates who are not your equal, show temperance in proportion to your opponents' weakness. If you leave such opponents alone they may rebut themselves. Do not challenge them to make yourself feel better or to vent your feelings. Contemptible is one who bullies uninformed subordinates. When other people will follow your advice, you will subdue your opponents through the judgment of others.

14. When among the people, attract supporters by earning their trust. Trustworthy persons speak in ways that do not distort what they think. Their conduct makes them superiors and owners of property....

17. If you are a superior, listen kindly when people make petitions to you. Do not interrupt petitioners until they have unburdened themselves and said what they came to say. Those who think they have suffered wrongs want to vent their feelings more than they want to win their cases. If you interrupt a petition, people will think you rejected it. You cannot grant every plea, but a good hearing soothes the heart.

25. If you hold an important position, earn respect through knowledge and through gentleness of speech. Do not issue commands unless they fit the business at hand. A superior who chafes gets into trouble. Do not act haughty lest you be humiliated. Do not keep silence, but be careful not to offend. When you run into someone who is fuming, avert your face, control yourself, and the flames of anger will sweep past and be gone....

30. If you become important after having been lowly, or gain wealth after having been poor, do not boast of your attainments and do not rely on your wealth. These came to you as gifts from the gods. Otherwise, you might look unworthy in comparison with others who have had similar success.

Being a Subordinate

Ptahhotep's Instruction assumes a sharply hierarchical society, and it implies that changes in social status and wealth lie outside the control of normal people, being determined instead by fate, gods, or the King. Because superiors exercised great power over their subordinates, and could even inflict death, subordinates had to behave carefully. The Instruction reminds subordinates of their dependency, and urges them to behave discreetly and loyally.

7. If you depend on an important person for largess, accept what your superior offers you. Focus on your responsibilities and do not covet a superior's; to annoy a superior tempts fate. Do not offer advice to a superior until asked for it, for you might displease the superior; but answer when a superior asks your advice, for your superior will then welcome it. When superiors are distributing rewards, they can do as they wish. Superiors reward those they favor, and it is fate that determines these decisions. Thus, the gods guide your welfare, and only a fool would complain about it.

15. State your business candidly. When your superior asks you to speak, say plainly what you know and do not know. A subordinate who reports fully and impartially will not find it hard to report and will not be asked 'How do you know such things?' What if a superior does challenge a subordinate's report? The subordinate should remain silent after saying merely 'I have told all I know'.

26. Do not oppose the actions of important superiors; do not vex the hearts of the burdened. Opposition will rouse their ill-will, whereas support draws their love. Your superiors are your providers, along with the gods, and what they desire should take place. Pacify superiors when they storm in anger. Just as opposition engenders ill-will, support nurtures love.

27. Tell an important superior what is useful; help your superior to win acceptance by other people. This will also benefit you, because your livelihood depends on your superior's success, which clothes your back, and your superior's help protects you. When your superior receives a promotion, your own desire for rank progresses toward fulfillment, as your superior gives you a helping hand. Thus, love will grow stronger among those who love you; it is goodwill that wants to listen.

31. Bow to the one who is over you, your superior who represents the King. In this way, you will preserve your household and earn your pay. Pitiful is one who opposes a superior, for you live only as long as your superior is indulgent. Showing respect does you no harm.

Keeping a Cool Head

Around 1500 BCE, Egyptians began to refer to their King as Pharaoh, and their schools replaced Ptahhotep's Instruction with a similar one composed by Amenemope. Amenemope was Pharaoh's Superintendent of Cereals, and he addressed his Instruction to his son, explaining that someone who followed its advice would be worthy to serve as an aide to Pharaoh.[6]

Amenemope strongly advocated rational behavior. He emphasized the desirability of being 'cool-headed' rather than 'hot-headed'. Cool-headed seems to denote a composite of considerate, slow to anger, temperate, socially concerned, thoughtful of others, and honest; whereas hot-headed appears to mean a composite of impetuous, quick to anger, rude, selfish, dishonest, and treacherous. Amenemope expected gods to punish hot-headed behavior.

3. Do not quarrel with hot-headed people, or provoke them with words. Act cautiously when dealing with an adversary, and bend to an attacker. Sleep on a response before speaking, for turmoil spreads like fire in hay. Control yourself around hot-headed people, when they appear. If you leave them alone, the gods will answer them.

9. Do not associate with the hot-headed people or consult them.

Control your tongue when answering your superiors, and be careful not to malign them. Beware that they may try to entrap you, so be not too free in your replies. Before replying to superiors, discuss the replies with people of your own station, and take care not to speak thoughtlessly....

12. Do not covet the property of a superior—do not fill your mouth extravagantly with too much food.

If a superior assigns you to manage property, respect the superior's interest, and yours will prosper too. Do not deal with the dishonest people, or associate with disloyal cow-orkers. If you are sent to transport grain, account for it correctly. People caught in dishonest transactions will never be employed again.

24. Do not listen to the words of your superior indoors and then repeat them outside. To have a clear conscience, do not air your opinions outside the office. A person's conscience is the gods' pointer to right and wrong, so heed it. An aide to an official should be nameless.

The Upside and Downside of Kingship

Whereas Ptahhotep framed proper actions by superiors in terms of how people would react, another Instruction from before 2000 BCE placed more emphasis on expectations set by gods. Composed around 2150–2050 BCE, this Instruction conveys advice from an unnamed king to his son, Merikare.[7]

Kings saw their worlds quite differently from their subordinates. Merikare's father saw himself as having gods' support: 'The ruler of [our kingdom] is wise. The ruler cannot act stupidly: The ruler receives advice from an entourage; the ruler is wise from birth; and the gods have chosen the ruler over millions of people.' At the same time, he admitted that he needed support from the gods, nobles, and populace. He placed emphasis on remaining in control, a complex task that requires balance between contrary needs. He indicated this balance by shifting back and forth between harshness and kindness, idealism and pragmatism, and eliciting support from different constituents.

Dissatisfied loudmouths make trouble. Suppress them, kill them, erase their names, destroy their kinsfolk, suppress the memory of them and their supporters who love them. Hot-headed rebels incite the citizens and divide the younger people into factions. If you find citizens adhering to them and their movements have grown beyond your control, accuse them publicly and suppress them.... Bend the multitude to your will and cool its hot heads.

Be lenient when you intercede.... Justify your acts ethically so that people will say that you punish in proportion to the crime.... A contented citizenry is a ruler's heaven, whereas the curses of the angry are harmful.

Be skillful in speech, that you may prevail. The tongue is a ruler's sword, and speaking is more powerful than fighting. No one can defeat a clever person through physical means. A wise ruler is a school for the nobles, and those who see the ruler's wisdom do not rebel.

Do not be cruel; kindness is good. Build a lasting monument in the citizens' love for you. Benefit the citizens; improve the nation. Then will the citizens praise the gods for your deeds and pray for your health.

Respect the nobles and keep your citizens safe. Strengthen your borders and your patrols in the disputed land beyond the border. It is an investment in the future, because enemies respect the foresighted whereas they attack the trusting. Do not go after your neighbors' lands; one who covets what others possess is a fool. Let your neighbors come to you because of your excellence as a ruler.

Make your nobles very wealthy so that they may carry out your laws. The rich will not be self-serving, for wealthy people do not crave more. The poor, on the other hand, may not speak truly: Those who say 'I wish I had' will be unfair, because they give favorable treatment to those who offer bribes.

Cultivate the young people so that the future citizens will love you. Win supporters among those who are going to replenish your towns. Young people happily follow their hearts for twenty years, but then they become the next generation of citizens and raise children themselves. Recognizing that the present comes from the past, I began enlisting the youth's support at my accession. Elevate the young nobles, and promote the young soldiers. Enrich the rising generation of your subordinates: Equip them with knowledge, endow them with lands, and reward them with cattle.

Do not favor the children of nobles over those commoners, but choose your aides because of their skills. To be a strong ruler, you will need to have all skills at your disposal. Guard your frontier and staff your fortresses, for troops are useful to their commander.

Yet another Instruction shows the downside of kingship. Although this Instruction describes itself as advice from King Amenemhet (Ammenemes) I to his son King Sesostris I, it was Sesostris who composed it. The Instruction says that after rebellious nobles murdered Amenemhet in 1965 BCE, Sesostris composed the Instruction 'as an accurate account' of Amenemhet's testimony 'as a god'.[8]

The Instruction restates the mistrust pervading superior–subordinate relationships, the threats arising from political agendas and shifting loyalties. It asserts that proper behavior and good deeds do not protect a ruler from rebellion by close associates. Self-servingly, Sesostris said nothing about the rebels' motives.

Be on your guard against all subordinates, because you cannot be sure who is plotting against you. Do not be alone with them. Trust no brothers; recognize no friends, make no intimates. Such trust does you no good. Keep your thoughts to yourself, even when you are relaxing. No King has allies when trouble comes.

I gave to the poor. I raised the lowly. I helped the poor and the rich alike. Yet, those who ate my food became my opponents. Those I embraced plotted against me. Those who wore my fine linen looked on me as a has-been. Those who put on my perfume undermined me....

They conspired against me without being heard and attacked me without being seen, even though I had adherents throughout the land. They fought me without regard for my good deeds in the past. Good fortune eludes one who overlooks those whom he should watch.

Protests in a Bureaucracy: 'Everything Is Going Well, and in Addition, . . .'

The Egyptian bureaucracy had few levels, and even slaves could seek hearings from senior officials in their cities or regions. Civic and regional administrators throughout Egypt sent reports directly to the Vizier. These reports show that the bureaucracy was plagued by rampant theft, inefficiency, waste, and interpersonal dislike. Thus, the reality of Egyptian bureaucracy seems to have violated the high-minded values preached by Ptahhotep and Amenemope.

Here are two examples of these reports.[9] Such letters followed a formula in which the reporter first states that all is well, and then adds, almost as an afterthought, that things are not entirely perfect.

Written between 1279 and 1212 BCE:

Chief of Police Mininuy communicates to his lord, the Mayor of the Capital and Vizier Khay.

Life, prosperity, and health!

This is a letter to inform my lord.

The important locality of Pharaoh that is under my lord's authority is in excellent order, and the guardposts around it are in good shape. We have received the yearly wages, which are in excellent condition, comprising firewood, vegetables, fish, and new pottery. I call upon all the gods to keep Pharaoh healthy and to keep my good lord in favor with Pharaoh every day.

In addition, I have been my lord's servant for many years. I ran ahead of Pharaoh's horses, held the reins for him, and harnessed them for him. I made various reports to him, and he praised me in front of the Council of Thirty. He never found fault in me.

I served as a police officer in Western Thebes, guarding the guardposts of this important locality of Pharaoh. Then I was promoted to a Chief of Police, as a reward for my flawless conduct.

Please note, however, that Chief of Police Nakhtsobeki has been ruining the important locality of Pharaoh in which I work. I am telling my lord of his failings. He has been bullying my police officers in conducting investigations. 'You are an old man and I am young', he says to me. 'Just keep the locality in order for me. You are a has-been', he says. He confiscated my fields in the countryside; he took away two fields planted with vegetables, the produce of which belonged to my lord as the Vizier's share. He gave these fields to Chief of Police Monturekh and to the high priest of Montu. He also appropriated grain I had stored in the countryside.

This is a letter to inform my lord.

Written between 1182 and 1151 BCE:

To the fan-bearer on Pharaoh's right, the Mayor of the Capital and Vizier To:
Scribe Neferhotep communicates to his lord.
Life, prosperity, and health!
This is a letter to inform my lord.
I call upon many gods to keep Pharaoh healthy and to let him celebrate many jubilees as the ruler of every land, while you continue in his favor every day.

We are working on the nobles' tombs, which my lord commanded us to build. We are working properly and superbly and producing excellent results. Let not my lord worry about the tombs, as we are laboring intensely and not slackening.

In addition, we are exceedingly impoverished. Our supplies—from the treasury, from the granary, and from the storehouse—are all gone. A load of stone is not light! Indeed, six measures of grain were taken away and returned to us as six measures of dirt.

Please, my lord, provide us with means to stay alive. We are starving, and we cannot continue to live if we receive nothing.

4. CHINA

As in Mesopotamia and Egypt, mass destruction, editing, and neglect erased a great majority of the ancient texts in China. Documents dating to 90 BCE blame some of this loss on Confucius, who died in 478 BCE. According to this legend, Confucius went through the king's library in the state of Chow, preserved by rewriting documents he regarded as important, and discarded the remainder. However, sources detailing Confucius' life indicate that he never visited Chow.

Much better documented is a mass destruction in 212 BCE. King Ch'eng, founding ruler of the Ch'in dynasty, wanted to replace the old feudal system with a new order, so he tried to erase traditions that had supported the old ways. He burned nearly all books and murdered nearly all literate people. Ironically, King Ch'eng ruled for just three more years after the burning and his dynasty lasted for only eight years after his death. Also many documents survived this destruction, as works were memorized by scholars, hidden in walls of houses and buried in graves of kings.

Even more losses have occurred since 200 BCE. Of 677 works in the imperial library of 0 CE, only 152 still exist. If destruction of old texts was often based on ideological criteria, so was their preservation. Many scholars rewrote texts, and with them, history. Some scholars seem to have attributed to their predecessors, texts that they themselves wrote.

Most surviving Chinese documents concern kings, presumably because it was kings who maintained libraries and supported scribes. The documents describe two fundamentally different approaches to rule: example setting and instrumental control.

Attracting Subordinates by Setting a Good Example

Before 230 BCE, China was not one nation but many feudal states, with smaller states depending on and subordinate to larger ones. These political structures aligned with clans—which are quite large extended families. Typically, one clan controlled each state, although some clans controlled no states. Also, cities often operated as independent political units.

One consequence was that larger states sought to acquire smaller affiliates. Of course, warfare was a method of gaining affiliates. Wars between states and revolts within them created an ever-changing political system. Another method, more talked about in ancient texts, was for a ruler to display virtuous behavior. For example, here is some advice that Prime Minister Kaou-yaou gave to King Yu around 2200 BCE.[10]

Kaou-yaou said, 'If rulers sincerely try to behave virtuously, they will receive intelligent advice and harmonious support.'

Yu said, 'That sounds right, but explain yourself further.'

Kaou-yaou replied, 'If rulers attend carefully to their personal improvement, with concern for the long-term, they will be able to show unselfish benevolence and to draw perceptive distinctions among the people in their service. Then, all intelligent people will exert themselves to serve the rulers; and through what is near, the rulers will be able to influence what is distant.' Yu acknowledged the wisdom of these admirable words, 'How true!'

Kaou-yaou counseled, 'Success as a ruler arises from knowing people and keeping people satisfied.'

Yu sighed, 'Alas, even King Yao found it difficult to attain both of these goals. When rulers know people, the rulers are wise and can assign people to positions that they fit. When rulers keep people satisfied, the rulers are kind and the people cherish them in their hearts. If rulers are both wise and kind, what reason would they have to worry about rebels? what reason to replace bad subordinates? what reason to fear people who have charming words, insinuating styles, and great cunning?'

Some 400 years later, around 1765–1768 BCE, T'ang the Successful led a revolution that made him a king. E Yin served as T'ang's Prime Minister and close advisor. T'ang ruled only twelve years, then two of his sons ruled for a total of seven years. E Yin, who remained extremely powerful, then designated the next king to be T'ang's eldest grandson, T'ae-këa. As the following excerpts show, E Yin thought T'ae-këa needed a lot of guidance.[11]

Around 1746 to 1750 BCE, E Yin offered a sacrifice to the former king [T'ang] and presented the heir to the throne respectfully to his ancestor. . . .

E Yin said, 'Of old, earlier rulers cultivated their virtue earnestly, and so Heaven inflicted no calamities. The spirits of the hills and rivers were all tranquil; and the birds and beasts, the fishes and tortoises, all enjoyed happy environments. But one king failed to follow his ancestors' example, with the result that Heaven sent down calamities, employing the services of King T'ang [to overthrow this evil king]. . . . Our king T'ang brilliantly displayed his distinguished ability. When for oppression, he substituted his high-minded gentleness, the millions of the people gave him their hearts.

'Now your Majesty is entering into the estate left by his virtue. Everything depends on how you begin your reign. To generate love, you must love your relations. To generate respect, you must respect your elders. These feelings arise in the clan and state and they consummate in the realm.

'The former king [T'ang] based his actions on careful attention to the bonds that hold people together: He listened to protests and did not seek to suppress them. He recognized the wisdom of bygone people. When occupying the highest position, he displayed intelligence; when occupying a subordinate position, he displayed loyalty. He allowed others to show their good qualities and did not expect them to have every talent. In governing his own behavior, he was never satisfied.

'It was through these qualities that he came to rule myriad regions. How painstaking was he in these things! He went to great lengths to seek out wise people, whom he expected to be helpful to his descendants and heirs. He defined punishments for wayward officials. . . .

The king would not reflect on these words, or listen to them. On seeing this, E Yin said, 'To develop broad and clear views, the former king meditated in the early morning. He also sought on every side for people of ability and virtue to instruct him and guide his future. Do not frustrate his charge to me and bring on yourself your own overthrow. Be careful to strive for the virtue of self-restraint, and value long-term results. Be like an archer, who looks to see where the arrow is pointing, whether the arrow is aimed properly, and then lets go. Set serious goals for yourself, and follow the ways of your ancestor. If you do so, I will be delighted and be able to show that I have discharged my trust.'

The king was not yet able to change his course. E Yin said to himself, 'This is real unrighteousness, and it is becoming through practice a second nature. I cannot bear to be near such a disobedient fellow. I will build a place in the palace at T'ung, where he can reside quietly near the remains of the former king. This will be a lesson that will keep him from going astray for the rest of his life.' The king went accordingly to the palace at T'ung, and dwelt during the period of mourning.

In the end, [after having been confined for three years,] the king became sincerely virtuous.

Behaving as a Noble Should

One of the most learned people of his time, Confucius had many students during his lifetime and many thousands more since his death. Sayings by Confucius and his main students were collected in a book titled *The Analects*. The book's origin is murky, as the oldest copies date only to around 2 BCE whereas Confucius lived around 500 BCE. *The Analects* was probably compiled long after Confucius' death by his students and their students, and words that it attributes to Confucius probably reflect his students' esteem for him and their own ideas about what he would have said.

Nearly all biographic statements about Confucius were also written long after he died and they include assertions that contradict better established facts, including claims about his having held exalted positions. Reliable sources indicate that Confucius held minor positions in the state of Lu, including inventory clerk for livestock, and that he earned his living partly by tutoring sons of nobles. Most of Confucius' students aspired to become senior officials, and some did so. Confucius himself probably attained his highest rank as Lu's police commissioner around 501 BCE. In that role, he participated in a failed effort to demolish strongholds of three powerful clans. The Duke of Lu seems to have held Confucius responsible for this failure, because shortly afterward, Confucius left Lu unexpectedly and his stated reasons seem trivial. Over thirteen years, Confucius and three students visited the states of Wei, Sung, Ch'en, Ts'ai, and Wei again. However, they left Wei quickly after Confucius gave its duke an untactful response; they traveled through Sung in disguise to avoid harm; and they lived in extreme poverty in Ch'en. In 484 BCE, they returned to Lu, where the Duke appointed Confucius an official of the lowest rank.

Confucius greatly respected and learned from experiences of ancient rulers and their advisors. His sayings echo ancient teachings about attracting followers by ruling well and leading by setting good examples, although he added his own emphases and sentiments. He extended prescriptions that had been formulated for rulers to all nobles. His teachings focus on nobility, his dominant and never-ending theme being that nobles should behave properly, should follow The Way. We use the phrase 'behave as a noble should' to denote this complex idea. Although Confucius saw The Way as a guide to life in general, not to super-visor–subordinate relations as such, some of his sayings speak to these relations. Indeed, *The Analects* affords the main surviving source about the advice that may have been given to government officials other than rulers.

We offer exemplary passages from *The Analects* on three topics: proper behav-ior for nobles, leadership, and superior–subordinate relations.[12]

How a Noble Should Behave

2: 3. Confucius said, 'If you guide people with commands and use punishment to keep them in line, they will avoid serving you and those who do serve you will have no self-respect. If you guide people through proper behavior and regulate them by behaving as a noble should, they will serve you voluntarily and retain their self-respect.'

13: 13. Confucius said, 'People who are able to manage themselves properly should find no difficulty in filling any administrative position. But if people cannot manage themselves properly, how can they hope to manage others properly?'

17: 6. Tzu-chang asked Confucius about noble behavior. Confucius said, 'A leader who would practice five principles could induce noble behavior every-where.' Tzu-chang asked, 'What are these five principles?' Confucius said, 'Re-spect, tolerance, truth, diligence and kindness. People respect one who is respectful; the multitude give support to one who is tolerant; people trust one who speaks truthfully; success comes to one who is diligent; people willingly serve one who is kind.'

Leading

13: 6. Confucius said, 'If a leader behaves as a noble should, all goes well even though the leader gives no orders. But if a leader does not behave as a noble should, people will not even obey when the leader gives orders.'

20: 2. Tzu-chang asked Confucius, 'What must one do to be fit to govern the land?' Confucius said, 'A leader should pay attention to five lovely things and avoid four ugly things.' Tzu-chang asked, 'What are these five lovely things?' Confucius said, 'An effective leader can show generosity without falling into extravagance, can assign people work without arousing resentment, can achieve ambitions without acting selfishly, can feel pride without being arrogant, and can inspire awe without displaying ferocity.'

Tzu-chang asked, 'What do you mean by "show generosity without falling into extravagance"?' Confucius said, 'If a leader gives to people only those advantages that are really advantageous to them, is the leader not showing generosity without falling into extravagance? If a leader assigns to people only those tasks that they can perform well, is the official not assigning work without arousing resentment? If a leader aspires to proper behavior, who can say that the official is selfish? An effective leader, whether dealing with many people or few, with the insignificant or the great, never presumes to slight people. Is not this indeed feeling pride without being arrogant? A properly behaved official wears clothes and hats so elegantly and maintains such a dignified demeanor that people are in awe as soon as they see the official from afar. Is not this inspiring awe without displaying ferocity?'

Tzu-chang asked, 'What are the four ugly things?' Confucius said, 'To put people to death without first having tried to reform them, that is savagery. To demand results without first having given due warning, that is tyranny. To enforce an early deadline after having been tardy in ordering work, that is tormenting. And similarly, to be grudging about letting a person have something that one knows they should have, that is acting like a petty functionary.'

Superiors and Subordinates

3: 18. Confucius said, 'Were anyone to obey all the established procedures when serving a superior, the subordinate would be thought servile.'

3: 19. Duke Ting asked, 'How should a superior use subordinates and how should subordinates serve their superior?' Confucius replied, 'In employing subordinates, a superior should adhere strictly to established procedures. Subordinates should devote themselves sincerely to their superior's service.'

10: 2. At court, when conversing with junior ministers, Confucius was affable; when conversing with senior ministers, he was respectful and courteous. When the ruler was present, his attitude was constant alertness and solemn readiness.

14: 23. Tzu-lu asked him how to serve a superior. Confucius said, 'Don't oppose covertly. Resist overtly.'

Controlling Subordinates Through Laws, Competition, Rewards, and Punishments

Around 350 BCE, the small state of Ch'in began to grow larger and more powerful. At that time, Ch'in's prime minister was Shang Yang, a believer in total control of the populace. Shang Yang's ideas about supervision diverged strikingly from the ancient advice given to kings.[13] For example:

If a ruler employs virtuous officials, the people will place primary importance on their social relations; but if a ruler employs wicked officials, the people will place primary importance on the statutes. The virtuous respond to others and seek agreement; the wicked spy upon others and argue with them. When the virtuous monitor others' behavior, they overlook crimes; when the wicked monitor others' behavior, they punish crimes. In the former case, the people are stronger than the law; in the latter case, the law is stronger than the people. When the people are the stronger, there is lawlessness; when the law is the stronger, the state will be strong. Thus, it is said: 'Governing through good people leads to lawlessness and weakness; governing through wicked people leads to order and strength.'

Shang Yang urged rulers to support laws with rewards, punishments, and ideologies.

Historians credit Shang Yang with initiating the totalitarian rule that enabled Ch'in to dominate the entire civilized world (as ancient Chinese viewed the world). Shang Yang himself believed that he had found a formula for total domination, and by 221 BCE, his state conquered or otherwise seized every state in feudal China. King Ch'eng, who ruled from 246 BCE until 210 BCE, called himself First August Emperor of the Ch'in.

One influence on the First August Emperor was Han Fei Tzu, who admired the works of Shang Yang. The only noble among the renowned Chinese philosophers, Han Fei belonged to the ruling clan in the small and unwealthy state of Han. He was unhappy about his state's condition, but felt he could not present his ideas in person because he stuttered so badly. Therefore, he frequently sent letters of advice to his king. When the king ignored his letters, Han Fei wrote a book. His king also ignored his book.

Although his own king ignored Han Fei's writings, one important ruler did appreciate them—King Ch'eng of Ch'in. When Ch'in attacked Han, the king of Han dispatched Han Fei as a goodwill envoy to Ch'in. However, the suspicious King Ch'eng committed Han Fei to prison, where he committed suicide.

Han Fei wanted to give rulers practical advice about how to strengthen their control and how to remain in power. His ideas differed from traditional ones. He certainly did not intend that his advice should apply to subordinate officials as well as rulers. He never addressed advice to officials, and he told rulers to behave very unlike their subordinates.

Han Fei saw his contribution as expediting adaptation to changing social values and changing economic conditions: 'People of antiquity strove to be known as moral and virtuous. Those of the middle ages struggled to be known as wise and resourceful. People of today fight for the reputation of being vigorous and powerful.' 'People of old made light of goods, not because they were benevolent, but because goods were abundant. People of today quarrel and pillage, not because they are brutish, but because goods are scarce.'

One of Han Fei's themes was pervasive conflict between superiors and subordinates. He advised rulers to distrust subordinates, to conceal their thoughts and intentions, and to inspire fear in their subordinates.[14]

It is said: 'A ruler must not reveal desires; for if a ruler reveals desires, the officials put on facades that please the ruler. A ruler must not reveal personal views, because if a ruler does so, the officials show false faces.' Similarly, it is said: 'If a ruler does away with likes and dislikes, the officials show their true feelings. If a ruler shuns wile and cunning, the officials watch their steps....'
Rulers stand in danger of being undercut in five ways:
    officials can block their rulers' plans,
    officials can control the wealth and resources of the state,

officials can issue any orders they please,
officials can take the credit for doing good deeds, and
officials can build up cliques.

If officials can block rulers, the rulers lose the control. If officials can control the wealth and resources, rulers cannot dispense bounty to others. If officials can issue any orders they please, the rulers lose authority. If officials can take credit for good deeds, the rulers lose the claim to providing benefits. If officials can build up cliques of their own, the rulers lose supporters. Rulers alone should exercise these powers; the powers should never pass into the hands of officials. . . .

To control scheming subordinates, rulers should apply rewards and punishments.

Astute rulers control their officials by means of two handles alone. The two handles are punishment and reward. What do I mean by punishment and reward? To inflict mutilation and death on people is to punish; to bestow honor and favor is to reward.

Officials fear punishments and hope for rewards. Hence, if rulers wield the handles of punishment and reward, officials will fear the rulers' sternness and hope to receive the rulers' generosity. However, the evil officials of this age are different. They would take the handle of punishment from their rulers so they can inflict punishments on people they hate, and they would take the handle of reward from their rulers so they can bestow rewards on people they like. If rulers do not reserve to themselves the power to dispense rewards and punishments and instead allow officials to hand these out, then the people fear the officials while holding the rulers in contempt, and they attend to the officials and turn away from the rulers. This is the calamity that results when rulers yield control of punishments and rewards. . . .

Yet another contributor to Ch'in's rise was Li Ssu, who became its prime minister sometime between 219 BCE and 213 BCE and who was as ruthless as his Emperor. On Li Ssu's advice, the First August Emperor abolished the feudal nobility, replaced the feudal states with administrative districts, burned almost all books, standardized weights and measures and writing, built better roads, relocated masses of people, and began building the Great Wall.

Li Ssu had no use for rewards and his approach to punishment made Han Fei's seem gentle. Whereas Han Fei said, 'astute rulers never use wise officials or virtuous people for selfish purposes', Li Ssu told his emperor to use his power for personal enjoyment:[15]

Astute rulers should be able to fulfill their duties and use the technique of punishment. Under threat of punishment, officials have to exert their abilities in utmost devotion to their rulers. When rulers define their statuses relative to officials unmistakably, and they make clear the duties of subordinates to superiors, then no one in their empires, whether worthy or unworthy, will dare do otherwise than exert their strength and fulfill their duties in devotion to their rulers. Thus, rulers can control their empires single-handedly and cannot be controlled by anyone. As a result, rulers can enjoy themselves to the utmost. How can talented and astute rulers afford not to pay attention to this point? . . .

When rulers use punishment effectively, they have no corrupt officials. When rulers have no corrupt officials, their empires are peaceful. When their empires are peaceful, the rulers are venerated and exalted. When rulers are venerated and exalted, they are using punishment without fail. When rulers use punishment without fail, they obtain what they seek. When they obtain what they seek, their states are wealthy. When their states are wealthy, the rulers enjoy abundant pleasures. Therefore, when rulers apply the skill of punishment, they get everything they desire. The officials and the people are so busy trying to correct their faults that they have no time to devise trouble.

5. STRUGGLING WITH INCONSISTENCIES

Even the most ancient documents show awareness of difficult relations between superiors and subordinates. Superiors distrust their subordinates, and subordinates distrust their superiors, yet each has to depend on the other.

One result has been ambivalence. Mesopotamians, for instance, viewed leadership as essential to effective work and leadership skills as distinctive to particular people, but they also joked that rulers' are unable to support themselves. The Egyptian Instruction of Merikare oscillates between harshness and kindness, between idealism and pragmatism. Chinese writer Han Fei advised rulers not to trust their subordinates and yet to rely on them to solve problems.

Managers who rise to high positions need to recognize that their subordinates are almost certain to complain and make jokes about their actions and decisions. Fault finding and ridicule are pervasive responses to control by someone else. It is clear that subordinates do not always appreciate their superiors' contributions to organizations and societies. Even when subordinates do acknowledge their superiors' contributions, they also see deficiencies.

Quite a few writers sought to lessen abrasions between superiors and subordinates. They urged superiors to restrain their exercise of power, to focus on behaving properly themselves, to be just and considerate, and to cultivate support of the populace over the long run. They urged subordinates to accept subordination, to demonstrate respect, to act honestly and forthrightly, and to pursue their superiors' best interests rather than their own. On the other hand, other writers advised superiors to be wary of their subordinates, to deal harshly with dissenters and rebels, to pit subordinates against one another, and to manipulate subordinates by means of rewards and punishments. Tales of violent insurrection show that subordinates did not always accept control from above. Although it may have been King Ch'eng's harsh methods that enabled him to unite China, his empire survived him for only four years.

Superiors' control of armed force enabled them to seize property, to alter people's statuses, and even to inflict death, so their subjects had reason to fear them and to avoid actions that might arouse superiors' displeasure. Mesopotamians enlisted gods to help them protest a ruler's actions. Egyptian schoolboys were taught to be submissive, circumspect, and wary. Although low-level personnel could appeal directly to Egypt's Vizier, they did so in a stylized fashion that portrayed their complaints as afterthoughts. Confucius urged subordinates to devote themselves to their superiors. One ancient Chinese legend explains that a powerful Prime Minister confined his young king in an isolated palace for three years, until 'the king became sincerely virtuous' and followed the Prime Minister's advice.

Superiors' powers generally increased with their hierarchical positions, but so did the political pressures with which they had to contend. Almost all the documents authored by rulers talk about the need for political support from the populace at large and especially from nobles. Many documents also say that rulers need support of gods. For instance, Prime Minister Kaou-yaou told his king: 'Heaven hears and sees as our people hear and see. Heaven discerningly judges our actions and displays its terrors, as our people discerningly judge our actions and can awe us: Such strong connections there are between Heaven and earth! How careful ought to be the rulers of the earth!'

Since differing political interests may make contrary claims, remaining in control required an ability to make the inconsistent less so. The Egyptians and Chinese used schooling to inculcate shared values and acceptance of existing social hierarchies. Such schooling focused on the sons of nobles. However, the Chinese records do contain examples of superiors seeking out unusually able commoners and promoting them to high positions. Indeed, one of the oldest Chinese stories tells how King Yao sought out 'one of the lowly and insignificant who deserves to rise higher' and ultimately made this man his successor.

The roles of superiors and subordinates are complex ones. It is often unclear what actions one should take, what words one should say, what emotions one should feel. All strategies for control entail advantages and disadvantages, as do all strategies for subordination. Clearly, ancient people saw these trade-offs and recognized their complexity. A good example is Confucius' attempt to state the essence of successful leadership. He told leaders to try to see issues from their subordinates' viewpoints and to beware of traps created by power:

13: 15. Duke Ting asked, 'Is there a single phrase that summarizes what makes a ruler succeed?' Confucius replied, 'No single phrase could ever do that. But there is a phrase that comes near to it. It is the saying: "It is hard to be a ruler and not easy to be a subject either." If a ruler really understands the difficulties of rule, would not this understanding be almost enough to produce success?'

Duke Ting asked, 'Is there a single phrase that summarizes what makes a ruler fail?' Confucius replied, 'No single phrase could ever do that. But there is a phrase that comes near to it. It is the saying: "The greatest pleasure in being a ruler is that one can say whatever one chooses and no one dares to disagree." If what a ruler says is good, it is of course all right that the ruler should be obeyed. But if what a ruler says is bad, would not obedience be almost enough to produce failure?'

NOTES

1. Our rendition of Atrahasis's story is based on translations by Ferry (1992), Foster (1993), Gardner and Maier (1984), Heidel (1970), Kovacs (1985), Lambert and Millard (1969), Leonard (1934), and Tigay (1982).) Because translations of ancient works differ, the quotations in this chapter are our own interpretations compiled from several translations. These interpretations rely more strongly on translations with

better scholarly documentation, and they use terminology of the late twentieth century.

2. Analysts may produce quite different estimates of the dates of ancient documents. Thus, most dates are approximate and some are very inexact. 253 BCE might mean 'between 265 and 240 BCE' or 'between 300 and 200 BCE'.

3. These interpretations of sayings integrate translations by Foster (1993), Gordon (1968), and Lambert (1960).

4. This interpretation of the protest relies on translations by Foster (1993) and Lambert (1960).

5. These excerpts from Ptahhotep's Instruction are based on translations by Erman and Blackman (1927), Faulkner, Wente, and Simpson (1972), Foster (1992), and Lichtheim (1973). The numbers preceding paragraphs indicate their positions in the Instruction.

6. These excerpts from the Instruction of Amenemope are based on translations made by Faulkner, Wente, and Simpson (1972) and Griffith (1926). The numbers preceding paragraphs indicate their positions in the Instruction.

7. These excerpts from the Instruction of Merikare are based on translations made by Erman and Blackman (1927), Faulkner, Wente, and Simpson (1972), Foster (1992), and Lichtheim (1973).

8. These excerpts from the Instruction of Amenemhet derive from translations made by Breasted (1962), Erman and Blackman (1927), Faulkner, Wente, and Simpson (1972), Foster (1992), and Lichtheim (1973).

9. These letters interpret translations by Wente (1990).

10. This version of Kaou-yaou's advice interprets a translation by Legge (1865).

11. This interpretation of E Yin's advice builds upon translations by Legge (1865) and Wu (1928).

12. These interpretations of *The Analects* integrate translations by Chan (1963), Lau (1979), Pound (1951), and Waley (1938). The numbers preceding paragraphs designate their positions in *The Analects*.

13. This rendition of Shang Yang's writings is based on Duyvendak's (1928) translation.

14. This version of Han Fei's writings is based on translations by Liao (1959), Peerenboom (1993), and Watson (1963).

15. This interpretation of Li Ssu's writings is based on a translation by de Bary, Chan, and Watson (1960).

19

Ancient Chinese Theories of Control

Coauthored with Violina P. Rindova

1. EXPLORING BCE

This chapter grows out of efforts to find and make sense of texts describing managerial practices Before the Christian Era (BCE). We undertook this project, not to prove any hypotheses or to justify a theory, but to find out what data exist about ancient management and organizations. How did ancient management practices differ from modern ones? How were they similar to modern practices? How did ancient organizations organize?

There are many reasons why the ancient management practices should have differed greatly from contemporary ones. Since the people of 4,000 years ago faced different economic and technological challenges than contemporary people, they understood their worlds differently. Travel was difficult, communication slow and error-filled, timekeeping very imprecise (Loewe 1968). The ancient social systems about which data exist—states, governments, armies—were very different from their modern counterparts, and very few data exist about ancient business organizations (Swann 1950). Perhaps, some modern ideas about managing are recent inventions, or at least inventions of the last 2,000 years.

Whether or not people of 4,000 years ago faced different problems than do people today, they evidently had as much intellectual ability as people today. Insofar as evolution has produced changes, the more recent changes have been too slow to produce results in a period as short as 4,000 years. After reviewing the paleoanthropological evidence, Cartmill, Pilbeam, and Isaac (1986: 419) concluded:

For the past 40,000 years, most hominids have been characterized by modern human morphology and by archeological traits demonstrating characteristically modern behavior patterns and potential. Unprecedented increases in the amount and rate of technological innovation accompany the appearance of anatomically modern hominids in Europe at the beginning of this period, and similar transitions are known, although less well documented in the archeological record, from other parts of the world. These and related facts—for instance, the first appearance of representational art at or soon after this horizon—suggest an enhanced capacity for the manipulation of symbols.

Although capable of diverse behaviors, people may have consistent behavioral tendencies—such as reactions to reward and punishment, or feelings about hierarchical domination—that would cause ancient management practices to face the same basic issues as modern ones. Similarly, some properties of human activities—such as coordination, division of labor, exchange, and leadership—may be so generic that they occur in all societies (Becker and Barnes 1961; Udy 1959*b*). Finally, since modern managers and modern organizations face very diverse technologies and cultures, there could be considerable overlap between the distributions of ancient and modern practices.

We have examined ancient texts from the areas now called China, Egypt, Greece, India, Israel, Iraq, and Italy (Rindova and Starbuck 1997). This chapter concentrates on China because China offers more texts that go back several thousand years, the Chinese texts are more elaborate, and they address issues regarding more complex political structures. However, we believe we understand ancient Chinese texts better because we also studied ancient texts from other areas. For example, the Nile River gave Egypt comparatively fast and reliable transportation, which enabled its rulers to establish and maintain simple, centralized hierarchies (Kees 1961). In contrast, until 250 BCE, China consisted of many states with differing sizes and resources (Bodde 1986; Ebrey 1981); these provide a loose parallel to modern large corporations with many divisions and subsidiaries. Between 250 BCE and 206 BCE, China became a centralized empire that exemplified tight authoritarian control, such as one also finds in some modern firms (Bodde 1986).

As much as possible, we are trying to learn what managers *did* do rather than what scholars advised them to do. Consequently, this article does not encompass texts by philosophers such as Mo Tzu and Lao Tzu, highly regarded as thinkers, because we have been unable to find evidence that actual practices followed their ideas until after the Christian Era (CE) began. Nearly all of our sources are texts created by practicing managers for the instruction of practicing managers, so they are didactic and prescriptive and sometimes pragmatic. These texts are very unlike modern empirical descriptions written by social scientists.

This chapter focuses on ideas about managerial control—relations between superiors and subordinates, leadership, socialization, rules, procedures, rewards, and punishments. It touches on political history, the feudal system, and the evolution of formal roles only insofar as these topics may relate to managerial practices. To help readers understand ancient practices, the chapter occasionally draws parallels to modern theories or research about management in Europe and North America. However, these citations are merely examples, as one chapter cannot realistically encompass both modern and ancient.

The first section discusses the evidence and our interpretations of it. Evidence is scarce and biased toward the interests of rulers and senior officials. Because translations sometimes differ significantly, the quotations appearing in this chapter are our interpretations. The second section recounts how the very ancient Chinese conceived the interdependencies between micro and macro social relations, how interpersonal dyads relate to organizations and states. Because managerial practices shifted dramatically around 350–200 BCE, the third section focuses on the control practices before this shift. After reviewing concepts about leadership, it describes part of a bureaucracy that existed around 1100 BCE. Finally, it discusses recommendations for how subordinates ought to behave.

The fourth section turns to the very different control practices guiding the creation of the Empire around 350–200 BCE. This period emphasized tight control from the top, achieved through laws, rewards, and punishments. The final section summarizes the chapter.

2. THE EVIDENCE

We started with anthologies of ancient Chinese texts and books about Chinese history before 0 BCE, of which there are not many. As Loewe (1986: 3) remarked in volume 1 of *The Cambridge History of China*:

> In general, the historian of this period has perforce to rely almost exclusively on sources compiled in the peculiarly Chinese form of the Standard History (*cheng-shih*). Only exceptionally is it possible to call on other written evidence with which to identify a document on which the compilers of these works drew, to check the accuracy of their statements of fact, to examine questions of authenticity, or to balance their opinions and judgments.

These initial sources pointed to works that discuss topics such as management, administration, government, business, economics, politics, and law. Then we searched the card catalogs of the Library of Congress and the Research Libraries (RLIN) for translations of the original source documents, and borrowed as many of these as possible. Ultimately, we were able to examine several thousand documents in several hundred books. The references cited in this chapter comprise only a minute fraction of the reading we did over three years. Table 19.1 associates dates with the main sources quoted.

Looking into the distant past is somewhat like looking at foreign cultures, but it is also more difficult and treacherous. We have depended upon modern scholars of Chinese history and philosophy who publish in English, and these scholars emphasize the texts that they regard as most important or most interesting. No writing survives from before 3000 BCE. The ancient methods of writing leave much ambiguous, perhaps because laborious writing processes led people to write fewer words, and one cannot interact with the original authors to clarify

Table 19.1. Dates associated with key sources

2500–1121 BCE	'The Great Plan'	Treatise
Around 2200 BCE	Kaou-yaou	Prime minister to King Yu
After 1750 BCE	E Yin	Prime minister to a ruler and regent to a young ruler-to-be
Soon after 1100 BCE	King Ching	Ruler
Around 1100 BCE	'The Officials of Chou'	Government document
Around 500 BCE	Confucius	Official and scholar
Around 350 BCE	Shang Yang	Prime minister
250–233 BCE	Han Fei Tzu	Scholar
246–216 BCE	Li Ssu	Official and prime minister

what they meant or what assumptions they were making. The surviving texts represent only a small fraction of what once existed, and they are nonrandom samples. The catalog of the imperial library of 0 BCE lists 677 works, of which only 152 still exist (Bodde 1986). The destruction of old texts has often been selective, based on ideological criteria. Some scholars appear to have attributed to their predecessors, texts that they themselves wrote. Many scholars rewrote texts, and with them, history. In 212 BCE, the first Chinese emperor burned nearly all the extant books and murdered nearly all the literate people. Intending to end the old feudal system and to replace it with a new order, he sought to erase the traditions that had supported the old ways. But some works did survive this destruction. One scholar hid 29 important works; other works were found hidden in the walls of houses or in the graves of kings.

The dates and authors associated with the very oldest texts can be debated because authors sometimes sought to give their own words more authority by attributing them to historical figures. Since old works were recopied to preserve them, it is impossible to sort out older from newer contributions. The dates we report are generally the ones in the texts themselves.

Not surprisingly, the oldest texts are speeches by rulers or advice addressed to rulers. However, the advice offered to rulers generally applied to their officials as well. We have found no texts used for educating future administrators. This is strange, given that the Chinese developed schools for training future officials and procedures for assigning graduates to appropriate administrative positions.

Despite the fragmentary evidence, this project has yielded valuable findings. First, we have found some texts that have previously been unknown to management scholars. This chapter discusses one document that has never before been translated into English, and that went out of print in other languages over 140 years ago. This document, 'The Officials of Chou', shows that ancient organizations could be complex, well defined, and bureaucratic, in contrast to beliefs that complex bureaucracies are a modern phenomenon. Second, the records show that ancient people had interesting and diverse theories about human behavior and management. These theories are simultaneously very like the theories of today and very unlike them. Some managerial philosophies popular today have clear antecedents running back 4,000 years. Third, in a few instances, ancient texts seem more insightful and useful than today's textbooks on related topics. For instance, many ancient Chinese asserted that holding a position of authority obliges one to work on improving one's personal qualities.

Our Interpretations

After examining documents from several societies, we have inferred that ancient forms of writing—including Chinese ideograms—leave much ambiguous. Contrasting translations indicate that pronouns often have unclear antecedents; active verbs are often indistinguishable from passive verbs; the subjects of sentences are often implicit, as may be the verbs. Different translations may bear weak resemblance to each other, and they occasionally make no sense. Where two translations do say very much the same things, it typically turns out that one translator looked at the work of a predecessor. The oldest texts rarely survive in their original forms: what survive are copies made to replace rotting forerunners. There are often places in which successive copyists appear to have compounded their predecessors' errors. The copyists sometimes modernized the texts as well as copied them.

The quotations in this chapter are our own interpretations, compiled by comparing several translations. Although we did consider translations into other languages, all but one of the translations that we used are in English because we intended our interpretations to be in English. After discovering that translations differ, sometimes differ greatly, we concluded that any single source may be unreliable. So whenever possible, we compared several translations and constructed composite 'interpretations'. One very helpful source has been a book in which Karlgren (1970) compared all commentaries in Chinese and translations to other languages of the oldest documents.

Our primary goal was to develop interpretations that would make the best sense to late-twentieth-century readers. The many differences among translations reflect, among other things, the immense differences between languages, historical periods, societies, beliefs and expectations, and cultures. Where translations diverged, we read footnotes, read the materials to which footnotes referred, and made judgments about which words made better sense in terms of management or administration. Of course, some sources elicited more confidence than others because of their careful scholarship; in particular, we have relied more heavily on the translations and documentation by Karlgren (1950) and Legge (1865). Table 19.2 illustrates our interpretation process, showing three translations of a passage from Confucius, our interpretation of this passage, and our rationale for this interpretation.

Our interpretations are integral parts of the text of this chapter, not merely quotations to illustrate points made in the text. Were they quotations, we would have to explain what the quotations mean to us. But instead, we have worded these interpretations carefully to express what we think they mean. In effect, the interpretations often contain points we would otherwise make in our text.

To make it easier to see the relevance of old ideas to today, our interpretations depart from the original sources in two ways. First, the ancient texts very rarely speak of women holding positions with formal authority. Since this is no longer the case, we have removed references to gender, changing man to person, men to people, king to ruler, and so forth. These changes have sometimes entailed using plural nouns rather than singular ones. The changes have not, however, altered the texts in essence because (*a*) men created the texts for consumption by men and (*b*) a reader can convert our interpretations by substituting man for person, king for ruler, and so on.

Second, our interpretations depart from the original sources in the titles used to denote managers. The original works used Chinese titles that most translators have translated as king, prince, emperor, or duke. Even within the context of one geographic area, a term such as 'king' has different meanings at different times

Table 19.2. Three translations and our interpretation

Lau (1979: 74): The Master said, 'If a man is able to govern a state by observing the rites and showing deference, what difficulties will he have in public life? If he is unable to govern a state by observing the rites and showing deference, what good are the rites to him?'

Pound (1951: 207): He said: 'Can with ceremony and politeness manage a state, what difficulty will he have; unable to govern a state with ceremonies and courtesy, what ordered enlightenment has he?'

Waley (1938: 104): The Master said, 'If it is really possible to govern countries by ritual and yielding, there is no more to be said. But if it is not really possible, of what use is ritual?' (The saying can be paraphrased as follows: If I and my followers are right in saying that countries can be governed solely by correct carrying out of ritual and its basic principle of 'giving way to others', there is obviously no case to be made out for any other form of government. If on the other hand we are wrong, then ritual is useless. To say, as people often do, that ritual is all very well so long as it is not used as an instrument of the government, is wholly to misunderstand the purpose of ritual.)

Our interpretation: Confucius said, 'If an official can follow procedures and be considerate, what other abilities could the official possibly need? But if an official cannot operate in this way, what use has the official for procedures?'

Note: Rites, ceremonies, or rituals may have included religious ceremonies. In 500 BCE, a ruler of a state would very likely have seen religious ceremonies as intertwined with governmental activities. However, rites, ceremonies, or rituals are not limited to religious ceremonies and etiquette associated with differences in social ranks. Indeed, Confucius placed great importance on ceremonies of all sorts. Thus, this quotation probably embraces all types of formalized practices, whether traditional or established by leaders. The modern term denoting the whole range of formalized practices is 'procedures'. Modern managers do not use the terms rites, ceremonies, or rituals to denote diverse behaviors; if they use these terms, it is solely to denote symbolic activities.

The other key element in this saying is translated as showing deference, politeness, and courtesy; yielding; or giving way to others. Courtesy or politeness may entail giving way to others, but it is possible to be polite without giving way to others. Conversely, yielding need not involve politeness. We chose 'consideration' as expressing this compound Confucian idea, partly because the Ohio State leadership studies have given 'consideration' special significance.

that make it difficult for people from one period to understand the viewpoints of people from another period. For example, a fourteenth-century English duke had quite different prerogatives and status from a twentieth-century English duke. When such terms not only cross thousands of years but large geographic and cultural distances, there is need for extreme caution. Therefore, we have replaced specific titles with generic ones such as commander, leader, official, and ruler. Karlgren (1950), one of the most thorough twentieth-century scholars, made similar word choices. Of course, we have retained the original terminology where it is crucial to the meaning.

3. SOCIAL RELATIONS

We use the term social relations to encompass both social structures and the interactions that occur within and between them. Social structures determine the available and most effective channels of managerial control; they set boundaries on communities. Social processes communicate norms and values, define duties and proper behavior, and administer rewards and punishments. Social relations provide contexts in which individuals may pursue their self-interest and personal objectives.

Kaou-yaou, a prime minister around 2200 BCE, made one of the rare, very ancient statements about social relations. He said,

The work is Heaven's, but people carry it out. Heaven has defined social arrangements with their respective duties: It is up to us to fulfill those five duties, and so we have five modes of charitable conduct. Heaven has defined social ranks with their respective ceremonies: It is up to us to observe those five ceremonies, and so we practice them regularly. When ruler and ministers show a common reverence and respect for these [duties and ceremonies], do they not harmonize the moral nature of the people? (Karlgren 1950, 1970; Legge 1865)

Kaou-yaou distinguished between micro and macro social relations. His social arrangements focus on small social units that are more concrete—essentially dyads; they require people to fulfill duties: that is, to behave in ways that produce results. For the ancient Chinese, the number five both designated a specific quantity and symbolized 'some' or 'several'. Thus, Kaou-yaou may have been speaking of several duties, several modes of charitable conduct, several ceremonies, and so forth. But the ancient Chinese did conventionally identify five social arrangements: ruler and subject, husband and wife, parent and child, elder and younger sibling, and friend and friend. It is unclear whether these were regarded as exhaustive.

Kaou-yaou's social ranks focus on large social units that are more abstract— essentially social strata in the feudal system. These call for ceremonial etiquette, behaviors that may have no immediate, tangible results. As Kaou-yaou indicated, each social arrangement entailed corresponding duties, and each social rank called for corresponding ceremonial etiquette. It seems quite improbable that Kaou-yaou believed there should be no ceremonial etiquette in social arrangements such as ruler–subject or husband–wife; it also seems improbable that Kaou-yaou believed there should be no duties between social ranks. Hence, Kaou-yaou was describing continuous variables rather than dichotomous ones.

Kaou-yaou also pointed to the usefulness of duties and ceremonial etiquette as means to increase social integration (to harmonize the moral nature of the people). This emphasis may reflect the fragmentation of power across Chinese feudal society (Bodde 1986; Ebrey 1981). Rebels overthrew several kings, and neighboring states often waged wars. Kaou-yaou made no mention of military force: As he portrayed it, social control was to be achieved through moral leadership, adherence to tradition, and capable, sincere government.

Kaou-yaou's view differs from contemporary Western views in placing the ruler-and-subject relation in the same cognitive domain with husband-and-wife and friend-and-friend. Although contemporary categories portray ruler-and-subject as a formalized hierarchical role relation, they portray husband-and-wife and friend-and-friend as egalitarian personal relations. Indeed, each of Kaou-yaou's five relations, with the disputable exception of friend-and-friend, expresses a distinct inequality. Ruler was superior to subject, husband was superior to wife, parent was superior to child, elder sibling was superior to younger. Thus, social hierarchy pervaded micro social relations in ancient China.

Five hundred years later, another prime minister, E. Yin, continued to emphasize the importance of micro relations. He advised his ruler to make them the foundation for political structures.

To generate love, you must love your relations. To generate respect, you must respect your elders. These feelings arise in the clan and state and they consummate in the kingdom. The former king (whom E Yin admired) based his actions on careful attention to the bonds that hold people together. (Legge 1865; Wu 1928)

In saying macro relations rest upon micro ones, E. Yin was participating in an ongoing debate that has continued to the present day. For example, Durkheim said that societies derive their cohesion and shared values from primary groups such as families, whereas Marx said that general societal properties strongly influence the relations between individuals and groups (Alexander 1988). Dreeben's (1968) analysis of schooling affords a more recent example of thinking similar to E. Yin's. Dreeben argued that schools' main function is to prepare people to behave appropriately as citizens and workers. They do this, he said, by progressively generalizing the norms and 'principles of conduct' that children have learned through family life.

4. MANAGERIAL CONTROL BEFORE UNIFICATION—FROM 2300 BCE to 250 BCE

The 2000 years from 2300 BCE to 350 BCE were turbulent ones. China was composed of many states that often attacked each other. The bronze age gave way to the iron age. Improvements in agriculture fostered population growth and urbanization. Nevertheless, according to the surviving texts, the Chinese ideas about management supposedly remained rather consistent throughout this period. Today, no one can determine whether this consistency existed at the time or it arose through later revisions of history.

The traditional ideas about management generally emphasized managers' personal virtues and self-development, moral leadership, and achieving social harmony. The first two subsections outline two theories of leadership. The first of these prescribes both tight and loose managerial control, saying that an effective ruler should behave in different ways in different situations. The second theory seems to say that managers can gain effectiveness by consistently setting good examples. The third subsection surveys some of the managerial controls prescribed for a prime minister. This description shows the sophistication of the ancient Chinese grasp of control options and of bureaucratic organization. The last subsection summarizes a few prescriptions for subordinate officials.

Leadership Styles: A Contingency Approach

'The Great Plan' is a document that combines astrology, moral principles, physics, politics, and religion. A mixture of ideas from various eras, the text itself mentions 1121 BCE but includes passages that scholars judge to be older than 2200 BCE. One passage states a contingency theory of leadership. The ambiguities of ancient writing have led experts to make two interpretations of this passage. One interpretation focuses on different types of subordinates:

The three virtues are rules, firmness, and gentleness. Spell out rules for peaceful people; deal firmly with violent and offensive people; deal gently with amenable and friendly people. Employ firm supervision with those who shirk or lack initiative, gentle supervision with those who are distinguished by their talents and good dispositions. (Karlgren 1950, 1970)

This interpretation advises managers to consider two dimensions of people—their attitudes toward social order and their attitudes toward work.

This interpretation of 'The Great Plan' articulates a prescriptive theory about how leaders should behave that loosely resembles the leader's side of Liden and Graen's descriptive Vertical Dyad Linkage model. Liden and Graen (1980) said leaders reward subordinates who show commitment and expend a lot of effort by showing consideration, trusting them and giving them information. Toward other subordinates, leaders act impersonally and rigidly.

A second interpretation of 'The Great Plan' focuses on different situations:

The three virtues are correct procedure, strong management, and mild management. Adhere to correct procedure in situations (times) of peace and tranquillity; use strong management in situations of violence and disorder; apply mild management in situations of harmony and order. Employ strong supervision with people who lack initiative, mild supervision with the honorable and intelligent. (Chan 1963; Karlgren 1970; Legge 1865)

This interpretation advises managers to consider two kinds of contingencies—the social context and the people who are being supervised.

Some modern writers credit Fiedler with having developed the contingency model of leadership (Fiedler 1967; Ivancevich and Matteson 1993; Luthans 1995). Fiedler distinguishes between task-directed and human-relations-directed leadership styles, arguing that leadership styles should match 'situational favorableness'. Situational favorableness combines leader–member relationship, degree of task structure, and a leader's formal authority. Table 19.3 compares 'The Great Plan's' situational interpretation with Fiedler's theory. His task-directed and human-relations-directed styles are not very different from the strong and mild styles in 'The Great Plan'. As we interpret 'The Great Plan', Fiedler's very unfavorable situations resemble situations of violence and disorder because these are times of low trust in leaders, low authority and power of leaders, and changing tasks. Fiedler's very favorable situations resemble situations of peace and tranquillity because the opposite conditions hold. Fiedler's moderately favorable situations resemble situations of harmony and order because these are situations of controlled moderate change that does not disrupt political leadership.

Table 19.3. Two theories of leadership: 'The Great Plan' versus Fiedler

Situation	'The Great Plan's' style	Fiedler's style
Very unfavorable Violence and disorder	Strong	Task-directed
Moderately favorable Harmony and order	Mild	Human-relations-directed
Very favorable Peace and tranquillity	Correct procedure	Task-directed

Both theories take account of the same kinds of contingencies. They differ in their prescriptions for one type of situation. Fiedler recommends that leaders in very favorable situations use a task-directed style. 'The Great Plan' recommends that leaders in periods of peace and tranquillity depersonalize their leadership and rely on correct procedures. According to 'The Great Plan,' Fiedler's prescription would lead superiors to overmanage.

Leadership Styles: Leading by Example

The older texts emphasized the importance of rulers' improving themselves and leading by example rather than giving instructions to subordinates or controlling them directly. They also emphasized that retaining one's position as a ruler depends on satisfying the populace. Consider, for instance, a conversation between prime minister Kaou-yaou and his ruler, Yu:

Kaou-yaou said, 'If rulers sincerely try to behave virtuously, they will receive intelligent advice and harmonious support.'

Yu said, 'That sounds right, but explain yourself further.'

Kaou-yaou replied, 'If rulers attend carefully to their personal improvement, with concern for the long-term, they will be able to show unselfish benevolence and to draw perceptive distinctions among people. Then, all intelligent people will exert themselves to serve their rulers; and through what is near, the rulers will be able to influence what is distant.'

Yu acknowledged the wisdom of these admirable words, 'How true!'

Kaou-yaou counseled, 'Success as a ruler arises from knowing people and keeping people satisfied.'

Yu sighed, 'Alas, even King Yao found it difficult to do both of these. When rulers know people, the rulers are wise and can assign people to positions that they fit. When rulers keep people satisfied, the rulers are kind and the people cherish them in their hearts. If rulers are both wise and kind, what reason would they have to worry about rebels? what reason to replace bad subordinates? what reason to fear people who have charming words, insinuating appearance, and great cunning?' (Karlgren 1950, 1970; Legge 1865)

This approach to leadership seems to have suited the social system and existing technologies. Until 1100 BCE, China's clans were rather loosely connected; then warfare, revolt, and conquest began to create hierarchical relations among clans.

However, clans continued to control lands, wealth, and many administrative positions. Because there were several strong clans with their own armies, some clans could limit a ruler's power to enforce orders. Indeed, several rulers faced revolts that overthrew them, and the usurpers declared that they had acted because the former rulers had been behaving improperly (Legge 1865). Higher-level rulers had to delegate much control because transport and communication were slow and difficult; rulers had trouble merely finding out what was happening in distant lands.

E Yin also pointed out ways to elicit support from the populace, ways to make societies more cohesive, and requisites of good leadership. He devoted special attention to the need for powerful leaders to consider subordinates' viewpoints. In doing so, he expressed refined ideas about cognition.

Do not slight the concerns of the people: Think of their difficulties. Do not yield to a feeling of ease on your throne: Think of its perils. Be careful to think about the end at the beginning. When you hear words against which your mind sets itself, you must inquire whether these words are not right. When you hear words that agree with your own thinking, you must ask whether these words are not wrong. What attainment can be made without anxious thought? What achievement can be made without earnest effort? (Legge 1865; Wu 1928)

Seventeen hundred years later, Confucius voiced similar ideas to those of Kaou-yaou and E Yin. One of the most learned people of his time, and one of the most honored philosophers of all time, Confucius exerted little influence on manager-ial practices during his lifetime (Lau 1979). However, Confucian philosophy became one of two influential viewpoints between 206 BCE and 220 CE. Then, following 1000 CE, Confucianism began to gain renewed prominence. Confu-cius's ideas, and implicitly the ancient ideas he so respected, continue to influence managerial behaviors today, primarily in China, Korea, Japan, and Vietnam.

Confucius held minor positions in the state of Lu, including inventory clerk for livestock and police commissioner, and he earned his living partly by tutoring the sons of nobles. Most of Confucius's students aspired to become senior officials, and some did so.

Several hundred years after his death, Confucian scholars wrote that Confucius had gone through the Chou dynasty's royal library, discarding worthless texts and recopying valuable ones. Scholars have cited this editing to explain the strong convergence between Confucius's ideas and those of the ancients. However, since there were about 170 states at that time, Chou's was probably not the only library that held ancient texts. Also, the best-documented evidence indicates that Con-fucius never visited the state of Chou (Lau 1979: Appendix I). So this is probably a myth.

Confucius greatly respected and drew lessons from the experiences of ancient rulers and their advisors. His sayings echo the ancient teachings about attracting followers by ruling well, not abusing power, using power considerately, providing moral government, and leading by setting good examples. More than the an-cients, he advocated activist rule aimed at doing good for the populace. He focused his teachings on the nobility. The following quotations exemplify Confucius's approach to ruling. The first statement says that if leaders behave properly themselves, their followers will also behave properly:

Chi K'ang-tzu asked Confucius about the art of leadership. Confucius said, 'Leadership is a matter of correctness. If you lead by going down a correct path yourself, who will dare to take an incorrect one?' (Chan 1963; Lau 1979; Pound 1951; Waley 1938)

The following conversation again emphasizes proper behavior, pointing out that rulers should consider their subjects' viewpoints and that obedience as such should not be a ruler's goal:

Duke Ting asked, 'Is there a single phrase that summarizes what makes a ruler succeed?' Confucius replied, 'No single phrase could ever do that. But there is a phrase that comes near to it. It is the saying: "It is hard to be a ruler and not easy to be a subject either." If a ruler really understands the difficulties of rule, would not this understanding be almost enough to produce success?'

Duke Ting asked, 'Is there a single phrase that summarizes what makes a ruler fail?' Confucius replied, 'No single phrase could ever do that. But there is a phrase that comes near to it. It is the saying: "The greatest pleasure in being a ruler is that one can say whatever one chooses and no one dares to disagree." If what a ruler says is good, it is of course all right that the ruler should be obeyed. But if what a ruler says is bad, would not obedience be almost enough to produce failure?' (Chan 1963; Lau 1979; Pound 1951; Waley 1938)

The traditional Chinese ideas about leadership resemble both contemporary 'transformational leadership' and 'charismatic leadership'. Table 19.4 compares the traditional Chinese ideas about leadership with one contemporary characterization—Tichy and Devanna's (1986) version of 'transformational leadership'. Tichy and Devanna's framework offers both similarities and striking differences from the Chinese ideas. In particular, Tichy and Devanna argued that their framework describes effective change agents, whereas the ancient Chinese did not seek change as such. On the one hand, the rulers wanted to expand their kingdoms and to avoid rebellion. On the other hand, they used the past as a vision about the future that they should seek. It is unclear to what degree the actual past shaped visions of the future and to what degree visions of the future shaped partly mythical stories about past events.

Although Table 19.4 does show many similarities, it seems more useful to portray the Chinese model as another alternative—moral leadership. Moral leadership combines charisma with ideology. It aims to attract voluntary followers, who join because of both the leader's very unusual overall excellence and the leader's moral uprightness.

Control of and through Bureaucracy

Written around 1100 BCE, 'The Officials of Chou' was composed at the behest of either King Ching of Chou or the Duke of Chou, who served as Regent during

Table 19.4. Comparison of traditional Chinese leadership values with the transformational leader

The transformational leader (Tichy and Devanna 1986)	Statements by Kaou-yaou, E Yin, King Ching, and Confucius
They identify themselves as change agents.	Kaou-yaou: . . . ingenuity in management combined with reverence for tradition. 　　E Yin: Heaven took notice of his virtue, and bestowed its great commission on him, that he should soothe and tranquilize the myriad regions.
They are courageous individuals.	Kaou-yaou: . . . adaptability combined with boldness. 　　Kaou-yaou: . . . audacity combined with uprightness.
They believe in people.	Kaou-yaou: Success as a ruler arises from knowing people and keeping people satisfied. 　　E Yin: Do not slight the concerns of the people: Think of their difficulties. 　　E Yin: A minister . . . ought to seek good for the people below.
They are value-driven.	Kaou-yaou: If rulers sincerely try to behave virtuously, they will receive intelligent advice and harmonious support. 　　Confucius said, Leadership is a matter of correctness. If you lead by going down a correct path yourself, who will dare to take an incorrect one? 　　Confucius: If their leaders cherish procedures, then the populace will not dare to be disrespectful. If their leaders cherish justice, then the populace will not dare to be disobedient. If their leaders cherish truth, then the populace will not dare to lie. 　　Confucius: If you show respect [for tradition and ancestors], the populace will respect you. If you promote the worthy and teach the backward, the populace will try their best.
They are life-long learners.	Kaou-yaou: If rulers attend carefully to their personal improvement, with concern for the long-term, they will be able to show unselfish benevolence and to draw perceptive distinctions among the people in their service. 　　E Yin: Of old, earlier rulers cultivated their virtue earnestly, and so Heaven inflicted no calamities. 　　King Ching: Without study, you stand facing a wall and your management of affairs will run into trouble.
They have the ability to deal with complexity, ambiguity, and uncertainty.	Kaou-yaou: People who display just three of these virtues daily can effectively manage and guide units of the government. People who thoughtfully and earnestly cultivate six of these virtues every day can brilliantly conduct important affairs of government.

Table 19.4. (*Cont'd*) Comparison of traditional Chinese leadership values with the transformational leader

The transformational leader (Tichy and Devanna 1986)	Statements by Kaou-yaou, E Yin, King Ching, and Confucius
	E Yin: Be careful to think about the end at the beginning. When you hear words against which your mind sets itself, you must inquire whether these words are not right. When you hear words that agree with your own thinking, you must ask whether these words are not wrong. What attainment can be made without anxious thought? What achievement can be made without earnest effort?
They are visionaries.	E Yin: When the ruler does not with disputatious words throw the old rules of government into confusion, and when the minister will not, for favor and gain, continue to occupy a position whose work is done, then the nation will lastingly and surely enjoy happiness.
	King Ching: I...look up to those former dynasties, and seek to imitate them when I instruct and direct you, my officials.
	E Yin: A truly intelligent ruler, at last as at first, chooses carefully to whom to listen and what advice to follow.

King Ching's youth. Like earlier texts, it says a king should lead by setting a good example. But it also details an elaborate organizational structure for the 'royal domain', which was a combination of the government and the king's household staff. 'The Officials of Chou' is a long, exhaustive, and detailed list of job descriptions for the multitude officials in the king's service, ranging from the prime minister to household servants (Biot 1851; Gingell 1852). Although concise, these job descriptions reveal a refined understanding of large-scale social control, of organizational essentials, and of rewards and punishments. They show a very well developed concept of bureaucracy. The longest section, which spells out the rights, powers, and obligations of the prime minister, suggests control methods in three domains: government officials, the populace, and affiliated feudal states and the cantons.

According to the book, the prime minister could use rules (*a*) to define departments, (*b*) to allocate responsibilities among departments, (*c*) to specify coordination links among officials, (*d*) to define standard operating procedures and exceptions to these, and (*e*) to audit officials' performance. Standardizing operating procedures would enhance efficiency and formalizing procedures would ensure stability. The available incentives included ranks of positions, compensation, recognition, favors from the sovereign, reappointment, fines, removal from office, and reprimand. Legal offenses or grave mistakes called for removal, whereas abuses of power or minor mistakes called for reprimand.

The book pointed out that the prime minister could control the populace and restrain conflicts through social norms, symbolic appointments of leaders, and assignments of people to occupations. The prime minister should reinforce the norms that told people to love their kinfolk and to respect the elderly. The prime minister should also promote worthy people, assign responsibilities to capable people, protect those who serve the state well, honor high ability, age, rank, or wealth, and respect the customs of foreign visitors. Respecting the customs of foreign visitors would teach the populace to love humanity and to stay on good terms with neighbors.

The prime minister should also use the sociopolitical structure and resource allocations to maintain control. Rulers of feudal states bind people through landholdings. Heads of cantons with distinguished reputations unite people through shared respect. Leaders who understand feelings and abuses satisfy people. Teachers connect people through shared wisdom, scholars through showing the right way. Clans link people through kinship. Officials unite people through administration. Friendships bond people through mutual assistance. Allotting enough pastures, rice paddies, and sources of brushwood pacifies people by assuring plentiful supplies. Finally, 'The Officials of Chou' pointed out many means with which the prime minister could influence the governance of affiliated feudal states and independent cantons. These ranged from ceremonies and sacrifices, through appointments of officials, to grants to students.

'The Officials of Chou' contradicts the widespread but undocumented idea that bureaucracy is a development of recent times. For example, Weber (Gerth and Mills 1946: 197) stated, 'Bureaucracy...is fully developed in political and ecclesiastical communities only in the modern state, and, in the private economy, only in the most advanced institutions of capitalism.' Similarly, Bennis (1966: 3) said, 'Bureaucracy...is a social invention, perfected during the Industrial Revolution to organize and direct the activities of the firm.'

Hall (1963) noted that different writers have defined bureaucracy in terms of eleven distinct properties, but he pointed to six properties as being especially important: (*a*) division of labor based on functional specialization; (*b*) a well-defined hierarchy of authority; (*c*) rules about the rights and duties associated with positions; (*d*) work procedures; (*e*) impersonal relations among people performing roles; and (*f*) promotion and employment based on technical competence. The government of Chou exhibited all of these, as Table 19.5 shows.

How To Be an Effective Subordinate

In a speech to his officials around 1100 BCE, King Ching of Chou reiterated the long-standing themes of self-improvement and proper behavior, especially

Table 19.5. Bureaucracy in 1100 BCE: Examples from 'The Officials of Chou'

Six key properties of bureaucracy	Examples
Division of labor based on functional specialization	The prime minister was to create six ministries: administration, education, customs and ceremonies, war, punishments, public works.
Well-defined hierarchy of authority	The ministry of administration was to direct officials of all ranks. Each ministry had a titular minister, an operational minister, and nominally sixty subordinate officials. The subordinates were told to refer important issues to their minister.
Rules about the rights and duties associated with positions	The prime minister was to promulgate rules to allocate responsibilities among departments, to coordinate the administration of diverse offices, to specify work procedures, and to set punishments for errant officials.
Work procedures	The prime minister's rules were supposed to make operating procedures efficient by standardizing them, to make procedures stable by formalizing them, to accommodate exceptions by granting discretion, and to assure control by defining auditing procedures.
Impersonal relations among people performing roles	Officials were required to behave in accordance with the rules and procedures and they were punished for deviations. However, the prime minister was also told to use kinship and friendship as means of social control.
Promotion and employment based on technical competence	The Prime Minister was to appoint (*a*) rulers of feudal states who had landholdings, (*b*) heads of cantons who had distinguished reputations, (*c*) teachers who had wisdom, (*d*) scholars who would show the people 'the right way', (*e*) leaders who understood how to make people content, and (*f*) secondary officials who were competent administrators. The prime minister was also admonished to promote worthy people, to assign responsibilities to capable people, to protect those who had served the state well, to honor high ability, age, rank, or wealth, and to recognize secondary officials who have performed well.

sincerity. But he also gave advice about goal-setting, decision-making, and selecting and promoting competent subordinates. Table 19.6 lists the King's admonitions, not in the sequence in which they appear in his speech, but categorized.

King Ching assumed that his subordinates had two kinds of goals: to manage effectively and to attain personal benefits such as status, pay, and peace of mind. He gave no indication that he thought his officials might enjoy holding authority

Table 19.6. King Ching's rules of good management

Personal qualities
- To be lazy and indifferent undermines your management.
- Let carefulness and economy be sincere virtues, and do not show them hypocritically. If you practice them sincerely, your minds will be at ease and you will daily become more admirable. If you practice them hypocritically, your minds will be stressful and you will daily become more tiresome.

Self-improvement
- Study history in order to perform your offices well; such study will make your arts of management free from error.
- Without study, you stand facing a wall and your management of affairs will run into trouble.

Effects of goals on behavior
- ... high achievement comes from high aims, and higher positions come only through diligence.
- Extinguish all selfish aims and the people will have confidence in you and obey gladly.

Effects of rewards on behavior
- With high rank, pride comes unnoticed; and with high pay, extravagance comes unseen.
- In the enjoyment of favored positions, think of risk and be ever cautious. Those who act without such caution find themselves amidst what they should have feared.

Decisions and actions
- By means of bold decisions you can avoid future difficulties.
- To build up uncertainty undermines your plans.
- Be careful about the commands you issue, for once issued, they must be put into effect and not retracted.

Conformity to rules
- Follow the statutes of our kingdom, and do not use artful language to introduce discretion into your offices.

Promoting subordinates
- Push forward the worthy and make room for the able, and harmony will prevail among your subordinates. When they are not harmonious, the government becomes a tangled confusion. If those whom you promote show ability in their offices, the ability is yours as well. If you promote the unqualified, you are unequal to your responsibility.

---

or dominating other people. He also emphasized that his subordinates should follow rules and procedures; at no point does he tell them to obey orders.

In contrast to the ideas about management enunciated by rulers or prime ministers, Confucius spoke to future officials from the viewpoint of a subordinate. His ideas about how subordinates should behave may have embodied the assumption that superior and subordinate both belong to the same social stratum, and hence that they could interact as social equals.

This assumption might explain why Confucius saw subordination as laden with ambivalence. He expressed ambivalence about forthrightness by subordinates. In the first of these two quotations, he advises circumspection, and in the second one, forthrightness.

Tzu-chang was studying in hope of becoming an official. Confucius told him, 'Listen carefully and discard unreliable information; be cautious when repeating the rest and you will rarely get into trouble. Look around carefully and overlook what it is dangerous to see; be cautious when acting on the rest and you will rarely be sorry. If your speech rarely gets you into trouble and your actions rarely make you sorry, success as an official will follow as a matter of course.'

Tzu-lu asked him how to serve a superior. Confucius said, 'Don't oppose covertly. Resist overtly.' (Chan 1963; Lau 1979; Pound 1951; Waley 1938)

Confucius also expressed ambivalence about whether officials should follow procedures. First, officials should both adhere to procedures and be considerate. If procedures make consideration impossible, the procedures will not work properly.

Confucius said, 'If an official can follow procedures and be considerate, what other abilities could the official possibly need? But if an official cannot operate in this way, what use has the official for procedures?' (Chan 1963; Lau 1979; Pound 1951; Waley 1938)

Second, procedures should restrict the behaviors of superiors but not of subordinates as long as the subordinates are trying sincerely to serve their superiors:

Confucius said, 'Were anyone to obey all the established procedures when serving a superior, the subordinate would be thought servile.'

Duke Ting asked, 'How should a superior use subordinates and how should subordinates serve their superior?' Confucius replied, 'In employing subordinates, a superior should adhere strictly to established procedures. Subordinates should devote themselves sincerely to their superior's service.' (Chan 1963; Lau 1979; Pound 1951; Waley 1938)

Evidently, superiors should adhere to procedures because people are comfortable with procedures.

Confucius said, 'As long as a ruler follows procedures, the populace will be easy to govern.' (Chan 1963; Lau 1979; Pound 1951; Waley 1938)

Among twentieth-century analysts, Merton (1940) and Gouldner (1954) have written about the reasons for and consequences of procedures in bureaucracies. Merton pointed out what Confucius appears to have observed, that procedures make relationships more impersonal and that officials may follow procedures even when they are dysfunctional. Also discussing a topic that interested Confucius, Gouldner said that the use of general and impersonal procedures makes supervisory authority more legitimate.

5. MANAGERIAL CONTROL DURING UNIFICATION—FROM 350 BCE to 206 BCE

Around 350 BCE, the small state of Ch'in began to grow larger and more powerful. At that time, Ch'in's prime minister was Shang Yang, a believer in total control of the populace. Shang Yang's approach has been labeled *Legalism* because it emphasized the use of laws. However, he advocated using laws to undercut social relations and thus to break down the sense of community.

If a ruler employs virtuous officials, the people will place primary importance on their social relations; but if a ruler employs wicked officials, the people will place primary importance on the statutes. The virtuous sympathize with others and seek agreement; the wicked spy upon others and argue with them. When the virtuous supervise others' behavior, they overlook crimes; when the wicked supervise others' behavior, they punish crimes. In the former case, the people are stronger than the law; in the latter case, the law is stronger than the people are.

To make laws effective requires support from incentives and ideologies.

A wise ruler uses consistent rewards, consistent punishments, and consistent ideologies.... What I mean by consistent rewards is that profits and incomes, positions and ranks should depend solely on how much a person contributes to the state; there should not be diverse rationales for allocating rewards.... What I mean by consistent punishments is that they should not vary with status or rank. From ministers of state and generals down to minor officials and ordinary folk, all should be sentenced to death if they disobey the ruler or violate prohibitions.... What I mean by consistent ideologies is that advocates of free thought should be excluded from wealth, honor, and power. (Duyvendak 1928)

Later scholars have credited Shang Yang with initiating the totalitarian rule that enabled Ch'in to dominate the entire civilized world (as the ancient Chinese viewed the world). Certainly, Shang Yang himself believed that he had found the formula for total domination, and by 221 BCE, Ch'in had conquered or otherwise taken control of every state in feudal China. King Ch'eng, who ruled from 246 BCE until 210 BCE, took the title of First August Emperor of the Ch'in.

One influence on the First August Emperor was Han Fei Tzu, who admired the works of Shang Yang. The only noble among the renowned Chinese philosophers, Han Fei was a member of the ruling clan in the small and unwealthy state of Han. Unhappy about the condition of his state, he sent frequent letters of advice to his king. When the king ignored his letters, Han Fei wrote a book. His king also ignored the book. But another, more important ruler did appreciate Han Fei's ideas—King Ch'eng of Ch'in.

Han Fei endeavored to give rulers practical advice about how to strengthen their control and how to remain in power. Not only were his ideas very different from those of Confucius and the traditional literature, his views often contradicted the traditional views. He certainly did not intend that his advice should apply to subordinate officials as well as rulers. He never addressed advice to officials, and he told rulers to behave very unlike their subordinates.

Han Fei's approach made him a supreme exponent of Legalism. However, Han Fei's rationale for relying on laws differed from Shang Yang's. Han Fei emphasized the impersonality of laws and their capacity to eliminate favoritism, as well as the leverage laws confer in allowing rulers to exert more influence with less effort.

Truly astute rulers use laws to select people for positions; the rulers do not choose people personally. Astute rulers use laws to weigh candidates' merits; the rulers do not attempt to judge them personally. As a result, candidates of true virtue cannot hide their talents or bad candidates gloss over their faults. People cannot advance because of false praise or be driven from office by slander. Accordingly, the rulers and the officials share clear understandings of goals and methods, and they can easily bring order to their states. The rulers need only scrutinize the laws. (Liao 1959; Watson 1963)

Han Fei himself portrayed his contribution as facilitating adaptation to changing social values and changing economic conditions:

People of antiquity strove to be known as moral and virtuous. Those of the middle ages struggled to be known as wise and resourceful. People of today fight for the reputation of being vigorous and powerful.... People of old made light of goods, not because they were benevolent, but because goods were abundant. People of today quarrel and pillage, not because they are brutish, but because goods are scarce. (Peerenboom, 1993)

Although some authors have likened Han Fei to Machiavelli, his texts resemble Machiavelli's mainly in seeking to foster the interests of rulers. Han Fei's vision of society resembles that of Adam Smith: People are amoral, selfish, calculating, and opportunistic. Competition fosters high performance. Opposing interests bring out the best in each other. High achievement comes from an effective system rather than from effective individuals. And Han Fei's vision of organization resembles the bureaucracy of Weber in that impersonal rules and procedures bring consistency and counteract the bad effects of selfishness and ambition. For Han Fei, the notion of laws encompassed rules, regulations, formal procedures, and formal standards as long as a ruler decreed them, rather than officials.

One of Han Fei's basic themes was the pervasive conflict between superiors and subordinates. He advised rulers to distrust subordinates, to conceal their thoughts and intentions, and to inspire fear by their subordinates.

It is said: 'A ruler must not reveal desires; for if a ruler reveals desires, the officials put on facades that please the ruler. A ruler must not reveal personal views, because if a ruler does so, the officials show false faces.' Similarly, it is said: 'If a ruler does away with likes and dislikes, the officials show their true feelings. If a ruler shuns wile and cunning, the officials watch their steps.'

There is also a saying: 'It is so still that it seems to be nowhere, so empty that no one can find it.' While astute rulers repose motionless above, their officials tremble with fear below....

Rulers stand in danger of being undercut in five ways:

> officials can block their rulers' plans,
> officials can control the wealth and resources of the state,
> officials can issue any orders they please,
> officials can take the credit for doing good deeds, and
> officials can build up cliques.

If officials can block rulers, the rulers lose the control. If officials can control the wealth and resources, rulers cannot dispense bounty to others. If officials can issue any orders they please, the rulers lose authority. If officials can take credit for good deeds, the rulers lose the claim to providing benefits. If officials can build up cliques of their own, the rulers lose supporters. Rulers alone should exercise these powers; the powers should never pass into the hands of officials.... (Liao 1959; Watson 1963)

Han Fei placed strong reliance on control through rewards and punishments.

Astute rulers control their officials by means of two handles alone. The two handles are punishment and reward....

Officials fear punishments and hope for rewards. Hence, if rulers wield the handles of punishment and reward, officials will fear the rulers' sternness and hope to receive the rulers' generosity. However, the evil officials of this age are different. They would take the handle of punishment from their rulers so they can inflict punishments on people they hate, and they would take the handle of reward from their rulers so they can bestow rewards on people they like. If rulers do not reserve to themselves the power to dispense rewards and punishments and instead allow officials to hand these out, then the people fear the officials while holding the rulers in contempt, and they attend to the officials and turn away from the rulers. This is the calamity that results when rulers yield control of punishments and rewards.... (Liao 1959; Watson 1963)

Yet another significant contributor to the rise of Ch'in was Li Ssu, who became the prime minister sometime between 219 and 213 BCE and who was as ruthless as his Emperor. Li Ssu had been a student together with Han Fei Tzu, and he also espoused Legalist views. With Li Ssu's advice, the First August Emperor abolished the feudal nobility, replaced the feudal states with administrative districts, burned almost all books, standardized weights and measures and writing, built better roads, relocated masses of people, and began building the Great Wall. Li Ssu advised the Emperor to burn almost all books so that opponents could not base their opposition on tradition. Literature, he argued, contains justification for many schools of thought, many ideas about what should be. This diversity spawns criticism of the government and promotes political factions. 'People wishing to pursue learning should turn to the officials as their teachers' (de Bary, Chan, and Watson 1960).

Whereas Han Fei said, 'astute rulers never use wise officials or virtuous people for selfish purposes', Li Ssu told his emperor to use his power for personal enjoyment:

Suppose that contemporary rulers fail to practice the astute methods of Shen Pu-hai and Han Fei Tzu and do not apply techniques of punishment to exploit their empires for their own pleasure, but on the contrary, pointlessly torture their bodies and waste their minds in devotion to the people. Then such rulers become the slaves of the common people instead of the tamers of their empires.... (de Bary, Chan, and Watson 1960)

Li Ssu had no use for rewards and his approach to punishment made Han Fei's approach look gentle.

According to the laws of Lord Shang [Shang Yang], the scattering of ashes in the streets called for corporal punishment. Now, the scattering of ashes is a minor offense, whereas corporal punishment is a severe penalty. Only the astute rulers have the insight to apply severe punishments for minor offenses. If a minor offense is punished severely, people can imagine what will be done against a serious offense! Thus, people do not dare to violate the laws. (de Bary, Chan, and Watson 1960)

Chan (1963: 251) has expressed one prevalent interpretation of the relationship between Legalist doctrines and the Ch'in empire:

...the Legalists were primarily interested in the accumulation of power, the subjugation of the individual to the state, uniformity of thought, and the use of force. It is not surprising that they were instrumental in setting up the dictatorship of Ch'in (221–206 BCE), in unifying

China in 221 BCE, and in instituting the tightest regimentation of life and thought in China's history. The brutality and violence of the Ch'in brought its early downfall in 206 BCE.

Legalism articulated a how-to-do-it manual for total control. This is not an ancient version of Theory X. McGregor (1960: 34) did say Theory X assumes that 'most people must be coerced, controlled, directed, or threatened with punishment to get them to put forth adequate effort toward the achievement of organizational objectives'. However, McGregor was discussing supervision of blue-collar factory workers, and he said Theory X assumes such people are lazy. By contrast, Legalism aimed at controlling subordinates at all levels of a hierarchy, and it assumed that people are energetic, intelligent, and capable, but entirely too independent, self-interested, and deceitful.

Although the first Empire lasted for only a few years, Legalist philosophy, however, did not vanish magically in 206 BCE. Rather, the Chinese bureaucracy continued to espouse Legalist principles, and the period from 206 BCE to 220 CE witnessed a continuing contest between Legalism and Confucian values (Weiming 1993). In the long run, neither side won this contest, and the contest continues today.

Barley and Kunda (1992: 364) argued that American 'managerial discourse appears to have alternated repeatedly between ideologies of normative and rational control'. To establish their proposition, they incorporated data going back to 1870. Based on a view of organizations as collectives, normative control involves 'shaping workers' identities, emotions, attitudes, and beliefs' (1992: 384). Based on a view of organizations as mechanistic systems, rational control treats workers as self-interested individuals who 'either...understand the economic advantages of an efficient system or [are] powerless to resist a well-designed structure'. Thus, rational control corresponds closely to Legalism and normative control to the ancient Chinese theories of management explicated by Kaou-yaou, E Yin, and Confucius.

6. CONCLUSION

Summary

This chapter focuses on ancient Chinese theories about managerial control—how superiors and subordinates should relate, and how to control, lead and motivate people. It tries to describe the prescriptions followed by practicing managers rather than scholarly thought. China offers very old, elaborate texts that address issues arising in complex political structures. Until 250 BCE, China consisted of many states with differing sizes and resources. After 250 BCE, China became a centralized empire with tight authoritarian control.

The ancient Chinese sought to use duties and ceremonial etiquette to increase social integration. They tried to build macro social relations upon micro ones. The macro relations included organizations and social strata as defined by the feudal hierarchy. The micro relations were dyads such as husband–wife and ruler–subject.

By 1100 BCE, the state of Chou's government had developed into a well-articulated bureaucracy. There were departments, coordination links among officials, standard operating procedures, and audits of officials' performance. Documents from this bureaucracy disclose sophisticated understanding or rewards and punishments, social norms, symbolic actions, and resource allocation.

Before 250 BCE when China became an Empire, the Chinese concept of effective leadership emphasized self-improvement. Leaders should lead by example rather than give orders, and should elicit support from their subordinates and from the populace. Subordinates should serve their superiors sincerely, balancing obedience with autonomy.

Another regime of managerial practice began to rise around 350 BCE, when the small state of Ch'in began to expand, eventually uniting China as one empire. A key element is this unification was a managerial approach—*Legalism*—that emphasized the use of laws.

Legalism's purpose was to help rulers strengthen their control and remain in power. It stressed the use of incentives and ideological control. One basic theme was the pervasive conflict between superiors and subordinates: Superiors should distrust subordinates and inspire fear by their subordinates.

What's Interesting?

The ancient texts disclose diverse ideas about human behavior, control, leadership, management, and organization. Five of these ideas deserve special attention.

First, one interpretation of 'The Great Plan' articulates a contingency theory of leadership that resembles Fiedler's. Both theories make similar prescriptions for two types of situations; they make different prescriptions for one type of situation. Fiedler says leaders in very favorable situations should use a task-directed style. 'The Great Plan' recommends that in periods of peace and tranquillity, leaders should depersonalize their leadership and rely on correct procedures.

Another interpretation of 'The Great Plan' resembles the leader's side of Liden and Graen's descriptive Vertical Dyad Linkage model. Liden and Graen (1980) said leaders favor and trust subordinates who expend effort, even as they act aloofly toward less committed subordinates. 'The Great Plan' can be interpreted as advising leaders to behave this way.

Second, at first glance, it is surprising to discover that ancient bureaucracies were as well articulated as 'The Officials of Chou'. But at second look, one wonders 'Why not?' The only technological prerequisite for bureaucracy is an ability to write, so as to record rules and procedures, assignments, and transactions.

Third, the very ancient Chinese ideas about leadership resemble contemporary 'transformational leadership'. However, it seems more useful to portray the

Chinese model as a distinct alternative—moral leadership. Moral leadership combines charisma with ideology. It aims to attract voluntary followers, who join because of both the leader's very unusual overall excellence and the leader's moral uprightness.

Fourth, Legalism synthesized a how-to-do-it manual for total control. It assumed that subordinates are independent, self-interested, and deceitful, so superiors must pit subordinates against each other, define behavioral limits, and use rewards and punishments to obtain desired behaviors. The surviving records seem to portray Legalism as a managerial innovation that came into prominence after 350 BCE and that helped the Ch'in to unite many states into one empire. However, there are many references to the uses of rewards, punishments, and strict rules throughout the ancient documents, and so Legalism was probably creating a philosophical framework for practices as old as human beings.

Overall, it seems that the similarities between ancient and contemporary are at least as great as the differences. The differences seem to fit a model that says people from different times have to restate knowledge anew, in their own language and citing current examples. The similarities suggest that modern people can understand and appreciate the insights of their ancestors. The ancient theories are as complex as modern ones and supported by reasoning that we can appreciate even when it differs quite a bit from our own.

ACKNOWLEDGMENTS

This chapter benefits from the helpful suggestions of Joan Dunbar, Roger Dunbar, Richard Freedman, Peter Friesen, Raghu Garud, Maxine Garvey, Jerome Kuperman, and Gilbert Mattos.

Part VII

Perceptions and Learning Part 2

20

How Organizations Learn from Success and Failure

Coauthored with Bo L. T. Hedberg

1. INTRODUCTION

Grinyer and Norburn (1975) made a careful study that they had expected to document the beneficial consequences of formal strategic planning. They did find a positive correlation between profitability and the use of formal planning, but the correlation was very weak. Profitable firms were nearly as likely to plan informally as formally, and the same was true of unprofitable firms. This suggests that efforts to forge consensus among managers around rationalizations about effective behavior are unlikely to produce the benefits sought. Furthermore, Grinyer and Norburn found that profitability correlated inconsistently and meaninglessly with the degrees to which senior executives agreed about their firms' objectives or about their personal responsibilities. Since such disagreements indicate that some executives have misperceived, this suggests that greater perceptual accuracy may not make effective behavior more likely.

These findings illustrate a family of interesting questions: To what degrees do misperceptions prevent organizations from learning effectively? How can organizations learn from feedback if they are making faulty judgments about their performance? How can organizations adapt effectively to outside conditions that they misread? Some theories say that these are central and important issues. Other theories say it really does not matter whether people perceive accurately or analyze well because learning is imposed by external forces.

To show that perceptual errors need to be taken seriously, this chapter begins by describing research about managers' perceptions. Then the chapter contrasts two complementary approaches to learning—the behavioral and the cognitive (Glynn, Lant, and Milliken 1994; Leroy and Ramanantsoa 1997). Two examples illustrate these approaches. The first illustrates how evolutionary learning led to the Challenger disaster. The second describes how changing conditions first created a successful growth industry and then devastated it. The chapter concludes with reflections about the integration of behavioral and cognitive approaches.

This chapter has benefited from suggestions by Joel Baum, Philippe Baumard, George Huber, Li Malmström, Danny Miller, and Anne Miner.

2. HOW WELL DO PEOPLE AND ORGANIZATIONS UNDERSTAND THEIR ENVIRONMENTS?

Research studies have found large errors and biases in people's perceptions both of their organizations' environments and of their organizations. How can organizations improve their behavior if they misunderstand their own capabilities or their environments? Or how should an organization proceed if different people in the organization hold radically different perceptions of their organization and its environments?

Psychological studies of human perception have revealed many biases. Bazerman (1997) lists more than a dozen biases, most of which assert that people do not behave as statisticians recommend. People also update their cognitions more slowly than statistical models recommend, and they see patterns or correlations in random data (Edwards 1968; Singer and Benassi 1981). People search for information in ways that tend to confirm their prior beliefs. Brains involuntarily alter memories to fit new information, and vice versa (Kiesler 1971; Loftus 1979). Brains also invent memories of events that never occurred. Nisbett and Wilson (1977) concluded that, by and large, people's introspections into their own thoughts are not true insights.

The 'fundamental attribution bias' is a propensity for people to overestimate their own influence on events and to underestimate external or situational influences. For instance, Meindl and Ehrlich (1987) and Meindl, Ehrlich, and Dukerich (1985) argued that both researchers and the general populace attribute too much control and influence to leaders. Based on the behaviors of college students, they inferred that these attributions become more frequent after especially successful performances. Rotter (1966) said that individual people show consistent tendencies either to perceive themselves as causes of events or to see causes arising in their environments.

The 'self-serving bias' denotes a propensity for people to overestimate their own influence on successes and to overestimate external or situational influences on failures (Heider 1958). People also tend to exhibit the opposite biases when interpreting other people's successes and failures. Wagner and Gooding (1997) found that managers who face equivocal information about their own businesses tend to attribute positive outcomes to strengths in their own organizations, while they blame negative outcomes on environmental circumstances. However, when managers are asked to interpret information about businesses managed by others, they attribute positive outcomes to opportunities in the environment and negative outcomes to organizational weakness. Similarly, Huff and Schwenk (1990) observed that Chrysler executives attributed negative company performance mainly to environmental causes while they tied positive performance to forceful managerial actions.

Lawrence and Lorsch (1967) initiated research into the accuracy of managers' perceptions inadvertently. They inferred that firms perform better when their organizational properties match the properties of their market environments.

But, Lawrence and Lorsch relied on managers' perceptions, and other researchers wondered how dependable such data might be. Two groups of researchers (Tosi, Aldag, and Storey 1973; Downey, Hellriegel, and Slocum 1975) asked middle and top managers to describe their firms' markets, and then compared these perceptions with financial reports and industry statistics. The correlations between managers' perceptions and objective measures were all near zero and were negative more often than positive. Thus, on average, managers' perceptions of environmental properties did not correlate with objective measures of those properties.

Obtaining data from middle managers in several companies, Mezias and Starbuck (2003) found considerable variation in perceptual errors. For the most accurately perceived variable, 39 percent of the managers made errors below 50 percent, whereas for the least accurately perceived variable, 31 percent of the managers made errors exceeding 200 percent. Very large errors were prevalent. Furthermore, contrary to the researchers' expectation, managers with sales experience had no more accurate perceptions of sales-related variables than did managers without such experience. One reason for this, the researchers conjectured, may be that people define their responsibilities and their environments very narrowly. Large organizations divide responsibilities into small compartments, and small organizations focus on small market segments.

Other research suggests that people are ignorant about or misperceive their own organizations. Mezias and Starbuck (2003) also observed managers' perceptions of quality performance by their business units. This company's top management said quality improvement was their top priority. Many personnel had attended training courses, each business unit had a department that focused on quality improvement, and quality measures were distributed to all managers frequently. Yet, 49–91 percent of the managers reported 'I don't know' when asked about current levels of quality performance.

After reviewing many studies in which people described their organizations' structures and cultures, Payne and Pugh (1976: 1168) drew three conclusions: (*a*) Different employees of the same organization disagree so strongly with each other that it makes no sense to talk about an average perception. 'Perceptual measures of each of the structural and climate variables have varied so much among themselves that mean scores were uninterpretable.' (*b*) Except for organizational size, employees' perceptions of organizational properties correlate weakly with objective measures of those properties. (*c*) Differences among employees' perceptions of organizational properties correspond with employees' jobs and hierarchical statuses. For instance, higher-status employees view their organizations more favorably.

Starbuck (1983) gave several reasons why top managers are especially prone to misperceive events and to resist changes (see also Glynn, Lant, and Milliken 1994): They have strong vested interests. They become the targets for blame when current behaviors are judged ineffective. Significant strategic reorientations threaten their dominance. Their high statuses lead them to think they have more expertise than their subordinates. Their expertise tends to be out-of-date.

They receive much information through biased channels that conceal or de-emphasize information that might displease them.

Normann (1971) pointed out that people can understand and readily respond to stimuli in domains where they have experience, and that they are likely to misperceive stimuli in unfamiliar domains, or to have difficulty responding to them. Since different parts of an organization have experience with different domains, organizational perceptions interact with politics and control structures. Starbuck, Greve, and Hedberg (1978) observed that some top managers prevent their organizations from dealing effectively with serious crises, either because they do not understand the situations faced by their firms or because they fear losing their high statuses. Thus, organizations typically welcome the small 'variations' on their recent activities but they resist dramatic 'reorientations' (Normann 1971; Starbuck 1983).

Organizations find it especially difficult to recognize and confront failure. Not seeing and not acting can result from slow sense-making processes or from ineffective information systems (Hodgkinson 1997). Slow sense-making processes and ineffective information systems make it more difficult for organizations to make sense of early warning signals and to recognize gradual transitions.

Overall, the evidence justifies caution about the accuracy of learners' perceptions. Although some people have accurate perceptions of some variables, most people have inaccurate perceptions of most variables, and an observer cannot distinguish accurate perceivers from inaccurate ones by their behaviors. As a result, theories of learning need to explain how learning can occur despite large perceptual errors.

Theories of learning fall into two broad classes that make very different assumptions about human capabilities and the complexity of learning processes. One of these approaches, behavioral learning, places little reliance on the perceptions of decision-makers. The second approach, cognitive learning, emphasizes the perceptions of decision-makers. Each approach has weaknesses, and each approach explains some phenomena that the other cannot. Using both approaches together gives a more complete picture, as the two approaches complement each other (Leroy and Ramanantsoa 1997).

3. ONE FRAMEWORK: BEHAVIORAL LEARNING

An ancient debate in social science echoes an ageless philosophical debate about free will. Must models of human behavior allow for choice, or is choice merely an illusion that disguises environmental control? Do organizations control their destinies, or do environments compel certain behaviors?

Theorists on the behavioral side of this debate seek to explain as much behavior as possible without injecting conscious thought or decision processes as controls. According to this approach, learning arises from automatic reactions to performance feedback, and learners' cognitions have weak effects. Figure 20.1 diagrams such a loop.

Behavioral approaches portray learning as a mechanistic and involuntary process over which learners can exert little control. Behavioral psychologists assume that actions are determined by hypothetical stimulus–response links. Pleasant outcomes (rewards, successes) strengthen the stimulus–response links and make the corresponding actions more likely to recur. Unpleasant outcomes (punishments, failures) weaken the stimulus–response links and make the corresponding actions less likely to recur. Behavioral organization theorists sometimes speculate about decision-makers' rationales, but they do not obtain data about these rationales and they do not study changes in perceptions or thought processes. They are satisfied to assume that good outcomes allow behaviors to persist or organizations to survive, that bad outcomes provoke behavioral changes or organizational failures.

One great advantage of behavioral theories is that they can explain how behaviors can improve even though learners misunderstand their environments or misunderstand the causal relations between actions and outcomes. Learners' erroneous perceptions do not become barriers to improved performance because learning is involuntary and noncognitive.

Behavioral theories can also explain why people and organizations may learn elaborate routines in which many components seem to have no instrumental effects. Over time, simple stimulus–response links aggregate into complex repertoires of habits that evolve, generalize, lose relevance, grow dysfunctional, and so forth. Since the behavioral theories do not require people or organizations to appraise the rationality of their behaviors, repertoires can include irrelevant behaviors that persist as long as rewards continue.

Because behavioral theories emphasize repetition of the same stimuli, they are less persuasive as descriptions of behavior in changing environments. Indeed, many psychologists refuse to apply the term learning to behavioral changes that occur in response to environmental changes; they restrict the term learning to performance improvements in response to the same or similar stimuli (Weick 1991). This restriction cannot be enforced strictly, as learning experiments always begin by presenting learners with new stimuli, but environmental change does

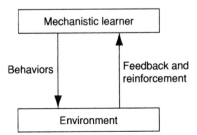

Figure 20.1. Behavioral learning

obscure the notion of performance improvement (Levinthal 1994). An unstable environment makes it difficult to evaluate consequences of behavior, and one must evaluate consequences before judging whether performance has improved. Weick (1991) submitted that changing stimuli are so pervasive in organizations that there is need for a different definition of learning in organizations.

Similarly, behavioral theories cannot explain how people and organizations suddenly act in dramatically novel ways. Successes reinforce prior behaviors, failures inhibit prior behaviors, and actions do not reflect learners' global understanding, so exploration and innovation remain mysterious and inexplicable.

Another problem is that a purely behavioral approach becomes difficult to sustain because rewards and punishments are subject to interpretation. When does a learner find an outcome rewarding? Different people find pleasure in different results. Different organizations have different standards for success.

As the ensuing subsections explain, behavioral studies have concentrated on learning by individual people or by populations of organizations. They have said little about learning by individual organizations.

Learning by Individual People

Much organizational learning involves learning by people within the organizations. Countless studies have applied behavioral-learning frameworks to individual people (Estes 1975–78; Hilgard 1948). These studies generally show that pleasant outcomes (successes) reinforce stimulus–response links whereas unpleasant outcomes (failures) break stimulus–response links. As a result, pleasant outcomes are much more effective at teaching new behaviors, whereas unpleasant outcomes are much more effective at discouraging existing behaviors. Also, extremely unpleasant outcomes often evoke aggression toward others.

Reinforcement frequency affects the speed of learning and the retention of learned behaviors. Reinforcements that occur after every repetition of a specific behavior produce fast learning but the learned behaviors are readily unlearned. Reinforcements that occur randomly after some repetitions but not all produce slow learning but the learned behaviors are difficult to unlearn later.

Complexity Theory (Schroder, Driver, and Streufert 1967) says the quality and sophistication of an individual's responses depend on the frequency of problematic stimuli. However, very high frequencies may produce information overload. Streufert (1973) later showed that negative feedback tends to make the performance peak earlier and at a lower level. Thus, negative feedback (failure) fosters simpler, less improved, responses than positive feedback (success) does.

Learning by Individual Organizations

Although organizations may learn when their members learn, it is possible for learning by individual members to have no effect on organizational behavior, as occurs when new members learn to follow established routines. Also, organizations can add new behaviors to their repertoires by adding new members without either the new or continuing members learning new behaviors.

Industrial learning curves afford one analog to behavioral learning by organizations. These curves describe how production costs decline when a manufacturing process is repeated. For example, the BCG Matrix, developed by the Boston Consulting Group and used globally as a prescriptive strategic model, relies heavily on the assumption that a production line becomes more efficient with the number of repeats and that overall efficiency depends on the number of items sold. The cost decreases have many sources that include both learning by individual workers and learning by the organization as an entity (Epple, Argote, and Devadas 1991; Levitt and March 1988). Possibly because industrial learning curves have been studied from macroscopic perspectives, theories about them say that improvements come from repetition alone, and the theories have not distinguished between successes and failures.

Evolutionary studies resemble behavioral learning theories insofar as they examine the results of change without describing processes inside learners. Although they acknowledge that organizations make choices, they do not describe choice processes or communications between people within an organization. They seek to relate the properties of behaviors to their survival or disappearance. However, most modern evolutionary theories do not assume that change implies improvement; behaviors that survive are not necessarily 'better' than those that disappear. In this respect, evolutionary theories differ from the behavioral theories of psychologists.

A very few evolutionary studies have focused on changes within or by one organization. However, Miner (1991) analyzed turnover of jobs in a university. Some jobs disappeared soon after they had appeared; others lasted for decades. Jobs created in larger departments lasted longer. Jobs created for specific people tended to disappear quickly.

Learning by Populations of Organizations

Most evolutionary studies have looked at populations of similar organizations in similar environments (Miner and Haunschild 1995). For instance, Milliken, Lant, and Batra (1992) interpreted data about two industries as showing that most poorly performing firms persist in their strategic orientations.

Nelson and Winter (1982) characterized organizational change as an evolutionary process in which standardized routines survive or disappear. The routines are not confined to single organizations because organizations imitate each other. Many studies have examined how managerial practices spread through interorganizational networks (Burns and Wholey 1993; Davis 1991; Haunschild 1993; Ingram and Baum 1997a; Powell, Koput, and Smith-Doerr 1996; Spender 1989). Such evolutionary theories have not, however, incorporated interorganizational communication processes. As Winter (1994: 100) stated the position, 'Evolutionary theory emphasizes that much of the knowledge that underlies organizational capabilities is tacit knowledge; it is not understood or communicable in symbolic form.'

Prevalent theories make drastic failure the main mechanism for learning in organizational populations. Organizations disappear if they act inappropriately or ineffectively, so the surviving organizations act appropriately and effectively. Miner et al. (1996) reviewed more subtle effects on an organizational population of failure by one organization or possibly a few. One effect can be the freeing of resources for other uses, either within the same population or in others. Other effects can include changes made to prevent additional failures, such as changes in government policies, industry practices, and organizational structures. Still another effect can be more experimentation by the surviving organizations, which makes the population more heterogeneous.

In a study of decisions to hire investment banks, Haunschild and Miner (1997) observed that firms were more likely to imitate more frequent events rather than less frequent events, to imitate larger and more profitable firms rather than smaller and less profitable firms, and to imitate successes rather than failures. However, although firms were more likely to hire investment banks that had been involved in more profitable acquisitions, they seemingly did not avoid hiring banks that had been involved in less profitable acquisitions.

Learning across a population of competing organizations creates the Red Queen effect. Barnett and Hansen (1996: 139) summarized this effect as follows:

An organization facing competition is likely to engage in a search for ways to improve performance. When successful, this search results in learning that is likely to increase the organization's competitive strength, which in turn triggers learning by its rivals—consequently making them stronger competitors and so again triggering learning in the first organization.

They inferred that historical data about some banks are consistent with the Red Queen effect. Ingram and Baum (1997b) inferred that hotel chains grew less likely to fail as they observed (a) more other hotel chains and (b) more failures by other hotel chains. Barnett (1997) argued that data on breweries and telephone companies say smaller firms need more competitive strength to survive than do larger firms; larger firms can survive without being as effective as smaller firms. As a result, large firms become increasingly vulnerable over time.

A few researchers have modeled learning across organizational populations as races in which organizations that learn a new method sooner gain greater advantages. For instance, Amburgey, Dacin, and Singh (2000) analyzed strategic alliances among biotechnology firms in such a framework.

Thus, behavioral approaches interpret learning as being strongly dependent on rewards or punishments that arise in the environment. For learning to occur, a learner and an environment must be tightly linked, but the environment exerts much more influence on a learner than vice versa. This asymmetric interdependence creates a puzzle at the population level, where the environment is largely composed of learners who are all learning from each other.

4. A SECOND FRAMEWORK: COGNITIVE LEARNING

The second approach describes learners as cognitive beings that perceive, analyze, plan, and choose. According to this approach, learning modifies cognitive maps that form the bases for analysis, and analysis guides action. Figure 20.2 diagrams such a loop.

Cognitive learning incorporates perception, analysis, and choice. Learners' mental processes integrate and interpret perceptions, analyze situations, and propose alternative behaviors. Schroder, Driver, and Streufert (1967) described how people build increasingly complex cognitive structures to analyze situations and to form responses to recurring problems. To varying degrees, learners can choose what to perceive, how to interpret perceptions, and which actions to take. Thus, the effectiveness of their behaviors depends on how well they read their environments and upon how rapidly they discover changes. Reading environments and rapidly discovering changes, in turn, depend upon factors such as curiosity, playfulness, willingness to experiment, and analytic skill (March 1971).

A great advantage of cognitive theories is that they can explain how people and organizations are able suddenly to act in dramatically novel ways. Cognitive maps allow people and organizations to try to predict behaviors they have never tried. Thus, they can find opportunities, threats, and shortcuts, and they can conceive innovations.

The weak spots of cognitive learning theories are the degrees to which behaviors depend upon realistic understanding and the theories' inability to explain how learners can improve even though they misunderstand their environments or misunderstand the causal relations between actions and outcomes. Because learners' perceptions form the bases for analysis, choice, and interpretation, erroneous perceptions become barriers to improvement. March and Olsen (1979: 32) reported a case in which the 'solutions' that an organization consid-

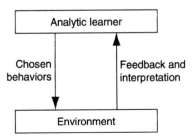

Figure 20.2. Cognitive learning

ered adopting were very weakly related to the 'problems' the organization had identified. They applied the label 'superstitious learning' to changes that are based on very precarious interpretations of environmental events.

Rapid environmental changes create a paradox for cognitive theories. On the one hand, rapid changes stimulate cognitive processes. Because people are likely to notice more events and to engage in more sense-making while they are adapting to changes, they tend to think they are doing more problem-solving and to credit themselves with any ensuing benefits. On the other hand, rapid changes amplify perceptual errors and foster more innovation. While they are adapting to changes, people tend to make worse choices, to create poorer solutions, and to learn inferior behaviors than they would in stable environments. As various authors have remarked, successful use of inferior behavior reinforces use of that behavior even though much more effective behaviors would be possible (Ginsberg and Baum 1994; Levitt and March 1988). Horvath (1996) argued that rapid environmental changes and uncertainty about future conditions lead managers to rely on their memories and to de-emphasize the significance of new data, to refine their knowledge rather than to reformulate it.

When learners model their situations, their models include noticed phenomena and omit unnoticed phenomena (Zebrowitz 1990). Learning usually changes what is noticed (Starbuck and Milliken 1988a). Noticing may be either involuntary or volitional. Voluntary noticing tends to depend on mental models that say some phenomena have relevance or importance; small stimuli or unimportant ones generally escape notice. For instance, people are more likely to notice words that relate to succeeding or failing immediately after they find out that they have succeeded or failed than at other times (Postman and Brown 1951).

Sense-making frameworks categorize data, fill in data that should exist, and edit out dissonant data. For instance, Milliken (1990) surmised that managers are less likely to interpret environmental changes as threatening when they perceive their organizations to be performing well than when they perceive their organizations to be performing poorly. Krull and Anderson (1997) reviewed some ways people's goals influence their choices among alternative sense-making frameworks. Watzlawick, Weakland, and Fisch (1974) pointed out that all perceptual frameworks have blind spots that prevent people from solving problems and that link behaviors into self-reinforcing cycles. When blind spots make problems unsolvable, people need new sense-making frameworks that portray situations differently. Watzlawick, Weakland, and Fisch (1974) proposed various strategies for reframing such situations.

Because social processes typically incorporate opposing effects, learning is much more likely to add sense-making frameworks than to eliminate them. Starbuck and Milliken (1988a: 59) remarked:

A process that tends to displace a social system from its current state gets offset by processes that tend to restore the current state; a process that tends to eliminate some characteristics gets offset by processes that tend to preserve the existing characteristics or to add new ones.

Thus, people and organizations face complex, contradictory environments, and they need enough, diverse sense-making frameworks to allow them to make sense of almost any situation.

Cognitive studies have concentrated on learning by individual people or organizations. They have paid little attention to learning by organizational populations. As is the case for behavioral learning, it is possible for learning by individuals and learning by organizations to link weakly: Individual members of organizations can develop new perceptions without changing their actions or communicating their new perceptions to other members. When this occurs, individuals learn without their organizations also learning. Nonaka (1994) argued that individuals often acquire knowledge tacitly and this tacit knowledge does not become organizational knowledge until it becomes explicit. As well, organizations can add new personnel who have distinctive expertise that they do not communicate to other members, so that the organizations learn in the sense that they add new expertise without individual members learning.

Learning by Individual People

Cameron (1984) remarked that people find it easier to establish criteria for ineffectiveness than criteria for effectiveness. However, a large body of research indicates that people set 'levels of aspiration' for successful performance (Starbuck 1963a, 1963b). Performance above a level of aspiration elicits pleasure; performance below a level of aspiration elicits disappointment. Levels of aspiration reflect experience, but people avoid setting them either too low or too high. Goals elicit the most effort if they are difficult but achievable, and performances produce the most satisfaction when they exceed difficult goals (Locke and Latham 1990). People are also more likely to feel satisfaction with their performances when they have devoted more effort to the tasks (Conway and Ross 1984).

Staw (1976) and colleagues (Staw and Fox 1977; Staw and Ross 1978) studied the tendency for college students to increase their commitments to unsuccessful courses of action in simulated tasks. That is, indications of failure may induce people to allocate more effort or resources to their current behavioral strategies rather than to adopt new behaviors. Milliken and Lant (1991: 131) argued that 'a number of forces push managers toward persistence after experiences of both success and failure' although these forces are stronger after success than after failure. The forces fostering persistence include the self-serving bias.

Some theorists have represented thought with computer programs that implement decision rules (Newell and Simon 1972). Some of these programs have accurately reproduced habitual routines, and some programs have learned in two senses: (a) they have searched for action alternatives and (b) they have adapted their response frequencies to match the frequencies of stimuli. They have not, however, shown holistic understanding or an ability to adapt to new circumstances, and they have been quite blind to their own limitations (Dreyfus and Dreyfus 1986; Stanfill and Waltz 1986). That is, programs have not been able to recognize that circumstances have changed in ways that make entrenched responses inappropriate.

Another, more prevalent approach portrays thought as mainly computational processes for choosing among already visible alternatives (Hogarth 1987; Mitchell 1974). These theories support three types of learning: (*a*) changes in perceived likelihoods of events, (*b*) changes in valuations of outcomes, and (*c*) changes in ability to discriminate among stimuli. However, their predictive accuracy has been low, partly because people do not always behave in logically consistent ways.

Cognitive phenomena vary across organizations and cultures. For instance, Dutton and Starbuck (1971) told how the problem-solving of a scheduler reflected the sense-making framework used by the scheduler's colleagues. If the scheduler had joined a different workgroup, his problem-solving would have reflected an alternative sense-making framework. Berthoin Antal, Dierkes, and Hähner (1997) described the effects of a company culture on the firm's perceptions of its environment and its readiness to respond to perceived issues. A company with a different culture would have different perceptions, would have perceived different issues, and would have responded differently to perceived issues. Nam (1991) presented evidence that Korean managers tend to take personal responsibility for poor performances by the groups they lead. Managers in a different society might blame poor performances on their subordinates or on uncontrollable external forces.

Learning by Individual Organizations

Dunbar, Garud, and Raghuram (1996*a*) argued that managers should manage the processes by which their firms acquire new sense-making frameworks. Porac and Rosa (1996: 35) contested this assertion, arguing that firms succeed without adapting to their environments: 'A frame's fit with the external environment is largely irrelevant' because a firm succeeds by imposing its frame on its environment. 'Success', they (1996: 40) said, 'is more a function of energy and persistence than of the repeating cycles of belief and discrediting proposed by Dunbar et al.'. Dunbar, Garud, and Raghuram (1996*b*) answered by saying that merely adhering to consistent strategies without attempting to adapt leaves survival up to natural selection.

Hedberg (1981: 10) emphasized the choices implicit in organizational learning: 'Reality is only the provider of potential inputs to a learner. Reality offers ranges of alternative environments from which an organization selects and enacts one from time to time.'

Some cognitive learning theories explicitly acknowledge communication within organizations. For instance, Clark (1972) wrote about shared 'sagas' that help colleges develop and preserve distinctive cultures, and Jönsson and Lundin (1977) described the waves of enthusiasm for successive business models pursued by politicians and administrators in city councils.

Other studies consider the use of communication to explicate tacit knowledge (Polanyi 1966; Weick 1995). These theories assert that organizations contain much more knowledge than people can express. Some knowledge is explicit and available; other is impossible to access or articulate at the moment. Thus, latent knowledge is waiting to be transformed, voiced, and interpreted. Processes of socialization, externalization, infusion, and diffusion transform tacit knowledge into explicit knowledge, and knowledge in individuals into knowledge in groups. For instance, Nonaka and Takeuchi (1995: 45–6) asserted: '[Knowledge-creating] organizations continuously create new knowledge by reconstructing existing perspectives, frameworks, or premises on a daily basis. In other words, the capacity for double-loop learning is built into the knowledge-creating organizations without the unrealistic assumption of the existence of a "right" answer.'

Baumard (1995, 1996, 1999), on the other hand, argued that knowledge need not be explicit to be useful. Not only can organizations exploit knowledge that has not been made explicit, but explication may fossilize knowledge, especially in turbulent settings. He interpreted four case studies as examples of how managerial groups can understand and manage tacit knowledge by experimenting with its borders.

On the ground that people are better able to generate appropriate responses to moderate successes and failures, Weick (1984) urged people to define problems in ways that will allow 'small wins' and 'small flops'.

Moderate Success

Cyert and March (1963) laid out a behavioral model in which decision rules govern actions, and successes and failures change the parameters in these decision rules. When actions yield apparently good results, organizations tend to repeat them, and repeated actions eventually become standard operating procedures. Starbuck (1983, 1985) observed that standard operating procedures frequently induce organizations to act unreflectively and automatically, and that they may invent 'problems' to justify their actions. Weick (1991) too argued that organizations tend to emit the same responses despite unstable and changing stimuli.

Success does not always induce organizations to standardize operating procedures, however. To explain firms' slowness in adapting to environmental changes, Cyert and March (1963: 36–38) introduced the concept of 'organizational slack', which is the difference between the resources available and the resources necessary to keep a firm in existence. Successes increase slack, which encourages risk taking and experimentation. The experiments can become launch platforms for new strategies, proactive actions, and market leadership. Furthermore, there are industries and professional cultures where creativity norms prohibit repetition of past successes. For example, a well-reputed advertising agency is unlikely to repeat a successful ad campaign. IKEA, the worldwide chain of furniture stores, has a strong culture (Salzer 1994) that seems to foster renewal. Whenever a product line, or a way of organizing, becomes routine, they change it. A similar culture of change seems to be present in the 3M Company, which creates 'garage projects' to foster new ideas. 3M employees can use 15 percent of their working hours to develop new ideas, to challenge present practices, and to innovate.

Success provides discretion and it facilitates fine-tuning and elaboration of strategies, but it also diverts attention from the environment and from the future. It makes organizations confident and homogeneous (Sitkin 1992). Levinthal and March (1993) emphasized the shortsightedness of organizational learning and the subjectivity of performance evaluations. They said, 'Organizational learning oversamples successes and undersamples failures' because successes and failures are defined by the organizations (1993: 109). Because learning appears to eliminate failures, it fosters optimistic expectations. Because organizations promote people who participated in successful activities, leaders are optimistic people.

During periods of repeated success, evolutionary learning in small steps seems to work better than does revolutionary learning. Continuous improvement, the daily challenging of status quo, supports the notion that everything can be improved. For instance, Asea Brown Boveri used simple benchmarks to challenge workers to cut lead times in half despite many years of success. The Japanese tradition of continuous improvement has demonstrated viability through long periods of daily-learning-at-work, particularly in manufacturing. Numerous Japanese companies, successful and not so successful, have implemented continuous improvement as a way of working life.

Nonaka and Takeuchi (1995) maintained that Japanese companies have considerably greater ability to learn, improve, and restructure in spite of success than do Western companies. Japanese shop-floor management has been very successful in supporting everyday learning and continuous improvement, mainly in manufacturing firms, but there seems to be no evidence that these principles have been applied successfully on management levels and to strategy reformulation. Indeed, Barker and Duhaime (1997) presented evidence that continuous improvement has little potential to drive organizational learning towards strategic turnarounds. They found that a few turnarounds succeed while most do not, and that substantial strategic changes, often CEO changes, must occur before reorientations begin.

Chronic Success

Empirical research suggests that long-term success weakens the ability to unlearn radically and to reorient strategically (Grinyer and Norburn 1975; Starbuck and Hedberg 1977; Hedberg and Jönsson 1977; Sitkin 1992). Chronically successful organizations develop introverted complacency and they tell stories about victories and heroes of the past. They elaborate and reinforce their cognition structures. They expect success to continue and stop scanning their environments for signals that they believe to be irrelevant (Hedberg, Nystrom, and Starbuck

1976; Sitkin 1992). On the other hand, Dougherty and Hardy (1996) studied sustained product innovation in fifteen firms that averaged ninety-six years of age and that had been quite successful. They concluded that a major obstacle to organizational change lay in innovators' inability to access power and to restructure resource flows rather than their inability to discover environmental threats and to exploit strategic opportunities. What product innovation did occur happened in spite of mature industrial organization, not because of it.

Miller (1990: 3) likened chronically successful organizations to Icarus, who flew so near the Sun that his wings melted: 'Success leads to specialization and exaggeration, to confidence and complacency, to dogma and ritual.... Robust, superior organizations evolve into flawed purebreds; they move from rich character to exaggerated caricature, as all subtlety, all nuance, is gradually lost.' He described four prototypic developmental trajectories corresponding to four formulas for success. After analyzing the histories of thirty-six firms, Miller (1993, 1994) inferred that lengthy periods of success foster (*a*) structural and strategic inertia, (*b*) extreme process orientations, (*c*) inattention, and (*d*) insularity. Success breeds simplicity and purity, not complexity. A focus on core competence and competitive edge, which initially make an organization successful, tends to grow even more narrow and specialized over time. Positive feedback reinforces simplicity to a point where the organization loses requisite variety. Thus, simplicity yields benefits during the first phases of success, but turns into a liability.

Moderate Failure

In their model, Cyert and March (1963) said actual or expected failures induce a firm to make parameter changes. If these parameter changes prove inadequate to allow forecasts of success, the firm searches its environments for new alternatives. Similarly, Sitkin (1992) argued that moderate levels of failure draw attention to potential problems and stimulate searches for potential solutions. He (1992: 243) set forth criteria for 'intelligent failure'. People should plan their actions (*a*) to yield diagnostic information, (*b*) to limit the costs of failure, (*c*) to generate feedback quickly, and (*d*) to focus on familiar domains so that they will be able to analyze what happened. He also listed organizational properties that foster intelligent failure.

The proposition that failure fosters experimentation contrasts with the findings from studies of individual people, which indicate that unpleasant consequences can stop existing behaviors without stimulating learners to try new behaviors. Also, Hedberg (1981) pointed out that organizational inertia often delays or counteracts problem-solving.

Burgelman (1994) portrayed moderate failure as a source of information. In a study of Intel Corporation, he analyzed the development of strategies as evolutionary processes. Top managers, he said, create 'an internal selection environment' of rules for choosing among courses of action. For such selection rules to be effective, they have to match prevailing pressures in the firm's environment.

This match depends, in turn, on middle managers' generating appropriate strategic initiatives and on top managers' having 'strategic recognition capability'. Failure in a line of business gives top managers better understanding of the relations between the firm's 'distinctive competence' and 'the basis of competition in the industries in which they remain active' (1994: 52).

Chronic Failure

Organizations' resistance to dramatic reorientations creates a need for explicit unlearning. Organizations, especially older ones, find it hard to ignore their current knowledge and their current operating procedures because they build up explicit justifications for their actions and they associate specific people with specific policies (Hedberg 1981). As one result, organizations integrate their knowledge and procedures into rigid, coherent structures in which ideas and politics buttress each other. External attributions for failure prevent organizations from questioning their key assumptions (Virany, Tushman, and Romanelli 1992). Before attempting radical changes, they must dismantle parts of their current ideological and political structures. Before they will contemplate dramatically different procedures, policies, and strategies, they must lose confidence in their current procedures, policies, strategies, and top managers. Several authors have argued that change in top management may be a prerequisite for strategic change (Starbuck 1983; Virany, Tushman, and Romanelli 1992).

Chronic organizational failure is painful and destructive (Starbuck, Greve, and Hedberg 1978). Coworkers depart, and those who remain wonder if everyone with job options and ambition is going. Those remaining are working harder and shouldering unfamiliar tasks, they may be receiving less pay, and their promotion chances seem dim. Budgets decline. As departments fight to preserve their shares, trust erodes. Central control exposes the top managers' inability to produce success: If the top managers knew what to do, their organizations would not remain in such serious trouble. Moreover, the top managers have probably declared many times over that better times are at hand. When the better times do not appear, such declarations underline the top managers' impotence and unreliability. In many cases, morale drops to such a low state that many organizations cannot go on. Like punishment, unlearning ends behavior without substituting new behavior, so many organizations discover that their procedures, policies, and strategies do not work and they lack the ability to replace them.

Learning by Populations of Organizations

Organizations transmit knowledge to each other via joint ventures, educational institutions, consultants, lawyers, venture capitalists, trade and popular periodicals, conventions, and personnel who change jobs (Levitt and March 1988, Miner et al. 1996). Hodgkinson (1997: 922) observed 'over time, strategists from rival firms develop highly similar (or "shared") mental models of the competitive arena due to the fact that they share similar technical and material problems and frequently exchange information'. Spender (1989) showed how recipes that had proven successful in one company spread to become industry-wide recipes. Sahlin-Andersson pictured such imitation as a process of 'editing success' (1996: 82). Firms can imitate with or without communicating with each other, with or without sharing a common rationale. As a result, the perceptual errors of each individual firm have less impact and shared misperceptions become even more powerful.

Tripsas (1997) portrayed imitation as partial and inefficient when she described three waves of change in the global typesetter industry from 1886 to 1990. She found that most of the established firms invested heavily in new, competence-destroying technologies even though their ability to implement these technologies profitably was hampered by their previous experience. The incumbents mostly survived change and managed to prevent new invaders from taking over. The incumbents had the advantage of specialized complementary assets such as team skills and strong sales and service networks, which served to buffer performance and to give time for slow learning processes.

Other studies have considered how performance affects learning. Miner et al. (1996) pointed out that failure by one organization often makes other organizations in the same population more alert to environmental changes. They also remarked that no such effect occurred in the Swiss watch industry. Miller and Chen (1994) analyzed data about U.S. airlines and inferred that, on average, high-revenue periods are followed by periods of inertia, and vice versa. Also, diversity of markets discouraged inertia. Later, they also inferred that, on average, high-revenue periods are followed by periods in which firms take fewer types of competitive actions, and vice versa (1996). They remarked:

Success may drive managers to whittle down their repertoires—to zero in on what they believe is the path to success. But the simplicity of that path may be at least in part a product of 'extrarational' factors such as a munificent environment, the complacency born of size, and perhaps even the attribution of merit to practices of little consequence. (1996: 434)

Thus, cognitive approaches allow learning to depend only weakly on rewards or punishments that arise in the environment. A learner and an environment can be loosely linked, a learner has much influence on the learning process, and indeed a learner can exert much influence on the environment.

The next two sections of this chapter describe illustrative cases of learning in real life. The first case shows the complexity of learning processes within both of two interdependent organizations. The second case broadens the horizon to an organizational population. Both cases indicate how greatly organizations depend on each other and how the slowness of learning influences what is learned. Both cases suggest that cognitive and behavioral learning occur at the same time.

5. THROUGH EVOLUTIONARY LEARNING
TO THE CHALLENGER DISASTER

The National Aeronautics and Space Administration (NASA), coordinates a coalition of aerospace firms that operate the U.S. space program. In the mid 1970s, this coalition began building space shuttles. Their efforts illustrate some common properties of organizational efforts to learn from feedback. Development efforts generated incremental changes that took place in a noisy and complex environment. In each of two key organizations, some people interpreted the feedbacks from these changes as reassuring and others saw them as ominous. People misperceived events, they disagreed about interpretations, and they competed for control; communications were incomplete and biased by political agendas.

The space shuttles have rocket engines, but these do not have enough power for launch. The shuttles receive added lift during launch from Solid Rocket Boosters (SRBs). NASA chose Thiokol to build the SRBs. The SRBs are composed of interlocking cylinders. When SRBs ignite, they fill with fiery gases that must not leak through the joints between cylinders. Two O-rings in each joint were supposed to seal it tightly.

During the second shuttle launch in 1981, hot gases eroded an O-ring. The NASA personnel who saw this damage judged it so minor that they did not report it upward. Launches in 1982 produced no more evidence of problems.

During 1982, Thiokol proposed small changes to make the SRBs lighter and more powerful. After tests showed that these changes increased the probability of leakage, NASA reclassified the joints as more dangerous. However, Thiokol judged the threat to be small, and in 1983, NASA started using the modified SRBs.

During 1983, a static test and one launch damaged O-rings. In response, NASA changed the method for testing joints when it assembled SRBs. After another launch damaged an O-ring in February 1984, engineers from NASA and Thiokol speculated that the new test procedures were making the O-rings more vulnerable. A review commission ran laboratory tests that suggested the O-rings would seal tightly even if eroded as much as 0.241 centimeters, and it ran a computer simulation that implied the erosion would not exceed 0.229 centimeters. 'Therefore,' concluded the review commission, 'this is not a constraint to future launches' (Presidential Commission 1986: I-128–32). At this point, the NASA manager in charge of SRBs proposed that some damage was 'acceptable' because the O-rings embodied a safety factor. NASA's top managers approved this idea (Presidential Commission 1986: II-H1).

After a launch in April 1984 produced more O-ring damage, NASA's second-in-command asked for a thorough study of the O-rings. NASA gave this assignment to Thiokol, which proposed tests but did not make them and did not submit a report.

SRB joints were damaged during three of five launches in 1984, during eight of nine launches in 1985, and during the first launch in 1986. Two test firings also produced damage. Furthermore, the damage became more serious over time. The erosion grew larger and sometimes both O-rings in a joint suffered damage.

After the fifteenth launch in January 1985 produced especially severe damage, Thiokol proposed that a low ambient temperature during launch might have made the joints more vulnerable. But even more serious damage occurred during a launch in April 1985 when the ambient temperature was moderate, so the temperature hypothesis lost plausibility. In that April launch, one O-ring was eroded 0.434 centimeters, nearly twice the maximum predicted by NASA's earlier simulation.

On the evening before the Challenger launch in January 1986, managers and engineers from NASA and Thiokol confronted each other about the desirability of launching. Two Thiokol engineers argued that the launch should be postponed because low ambient temperatures existed at the launch site and low ambient temperatures were very probably a factor in O-ring erosion. Other Thiokol engineers advocated caution, but without fervor. The chief NASA engineer said he thought the Thiokol engineers were being excessively cautious. NASA's managers argued that the evidence about low ambient temperatures was unclear and that, since low ambient temperatures were common in winter, postponing this launch would imply that they should postpone all launches until spring brought warmer weather. Worried about maintaining amicable relations with NASA, Thiokol's managers overruled their engineers and endorsed launching.

The next day, Challenger disintegrated, killing its crew and shattering America's confidence in NASA's competence.

Cognitive Learning

The gradually escalating damage convinced engineers at NASA and Thiokol that the SRBs posed risks, but the engineers disagreed about the degree of risk. In July 1985, Thiokol ordered new SRB cases with three O-rings in each joint, but the supplier was given three years to produce these SRBs. In August 1985, Thiokol at last created a task force to make the study that NASA had requested 16 months earlier; this task force proposed numerous studies but it had few resources. In January 1986, engineers from NASA and Thiokol assembled to discuss hypotheses about O-ring damage. There were many hypotheses and much ambiguity, as the engineers debated the alternative hypotheses.

The events that were causing engineers to worry were leading key managers at NASA and Thiokol to infer that the SRB joints posed only small risks. These managers observed that the SRBs had suffered no serious harm even though O-rings had been damaged in almost every recent launch. Indeed, the joints had sealed adequately even when the O-rings had sustained damage that greatly exceeded the direst forecast. Not only did the engineers seem to have overstated the risks but 'O-ring erosion was accepted and indeed expected' (Bell and Esch 1987: 43). After a briefing in August 1985, NASA's top management concluded, 'it is safe to continue flying' (Presidential Commission 1986: I-140).

An investigation after the disaster found much to blame in the behavior of NASA and Thiokol managers, but it did not yield a definitive explanation for the disaster. Indeed, the investigators introduced two hypotheses about causes for the disaster that no one had posed earlier. Many hypotheses remain plausible to this day (Starbuck and Milliken 1988b).

Two years after the disaster, an astronaut observed that the disaster had taught lessons that NASA would probably have to learn again and again. Although the astronaut did not explain what lessons he thought NASA had learned, different people, inside and outside NASA, might deem different lessons to be the appropriate ones.

Behavioral Learning

The Challenger disaster halted much of the behavior that preceded it, and it instigated widespread changes in NASA, in Thiokol, and in the space shuttle. Many managers were replaced in both organizations, including almost everyone who participated in the decision to launch Challenger. The replaced personnel may have behaved differently in their new jobs or in retirement but no data are available. NASA changed many procedures.

NASA made no further launches until Thiokol received new SRB cases; these were the cases that had been ordered in July 1985 except that they had three O-rings in each joint. During the launch hiatus, suppliers modified many components of the space shuttle, seeking to make them safer.

Later, NASA solicited SRB-design proposals from potential suppliers other than Thiokol. As is generally true of behavioral changes that follow failures, changes in design or supplier could introduce unforeseen problems or yield unexpected benefits.

6. BUILDING INERTIA IN THE SWEDISH CONSTRUCTION INDUSTRY

Events in the Swedish construction industry illustrate population-level learning. As the industry went through a cycle of success, crisis, and recovery, there was change in the kinds of firms in the population and in their interdependencies. Mainly, the industry lost diversity. The surviving firms had behaved differently from those that failed. They had had more financial resources initially and had remained financially stronger throughout the changes, partly because they had been slower to adopt changing industry recipes.

The construction industry, consisting of construction firms, real-estate firms, and combinations thereof, was a favorite at the Stockholm Stock Exchange during the 1980s. Deregulation of rents and of the banking system, an oversupply of credit from an expanding service industry, and low interest rates fueled a boom. Between 1983 and 1988, the property index increased more than 1500 percent, property prices grew an average of 25 percent per annum, and the thirty-five listed firms increased their joint market value enormously. In 1988, several listed firms hit all-time highs, and more than half of them increased their adjusted net asset value by more than 50 percent during that year alone.

Malmström (1995) and Hedberg and Malmström (1997) traced the histories of the listed firms over 1982–92. They gathered economic indicators, strategies, and CEOs' statements in annual reports. Initially, the industry had subgroups with distinct performances and strategies. Some firms were mainly construction firms whereas others focused on ownership, maintenance, and rental of apartments and commercial buildings. However, as the boom developed, the firms elaborated their core businesses and imitated each other's strategies. Towards the end of the period, most firms focused on a few industry recipes and the industry exhibited much less heterogeneity. The CEOs expressed similar values and expectations in annual reports. The firms linked through interlocking ownership, and they formed a network that encompassed real-estate firms, construction firms, and the independent institutes that assessed and certified property values. Assuming that the Swedish market was becoming saturated, twenty-three of the twenty-nine firms began to invest in Brussels, Amsterdam, Antwerp, and London during 1988–89. By these firms' standards, these markets were undervalued and offered good bargains.

Warning signals of oversupply, boosted valuations, and sagging rental development arrived in 1987 and 1988. These signals were first neglected, then recognized but not acted upon. For a short period also, firms attributed growing turbulence to 'the Saddam effect' in connection with the Gulf invasion. House rentals began stagnating early in 1989, but investments continued and the price index of commercial property increased by another 15 percent during 1989. Seeing but not acting might have been a result of slow sense-making or of difficulties unlearning previously successful behaviors. Even when firms acted, time delays and inertia led to the initiation of new building projects at a time when property could not be sold or rented.

In September 1990, a once-highly-successful real-estate firm declared bankruptcy. This triggered an unprecedented crisis in the Swedish real-estate markets, and the crisis spread to the banks and to the financial institutions. Some fifty firms went bankrupt each month during the fall of 1990 and the property index declined by 50 percent by year's end. The firms' total market value, which had more than quintupled between 1985 and 1990, fell one-third in less than two years and then continued to decline until it reached half of its peak value. Sweden struggled with economic turmoil for several years, as the crisis shattered financial institutions.

In retrospect, one can see clear and strong warning signals that might have heralded the approaching crisis. The warning signals that construction firms neglected include: (*a*) growing vacancy rates that signaled oversupply of commercial property; (*b*) reports showing that Swedish property yields were very low in comparison with yields in other countries; (*c*) a severe real-estate crisis in Norway that caused turbulence in banking; (*d*) construction costs that continued to rise dramatically; (*e*) a halt in new construction of commercial buildings by the Swedish government to cool down the economy; (*f*) two consecutive deregulations of the Swedish currency system; and (*g*) Sweden's application to join the European Union and beginning attempts to harmonize the Swedish economy with that of the EU. True enough, some CEOs did predict as early as 1987 and 1988 that their industry would stagnate, but even these firms continued to expand and invest. None of these CEOs predicted that property values would be cut in half and that almost all business activities would stop.

Cognitive Learning

As the industry grew and prospered, the firms shared their cognitive models; most firms focused on a very few industry recipes. With few exceptions, the firms' annual reports described similar expectations about the future. Firms developed and changed their assessment and accounting criteria with striking coordination. They also identified promising investment opportunities in the UK, in Holland and in Belgium at about the same time. In short, their cognitive models became more and more homogeneous.

It took several years of mounting crises to reframe these mental models. When warning signals appeared they were first overlooked and then recognized, but the firms were slow in changing their strategies. The changing stimuli did not elicit behavioral change until very late, and the firms' public statements and analyses of the crisis bore weak relations to their behaviors.

There were no distinctly better learners. There were no firms that discovered early warning signals and reacted in timely fashion. The survivors may have had less-than-average propensities to imitate others.

Behavioral Learning

Success led to repeated behavior and, later, to unification of industry recipes. An initial population of quite diverse firms became much more homogeneous as firms imitated each other. This homogeneity, in turn, contributed to a build-up of organizational inertia across the industry. Inertia arose partly from complexity, as the firms integrated via interlocking ownership and created a network that spanned real-estate firms, construction firms, and property-valuation institutes.

Learning did not prepare the firms for a market downturn; instead it led to unfortunate delays and a collapsing market. Inertia in production systems made it difficult to halt new investments. Organizational inertia made strategic changes very difficult. Many construction firms went bankrupt, most firms suffered badly, and only a few firms came out of the turbulence with adequate performance. The firms that survived were ones that had had initial financial strength, that ran diverse operations, and that adopted industry recipes slowly; they may have reacted to warning signals more rapidly, although not rapidly enough. The survivors that have continued to do well subsequently have maintained diversity of operations and have focused on well-defined geographic regions and on certain types of housing projects. They have also sold most of their foreign investments.

7. INTEGRATING BEHAVIORAL AND COGNITIVE LEARNING

The foregoing cases suggest that cognitive and behavioral learning occur in combinations that are difficult to disentangle. Perhaps this mutual entanglement is why theories of learning are filled with ironic contradictions. Extreme advocates of behavioral learning have asserted that cognition plays an unimportant role in behavioral change, whereas extreme advocates of cognitive learning have asserted that all behavioral change follows cognitive dictates. Yet each approach seems to find it difficult to ignore the other. Those who study behavioral learning often explain hypotheses in terms of peoples' motives and thoughts; the fundamental concepts of success and failure cannot be separated from people's interpretations of outcomes. Those who study cognitive learning often speak of reinforcement effects or of unconscious processes; the routines that people use when perceiving or deciding may be established through mechanistic processes.

Loose Links

Although people perceive that their thinking controls their behavior, neither theory nor empirical evidence is consistent with tight cognitive control. The links between behavior and cognition must be loose. Even cognitive theories assert that learning can be occurring while outsiders can see no behavioral changes. For instance, in their study of a merger, Leroy and Ramanantsoa (1997) noted that cognitive changes both began and ended before observable changes in behavior.

Behaviors have many determinants in addition to cognitive ones. Firstly, many behaviors occur automatically without continuing reflection, which implies that cognitive controls operate intermittently if at all. Secondly, external forces dictate many behaviors. For instance, in hierarchical organizations, subordinates have to obey orders and rules, and their compensation and promotions depend on their conformity. Thirdly, people sometimes imitate successful behaviors or the behaviors of respected people even though they do not know why their models acted as they did. Some imitated behaviors yield benefits solely or mainly because they conform to societal norms.

There is abundant evidence that cognitions adapt to actual behavior (Kiesler 1971). Involuntary perceptual changes make behaviors seem more rational, and these changes occur even when external forces have compelled the behavior. Festinger (1962) theorized that forced compliance generates less and less cognitive dissonance as rewards or punishments grow larger. That is, people's actions cause little dissonance for them when their actions seem to promote enormous success or to prevent dreadful failure. Festinger also suggested that perceptions of successes and failures change to reduce the dissonance created by forced compliance (see also Conway and Ross 1984). Sproull (1981) conjectured that cognitions correlate with behaviors in situations that appear familiar, but that novel situations induce people to innovate and subsequently to revise their cognitions to match the new behaviors.

Causal theories that people construct from their experience may be so erroneous that they afford no useful bases for behavioral control (Anderson, Krull, and Weiner 1996). That is, they may lead to very inaccurate predictions about the effects of actions on outcomes. As a result, behavior that appears optimal on the basis of cognitions can be foolhardy.

The hypothesis that cognitions determine behaviors has shown such weak predictive power that some psychologists regard it as having been disconfirmed (Broadbent 1961; Skinner 1974). For instance, people's stated perceptions of their leaders predict poorly their actions with respect to their leaders (Kerr and Slocum 1981). Nystrom and Starbuck (1984) concluded that, in general, behaviors exert stronger influence on cognitions than cognitions exert on behaviors. They (1984: 284) prescribed: 'Change beliefs by changing peoples' behaviors rather than by ideological education, propaganda, or structural interventions. Focus on behaviors as causes of beliefs rather than the other way around.'

Festinger (1962) framed the issue of behavioral control versus cognitive control in terms of the difficulty of making different kinds of changes. Some behaviors are easy to change and others hard to change; and likewise, some cognitions are easy to change and others hard to change.

Organizations tend to have looser connections between behaviors and cognitions than do individual people. Firstly, organizations frequently concretize their cognitions as stable behavior programs that continue even as environmental and social conditions evolve. Starbuck (1982, 1983, 1985) asserted that organizations often amend their cognitions to fit with actions that they have already taken or that they take programmatically and nonreflectively. Secondly, organizational political processes loosen the connections between specific cognitions and specific behaviors. March and Olsen (1979: 26) likened organizational decision settings to 'garbage cans' filled with diverse actors, diverse problems, and diverse potential solutions. Starbuck, Greve, and Hedberg (1978) said top managers' efforts to retain their positions often prevent their organizations from taking actions needed to deal with crises. Thirdly, organizations often wait too long to respond to external forces, then make dramatic responses. Fourthly, most organizations follow institutionalized rituals in order to win societal support (Meyer and Rowan 1977).

Duality

Studies of learning by individual organizations show a puzzling imbalance. Almost all of these studies have taken a cognitive approach and very few a behavioral one. Yet the theories arising from these studies emphasize the importance of standard operating procedures, as well as behavior programs that are not formalized.

Likewise, studies of learning by populations of organizations show an imbalance of a different sort. Most of these studies have taken a behavioral approach and very few a cognitive one. The latter have focused on imitation and they have de-emphasized rational thought. The former have often explained their theories in cognitive terms even though they did not gather evidence about cognitions.

That such incongruities not only exist but also exist without bothering researchers poses yet another puzzle. Perhaps the distinction between behavior and cognition is an abstraction that does not exist in the realities of daily life?

> ... we are only able to perceive the environment as composed of separate things by suppressing our recognition of the nonthings which fill the interstices.
> — Edmund Leach (1964: 37)

21

The Accuracy of Managers' Perceptions: A Dimension Missing from Theories about Firms

Coauthored with Susan R. Salgado and John M. Mezias

1. INTRODUCTION

This chapter looks at some evidence about the accuracy—or rather the inaccuracy—of managers' perceptions. With few exceptions, academic theorists assume that managers perceive accurately. Some theorists, mainly economists, even assume that managers have precisely correct expectations about future events. But managers often perceive inaccurately. They often make perception errors when they are dealing with phenomena that they run into daily in their jobs; they make larger errors and make them more often when they encounter novel phenomena. Yet academics often base studies on managers' perceptions of phenomena that are unfamiliar to the managers and do not fit into their daily experiences. As a result, academics generate noisy data that have very different meanings for managers than for academics.

Section 2 reviews debates about the theory of the firm because these debates center on the need for theorists to know what managers perceive, how they reason, and how they make decisions. Some theorists hold that these processes are unimportant, others that they are very important. Thus these debates set a theoretical context for considering the usefulness of understanding managers' perceptions. Section 3 describes some studies that suggest managers make significant perception errors, and it inventories some of the factors affecting the accuracy of managers' perceptions. The final section extracts implications for research about the behavior of firms.

2. HOW REALISTIC SHOULD A THEORY BE?

'Neoclassical economists take the position that "If the world is not like the model, so much the worse for the world".'
—Sir John L. Eatwell, in a speech at The New School for Social Research,
New York (1994)

The economic 'theory of the firm' assumes that firms maximize long-run profits. This assumption limits discussion of a firm's decisions about prices and quantities by ruling out almost all of the actions that the firm might consider taking. In fact, economic theorists usually add assumptions that rule out all actions but one. These theorists can then analyze the sensitivity of this unique optimal action to conjectured changes in factors such as costs, market conditions or taxes.

Complaints about the realism of the theory of the firm have a long history. Some of these complaints have emphasized logical problems within the framework of the theory itself. For instance, Tintner (1941) reasoned that a firm could have only a single goal—to maximize profits—only if the firm has perfect knowledge of the future. If a firm has uncertainty about the future, it has to regard the outcomes of its possible actions as probability distributions. But it is not possible to maximize a probability distribution: an evaluation of a distribution must take account of all of the properties of the distribution—its mean, its variance, its skewness, and so forth.

However, the most plentiful complaints have concerned the apparent divergence between the assumption of profit maximization and the actions taken by real-life managers. These complaints gained impetus from an empirical study conducted by researchers at Oxford University in 1938–39. They (Hall and Hitch 1939; Harrod 1939: 4–5) found that business managers 'were in profound ignorance' concerning the elasticity of demand for their products, that managers had little confidence in their knowledge of marginal costs, and that firms set prices not by optimizing but by applying traditional markup rules. Harrod (1939) proposed that economists should pay more attention to what managers actually do rather than to deductions from economic theories.

Complaints escalated in the late 1940s and 1950s. Lester (1946: 72) made an empirical study that echoed the Oxford study; 'most entrepreneurs do not tend to think in terms of marginal variable cost'. Gordon (1948) called for a radically different theory of the firm. He asserted that firms follow accepted maxims that bear no obvious relationships to profit maximization; for example, in the short run, firms seek only to attain satisfactory profits. Andrews (1949) pointed out that, because some costs appear to be 'fixed', firms might expand in pursuit of cost savings that never materialize. Cooper (1949) complained that the theory of the firm did not view firms as organizations. Papandreou (1952) argued that firms develop strategic plans and organization designs and that these plans reflect the interests of different stakeholders. Penrose (1952) pointed out that managers try to alter the environments in which their businesses operate, and thereby to extract success from whatever actions they prefer to take. Simon (1955: 104) contended 'that there is a complete lack of evidence that, in actual human choice situations of any complexity', people make the calculations that would be necessary in order to make optimal choices. People have 'limited' or 'approximate' rationality (1955: 113–114): they do not know all possible outcomes of their potential actions; they engage in limited searches to investigate such outcomes; and they categorize outcomes crudely as satisfactory or unsatisfactory. Making arguments similar to Simon's, Margolis (1958: 189) pointed out that firms use 'non-profit-maximizing goals and business rules' because managers do not have the information they would need to make 'fully rational' decisions. Margolis charged that efforts to apply the theory of the firm to practical problems require 'extra-economic' assumptions.

Of course, the protests against conventional economic theory evoked responses. Machlup (1946) criticized the empirical studies by the Oxford University researchers and by Lester. These researchers, he said, did not allow for the fact that the theory of the firm deals with expectations about the future rather than actual experiences, and they had assumed that entrepreneurs understand concepts such as marginal cost and elasticity of demand. Furthermore, Lester had relied on mailed questionnaires: 'A set formulation of questions will hardly fit any large number of business men in different fields and, hence, questionnaires to be filled out by them will rarely yield useful results' (1946: 537).

Alchian (1950: 217) concurred 'that empirical investigations via questionnaire methods, so far used, are incapable of evaluating the validity of marginal productivity analysis'. However, he argued, economists do not have to look at actual decision processes in order to predict the behaviors that survive in the long run. No matter what decision rules firms might use, they can survive only by earning positive profits; firms that lose money go out of business. Also, firms that behave more optimally have higher probabilities of survival. As a result, an economist 'can state what types of firms or behavior relative to other possible types will be more viable, even though the firms themselves may not know the conditions or even try to achieve them' (1950: 216). However, Alchian (1950: 220) stopped short of the extreme inference that the long-run results would be profit-maximizing: 'The economist may be pushing his luck too far in arguing that actions... will converge... toward the optimum action that should have been selected if foresight had been perfect.'

Less cautious than Alchian, Friedman (1953) maintained that evolution would produce profit maximization in the long run. He also opined that economic theory does not have to describe firms' behaviors as long as it helps economists to analyze these behaviors. Thus it is more important for the theory of the firm to meet the intellectual needs of economists than for it to describe firms' behaviors.

Alchian and Friedman framed their defenses around long-run outcomes across populations of competing firms, an orientation that illustrates two differences that have powered and confounded the debates between critics and defenders. One difference is the level of aggregation that the theory of the firm ought to address: is it one firm or a population of competing firms? Although the theory's label speaks of 'the firm' as if the theory deals with a single organization, the theory actually says little about activities within a single organization. Attempts to apply the theory have typically concerned events involving many firms, and very few economists have shown interest in events within a single firm. The second difference is the time period that the theory ought to address. Is it the short run or the long run? The conventional theory does not attempt to describe short-run outcomes; it speaks only of equilibrium states that might be reached in the long run, if ever. By contrast, critics of the conventional theory framed their arguments in terms of short-run activities within a single organization. Proponents of 'a theory of one firm in the short run' were criticizing 'a theory of long-run outcomes across a population of firms'.

The foregoing debates motivated three lines of development during the late 1950s and early 1960s. Focusing on populations of competing firms in the long run, Winter (1964) followed up on Alchian's evolutionary viewpoint, but he expressed much more skepticism about the effectiveness of evolutionary processes in selecting profitable firms. He inferred that there are many reasons why unprofitable firms might survive indefinitely despite evolutionary selection. Since firms mainly compete with similar firms, selection processes are weak. There is no evidence that any firm has discovered and is capable of using decision rules that will maximize profits. Some firms might use suboptimal decision rules that produce profit-maximizing behaviors in their current environments, but as the environments change, the suboptimal rules would become inappropriate. Because stakeholders do not shift their commitments rapidly, a suboptimal firm can survive for a very long time. Stakeholders might erroneously support firms that maximize short-run profits, while withholding support from the long-run profit maximizers and thereby driving them out of business.

The second and third lines of development focused on a single firm in the short run. Penrose (1959) argued that profitability might come from short-run processes of change rather than from long-run end states achieved through change.

The growth of firms may be consistent with the most efficient use of society's resources; the result of past growth—the size attained at any time—may have no corresponding advantages. Each successive step in its growth may be profitable to the firm and, if otherwise under-utilized resources are used, advantageous to society. But once any expansion is completed, the original justification for the expansion may fade into insignificance as new opportunities for growth develop and are acted upon. (1959: 103)

Cyert and March (1963) attempted to launch 'a behavioral theory of the firm'. They (1963: 19) wanted to create a theory that would make predictions about the behaviors of a single firm and would base these predictions on 'the actual process of organizational decision making'. To illustrate what they meant by predictions based on 'the actual process of organizational decision making', Cyert and March developed models of decision-making about prices and quantities in a department store. These models involved very detailed rules of thumb, and so tests of the models were essentially tests of how closely human beings adhered to the described rules. Although these models were quite accurate, the models described routine, microscopic decisions that occurred over and over again. Only routine, repeated decisions are codified as rules that decision-makers can articulate.

Cyert and March championed various generalizations that describe entire organizations macroscopically over long periods. First, organizations pursue conflicting goals; long-run profit maximization is not the sole goal. Second, organizations avoid uncertainty by concentrating on pressing problems, by attempting to control their environments, and by retaining 'organizational slack', meaning resources that are not fully utilized. Third, organizations do not see all alternatives; they have to search for alternatives, and they undertake these searches primarily in response to problems. Fourth, organizations learn: they change their goals and forecasts in reaction to experience; they change their decision rules to suit new circumstances. Finally, organizations' estimates of current and future parameters embody biases. However, Cyert and March's book said little about how these macroscopic properties of organizations do or might relate to the routine, repeated decisions that they actually modeled. The macroscopic properties seem to involve perception of abstract concepts, analysis, and debate, whereas the microscopic decision rules seem to act mechanistically in reaction to immediate, concrete events. For example, what is the relation between a long-run pricing strategy and a decision about the price of one specific product right now? Do the routine microscopic behaviors express macroscopic rationales or are people merely repeating programs that they have learned?

Two decades later, Nelson and Winter (1982) produced a second-generation behavioral theory of the firm that partly reconciles the disparity between microscopic current behaviors and macroscopic long-run behaviors. Nelson and Winter described organizational development as an evolutionary process in which standardized behavioral routines survive or disappear; some behavioral routines survive for long periods and others do not. Moreover, a given routine may occur in many organizations, and the entities that develop are populations of organizations that often imitate each other. This view aggregates current, microscopic behaviors, which may apply to very small parts of organizations, into long-run patterns that cross many organizations. However, it also seems to relegate human cognition to very minor roles, as an invisible hand steers development.

Managers and Management Scholars See It Differently

The foregoing theories of the firm reflect their roots in economics and in academe. Economists have emphasized different phenomena than have management scholars. Academics have emphasized different phenomena than managers.

Economists Versus Management Scholars

With the exception of Cyert and March's and Penrose's behavioral theories, the economic theories are not about a firm's behavior in the immediate future, but about industry-level phenomena over the very long run. An aggregate, long-run perspective may have advantages for economists. Behaviors may converge toward consistent patterns over the long run. Firms attend to the actions of their competitors, imitate each other, learn from each other, and form alliances. Also, in the long run, one firm's behaviors may induce changes in the parameters framing an entire industry, such as government policies or resource availability (Miner et al. 1996). However, long-run phenomena must be studied retrospectively, so long-run theories offer little to managers who face immediate problems.

For such reasons, some management scholars, mainly organization theorists, have shifted their attention toward populations of organizations. However, most management scholars are not satisfied to describe or analyze industry-level phenomena over the very long run. They seek theories that address organizational-level issues that exist now. Such theories need to incorporate the kinds of data that are currently available to managers, including the managers' perceptions.

All versions of the economic theory of the firm have a narrow focus on prices and quantities. This narrow focus may have advantages for economists, especially those who like mathematical theories. Simplicity makes theories easier to understand. To exist for long periods, firms must ultimately appear to generate some profits. Prices and quantities may be much more important for generating long-run profits than factors such as advertising, human resources, product quality, or innovation.

By contrast, management theories incorporate many variables because management scholars believe that many factors influence firms' successes in both the short run and the long run. Management prescriptions for organizational design and strategy include abstract variables such as centralization, distinctive competence, environmental dynamism, expertise, formalization, and resource munificence. Management scholars regard such variables as relevant because they look upon firms as being complex. For management scholars, firms have many stakeholders, such as employees, customers, suppliers and neighbors, in addition to stockholders. Management scholars also view firms as having diverse legitimate goals in addition to long-run profits, because firms are places to work, to learn, and to pursue careers and they are partners in alliances and citizens in communities.

Academics Versus Managers

Academic theorists discuss abstract worlds that are strange to managers. The disjunctures between abstract academic perspectives and concrete managerial perspectives become especially large when management scholars ask managers about macroscopic variables such as centralization, environmental dynamism, and resource munificence. Managers work in concrete worlds and they focus on the data about their daily tasks: what do I have to do right now? Do we have enough inventory to fill this order? Boland and his colleagues (2001) concluded that managers make better decisions when they focus on concrete stimuli. Goals with very distant time horizons have little meaning for managers. Indeed, many managers expect to move to another assignment every two or three years, and many of the projects undertaken by firms have similarly short time horizons, so time horizons of two to three years seem realistic to them.

Also, both the theory of the firm and management theories view events macroscopically in comparison with the microscopic worlds in which nearly all managers work. For example, academics classify industries by Standard Industrial Classification codes (SIC codes) and assume that managers see their industries on similarly large scales. Very few managers, however, define their industries in such broad terms; nearly all managers focus on market segments so small that no statistics exist about them. Many managers have little perspective on worlds other than their own. They have had experience in only one work organization and only one functional specialty. When they are asked to compare their organizations with others, their statements are based largely on hearsay or fantasy.

These disparities between the theoretical worlds of management academics and the practical worlds of business managers are both important and difficult to reconcile. The disparities are important because management academics ought to be able to explain how their theories relate to observable phenomena, how managers' actions in microscopic, concrete worlds translate into concepts in macroscopic, abstract theories. They are also important because they impede communication between academics and managers; the questions academics ask of managers and the responses managers give are often not parallel to one another. The disparities are difficult to reconcile because such explanations do not come easily. For instance, Baumol and Quandt (1964) attempted to study the effectiveness of rules of thumb as ways to approximate optimal behavior; they concluded that this is a 'surprisingly difficult' problem (1964: 41). Winter (1964) showed that one should not rely on evolutionary selection to produce short-run behavior that has long-run benefits. In fact, when organizations imitate each other, there is no reason to believe that any organization can gain a survival advantage by discovering a better way to behave (Starbuck 1994). But even if evolutionary selection were effective, it would produce long-run consistency between managers' actions and survival conditions, not consistency between managers' actions and the abstract concepts of organizational form or strategic policy that appear in management theories.

In order to reconcile managers' actions with management theories, academics need to understand the disparities that require reconciliation. The arguments above suggest that these disparities have at least four dimensions: (1) long-run versus short-run orientation; (2) a population of organizations versus one organization; (3) degree of generality versus specificity; and (4) degree of abstraction versus concreteness.

This chapter adds a fifth dimension that interacts with the other four: the degree to which managers perceive their worlds accurately. With only a few exceptions, both economic theorists and management theorists have assumed that managers perceive accurately. But quite a lot of evidence indicates that this is simply not so. All people, including managers, make perception errors frequently. They make errors even when perceiving phenomena that they encounter daily. They make bigger errors and make errors more often when they are being asked to perceive unfamiliar phenomena.

If theories are going to be helpful to managers, the theories need to allow for perception errors. Theories are unlikely to provide useful guidance if they make very unrealistic assumptions about the accuracy of the information flowing into decisions. Similarly, researchers who gather data from managers need to allow for perception errors. Researchers have tended to ask managers for their perceptions of unfamiliar phenomena—the long run, the population of firms, the general, the abstract—which are precisely the perceptions that are least likely to be accurate.

The next section reviews some studies that suggest that managers do not perceive accurately and that their perception errors may affect the performance of their firms.

3. HOW ACCURATE ARE MANAGERS' PERCEPTIONS OF THEIR WORLDS?

The literatures on decision-making and managerial sense-making rely heavily on the assumption that managers are aware of and understand their organizations' environments in terms of the kinds of macroscopic variables that appear in prescriptions for organizational design and strategizing. Almost no research has examined the accuracy of such perceptions (Starbuck and Mezias 1996). However, a few research studies have compared objective and perceptual data. Disconcertingly, these studies found large errors and biases in managers' perceptions, both of their organizations and of the environments in which the organizations operate. Managers' responses to academics' questions indicate that they live in microscopic, immediate worlds, and have little awareness of long-run issues, of changes from year to year, of comparisons among firms, or of differences among market environments.

In 1967, Lawrence and Lorsch inferred that organizations whose properties match their market environments perform better than firms not aligned with their environments. Their research relied on managers' perceptions of both organizational properties and the environments. The key variable they discussed was environmental uncertainty. However, two later studies presented questions about the accuracy of managerial perceptions of environmental uncertainty. Both studies compared top managers' perceptions of their firms' markets to financial reports and industry statistics. In both studies, the correlations between the two were near zero and were as likely to be negative as positive. Tosi, Aldag, and Storey (1973) studied 102 middle and top managers from diverse firms and found correlations from -0.29 to $+0.04$ between managers' beliefs about environmental uncertainty and stability indices. Similarly, Downey, Hellriegel, and Slocum (1975) collected data from 51 heads of the divisions of a large conglomerate and found correlations from -0.17 to $+0.11$ between managers' beliefs about environmental uncertainty and stability indices.

In their 1975 study, Grinyer and Norburn found that profitability correlated only very weakly with strategic planning ($r = 0.22$). Strategic planning is a double-edged sword that is as likely to reduce profits as to raise them. Strategies that reflect accurate forecasts and assessments of the environment enable organizations to work toward the achievement of appropriate goals, while ignoring irrelevant distractions. But strategies based on inaccurate forecasts and assessments lead to work toward the wrong goals, while overlooking unexpected

opportunities. Since negative outcomes occur nearly as often as positive outcomes, strategic planning has negligible effects on the average.

Grinyer and Norburn's study suggests not only that managers misperceive
their environments, but also their organizations. They found inconsistent and
meaningless correlations between profitability and consensus among executives
about their firms' goals or about their personal responsibilities. The correlations
ranged from -0.40 to $+0.40$, indicating that agreement on perceptions did not
increase profitability. The fact that there was disagreement implies that some
executives misperceived, which highlights the fact that even if consensus is
achieved, there is no way of knowing whether or not the consensus is correct.
Therefore, achieving consensus on inaccurate perceptions is as likely to lead to
unprofitability as not achieving consensus on accurate perceptions. Depending
on whether perceptions are accurate, consensus (or lack thereof) can be as
harmful as beneficial.

Further evidence about misperceptions of organizational characteristics comes
from Payne and Pugh's 1976 review of more than 100 studies. Payne and Pugh
examined subjective and objective measures of organizational structures and
climates. They drew three conclusions: (*a*) Employees in the same organization
disagree so strongly with each other that it makes no sense to talk about an
average perception. 'Perceptual measures of each of the structural and climate
variables have varied so much among themselves that mean scores were uninterpretable' (1976: 1168). (*b*) Except for organizational size, employees' perceptions
of organizational properties correlate weakly with objective measures of those
properties. (*c*) Differences among employees' perceptions of organizational properties correspond with employees' jobs and hierarchical statuses. For instance,
higher-status employees view their organizations more favorably.

Overall, these early studies showed that perceptual data correlate very weakly
with objective data. However, perceptual data seem to be mutually consistent.
Lawrence and Lorsch (1967) observed that perceptions of organizations fit
logically with perceptions of the organizations' environments. Payne and Pugh
(1976) found that perceptions of different organizational characteristics fit together logically. Thus, although people make sense of their organizational environments, the sense that they make seems to have weak correspondence to
objective measures of their organizations. The sense that people make may
be the result of (*a*) human brains imposing logic on ambiguous stimuli or
(*b*) collective sense-making processes within organizations.

Mezias and Starbuck (2003) conjectured that these old studies had to be
misleading because managers could not possibly be so far out of touch with
their environments. Because the studies had not been designed to access perceptual accuracy, research methodology might have manufactured the inconsistencies between perceptual and objective data: in particular, the 'objective' measures
in some of these studies had been rather ad hoc.

Therefore Mezias and Starbuck decided to gather data to assess perceptual
accuracy, believing that they would find much smaller perception errors. In their
first study, they were very disappointed to find large perceptual errors in data

collected from managers in several companies. In the best case, 39 percent of managers' perceptions of a given variable were within 50 percent of the objective measure. In the worst case, 31 percent of managers' perceptions exceeded 200 percent of the objective value. Most surprising was that managers' perceptions of variables specifically related to their areas of expertise were no more accurate than other managers' perceptions of those same variables. That is, managers with sales experience were as inaccurate in their estimates of sales-related variables as managers without sales experience.

In a second study, Mezias and Starbuck observed senior managers' perceptions of quality performance in four divisions of a company whose top management said that quality improvement was a top priority. The company had been training all managers in quality, and each business unit had a quality improvement department. The company distributed quality measures to all managers on a regular basis, and managers met to discuss quality performance in their divisions. Yet 49–91 percent of the managers reported 'I don't know' when asked about current levels of quality performance. Although the managers who thought they knew the current levels of quality performance were often fairly accurate, the managers who specialized in quality were no more accurate than the nonspecialists.

Because research and managerial prescriptions so often assume that managers perceive accurately, it seems useful to remind people of the many sources of perceptual errors. Indeed, perceptual errors have so many sources that we can list only some of the main ones. We place errors in four categories according to whether they occur during noticing or during sense-making, and whether they reflect properties of stimuli or properties of perceivers.

Errors Due to Noticing

> It's not like information comes with a little flag on it that says, 'Look at me;
> I'm your proactive piece of data.' The people in this world who make money
> are the people who see things in information that other people don't see.
> — Leonard M. Fuld, as quoted by Buchanan (1995)

Noticing is a matter of detecting stimuli and distinguishing meaningful information from noise (Starbuck and Milliken 1988a). Noticing usually exerts strong influence on cognition because it determines whether people even consider responding to events. Noticing also takes precedence over sense-making. If events have been noticed, people can try to make sense of them, but if events have not been noticed, they cannot affect sense-making.

Some stimuli are more likely to attract attention, and some people are more likely to pay attention to particular stimuli. As a result, errors due to noticing fall into two categories: problems with stimuli and problems with perceivers. Important stimuli may be difficult to perceive; people's biases may lead them to notice the wrong stimuli.

Problems with Stimuli

People tend either to ignore changes over time or to underestimate vastly their magnitudes. Changes are more likely to be noticed if they are large or dramatic, less likely to be noticed if they are small or incremental. For example, Microsoft's surprising ignorance of the Internet's emergence and growth illustrates how an industry leader can greatly underestimate changes in the year-to-year growth rate of an important industry segment. Considerable evidence indicates that Microsoft's top managers greatly underestimated the rapid growth and profound implications of the Internet. Rob Glaser, who joined Microsoft in 1983, repeatedly warned Microsoft's top managers not to underestimate the importance of the Internet and to develop a browser immediately. As late as January of 1995, Microsoft had very few people working to develop its own Internet browser (Wallace 1997).

In unfamiliar circumstances, people feel that they are being inundated with stimuli because the stimuli are difficult to classify. That is, unfamiliar stimuli create the problem of not knowing what to notice because it is difficult to know what is important. After repeated exposure to the same stimuli, some stimuli become familiar and people learn to ignore the stimuli that have had less influence. For example, Gersick and Hackman (1990) discussed how routinized information processing produces insensitivity to unfamiliar stimuli. They examined the crash of a flight that took off from Washington, DC. The Florida-based crew had filtered out unfamiliar stimuli (ice on the wings) when they were going through the all-too-familiar takeoff checklist.

In the U.S., just three industries—chemicals, petroleum, and plastics—account for about half of the forecasts made about manufacturing. Thus managers in these industries receive frequent reminders that they should be thinking about the future. Furthermore, on average, the forecasts made about chemicals and plastics have been distinctly optimistic whereas the forecasts made about other manufacturing industries have been unbiased. Thus managers in the chemicals and plastics industries receive stimuli that encourage overproduction and overinvestment.

Overly abundant stimuli create obstacles in processing information effectively, such that some stimuli are overlooked. Managers often feel that they are drowning in data. Corporate information systems produce reports whether or not the reports are relevant to current issues, so managers learn to ignore nearly all of the data they receive. A study by The Institute For The Future and the Gallup Organization described office workers as being deluged by communications and technology. For example, an average UK office worker receives 48 telephone calls, 23 e-mails, 11 voice mails, 20 letters, 15 internal memos, 11 faxes, 13 Post-it notes and eight mobile phone calls per day. An average U.S. manager in Fortune 1000 companies is sending and receiving about 180–200 documents a day through various media. 'Today's corporate staffs are inundated with so many communications tools—fax, electronic mail, teleconferencing, postal mail, inter-office mail, voice mail—that sometimes they don't know where to turn for the simplest tasks' (Institute For The Future 1997).

Problems with Perceivers

Like other people, managers are prone to seek out data that confirm their beliefs, and analogously, managers' beliefs about what is relevant guide organizational information-gathering operations. Of course, such beliefs have roots in experience, which may be a poor guide to current events. For example, the Facit company was a dominant manufacturer of mechanical calculators in 1969 when electronic calculators first appeared in their market (Starbuck, Greve, and Hedberg 1978). To assess this threat, Facit's managers instructed sales personnel to ask customers whether they intended to continue purchasing mechanical calculators or whether they intended to switch to electronic calculators. Month after month, the sales personnel reported back that nearly 100 percent of the customers liked mechanical calculators and intended to continue using them. But month after month, there were fewer and fewer customers for the sales personnel to interview.

Involvement in a course of action focuses one's attention. Elaborate strategic planning produces blindness to stimuli that fall outside the plans. This is partly a result of the planners' psychological investments in their plans and partly the result of the information gathering that they set up to implement their plans. For example, Microsoft may have overlooked the development of the Internet because it had all of its resources committed to desktop products such as Office and the Windows operating systems. Similarly, Merrill Lynch fell victim to its commitment to a course of action. To deter insider trading, Merrill required employees to have their brokerage accounts exclusively with the company. But because employees were unable to trade on Internet sites, they were unfamiliar with Internet trading, and ill-equipped to deal with the online trading explosion. Spiro (1999: 256) remarked that 'the proud firm earned an unwanted reputation as the case study for Internet anxiety by arriving at the on-line trading party more than two years late'.

Organizational and societal cultures blind people to some stimuli while emphasizing others. To support its effort to be the dominant manufacturer of mechanical calculators, Facit hired the best mechanical engineers and promoted them to senior management positions. The mechanical engineers focused on developments in mechanical design and attached little significance to developments in other fields of engineering. One result was that they greatly underestimated the significance of electronic calculators. Miller (1990) has documented many similar cases in which firms focused so intently on what they perceived as being their strategic strengths that they did not see important developments outside the range of their vision. Cyert and March (1963) asserted that organizations are more likely to respond to threats than to opportunities, which implies that managers should pay more attention to threats. Jackson and Dutton (1988) speculated that managers are indeed more sensitive to threat-consistent information than to opportunity-consistent information, and conversely, that they are less sensitive to threat-discrepant information than to opportunity-discrepant information.

Managers focus on stimuli that they think are immediately relevant to their jobs, and they screen out other stimuli. For example, when Starbuck and Mezias (1996) asked managers to describe their industries, only five of seventy managers gave descriptions that approximated the national industries that appear in government reports. Most managers regarded national industries as too large to be relevant for their business units. Many managers described their business units as competing in local or regional markets, not the entire United States. Many other managers described their competitive environments with phrases such as 'Jewish in-ground burial on Long Island', 'entertainment advertising', 'radio air personality', 'alkaline batteries', and 'industrial sorbents for oil-spill clean-up and chemical-spill clean-up'.

Errors Due to Sense-Making

Managers . . . must wade into the ocean of events that surround the organization and actively try to make sense of them

— Richard L. Daft and Karl E. Weick (1984: 286)

Sense-making involves placing stimuli into frameworks that reflect habits and beliefs. These frameworks help people to categorize and to interpret data, which often involves filling in missing data and editing out dissonant data (Starbuck and Milliken 1988*a*). Ambiguous stimuli are difficult to interpret, and people's biases lead them to interpret stimuli incorrectly. People are also subject to perceptual blind spots that may hinder decision-making and that generate self-reinforcing cycles (Watzlawick, Weakland, and Fisch 1974). Dunbar, Garud, and Raghuram (1996) advocated that managers should help their organizations to develop effective sense-making frameworks. But, managers' abilities to do this depend on the managers' knowing what good sense-making frameworks are.

Starbuck and Milliken (1988*a*) argued that people possess many sense-making frameworks, and that they can apply several, partially inconsistent frameworks to any specific situation. Furthermore, sense-making frameworks can be evaluated by many, partially inconsistent criteria, which makes it difficult to judge some frameworks as more effective than others except in retrospect.

Like errors in noticing, errors in sense-making arise from both problems with stimuli and problems with perceivers. It seems that perceivers present more problems than stimuli. The following sections outline the role of each in sense-making errors.

Problems with Stimuli

Managers in different industries make different sense-making errors because either the data change very rapidly or data do not exist. In stable industries, such as furniture or commodity foods, managers develop constricted sense-making frameworks based on long experience, so they have difficulty making sense of surprising developments. In volatile industries, such as capital goods or high-technology industries, managers must keep abreast of changing environmental conditions, so they develop sense-making frameworks that tolerate errors. Horvath (1996) argued that rapid environmental changes and uncertainty about future conditions lead managers to de-emphasize the significance of new data, to refine their knowledge rather than to reformulate it. Because adapting to changes induces people to notice more events and to engage in more sense-making, they tend to think they are doing more problem-solving and to credit themselves with any good results. Normann (1971) pointed out that managers perceive incremental changes more accurately than dramatic ones. Because incremental changes deviate only slightly from experience, managers can interpret them by modifying existing frameworks. Dramatic changes, on the other hand, force managers to adopt radically different frameworks, so they are prone to err.

Government agencies or trade associations publish data about some industries. In such industries, firms can use published data in their sense-making, whereas in other industries, no such data exist. Published data are useful mainly to firms in industries that are changing at moderate rates. In highly stable industries, firms have little need for data that are changing in miniscule increments. In rapidly changing industries, data become obsolete even before they are published, so firms have to develop other ways to gather information (Gulati 1999).

Top managers receive distorted information from subordinates who tell their bosses what they think the bosses want to hear or who seek to promote their own interests or favored projects. Dunbar and Goldberg (1978) surmised that such distortions play significant roles in top managers' awareness of developing crises. Top managers may also think they have more expertise than their subordinates, causing them to discount the subordinates' input. Thus managers of the space shuttle program thought that their subordinate engineers were exaggerating the significance of burn damage to O-rings in the Solid Rocket Boosters. According to the engineers, damage to O-rings was evidence that the space shuttle was unsafe; but according to the program managers, history had shown that the space shuttle could fly safely despite damage to O-rings. As a result, the managers overruled the engineers and went ahead with the launch of the Challenger (Starbuck and Milliken 1988*b*).

Problems with Perceivers

Several properties of perceivers may lead to errors in sense-making, including biases, vested interests, specialization, culture, and learning. Extensive research has revealed that people do not behave according to prescriptions for rational thought. Bazerman (1997) documented a list of more than a dozen biases that influence cognitive behavior. For instance, Milliken (1990) inferred that managers are less likely to interpret environmental changes as threatening when they perceive their organizations to be performing well than when they perceive their organizations to be performing poorly. Other research shows that people's brains invent memories of events that never occurred (Nisbett and Wilson 1977), and that people search for confirming evidence of their prior beliefs (Singer and Benassi 1981). Human cognition tends to edit out dissonant stimuli and to fill in missing stimuli automatically. Thus memories change to fit new information (Kiesler 1971; Loftus 1979).

Research on attributions indicates that people tend to overestimate their own impacts on events, and to underestimate the impacts of external forces. That is, people tend to see themselves as causing events. People especially tend to overestimate their own impacts when outcomes are successful. Conversely, people tend to see others' successes as resulting from the situations or environments (Heider 1958). For example, ambiguous stimuli may cause managers to attribute success to internal strengths of their organizations, and failures to environmental circumstances (Wagner and Gooding 1997). On the other hand, when interpreting stimuli about others' behaviors, managers are more likely to attribute success to environmental opportunities than to managers' competence, and failures to managers' incompetence than to environmental threats. For instance, Ragins, Townsend, and Mattis (1998) found that male chief executive officers (CEOs) and female executives hold very different perceptions of work environments in corporations. Whereas the females, all vice presidents or higher, 'were more than twice as likely as the CEOs to consider inhospitable work environments as a barrier to women's advancement' (1998: 35), the male CEOs attributed women's not advancing to a deficiency of general management or line experience.

Managers' sense-making also reflects their need to believe that their decisions will turn out to be correct. For example, Jill Barad, Chairwoman and CEO of Mattel demonstrated a need to believe that her purchase of The Learning Company would be profitable. After making the purchase, she repeatedly predicted that profits would rise in the next quarter even though profits had fallen in the previous quarter. After losses had totaled $183 million, shareholders lost faith in her credibility and she resigned her position.

Starbuck (1983) suggested that top managers' sense-making is especially prone to errors (see also Glynn, Lant, and Milliken 1994). Several factors make it difficult for top managers to interpret events accurately: First, as Payne and Pugh (1976) surmised, the higher up managers are, the more likely they are to perceive their organizations favorably and to perceive problems as benign. Second, because top managers are some distance from customers, first-line workers, and the latest production methods, they may not understand current circumstances. Third, top managers tend to see technological and social changes as threatening to their abilities to control their organizations because new technologies or new markets might require top managers having different expertise. Fourth, because stakeholders typically blame top managers for poor organizational performance, they are less likely to acknowledge that something is wrong (Starbuck, Greve, and Hedberg 1978).

Just as familiarity makes stimuli easier to process in noticing, familiarity of stimuli facilitates sense-making processes. People are better able to understand and respond to stimuli that resemble those with which they have experience, while they are more likely to misperceive unfamiliar stimuli (Normann 1971).

Managers' experiences in various job assignments give them specific expertise in specific domains. Therefore, someone working in production tends to be better equipped to make sense of production statistics, problems, and issues than someone who works in marketing.

At the same time, organizations cherish illusions of expertise. That is, people in production assume that people in marketing know more about marketing than they actually do. These illusions of expertise influence collective sense-making even in situations where experience may not produce expertise. Information systems also create illusions of expertise. Information systems store information that has been historically relevant, but data categories that were relevant in the past may overlook information that is important today. Further, past trends may bias information and cause people to misinterpret important changes in trends.

Social construction makes some stimuli more salient than others. As people talk to each other and share their perceptions, they invent a shared image of reality. Within the same environment, different subgroups of people construct different images of reality. For instance, explaining why men and women view workplaces differently, Ragins, Townsend, and Mattis (1998: 36) observed:

The [male] CEOs in this study were logical in their approach and viewed the problem of women's advancement in terms of what they can see and what they can count: the number of women in the pipeline and their years of experience. They have no way of understanding the corporate environment faced by their female employees because it is an environment that they do not currently experience, nor did they face in their rise to the top. As members of the majority, they were in environments designed by and for men.

4. CONCLUSION

While most academics and most managers assume that managers perceive accurately, managers often hold erroneous perceptions. Indeed, research on managerial perceptions has found large errors and biases in managers' perceptions, both of their organizations and of the environments in which they operate.

Perception errors arise during both noticing and sense-making. During noticing, stimuli foster errors because they are unfamiliar, changing slowly, or buried in the midst of voluminous data. Managers make errors during noticing because they tend to find data that confirm their prior beliefs; because they become too involved in courses of action to observe stimuli accurately; because their cultures blind them to some stimuli; or because they do not perceive stimuli to be relevant to their jobs. During sense-making, stimuli promote errors when data are inaccessible, changing at extreme rates, or distorted by subordinates. Managers make errors during sense-making because of their biases, vested interests, hierarchical positions, illusions of expertise, social environments, or strong needs to believe they made correct decisions.

Errors in noticing dominate errors in sense-making. Only events that have been noticed can affect sense-making. Also, noticing tends to be binary whereas sense-making offers many alternatives. People can apply multiple, partially inconsistent sense-making frameworks to any specific situation, and these sense-making frameworks can be evaluated by multiple, partially inconsistent criteria.

Relating Theories to Observations

Efforts to base theories on empirical evidence need to deal with the fact that managers make bigger errors about the phenomena that are most interesting to academics. Managers and academics notice different phenomena and interpret them differently: whereas managers notice and interpret events as participants in a social system, academics perceive these events as observers outside the social system. The most obvious implication of these differences is that academics need to be very careful about relying on managerial informants. Managers are more likely to perceive accurately short-run implications of their behaviors within a single firm than long-run implications of behaviors across a population of firms. Managers are more likely to perceive accurately specific and concrete phenomena than abstract or general concepts. Academics are more likely to ask managers about, or to interpret their responses as being relevant to, long-run behaviors across a population of firms than short-run behaviors within a single firm. Academics also are more likely to ask managers about, or to interpret their responses as being relevant to, abstract or general concepts than specific and concrete phenomena. Hence, literatures relying on managerial perceptions tend to expose managerial misperceptions, but these apparent errors are likely produced by the research methods.

Insofar as one is concerned with theoretically important behaviors, one needs to recognize that managers and academics notice very different phenomena. For example, managers rarely notice competitive behaviors outside the narrowly defined industries that they see as relevant to their jobs. At the same time, academics are unlikely to think that competitive behaviors in these narrowly defined industries are relevant to their theories. Thus, when Porac, Thomas, and Baden-Fuller (1989) asked managers in the Scottish knitwear industry about their competitors, the Scots described themselves as competing solely with other Scottish firms; one manager even represented that his only competitors were other firms in the same city. Consequently, the Scots did not pay attention to the strategic moves of knitwear producers outside of Scotland. Porac, Thomas, and Baden-Fuller (1989: 413) observed that academics define competitive groups very differently from the Scottish managers: 'many of the studies measuring strategic group membership have classified firms on the basis of attributes tangentially related to intended strategies. The resulting "strategic groups" are thus analytical abstractions of the researchers.'

Just as managers and academics notice very different phenomena, they interpret phenomena differently. Whereas managers interpret events as participants inside a social system, academics often interpret managers' behaviors as observers outside the social system. Thus, when Porac, Thomas, and Baden-Fuller (1989) asked managers in the Scottish knitwear industry about their competitors, one manager replied:

Quite honestly, there is not a lot of competition. The Italian industry is a different industry from ours. The Asian industry is a different industry from ours.... Basically it's pullovers and cardigans. It's classic type garments. In my opinion, it is quite clearly defined that people expect to buy the best cashmere pullovers from Scotland.

Porac, Thomas, and Baden-Fuller (1989: 414) contrasted such descriptions with the 'analytical abstractions' used by academics who write about strategic groups. Academics regard strategic groups as 'purely economic entities' that are defined in terms of factors such as cross-elasticities of demand, entry and mobility barriers, product differentiation, and pricing. Managers do not perceive 'purely economic entities' but rather 'primary groups' of firms that reflect sociological and psychological factors such as shared perceptions and cognitive models.

Opportunities

Although perception errors add to the yawning gulf between the behaviors of managers and academic theories, they do present some very interesting issues for investigation.

First, to what extent do perception errors introduce randomness into economic activity? The well-known 'random walk down Wall Street' is largely a result of competition between plausible alternative perceptions; some people perceive a stock to be undervalued and others perceive it to be overvalued. Nelson and Winter (1982: 370) pointed out 'that things always are changing in ways that could not have been fully predicted, and that adjustments always are having to be made to accommodate to or exploit those changes.... [T]hose adjustments and accommodations... do not lead to tightly predictable outcomes. For better or for worse, economic life is an adventure.' There are other causes of randomness, such as natural disasters and social turmoil, but the uncertainty arising from inaccurate perceptions may be the dominant factor in small-scale, frequent economic change.

Second, to what extent do managers correct for perception errors by turning their visions into reality? Porac and Rosa (1996) argued that any sense-making framework could be effective if a firm is able to impose its framework on its environments. A firm may also be able to elevate the importance of stimuli that its personnel do notice by acting as if these stimuli are important. Such outcomes imply that the firm exercises considerable power in comparison with elements in its environment, and firm size is not the only determinant of such power: a small firm may be powerful if it behaves effectively in its specialized niche. What conditions affect firms' abilities to construct the realities they perceive?

Third, when are perception errors beneficial rather than harmful? Although a rational model says that people will behave more appropriately if they appraise situations accurately, real life holds surprises. In particular, societies may benefit when the faulty perceptions of individuals encourage or deter actions. When does social and economic change depend on some individuals' being unusually optimistic or pessimistic? Entrepreneurs often remark that they would never have attempted to innovate if they had foreseen accurately how much difficulty they would have. Yet a classroom experiment induced Jackson and Dutton (1988: 385) to speculate that most managers are 'more likely to perceive an issue as a threat [than as an opportunity] unless there is strong evidence to do otherwise'; most managers must be 'convinced of the presence of opportunities'. The high prevalence of perceived threats might explain Cyert and March's (1963) observation that threats are more likely to induce firms to explore alternative behaviors than are opportunities.

Fourth, are some managers able to operate much more effectively than others in situations that they misperceive? If so, what distinguishes this ability? Many managers are utterly unaware that they are misperceiving, but those who are aware that they may be misperceiving see their environments as ambiguous and uncertain. Baumard (1999) has argued that rational problem-solving proves to be more harmful than merely ineffective in ambiguous, uncertain environments, but that some top managers have an ability to operate effectively in such environments. He described this ability as a pragmatic, creative cunning that enables managers to generate new sense-making frameworks. 'Strategy sometimes consists in establishing *temporary articulations* to avoid fossilizing knowledge into restrictive statements, and so as to take tactical advantage of their unfinished or mutable character' (Baumard 1999: 228). Thus, in addition to the traditional idea of strategizing as a process that appraises the present realistically and forecasts the future accurately, there may be a second mode of strategizing as a creator and exploiter of perception errors.

22

Studying the Accuracy of Managers' Perceptions: A Research Odyssey

Coauthored with John M. Mezias

1. INTRODUCTION

Both academic research and managerial practices depend on the accuracy of managers' perceptions. Many organizational practices assume that managers have accurate perceptions of their organizations or their organizations' environments. For example, strategic planning attempts to match organizations' properties to the contingencies in organizations' environments. Many research studies analyze data gathered from managers through questionnaires or interviews. But several research studies suggest that most managers have quite different perceptions and that many managers have inaccurate perceptions. What if most managers have very unrealistic perceptions of their organizations, of their organizations' environments, or of both? Or what if different managers in the same organization have very different perceptions of their organization or its environments?

This chapter reports a stream of research about managers' perceptions of the variables that academics say managers ought to consider when they strategize or design organizations. These variables are difficult to perceive accurately and less relevant for managers than for academics. In particular, academic theories talk about abstract, macroscopic variables such as centralization, environmental dynamism, and resource munificence, and these may have no concrete effects in the short-run. Managers focus on solving concrete problems that exist right now. In fact, Boland et al. (2001) surmised that managers make higher quality decisions when they focus on concrete stimuli. Thus, a manager may have very accurate perceptions of the documents on his desk but have only vague impressions of the variations in document flows over time.

Although this chapter reports the findings of two empirical studies, it treats these studies as two increments in a research process extending over two decades. Successive sections of the chapter divide this research process into four developmental stages: before 1990, around 1994 just before study 1, after study 1, and after study 2. Our own beliefs about managerial perceptions were different at each stage.

Perceptual phenomena incorporate several components, each of which can be labeled distinctly. We searched for appropriate terminology, considered alternatives such as awareness, belief, cognition, estimation and sense-making, and eventually concluded that the term 'perception' best denotes the entire complex of related phenomena. We recognize that this linguistic choice runs into differing professional conventions in biology, philosophy, several variants of psychology, and sociology. Within and between these groups, scholars disagree about the best terminology and definitions. We hope to sidestep these linguistic differences because we want to focus on the entire complex of related phenomena no matter what one calls this complex. Therefore, this chapter assumes that the term perception has its fundamental meaning: 'apprehension by means of the senses or of the mind'.

Accordingly, managerial 'perceptions' include everything that goes into managers' understanding of their work situations. When managers make decisions about their organizations or their business strategies, their analyses may be based on such diverse sources as formal corporate documents, on their personal experiences, on rumors they heard beside water coolers, on conversations during committee meetings, on articles they read in periodicals or on speeches by their CEOs. Managers cannot and do not rely solely on data that are in front of them. Not only are the incoming data insufficient to describe all of the variables the managers have to consider, but they make sense of incoming data by setting these data into the context of prior cognitions. Similarly, when managers meet to discuss organizational or strategic problems, they do not focus solely on data that are on the conference table. Indeed, there are often few data on the conference table. Such meetings rely heavily on the perceptions that the participants carried into the room.

Many variables affect managers' perceptions. First, perceptions depend on the subject matter. People are more likely to notice more recent events, larger changes, and more dramatic events (Arnold et al. 1998; Kahneman and Tversky 1972), but they may have more accurate perceptions of older changes, smaller changes, and prosaic events (Normann 1971). People are also better equipped to perceive sounds, symbols, or objects than abstract concepts or invisible processes. Whether visible or invisible, some processes are highly complex and dynamic and others are simple and slow changing (Dörner 1997). Second, human perceptual systems vary significantly across people. Some people hear, see or remember more accurately. Third, increased experience makes people both more likely to notice some stimuli and less likely to notice other stimuli (Helson 1964; Kagel and Levin 1986). Experienced and inexperienced managers perceive very different data. Fourth, a specific manager's training and job assignments increase experience in one domain even as they withhold experience in other domains. Someone who works in marketing likely learns more about customers and markets while learning less about costs, raw materials, and production processes. Fifth, to make sense of incoming data, people place them in the context of experience, and people find it easier to recall some experiences than others (Hogarth 1980). Memory is especially important for perceptions of variables that people assess by observing them over time—such as trends and long-run averages. Managers do (or should) consider such variables when developing strategies and policies. Sixth, a manager's interpersonal skills and demeanor may encourage colleagues and subordinates to report forthrightly or to conceal or dissimulate (Hargie 1986). Some managers want to find out what is wrong whereas others punish those who report deficiencies. Seventh, organizational information systems collect and disseminate some kinds of information while ignoring or obscuring other information. Ordinarily, formal information systems focus on variables that have appeared to be more relevant in the past, with the result that they tend to overlook new trends and variables that might become relevant in the future (Starbuck, Greve, and Hedberg 1978). Also, organization members often bias or conceal information to promote their own interests. Eighth, societal and organizational cultures focus attention on certain phenomena and de-emphasize others; shared perceptual frameworks may make it easy to discuss some events and impossible to discuss others (Harris and Moran 1996). For instance, many members of minorities complain that their organizations embody the biases of white male majorities. Ninth, managers near the tops of hierarchies perceive different organizational phenomena than do managers lower down. Studies typically find that higher-level managers see fewer, milder deficiencies in their organizations (Mezias, Grinyer, and Guth 2001; Payne and Pugh 1976). Tenth, some businesses have distinctive environments for which published data have little relevance whereas other businesses operate in environments that align closely with industries for which trade associations or government agencies publish data (Starbuck and Mezias 1996). Finally, some business environments are much more volatile than others, with the result that data become obsolete more quickly.

Indeed, we designed our own studies (reported below) to rule out direct observation and to emphasize the information managers carry around in their heads. It was our assumption (which later turned out to be naïve) that managers can read formal reports accurately. But managers typically do not read formal reports when they are being interviewed by academics or participating in group decision-making. Instead managers often rely on information they carry around in their heads, and this is the situation we wanted to simulate.

2. BEFORE 1990

This project sprouted from seeds planted by studies published during the 1970s. One seed was planted by two studies that tried to systematize the 'environmental uncertainty' variable proposed by Lawrence and Lorsch. Lawrence and Lorsch (1967) inferred that firms perform better when their organizational properties align with the 'environmental uncertainty' of their market environments. Several years later, two groups of researchers tried to construct questionnaires to measure environmental uncertainty (Downey, Hellriegel, and Slocum 1975; Tosi, Aldag, and Storey 1973). Both groups asked middle and top managers to describe their uncertainty about their firms' markets, and both groups compared the managers' questionnaire responses with volatility indices calculated from the firms' financial reports and industry statistics. Both groups found correlations between managers' perceptions and 'objective' measures that were near zero and negative more often than positive. Specifically, using data from 102 middle and top managers from 22 diverse firms, Tosi, Aldag, and Storey (1973) obtained correlations ranging from −0.29 to +0.07 between volatility indices and managers' uncertainty perceptions. Using data from 51 division heads in a large conglomerate, Downey, Hellriegel, and Slocum (1975) calculated three kinds of volatility indices and one index of competitiveness, and compared these with the managers' uncertainty perceptions; the correlations ranged from −0.24 to +0.21. As the researchers had recognized, the low and erratic correlations in these studies might have arisen from poor questionnaires or from poor 'objective' measures of volatility. However, another interpretation was more intriguing: These studies might be saying that, on average, managers' perceptions of their environments' stabilities do not correlate with 'objective' measures of those stabilities.

A second seed was planted by a review of research about employees' perceptions of organizational properties. After reviewing scores of studies in which people described their firms' structures and cultures, Payne and Pugh (1976) concluded: (a) Different employees of one firm disagree so strongly with each other that it makes no sense to talk about an average perception. 'Perceptual measures of each of the structural and climate variables varied so much among themselves that mean scores were uninterpretable' (1976: 1168). (b) Except for organizational size, employees' perceptions of their firms correlate weakly with 'objective' measures of their firms' properties. (c) Differences among employees' perceptions of their firms' properties seem to correspond with their jobs and hierarchical statuses. For example, higher-status employees view their organizations more favorably.

A third seed was planted by studies of organizations facing serious crises. Greve, Hedberg, Nystrom, and Starbuck studied several situations in which firms faced, or appeared to face, dissolution (Starbuck 1983; Starbuck, Greve, and Hedberg 1978). A consistent theme emerging from these studies was that the top managers of firms developed views of their firms and their market environments that diverged greatly from what an outsider might have considered to be realistic. One reason for this divergence was that the firms allocated information-gathering resources to the areas that appeared to be most important and in so doing, they blinded themselves to environmental events that deviated from their managers' beliefs and expectations. A second reason was that the top managers had much more confidence in their personal experiences than in information coming from their subordinates. In every studied crisis, the top managers received accurate warnings and diagnoses from some subordinates, but they paid no attention to these. Indeed, they sometimes laughed at them (Harrison 1991). In their study of twenty firms facing crises, Dunbar and Goldberg (1978) found that many top managers surrounded themselves with yes-sayers. These yes-sayers filtered out signs of trouble and warnings from middle managers who tried to report problems.

A fourth seed was planted by psychological studies of people's cognitions, which revealed numerous biases and fantasies (Bazerman 1997). Although few of these studies involved managers, their findings probably generalize to many managers. Some perceptual biases seem to arise in people's social environments. For example, Slovic, Fischhoff, and Lichtenstein (1980) surmised that people tend to overestimate the frequencies of events that the media cover extensively and to underestimate the frequencies of events that the media treat cursorily. Environments are especially likely to affect the so-called 'availability' heuristic, according to which people overestimate the frequencies of events that are easily called to mind, such as recent disasters or dramatic films (Slovic, Fischhoff, and Lichtenstein 1982). Many studies reported that organizational documents attempt to mislead their readers by emphasizing financial and numerical data, by highlighting successes and rationalizing failures, and by giving senior executives credit for good results (Altheide and Johnson 1980; Bettman and Weitz 1983; Boland 1982; Dunbar 1981; Edelman 1977; Hofstede 1967; Hopwood 1972; Staw, McKechnie, and Puffer 1983). Of course, people's overt behaviors are also intended to give observers desired impressions. For example, managers may shift revenues or expenditures between time periods so as to alter apparent profits (Kondra and Hinings 1998).

Other perceptual biases seem to arise within people as individuals. For example, the 'self-serving bias' says people inflate their own contributions to successes and overstate external or situational causes of failures. People tend to reverse these biases when explaining other people's successes and failures. Singer and Benassi (1981: 50) concisely summarized the findings from many laboratory studies as follows:

... subjects show strong tendencies to perceive order and causality in random arrays, to perceive a pattern or correlation which seems a priori intuitively correct even when the actual correlation in the data is counterintuitive, to jump to conclusions about the correct hypothesis, to seek confirmatory evidence, to construe evidence liberally as confirmatory, to fail to generate or to assess alternative hypotheses, and, having thus managed to expose themselves only to confirmatory instances, to be fallaciously confident of the validity of their judgments.

Stage 1: Starbuck's Conclusions Around 1990

By the late 1980s, the foregoing studies pushed Starbuck to several conclusions (Starbuck 1985, 1992). First, many managers, possibly most, have erroneous perceptions of both their organizations and their business environments. As a result, most managers are not capable of matching organizations to environments, and formal organizational analyses, carried out by groups of managers, are very likely to yield incorrect results. Successful strategizing requires not only accurate perceptions of current organizational and environmental properties but also good forecasts of future developments. Thus formal strategizing is as likely to cause harm as to yield benefits (Starbuck 1992).

The foregoing studies also cast doubt on many studies that had been and were being published in academic journals. These studies relied on interviews with managers or on questionnaires completed by managers, including many of the numbers in statistical databases. If most managers do not actually know the properties of their organizations or their market environments, their answers to questions are going to be based on their beliefs. Statistical analyses of such responses are going to highlight the beliefs that are shared by many managers—what one might call managerial folklore. These shared beliefs are very likely to incorporate logical relations among concepts, but these logical relations are ones that accord with common sense. Logical relations among shared beliefs may differ from relations among 'objective' variables.

3. AFTER 1990, MEZIAS ARRIVES

In 1993, Mezias, a doctoral student, asked Starbuck to suggest some readings about managers' perceptions, especially studies assessing the accuracy of managers' perceptions. After reading the suggested studies, Mezias asked Starbuck why he had only suggested studies from the 1970s. Where were the recent studies? Starbuck proposed that Mezias search for more recent studies. After searching several online databases, Mezias found only a few studies of college students (e.g. Blomqvist 1988), but students would likely differ significantly from experienced managers. He found no studies that both obtained data from managers and compared managers' perceptions with 'objective' measures. He did find a few studies that compared averages of subjective perceptions with 'objective' measures (Bourgeois 1985; Dess and Keats 1987; Jermier, Gaines, and McIntosh 1989; Sutcliffe 1994). Averaging across people misrepresents the accuracy of their individual perceptions because averaged perceptions can be quite accurate even though most individuals have inaccurate perceptions (Dawes 1977; Gordon 1924; Starbuck and Bass 1967; Zajonc 1967).

We were both astonished at this null result. Starbuck urged Mezias to search again, but again he found nothing that assessed the accuracy of individual managers' perceptions. We then searched together and still did not find studies of the accuracy of managers' perceptions. Of course, our searches may not have detected comparisons of subjective and 'objective' measures that studies did not report in their abstracts. However, Sutcliffe (1994) also searched and found no such studies.

Stage 2: Our Conclusions Around 1994

At this point, our analysis of the research left us debating what conclusions we ought to be drawing. The old studies from the 1970s had to be misleading, we thought, because managers could not possibly be so far out of touch with their environments. The studies were not designed to assess perceptual accuracy, and research methodology might have manufactured the observed perception errors. In particular, Downey, Hellriegel, and Slocum (1975) and Tosi, Aldag, and Storey (1973) debated whether to attribute the apparently very large errors in managers' answers to the managers or to the research methods, and their 'objective' measures were rather ad hoc. Although such debate arises about every empirical study, studies of perception errors do face some tough challenges (Starbuck and Mezias 1996).

We decided to gather data about perceptual accuracy. We conjectured that a study designed specifically to assess perceptual accuracy would find much smaller perception errors. In particular, we thought that we could obtain better 'objective' measures. We also expected to be able to discover patterns in the errors that would make it possible for organizations to minimize or compensate for the errors.

We were convinced that managers' perceptual accuracy is an important topic. Many research studies rely on managers' perceptions. Many practices in organizations rely on managers' perceptions. Yet, almost no research has examined the accuracy of these perceptions.

4. STUDY 1: MANAGERS IN EXECUTIVE MBA PROGRAMS

We formulated hypotheses about variables that would affect the sizes of perception errors, designed a study, gathered data, and analyzed them. We wanted data from experienced managers, not inexperienced students; we also wanted data from managers working in diverse industries so that there would be variation in the 'objective' measures. We enlisted the cooperation of managers in Executive MBA courses at Columbia University and New York University. These managers held different jobs in many industries, and they included the presidents of small companies, department heads in large firms, and technical specialists.

We asked these managers about their current jobs, their previous jobs, their sources of information, their business units, and the industry environments of their business units. However, our questions focused on variables we found in prescriptions about organization design and prescriptions about strategic planning. These variables describe either organizational properties or environmental properties. The questions about their organizations concerned properties such as number of employees, number of rules, use of formal versus informal communications, emphasis on numerical or non-numerical information, processes used for evaluating strategies and policies and stability of strategies. The questions about their environments concerned properties such as sales growth, industry concentration, industry homogeneity, industry growth, fluctuations in sales and their industries' Standard Industrial Classification (SIC) codes.

Because we wanted to simulate interviews by academics and group decision-making, we sought to prevent the managers from looking up data in corporate reports. We asked our questions when the managers were in their Executive MBA classrooms so that they would reply on the basis of the information they carried around in their heads.

Almost all the organizational properties that we attempted to investigate are socially constructed ones (Searle 1995), and almost none of them are 'measured' in ways that confer measurements with 'objectivity'. That is, 'objective' measures existed only insofar as there was consensus among organizations' members. Therefore, we asked the managers to give our questionnaire to five of their immediate colleagues, who were then supposed to mail it directly to us. Often we received data from only one or two colleagues (in addition to the original manager). To properly assess consensus, we decided that we needed data from at least three colleagues (a total of four people). As a result, we had a sample of twenty-two groups of colleagues. We spent many hours trying to discern patterns in these data, but we could see none.

Many aspects of organizations' environments are also socially constructed (Hodgkinson 2001; Porac, Thomas, and Baden-Fuller 1989). However, environmental variables are often 'measured' and reported by legitimating social institutions, and people treat these measurements as 'objective'. Thus, we expected that we would be able to find such 'objective' measures for most of the environmental variables, but we could find appropriate 'objective' data to match less than half of the environmental perceptions. We had just two sources of data: 10-K reports and government statistics. U.S. companies annually send the government 10-K reports, which provide aggregate data on the firms and on their largest divisions. However, many of our managers worked in divisions that were too small to be reported separately in 10-K reports. Government statistics are mainly available for the industries defined by four-digit SIC codes. Only five of our seventy managers equated their business units' competitive environments with SIC codes or used industry labels that correspond to SIC codes. Indeed, many managers asked, 'What is an SIC code?' Also, SIC codes describe the entire U.S., while many managers described their competitive environments as local or regional markets. Still other managers described their competitive environments with very specific phrases such as 'Jewish inground burial on Long Island', 'radio air personality', 'architecture and construction of custom homes', 'alkaline batteries', 'emergency health care', and 'industrial sorbents for oil-spill clean-up and chemical-spill clean-up'.

Our study disappointed us. First, the data were not consistent with most of our hypotheses, as discussed below. Even more disappointing to us, instead of finding that managers' perceptions are more accurate than prior studies suggested, the study basically confirmed the prevalence of very large perception errors. We will not belabor this point by graphing all the errors we found in managers' perceptions, but we do think it useful to give a few examples of the frequencies and magnitudes of systematic errors.

Table 22.1 shows the average errors and the frequencies of moderate and very large errors in all respondents' descriptions of four sales-related variables. We use these variables as illustration partly because they correspond to publicly reported 'facts'; managers learn about sales from the same information sources that provided our 'objective' measures. Also, these are numeric variables: Some research has been interpreted as indicating that people give more accurate answers to questions having numeric answers (Budescu, Weinberg and Wallsten 1988).

Table 22.1. Moderate and extreme errors in managers' perceptions of sales variables

	Errors under 50%	Errors over 200%	Average error (%)	Numbers of responses
Last year's sales by own business unit	35	24	475.7	17
Percent change in own industry's sales last year	14	31	303.0	35
Percent change in own industry's sales over the last 5 years	3	6	−64.6	32
Average year-to-year fluctuations in own industry sales	39	3	−29.8	35

The managers' most accurate descriptions dealt with the average year-to-year fluctuations in their industries' sales: 39 percent of the managers made errors below 50 percent, only 3 percent of the managers made errors exceeding 200 percent, and the average error was only −30 percent. At the other extreme, the managers' least accurate descriptions depicted the percentage change in their industry's sales last year: Only 14 percent of the managers made errors below 50 percent, 31 percent of the managers made errors exceeding 200 percent, and the average error was over 300 percent.

Figures 22.1, 22.2, 22.3, and 22.4 graph the errors for these four variables. Errors exceeding 200 percent are grouped and labeled Big. Many of these errors exceeded 1000 percent, and they went as high as 5000 percent. Although seventy managers told us their perceptions, not all managers answered every question, and we obtained complete responses from only sixty-two. More problematically, we could not get reliable objective data about some business units. Hence, Figures 22.2, 22.3, and 22.4 describe 32–36 managers, and Figure 22.1 describes only seventeen managers.

Figure 22.1 shows the errors in perceptions of sales by the managers' own business units. The managers' perceptions fell into three categories. About 35 percent of the managers had very accurate perceptions, with errors below 11 percent. About 35 percent of the managers greatly underestimated sales, with errors ranging from −75 percent to almost −100 percent. About 24 percent of the managers overestimated sales to extreme degrees, with errors ranging from 200 percent to 4800 percent. Overall, about two-thirds of the managers expressed unrealistic notions of their business units' sizes in monetary terms.

Figure 22.2 compares public data with managers' statements about recent changes in their industries' sales. They made two types of errors. First, about 31 percent of the managers gave extreme overestimates. Second, most of the less extreme errors were underestimates. Sixty-three percent of the errors fell between −32 percent and −124 percent, averaging −71 percent.

Figure 22.3 presents managers' perceptions of changes in industry sales over the last five years. Only 6 percent of the managers made very large errors when characterizing these longer-run changes, and 94 percent of the errors fell between −43 percent and −99 percent. These less extreme errors averaged −83 percent.

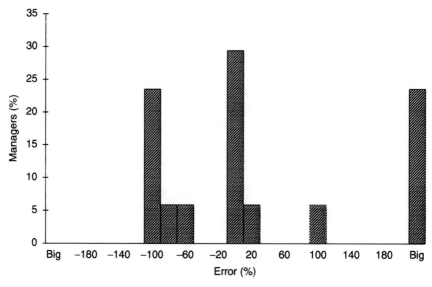

Figure 22.1. Error in perceived sales by own business unit last year

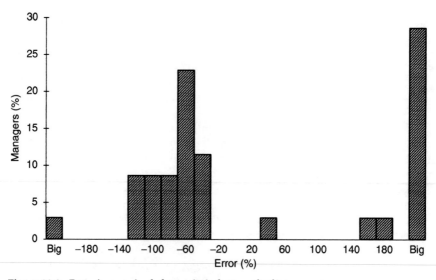

Figure 22.2. Error in perceived change in industry sales last year

Figure 22.4 shows the errors in managers' perceptions of average year-to-year fluctuations in industry sales. Although this is much the same idea as the data in Figures 22.2 and 22.3, extreme errors occurred less often. Only 3 percent of the managers made errors exceeding 200 percent: Compared to Figures 22.2 and 22.3, Figure 22.4 shows much less tendency to underestimate so these less extreme

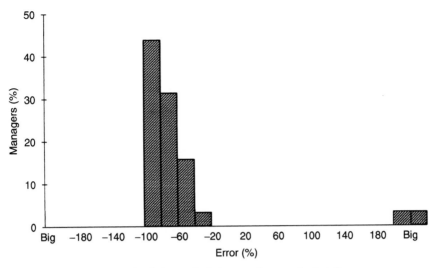

Figure 22.3. Error in perceived change in industry sales over the last five years

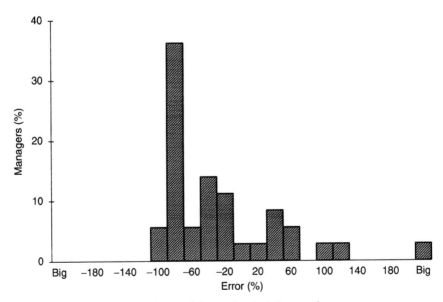

Figure 22.4. Error in perceived annual fluctuation in industry sales

errors averaged −34 percent. However, the less extreme errors did have high variance, ranging from −100 percent to +119 percent.

Normann (1971) pointed out that people better understand stimuli in domains where they have experience and they are likely to misperceive stimuli in unfamiliar domains. Therefore, we hypothesized that managers working in sales or with sales experience would have more accurate perceptions of sales-related variables. To our surprise, we found no meaningful differences between managers with sales experience and those without such experience.

One reason relevant experience does not improve accuracy may be that people tend to focus very, very narrowly. As mentioned above, when we asked managers to describe their competitive environments, many of them specified very small market segments—such as 'Jewish inground burial', 'alkaline batteries', and 'industrial sorbents for oil-spill clean-up and chemical-spill clean-up'. These narrow foci reflect the compartmentalization of modern organizations, especially large ones. This compartmentalization fosters tunnel vision about both organizational capabilities and environmental properties. That is, a manager who focuses on alkaline batteries thinks only about manufacturing processes and marketing efforts that relate to alkaline batteries; the manager is very likely to be unaware of technological developments or market demand for other power-source products. It may also make it very difficult for managers in different business units to discuss organizational capabilities and environmental properties and to evaluate the perceptions of other managers.

We also expected managers to have more accurate perceptions of events that are nearer to their immediate environments and everyday work. Thus, we hypothesized that managers would have more accurate perceptions of their own business units than of their industries, that the top row of Table 22.1 would show higher accuracy than the second row. Also, we hypothesized that managers would have more accurate perceptions of last year's sales than of changes in sales over the last five years, that the second row of Table 22.1 would show higher accuracy than the third row. According to the left-hand column of Table 22.1, the percentages of managers having rather accurate perceptions supported these hypotheses (although we also expected these percentages to be much larger than they were). However, the middle column in Table 22.1 shows that the percentages of managers having very inaccurate perceptions contradicted our hypotheses: The first two rows have similarly high percentages, and these are much higher than the percentage in the third row.

Our evidence says many managers greatly understate rates of change over time as well as period-to-period fluctuations. That is, the managers report much, much smaller changes than occur. We had expected the former result because some research has found that people underestimate the accumulated effects of percentage change (Bürkle 1979; Dörner 1997).

Stage 3: Our Conclusions After Study 1

There are serious communication gaps between managers and academics that are very difficult to bridge (Porac, Thomas, and Baden-Fuller 1989; Starbuck and Mezias 1996). Managers live in microworlds composed of concrete, immediate events. They focus on what is happening right now, in their specific jobs, in their specific business units, operating in very specific competitive environments (Boland et al. 2001). Academics, by contrast, frame their theories in terms of abstract concepts that generalize to many organizations and many environments. Even though we used terms from their Executive MBA courses, many managers either did not understand or poked fun at our terminology. For example, we asked where their business units fell on a continuum from 'machine-like' to 'organic'. The managers had read about and discussed mechanistic versus organic organizations during their MBA program, so we assumed they would understand this question. But this assumption was not valid for every manager. One manager replied, 'Do you mean do we make it or do we grow it?' Although this manager may have been joking, his response was appropriate. Another example of communication gaps concerns the term 'industry'. Responding to our question 'In what industry does your business unit operate?' one manager wrote: 'My unit doesn't operate in one industry. Instead each of the staff focuses on a specific industry/segment.' Thus, this manager conceived industries as groups of customers. Academics consistently think of industries as groups of competing firms.

Obviously, some managers have accurate perceptions. Our data suggest that for some variables, as many as 40 percent may have accurate perceptions. But managers with very inaccurate perceptions are more prevalent. For some variables, the likelihood of obtaining accurate information is very low. If organizations are going to base decisions and strategies on managers' perceptions they need to draw data from the managers with accurate perceptions while discarding data from the others. How to identify managers with accurate perceptions remains a problem for future research. Unfortunately, our studies say perceptual accuracy does not, on average, correlate with relevant job experience. This is a mystery that cries out for further research, and we later tried to examine it further in Study 2.

Big errors and frequent ones offer big and prevalent opportunities for improvement. In principle, organizations can produce significant increases in perceptual accuracy by educating managers and providing them with information. Some consultants who advise firms about strategic planning told us that many organizations have turned away from the mode in which managers pool their judgments and seek to develop strategies collectively. Instead, these organizations are using planning activities to educate managers about the actual properties of firms and market environments. Thus, management practice seems to be recognizing that there are gains to be had from educating and informing.

Although organizational information systems can enhance managers' perceptions, they can also degrade them. Automatic periodic reports dull senses and divert managers' attentions from what is important by inundating them with irrelevant or obsolete data (Normann 1971). Our studies and those by others indicate that managers could benefit by relying much less on their beliefs and relying on databases much more. Modern information technology can help to make data more objective and more up-to-date. Organizations can use information systems to gather and analyze objective data, to focus attention on important phenomena, and to provide prompt feedback about results. The fact that technological innovations are introducing new data and different viewpoints offers managers a rationale for abandoning past perceptions.

Perhaps the greatest challenge and the greatest opportunity is to design robust organizations and decision processes that act effectively despite their managers' inaccurate perceptions, just as aircraft designers try to anticipate pilot error. Based on Hedberg, Nystrom, and Starbuck (1976), Nystrom and Starbuck (1984) and Quinn (1980), robust organizations need at least three properties. First, they need to anticipate perceptual inaccuracy when they allocate data-gathering resources. Data-gathering resources and educational efforts should focus on crucial variables, and extra resources and backup systems should go where errors are most likely and the consequences of error harshest. Second, robust organizations need multifaceted feedback about performance outcomes. People who expect to make mistakes not only realize the value of information about their performances, they also recognize that the most useful information may relate to unpredicted outcomes. Third, robust organizations need to concentrate on incremental moves, avoiding drastic innovations. Smaller innovations entail smaller risks because they place less reliance on managers' understanding of their environments, and the outcomes from smaller innovations are more likely to resemble the predicted outcomes.

5. STUDY 2: SENIOR MANAGERS IN A LARGE FIRM

We were unhappy about the quality of our data in study 1. Some of the 'managers' in study 1 had had little managerial experience. Of course, any heterogeneous group of managers is likely to include some with little managerial experience, but we were surprised because we had taken the label 'Executive' too literally. Further, we asked these managers questions about their perceptions of diverse variables. They undoubtedly regarded some of these variables as important and relevant to their jobs and others as irrelevant or unimportant.

Therefore, we undertook another study in which it would be clear that (*a*) our respondents were experienced managers and (*b*) the variables we were studying were relevant and important to our respondents. We negotiated access to a large, multidivisional firm; because this firm is very large, its divisions are major companies in themselves. This firm said we could have access to its executives only if we would study variables relating to its quality-improvement program. The CEO declared that his highest priority was quality improvement, and much effort was going into identifying, gathering, and disseminating information about quality performance. Many managers attended training courses about quality improvement, each division had a department that focused on quality improvement, and quality measures were being distributed to all managers frequently. Respondents also confirmed the importance of quality improvement: 74 percent expected to receive large increases in their personal rewards if their divisions did achieve higher quality.

Corporate sponsorship had several benefits. Our respondents were senior managers in charge of four major divisions. A corporate vice president personally asked these divisional senior managers to answer our questions. We received responses from nearly 100 percent of the senior managers in each division. Each division's quality personnel helped us to tailor our questions to suit that division's quality-improvement program. This increased our confidence that the variables were relevant to our respondents and that our questionnaire used the same terminology our respondents themselves used.

Table 22.2 shows managers' responses concerning six numeric measures of quality performance. The managers receive quarterly reports about these measures. We asked each manager to give the numeric performance measure and also to classify this performance on a qualitative scale—for example, very good, good, fair, poor, very poor. From 9 to 51 percent of the managers stated their perceptions of the current numeric levels of quality performance, and 49–91 percent responded 'I don't know' the current numeric levels of quality performance. As Table 22.2 indicates, most managers marked qualitative-scale classifications even when answering 'I don't know' regarding the numeric measures. Our respondents gave very similar qualitative classifications about all areas of quality performance in their divisions, even though the actual numeric measures varied significantly across areas.

Our questions used sigmas where the divisions used sigmas in their internal reports, our questions used defects per million where the divisions used defects per million in their internal reports, and our questions used percentages where the divisions used percentages in their internal reports. However, respondents often replied in sigmas to questions that asked for defects per million. We discovered that using terminology that the managers actually used did not assure that they understood the terminology. In particular, there is evidence that very few managers understood the use of 'sigmas' as units of measure. The nonlinear sigma scale, widely used in quality-improvement programs, is a deceptive one in which small changes in the number of sigmas represents very large changes in defect rates. Table 22.3 shows the defect rates that correspond to several sigma values.

Table 22.2. Percentages of 47 managers responding

Measure of quality	Stating a quantitative response	Stating a qualitative response	Stating a qualitative response after saying 'I don't know' about the corresponding quantitative measure
1	51	86	74
2	49	92	85
3	42	95	91
4	36	77	66
5	19	63	57
6	9	56	52

Table 22.3. Defect rates corresponding to various sigma values

Number of sigmas	Defects per million
2	308,770.2
3	66,810.6
4	6209.7
5	232.7
6	3.4
7	0.0

Table 22.4 shows the average errors and the frequencies of moderate and very large errors in managers' descriptions of quality performance in their divisions. We calculated these errors using the same quarterly reports that the managers received. The most striking property of Table 22.4 is that when defect rates were stated as percentages or defects per million, managers had much more accurate perceptions than they did when defect rates were stated in sigmas. In fact, when defect rates were stated as percentages or defects per million, managers who were not quality specialists had about the same perceptions of quality performance as did the quality specialists. On the other hand, when defect rates were stated in sigmas, quality specialists were roughly twice as likely to have perceptions with only moderate errors. Furthermore, when defect rates were stated in sigmas, some managers had extremely large errors in their perceptions of quality performance. These extreme errors produce some very large average errors.

Figure 22.5 compares the perception errors when defect rates were stated as percentages or defects per million versus when defect rates were stated in sigmas. Figure 22.5 combines the data for all managers, both quality specialists and nonspecialists. It is evident that extreme errors occurred more often when defect rates were stated in sigmas, and that accurate perceptions occurred more often when defect rates were stated as percentages or defects per million. One reason people make fewer extreme errors with percentages is that people tend not to state very tiny or very large defect rates; the sigma scale leads people to state very tiny or very large defect rates without realizing they are doing so.

Table 22.4. Moderate and extreme errors in managers' perceptions of quality performance

		Errors under 50%	Errors over 200%	Average error (%)	Numbers of responses
Defect rates stated as percentages or as defects per million	Not quality specialists	68	19	3.4	31
	Quality specialists	73	7	14.8	15
Defect rates stated as sigmas	Not quality specialists	26	23	715.1	35
	Quality specialists	50	33	3724.0	12

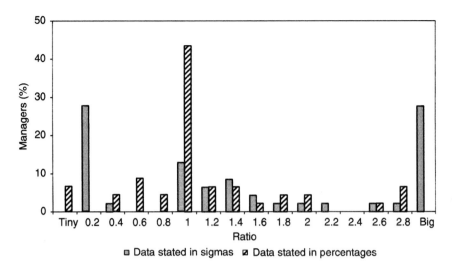

Figure 22.5. Ratios of managers' statements about defect rates to actual defect rates

We do think that study 2 was an improvement over study 1, and it does give us more confidence in managers' perceptions. In particular, Table 22.2 is consistent with the notion that managers know what they do not know. Of course, we have no way to verify that the 'I don't know' managers had inaccurate perceptions, but that seems plausible. Further, when performance was measured in percentages, 70 percent of the managers who believed they knew the performance measures were fairly accurate.

Hoping that a good hypothesis would be supported by better data, we once again hypothesized that specialists would have more accurate perceptions than nonspecialists. The mixed evidence in Table 22.4 does not support this hypothesis. This also suggests that managers may have inaccurate perceptions regarding information that is central to their jobs as well as about information they believe is someone else's responsibility.

We also hypothesized that perceptions would be more accurate after the program was older. However, when we returned for a follow-up study a year later, we were unable to obtain sufficient, dependable data.

Study 2 was not as perfect as we had hoped it would be. One reason corporate headquarters was very interested in our studying the quality-improvement program was that this program was rather new. When we gathered data the first time, the program had been on-going for one year. Organizations often do focus on new initiatives and so the conditions we studied are typical ones, but we were concerned that we might have gathered data too early in the program's life. Thus, we returned to the firm a year later. We discovered that the senior vice president who distributed our questionnaires previously was no longer visiting

Table 22.5. Seven managers' responses to a question about quality performance

Job assignment	Hours of quality training	Stated defects per million
Finance	1	207,668
Quality	17.5	207,668
Quality	50	162,695
Quality	30	162,695
Quality	30	162,000
Quality	25	160,000
Quality	Unknown	30,000

the divisions to discuss quality. We also had less support from the corporate headquarters. The senior vice president told us that (*a*) corporate headquarters worked hard to persuade divisions to take responsibility for the quality program so that, after two years, the pressure was coming from division managers, and (*b*) after two years, corporate headquarters figured out which metrics were good criteria for tracking progress without visible intervention.

The firm insisted that we study its quality-improvement program because this was a high priority for the corporate headquarters at that time. But it was not clear that the program was an equally high priority for the managers of the divisions; the divisions may have been feigning interest in this program. Our attempted follow-up study accidentally discovered that some managers could not read the quality-performance reports correctly even after the program had been operating for two years. Personnel in one division sent the managers our questionnaire without instructions: Table 22.5 shows seven of the answers we received, as well as the respondents' primary job assignments and the numbers of hours of training they received in quality improvement. Note that four respondents gave numerical answers having six significant digits! Obviously, these managers looked up the numbers in the quality-performance reports that they were then receiving monthly. Three of these four respondents were quality specialists, and two of these specialists gave the correct numbers. The other quality specialist and a finance manager gave the same extremely precise incorrect number. They had both pulled this number from the wrong section of the quality-performance report. Thus, even having written documents in front of them and having relevant training does not assure that managers will give accurate information.

Stage 4: Our Conclusions After Study 2

Organizations make measurements and discuss measurements to focus people's attentions. Although the sigma scale fostered very large perception errors, it also gave the program a scientific aura and it gave the quality specialists an area of expertise. Some quality specialists received only a few hours of training, which suggests that the specialist designation was symbolic (Johnson 1990).

Not only did our studies fail to confirm our hypotheses, they forced us to reconsider our assumptions about the importance of accurate perceptions. Only long after completing our studies and after considerable reflection, did we recognize that we had been assuming people need to perceive problems accurately in order to solve them. The prevalence of large perception errors made us aware of this assumption. Most managers we studied came from the world's best-known companies. If people in these companies were aware that perceptual errors were causing prevalent serious problems, the companies would surely have the resources to eliminate them. But these companies were not devoting significant resources to error correction.

Eventually, we realized that most problem-solving, possibly almost all problem-solving, does not depend on accurate knowledge of current situations. In most situations, people can act effectively without having accurate perceptions: They need only pursue general, long-term goals. Because they usually get prompt evidence about the effectiveness of their actions, at least in gross terms, their misperceptions cause only small errors. For example, managers' ability to improve product quality depends hardly at all on their knowledge of current quality measures. The managers mainly need to accept the idea that they should improve quality. There are many actions they can take that are likely to produce improvements, and it does not matter that they choose the actions that offer the greatest improvements. If a controversy develops that measurements might resolve, such as which aspects of quality are most deficient, the managers can then make measurements or examine measurements that already exist.

Perception errors that differ among individual managers create ambiguity that some managers can use to promote their interests. Kelemen (2000) has argued that managers take advantage of the ambiguous language of Total Quality Management to help them control lower-level employees. Walton and Dawson (2001) observed that when speaking of criteria for judging managerial performance, managers prefer to emphasize variables that they can control. An implication is that managers value ambiguity about variables they have trouble controlling. Baumard (1999) has argued that some top managers operate effectively in ambiguous, uncertain environments through a pragmatic, creative cunning that generates new sense-making frameworks. Thus, beyond the idea of management as a process that appraises the present realistically and forecasts the future accurately, another mode of management is creating and exploiting perception errors (Salgado, Starbuck, and Mezias 2002).

In almost all domains, acceptable managerial performance is comparative (Hinings and Greenwood 1988; Walgenbach and Hegele 2001). Managers have to perform as well or better than competitors; they need not take optimal actions, or even good actions, unless their competitors are taking equally effective actions (Salgado, Starbuck, and Mezias 2002). If most actions resemble the actions taken by others, the rationales for these actions do not matter. For internal evaluations, managers may not even have to perform as well as competitors, but merely better than before. Even when performance is lagging, a trend toward improvement is taken as a sign of promise for the future.

Porac and Rosa (1996) argued that any sense-making framework can be effective if a firm can impose this framework on its environments. Parallel arguments suggest that a firm can impose a shared sense-making framework on its internal properties and can direct the attentions of its personnel to important stimuli. Such arguments imply that perceptions shared by a dominant coalition would tend to be accurate. However, there are several reasons to doubt that such processes actually occur with sufficient strength to produce these effects. First, these arguments assume that a firm has considerable power in comparison with elements in its environment. Second, if these processes do produce accurate perceptions by most senior managers, then studies such as ours would not be finding low correlations between senior managers' perceptions and 'objective' measurements (Downey, Hellriegel, and Slocum 1975; Tosi, Aldag, and Storey 1973). Third, our Study 2 shows how difficult it is for a firm to direct the attentions of its personnel.

Nevertheless, an organization would be unrealistically optimistic to assume that misperceptions can never cause harm. Well-intended efforts to produce improvements can yield unexpected disappointments that waste resources or make troublesome situations worse. Managers who have inaccurate perceptions may lose out to competitors who see opportunities more clearly. The early studies that aroused our interest in this topic suggest that erroneous perceptions sometimes have dire consequences. And organizations can take steps to insure themselves against such losses if they will anticipate and allow for the perceptual errors (e.g. Nystrom and Starbuck 1984).

Although most managers know they do not know, recognizing that ignorance does not ensure that someone in the organization actually does have essential information. When forced to provide 'answers' about topics on which they lack definite facts, managers seem to be content to fill in the gaps with folklore that has been socially constructed. (We wonder if managers are especially likely to do this while they are being interviewed by academic researchers.) Furthermore, organizations cannot rely on internal specialists to provide expertise. The designation of specialists may be symbolic, and specialists do not show themselves to be reliably more accurate than nonspecialists.

We remain convinced that the accuracy of managers' perceptions is an important research topic. But it may be a topic that cannot be studied with large samples and statistics because the occasions when erroneous perceptions have serious consequences are unusual and because managers seem to be aware that there is a lot they do not know.

ACKNOWLEDGMENTS

The authors thank Susan Jackson, Steve Kerr, Bob Lamb, and Sheila Puffer for making helpful suggestions or providing useful information.

Part VIII

Strategizing Part 3

23

Which Dreams Come True? Endogeneity, Industry Structure, and Forecasting Accuracy

Coauthored with Michael L. Barnett and P. Narayan Pant

1. INTRODUCTION

Forecasting the future seems to me to be a fool's fantasy.
—James G. March (1996)

Forecasting holds endless fascination for people. The mass media devote multitude hours and pages to speculations about what is going to happen. People construct forecasts with horoscopes, statistical analyses, esteemed experts, simulation models, and Delphi techniques. Trade associations frequently publish cries of impending triumph or doom, and government agencies regularly publish authoritative trajectories.

Yet, forecasting has also had a record of abject failure. The most accurate forecasts are generally no more accurate than naive linear extrapolations that anyone can make (Pant and Starbuck 1990). Models having credible face validities make no more accurate forecasts than do ones having poor face validities. Simple, crude models tend to forecast more accurately than complex, subtle ones. Quite a few studies have found that an average of five or six forecasts is usually more accurate than any one of the component forecasts is, which implies 'that there is no such thing as a best model' (Makridakis and Winkler 1983). After assessing the performance evidence, Armstrong (1985: 91) advised: 'Do not hire the best expert you can—or even close to the best. Hire the cheapest expert.'

Failures are especially evident where forecasts span long intervals. The simple, linear extrapolations that tend to work well generally do so for only short intervals. After several periods, trends no longer adhere to linearity (Pant and Starbuck 1990). Thus, one reacts with surprise when one discovers a series of forecasts that have proven to be remarkably accurate for a very long period.

This chapter describes such an anomaly—Moore's Law. This anomaly suggests factors that might make forecasts more accurate, so we set out to investigate the possibility that these factors might be visible in large-scale data. The first sections of this chapter describe the history of Moore's Law and extract some inferences about the factors that have made it accurate. Then the ensuing sections describe our effort to find evidence of these factors at work in forecasts about U.S. manufacturing industries.

2. MOORE'S LAW: A CASE STUDY OF CONSCIOUS PARALLELISM

> Moore's Law has given us an extraordinary gift: we know how and when the future will arrive.
>
> —Intel (2002)

In 1965, Gordon Moore, then director of research and development at Fairchild Semiconductor, published a somewhat obscure four-page article in the trade magazine, *Electronics*. In this article, he noted that since 1959, the number of components that could be 'crammed' onto a silicon chip had doubled annually. Moore predicted that such annual doubling would continue through at least 1975. 'That means by 1975, the number of components per integrated circuit for minimum cost will be 65,000' (Moore 1965: 115). In 1975, Intel developed a silicon chip containing approximately 8,000 transistors and 65,000 components (Schaller 1997). Although Moore's prediction had spanned a decade and addressed a technologically complex phenomenon, the prediction had proven surprisingly accurate.

In 1975, in a paper presented at a major electronics-industry conference, Moore again reviewed recent developments and predicted the future of computing. Because of the increasing technical challenges of placing ever more components onto a single chip, the number of components on a chip was no longer doubling annually. Moore now predicted that doubling would occur every eighteen to twenty-four months over the foreseeable future (Intel 2002; Schaller 1997). Over the next several decades, up to today and beyond, Moore's prediction has been remarkably accurate. This consistent pace of innovation proved so reliable that people began to call it 'Moore's Law'.

Figure 23.1 shows the actual numbers for two kinds of chips from 1965 through 2000: the number of bits on a DRAM memory chip and the number of transistors on a microprocessor chip (Advanced Horizons 2002; Intel 2002; Moore 1965; Schaller 1997; Watson 2002). The shift that induced Moore to alter his prediction in 1975 is most apparent in the case of processors: slower evolution began around 1971. Figure 23.1 also presents lines that correspond to Moore's predictions as they apply to these two kinds of chips. Because Moore's 1975 prediction specified only a range of developmental speeds, we used regression to fit the two lines for the period after 1975 to the actual data. The fitted lines say that since 1975, the number of bits on a DRAM memory chip has doubled every 20.8 months and the number of transistors on a microprocessor has doubled every 25.9 months.

Given the difficulty of making accurate long-term predictions about even simplistic phenomena, how has Moore's prediction, which proposed continuous

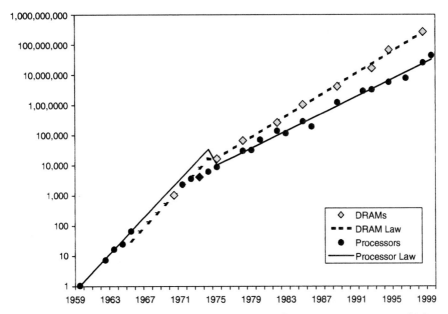

Figure 23.1. Moore's Law versus actual chips (Numbers of bits or transistors on one chip)

major advances, proven so accurate for nearly forty years? Moore is not an extraordinarily gifted soothsayer. According to Moore (Intel 2002: 3), 'I just blindly extrapolated.... I did not expect it to be accurate.... It was not intended to be a precise prediction at all, but only a guiding idea.'

3. FROM PREDICTION TO PRODUCTION

What made Moore's predictions accurate were characteristics both of the predicted phenomenon and of the semiconductor industry. Carver Mead observed that Moore's Law is 'not a law of physics, it's about human belief, and when people believe in something, they'll put energy behind it to make it come to pass' (Schaller 1996).

Moore's predictions became self-fulfilling prophecies (Howard-Grenville 2000; Intel 2002; Moore 1996; Schaller 1997). Over time, Moore's predictions began actually to drive the behavior that created the predicted outcomes. The Semiconductor Industry Association's *International National Technology Roadmap for Semiconductors* assumes continuous advancement at the pace of Moore's Law (Kostoff and Schaller 2001). Computer manufacturers and software firms schedule production cycles based on Moore's Law. The U.S. Congress bases economic planning on Moore's Law (Fixmer 2002).

Once the pace observed by Moore became accepted, it began to serve as the 'technological barometer' (Malone 1996) or 'time pacing' (Eisenhardt and Brown 1998) by which Intel, its rivals, its suppliers, its buyers, and the technology sector in general operate. The people whose actions make Moore's Law accurate believe that the Law accurately predicts the future, and so they make the necessary investments to produce the innovations that sustain the Law. As Moore put it: 'It really becomes a question of putting the track ahead of the train to stay on plan' (Korcynski 1997).

Moore helped to lay the track on which semiconductor technology has traveled predictably for four decades. That is, Moore exerted strong influence upon the subject of his prediction. First, as a founder of Fairchild Semiconductor and its director of research and development, Moore conducted and oversaw early research in semiconductor manufacturing. Then Moore and another Fairchild founder, Bob Noyce, grew frustrated with the ability of Fairchild to commercialize new technologies, so in 1968, they founded Intel (Jackson 1997). At Intel, Moore assembled and oversaw the world's brightest engineers working on semiconductor technology, and as CEO, he had a strong voice in the assumptions guiding Intel's investments. But Intel was far from alone. Engineers from Fairchild Semiconductor founded 150 firms.

The semiconductor industry confronted daunting technological challenges in doubling the number of components on a single chip every year up to 1975. However, the challenges after 1975 were more daunting. Moore noted, 'There is no room left to squeeze anything out by being clever' (Schaller 1997: 54). People had plucked all the low-hanging fruit in the early years. Putting more and more components on a single chip required fundamental advances in underlying technologies, not just cleverness in design.

Alone, Moore and his team at Intel would have faced difficulty creating all the advances necessary to keep pace with Moore's Law. While predicting that rapid advances would continue, Moore spread his research program to others in the semiconductor industry and in academia. According to Carver Mead, Moore 'really gave us permission to believe that it would keep going' (Mead 1992, as quoted in Schaller 1996). As belief in Moore's Law spread, more engineering talent was attracted to solving the problems necessary to break down barriers to continued achievement and more firms premised their investments on this forecast.

The continued success of Moore's Law depended on more than beliefs and innovation within the semiconductor industry. Increasingly powerful computer chips call for complementary devices and software and customer demand. In the late 1960s and early 1970s, the market for sophisticated semiconductor chips was largely limited to mainframe computers. To expand beyond this small market, semiconductor firms had to convince device manufacturers that semiconductor technology was functional. Eisenhardt and Brown (1998: 65) have remarked, 'If [Intel] designs chips for which there aren't enough uses, then Intel falters. So...Intel must create "new uses and new users"—which is, in fact, the company's slogan.' As manufacturers in other industries began to believe in Moore's Law, they began to design semiconductor technology into their current and future products. As Jackson (1997: 200) noted, 'If microprocessors doubled in power every eighteen months, then you could predict in advance when it would make economic sense to put a microprocessor inside a weighing machine, a digital watch, or a car.' In 1996, Steinberg observed, 'Computer manufacturers time their product cycles to coincide with the introduction of the next generation of microprocessors. Even software vendors take Moore's Law into account when planning what capabilities to add to future program versions.'

Belief in exponential innovation became so widespread outside the semiconductor industry that there has been some debate as to whether semiconductors have led or followed. Microsoft's chief technology officer, Nathan Myhrvold, asserted, 'So, we have increased the size and complexity of software even faster than Moore's Law. In fact, this is why there is a market for faster processors—software people have always consumed new capability as fast or faster than the chip people could make it available' (Brand 1995). Innovation in hard disk technology has both lagged that in semiconductors and led it. Figure 23.2 shows the speeds of hard disks produced by IBM; graphs for access time and the density of storage look very similar to Figure 23.2. The kinked line assumes that there have been three distinct developmental periods: before 1970, from 1970 to 1991, and since 1991. Thompson and Best (2000) attributed the abrupt acceleration that began in the early 1990s to a combination of factors, and they predicted that further acceleration is likely.

Although people in his industry respected Moore greatly (Jackson 1997), his 1965 prediction did not attain the status of 'law' quickly. Indeed, it did not even gain much attention when first published, and it was not controversial.

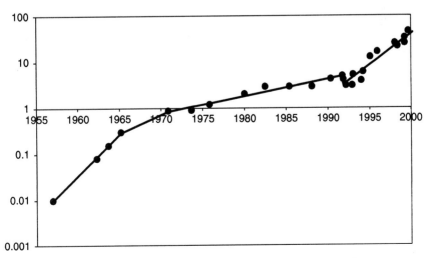

Figure 23.2. Internal data rates for IBM hard disks (megabytes per second)

Others in the semiconductor industry shared Moore's vision of the future (Schaller 1996). In 1972, Hoeneisen and Mead published a detailed and sophisticated academic argument as to why the trend noted by Moore would continue through 1975 and perhaps beyond. But, it was not until Intel dominated its industry that people came to consider Moore's prediction a 'law'. In 1975, Moore publicly reiterated, modified, and more thoroughly justified his prediction at the IEEE International Electron Devices Meeting. By this time, Intel had become a major player in the semiconductor industry, and Moore's beliefs held considerably more influence. As Intel's dominance grew, the personnel and organizations crucial to turn Moore's prediction into reality were more willing to follow Moore's lead. Sometime thereafter, Mead coined the term 'Moore's Law' (Intel 2002).

Competition has rarely challenged Intel's technology, and never to a serious degree. Because of the need to coordinate product development across industries, competition has emphasized confrontations between coalitions. The most visible example of a coalition challenging Intel has been the development of RISC processors by Sun Microsystems and its partners.

4. CONSCIOUS PARALLELISM AND FORECAST ACCURACY

The history of Moore's Law helps illustrate the influence of interfirm coordination on forecast accuracy. The doctrine of conscious parallelism notes that it is possible for firms to coordinate their activity without direct interaction and formal planning but rather by following parallel paths (Nye 1975; Scherer and Ross 1990). As Cyert and March (1963) pointed out, firms rely on standardized programs. Programs make the future more regular and predictable, in that distinct subunits of a firm can anticipate the actions of other subunits on which they depend. Predictability also facilitates parallel competitive actions. Such parallelism may result from conscious intentions, but it also tends to occur spontaneously as different firms share common routines. Nelson and Winter (1982) described the transmission of routines across firms, with one result being that industries evolve in harmony.

We infer that Moore's Law has functioned as a coordination mechanism that allowed personnel and organizations to act in parallel. Coordinated action was essential to survival and growth of the semiconductor industry. The rapid pace of technological progress set forth by Moore's Law was critical to legitimating semiconductors as the technology of choice for electronic products. Once established, Moore's Law set the competitive benchmark. As Moore stated,

Every company knows that unless they keep moving at that pace, they are going to fall behind. It has kind of become a guideline of how fast things have to continue to evolve. It has become the driver of what happens, because of people's recognition that you have to stay on it or ahead of it to be competitive. (Intel 2002: 4)

Moore's Law is 'so enmeshed in our daily lives, that it has become as omnipresent and as deeply felt as the seasons' (Malone 1998: 116; Howard-Grenville 2000). Firms within the industry and in complementary industries realized the importance of keeping Moore's Law on track, and so they channeled investments of time, energy, and resources on pace with this 'metronome driving the technology age' (Malone 1998: 116). With the exception of Sun's RISC venture, firms have not tried to deviate greatly from Moore's Law. The Law sets a technologically challenging pace and firms know that extreme deviations would encounter weak demand due to lack of complementary products. As a result, Moore's Law has proven very accurate.

Generalizing beyond Moore's Law, we believe several factors enable the sort of conscious parallelism that leads to improved accuracy of public forecasts. Obviously, firms find it easier to make outcomes match their forecasts where the forecasts concern variables over which the firms exert more control. Although no variable is entirely exogenous over a long period, some variables—say, legislation or international economic conditions—are determined by factors largely outside the direct control of any firm and possibly of an entire industry. Other variables— say, expenditures for R&D or capital investments—are largely under a firm's control, or at least the control of policies that firms share. For example, Moore was able to help his prediction come to fruition by marshaling the resources of Intel: 'The mission of Intel's technology development team is to continue to break down barriers to Moore's Law' (Intel website 2002).

Firms also find it easier to achieve their forecasts if most of the firms in an industry have an interest in acting in parallel. Moore's Law clearly benefited the entire semiconductor industry by helping to establish semiconductor technology as the technology of choice, and by expanding the market for semiconductors over time. Both economic theory and some evidence indicate that 'conscious parallelism of action' occurs mainly in oligopolies (Posner 1969; Scherer and Ross 1990). In the absence of coordination, the complexity of competitive interactions among firms in oligopolies would make their futures very unpredictable. Therefore, oligopolistic firms pursue coordination. For example, automobile companies appear to have constrained technological innovation, possibly to the detriment of long-term demand for their products. Firms in the electrical equipment industry have developed schemes to distribute orders among themselves—including illegal conspiracies in the United States and a legal cartel outside the United States. Thus, we conjecture that industry concentration makes futures more predictable.

In summary, we hypothesize that forecasts are more likely to prove accurate where (*a*) the forecasts concern variables over which firms exert control that is more direct and (*b*) industry concentration is higher.

Hypothesis 1: The more control firms exert over a variable, the more accurate predictions about this variable tend to be.

Hypothesis 2: The more concentrated an industry, the more accurate predictions about this industry tend to be.

5. A STATISTICAL STUDY OF INDUSTRY FORECASTS

We investigated our conjectures by examining forecasts about U.S. manufacturing industries. For many years, Predicast compiled and republished every forecast they could find concerning the U.S. economy. They also compiled and republished many of the outcome data needed to assess the accuracy of earlier forecasts.

We examine only long-range forecasts—ones that extended eight or more years into the future. Many techniques can produce accurate short-range forecasts, including linear extrapolation. As a result, short-range forecasts are unlikely to reflect factors such as industry concentration or firms' control over outcomes. Since we wanted to compare long-range forecasts with their eventual outcomes, we focused on forecasts published many years ago—from 1971 to 1977. For this period, Predicast had compiled 4,509 long-range forecasts about manufacturing industries, including 2-digit, 3-digit, and 4-digit industries. Table 23.1 presents four example forecasts.

The studied forecasts concerned outcomes that would occur from 1979 to 1990. We searched for these outcome data, and were able to find matches for 3,142 forecasts. After considering various possible biases, we have concluded that these 3,142 forecasts are a plausibly representative sample of the 4,509 forecasts in the population, except that the population includes some forecasts for which outcome data do not exist because no organization tracked them.

Forecasts fall into four basic types: expected rates of change, future quantities expressed in physical units such as tons or barrels, forecasts in current dollars that incorporate expected price changes, and forecasts in constant dollars that explicitly exclude price changes. Figure 23.3 describes the distribution of these four types. We had more success in finding outcomes for forecasts about rates of change (82%) and less success in finding outcomes for forecasts about physical quantities (62%).

To render forecasts and outcomes comparable, we converted them to percentage rates of change compounded annually. For example, in 1977, *Chemical Market Review* reported that the petroleum refining industry had expended $466 million on air-pollution control equipment in 1976, and forecast that this expenditure would escalate to $6 billion by 1985. We represented this forecast as

Table 23.1. Examples of forecasts

SIC 2091: In 1985, consumption of cotton will total 8,250,000 bales. Published by the U.S. Department of Agriculture in 1973

SIC 2800: In 1990, expenditures by the coal-gas industry for chemicals and allied products will equal 20 million 1974 $. Published by Chemical Engineering in 1975 but based on 1974 data

SIC 3534: In 1985, shipments of elevators and moving stairways will total 10 billion in current $. Published by U.S. Outlook in 1976 but based on 1975 data

SIC 3712: In 1984, 41 percent of automobiles will be in use by two-car families. Published by Plastics World in 1974

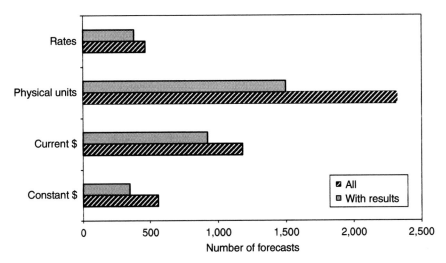

Figure 23.3. Distribution of types of forecasts

an average annual change of 124 percent. We then found that this industry expended only $169 million for air-pollution control equipment in 1985. We represented this outcome as an average annual change of −17 percent. The forecast was therefore in error by 141 percent.

Overall, the data give reason to doubt that many forecasts are even somewhat accurate. Computed across all 3,142 forecasts, the correlation between the forecasted rates of change and the actual rates of change was only 0.0043—very nearly zero. As a result, the error in forecasts and the actual rates of change correlated −0.9999—very nearly perfectly, but negatively. These correlations also suggest that the data pose challenges for regression calculations: Our dependent variable, the absolute error in forecasts, is the absolute difference between two variables that correlate very weakly.

Table 23.2 shows median rates of change for the four types of forecasts. We report medians because the distributions skew to the right and a few large rates distort the means. It is striking that the forecasted rates of change were nearly the

Table 23.2. Median rates of change by type of forecast

	Forecasted rate (%)	Actual rate (%)	Error in forecasts (%)
Rates	3.70	0.50	2.98
Physical units	4.12	0.32	3.87
Constant $	4.12	0.83	4.71
Current $	9.96	13.15	−3.75
Current $ deflated	3.96	2.68	1.58
All types	4.00	0.56	3.36

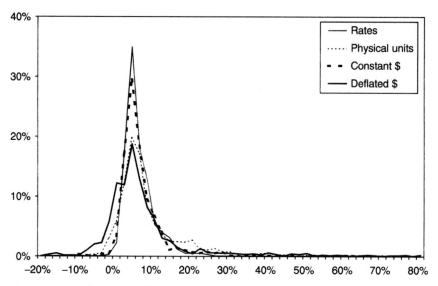

Figure 23.4. Distributions of forecasted rates of change by type of forecast

same for three types—rates, physical quantities, and constant dollars. Likewise, the actual rates of change were not very different for these three types, ranging from 0.32 percent to 0.83 percent. The median errors in these forecasts did differ slightly, the smallest median error occurring with rates and the largest with constant dollars.

The glaring deviate, of course, is forecasts stated in current dollars. Forecasters appear to have assumed that inflation would run around 6 percent, whereas the actual rates of inflation were much higher than 6 percent. Therefore, Table 23.2 also shows 'deflated current dollars', computed by subtracting the actual rates of inflation from both the forecasts and the actual outcomes.

Figure 23.4 graphs the distributions of forecasted rates of change for the four types of forecasts. These distributions are quite similar.

6. METHODOLOGY: OPERATIONALIZATIONS, CONTROL VARIABLES, AND REGRESSION WEIGHTS

To represent industry concentration, we used 4-firm concentration ratios averaged across 1972 and 1977, these being the two years within the period we studied when the *Census of Manufactures* reported concentration ratios. We chose the 4-firm ratios because they emphasize situations in which a few firms exert strong influence. However, for these industries during the period studied, 4-firm and 8-firm concentration ratios correlated 0.9696.

To represent the endogeneity of forecasted variables, we used a very crude, binary distinction. Because firms can control these variables directly, we classified as endogenous: employment, investments, wages, and imports. Forecasts about such variables comprised 38 percent of the forecasts for which we found outcome data. Because customers control these variables directly and firms cannot do so (except through 'creative accounting'), we classified as exogenous: sales, shipments, and exports. Forecasts about such variables comprised 62 percent of the forecasts for which we found outcome data.

Our regressions also take account of three control variables: length of forecast, industry's average growth rate, and the consistency of the industry's growth rate. We expected that forecasters probably make larger errors about longer periods, that forecasters probably make more optimistic forecasts about industries that grow more rapidly, and that forecasters probably make smaller forecasting errors about industries having more consistent growth rates. To represent growth rate and consistency of growth rate, we computed the mean and standard deviation of the annual percentage changes in the average of employment and deflated shipments.

Our primary dependent variable is the absolute value of the difference between the forecasted rate of change and the actual rate of change. Because it seems likely that the largest errors might be associated with very large forecasts or very large rates of change, we also consider a secondary dependent variable—the percentage absolute error. We computed this variable as $Abs(F-A)/Average(Abs(F), Abs(A), Abs(C))$ where F is the forecasted rate of change, A is the actual rate of change, and C is the average annual percentage change in the average of employment and deflated shipments. The denominator is an average of three variables because we want to avoid situations in which a very small denominator produces a very large ratio. By including four rates of change in the denominator, we assure that the denominator becomes very small only when all measures of change rate are very small.

Regression has at least two distinct uses: One may want to estimate the correlation that actually occurs in a population. In that case, one wants the independent variables to have distributions that closely resemble the population distributions. Alternatively, one may want, as we do, to estimate the strength of a relationship between the independent and dependent variables. To see an independent variable's effects, one needs for it to vary, so range-restriction of the independent variables is a key issue. If a variable exhibits very little variation, one cannot see its potential effect.

Our independent variables exhibit quite a bit of range restriction. As Figure 23.3 shows, we have noticeably more forecasts in physical quantities. Figure 23.5 graphs the distribution of 4-firm concentration ratios. These tend to fall between 20–35 percent; there are few industries with very low or very high ratios. Figure 23.6 graphs the distribution of forecast periods, which emphasizes periods of nine to eleven years. Figure 23.7 graphs the distribution of the standard deviation of industry rates of change, which emphasizes the range from 0.02 to 0.10.

Therefore, we weighted observations to approximate uniform distributions of the observations with respect to forecast type, forecast length, concentration

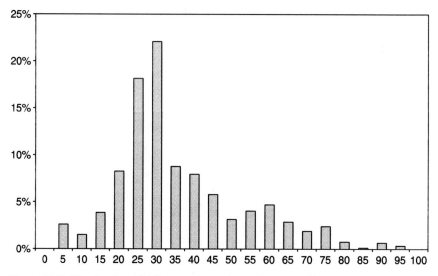

Figure 23.5. Distribution of 4-firm concentration ratios across forecasts

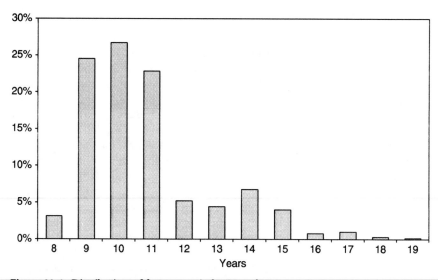

Figure 23.6. Distribution of forecast periods across forecasts

ratio, and the consistency of industry growth. In our regression calculations, an observation has the least weight if

• the forecast is in physical units,
• the forecast period is from nine to eleven years,
• the concentration ratio is from 24–31 percent, and
• the industry growth exhibits high consistency.

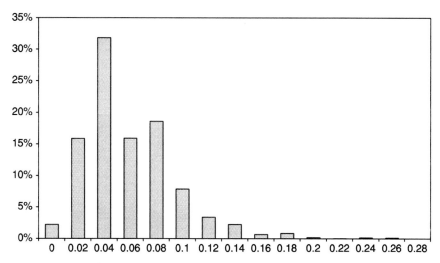

Figure 23.7. Distribution of the standard deviation of rates of changes across observations

Conversely, an observation has the greatest weight if

- the forecast period is either eight years or longer than eleven years,
- the concentration ratio is either low or high, and
- the industry growth exhibits very low consistency.

7. REGRESSION RESULTS

We do not know the error rate in the Predicast data, but studies of other large databases have shown that they incorporate quite a few errors—from 20 percent to 30 percent (Rosenberg and Houghlet 1974; San Miguel 1977). Although we were very careful, we also deem it likely that we committed errors when looking up and recording data, or when matching forecasts with actual outcomes. Thus, we used statistical methods that minimize the effects of egregious errors.

In addition, our interest focuses on the data that form the central core of the multivariate distribution, and a small fraction of the data are extreme outliers. For example, the mean value of the largest 2.5 percent absolute errors is approximately forty times the mean value of the other 97.5 percent of the absolute errors. Those extreme 2.5 percent of the observations are going to dominate any calculations that include them. The highly erroneous forecasts generally represented situations in which the forecasted variable was close to zero at the time of the forecast, so any predicted increase amounted to a very, very large rate of increase.

Table 23.3. Regression coefficients for the absolute error in forecasts

	97.5%	90%	80%	70%	60%	LTS 60%
☺ Industry Concentration (SD = 16.1%)	−0.09	−0.03	−0.28%	−0.32	−0.46	−0.32
☺ Endogeneity (Binary)	−1.29	−0.72	−0.71	−0.41	−0.40	−0.60
Length (SD = 1.97 years)	0.10	0.36	0.22	0.34	0.41	0.13
Change rate (SD = 2.56%)	−0.09	−0.44	−0.44	−0.48	−0.57	−0.41
Consistency of change (SD = 3.57%)	0.95	1.01	1.07	0.30	0.34	0.38
Percent of variation explained	6.49	8.05	8.86	15.15	24.86	26.58
Sample size	3,063	2,828	2,514	2,199	1,885	1,885

Note: SD = standard deviation.

In a few instances, increases did not occur; in most cases, increases did occur but at rates very different from those forecasted.

Therefore, we take two precautions. First, we use MM Robust regression, which limits the effects of extreme outliers and prevents them from dominating the regression results (Rousseeuw and Leroy 1987). The S-Plus statistical package estimates that the regression coefficients we present have negligible probabilities of bias whereas ordinary least-squares regression would be virtually certain to produce biased coefficient estimates. Second, we report coefficient estimates for different percentages of the data, from 97.5 percent down to 60 percent, where observations were chosen for their closeness to the regression equation. The estimates made with only 60 percent to 70 percent of the data are very unlikely to reflect data errors or aberrant observations, and our confidence in our inferences rises insofar as different percentages of the data produce similar coefficient estimates.

Table 23.3 presents the results of regression calculations in which the dependent variable is the absolute error. To facilitate comparison of the regression coefficients, we have standardized all of the independent variables except endogeneity. For example, when the forecast period increases by one standard deviation, which is 1.97 years, the absolute error in forecasts increases by 0.10 percent to 0.41 percent. The right-hand column in Table 23.3 gives coefficient estimates computed by least trimmed squares (LTS) regression using 60 percent of the data. Thus, the 60 percent column and the LTS column present the results of similar calculations that use different rules for selecting the most central 60 percent of the data and somewhat different procedures for computing regression coefficients. The 4,509 forecasts in Predicast constitute the entire population of forecasts published from 1971 to 1977, and the regression calculations in Tables 23.3 and 23.4 involve high percentages of this population.

Figure 23.8 breaks into three categories the distribution of the dependent variable and the regression estimates: The darkest points are the central 60 percent of the observations. The next darkest points are the observations outside the central 60 percent but within the central 80 percent. The lightest points are the observations outside the central 80 percent but within the central 97.5 percent. Figure 23.8 shows that the most extreme outliers, and hence the first observations

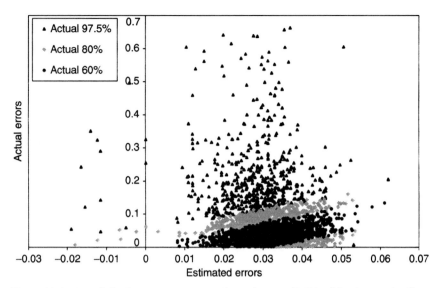

Figure 23.8. Actual absolute errors versus estimated errors (2.5% of the data omitted)

removed from regression analyses, correspond to forecasts that had very large errors. The central 60 percent and 80 percent of the observations correspond to forecasts with moderate errors. The range of the actual errors is much larger than the range of the estimates.

Table 23.4 shows the results of regressions with our secondary dependent variable, the absolute percentage error. These results resemble those for the absolute error (Table 23.3).

All of the regression coefficients in Tables 23.3 and 23.4 have the expected signs. Forecasts tended to be more accurate where forecasts covered shorter periods, industries grew more rapidly, industry growth was more consistent, industries were more concentrated, and firms had more control over the variable forecast. However, these effects are not dramatic. Whereas the median value of the absolute error is 4.81 percent, a one standard deviation change in an independent variable alters this error by roughly one twelfth.

Table 23.4. Regression coefficients for the absolute percentage error in forecasts

	97.5%	90%	80%	70%	60%	LTS 60%
☺ Industry Concentration (SD = 16.1%)	−11.94	3.56	−10.64	−10.68	−25.98	−0.89
☺ Endogeneity (Binary)	−24.19	−24.69	−17.13	−17.44	−22.42	−9.67
Length (SD = 1.97 years)	7.71	5.35	9.32	7.95	13.95	−1.70
Change rate (SD = 2.56%)	−20.69	−15.51	−14.76	−14.27	−51.16	−7.19
Consistency of change (SD = 3.57%)	−0.18	16.17	13.86	15.28	13.55	−9.23
Percent of variation explained	26.15	58.05	67.91	74.67	77.96	21.32
Sample size	3,063	2,828	2,514	2,199	1,885	1,885

Note: SD = standard deviation.

8. CONCLUSION

The statistical evidence supports the hypotheses that predictions about concentrated industries turn out to be more accurate, and that predictions about endogenous variables turn out to be more accurate. However, forecasts exhibit a lot of variation and to see these effects, one has to ignore some extreme forecasts. Nonetheless, in a business environment commonly described as increasingly turbulent, uncertain, and hypercompetitive, it is quite interesting to find evidence of predictability through interfirm coordination and control.

We see two ways to improve on our study. Firstly, future research might develop an empirically based and more subtle measure of the degree to which firms can control variables, and such a measure would likely show stronger effects. Secondly, the case of the semiconductor industry implies that the accuracy of forecasts ought to be higher where several industries link together and try to coordinate their activities. We would have included a hypothesis about inter-industry coordination if we had been able to find a good measure of the degree to which an industry has reason to coordinate with others. Future research might develop a measure of interindustry coordination.

We studied forecasts that occurred when U.S. antitrust policies were somewhat less tolerant of interfirm coordination than they have become more recently. In fact, rather than seeking to penalize interfirm coordination, the U.S. government now actively encourages some forms of it. In particular, the U.S. government has supported a widespread move toward 'industry self-regulation' (King, Lenox, and Barnett 2002; Gupta and Lad 1983; Maitland 1985). The numbers of consortia, networks, and trade associations have significantly increased since these forecasts appeared in the 1970s (Aldrich and Staber 1988). Thus, the forecasts published today seem more likely to facilitate coordinated behavior and so the historical effects we found may well underestimate current effects.

Overall, this study suggests interesting new directions for future studies of forecasting, and furthers an emerging trend in the field of strategic management. Forecasters should be able to make predictions that are more accurate by considering previously published forecasts together with endogeneity, industry concentration, and interindustry coordination. For strategic management, our findings enhance a recent push toward the study of firms' influence over environmental change (Hirsch and Lounsbury 1997: Ingram and Silverman 2002). Scholars have overlooked coordination through forecasting as a means of exerting control over the competitive environment and so forecasting offers opportunity for future studies. Utterly unexplored is the possibility that the effects we have observed might occur at the level of a single firm. Each firm faces repeated decisions about whether to benchmark forecasts and help to make them come true or whether to deviate in pursuit of competitive advantages.

References

Abegglen, J. C. (1958). *The Japanese Factory*. Glencoe, IL: Free Press.

Ackoff, R. L. (1967). 'Management Misinformation Systems', *Management Science*, 14: 6147–6156.

Advanced Horizons, Inc. (2002). 'Chips Explained'. Available at: http://www.ahinc.com/chips.htm.

Aguilar, F. J. (1967). *Scanning the Business Environment*. New York: Macmillan.

Aiken, M. and Hage, J. (1968). 'Organizational Interdependence and Intraorganizational Structure', *American Sociological Review*, 33: 912–930.

Alchian, A. (1950). 'Uncertainty, Evolution, and Economic Theory', *Journal of Political Economy*, 57: 211–221.

Alchian, A. A. (1949). 'An Airframe Production Function', Working paper, RAND Corporation, Paper P-108.

—— (1950). 'Uncertainty, Evolution, and Economic Theory', *Journal of Political Economy*, 58: 211–221.

—— (1959). 'Costs and Outputs', in M. Abramovitz et al. (eds.), *The Allocation of Economic Resources*. Stanford, CA: Stanford University Press, pp. 23–40.

Aldrich, H. and Staber, U. (1988). 'Organizing Business Interests: Patterns of Trade Association Foundings, Transformations, and Deaths', in G. Carroll (ed.), *Ecological Models of Organizations*. New York: Ballinger, pp. 111–126.

Alexander, E. R. (1979). 'The Design of Alternatives in Organizational Contexts: A Pilot Study', *Administrative Science Quarterly*, 24: 382–404.

Alexander, J. C. (1988). *Action and Its Environments*. New York: Columbia University Press.

Alfvén, H. (1985). 'Memoirs of a Dissident Scientist', in Y. Sekido and H. Elliot (eds.), *Early History of Cosmic Ray Studies*. Dordrecht, The Netherlands: Reidel, pp. 427–431.

Alland, A. Jr. (1970). *Adaptation in Cultural Evolution*. New York: Columbia University Press.

Altheide, D. L. and Johnson, J. M. (1980). *Bureaucratic Propaganda*. Boston, MA: Allan & Bacon.

Alvesson, M. (1991). 'Corporate Culture and Corporatism at the Company Level: A Case Study', *Economic and Industrial Democracy*, 12: 347–367.

—— (1992). 'Leadership as Social Integrative Action: A Study of a Computer Consultancy Company', *Organization Studies*, 13: 185–209.

Amburgey, T. L., Dacin, T., and Singh, J. V. (2000). 'Learning Races and Dynamic Capabilities', Working paper, University of Toronto.

Anderson, C. A., Krull, D. S., and Weiner, B. (1996). 'Explanations: Processes and Consequences', in E. T. Higgins and A. W. Kruglanski (eds.), *Social Psychology: Handbook of Basic Principles*. New York: Guilford Press, pp. 271–296.

Anderson, T. R. and Warkov, S. (1961). 'Organizational Size and Functional Complexity: A Study of Administration in Hospitals', *American Sociological Review*, 26: 23–28.

Andrews, P. W. S. (1949*a*). 'A Reconsideration of the Theory of the Individual Business', *Oxford Economics Papers*, 1: 54–89.

—— (1949*b*). *Manufacturing Business*. New York: St Martin's; London: Macmillan.

Ansoff, H. I. (1965). 'The Firm of the Future', *Harvard Business Review*, 43(5): 162–178.

Antonio, R. J. (1979). 'The Contradiction of Domination and Production in Bureaucracy: The Contribution of Organizational Efficiency to the Decline of the Roman Empire', *American Sociological Review*, 44: 895–912.

Argyris, C. (1957). *Personality and Organization*. New York: Harper.

—— and Schön, D. A. (1978). *Organizational Learning: A Theory of Action Perspective*. Reading, MA: Addison-Wesley.

Armstrong, J. S. (1982). 'The Value of Formal Planning for Strategic Decisions: Review of Empirical Research', *Strategic Management Journal*, 3: 197–211.

—— (1985). *Long-Range Forecasting: From Crystal Ball to Computer*, 2nd edn. New York: Wiley-Interscience.

Arnold, V., Collier, P. A., Leech, S. A., and Sutton, S. G. (1998). 'The Effect of Experience on Order and Recency Bias in Decision Making by Professional Accountants', Paper presented at the 1998 AAANZ Conference, Accounting Association of Australia and New Zealand. Adelaide, South Australia.

Ascher, W. (1978). *Forecasting: An Appraisal for Policy-Makers and Planners*. Baltimore, MD: Johns Hopkins University Press.

Ashby, W. R. (1960). *Design for a Brain*, 2nd edn. New York: Wiley.

Asher, H. (1956). *Cost-Quantity Relationships in the Airframe Industry*. Santa Monica, CA: RAND Corporation, Report R-291.

Astley, W. G. (1985). 'The Two Ecologies: Microevolutionary and Macroevolutionary Perspectives on Organizational Change', *Administrative Science Quarterly*, 30: 224–241.

—— and Fombrun, C. J. (1987). 'Organizational Communities: An Ecological Perspective', in S. Bacharach and N. DiTomaso (eds.), *Research in the Sociology of Organizations*, Vol. 5. Greenwich, CT: JAI Press, pp. 163–185.

Axelrod, R. M. (1976). 'Results', in R. M. Axelrod (ed.), *Structure of Decision: The Cognitive Maps of Political Élites*. Princeton, NJ: Princeton University Press, pp. 221–248.

Bain, J. S. (1954). 'Economies of Scale, Concentration, and the Condition of Entry in Twenty Manufacturing Industries', *American Economic Review*, 44: 15–39.

—— (1956). *Barriers to New Competition*. Cambridge, MA: Harvard University Press.

Baker, A. W. and Davis, R. C. (1954). *Ratios of Staff to Line Employees and Stages of Differentiation of Staff Functions*. Columbus, OH: Ohio State University, Bureau of Business Research. Research Monograph No. 72.

Bales, R. F. (1951). *Interaction Process Analysis*. Cambridge: Addison-Wesley.

Bargh, J. A. (1982). 'Attention and Automaticity in the Processing of Self-Relevant Information', *Journal of Personality and Social Psychology*, 43: 425–436.

Barker, R. G. (1968). *Ecological Psychology*. Stanford, CA: Stanford University Press.

Barker, V. L., III and Duhaime, I. M. (1997). 'Strategic Change in the Turnaround Process: Theory and Empirical Evidence', *Strategic Management Journal*, 18: 13–38.

Barley, S. R. and Kunda, G. (1992). 'Design and Devotion: Surges of Rational and Normative Ideologies of Control in Managerial Discourse', *Administrative Science Quarterly*, 37: 363–399.

Barnard, C. I. (1938). *The Functions of the Executive*. Cambridge, MA: Harvard University Press.

Barnett, W. P. (1997). 'The Dynamics of Competitive Intensity', *Administrative Science Quarterly*, 42: 128–160.

—— and Hansen, M. T. (1996). 'The Red Queen in Organizational Evolution', *Strategic Management Journal*, 17: 139–157.

Barth, J. R. (1991). *The Great Savings and Loan Debacle*. Washington, DC: AEI Press.

Baumard, P. (1995). *Organisations déconcertées: la gestion stratégique de la connaissance.* Paris: Masson.

—— (1996). 'Organizations in the Fog: An Investigation into the Dynamics of Knowledge', in B. Moingeon and A. Edmondson (eds.), *Organizational Learning and Competitive Advantage.* London: Sage, pp. 74–91.

—— (1999). *Tacit Knowledge in Organizations.* London: Sage.

Baumgartel, H. and Sobol, R. (1959). 'Background and Organizational Factors in Absenteeism', *Personnel Psychology,* 12: 431–443.

Baumol, W. J. (1959). *Business Behavior, Value and Growth.* New York: Macmillan.

—— (1962). 'On the Theory of Expansion of the Firm', *American Economic Review,* 52: 1078–1087.

—— and Quandt, R. E. (1964). 'Rules of Thumb and Optimally Imperfect Decisions', *American Economic Review,* 54: 23–46.

Bazerman, M. H. (1997). *Judgment in Managerial Decision Making,* 2nd edn. New York: Wiley.

BBRP (1958). *Small Business Bibliography.* Pittsburgh, PA: University of Pittsburgh, Bureau of Business Research.

Beach, L. R. (1966). 'Accuracy and Consistency in the Revision of Subjective Probabilities', *IEEE Transactions on Human Factors in Electronics,* HFE–7: 29–37.

Becker, H. and Barnes, H. E. (1961). *Social Thought from Lore to Science,* Vol. 1. New York: Dover.

Beer, S. (1972). *Brain of the Firm.* New York: Herder & Herder.

—— (1974). *Designing Freedom.* Toronto: CBC Publications.

Beesley, M. (1955). 'The Birth and Death of Industrial Establishments: Experience in the West Midlands Conurbation', *Journal of Industrial Economics,* 4: 45–61.

Belden, T. C. and Belden, M. R. (1962). *The Lengthening Shadow.* Boston, MA: Little, Brown.

Bell, G. D. (1974). 'Organizations and the External Environment', in J. W. McGuire (ed.), *Contemporary Management: Issues and Viewpoints.* Englewood Cliffs, NJ: Prentice-Hall, pp. 259–282.

Bell, T. E. and Esch, K. (1987). 'The Fatal Flaw in Flight 51-L', *IEEE Spectrum,* 24(2): 36–51.

Bendix, R. (1956). *Work and Authority in Industry.* New York: Wiley.

Bennis, W. G. (1963). 'A New Role for the Behavioral Sciences: Effecting Organizational Change', *Administrative Science Quarterly,* 8: 125–165.

—— (1965). 'The Decline of Bureaucracy and Organizations of the Future', *Trans-Action,* 2(5): 31–35.

—— (1966). *Changing Organizations: Essays on the Development and Evolution of Human Organization.* New York: McGraw-Hill.

—— (1970). 'A Funny Thing Happened on the Way to the Future', *American Psychologist,* 25: 595–608.

—— (1983). 'The Artform of Leadership', in S. Srivastva and Associates (eds.), *The Executive Mind: New Insights on Managerial Thought and Action.* San Francisco, CA: Jossey-Bass, 15–24.

—— Benne, K. D., and Chin, R. (1961). *The Planning of Change.* New York: Holt, Rinehart, & Winston.

Benston, G. J. (1985). *An Analysis of the Causes of Savings and Loan Association Failures.* New York: Salomon Brothers Center for the Study of Financial Institutions, Monograph 1985–4/5.

Berger, P. L. and Luckmann, T. (1966). *The Social Construction of Reality.* Garden City, NY: Doubleday.

Berkowitz, L. and Green, J. A. (1962). 'The Stimulus Qualities of the Scapegoat', *Journal of Abnormal and Social Psychology*, 64: 293–301.

Berle, A. A. and Means, G. C. (1932). *The Modern Corporation and Private Property*. New York: Macmillan.

—— —— (1967). *The Modern Corporation and Private Property*, (rev. edn.). New York: Harcourt, Brace & World.

Berlyne, D. E. (1960). *Conflict, Arousal and Curiosity*. New York: McGraw-Hill.

—— (1969). 'Laughter, Humor, and Play', in G. Lindzey and E. Aronson (eds.), *The Handbook of Social Psychology*, Vol. 3, 2nd edn. Reading, MA: Addison-Wesley, pp. 795–852.

Berthoin Antal, A. B., Dierkes, M., and Hähner, K. (1997). 'Business Perception of Contextual Changes: Sources and Impediments to Organizational Learning', *Business and Society*, 36(4): 387–407.

Bettman, J. R. and Weitz, B. A. (1983). 'Attribution in the Board Room: Causal Reasoning in Corporate Annual Reports', *Administrative Science Quarterly*, 28: 165–183.

Beyer, J. M. (1981). 'Ideologies, Values, and Decision Making in Organizations', in P. C. Nystrom and W. H. Starbuck (eds.), *Handbook of Organizational Design*, Vol. 2. New York: Oxford University Press, pp. 167–202.

Bhargava, N. (1990). 'Managing Knowledge Bases in Knowledge-Intensive Firms: An Empirical Study of Software Firms', Working paper, New York University.

Biot, E. (1851). *Le Tcheou-Li*. Paris: L'Imprimerie Nationale.

Blair, J. M. (1948). 'Technology and Size', *American Economic Review*, 38(2): 121–152.

Blankenship, L. V. and Elling, R. H. (1962). 'Organizational Support and Community Power Structure: The Hospital', *Journal of Health and Human Behavior*, 3: 257–269.

Blau, P. M. (1955). *The Dynamics of Bureaucracy*. Chicago, IL: University of Chicago Press.

—— (1957). 'Formal Organization: Dimensions of Analysis', *American Journal of Sociology*, 63: 58–69.

—— and Scott, W. R. (1962). *Formal Organizations*. San Francisco, CA: Chandler.

Blomqvist, H. C. (1988). 'Uncertainty and Predictive Accuracy: An Empirical Study', *Journal of Economic Psychology*, 9: 525–532.

Bobrow, D. G. and Norman, D. A. (1975). 'Some Principles of Memory Schemata', in D. C. Bobrow and A. Collins (eds.), *Representation and Understanding*. New York: Academic Press, pp. 131–149.

Bodde, D. (1986). 'The State and Empire of Ch'in', in D. Twitchett and M. Loewe (eds.), *The Cambridge History of China*, Vol. 1: *The Ch'in and Han Empires*. Cambridge: Cambridge University Press, pp. 21–102.

Boffey, P. M. (1986a). 'Space Agency Image: A Sudden Shattering', *New York Times*, 135(February 5): A1, A25.

—— (1986b). 'Analyst Who Gave Shuttle Warning Faults "Gung-ho, Can-do" Attitude', *New York Times*, 135(February 14): B4.

—— (1986c). 'Safety Assessment Hinged on Weather and Booster Seats', *New York Times*, 135(February 20), A1, D22.

Boland, R. J., Jr. (1982). 'Myth and Technology in the American Accounting Profession', *Journal of Management Studies*, 19: 109–127.

—— Singh, J., Salipante, P., Aram, J., Fay, S. Y., and Kanawattanachai, P. (2001). 'Knowledge Representations and Knowledge Transfer', *Academy of Management Journal*, 44: 393–417.

Bonini, C. P. (1963). *Simulation of Information and Decision Systems in the Firm*. Englewood Cliffs, NJ: Prentice-Hall.

Bossard, J. H. S. (1945). 'The Law of Family Interaction', *American Journal of Sociology*, 50: 292–294.

Bougon, M., Weick, K. E., and Binkhorst, D. (1977). 'Cognition in Organizations: An Analysis of the Utrecht Jazz Orchestra', *Administrative Science Quarterly*, 22: 606–639.

Boulding, K. E. (1953). *The Organizational Revolution*. New York: Harper.

Bourgeois, L. J. (1985). 'Strategic Goals, Perceived Uncertainty, and Economic Performance in Volatile Environments', *Academy of Management Journal*, 28: 548–573.

—— and Eisenhardt, K. M. (1988). 'Strategic Decision Processes in High Velocity Environments: Four Cases in the Microcomputer Industry', *Management Science*, 34: 816–835.

Bowman, R. F. Jr. (1982). 'A Pac-man Theory of Motivation: Tactical Implications For Classroom Instruction', *Educational Technology*, 22(9): 14–16.

Box, G. E. P. and Draper, N. R. (1969). *Evolutionary Operation*. New York: Wiley.

Brand, S. (1995). 'The Physicist' (interview with Nathan Myhrvold). *Wired Magazine*, 3(9): 152. Available at: http://www.wired.com/wired/archive/3.09/myhrvold.html.

Braybrooke, D. and Lindblom, C. E. (1963). *A Strategy of Decision*. New York: Free Press.

Breasted, J. H. (1962). *Ancient Records of Egypt*. New York: Russell & Russell.

Bresser, R. K. and Bishop, R. C. (1983). 'Dysfunctional Effects of Formal Planning: Two Theoretical Explanations', *Academy of Management Review*, 8: 588–599.

Brewer, E., Gittings, T., Gonczy, A. M., Merris, R., Mote, L., Nichols, D., and Reichert, A. (1980). 'The Depository Institutions Deregulation and Monetary Control Act of 1980', *Economic Perspectives*, 4(5): 3–23. (Chicago, IL: Federal Reserve Bank of Chicago.)

Brill, S. (1976). 'Two Tough Lawyers in the Tender-offer Game', *New York Times*, (June 21): 52–61.

Broad, W. J. (1986a). 'Changes in Rocket Strained Booster's Seals, Experts Say', *New York Times*, 135(February 17): A14.

—— (1986b). 'NASA Official Orders Review of 900 Shuttle Parts', *New York Times*, 135 (February 27): D27.

—— (1986c). 'NASA had Solution to Key Flaw in Rocket When Shuttle Exploded', *New York Times*, 135(September 22): Al, B8.

Broadbent, D. E. (1961). *Behaviour*. London: Eyre & Spottiswoode.

Brooks, F. P., Jr. (1975). *The Mythical Man-Month: Essays on Software Engineering*. Reading, MA: Addison-Wesley.

Brooks, J. N. (1963). *The Fate of the Edsel and Other Business Adventures*. New York: Harper & Row.

Brown, W. H. (1957). 'Innovation in the Machine Tool Industry', *Quarterly Journal of Economics*, 71: 406–425.

Brumbaugh, R. D. (1988). *Thrifts under Siege: Restoring Order to American Banking*. Cambridge, MA: Ballinger.

Brunsson, N. (1982). 'The Irrationality of Action and Action Rationality: Decisions, Ideologies, and Organisational Actions', *Journal of Management Studies*, 19: 29–44.

—— (1985). *The Irrational Organization: Irrationality as a Basis for Organizational Action and Change*. Chichester, UK: Wiley.

Buchanan, L. (1995). 'Scavenger Hunt', *CIO Magazine*, July 1.

Bucher, R. and Stelling, J. (1969). 'Characteristics of Professional Organizations', *Journal of Health and Social Behavior*, 10: 3–15.

Buck, V. E. (1966). 'A Model for Viewing an Organization as a System of Constraints', in J. D. Thompson (ed.), *Approaches to Organizational Design*. Pittsburgh, PA: University of Pittsburgh Press, pp. 103–172.

Budescu, D. V., Weinberg, S., and Wallsten, T. S. (1988). 'Decisions Based on Numerically and Verbally Expressed Uncertainties', *Journal of Experimental Psychology: Human Perception and Performance*, 14: 281–294.

Burgelman, R. A. (1994). 'Fading Memories: A Process Theory of Strategic Business Exit in Dynamic Environments', *Administrative Science Quarterly*, 39: 24–56.

Bürkle, A. (1979). 'Eine Untersuching über de Fähigkeit, exponentielle Entwicklungen su schätzen'. Working paper, Department of Psychology, University of Giessen.

Burns, L. R. and Wholey, D. R. (1993). 'Adoption and Abandonment of Matrix Management Programs: Effects of Organizational Characteristics and Interorganizational Networks', *Academy of Management Journal*, 36: 106–138.

Burns, T. and Stalker, G. M. (1961). *The Management of Innovation*. London: Tavistock.

Burtchen, I. (1987). 'Analysis of Spontaneous Play Activities in Everyday Situations With Mixed Aged Groups', in D. Gorlitz and J. F. Wohlwill (eds.), *Curiosity, Imagination, and Play*. Hillsdale, NJ: Erlbaum, pp. 259–280.

Camerer, C. F. and Johnson, E. J. (1991). 'The Process-Performance Paradox in Expert Judgment: How Can Experts Know So Much and Predict So Badly?', in K. A. Ericsson and J. Smith (eds.), *Toward a General Theory of Expertise: Prospects and Limits*. Cambridge: Cambridge University Press, pp. 195–217.

Cameron, K. S. (1984). 'The Effectiveness of Ineffectiveness', *Research in Organizational Behavior*, 6: 235–285.

Campbell, D. T. (1969). 'Reforms as Experiments', *American Psychologist*, 24: 409–429.

Caplow, T. (1957). 'Organizational Size', *Administrative Science Quarterly*, 1: 484–505.

Carroll, G. R. (1985). 'Concentration and Specialization: Dynamics of Niche Width in Populations of Organizations', *American Journal of Sociology*, 90: 1262–1283.

Carroll, J. M. and Carrithers, C. (1984). 'Training Wheels in a User Interface', *Communications of the ACM*, 27: 800–806.

—— and Thomas, J. C. (1988). 'Fun', *SIGCHI Bulletin*, 19(3): 21–24.

Carter, C. F. and Williams, B. R. (1959). *Science in Industry*. New York: Oxford University Press.

Carter, E. E. (1971). 'The Behavioral Theory of the Firm and Top-level Corporate Decisions', *Administrative Science Quarterly*, 16: 413–428.

Cartmill, M., Pilbeam, D., and Isaac, G. (1986). 'One Hundred Years of Paleoanthropology', *American Scientist*, 74: 410–420.

Cartwright, T. J. (1973). 'Problems, Solutions and Strategies: A Contribution to the Theory and Practice of Planning', *Journal of the American Institute of Planners*, 39: 179–187.

Caves, R. (1967). *American Industry*, 2nd edn. Englewood Cliffs, NJ: Prentice-Hall.

Central Intelligence Agency. Report CS-3/467: 630.

—— Report CS-3/470: 587.

Chakravarthy, B. and Lorange, P. (1991). *Managing the Strategy Process*. Englewood Cliffs, NJ: Prentice-Hall.

Chalk, R., Frankel, M. S., and Chafer, S. B. (1980). *Professional Ethics Activities in the Scientific and Engineering Societies*. Washington, DC: American Association for the Advancement of Science.

Chamberlin, E. H. (1948). 'Proportionality, Divisibility and Economies of Scale', *Quarterly Journal of Economics*, 62: 229–262. Reprinted as 'The Cost Curve of the Individual Producer', in Chamberlin (1950), 230–259.

—— (1950). *The Theory of Monopolistic Competition*, 6th edn. Cambridge, MA: Harvard University Press.

Chan, W. T. (1963). *Source Book in Chinese Philosophy*. Princeton, NJ: Princeton University Press.

Chandler, A. D., Jr. (1962). *Strategy and Structure*. Cambridge, MA: MIT Press.

—— (1962). *Strategy and Structure*. Boston, MA: MIT Press.

Chang, Y. N. and Campo-Flores, F. (1980). *Business Policy and Strategy*. Santa Monica, CA: Goodyear.

Chapin, F. S. (1957). 'The Optimum Size of Institutions: A Theory of the Large Group', *American Journal of Sociology*, 62: 449–460.

Chatov, R. (1971). 'The Problem of Independent Regulatory Agency Behavior: A Sociological Systemic and Equilibrium Approach'. Working paper, University of California, Berkeley.

—— (1979). *An Analysis of Corporate Statements on Ethics and Behavior*. San Francisco, CA: The California Roundtable.

Chester, T. E. (1961). *A Study of Post-War Growth in Management Organizations*. Paris: European Productivity Agency (OEEC), Project 347.

Chi, T. and Nystrom, P. C. (1998). 'An Economic Analysis of Matrix Structure, Using Multinational Corporations as an Illustration', *Managerial and Decision Economics*, 19: 141–156.

Child, J. (1969). *The Business Enterprise in Modern Industrial Society*. London: Collier-Macmillan.

—— (1972). 'Organizational Structure, Environment and Performance: The Role of Strategic Choice', *Sociology*, 6: 1–22.

Chiles, J. R. (1985). 'Learning from the Big Blackouts', *American Heritage of Invention and Technology*, 1(2): 27–30.

Chowdhry, K. and Pal, A. K. (1957). 'Production Planning and Organizational Morale', *Human Organization*, 15(4): 11–16

Christensen, C. R. (1953). *Management Succession in Small and Growing Enterprises*. Boston, MA: Harvard University, Graduate School of Business Administration, Division of Research.

—— Berg, N. A., and Salter, M. S. (1980). *Policy Formulation and Administration*, 8th edn. Homewood, IL: Irwin.

Churchman, C. W. (1971). *The Design of Inquiring Systems*. New York: Basic Books.

Clark, B. R. (1956). *Adult Education in Transition*. Berkeley, CA: University of California Press.

—— (1962). *Educating the Expert Society*. San Francisco, CA: Chandler.

—— (1965). 'Interorganizational Patterns in Education', *Administrative Science Quarterly*, 10: 224–237.

—— (1970). *The Distinctive College*. Chicago, IL: Aldine.

—— (1972). 'The Organizational Saga in Higher Education', *Administrative Science Quarterly*, 17: 178–184.

Cobb, C. W. and Douglas, P. H. (1928). 'A Theory of Production', *American Economic Review*, 18 (suppl.): 139–165.

Coch, L. and French, J. R. P., Jr. (1948). 'Overcoming Resistance to Change', *Human Relations*, 1: 512–532.

Coffey, W. (1983). *303 of the World's Worst Predictions*. New York: Tribeca.

Cohen, A. M. (1961). 'Changing Small Group Communication Networks', *Journal of Communication*, 11: 116–124 and 128.

Cohen, M. D., March, J. G., and Olsen, J. P. (1972). 'A Garbage Can Model of Organizational Choice', *Administrative Science Quarterly*, 17: 1–25.

—— —— —— (1976). 'People, Problems, Solutions and the Ambiguity of Relevance', in J. G. March and J. P. Olsen, (eds.), *Ambiguity and Choice in Organizations*. Bergen, Norway: Universitetsforlaget, pp. 24–37.

Cohen, R. (1991). 'Denting a Legal Galahad's Armor', *New York Times*, October 16: D1, D6.

Coleman, J. S. (1960). 'The Mathematical Study of Small Groups', in H. Solomon (ed.), *Mathematical Thinking in the Measurement of Behavior*. Glencoe, IL: Free Press.

—— and James, J. (1961). 'The Equilibrium Size Distribution of Freely-forming Groups', *Sociometry*, 24: 36–45.

Collins, J. (1989). 'Creativity and the Personal Computer', *The Wall Street Journal National Business Employment Weekly*, Winter/Spring: 10–11.

Comanor, W. S., Kover, A. J., and Smiley, R. H. (1981). 'Advertising and its Consequences', in P. C. Nystrom and W. H. Starbuck (eds.), *Handbook of Organizational Design*, Vol. 2. New York: Oxford University Press, pp. 429–439.

Committee on the Budget (1983). *Hearing before the Committee on the Budget, House of Representatives, Ninety-Eighth Congress, March 8, 1983*. Washington, DC: U.S. Government Printing Office, Serial No. 98–5.

Conway, M. and Ross, M. (1984). 'Getting What you Want by Revising What you Had', *Journal of Personality and Social Psychology*, 47: 738–748.

Cooper, W. W. (1949). 'Theory of the Firm: Some Suggestions for Revision', *American Economic Review*, 39: 1204–1222.

—— and Charnes, A. (1954). 'Silhouette Functions of Short-run Cost Behavior', *Quarterly Journal of Economics*, 68: 131–150.

Copeland, M. T. (1955). *The Executive at Work*. Cambridge, MA: Harvard University Press.

Coser, L. A. (1956). *The Functions of Social Conflict*. Glencoe, IL: Free Press.

Crozier, M. (1972). 'The Relationship Between Micro- and Macrosociology', *Human Relations*, 25: 239–251.

Crum, W. L. (1939). *Corporate Size and Earning Power*. Cambridge, MA: Harvard University Press.

—— (1953). *The Age Structure of the Corporate System*. Berkeley, CA: University of California Press.

Csikszentmihalyi, M. (1975). *Beyond Boredom and Anxiety*. San Francisco, CA: Jossey-Bass.

—— and LeFevre, J. (1989). 'Optimal Experience in Work and Leisure', *Journal of Personality and Social Psychology*, 56: 815–822.

Cyert, R. M. and March, J. G. (1963). *A Behavioral Theory of the Firm*. Englewood Cliffs, NJ: Prentice-Hall.

—— Feigenbaum, E. A., and March, J. G. (1959). 'Models in a Behavioral Theory of the Firm', *Behavioral Science*, 4: 81–95. The central model is reprinted in Cyert and March (1963), 84–98.

—— Simon, H. A., and Trow, D. B. (1956). 'Observation of a Business Decision', *Journal of Business*, 29: 237–248.

Daft, R. L. and Weick, K. E. (1984). 'Toward a Model of Organizations as Interpretation Systems', *Academy of Management Review*, 9: 284–295.

Dale, E. (1952). *Planning and Developing the Company Organization Structure*. New York: American Management Association, Research Report No. 20, particularly 66–82.

Damanpour, F. (1992). 'Organizational Size and Innovation', *Organization Studies*, 13: 375–402.

Danet, B. (1981). 'Client-organization Relationships', in P. C. Nystrom and W. H. Starbuck (eds.), *Handbook of Organizational Design*, Vol. 2. New York: Oxford University Press, pp. 382–428.

Davis, F. D., Jr. (1986). 'A Technology Acceptance Model for Empirically Testing New End-User Information Systems: Theory and Results'. Ph.D. thesis, Massachusetts Institute of Technology.

—— (1989). 'Perceived Usefulness, Perceived Ease of Use and User Acceptance of Information Technology', *MIS Quarterly*, 13: 319–342.

—— Bagozzi, R. P., and Warshaw, P. R. (1989). 'User Acceptance of Computer Technology: A Comparison of Two Theoretical Models', *Management Science*, 35: 982–1003.

Davis, G. F. (1991). 'Agents Without Principles? The Spread of the Poison Pill Through the Intercorporate Network', *Administrative Science Quarterly*, 36: 583–613.

Davis, R. C. (1951). *The Fundamentals of Top Management*. New York: HarperCollins.

Dawes, R. M. (1977). 'Suppose we Measured Height with Rating Scales Instead of Rulers', *Applied Psychological Measurement*, 1: 267–273.

Day, H. I. (1981). 'Play', in H. I. Day (ed.), *Advances in Intrinsic Motivation and Aesthetics*. New York: Plenum, pp. 225–250.

Day, R. H. and Tinney, E. H. (1968). 'How to Cooperate in Business Without Really Trying: A Learning Model of Decentralized Decision Making', *Journal of Political Economy*, 76: 583–600.

—— Aigner, D. J., and Smith, K. R. (1971). 'Safety Margins and Profit Maximization in the Theory of the Firm', *Journal of Political Economy*, 79: 1293–1301.

de Bary, W. T., Chan, W. T., and Watson, B. (eds.) (1960). *Sources of Chinese Tradition*. New York: Columbia University Press.

Deal, T. and Kennedy, A. (1982). *Corporate Cultures*. Reading, MA: Addison-Wesley.

Dean, L. R. (1954–1955). 'Social Integration, Attitudes, and Union Activity', *Industrial and Labor Relations Review*, 8: 48–58.

Dearborn, D. C. and Simon, H. A. (1958). 'Selective Perception: A Note on the Departmental Identifications of Executives', *Sociometry*, 21: 140–144.

Deci, E. L. and Ryan, R. M. (1985). *Intrinsic Motivation and Self-Determination in Human Behavior*. New York: Plenum.

Degeorge, F., Patel, J., and Zeckhauser, R. (1999). 'Earnings Management to Exceed Thresholds', *Journal of Business*, 72: 1–33.

Denhardt, R. B. (1969). 'Bureaucratic Socialization, and Organizational Accommodation', *Administrative Science Quarterly*, 13: 441–450.

Dent, J. K. (1959). 'Organizational Correlates of the Goals of Business Managements', *Personnel Psychology*, 12: 365–393.

Dess, G. G. and Keats, B. W. (1987). 'Environmental Assessment and Organizational Performance: An Exploratory Field Study', *Academy of Management, Proceedings of the Annual Meeting, 1987*: 21–25.

Diamond, S. (1958). 'From Organization to Society: Virginia in the Seventeenth Century', *American Journal of Sociology*, 63: 457–475.

—— (1986a). 'Study of Rockets by Air Force Said Risks Were 1 in 35', *New York Times*, 135(February 11): Al, A24.

—— (1986b). 'NASA Wasted Billions, Federal Audits Disclose', *New York Times*, 135(April 23): Al, A14–A15.

—— (1986c). 'NASA Cut or Delayed Safety Spending', *New York Times*, 135(April 24): Al, B4.

Dill, W. R. (1958). 'Environment as an Influence on Managerial Autonomy', *Administrative Science Quarterly*, 2: 409–443.

—— (1962). 'The Impact of Environment on Organizational Development', in S. Mailick and E. H. Van Ness (eds.), *Concepts and Issues in Administrative Behavior*. Englewood Cliffs, NJ: Prentice-Hall, pp. 94–109.

Ditton, J. (1979). *Controlology*. London: Macmillan.

Dixon, R. L. (1953). 'Creep', *Journal of Accountancy*, 96: 48–55.

Donaldson, G. and Lorsch, J. W. (1983). *Decision Making at the Top: The Shaping of Strategic Direction*. New York: Basic Books.

Dörner, D. (1997). *The Logic of Failure*, translated by R. and R. Kimber. Reading, MA: Addison-Wesley.

Dougherty, D. and Hardy, C. (1996). 'Sustained Product Innovation in Large, Mature Organizations: Overcoming Innovation-to-organization Problems', *Academy of Management Journal*, 39: 1120–1153.

Downey, H. K., Hellriegel, D., and Slocum, J. W. Jr. (1975). 'Environmental Uncertainty: The Construct and its Application', *Administrative Science Quarterly*, 20: 613–629.

—— Hellriegel, D., and Slocum, J. W. Jr. (1977). 'Individual Characteristics as Sources of Perceived Uncertainty', *Human Relations*, 30: 161–174.

Downie, J. (1958). *The Competitive Process*. London: Gerald Duckworth.

Draper, J. and Strother, G. B. (1963). 'Testing a Model for Organizational Growth', *Human Organization*, 22: 180–194.

Dreeben, R. (1968). *On What Is Learned in School*. Reading, MA: Addison-Wesley.

Dreyfus, H. L. and Dreyfus, S. E. (1986). *Mind over Machine*. New York: Free Press.

Drucker, P. F. (1958). 'Business Objectives and Survival Needs: Notes on a Discipline of Business Enterprise', *Journal of Business*, 31: 81–99.

DSIR (1958). *Estimates of Resources Devoted to Scientific and Engineering Research and Development in British Manufacturing Industry, 1955*. London: Department of Scientific and Industrial Research.

Dubin, R. (1959). 'Stability of Human Organizations', in M. Haire (ed.), *Modern Organization Theory*. New York: Wiley, pp. 218–253.

Dunbar, R. L. M. (1971). 'Budgeting for Control', *Administrative Science Quarterly*, 16: 88–96.

—— (1981). 'Designs for Organizational Control', in P. C. Nystrom and W. H. Starbuck (eds.), *Handbook of Organizational Design*, Vol. 2. New York: Oxford University Press, pp. 85–115.

—— and Goldberg, W. H. (1978). 'Crisis Development and Strategic Response in European Corporations', *Journal of Business Administration*, 9(2): 139–149.

—— Dutton, J. M., and Torbert, W. R. (1982). 'Crossing Mother: Ideological Constraints on Organizational Improvements', *Journal of Management Studies*, 19: 91–108.

—— Garud, R., and Raghuram, S. (1996a). 'A Frame for Deframing in Strategic Analysis', *Journal of Management Inquiry*, 5: 23–34.

—— —— —— (1996b). 'Run, Rabbit, Run! But Can You Survive?', *Journal of Management Inquiry*, 5: 168–175.

Duncan, R. B. (1972). 'Characteristics of Organizational Environments and Perceived Environmental Uncertainty', *Administrative Science Quarterly*, 17: 313–327.

—— (1973). 'Multiple Decision-making Structures in Adapting to Environmental Uncertainty: The Impact on Organizational Effectiveness', *Human Relations*, 26: 273–291.

Dutton, J. E. and Jackson, S. E. (1987). 'Categorizing Strategic Issues: Links to Organizational Action', *Academy of Management Review*, 12: 76–90.

Dutton, J. M. and Starbuck, W. H. (1971*a*). 'Finding Charlie's Run-time Estimator', in J. M. Dutton and W. H. Starbuck (eds.), *Computer Simulation of Human Behavior*. New York: Wiley, pp. 218–242.

—— —— (1971*b*). *Computer Simulation of Human Behavior*. New York: Wiley.

—— and Thomas, A. (1984). 'Treating Progress Functions as a Managerial Opportunity', *Academy of Management Review*, 9: 235–247.

Duyvendak, J. J. L. (1928). *The Book of the Lord Shang*. London: Arthur Probsthain.

Ebrey, P. B. (1981). *Chinese Civilization and Society*. New York: Free Press.

Eckstein, H. (1958). *The English Health Service*. Cambridge, MA: Harvard University Press.

Edelman, M. (1977). *Political Language: Words That Succeed and Policies That Fail*. New York: Academic Press.

Edwards, W. (1968). 'Conservatism in Human Information Processing', in B. Kleinrnuntz (ed.), *Formal Representation of Human Judgement*. New York: Wiley, pp. 17–52.

Eichler, N. (1989). *The Thrift Debacle*. Berkeley, CA: University of California Press.

Eisenhardt, K. M. and Brown, S. L. (1998). 'Time Pacing: Competing in Markets that Won't Stand Still', *Harvard Business Review*, 76(March–April 2): 59–69.

Eiteman, W. J. and Guthrie, G. E. (1952). 'The Shape of the Average Cost Curve', *American Economic Review*, 42: 832–838.

Ekstedt, E. (1988). *Human Capital in an Age of Transition: Knowledge Development and Corporate Renewal*. Stockholm: Allmänna Förlaget.

—— (1989). 'Knowledge Renewal and Knowledge Companies', *Uppsala Papers in Economic History*, Report 22, Department of Economic History. University of Uppsala.

Elling, R. H. and Halebsky, S. (1961). 'Organizational Differentiation and Support: A Conceptual Framework', *Administrative Science Quarterly*, 6: 185–209.

Elliott, J. W. (1973). 'A Direct Comparison of Short-run GNP Forecasting Models', *Journal of Business*, 46: 33–60.

Ellis, M. J. (1973). *Why People Play*. Englewood Cliffs, NJ: Prentice-Hall.

Emery, F. E. and Thorsrud, E. (1969). *The Form and Content in Industrial Democracy*. London: Tavistock.

—— and Trist, E. L. (1965). 'The Causal Texture of Organizational Environments', *Human Relations*, 18: 21–32.

English, H. B. and English, A. C. (1958). *A Comprehensive Dictionary of Psychological Terms: A Guide To Usage*. New York: Longmans, Green.

Enke, S. (1951). 'On Maximizing Profits: A Distinction Between Chamberlin and Robinson', *American Economic Review*, 41: 566–578.

Entwisle, Doris, R. and Walton, J. (1961). 'Observations on the Span of Control', *Administrative Science Quarterly*, 5: 522–533.

Epple, D., Argote, L., and Devadas, R. (1991). 'Organizational Learning Curves: A Method for Investigating Intra-plant Transfer of Knowledge Acquired Through Learning by Doing', *Organization Science*, 2: 58–70.

Erikson, E. H. (1972). 'Play and Actuality', in M. W. Piers (ed.), *Play and Development*. New York: W. W. Norton.

Erman, A. and Blackman, A. M. (1927). *The Literature of the Ancient Egyptians*. New York: E. P. Dutton.

Esposito, L. and Esposito, F. F. (1971). 'Foreign Competition and Domestic Industry Profitability', *Review of Economics and Statistics*, 53: 343–353.

Estes, W. K. (1975–78). *Handbook of Learning and Cognitive Processes*. Hillsdale, NJ: Erlbaum.

Etzioni, A. (1968). *The Active Society*. New York: Free Press.

Evan, W. M. (1965). 'Toward a Theory of Interorganizational Relations', *Management Science*, 11: B-217–B-230.

—— (1966). 'The Organization-set: Toward a Theory of Interorganizational Relations', in J. D. Thompson (ed.), *Approaches to Organizational Design*. Pittsburgh, PA: University of Pittsburgh Press, pp. 174–191.

Faltermayer, E. K. (1961). 'Executive Austerity', *Wall Street Journal*, January 26, 1: 4.

Faulkner, R. O., Wente, E. F., Jr., Simpson, W. K. (1972). *The Literature of Ancient Egypt*. New Haven, CT: Yale University Press.

Faunce, W. A. (1958). 'Automation in the Automobile Industry: Some Consequences for In-plant Social Structure', *American Sociological Review*, 23: 401–407.

Fayol, H. (1949). *General and Industrial Management*. London: Pitman.

Feller, W. (1950). *An Introduction to Probability Theory and Its Applications*, Vol. 1. New York: Wiley, 379–383.

Ferry, D. (1992). *Gilgamesh: A New Rendering in English Verse*. New York: Farrar, Straus & Giroux.

Festinger, L. (1962). *A Theory of Cognitive Dissonance*. Stanford, CA: Stanford University Press.

—— Riecken, H. W., and Schachter, S. (1956). *When Prophecy Fails*. Minneapolis, MN: University of Minnesota Press.

Feynman, R. P. (1986). 'Personal Observations on Reliability of Shuttle', *Report of the Presidential Commission on the Space Shuttle Challenger Accident*, Vol. II, Appendix F. Washington, DC: U.S. Government Printing Office.

Fiedler, F. E. (1967). *A Theory of Leadership Effectiveness*. New York: McGraw-Hill.

Filley, A. C. (1963). 'A Theory of Business Growth'. Working paper, University of Wisconsin, School of Commerce.

Finkel, S. I. (1990). 'Psychotherapy, Technology and Aging', *International Journal of Technology and Aging*, 3: 57–61.

Finkelstein, S. and Hambrick, D. C. (1990). 'Top-management-team Tenure and Organizational Outcomes: The Moderating Role of Managerial Discretion', *Administrative Science Quarterly*, 35: 484–503.

Fischhoff, B. (1975). 'Hindsight or Foresight: The Effect of Outcome Knowledge on Judgment Under Uncertainty', *Journal of Experimental Psychology: Human Perception and Performance*, 1: 288–299.

—— (1980). 'For Those Condemned to Study the Past: Reflections on Historical Judgment', in R. A. Shweder and D. W. Fiste (eds.), *New Directions for Methodology of Behavioral Science*. San Francisco, CA: Jossey-Bass, pp. 79–93.

—— and Beyth R. (1975). 'I Knew it Would Happen: Remembered Probabilities of Once-future Things', *Organizational Behavior and Human Performance*, 13: 1–16.

Fisher, B. A. (1980). *Small Group Decision Making*. New York: McGraw-Hill.

Fiske, D. W. and Maddi, S. R. (1961). *Functions of Varied Experience*. Homewood, IL: Dorsey.

Fixmer, R. (2002). 'Internet Insight: Moore's Law & Order', *eWeek*, April 15.

Fleming, T. (1995). 'Tanks', *American Heritage of Invention and Technology*, 10(3): 54–63.

Florence, P. S. (1953). *The Logic of British and American Industry*. Chapel Hill, NC: University of North Carolina Press.

Fombrun, C. J. and Starbuck, W. H. (1987). 'Variations in the Evolution of Organizational Ecology', Working paper, New York University.

Fordham, S. (1957–1958). 'Organization Efficiency', *Journal of Industrial Economics*, 6: 209–215.

Form, W. H. and Miller, D. C. (1960). *Industry, Labor, and Community*. New York: Harper.

Foster, B. R. (1993). *Before the Muses: An Anthology of Akkadian Literature*. Bethesda, MD: CDL Press.

Foster, J. L. (1992). *Echoes of Egyptian Voices*. Norman, OK: University of Oklahoma Press.

Frankel, A. (2000). 'Edifice Lex', *The American Lawyer*, July 5, 2000.

Frankenberg, R. J. (1972). 'Taking the Blame and Passing the Buck, or, the Carpet of Agamemnon', in M. Gluckman (ed.), *The Allocation of Responsibility*. Manchester: Manchester University Press, pp. 257–280.

Fredrickson, J. W. (1985). 'Effects of Decision Motive and Organizational Performance Level on Strategic Decision Processes', *Academy of Management Journal*, 28: 821–843.

Friedel, R. (1994). 'The History of the Zipper', *American Heritage of Invention and Technology*, 10(1): 8–16.

Friedlander, F. and Pickle, H. (1968). 'Components of Effectiveness in Small Organizations', *Administrative Science Quarterly*, 13: 289–304.

Friedman, M. (1953). *Essays in Positive Economics*. Chicago, IL: University of Chicago Press.

Friend, I. (1969). *Study of the Savings and Loan Industry*. Washington, DC: Federal Home Loan Bank Board.

Friesema, H. P. (1970). 'Interjurisdictional Agreements in Metropolitan Areas', *Administrative Science Quarterly*, 15: 242–252.

Galanter, M. and Palay, T. M. (1991). *Tournament of Lawyers: The Transformation of the Big Law Firm*. Chicago, IL: University of Chicago Press.

Galbraith, J. K. (1952). *American Capitalism*. Boston, MA: Houghton Mifflin.

—— (1957). 'Many Hands Make Heavy Work', *Reporter*, 17(6): 46–47.

—— (1973). *Economics and the Public Purpose*. New York: Houghton Mifflin.

Galbraith, J. R. (1973). *Organizational Design*. Reading, MA: Addison-Wesley.

Garcia, G., Baer, H., Brewer, E., Allardice, D. R., Cargill, T. F., Dobra, J., Kaufman, G. G., Gonczy, A. M. L., Laurent, R. D., and Mote, L. R. (1983). 'The Garn-St. Germain Depository Institutions Act of 1982', *Economic Perspectives*, 7(2): 3–31. (Chicago, IL: Federal Reserve Bank of Chicago.)

Gardner, B. B. and Moore, D. G. (1955). *Human Relations in Industry*, 3rd edn. Homewood, IL: Irwin.

Gardner, D. G. (1986). 'Activation Theory and Task Design: An Empirical Test of Several New Predictions', *Journal of Applied Psychology*, 71: 411–418.

Gardner, E. P., Young, P., and Ruth, S. R. (1989). 'Evolution of Attitudes Toward Computers: A Retrospective Review', *Behaviour and Information Technology*, 8: 89–98.

Gardner, J. and Maier, J. (1984). *Gilgamesh*. New York: Knopf.

Garfinkel, H. (1967). *Studies in Ethnomethodology*. Englewood Cliffs, NJ: Prentice-Hall.

Garson, B. (1977). *All the Livelong Day*. New York: Penguin.

General Accounting Office (1987). *Financial Audit, Federal Savings and Loan Insurance Corporation's 1986 and 1985 Financial Statements*. Washington, DC: U.S. Government Printing Office, GAO/AFMD-87–41.

—— (1989). *Thrift Failures: Costly Failures Resulted from Regulatory Violations and Unsafe Practices*. Washington, DC: U.S. Government Printing Office, GAO/AFMD-89–62.

George, C. S. Jr. (1968) *The History of Management Thought*. Englewood Cliffs, NJ: Prentice-Hall.

Gershefski, G. W. (1969). 'Building a Corporate Financial Model', *Harvard Business Review*, 4714: 61–72.

Gersick, C. J. and Hackman, J. R. (1990). 'Habitual Routines in Task-performing Groups', *Organizational Behavior and Human Decision Processes*, 47: 65–97.

Gerth, H. H. and Mills, C. W. (1946). *From Max Weber: Essays in Sociology*. New York: Oxford University Press.

Gerwin, D. (1981). 'Relationships Between Structure and Technology', in P. C. Nystrom and W. H. Starbuck (eds.), *Handbook of Organizational Design*, Vol. 2. New York: Oxford University Press, pp. 3–38.

Gezelius, G. and Otterbeck, L. (1977). *Kalmar Verkstad AB*. Stockholm: Institutet för Företagsledning, Stockholm School of Economics (teaching case).

Ghani, J. A. (1990). 'Factors Leading to Playful Interactions with Computers in the Workplace', paper presented at the Academy of Management Meetings, San Francisco.

—— (1991). 'Flow in Human-computer Interactions: Test of a Model', in J. M. Carey (ed.), *Human Factors in Information Systems: An Organizational Perspective*. Norwood, NJ: Ablex.

Gibson, E. (1953). 'Improvement in Perceptual Judgments as a Function of Controlled Practice or Training', *Psychological Bulletin*, 50: 401–431.

Giddens, A. (1979). *Central Problems in Social Theory: Action, Structure and Contradiction in Social Analysis*. London: Macmillan.

Gilmore, F. F. and Brandenburg, R. G. (1962). 'Anatomy of Corporate Planning', *Harvard Business Review*, 40, 61: 61–69.

Gilson, R. J. and Mnookin, R. H. (1985). 'Sharing Among the Human Capitalists: An Economic Inquiry into the Corporate Law Firm and How Partners Split Profits', *Stanford Law Review*, 37: 313–392.

—— —— (1989). 'Coming of Age in a Corporate Law Firm: The Economics of Associate Career Patterns', *Stanford Law Review*, 41: 567–595.

Gingell, W. R. (1852). *The Ceremonial Usages of the Chinese, B.C. 1121, as Prescribed in the 'Institutes of the Chow Dynasty Strung as Pearls', or Chow Le Kwan Choo*. London: Elder.

Ginsberg, A. and Baum, J. A. C. (1994). 'Evolutionary Processes and Patterns of Core Business Change', in J. A. C. Baum and J. V. Singh (eds.), *Evolutionary Dynamics of Organizations*. New York: Oxford University Press, pp. 127–151.

Ginzberg, E. and Reilley, E. W. (1957). *Effecting Change in Large Organizations*. New York: Columbia University Press.

Glover, J. D. (1954). *The Attack on Big Business*. Boston, MA: Harvard University, Graduate School of Business Administration, Division of Research.

Glynn, M. A. (1988). 'The Perceptual Structuring of Tasks: A Cognitive Approach to Understanding Task Attitudes and Behavior', Ph.D. thesis, Columbia University.

—— Lant, T. K., and Milliken, F. J. (1994). 'Mapping Learning Processes in Organizations', *Advances in Managerial Cognition and Organizational Information Processing*, 5: 43–93.

Golding, D. (1980). 'Establishing Blissful Clarity in Organizational Life: Managers', *Sociological Review*, 28: 763–782.

Goldstein, K. M. and Blackman, S. (1978). *Cognitive Style: Five Approaches and Relevant Research*. New York: Wiley.

Goleman, D. (1985). *Vital Lies, Simple Truths: The Psychology of Self-Deception*. New York: Simon & Schuster.

Gordon, E. I. (1968). *Sumerian Proverbs: Glimpses of Everyday Life in Ancient Mesopotamia*. New York: Greenwood Press.

Gordon, G. and Marquis, S. (1966). 'Freedom, Visibility, of Consequences, and Scientific Innovation', *American Journal of Sociology*, 72: 195–202.

Gordon, K. (1924). 'Group Judgments in the Field of Lifted Weights', *Journal of Experimental Psychology*, 7: 398–400.

Gordon, R. A. (1945). *Business Leadership in the Large Corporation*. Washington, DC: Brookings.

—— (1948). 'Short Period Price Determination in Theory and Practice', *American Economic Review*, 38: 265–288.

—— (1961). *Business Leadership in the Large Corporation*, 2nd edn. Berkeley, CA: University of California Press.

Gould, S. J. (1987). 'The Panda's Thumb of Technology', *Natural History*, 96(1): 14–23.

Gouldner, A. W. (1954) *Patterns of Industrial Bureaucracy*. Glencoe, IL: Free Press.

Graicunas, V. A. (1933). 'Relationship in Organization', *Bulletin of the International Management Institute*, 7: 39–42. Reprinted in Gulick and Urwick (1937), 183–187.

Greenberger, M., Crenson, M. A., and Crissey, B. L. (1976). *Models in the Policy Process: Public Decision-Making in the Computer Era*. New York: Russell Sage Foundation.

Greenwald, A. G. (1980). 'The Totalitarian Ego: Fabrication and Revision of Personal History', *American Psychologist*, 35: 603–618.

Greenwood, R., Hinings, C. R., and Brown, J. L. (1990). ' "P²-Form" Strategic Management: Corporate Practices in Professional Partnerships', *Academy of Management Journal*, 33: 725–755.

Greist, J. H. (1989). 'Computer-administered Behavior Therapies', *International Review of Psychiatry*, 1: 267–274.

Griffin, C. E. (1949). *Enterprise in a Free Society*. Homewood, IL: Irwin.

Griffith, F. L. (1926). *Journal of Egyptian Archaeology*, XII: 191–231.

Grinyer, P. H. and Norburn, D. (1975). 'Formal Strategizing for Existing Markets: Perceptions of Executives and Financial Performance', *Journal of the Royal Statistical Society, Series A*, 138: 70–97.

Grusky, O. (1961). 'Corporate Size, Bureaucratization, and Managerial Succession', *American Journal of Sociology*, 67: 261–269.

Guetzkow, H. (1966). 'Relations Among Organizations', in R. V. Bowers (ed.), *Studies on Behavior in Organizations*. Athens: University of Georgia Press, pp. 13–44.

Gulati, R. (1999). 'Network Location and Learning: The Influence of Network Resources and Firm Capabilities on Alliance Formation', *Strategic Management Journal*, 20: 397–420.

Gulick, L. and Urwick, L. (eds.) (1937). *Papers on the Science of Administration*. New York: Columbia University, Institute of Public Administration.

Gundhus, P. (1977). 'Bedrift i krise: hvordan avslöres i tide?', *Bedriftsökonomen*, 7: 328–331.

Gupta, A. and Lad, L. (1983). 'Industry Self-regulation: An Economic, Organizational, and Political Analysis', *Academy of Management Review*, 8(3): 416–425.

Haas, E., Hall, R. H., and Johnson, N. J. (1963). 'The Size of the Supportive Component in Organizations: A Multi-organizational Analysis', *Social Forces*, 42: 9–17.

Haire, M. (1959). 'Biological Models and Empirical Histories of the Growth of Organizations', in M. Haire (ed.), *Modern Organization Theory*. New York: Wiley, pp. 272–306.

—— Ghiselli, E. E., and Porter, L. W. (1966). *Managerial Thinking*. New York: Wiley.

Halberstam, D. (1972). *The Best and the Brightest*. New York: Random House.

Hall, D. T. and Mansfield, R. (1971). 'Organizational and Individual Response to External Stress', *Administrative Science Quarterly*, 16: 533–547.

Hall, P. M. and Hewitt, J. P. (1970). 'The Quasi Theory of Communication and the Management of Dissent', *Social Problems*, 18: 17–27.

Hall, R. H. (1963). 'The Concept of Bureaucracy: An Empirical Assessment', *American Journal of Sociology*, 69: 32–40.

Hall, R. I. (1976). 'A System Pathology of an Organization: The Rise and Fall of the Old *Saturday Evening Post*', *Administrative Science Quarterly*, 21: 185–211.

Hall, R. L. and Hitch C. J. (1939). 'Price Theory and Business Behavior', *Oxford Economic Papers*, 2: 12–45.

Hall, W. K. (1980). 'Survival Strategies in a Hostile Environment', *Harvard Business Review*, 58(September–October): 75–85.

Hamilton, I. (1921). *The Soul and Body of an Army*. London: Arnold.

Hammer, M. and Champy, J. (1993). *Reengineering the Corporation*. New York: Harper Business.

Hand, L. (1945). *Opinion in United States v. Aluminum Company of America et al*. New York: United States Circuit Court of Appeals for the Second District, Vol. 144. Reprinted in *Trade Cases 1944–1945*, Case 57342. Chicago, IL: Commerce Clearing House, 1948, 57676–57700.

Hanson, R. C. (1961). 'Administrator Responsibility in Large and Small Hospitals in a Metropolitan Community', *Journal of Health and Human Behavior*, 2: 199–204.

Harbison, F. H. and Myers, C. A. (1959). *Management in the Industrial World*. New York: McGraw-Hill.

—— Kochling, E., Cassell, F. H., and Ruebmann, H. C. (1955). 'Steel Management on Two Continents', *Management Science*, 2: 31–39.

Hargie, O. (1986). *A Handbook of Communication Skills*. London: Croom Helm.

Harris, P. R. and Moran, R. T. (1996). *Managing Cultural Differences*. Houston, TX: Gulf Publishing.

Harrison, E. F. (1991). 'Strategic Control at the CEO Level', *Long Range Planning*, 24(6): 78–87.

Harrod, R. F. (1939). 'Price and Cost in Entrepreneurs' Policy', *Oxford Economic Papers*, 2: 1–11.

Hart, J. A. (1976). 'Comparative Cognition: Politics of International Control of the Oceans', in R. M. Axelrod (ed.), *Structure of Decision: The Cognitive Maps of Political Elites*. Princeton, NJ: Princeton University Press, pp. 180–217.

—— (1977). 'Cognitive Maps of Three Latin American Policy Makers', *World Politics*, 30: 115–140.

Hart, P. E. and Prais, S. J. (1956). 'The Analysis of Business Concentration', *Journal of the Royal Statistical Society, Series A*, 119(II): 150–190.

Hastie, R. (1981). 'Schematic Principles in Human Memory', in E. T. Higgins, C. P. Herman, and M. P. Zanna (eds.), *Social Cognition, The Ontario Symposium*, Vol. 1. Hillsdale, NJ: Erlbaum, pp. 39–88.

Haunschild, P. R. (1993). 'Interorganizational Imitation: The Impact of Interlocks on Corporate Acquisition Activity', *Administrative Science Quarterly*, 38: 564–592.

—— and Miner, A. S. (1997). 'Modes of Interorganizational Imitation: The Effects of Outcome Salience and Uncertainty', *Administrative Science Quarterly*, 42: 472–500.

Hawkins, H. A. and Hastie, R. (1986). 'Hindsight: Biased Processing of Past Events in Response to Outcome Information'. Working paper, Carnegie-Mellon University and Northwestern University.

Hayek, F. A. von (1974). *The Pretence of Knowledge*. Stockholm: The Nobel Foundation.

Healey, J. H. (1956). 'Coordination and Control of Executive Functions', *Personnel*, 33: 106–117.

Hedberg, B. L. T. (1973a). 'Uncertainty Reduction and Action Programs in Organizational Transition from Growth to Non-Growth', Working paper, International Institute of Management, Berlin.

—— (1973*b*). 'Organizational Stagnation and Choice of Strategy', Working paper, International Institute of Management, Berlin.

—— (1974). 'Refraining as a Way to Cope with Organizational Stagnation: A Case Study', Working paper, Preprint 1/74–71, International Institute of Management, Berlin.

—— (1975*a*). 'Growth Stagnation as a Managerial Discontinuity', in *Proceedings of the INSEAD Seminar on Management Under Discontinuity*. Brussels: European Institute for Advanced Studies in Management, 34–59.

—— (1975*b*). 'Computer Systems to Support Industrial Democracy', in E. Mumford and H. Sackman (eds.), *Human Choice and Computers*. Amsterdam: North-Holland, pp. 211–230.

—— (1981). 'How Organizations Learn and Unlearn', in P. C. Nystrom and W. H. Starbuck (eds.), *Handbook of Organizational Design*, Vol. 1. New York: Oxford University Press, pp. 3–27.

—— and Jönsson, S. A. (1977). 'Strategy Formulation as a Discontinuous Process', *International Studies of Management & Organization*, 7: 89–109.

—— —— (1978). 'Designing Semi-confusing Information Systems for Organizations in Changing Environments', *Accounting, Organizations and Society*, 3: 47–64.

—— and Malmström, L. (1997). *Building Organizational Inertia: How the Swedish Real-Estate Industry Turned Tents into Palaces in the Decade of 1982–1992*. Stockholm: Stockholm University, School of Business, Research series.

—— Nystrom, P. C., and Starbuck, W. H. (1976). 'Camping on Seesaws: Prescriptions for a Self-designing Organization', *Administrative Science Quarterly*, 21: 41–65.

Heidel, A. (1970). *The Gilgamesh Epic and Old Testament Parallels*, 2nd edn. Chicago, IL: University of Chicago Press.

Heider, F. (1958). *The Psychology of Interpersonal Relations*. New York: Wiley.

Heller, W. W. (1951). 'The Anatomy of Investment Decisions', *Harvard Business Review*, 29(2): 95–103.

Helson, H. (1964). *Adaptation-Level Theory: An Experimental and Systematic Approach to Behavior*. New York: Harper & Row.

Herald, D. M. (1972). 'Long-range Planning and Organizational Performance: A Cross-valuation Study', *Academy of Management Journal*, 15: 91–102.

Herbst, P. G. (1957). 'Measurement of Behaviour Structures by Means of Input-output Data', *Human Relations*, 10: 335–346.

Hewitt, J. P. and Hall, P. M. (1973). 'Social Problems, Problematic Situations, and Quasi-Theories', *American Sociological Review*, 38: 367–374.

—— and Stokes, R. (1975). 'Disclaimers', *American Sociological Review*, 40: 1–11.

Hickman, C. A. and Kuhn, M. H. (1956). *Individuals, Groups, and Economic Behavior*. New York: Dryden.

Hiemstra, G. (1983). 'You Say you Want a Revolution? "Information Technology", in organizations', *Communication Yearbook*, 7: 802–827.

Hilgard, E. R. (1948). *Theories of Learning*. New York: Appleton-Century-Crofts.

Hill, T., Smith, N. D., and Mann, M. F. (1987). 'Role of Efficacy Expectations in Predicting the Decision to use Advanced Technologies: The Case of Computers', *Journal of Applied Psychology*, 72: 307–313.

Hinings, C. R. and Greenwood, R. (1988). 'The Normative Prescription of Organizations', in L. G. Zucker (ed.), *Institutional Patterns and Organizations: Culture and Environment*. Cambridge, MA: Ballinger.

—— Brown, J. L., and Greenwood, R. (1991). 'Change in an Autonomous Professional Organization', *Journal of Management Studies*, 28: 375–393.

Hirsch, P. M. (1972). 'Processing Fads and Fashions: An Organization-set Analysis of Cultural Industry Systems', *American Journal of Sociology*, 77: 639–659.

—— and Lounsbury, M. (1997). 'Ending the Family Quarrel: Toward a Reconciliation of "Old" and "New" Institutionalisms', *American Behavioral Scientist*, 40: 406–418.

Hirsch, W. Z. (1952). 'Manufacturing Progress Functions', *Review of Economics and Statistics*, 34: 143–155.

Hirschman, A. O. (1970). *Exit, Voice and Loyalty*. Cambridge, MA: Harvard University Press.

Hitch, C. J. (1966). *Decision-Making for Defense*. Berkeley, CA: University of California Press.

Hodgkinson, G. P. (1997). 'Cognitive Inertia in a Turbulent Market: The Case of the UK Residential Estate Agents', *Journal of Management Studies*, 34: 921–945.

—— (2001). 'The Psychology of Strategic Management: Diversity and Cognition Revisited', in C. L. Cooper and I. T. Robertson (eds.), *International Review of Industrial and Organizational Psychology*, Vol. 16. London: Wiley, pp. 65–119.

Hoeneisen, B. and Mead, C. A. (1972). 'Fundamental Limitations on Microelectronics I: MOS Technology', *Solid-State Electronics*, 15: 819–829.

Hofer, C. W. and Schendel, D. (1978). *Strategy Formulation*. St. Paul, MN: West.

Hofstede, G. H. (1967). *The Game of Budget Control*. Assen, The Netherlands: Van Gorcum.

Hogarth, R. M. (1980). *Judgment and Choice*. New York: Wiley.

—— (1987). *Judgement and Choice: The Psychology of Decision*. New York: Wiley.

—— and Makridakis, S. (1981). 'Forecasting and Planning: An Evaluation', *Management Science*, 27: 115–138.

Hoiberg, E. O. and Cloyd, J. S. (1971). 'Definition and Measurement of Continuous Variation in Ecological Analysis', *American Sociological Review*, 36: 65–74.

Holt, C. C., Modigliani, F., Muth, J. F., and Simon, H. A. (1960). *Planning Production, Inventories, and Work Force*. Englewood Cliffs, NJ: Prentice-Hall, esp. chs. 2, 3, 8.

Hopwood, A. G. (1972). 'An Empirical Study of the Role of Accounting Data in Performance Evaluation', *Empirical Research in Accounting: Selected Studies* (supplement to the *Journal of Accounting Research*), 10: 156–182.

Horvath, J. A. (1996). 'Managerial Learning: An Inductive Systems Perspective', Working paper, Yale University.

Hounshell, D. A. and Smith, J. K., Jr. (1988). 'The Nylon Drama', *American Heritage of Invention and Technology*, Fall: 40–55.

Howard-Grenville, J. A. (2000). 'Inside Out: A Cultural Study of Environmental Work in Semiconductor Manufacturing'. Ph.D. thesis, Massachusetts Institute of Technology.

Huff, A. and Schwenk, C. R. (1990). 'Bias and Sensemaking in Good Times and Bad', in A. Huff (ed.), *Mapping Strategic Thought*. New York: Wiley, pp. 98–108.

Huizinga, J. (1950). *Homo ludens*. Boston, MA: Beacon Press.

Ijiri, Y. and Simon, H. A. (1964). 'Business Firm Growth and Size', *American Economic Review*, 54: 77–89.

Indik, B. P. (1963). 'Some Effects of Organization Size on Member Attitudes and Behavior', *Human Relations*, 16: 369–384.

Ingram, P. and Baum, J. A. C. (1997*a*). 'Chain Affiliation and the Failure of Manhattan Hotels, 1898–1980', *Administrative Science Quarterly*, 42: 583–613.

—— —— (1997*b*). 'Opportunity and Constraint: Organizations' Learning from the Operating and Competitive Experience of Industries', *Strategic Management Journal*, 18: 75–98.

—— and Silverman, B. (2002). 'The New Institutionalism in Strategic Management', *Advances in Strategic Management*, 19: 1–30.

Institute For The Future (1997). *Managing Corporate Communications in the Information Age*. Menlo Park, CA: The Institute For The Future, SR–619.

Intel (2002). 'Expanding Moore's Law: The Exponential Opportunity', Intel Corporation, Publication TL_001: Santa Clara, CA.

Intel website (2002). 'Moore's Law'. Available at: http://www.intel.com/research/silicon/mooreslaw.htm.

Ittelson, W. H., Franck, K. A., and Timothy, J. O. (1976). 'The Nature of Environmental Experience', in S. Wapner, S. Cohen, and B. Kaplan (eds.), *Experiencing the Environment*. New York: Plenum, pp. 187–206.

Ivancevich, J. M. and Matteson, M. T. (1993) *Organizational Behavior and Management*, 3rd edn. Homewood, IL: Irwin.

Jackson, S. E. and Dutton, J. E. (1987). 'What do "Threat" and "Opportunity" Mean? A Complex Answer to a Simple Question'. Working paper, New York University. (A related article is Jackson, S. E. and Dutton, J. E. (1987). 'Discerning Threats and Opportunities', *Administrative Science Quarterly*, 33: 370–387.)

—— —— (1988). 'Discerning Threats and Opportunities', *Administrative Science Quarterly*, 33: 370–387.

Jackson, T. (1997). *Inside Intel: Andy Grove and the Rise of the World's Most Powerful Chip Company*. New York: Dutton.

James, J. (1951). 'A Preliminary Study of the Size Determinant in Small Group Interaction', *American Sociological Review*, 16: 474–477.

—— (1953). 'The Distribution of Free-forming Small Group Size', *American Sociological Review*, 18: 569–570.

Janis, I. L. (1972). *Victims of Groupthink*. Boston, MA: Houghton Mifflin.

Jaques, E. (1961). *Equitable Payment*. New York: Wiley.

Jarvenpaa, S. L. and Dickson, G. W. (1988). 'Graphics and Managerial Decision Making: Research Based Guidelines', *Communications of the ACM*, 31: 764–774.

Jermier, J. M., Gaines, J., and McIntosh, N. J. (1989). 'Reactions to Physically Dangerous Work: A Conceptual and Empirical Analysis', *Journal of Organizational Behavior*, 10: 15–33.

Jervis, R. (1976). *Perception and Misperception in International Politics*. Princeton, NJ: Princeton University Press.

Jewkes, J., Sawers, D., and Stillerman, R. (1959). *The Sources of Invention*. New York: St Martin's.

Johnson, G. (1990). 'Managing Strategic Change: The Role of Symbolic Action', *British Journal of Management*, 1: 183–200.

Johnston, J. (1955–1956). 'Scale, Costs and Profitability in Road Passenger Transport', *Journal of Industrial Economics*, 4: 207–223.

Jönsson, S. A. (1973). *Decentralisering och utveckling: en fältstudie av utvecklingsbolagens planeringsproblem*. Gothenburg, Sweden: Business Administration Studies (BAS) No. 21.

—— and Lundin, R. A. (1977). 'Myths and Wishful Thinking as Management Tools', in P. C. Nystrom and W. H. Starbuck (eds.), *Prescriptive Models of Organizations*. Amsterdam: North-Holland, pp. 157–170.

Kabanoff, B. (1980). 'Work and Nonwork: A Review of Models, Methods, and Findings', *Psychological Bulletin*, 88: 60–77.

Kagel, J. H. and Levin, D. (1986). 'The Winner's Curse and Public Information in Common Value Auctions', *American Economic Review*, 76: 894–920.

Kahn, R. L., Wolfe, D. M., Quinn, R. P., Snoek, J. D., and Rosenthal, R. A. (1964). *Organizational Stress.* New York: Wiley.

Kahneman, D. and Tversky, A. (1972). 'Subjective Probability: A Judgment of Representativeness', *Cognitive Psychology,* 3: 430–454.

Kamouri, A. L., Kamouri, J., and Smith, K. H. (1986). 'Training by Exploration: Facilitating the Transfer of Procedural Knowledge Through Analogical Reasoning', *International Journal of Man-Machine Studies,* 24: 171–192.

Kane, E. J. (1985). *The Gathering Crisis in Federal Deposit Insurance.* Cambridge, MA: MIT Press.

—— (1989). *The S&L Insurance Mess: How Did It Happen?* Washington, DC: Urban Institute.

Kaplan, A. D. H. (1948). *Small Business: Its Place and Problems.* New York: McGraw-Hill.

Kaplan, H. B. (1967). 'Implementation of Program Change in Community Agencies', *Milbank Memorial Fund Quarterly,* 45: 321–332.

Karlgren, B. (1950). *The Book of Documents.* Stockholm: Museum of Far Eastern Antiquities.

—— (1970). *Glosses on the Book of Documents.* Stockholm: Museum of Far Eastern Antiquities.

Katona, G. (1951). *Psychological Analysis of Economic Behavior.* New York: McGraw-Hill.

Katz, D. and Kahn, R. L. (1966). *The Social Psychology of Organizations.* New York: Wiley.

Katz, J. A. (1987). 'Playing at Innovation in the Computer Revolution', in M. Frese, E. Ulich, and W. Dzida (eds.), *Psychological Issues of Human Computer Interaction in the Work Place.* Amsterdam: North-Holland, pp. 97–112.

Kaufman, H. (1960). *The Forest Ranger.* Baltimore, MD: Johns Hopkins Press.

Kay, A. (1977). 'Microelectronics and the Personal Computer', *Scientific American,* 237(3): 230–244.

—— (1985). 'Software's Second Act', *Science Magazine,* 85(November): 122–126.

Kees, H. (1961). *Ancient Egypt.* Chicago, IL: University of Chicago Press.

Keleman, M. (2000). 'Too Much or Too Little Ambiguity: The Language of Total Quality Management', *Journal of Management Studies,* 37: 483–498.

Kephart, W. M. (1950). 'A Quantitative Analysis of Intragroup Relationships', *American Journal of Sociology,* 55: 544–549.

Kepner, C. H. and Tregoe, B. B. (1965). *The Rational Manager.* New York: McGraw-Hill.

Kerr, S. and Slocum, J. W. Jr. (1981). 'Controlling the Performances of People in Organizations', in P. C. Nystrom and W. H. Starbuck (eds.), *Handbook of Organizational Design,* Vol. 2. New York: Oxford University Press, pp. 116–134.

Khandwalla, P. N. (1972a). 'Environment and its Impact on the Organization', *International Studies of Management and Organization,* 2: 297–313.

—— (1972b). 'Uncertainty and the "Optimal" Design of Organizations', Working paper, McGill University, Montreal.

—— (1973). 'Viable and Effective Organizational Designs of Firms', *Academy of Management Journal,* 16: 481–495.

—— (1974). 'Mass Output Orientation of Operations Technology and Organizational Structure', *Administrative Science Quarterly,* 19: 74–97.

Kiesler, C. A. (1971). *The Psychology of Commitment.* New York: Academic Press.

—— and Sproull, L. S. (1982). 'Managerial Responses to Changing Environments: Perspectives on Problem Sensing from Social Cognition', *Administrative Science Quarterly,* 27: 548–570.

Kimberly, J. R. (1981). 'Managerial Innovation', in P. C. Nystrom and W. H. Starbuck (eds.), *Handbook of Organizational Design,* Vol. 1. New York: Oxford University Press, pp. 84–104.

King, A. S. (1974). 'Expectation Effects in Organizational Change', *Administrative Science Quarterly*, 19: 221–230.

King, A., Lenox, M., and Barnett, M. (2002). 'Strategic Responses to the Reputation Commons Problem', in A. Hoffman and M. Ventresca (eds.), *Organizations, Policy and the Natural Environment: Institutional and Strategic Perspectives*. Stanford, CA: Stanford University Press, pp. 393–406.

Kling, R. (1980). 'Social Analyses of Computing: Theoretical Perspectives in Recent Empirical Research', *Computing Surveys*, 12(1): 61–110.

Klinger, E. (1969). 'Development of Imaginative Behavior: Implications of Play for a Theory of Fantasy', *Psychological Bulletin*, 72: 277–298.

Kondra, A. Z. and Hinings, C. R. (1998). 'Organization Diversity and Change in Institutional Theory', *Organization Studies*, 19(5): 743–767.

Korcynski, E. (1997). 'Moore's Law Extended: The Return of Cleverness', *Solid State Technology*, 40(7): 359–364.

Kormendi, R. C., Bernard, V. L., Pirrong, S. C., and Snyder, E. A. (1989). *Crisis Resolution in the Thrift Industry*. Boston, MA: Kluwer.

Kostoff, R. N. and Schaller, R. R. (2001). 'Science and Technology Roadmaps', *IEEE Transactions on Engineering Management*, 48(2): 132–143.

Kovacs, M. G. (1985). *The Epic of Gilgamesh*. Stanford, CA: Stanford University Press.

Krull, D. S. and Anderson, C. A. (1997). 'The Process of Explanation', *Current Directions in Psychological Science*, 6(1): 1–5.

Kudla, R. J. (1980). 'The Effects of Strategic Planning on Common Stock Returns', *Academy of Management Journal*, 23: 5–20.

Kuhn, T. S. (1962). *The Structure of Scientific Revolutions*. Chicago, IL: University of Chicago Press.

Kusterer, K. C. (1978). *Know-How on the Job: The Important Working Knowledge of "Unskilled" Workers*. Boulder, CO: Westview.

Kusyszyn, I. (1977). 'How Gambling Saved me From a Misspent Sabbatical', *Journal of Humanistic Psychology*, 17: 19–34.

Lambert, W. G. (1960). *Babylonian Wisdom Literature*. Oxford: Oxford University Press.

—— and Millard, A. R. (1969). *Atrahasis: The Babylonian Story of the Flood*. Oxford: Clarendon.

Landau, M. (1973). 'On the Concept of a Self-correcting Organization', *Public Administration Review*, 33: 533–542.

Langer, E. J. (1975). 'The Illusion of Control', *Journal of Personality and Social Psychology*, 32: 311–328.

—— and Roth, J. (1975). 'Heads I Win, Tails it's Chance: The Illusion of Control as a Function of the Sequence Outcomes in a Purely Chance Task', *Journal of Personality and Social Psychology*, 32: 951–955.

Lau, D. C. (1979). *Confucius: The Analects*. Harmondsworth: Penguin.

Laudon, K. C. and Laudon, J. P. (1991). *Business Information Systems: A Problem Solving Approach*. Hinsdale, IL: Dryden.

Lawrence, P. R. and Lorsch, J. W. (1967). *Organization and Environment*. Cambridge, MA: Graduate School of Business Administration, Harvard University.

—— —— (1967). *Organization and Environment*. Boston, MA: Graduate School of Business Administration, Harvard University.

Leach, E. R. (1964). 'Anthropological Aspects of Language: Animal Categories and Verbal Abuse', in Eric H. Lenneberg (ed.), *New Directions in the Study of Language*. Cambridge, MA: MIT Press, pp. 23–63.

Lederman, L. (1992). *Tombstones: A Lawyer's Tales from the Takeover Decades*. New York: Farrar, Straus & Giroux.

Lee, K. and Pennings, J. M. (2002). 'Mimicry and the Market: Adoption of a New Organizational Form', *Academy of Management Journal*, 45: 144–162.

Legge, J. (1865). *The Chinese Classics*. Oxford: Oxford University Press.

Leonard, W. E. (1934). *Gilgamesh: Epic of Old Babylonia*. New York: Viking Press.

Leroy, F. and Ramanantsoa, B. (1997). 'The Cognitive and Behavioral Dimensions of Organizational Learning in a Merger: An Empirical Study', *Journal of Management Studies*, 34: 871–894.

Lester, R. A. (1946). 'Shortcomings of Marginal Analysis for Wage-employment Problems', *American Economic Review*, 36: 62–82.

Levine, J. H. (1972). 'The Sphere of Influence', *American Sociological Review*, 37: 14–27.

Levine, S. and White, P. E. (1961). 'Exchange as a Conceptual Framework for the Study of Inter-organizational Relationships', *Administrative Science Quarterly*, 5: 583–601.

Levins, R. (1968). *Evolution in Changing Environments*. Princeton, NJ: Princeton University Press.

Levinthal, D. (1994). 'Surviving Schumpeterian Environments: An Evolutionary Perspective', in J. A. C. Baum and J. V. Singh (eds.), *Evolutionary Dynamics of Organizations*. New York: Oxford University Press, pp. 167–178.

—— and March, J. G. (1993). 'The Myopia of Learning', *Strategic Management Journal*, 14: 95–112.

Levitt, B. and March, J. G. (1988). 'Organizational Learning', *Annual Review of Sociology*, 14: 319–340.

Levy, J. (1983). *Play Behavior*. Malabar, FL: Robert E. Krieger Publishing.

Lewin, A. Y. and Wolf, C. (1972). 'Organizational Slack: A Test of the General Theory'. Working paper, New York University.

Lewis, M. M. (1989). *Liar's Poker: Rising Through the Wreckage of Salomon Brothers*. New York: W. W. Norton.

Liao, W. K. (1959). *The Complete Works of Han Fei Tzu*. London: Arthur Probsthain.

Lichtheim, M. (1973). *Ancient Egyptian Literature: A Book of Readings*. Berkeley, CA: University of California Press.

Liden, R. C. and Graen, G. (1980). 'Generalizability of the Vertical Dyad Linkage Model of Leadership', *Academy of Management Journal*, 23: 451–465.

Lieberman, J. N. (1977). *Playfulness*. New York: Academic Press.

Likert, R. (1961). *New Patterns of Management*. New York: McGraw-Hill.

Lincoln, J. R., Olson, J., and Hanada, H. (1978). 'Cultural Effects on Organizational Structure: The Case of Japanese Firms in the United States', *American Sociological Review*, 43: 829–847.

Lindblom, C. E. (1959). 'The Science of "Muddling Through" ', *Public Administration Review*, 19: 79–88.

Lippitt, R., Watson, J., and Westley, B. (1958). *The Dynamics of Planned Change*. New York: Harcourt Brace & World.

Lippman, S. A. and Rumelt, R. P. (1982). 'Uncertain Imitability: An Analysis of Interfirm Differences in Efficiency Under Competition', *Bell Journal of Economics*, 13: 418–438.

Lipset, S. M., Trow, M. A., and Coleman, J. S. (1956). *Union Democracy*. Glencoe, IL: Free Press.

Lipton, M. (1990). 'The Firm at Twenty-five'. Unpublished document.

Litwak, E. and Hylton, L. F. (1962). 'Interorganizational Analysis: A Hypothesis on Co-ordinating Agencies', *Administrative Science Quarterly*, 6: 395–420.

Locke, E. A. (1968). 'Toward a Theory of Task Motivation and Incentives', *Organizational Behavior and Human Performance*, 3: 157–189.

—— and Latham, G. P. (1990). *A Theory of Goal Setting and Task Performance*. Englewood Cliffs, NJ: Prentice-Hall.

Loewe, M. (1968). *Everyday Life in Early Imperial China during the Han Period, 202 B.C. – A.D. 220*. London: Batsford; New York: Putnam.

—— (1986). 'Introduction', in D. Twitchett and M. Loewe (eds.), *The Cambridge History of China*, Vol. 1: *The Ch'in and Han Empires*. Cambridge: Cambridge University Press, pp. 1–20.

Loftus, E. F. (1979). 'The Malleability of Human Memory', *American Scientist*, 67: 312–320.

Lorsch, J. W. and Allen, S. A., III (1973). *Managing Diversity and Interdependence*. Boston, MA: Graduate School of Business Administration, Harvard University.

Luce, R. D. and Galanter, E. (1963). 'Discrimination', in R. D. Luce, R. A. Bush, and E. Galanter (eds.), *Handbook of Mathematical Psychology*, Vol. 1. New York: Wiley, pp. 191–243.

Luthans, F. (1995). *Organizational Behavior*. New York: McGraw-Hill.

Lyles, M. A. and Mitroff, I. I. (1980). 'Organizational Problem Formulation: An Empirical Study', *Administrative Science Quarterly*, 25: 102–119.

Machlup, F. (1946). 'Marginal Analysis and Empirical Research', *American Economic Review*, 36: 519–554.

—— (1962). *The Production and Distribution of Knowledge in the United States*. Princeton, NJ: Princeton University Press.

Magnuson, E. (1986). 'Fixing NASA', *Time*, 127 (June 23, 9): 14–18, 20, 23–25.

Mahoney, M. J. (1977). 'Publication Prejudices: An Experimental Study of Confirmatory Bias in the Peer Review System', *Cognitive Therapy and Research*, 1: 161–175.

—— (1979). 'Psychology of the Scientist: An Evaluative Review', *Social Studies of Science*, 9(3): 349–375.

Maier, N. R. F. (1963). *Problem-Solving Discussions and Conferences: Leadership Methods and Skills*. New York: McGraw-Hill.

Maister, D. H. (1985). 'The One-firm Firm: What Makes it Successful', *Sloan Management Review*, 27(1), 3–13.

Maitland, I. (1985). 'The Limits of Business Self-regulation', *California Management Review*, 27(3): 132–147.

Makridakis, S. and Hibon, M. (1979). 'Accuracy of Forecasting: An Empirical Investigation', *Journal of the Royal Statistical Society, Series A*, 142: 97–145.

—— and Winkler, R. L. (1983). 'Averages of Forecasts: Some Empirical Results', *Management Science*, 29: 983–996.

—— Andersen, A., Carbone, R., Fildes, R., Hibon, M., Lewandowski, R., Newton, J., Parzen, E. and Winkler, R. (1982). *The Forecasting Accuracy of Major Time Series Methods*. Chichester, UK: Wiley.

Malik, Z. A. and Karger, D. W. (1975). 'Does Long-range Planning Improve Company Performance?', *Management Review*, 64(9): 27–31.

Malmström, L. (1995). 'Lärande organisationer? Krisen på den svenska fastighetsmarknaden (Learning Organizations? The Crisis in the Swedish Real-Estate Market)'. Ph.D. thesis, Stockholm University.

Malone, M. (1996). 'Chips Triumphant', *Forbes ASAP*, February 26: 53–82.

Malone, M. (1998). 'To Infinity and Beyond', in R. Smolan and J. Erwitt (eds.), *One Digital Day*. New York: Times Books, pp. 115–120.

Malone, T. W. (1981). 'Toward a Theory of Intrinsically Motivating Instruction', *Cognitive Science*, 4: 333–369.

Maniha, J. and Perrow, C. (1965). 'The Reluctant Organization and the Aggressive Environment', *Administrative Science Quarterly*, 10: 238–257.

Mann, F. C. and Neff, F. W. (1961). *Managing Major Change in Organizations*. Ann Arbor, MI: Foundation for Research on Human Behavior.

Mann, H. M. (1966). 'Seller Concentration, Barriers to Entry, and Rates of Return in the Thirty Industries, 1950–1960', *Review of Economics and Statistics*, 48: 296–307.

Manning, P. K. (1977). 'Rules in Organizational Context: Narcotics Law Enforcement in Two Settings', *Sociological Quarterly*, 18: 44–61.

Mansfield, E. (1962). 'Entry, Gibrat's Law, Innovation, and the Growth of Firms', *American Economic Review*, 52: 1023–1051.

—— (1963*a*). 'Intrafirm Rates of Diffusion of an Innovation', *Review of Economics and Statistics*, 45: 348–359.

—— (1963*b*). 'The Speed of Response of Firms to New Techniques', *Quarterly Journal of Economics*, 77: 290–311.

—— (1963*c*). 'Size of Firm, Market Structure, and Innovation', *Journal of Political Economy*, 71(6): 556–576.

—— (1964). 'Industrial Research and Development Expenditures: Determinants, Prospects, and Relation to Size of Firm and Inventive Output', *Journal of Political Economy*, 72(4): 319–340.

Marbach, W. D. et al. (1986). 'What Went Wrong?', *Newsweek*, 107(February 10): 32–34.

March, J. G. (1971). 'The Technology of Foolishness', *Civiløkonomen* (Copenhagen), 18 (4): 4–12 (republished in several books).

—— (1996). 'A Scholar's Quest', Remarks prepared for a faculty seminar, June 1996, Stanford University. Available at: http://www.gsb.stanford.edu/community/bmag/sbsm0696/ascholar.htm.

—— and Simon, H. A. (1958). *Organizations*. New York: Wiley.

—— and Olsen, J. P. (1976). *Ambiguity and Choice in Organizations*. Bergen, Norway: Universitetsforlaget.

Marcis, R. G. and Riordan, D. (1980). 'The Savings and Loan Industry in the 1980's', *Federal Home Loan Bank Board Journal*, 13(5): 3–15.

Marcus, M. (1967). 'Firms' Exit Rates and Their Determinants', *Journal of Industrial Economics*, 16: 10–22.

Margolis, J. (1958). 'The Analysis of the Firm: Rationalism, Conventionalism, and Behaviorism', *Journal of Business*, 31: 187–199.

Marschak, J. and Andrews, W. H., Jr. (1944). 'Random Simultaneous Equations and the Theory of Production', *Econometrica*, 12: 143–205.

Marshall, A. (1920). *Principles of Economics*, 8th edn. New York: Macmillan.

Martin, J. (1992). *Cultures in Organizations: Three Perspectives*. New York: Oxford University Press.

Marx, K. (1904). [1859] *A Contribution to the Critique of Political Economy*. Chicago, IL: Kerr.

Mason, R. O. (1969). 'A Dialectical Approach to Strategic Planning', *Management Science*, 15: B-403-B-414.

Masuch, M. (1985). 'Vicious Circles in Organizations', *Administrative Science Quarterly*, 30: 14–33.

Maurer, H. (1955). *Great Enterprise, Growth and Behavior of the Big Corporation.* New York: Macmillan.

McArthur, L. Z. (1981). 'What Grabs You? The Role of Attention in Impression Formation and Causal Attribution', in E. T. Higgins, C. P. Herman, and M. P. Zanna (eds.), *Social Cognition, The Ontario Symposium*, Vol. 1. Hillsdale, NJ: Erlbaum, pp. 201–246.

McCall, M. W., Jr. (1977). 'Making Sense with Nonsense: Helping Frames of Reference Clash', in P. C. Nystrom and W. H. Starbuck (eds.), *Prescriptive Models of Organizations.* Amsterdam: North-Holland, pp. 111–123.

McClelland, D. C., Atkinson, J. W., Clark, R. A., and Lowell, E. L. (1953). *The Achievement Motive.* New York: Appleton-Century-Crofts.

McGregor, D. (1960). *The Human Side of Enterprise.* New York: McGraw-Hill.

McGuire, J. W. (1963). *Factors Affecting the Growth of Manufacturing Firms.* Seattle, WA: University of Washington, Bureau of Business Research.

—— Chiu, J. S. Y., and Elbing, A. O. (1962). 'Executive Incomes, Sales, and Profits', *American Economic Review*, 52: 753–761.

McNulty, J. E. (1956–1957). 'Administrative Costs and Scale of Operations in the US. Electrical Power Industry: A Statistical Study', *Journal of Industrial Economics*, 5: 30–43.

—— (1962). 'Organizational Change in Growing Enterprises', *Administrative Science Quarterly*, 7: 1–21.

McWhinney, W. H. (1968). 'Organizational Form, Decision Modalities and the Environment', *Human Relations*, 21: 269–281.

Mead, C. A. (1992). 'How Things Really Work: Two Inventors on Innovation, Gordon Bell and Carver Mead'. Video recording, University Video Communications: Stanford, CA.

Meadows, D. H., Meadows, D. L., Randers, J., and Behrens, W. W. III (1972). *The Limits to Growth.* New York: Universe Books.

Mehan, H. (1984). 'Practical Decision Making in Naturally Occurring Institutional Settings', in B. Rogoff and J. Lave (eds.). *Everyday Cognition: Its Development in Social Context.* Cambridge, MA: Harvard University Press.

Mehrabian, A. and Wixen, W. J. (1986). 'Preferences for Individual Video Games as a Function of their Emotional Effects on Players', *Journal of Applied Social Psychology*, 16: 3–15.

Meindl, J. R. and Ehrlich, S. B. (1987). 'The Romance of Leadership and the Evaluation of Organizational Performance', *Academy of Management Journal*, 30: 91–109.

—— —— and Dukerich, J. M. (1985). 'The Romance of Leadership', *Administrative Science Quarterly*, 30: 78–102.

Melman, S. (1951). 'The Rise of Administrative Overhead in the Manufacturing Industries of the United States 1899–1947', *Oxford Economic Papers*, 3: 62–112.

—— (1956). *Dynamic Factors in Industrial Productivity.* New York: Wiley, esp. 159–162.

—— (1958). *Decision-Making and Productivity.* New York: Wiley.

Merriam (1971). *Webster's Third New International Dictionary of the English Language* (unabridged). Springfield, MA: Merriam.

Merton, R. K. (1940). 'Bureaucratic Structure and Personality', *Social Forces*, 18: 560–568.

—— (1957). *Social Theory and Social Structure*, (rev. edn.). Glencoe, IL: Free Press.

Messinger, S. L. (1955). 'Organizational Transformation: A Case Study of a Declining Social Movement', *American Sociological Review*, 20: 3–10.

Meyer, A. D. (1982). 'How Ideologies Supplant Formal Structures and Shape Responses to Environments', *Journal of Management Studies*, 19: 45–61.

—— and Starbuck, W. H. (1993). 'Interactions Between Politics and Ideologies in Strategy Formation', in K. Roberts (ed.), *New Challenges to Understanding Organizations.* New York: Macmillan, pp. 99–116.

Meyer, J. W. and Rowan, B. (1977). 'Institutionalized Organizations: Formal Structure as Myth and Ceremony', *American Journal of Sociology*, 83: 340–363.

Mezias, J. M. and Starbuck, W. H. (2003a). 'Studying the Accuracy of Managers' Perceptions: A Research Odyssey', *British Journal of Management*, 14: 3–17.

—— —— (2003b). 'What do Managers Know, Anyway? A Lot Less Than They Think: But Now, the Good News', *Harvard Business Review*, 81(May 5), Forethought section, pages 16–17.

—— Grinyer, P., and Guth, W. D. (2001). 'Changing Collective Cognition: A Process Model for Strategic Change', *Long Range Planning*, 34: 71–93.

Milgram, S. (1974). *Obedience to Authority*. New York: Harper & Row.

Millar, S. (1968). *The Psychology of Play*. Harmondsworth: Penguin.

Miller, D. (1982). 'Evolution and Revolution: A Quantum View of Structural Change in Organizations', *Journal of Management Studies*, 19: 131–151.

—— (1990). *The Icarus Paradox: How Exceptional Companies Bring about Their Own Downfall*. New York: HarperCollins.

—— (1993). 'The Architecture of Simplicity', *Academy of Management Review*, 18: 116–138.

—— (1994). 'What Happens After Success: The Perils of Excellence', *Journal of Management Studies*, 31: 325–358.

—— and Mintzberg, H. (1974). 'Strategy Formulation in Context: Some Tentative Models', Working paper, McGill University, Montreal.

—— and Chen, M.-J. (1994). 'Sources and Consequences of Competitive Inertia: A Study of the U.S. Airline Industry', *Administrative Science Quarterly*, 39: 1–23.

—— —— (1996). 'The Simplicity of Competitive Repertoires: An Empirical Analysis', *Strategic Management Journal*, 17: 419–439.

Miller, E. J. (1959). 'Technology, Territory, and Time', *Human Relations*, 12: 243–272.

Miller, J. G. (1972). 'Living Systems: The Organization', *Behavioral Science*, 17: 1–182.

Miller, S. (1973). 'Ends, Means, and Galumphing: Some Leitmotifs of Play', *American Anthropologist*, 75: 87–98.

Milliken, F. J. (1990). 'Perceiving and Interpreting Environmental Change: An Examination of College Administrators' Interpretations of Changing Demographics', *Academy of Management Journal*, 33: 42–63.

—— and Lant, T. K. (1991) 'The Effect of an Organization's Recent Performance on Strategic Persistence and Change', *Advances in Strategic Management*, 7: 129–156.

—— —— and Batra, B. (1992). 'The Role of Managerial Learning and Interpretation in Strategic Persistence and Reorientation: An Empirical Exploration', *Strategic Management Journal*, 13: 585–608.

Mills, C. W. (1940). 'Situated Actions and Vocabularies of Motive', *American Sociological Review*, 5: 904–913.

Miner, A. S. (1991). 'Organizational Evolution and the Social Ecology of Jobs', *American Sociological Review*, 56: 772–785.

—— and Haunschild, P. R. (1995). 'Population Level Learning', *Research in Organizational Behavior*, 17: 115–166.

—— Kim, J.-Y., Holzinger I. W., and Haunschild, P. (1996). 'Fruits of Failure: Organizational Failure and Population Level Learning', *Best Papers Proceedings, Academy of Management*, 239–243.

Mintzberg, H. (1972). 'Research on Strategy-making', *Academy of Management Proceedings*, 90–94.

—— (1973). *The Nature of Managerial Work*. New York: Harper & Row.

—— (1994). *The Rise and Fall of Strategic Planning: Reconceiving Roles for Planning, Plans, Planners.* New York: Free Press.

—— Raisinghani, D., and Théorêt, A. (1976). 'The Structure of "Unstructured" Decision Processes', *Administrative Science Quarterly*, 21: 246–275.

Mischel, W. (1968). *Personality and Assessment.* New York: Wiley.

Mitchell, T. R. (1974). 'Expectancy Models of Job Satisfaction, Occupational Preference, and Effort: A Theoretical, Methodological, and Empirical Appraisal', *Psychological Bulletin*, 81: 1053–1077.

Mitroff, I. I. and Betz, F. (1972). 'Dialectical Decision Theory: A Metatheory of Decision-making', *Management Science*, 19: 11–24.

—— and Featheringham, T. R. (1974). 'On Systematic Problem Solving and the Error of the Third Kind', *Behavioral Science*, 19: 383–393.

—— and Kilmann, R. H. (1976). 'On Organizational Stories: An Approach to the Design and Analysis of Organizations Through Myths and Stories', in R. H. Kilmann, L. R. Pondy, and D. P. Slevin (eds.), *The Management of Organization Design*, Vol. I, *Strategies and Implementation.* New York: Elsevier, pp. 189–207.

—— and Kilmann R. H. (1984). *Corporate Tragedies: Product Tampering, Sabotage, and Other Catastrophes.* New York: Praeger.

Mohr, L. B. (1969). 'Determinants of Innovation in Organizations', *American Political Science Review*, 63: 111–126.

Montagna, P. D. (1968). 'Professionalization and Bureaucratization in Large Professional Organizations', *American Journal of Sociology*, 73: 138–145.

Mooney, J. D. and Reiley, A. C. (1931). *Onward Industry!* New York: Harper.

Moore, D. G. (1959). 'Managerial Strategies', in W. L. Warner and N. H. Martin (eds.), *Industrial Man.* New York: Harper, pp. 219–226.

Moore, G. E. (1965). 'Cramming More Components Onto Integrated Circuits', *Electronics*, 38(8): 114–117.

—— (1996). 'Intel: Memories and the Microprocessor', *Daedalus*, 125(2): 55–80.

Moore, W. E. and Tumin, M. M. (1949). 'Some Social Functions of Ignorance', *American Sociological Review*, 14: 787–795.

Morison, E. (1966). *Men, Machines and Modern Times.* Cambridge, MA: MIT Press.

Nadler, G. and Smith, W. D. (1963). 'Manufacturing Progress Functions for Types of Processes', *International Journal of Production Research*, 2: 115–135.

Nam, S. (1991). 'Cultural and Managerial Attributions for Group Performance'. Ph.D. thesis, University of Oregon.

Nash, J. E. (1990). 'Working at and Working: Computer Fritters', *Journal of Contemporary Ethnography*, 19: 207–225.

Nayak, P. R. and Ketteringham, J. M. (1986). *Breakthroughs!* New York: Rawson.

Neisser, U. (1981). 'John Dean's Memory: A Case Study', *Cognition*, 9: 1–22.

Nelson, R. L. (1988). *Partners with Power: The Social Transformation of the Large Law Firm.* Berkeley, CA: University of California Press.

—— (1992). 'Of Tournaments and Transformations: Explaining the Growth of Large Law Firms', *Wisconsin Law Review*, 733–750.

Nelson, R. R. (1959). 'The Economics of Invention: A Survey of the Literature', *Journal of Business*, 32: 101–127.

—— (1972). 'Issues and Suggestions for the Study of Industrial Organization in a Regime of Rapid Technical Change', in V. R. Fuchs (ed.), *Policy Issues and Research Opportunities in Industrial Organization.* New York: National Bureau of Economic Research, pp. 34–58.

Nelson, R. R. and Winter, S. G. Jr. (1982). *An Evolutionary Theory of Economic Change*. Cambridge, MA: Belknap.

Newell, A. and Simon, H. A. (1972). *Human Problem Solving*. Englewood Cliffs, NJ: Prentice-Hall.

Newman, W. H. and Logan, J. P. (1955). *Management of Expanding Enterprises*. New York: Columbia University Press.

—— —— (1981). *Strategy, Policy, and Central Management*, 8th edn. Cincinnati, OH: South-Western.

Nielsen, S. L. and Sarason, I. G. (1981). 'Emotion, Personality, and Selective Attention', *Journal of Personality and Social Psychology*, 41: 945–960.

Nisbett, R. E. and Ross, L. (1980). *Human Inference: Strategies and Shortcomings of Social Judgment*. Englewood Cliffs, NJ: Prentice-Hall.

—— and Wilson, T. D. (1977). 'Telling More Than we Can Know: Verbal Reports on Mental Processes', *Psychological Review*, 84: 231–259.

Nonaka, I. (1994). 'A Dynamic Theory of Organizational Knowledge Creation', *Organization Science*, 5: 14–37.

—— and Takeuchi, H. (1995). *The Knowledge-Creating Company: How Japanese Companies Create the Dynamics of Innovation*. New York: Oxford University Press.

Normann, R. (1969). Organization, Mediation and Environment. Stockholm: Swedish Institute for Administrative Research, Report No. UPM-RN-91.

—— (1971). 'Organizational Innovativeness: Product Variation and Reorientation', *Administrative Science Quarterly*, 16: 203–215.

Nourse, E. G. (1944). *Price Making in a Democracy*. Washington, DC: Brookings.

NSF (1956). *Science and Engineering in American Industry*. Washington, DC: National Science Foundation.

—— (1959). *Funds for Research and Development in Industry*. Washington, DC: National Science Foundation.

Nye, S. (1975). 'Can Conduct-oriented Enforcement Inhibit Conscious Parallelism?', *Antitrust Law Journal*, 44(2): 206–230.

Nystrom, P. C. (1975). 'Input-output Processes of the Federal Trade Commission', *Administrative Science Quarterly*, 20: 104–113.

—— (1977). 'Managerial Resistance to a Management System', *Accounting, Organizations, and Society*, 2: 317–322.

—— and Starbuck, W. H. (1984). 'To Avoid Organizational Crises, Unlearn', *Organizational Dynamics*, 12(4): 53–65.

—— Hedberg, B. L. T., and Starbuck, W. H. (1976). 'Interacting Processes as Organization Designs', in R. H. Kilmann, L. R. Pondy, and D. P. Slevin (eds.), *The Management of Organization Design*, Vol. 1. New York: North-Holland, pp. 209–230.

—— Ramamurthy, K., and Wilson, A. L. (2002). 'Organizational Context, Climate and Innovativeness: Adoption of Imaging Technology', *Journal of Engineering and Technology Management*, 19: 221–247.

O'Reilly, C. A. III (1983). 'The Use of Information in Organizational Decision Making: A Model and Some Propositions', in L. L. Cummings and B. M. Staw (eds.), *Research in Organizational Behavior*, Vol. 5. Greenwich, CT: JAI Press, pp. 103–139.

Olofsson, C., Schlasberg, J., and Swalander, P.-A. (1973). 'Sjukvårdens nyfattigdom', *Läkartidningen*, 70: 2312–2314.

Ord, J. G. (1989). 'Who's Joking? The Information System at Play', *Interacting with Computers*, 1: 118–128.

Orlikowski, W. J. (1988). 'Information Technology in Post-Industrial Organizations: An Exploration of the Computer Mediation of Production Work', Ph.D. thesis, New York University.

Osborn, R. C. (1951). 'Efficiency and Profitability in Relation to Size', *Harvard Business Review*, 29(2): 82–94.

Pant, P. N. (1991). 'Strategies, Environments, Effectiveness: Savings and Loan Associations, 1978–1989'. Ph.D. thesis, New York University.

—— and Starbuck, W. H. (1990). 'Innocents in the Forest: Forecasting and Research Methods', *Journal of Management*, 16(2): 433–460.

Papandreou, A. G. (1952). 'Some Basic Problems in the Theory of the Firm', in B. F. Haley (ed.), *A Survey of Contemporary Economics*, Vol. II. Homewood, IL: Irwin, pp. 183–219.

Papert, S. (1980). *Mindstorms*. New York: Basic Books.

Parkinson, C. N. (1957). *Parkinson's Law*. Boston, MA: Houghton Mifflin, 2–13.

Patton, A. (1961). *Men, Money and Motivation*. New York: McGraw-Hill.

Payne, R. L. and Pugh, D. S. (1976). 'Organizational Structure and Climate', in M. D. Dunnette (ed.), *Handbook of Industrial and Organizational Psychology*. Chicago, IL: Rand McNally, pp. 1125–1173.

Pear, R. (1986). 'Senator Says NASA Cut 70% of Staff Checking Quality', *New York Times*, 135(8 May): A1, B25.

Peerenboom, R. P. (1993). *Law and Morality in Ancient China: The Silk Manuscripts of Huang-Lao*. Albany, NY: State University of New York Press.

Penrose, E. T. (1952). 'Biological Analogies in the Theory of the Firm', *American Economic Review*, 42: 804–819.

—— (1955). 'Limits to the Growth and Size of Firms', *American Economic Review*, 45(2): 531–543. Also see the discussion by W. W. Cooper, 559–565.

—— (1959). *The Theory of the Growth of the Firm*. New York: Wiley.

Perrow, C. (1961a). 'Organizational Prestige: Some Functions and Dysfunctions', *American Journal of Sociology*, 66: 335–341.

—— (1961b). 'The Analysis of Goals in Complex Organizations', *American Sociological Review*, 26: 854–866.

—— (1984). *Normal Accidents: Living with High-Risk Technologies*. New York: Basic Books.

Peters, T. J. (1980). 'Putting Excellence Into Management', *Business Week*, 2646 (July 21): 196–197, 200, 205.

—— and Waterman, R. H., Jr. (1982). *In Search of Excellence*. New York: Harper & Row.

Petroski, H. (1992). *To Engineer Is Human*. New York: Vintage.

—— (1996). 'Harnessing Steam', *American Scientist*, 84(1): 15–19.

Pettigrew, A. N. (1973). *The Politics of Organizational Decision-Making*. London: Tavistock.

—— (1974). 'Internal Politics and the Emergence and Decline of Departmental Groups', Working paper, London Graduate School of Business Studies.

—— (1979). 'On Studying Organizational Cultures', *Administrative Science Quarterly*, 24: 570–581.

Pfeffer, J. (1971). 'Organizational Ecology: A System Resource Approach', Working paper, Stanford University.

—— (1972). 'Size and Composition of Corporate Boards of Directors: The Organization and Its Environment', *Administrative Science Quarterly*, 17: 218–228.

Phelps Brown, E. H. (1957). 'The Meaning of the Fitted Cobb-Douglas Function', *Quarterly Journal of Economics*, 71: 546–560.

Phillips, A. (1956). 'Concentration, Scale and Technological Change in Selected Manufacturing Industries 1899–1939', *Journal of Industrial Economics*, 4: 179–193.

Phillips, L. D., Hays, W. L., and Edwards, W. (1966). 'Conservatism in Complex Probabilistic Inference', *IEEE Transactions on Human Factors in Electronics*, HFE-7: 7–18.

Piaget, J. (1962). *Play, Dreams, and Imitation in Childhood*. New York: W. W. Norton.

Pock, J. C. (1972). 'Definition and Maintenance of Organizational Boundaries', Working paper, Reed College.

Polanyi, M. (1966). *The Tacit Dimension*. London: Routledge & Kegan Paul.

Pondy, L. R. (1969). 'Effects of Size, Complexity, and Ownership on Administrative Intensity', *Administrative Science Quarterly*, 14: 47–60.

Porac, J. F. and Rosa, J. A. (1996). 'In Praise of Managerial Narrow-mindedness', *Journal of Management Inquiry*, 5: 35–42.

—— Thomas, H., and Baden-Fuller, C. (1989). 'Competitive Groups as Cognitive Communities: The Case of Scottish Knitwear Manufacturers', *Journal of Management Studies*, 26: 397–416.

Porter, L. W. and Roberts, K. H. (1976). 'Communication in Organizations', in M. D. Dunnette (ed.), *Handbook of Industrial and Organizational Psychology*. Chicago, IL: Rand McNally, pp. 1553–1589.

Posner, R. (1969). 'Oligopoly and the Antitrust Laws: A Suggested Approach', *Stanford Law Review*, 212: 1562–1606.

Postman, L. and Brown, D. R. (1951). 'The Perceptual Consequences of Success and Failure', *Journal of Abnormal and Social Psychology*, 47: 213–221.

Pound, E. (1951). *Confucius*. New York: New Directions.

Powell, M. J. (1993). 'Professional Innovation: Corporate Lawyers and Private Lawmaking', *Law and Social Inquiry*, 18(3): 423–452.

Powell, W. W., Koput, K. W., and Smith-Doerr, L. (1996). 'Interorganizational Collaboration and the Locus of Innovation: Networks of Learning in Biotechnology', *Administrative Science Quarterly*, 41: 116–145.

Presidential Commission (1986). *Report of the Presidential Commission on the Space Shuttle Challenger Accident*. Washington, DC: U.S. Government Printing Office.

Pressman, J. L. and Wildavsky, A. B. (1973). *Implementation*. Berkeley, CA: University of California Press.

Pugh, D. S. (1981). 'The Aston Program of Research: Retrospect and Prospect', in A. Van de Ven and W. Joyce (eds.), *Perspectives on Organization Design and Behavior*. New York: Wiley, pp. 135–166.

—— Hickson, D. J., Hinings, C. R., and Turner, C. (1968). 'Dimensions of Organization Structure', *Administrative Science Quarterly*, 13: 65–105.

—— —— —— (1969). 'The Context of Organization Structures', *Administrative Science Quarterly*, 14: 91–114.

Qualls, D. (1972). 'Concentration, Barriers to Entry, and Long Run Economic Profit Margins', *Journal of Industrial Economics*, 20: 146–158.

Quinn, J. B. (1980). *Strategies for Change: Logical Incrementalism*. Homewood, IL: Irwin.

Ragins, B. R., Townsend, B., and Mattis, M. (1998). 'Gender Disparity in the Executive Suite: CEOs and Female Executives Report on Breaking the Glass Ceiling', *Academy of Management Executive*, 12(1): 28–42.

Reilly, M. (1974). 'An Explanation of play', in M. Reilly (ed.), *Play as Exploratory Learning*. Beverly Hills, CA: Sage, pp. 117–149.

RERP (1959). *Industrial Location Bibliography*. Los Angeles, CA: University of California, Graduate School of Business Administration, Real Estate Research Program.

Revans, R. W. (1958). 'Human Relations, Management and Size', in E. M. Hugh-Jones (ed.), *Human Relations and Modern Management*. Amsterdam: North-Holland, pp. 177–220.

Rhenman, E. (1973). *Organization Theory for Long-Range Planning*. London: Wiley.

Richardson, F. L. W., Jr. and Walker, C. R. (1948). *Human Relations in an Expanding Company*. New Haven, CT: Yale University, Labor and Management Center.

Richman, B. M. and Copen, M. (1972). *International Management and Economic Development*. New York: McGraw-Hill.

Rindova, V. P. and Starbuck, W. H. (1997). 'Distrust in Dependence: The Ancient Challenge of Superior-subordinate Relations', in T. A. R. Clark (ed.), *Advancements in Organization Behaviour: Essays in Honour of Derek Pugh*. Aldershot, UK: Dartmouth Publishing, forthcoming.

Ritzer, G. and Walczak, D. (1986). *Working: Conflict & Change*, 3rd edn. Englewood Cliffs, NJ: Prentice-Hall.

Roberts, D. R. (1956). 'A General Theory of Executive Compensation Based on Statistically Tested Propositions', *Quarterly Journal of Economics*, 20: 270–294.

—— (1959). *Executive Compensation*. Glencoe, IL: Free Press.

Robey, D. (1979). 'User Attitudes and Management Information System Use', *Academy of Management Journal*, 22: 527–538.

Robinson, E. A. G. (1934). 'The Problem of Management and the Size of Firms', *Economic Journal*, 44: 242–257.

Robinson, W. S. (1950). 'Ecological Correlations and the Behavior of Individuals', *American Sociological Review*, 15: 352–357.

Rosenberg, B. and Houghlet, M. (1974). 'Error Rates in CRSP and Compustat Data Bases and Their Implications', *Journal of Finance*, 29: 1303–1310.

Rosenhan, D. L. (1978). 'On Being Sane in Insane Places', in J. M. Neale, G. C. Davison and K. P. Price (eds.), *Contemporary Readings in Psychopathology*. New York: Wiley, pp. 29–41.

Ross, A. M. (1947). 'The Trade Union as a Wage-fixing Institution', *American Economic Review*, 37: 566–588.

Ross, J. and Staw, B. M. (1986). 'Expo 86: An Escalation Prototype', *Administrative Science Quarterly*, 31: 274–297.

Ross, N. S. (1952–1953). 'Management and the Size of the Firm', *Review of Economic Studies*, 19(3): 148–154.

Rostas, L. (1948). *Comparative Productivity in British and American Industry*. Cambridge: Cambridge University Press.

Rothschild, K. W. (1947). 'Price Theory and Oligopoly', *Economic Journal*, 57: 299–320.

Rotter, J. B. (1966a). 'Generalized Expectancies for Internal Versus External Control of Reinforcement', *Psychological Monographs*, 60(1): 1–28.

—— (1966b). 'Generalized Expectancies for Internal Versus External Control of Reinforcement', *Psychological Monographs*, 80: 1–28.

Rousseau, D. M. (1986). 'Choosing an Appropriate Level of Technology for Studying Computerized Work Systems', paper presented at the Academy of Management Annual Meetings, Chicago.

Rousseeuw, P. J. and Leroy, A. M. (1987). *Robust Regression and Outlier Detection*. New York: Wiley.

Roy, D. F. (1960). ' "Banana Time": Job Satisfaction and Informal Interaction', *Human Organization*, 18: 158–168.

Rue, L. W. and Fulmer, R. M. (1974). 'Is Long-range Planning Profitable?' *Academy of Management Proceedings, Thirty-third Annual Meeting, Boston*, 1974: 66–73.

Sage, A. P. (1981). 'Designs for Optimal Information Filters', in P. C. Nystrom and W. H. Starbuck (eds.), *Handbook of Organizational Design*, Vol. 1. New York: Oxford University Press, pp. 105–121.

Sahlin-Andersson, K. (1996). 'Imitating by Editing Success: The Construction of Organizational Fields', in B. Czarniawska-Joerges and G. Sévon (eds.), *Translating Organizational Change*. Berlin: de Gruyter, pp. 69–92.

Sahlins, M. D. and Service, E. R. (eds.) (1960). *Evolution and Culture*. Ann Arbor, MI: University of Michigan Press.

Salancik, G. R. (1977). 'Commitment and the Control of Organizational Behavior and Belief', in B. M. Staw and G. R. Salancik (eds.), *New Directions in Organizational Behavior*. Chicago, IL: St. Clair, pp. 1–54.

Salgado, S. R., Starbuck, W. H., and Mezias, J. M. (2002). 'The Accuracy of Managers' Perceptions: A Dimension Missing from Theories About Firms', in M. Augier and J. G. March (eds.), *The Economics of Choice, Change, and Organizations: Essays in Memory of Richard M. Cyert*. Cheltenham, UK: Edward Elgar, pp. 168–185.

Salzer, M. (1994). 'Identity Across Borders: A Study in the "IKEA-World" ', Ph.D. thesis, Linköping University.

Samuelson, S. S. and Jaffe, L. J. (1990). 'A Statistical Analysis of Law Firm Profitability', *Boston University Law Review*, 70: 185–211.

San Miguel, J. G. (1977). 'The Reliability of R&D Data in Compustat and 10-K Reports', *Accounting Review*, 52: 638–641.

Sandelands, L. E. (1988). 'Effects of Work and Play Signals on Task Evaluation', *Journal of Applied Social Psychology*, 18: 1032–1048.

—— and Buckner, G. C. (1989). 'Of Art and Work: Aesthetic Experience and the Psychology of Work Feelings', in L. L. Cummings and B. M. Staw (eds.), *Research in Organizational Behavior*, Vol. 11. Greenwich, CT: JAI Press, pp. 105–131.

—— Ashford, S. J., and Dutton, J. E. (1983). 'Reconceptualizing the Overjustification Effect: A Template-matching Approach', *Motivation and Emotion*, 7: 229–255.

Sander, R. H. and Williams, E. D. (1992). 'A Little Theorizing About the Big Law Firm: Galanter, Palay, and the Economics of Growth', *Law and Social Inquiry*, 17: 391–414.

Sanger, D. E. (1986a). 'Panel Questioned Shuttle Schedule', *New York Times*, 135(February 13): 2.

—— (1986b). 'Shuttle Data Now Emerging Show that Clues to Disaster were There', *New York Times*, 135(February 16): 1, 32.

—— (1986c). 'Challenger Report is Said to Omit Some Key Safety Issues for NASA', *New York Times*, 135(June 8): 1, 36.

—— (1986d). 'NASA Pressing Shuttle Change Amid Concerns', *New York Times*, 135 (September 23): A1, C10.

—— (1986e). 'Top NASA Aides Knew of Shuttle Flaw in '84', *New York Times*, 135 (December 21): 1, 34.

—— (1986f). 'Shuttle Changing in Extensive Ways to Foster Safety', *New York Times*, 135(December 28): 1, 22.

—— (1986g). 'Rebuilt NASA "On Way Back" as an Array of Doubts Persist', *New York Times*, 135(December 29): A1, B12.

Sapolsky, H. H. (1972). *The Polaris System Development*. Cambridge, MA: Harvard University Press.

Savings & Community Bankers of America (1994). *1994 Sourcebook*. Washington, DC: Savings & Community Bankers of America.

Schaller, R. R. (1996). 'The Origin, Nature, and Implications of "Moore's Law": The Benchmark of Progress in Semiconductor Electronics'. Working paper, George Mason University. Available at: http://mason.gmu.edu/~rschalle/moorelaw.html.

—— (1997). 'Moore's Law: Past, Present, and Future', *IEEE Spectrum*, 34(6, June): 52–59.

Schank, R. C. (1975). 'The Structure of Episodes in Memory', in D. G. Bobrow and A. Collins (eds.), *Representations and Understanding*. New York: Academic Press, pp. 237–272.

Schell, J. (1982). *The Fate of the Earth*. New York: Knopf.

Schendel, D. and Hatten, K. (1977). 'Heterogeneity Within an Industry: Firm Conduct in the US Brewing Industry', *Journal of Industrial Economics*, 25: 97–113.

—— and Patton, R. (1978). 'A Simultaneous Equation Model of Corporate Strategy', *Management Science*, 24: 1611–1621.

—— —— and Riggs, J. (1975). 'Corporate Turnaround Strategies', Working paper, Purdue University.

Scherer, F. M. (1970). *Industrial Market Structure and Economic Performance*. Chicago, IL: Rand McNally.

—— and Ross, D. (1990). *Industrial Market Structure and Economic Performance*, 3rd edn. Boston, MA: Houghton Mifflin.

Schiffrin, D. (1977). 'Opening Encounters', *American Sociological Review*, 42: 679–691.

Schneider, L. (1962). 'The Role of the Category of Ignorance in Sociological Theory: An Exploratory Statement', *American Sociological Review*, 27: 492–508.

Schriesheim [Fulk] J., Von Glinow, M. A., and Kerr, S. (1977). 'Professionals in Bureaucracies: A Structural Alternative', in P. C. Nystrom and W. H. Starbuck (eds.), *Prescriptive Models of Organizations*. Amsterdam: North-Holland, pp. 55–69.

Schroder, H. M., Driver, M. J., and Streufert, S. (1967). *Human Information Processing*. New York: Holt, Rinehart & Winston.

Schwartz, H. S. (1987). 'On the Psychodynamics of Organizational Disaster: The Case of the Space Shuttle Challenger', *Columbia Journal of World Business*, 22(1): 59–67.

Schweitzer, M. D., Ordóñez, L., and Douma, B. (2004). 'Goal Setting as a Motivator of Unethical Behavior', *Academy of Management Journal*, 47: 422–432.

Scott, W. E. (1966). 'Activation Theory and Task Design', *Organizational Behavior and Human Performance*, 1: 3–30.

Scott, W. R. (1995). *Institutions and Organizations*. Thousand Oaks, CA: Sage.

Searle, A. D. and Gody, C. S. (1945). 'Productivity Changes in Selected Wartime Shipbuilding Programs', *Monthly Labor Review*, 61: 1132–1147.

Searle, J. R. (1995). *The Construction of Social Reality*. New York: Free Press.

Seashore, S. E. and Yuchtman, E. (1967). 'Factorial Analysis of Organizational Performance', *Administrative Science Quarterly*, 12: 377–395.

Selznick, P. (1943). 'An Approach to a Theory of Bureaucracy', *American Sociological Review*, 8: 47–54.

—— (1949). *TVA and the Grass Roots*. Berkeley, CA: University of California Press.

Sheppard, S. B., Bailey, J. W., and Bailey [Kruesi], E. (1984). 'An Empirical Evaluation of Software Documentation Formats', in J. C. Thomas and M. L. Schneider (eds.), *Human Factors in Computer Systems*. Norwood, NJ: Ablex, pp. 135–164.

Sheppard, S. B., Bailey, J. W., and Kruesi [Bailey], E., and Curtis, B. (1980). *The Effects of Symbology and Spatial Arrangement on the Comprehension of Software Specifications*. Arlington, VA: General Electric Company, TR-80–388200–2.

Sills, D. L. (1957). *The Volunteers*. Glencoe, IL: Free Press.

Silver, M. S. (1988). 'User Perceptions of Decision Support System Restrictiveness: An Experiment', *Journal of Management Information Systems*, 5: 51–65.

Simon, H. A. (1953). 'Birth of an Organization: The Economic Cooperation Administration', *Public Administration Review*, 13: 227–236.

—— (1955a). 'A Behavioral Model of Rational Choice', *Quarterly Journal of Economics*, 69: 99–118.

—— (1955b). 'On a Class of Skew Distribution Functions', *Biometrica*, 42: 425–440.

—— (1956). 'Rational Choice and the Structure of the Environment', *Psychological Review*, 63: 129–138.

—— (1957a). *Administrative Behavior*, 2nd edn. New York: Macmillan.

—— (1957b). 'The Compensation of Executives', *Sociometry*, 20: 32–35.

—— and Bonini, C. P. (1958). 'The Size Distribution of Business Firms', *American Economic Review*, 48: 607–617.

Simpson, R. L. (1959). 'Vertical and Horizontal Communication in Formal Organizations', *Administrative Science Quarterly*, 4: 188–196.

Singer, B. and Benassi, V. A. (1981). 'Occult Beliefs', *American Scientist*, 69(1): 49–55.

Sitkin, S. B. (1992). 'Learning Through Failure: The Strategy of Small Losses', *Research in Organizational Behavior*, 14: 231–266.

Skinner, B. F. (1974). *About Behaviorism*. New York: Knopf.

Slichter, S. H., Healy, J. J., and Livernash, E. R. (1960). *The Impact of Collective Bargaining on Management*. Washington, DC: Brookings.

Slovic, P., Fischhoff, B., and Lichtenstein, S. (1980). 'Risky Assumptions', *Psychology Today*, 14(June): 44–48

—— —— —— (1982). 'Fact Versus Fears: Understanding Perceived Risk', in D. Kahneman, P. Slovic and A. Tversky (eds.), *Judgment under Uncertainty: Heuristics and Biases*. Cambridge: Cambridge University Press.

Smelser, N. J. (1959). *Social Change in the Industrial Revolution*. Chicago, IL: University of Chicago Press.

Smigel, E. O. (1964). *The Wall Street Lawyer: Professional Organization Man?* New York: Free Press.

Smith, C. G. (1966). 'A Comparative Analysis of Some Conditions and Consequences of Intraorganizational Conflict', *Administrative Science Quarterly*, 10: 504–529.

Snyder, M. (1981). 'Seek, and ye Shall Find: Testing Hypotheses about Other People', in E. T. Higgins, C. P. Herman, and M. P. Zanna (eds.), *Social Cognition, The Ontario Symposium*, Vol. 1. Hillsdale, NJ: Erlbaum, pp. 277–303.

—— and Uranowitz, S. W. (1978). 'Reconstructing the Past: Some Cognitive Consequences of Person Perception', *Journal of Personality and Social Psychology*, 36: 941–950.

Soemardjan, S. (1957). 'Bureaucratic Organization in a Time of Revolution', *Administrative Science Quarterly*, 2: 182–199.

Sofer, C. (1961). *The Organization from Within*. London: Tavistock.

Spender, J.-C. (1989). *Industry Recipes: The Nature and Sources of Managerial Judgement*. Oxford: Basil Blackwell.

Spinrad, W. (1960). 'Correlates of Trade Union Participation: A Summary of the Literature', *American Sociological Review*, 25: 237–244.

Spiro, L. N. (1999). 'Merrill's e-battle', *Business Week*, November 15: 256–268.

Sproull, L. S. (1981). 'Beliefs in Organizations', in P. C. Nystrom and W. H. Starbuck (eds.), *Handbook of Organizational Design*, Vol. 2. New York: Oxford University Press, pp. 203–224.

Staehle, H. (1942). 'The Measurement of Statistical Cost Functions: An Appraisal of Some Recent Contributions', *American Economic Review*, 32: 321–333.

Stanfill, C. and Waltz, D. (1986). 'Toward Memory-based Reasoning', *Communications of the ACM*, 29: 1213–1228.

Starbuck, W. H. (1963a). 'Level of Aspiration', *Psychological Review*, 70: 51–60.

—— (1963b). 'Level of Aspiration Theory and Economic Behavior', *Behavioral Science*, 8: 128–136.

—— (1965). 'Organizational Growth and Development', in J. G. March (ed.), *Handbook of Organizations*. Chicago, IL: Rand McNally, pp. 451–533.

—— (1966). 'The Efficiency of British and American Retail Employees', *Administrative Science Quarterly*, 11: 345–385.

—— (1968a). 'Organizational Metamorphosis', in R. W. Millman and M. P. Hottenstein (eds.), *Promising Research Directions*. State College, PA: Academy of Management, pp. 113–122.

—— (1968b). 'Some Comments, Observations, and Objections Stimulated by "Design of Proof in Organizational Research" ', *Administrative Science Quarterly*, 13: 135–161.

—— (1973). 'Tadpoles into Armageddon and Chrysler into Butterflies', *Social Science Research*, 2: 81–109.

—— (1974a). 'Systems Optimization with Unknown Criteria', *Proceedings of the 1974 International Conference on Systems, Man and Cybernetics*. New York: Institute of Electrical and Electronics Engineers, 67–76.

—— (1974b). 'The Current State of Organization Theory', in J. W. McGuire (ed.), *Contemporary Management: Issues and Viewpoints*. Englewood Cliffs, NJ: Prentice-Hall, pp. 123–139.

—— (1975). 'Information Systems for Organizations of the Future', in E. Grochla and N. Szyperski (eds.), *Information Systems and Organizational Structure*. Berlin: de Gruyter, pp. 217–229.

—— (1976). 'Organizations and their Environments', in M. D. Dunnette (ed.), *Handbook of Industrial and Organizational Psychology*. Chicago, IL: Rand McNally, pp. 1069–1123.

—— (1981). 'A Trip to View the Elephants and Rattlesnakes in the Garden of Aston', in A. H. Van de Ven and W. F. Joyce (eds.), *Perspectives on Organization Design and Behavior*. New York: Wiley-Interscience, pp. 167–198.

—— (1982). 'Congealing Oil: Inventing Ideologies to Justify Acting Ideologies Out', *Journal of Management Studies*, 19: 3–27.

—— (1983). 'Organizations as Action Generators', *American Sociological Review*, 48: 91–102.

—— (1985). 'Acting First and Thinking Later: Theory Versus Reality in Strategic Change', in J. M. Pennings and Associates (eds.), *Organizational Strategy and Change: New Views on Formulating and Implementing Strategic Decisions*. San Francisco, CA: Jossey-Bass, pp. 336–372.

—— (1987). 'Sharing Cognitive Tasks Between People and Computers in Space Systems', in T. B. Sheridan, D. S. Kruser, and S. Deutsch (eds.), *Human Factors in Automated and Robotic Space Systems: Proceedings of a Symposium*. Washington, DC: National Research Council, pp. 418–443.

—— (1989). 'Why Organizations Run into Crises...and Sometimes Survive Them', in K. Laudon and J. Turner (eds.), *Information Technology and Management Strategy*. Englewood Cliffs, NJ: Prentice-Hall, pp. 11–33.

Starbuck, W. H. (1990). 'Knowledge-intensive Firms: Learning to Survive in Strange Environments', in L. Lindmark (ed.), *Kunskap som kritisk resurs* (Knowledge as a critical resource). Umeaa, Sweden: University of Umeaa, Department of Business Administration, pp. 10–20.

—— (1992a). 'Learning by Knowledge-intensive Firms', *Journal of Management Studies*, 29(6): 713–740.

—— (1992b). 'Strategizing in the Real World', *International Journal of Technology Management, Special Publication on Technological Foundations of Strategic Management*, 8(1/2): 77–85.

—— (1994). 'On Behalf of Naïveté', in J. A. C. Baum and J. V. Singh (eds). *Evolutionary Dynamics of Organizations*. London: Oxford University Press, pp. 205–220.

—— and Bass, F. M. (1967). 'An Experimental Study of Risk-taking and the Value of Information in a New Product Context', *Journal of Business*, 40, 155–165.

—— and Dutton, J. M. (1973). 'Designing Adaptive Organizations', *Journal of Business Policy*, 3(4): 21–28.

—— and Hedberg, B. L. T. (1977). 'Saving an Organization from a Stagnating Environment', in H. B. Thorelli (ed.), *Strategy + Structure = Performance*. Bloomington, IN: Indiana University Press, pp. 249–258.

—— and Mezias, J. M. (1996). 'Opening Pandora's Box: Studying the Accuracy of Managers' Perceptions', *Journal of Organizational Behavior*, 17(2): 99–117.

—— Milliken, F. J. (1988a). 'Executives' Perceptual Filters: What They Notice and How They Make Sense', in D. Hambrick (ed.), *The Executive Effect: Concepts and Methods for Studying Top Managers*. Greenwich, CT: JAI Press, pp. 35–65.

—— —— (1988b). 'Challenger: Changing the Odds Until Something Breaks', *Journal of Management Studies*, 25: 319–340.

—— and Nystrom, P. C. (1981a). 'Designing and Understanding Organizations', in P. C. Nystrom and W. H. Starbuck (eds.), *Handbook of Organizational Design*, Vol. 1. New York: Oxford University Press, pp. ix–xxii.

—— —— (1981b). 'Why the World Needs Organizational Design', *Journal of General Management*, 6(1): 3–17.

—— —— (1983). 'Pursuing Organizational Effectiveness that is Ambiguously Specified', in K. Cameron and D. A. Whetten (eds.), *Organizational Effectiveness*. New York: Academic Press, 135–161.

—— Greve, A., and Hedberg, B. L. T. (1978). 'Responding to Crises,' *Journal of Business Administration*, 9(2): 111–137.

Staw, B. M. (1976). 'Knee-deep in the Big Muddy: A Study of Escalating Commitment to a Chosen Course of Action', *Organizational Behavior and Human Performance*, 16: 27–44.

—— (1980). 'Rationality and Justification in Organizational Life', in B. M. Staw and L. L. Cummings (eds.), *Research in Organizational Behavior*, Vol. 2. Greenwich, CT: JAI Press, 45–80.

—— and Epstein, L. D. (2000). 'What Bandwagons Bring: Effects of Popular Management Techniques on Corporate Performance, Reputation, and CEO Pay', *Administrative Science Quarterly*, 45: 523–556.

—— and Fox, F. V. (1977). 'Escalation: Some Determinants of Commitment to a Previously Chosen Course of Action', *Human Relations*, 30: 431–450.

—— and Ross, J. (1978). 'Commitment to a Policy Decision: A Multi-theoretical Perspective', *Administrative Science Quarterly*, 23: 40–64.

—— McKechnie, P. I., and Puffer, S. M. (1983). 'The Justification of Organizational Performance', *Administrative Science Quarterly*, 28: 582–600.

Steinberg, S. G. (1996). 'Chip Improvements and the Real Truth of Moore's Law', *The Los Angeles Times*, April 15: 7.

Steindl, J. (1945). *Small and Big Business*. Oxford: Blackwell.

—— (1952). *Maturity and Stagnation in American Capitalism*. Oxford: Blackwell.

—— (1965). *Random Processes and the Growth of Firms*. London: Charles Griffin.

Steiner, G. A. (1969). *Top Management Planning*. New York: Macmillan.

Stephan, F. and Mishler, E. G. (1952). 'The Distribution of Participation in Small Groups: An Exponential Approximation', *American Sociological Review*, 17: 598–608.

Stevens, P., Jr. (1980). 'Play and Work: A False Dichotomy?', in H. B. Schwartzman (ed.), *Play and Culture*. West Point, NJ: Leisure Press, pp. 316–324.

Stigler, G. J. (1950). 'Monopoly and Oligopoly by Merger', *American Economic Review, Proceedings*, 40: 23–34.

—— (1968). *The Organization of Industry*. Homewood, IL: Irwin.

Stinchcombe, A. L. (1959). 'Bureaucratic and Craft Administration of Production', *Administrative Science Quarterly*, 4: 168–187.

Stinchcombe, A. L. (1965). 'Social Structure and Organizations', in J. G. March (ed.), *Handbook of Organizations*. Chicago, IL: Rand McNally, pp. 142–193.

—— (1974). *Creating Efficient Industrial Administrations*. New York: Academic Press.

—— and Heimer, C. A. (1988). 'Interorganizational Relations and Careers in Computer Software Firms', in I. H. Simpson and R. L. Simpson (eds.), *Research in the Sociology of Work*, Vol. 4: *High Tech Work*. Greenwich, CT: JAI Press, pp. 179–204.

Stocking, G. W. and Mueller, W. F. (1957). 'Business Reciprocity and the Size of Firms', *Journal of Business*, 30: 73–95.

Streufert, S. (1973). 'Effects of Information Relevance on Decision Making in Complex Environments', *Memory and Cognition*, 1: 224–228.

Strunk, N. and Case, F. (1988). *Where Deregulation Went Wrong: A Look at the Causes Behind Savings and Loan Failures in the 1980s*. Chicago, IL: U.S. League of Savings Institutions.

Suojanen, W. W. (1955). 'The Span of Control: Fact or Fable?', *Advanced Management*, 20(11): 5–13.

Sutcliffe, K. (1994). 'What Executives Notice: Accurate Perceptions in Top Management Teams', *Academy of Management Journal*, 37: 1360–1378.

Sveiby, K. E. and Lloyd, T. (1987). *Managing Knowhow*. London: Bloomsbury.

—— and Risling, A. (1986). *Kunskapsföretaget: Seklets viktigaste ledarutmaning?* (The Knowledge Firm: This Century's Most Important Managerial Challenge?). Malmö, Sweden: Liber AB.

Swaine, R. T. (1946–1948). *The Cravath Firm and Its Predecessors, 1819–1947*, 2 vols. New York: Privately printed.

Swann, N. L. (1950). *Food & Money in Ancient China*. Princeton, NJ: Princeton University Press.

Talacchi, S. (1960). 'Organization Size, Individual Attitudes and Behavior: An Empirical Study', *Administrative Science Quarterly*, 5: 398–420.

Tannenbaum, A. S. and Kahn, R. L. (1958). *Participation in Union Locals*. Evanston, IL: Row, Peterson.

TAST (1953). *Size and Morale*, Part I. London: Acton Society Trust.

—— (1957). *Size and Morale*, Part II. London: Acton Society Trust.

Taylor, S. E. and Crocker, J. (1981). 'Schematic Bases of Social Information Processing', in E. T. Higgins, C. P. Herman, and M. P. Zanna (eds.), *Social Cognition, The Ontario Symposium*, Vol. 1. Hillsdale, NJ: Erlbaum, pp. 69–134.

Terkel, S. (1974). *Working*. New York: Ballantine.

Terreberry, S. (1968). 'The Evolution of Organizational Environments', *Administrative Science Quarterly*, 12: 590–613.

Terrien, F. W. and Mills, D. L. (1955). 'The Effect of Changing Size Upon the Internal Structure of Organizations', *American Sociological Review*, 20: 11–13.

Thomas, E. J. (1959). 'Role Conceptions and Organizational Size', *American Sociological Review*, 24: 30–37.

Thompson, D. A. and Best, J. S. (2000). 'The Future of Magnetic Data Storage Technology', *IBM Journal of Research and Development*, 44(3): 311–322. Available at: http://www.research.ibm.com/journal/rd/443/thompson.html.

Thompson, J. D. (1962). 'Organizations and Output Transactions', *American Journal of Sociology*, 68: 309–324.

—— (1967). *Organizations in Action*. New York: McGraw-Hill.

—— and Bates, F. L. (1957). 'Technology, Organization, and Administration', *Administrative Science Quarterly*, 2: 325–343.

—— and McEwen, W. J. (1958). 'Organizational Goals and Environment: Goal-setting as an Interaction Process', *American Sociological Review*, 23: 23–31.

Thorndike, E. L. (1939). 'On the Fallacy of Imputing the Correlations Found for Groups to the Individuals or Smaller Groups Composing Them', *American Journal of Psychology*, 52: 122–124.

Thornton, P. H. (2002). 'The Rise of the Corporation in a Craft Industry: Conflict and Conformity in Institutional Logics', *Academy of Management Journal*, 45: 81–101.

Thune, S. S. and House, R. J. (1970). 'Where Long-range Planning Pays Off', *Business Horizons*, 13(4): 81–87.

Tichy, N. M. and Devanna, M. A. (1986). *The Transformational Leader*. New York: Wiley.

Tigay, J. H. (1982). *The Evolution of the Gilgamesh Epic*. Philadelphia, PA: University of Pennsylvania Press.

Tintner, G. (1941). 'The Theory of Choice Under Subjective Risk and Uncertainty', *Econometrica*, 9 (3/4): 298–304.

TNEC (1941). *Relative Efficiency of Large, Medium-Sized and Small Business*. Washington, DC: Temporary National Economic Committee, Monograph No. 13. (Prepared by the Federal Trade Commission.)

Tosi, H., Aldag, R. and Storey, R. (1973). 'On the Measurement of the Environment: An Assessment of the Lawrence and Lorsch Environmental Uncertainty Subscale', *Administrative Science Quarterly*, 18: 27–36.

Tripsas, M. (1997). 'Unraveling the Process of Creative Destruction: Complementary Assets and Incumbent Survival in the Typesetter Industry', *Strategic Management Journal*, 18 (Special Issue, Summer): 119–142.

Trist, E. L. and Bamforth, K. W. (1951). 'Social and Psychological Consequences of the Longwall Method of Coal-getting', *Human Relations*, 4: 3–38.

Tsouderos, J. E. (1955). 'Organizational Change in Terms of a Series of Selected Variables', *American Sociological Review*, 20: 206–210.

Tuchman, G. (1973). 'Making News by Doing Work: Routinizing the Unexpected', *American Journal of Sociology*, 79: 110–131.

Tufte, E. R. (1983). *The Visual Display of Quantitative Information*. Cheshire, CT: Graphics Press.

Turkle, S. (1984). *The Second Self*. New York: Simon & Schuster.

Tushman, M. L. and Anderson, P. (1986). 'Technological Discontinuities and Organizational Environments', *Administrative Science Quarterly*, 31: 439–465.

—— and Romanelli, E. (1985). 'Organizational Evolution: A Metamorphosis Model of Convergence and Reorientation', *Research in Organizational Behavior*, 7. Greenwich, CT: JAI Press.

—— Newman, W. H., and Romanelli, E. (1986). 'Convergence and Upheaval: Managing the Unsteady Pace of Organizational Evolution', *California Management Review*, 29(1): 29–44.

Tversky, A. and Kahneman, D. (1974). 'Judgement under Uncertainty: Heuristics and Biases', *Science*, 185: 124–131.

Tyre, M. J. and Orlikowski, W. J. (1994). 'Windows of Opportunity: Temporal Patterns of Technological Adaptation in Organizations', *Organization Science*, 5(1): 98–118.

Udy, S. H., Jr. (1959*a*). ' "Bureaucracy" and "Rationality" in Weber's Organization Theory: An Empirical Study', *American Sociological Review*, 24: 791–795.

—— (1959*b*). *Organization of Work*. New Haven, CT: Human Relations Area Files Press.

Ungson, G. R., Braunstein, D. N., and Hall, P. D. (1981). 'Managerial Information Processing: A Research Review', *Administrative Science Quarterly*, 26: 116–134.

Urwick, L. F. (1956). 'The Manager's Span of Control', *Harvard Business Review*, 34(3): 39–47.

Van Maanen, J. (1976). 'Breaking In: Socialization to Work', in C. Dubin (ed.), Handbook of Work, Organization, and Society. Chicago, IL: Rand McNally, pp. 67–130.

—— and Kunda, G. (1989). 'Real Feelings: Emotional Expression and Organizational Culture', *Research in Organizational Behavior*, 11, 43–103.

Vickers, G. (1959). 'Is Adaptability Enough?', *Behavioral Science*, 4: 219–234.

Virany, B., Tushman, M. L., and Romanelli, E. (1992). 'Executive Succession and Organization Outcomes in Turbulent Environments: An Organization Learning Approach', *Organization Science*, 3: 72–91.

Voss, H.-G. (1987). 'Possible Distinctions Between Exploration and Play', in D. Gorlitz and J. F. Wohlwill (eds.), *Curiosity, Imagination, and Play*. Hillsdale, NJ: Erlbaum, pp. 44–58.

Wagner, J. A. III and Gooding, R. Z. (1997). 'Equivocal Information and Attribution: An Investigation of Patterns of Managerial Sensemaking', *Strategic Management Journal*, 18: 275–286.

Waley, A. (1938). *The Analects of Confucius*. London: George Allan & Unwin.

Walgenbach, P. and Hegele, C. (2001). 'What Can an Apple Learn from an Orange? Or: What do Companies Use Benchmarking For?', *Organization*, 8: 121–144.

Walker, C. R. and Guest, R. H. (1952). 'The Man on the Assembly Line', *Harvard Business Review*, 30(3): 71–83.

Wallace, J. (1997). *Overdrive: Bill Gates and the Race to Control Cyberspace*. New York: Wiley.

Walton, E. J. and Dawson, S. (2001). 'Managers' Perceptions of Criteria of Organizational Effectiveness', *Journal of Management Studies*, 38: 173–199.

Wang, G. H. K., Sauerhaft, D., and Edwards, D. (1987). 'Predicting Thrift-Institution Examination Ratings'. Working paper, Washington, DC: Office of Policy and Economic Research, Federal Home Loan Bank Board 131.

Ward, J. K. (1989). 'The Future of an Explosion', *American Heritage of Invention and Technology*, 5(1): 58–63.

Warner, W. L. and Low, J. O. (1947). *The Social System of the Modern Factory*. New Haven, CT: Yale University Press.

Watson, B. (1963). *Basic Writings of Mo Tzu, Hsün Tzu, and Han Fei Tzu*. New York: Columbia University Press.

Watson, G. H. (2002). 'Moore's Law for Intel CPUs'. Available at: http://www.physics.udel.edu/~watson/scen103/intel.html.

Watzlawick, P., Weakland, J. H., and Fisch, R. (1974). *Change: Principles of Problem Formation and Problem Resolution.* New York: W. W. Norton.

Weber, C. E. (1959) 'Change in Managerial Manpower with Mechanization of Data-processing', *Journal of Business,* 32: 151–163.

Webster, E. J. (1989). 'Playfulness and Computers at Work'. Ph.D. thesis, New York University.

—— and Starbuck, W. H. (1988). 'Theory Building in Industrial and Organizational Psychology', in C. L. Cooper and I. Robertson (eds.), *International Review of Industrial and Organizational Psychology 1988.* London: Wiley, pp. 93–138.

—— Heian, J., and Michelman, J. (1990). 'Computer Training and Computer Anxiety in the Educational Process: An Experimental Analysis', in J. I. DeGross, M. Alavi, and H. Oppelland (eds.), *Proceedings of the Eleventh International Conference on Information Systems.* Copenhagen, Denmark: ICIS, pp. 171–182.

Weick, K. E. (1969). *The Social Psychology of Organizing.* Reading, MA: Addison-Wesley.

—— (1979). *The Social Psychology of Organizing,* 2nd edn. Reading, MA: Addison-Wesley.

—— (1983). 'Managerial Thought in the Context of Action', in S. Srivastva and Associates (eds.), *The Executive Mind: New Insights on Managerial Thought and Action.* San Francisco, CA: Jossey-Bass, pp. 221–242.

—— (1984). 'Small Wins: Redefining the Scale of Social Problems', *American Psychologist,* 39/1: 40–49.

—— (1987*a*). 'Perspectives on Action in Organizations', in J. W. Lorsch (ed.), *Handbook of Organizational Behavior.* Englewood Cliffs, NJ: Prentice-Hall, pp. 10–28.

—— (1987*b*). 'Organizational Culture and High Reliability', *California Management Review,* 29: 112–127.

—— (1991). 'The Nontraditional Quality of Organizational Learning', *Organization Science,* 2: 116–123.

—— (1995). *Sensemaking in Organizations.* Thousand Oaks, CA: Sage.

Weigand, R. E. (1963). 'The Marketing Organization, Channels, and Firm Size', *Journal of Business,* 36: 228–236.

Wei-ming, T. (1993). *Way, Learning, and Politics: Essays on the Confucian Intellectual.* Albany, NY: State University of New York Press.

Weinshall, T. D. (1960–1961). 'Problems of Change in Organizational Structure in Growing Enterprises'. Ph.D. thesis, Harvard University.

Weiss, L. W. (1965). 'An Evaluation of Mergers in Six Industries', *Review of Economics and Statistics,* 47: 172–181.

Weiss, R. S. (1956). *Processes of Organization.* Ann Arbor, MI: University of Michigan, Survey Research Center.

Wente, E. F. (1990). *Letters from Ancient Egypt.* Atlanta, GA: Schools Press.

Westerlund, G. and Sjöstrand, S. E. (1979). *Organizational Myths.* London: Harper & Row.

Westphal, J. D. and Zajac, E. J. (1998). 'The Symbolic Management of Stockholders: Corporate Governance Reforms and Shareholder Reactions', *Administrative Science Quarterly,* 43: 127–153.

White, C. M. (1960). 'Multiple Goals in the Theory of the Firm', in K. E. Boulding and W. A. Spivey (eds.), *Linear Programming and the Theory of the Firm.* New York: Macmillan, pp. 181–201.

White, H. (1962). 'Chance Models of Systems of Casual Groups', *Sociometry,* 25: 153–172. See also the discussion by J. S. Coleman, 172–176.

White, L. J. (1986). 'The Partial Deregulation of Banks and Other Depository Institutions', in L. W. Weiss and M. W. Klass (eds.), *Regulatory Reform: What Actually Happened*. Boston, MA: Little Brown, pp. 169–209.

—— (1991). *The S&L Debacle: Public Policy Lessons for Bank and Thrift Regulation*. New York: Oxford University Press.

White, O. F., Jr. (1969). 'The Dialectical Organization: An Alternative to Bureaucracy', *Public Administration Review*, 29: 32–42.

White, R. W. (1959). 'Motivation Reconsidered: The Concept of Competence', *Psychological Review*, 66: 297–333.

Whitin, T. M. and Peston, M. H. (1954). 'Random Variations, Risk, and Returns to Scale', *Quarterly Journal of Economics*, 68: 603–612.

Whyte, W. F. (1948). *Human Relations in the Restaurant Industry*. New York: McGraw-Hill.

—— (1961). *Men at Work*. Homewood, IL: Dorsey.

Whyte, W. H., Jr. (1956). *The Organization Man*. New York: Simon & Schuster.

Wickesberg, A. K. (1961). *Organizational Relationships in the Growing Small Manufacturing Firm*. Minneapolis MN: University of Minnesota.

Wilcox, C. (1955). *Public Policies Toward Business*. Homewood, IL: Irwin.

Wildavsky, A. B. (1972). 'The Self-evaluating Organization', *Public Administration Review*, 32: 509–520.

Williamson, O. E. (1963). 'A Model of Rational Managerial Behavior', in R. M. Cyert and J. G. March (eds.), *A Behavioral Theory of the Firm*. Englewood Cliffs, NJ: Prentice-Hall, pp. 237–252.

Wilson, J. O. (1966). 'Innovation in Organization: Notes Toward a Theory', in J. D. Thompson (ed.), *Approaches to Organizational Design*. Pittsburgh, PA: University of Pittsburgh Press, pp. 193–218.

Winter, S. G. Jr. (1964). 'Economic "Natural Selection" and the Theory of the Firm', *Yale Economic Essays*, 4: 225–272.

—— (1971). 'Satisficing, Selection, and the Innovating Remnant', *Quarterly Journal of Economics*, 85: 237–261.

—— (1987). 'Knowledge and Competence as Strategic Assets', in D. J. Teece (ed.), *The Competitive Challenge: Strategies for Industrial Innovation and Renewal*. Cambridge, MA: Ballinger, pp. 159–184.

—— (1994). 'Organizing for Continuous Improvement: Evolutionary Theory Meets the Quality Revolution', in J. A. C. Baum and J. V. Singh (eds.), *Evolutionary Dynamics of Organizations*. New York: Oxford University Press, pp. 90–108.

Winterbotham, F. W. (1975). *The Ultra Secret*. New York: Dell.

Witte, E. (1972). 'Field Research on Complex Decision Making Processes: The Phase Theorem', *International Studies on Management & Organization*, 2: 156–182.

Wohlwill, J. F. and Kohn, I. (1976). 'Dimensionalizing the Environmental Manifold', in S. Wapner, S. Cohen, and B. Kaplan (eds.), *Experiencing the Environment*. New York: Plenum, 19–54.

Wolf, D. P. (1984). 'Repertoire, Style and Format: Notions Worth Borrowing From Children's Play', in P. K. Smith (ed.), *Play in Animals and Humans*. Oxford: Blackwell, pp. 175–193.

Wolff, E. N. and Baumol, W. J. (1989). 'Sources of Postwar Growth of Information Activity in the United States', in L. Osberg, E. N. Wolff, and W. J. Baumol (eds.), *The Information Economy and the Implications of Unbalanced Growth*. Ottawa, Canada: Institute for Research on Public Policy, pp. 17–46.

Wood, D. R., Jr. and LaForge, R. L. (1979). 'The Impact of Comprehensive Planning on Financial Performance', *Academy of Management Journal*, 22: 516–526.

Woodruff, A. M. and Alexander, T. G. (1958). *Success and Failure in Small Manufacturing*. Pittsburgh, PA: University of Pittsburgh Press.

Woodward, J. (1958). *Management and Technology*. London: Her Majesty's Stationery Office.

World (1960). *Webster's New World Dictionary of the American Language* (college edition). Cleveland, OH: World.

Worthy, J. C. (1950a). 'Factors Influencing Employee Morale', *Harvard Business Review*, 28(1): 61–73.

—— (1950b). 'Organizational Structure and Employee Morale', *American Sociological Review*, 15: 169–179.

Wu, K. C. (1928). *Ancient Chinese Political Theories*. Shanghai: The Commercial Press, Limited.

Wuthnow, R. and Shrum, W. (1983). 'Knowledge Workers as a "New Class": Structural and Ideological Convergence Among Professional-technical Workers and Managers', *Work and Occupations*, 10: 471–487.

Wynia, B. L. (1972). 'Executive Development in the Federal Government', *Public Administration Review*, 32: 311–317.

Yasai-Ardekani, M. and Nystrom, P. C. (1996). 'Designs for Environmental Scanning Systems: Tests of a Contingency Theory', *Management Science*, 42: 187–204.

Yuchtman, E. and Seashore, S. E. (1967). 'A System Resource Approach to Organizational Effectiveness', *American Sociological Review*, 32: 891–903.

Zajonc, R. B. (1967). *Social Psychology: An Experimental Approach*. Belmont, CA: Brooks/ Cole.

Zald, M. N. and Denton, P. (1963). 'From Evangelism to General Service: The Transformation of the YMCA', *Administrative Science Quarterly*, 8: 214–234.

Zebrowitz, L. A. (1990). *Social Perception*. Pacific Grove, CA: Brooks/Cole.

Index